Lecture Notes  Science

Edited

Advisor Stoer

T0190064

Lecture Notes in Computer Science 729

Edited by G. Goos and J. Hartmanis

Advisory Board: W. Brauer   D. Gries   J. Stoer

Lorenzo Donatiello · Randolph Nelson (Eds.)

Performance Evaluation of Computer and Communication Systems

Joint Tutorial Papers of
Performance '93 and Sigmetrics '93

Springer-Verlag

Berlin Heidelberg New York
London Paris Tokyo
Hong Kong Barcelona
Budapest

Lorenzo Donatiello   Randolph Nelson (Eds.)

Performance Evaluation of Computer and Communication Systems

Joint Tutorial Papers of
Performance '93 and Sigmetrics '93

Springer-Verlag
Berlin Heidelberg New York
London Paris Tokyo
Hong Kong Barcelona
Budapest

Series Editors

Gerhard Goos
Universität Karlsruhe
Postfach 69 80
Vincenz-Priessnitz-Straße 1
D-76131 Karlsruhe, Germany

Juris Hartmanis
Cornell University
Department of Computer Science
4130 Upson Hall
Ithaca, NY 14853, USA

Volume Editors

Lorenzo Donatiello
Dipartimento di Matematica, Università di Bologna
Piazza di Porta San Donato 5, I-40127 Bologna, Italia

Randolph Nelson
IBM T. J. Watson Research Center
P. O. Box 704, Yorktown Heights, N. Y. 10598, USA

CR Subject Classification (1991): C.4, D.4.8, I.6

ISBN 3-540-57297-X Springer-Verlag Berlin Heidelberg New York
ISBN 0-387-57297-X Springer-Verlag New York Berlin Heidelberg

This work is subject to copyright. All rights are reserved, whether the whole or part
of the material is concerned, specifically the rights of translation, reprinting, re-use
of illustrations, recitation, broadcasting, reproduction on microfilms or in any other
way, and storage in data banks. Duplication of this publication or parts thereof is
permitted only under the provisions of the German Copyright Law of September 9,
1965, in its current version, and permission for use must always be obtained from
Springer-Verlag. Violations are liable for prosecution under the German Copyright
Law.

© Springer-Verlag Berlin Heidelberg 1993
Printed in Germany

Typesetting: Camera-ready by author
Printing and binding: Druckhaus Beltz, Hemsbach/Bergstr.
45/3140-543210 - Printed on acid-free paper

Foreword

The present volume contains the complete set of tutorial papers presented at the 16th IFIP Working Group 7.3 International Symposium on Computer Performance Modeling, Measurement and Evaluation held in Rome, September 27 to October 1, 1993 and a number of tutorial papers presented at the 1993 ACM SIGMETRICS Conference on Measurement and Modeling of Computer Systems held in Santa Clara, California, May 10 to 14, 1993.

The principal goal of this publication is to present an overview of recent results in the field of modeling and performance evaluation of computer and communication systems. The wide diversity of application and methodologies included in the tutorials attests to the breadth and richness of current research in the area of performance modeling.

The tutorials herein may serve to introduce the reader to an unfamiliar research area, to unify material already known, or simply to illustrate the diversity of research found in the field. The extensive bibliographies found in the tutorials guide the reader to additional sources for future reading.

We would like to thank all the authors for their effort, dedication and cooperation.

August 1993   L. Donatiello
                                                           R. Nelson

Table of Contents

PARALLEL SIMULATION

Rassul Ayani

Department of Teleinformatics, Computer Systems Laboratory

Royal Institute of Technology (KTH)

Stockholm, Sweden

Abstract

This tutorial surveys various approaches to executing discrete event simulation programs on a parallel computer. The tutorial is focused on *asynchronous* simulation programs where different processes may advance asynchronously in simulated time. Parallelization of discrete event simulation programs requires adequate synchronization scheme. We review several synchronization schemes that have appeared in the literature in recent years. The performance result of these schemes will be surveyed and some application areas will be discussed.

1. Introduction

The analysis of large and complex systems by analytical techniques is often very difficult. The availability of low cost microcomputers has introduced simulation to many real life applications. Simulation of a system may have several objectives, including: (i) understanding behavior of a system; (ii) obtaining estimates of performance of a system; (iii) guiding the selection of design parameters; (iv) validation of a model. Simulation has been used in many areas, including manufacturing lines, communication networks, computer systems, VLSI design, design automation, air traffic and road traffic systems, among others.

Two separate classes of methodologies, called *continuous* time and *discrete* time simulation, have emerged over the years and are widely used for simulating complex systems. As the terms indicate, in a continuous simulation changes in the state of the system occur continuously in time, whereas in a discrete simulation changes in the system take place only at selected points in time. Thus, in a discrete-event simulation (DES) events happen at discrete points in time and are instantaneous. One kind of discrete simulation is the fixed time increment, or the *time-stepped* approach, the other kind is the *discrete-event* method. A typical DES algorithm is based on an ordered list of events, called *event-list*, or future-event-set. The algorithm repeatedly performs the following steps:(1) removes the event with the minimum simulation time from the event-list, (2) evaluates the event and possibly, and (3) inserts new event(s), generated by step 2, in the event-list.

The traditional DES, as described above, is sequential. However, many practical simulations, e.g. in engineering applications, consume several of hours (and even days) on a sequential machine. Parallel computers are attractive tools to be used to reduce execution time of such simulation programs.

In practice, a simulation program is run with several parameter settings. For instance, to design a system various parameters must be tested to determine the most appropriate ones. One may suggest to run *replication* of a simulator on separate processors of a multiprocessor computer. The replication approach is reasonable, if the experiments are independent. However, in many practical situations parameters of an experiment is determined based on outcome of the previous experiments and thus the replication approach is not applicable. An alternative solution would be to parallelize a single run of a simulator.

In this tutorial, we discuss cases where several processors of a multiprocessor system cooperate to *execute a single simulation program* and complete it in a fraction of the time one processor would need. There are several approaches to parallel simulation some of which are briefly reviewed below (see e.g. [56] for more detail).

A. *Functional decomposition*: In this approach, the simulation support tasks (such as random number generation, event set processing and statistics collection) are performed by different processors. Generally, the time needed to execute different tasks is different and thus load balancing is a problem in this approach. Moreover, the number of support functions is limited and thus this method cannot use large multiprocessors efficiently.

B. *Time-stepped simulation*: In a time-stepped simulation, simulated time is advanced in fixed increments and ach process simulates its components at these fixed points. The time step must be short to guarantee accuracy of the simulation result. This method is inefficient if there occur few events at each point. A case where good speed can be obtained has been reported by Goli et al. [25]).

C. *Asynchronous parallel simulation*: In this paper, we focus on asynchronous parallel simulation, where each process maintains its own local clock and the local time of different processes may advance asynchronously.

The rest of this tutorial is organised as following: Some basic concepts are reviewed in Section 2 and the use of parallel simulation is argued in Section 3. We review conservative parallel simulation schemes in Section 4 and optimistic methods in Section 5. Some hybrid approaches are highlighted in Section 6. Finally, concluding remarks are given in Section 7.

2. Preliminaries

Real time is the actual time needed to run a simulator, whereas the occurrence time of events in the actual system is denoted by *simulated time*.

Event list is a list that contains all scheduled, but not yet processed events.

Timestamp of an event denotes the time the event occurs in the actual system.

State variables describe the state of the system. In the process of developing a simulation model, state variables are identified. The value of the state variables represent the essential features of a system at specific points in time. For instance, in a network, state variables represent queue length and waiting time, among others.

Causality error may occur if an event E_2 depends on another event E_1 in the actual system, but it is processed before E_1 in the simulation program. In the sequential DES described in Section 1, it is crucial to remove the event with the *minimum* simulation time from the event list to avoid causality error.

Speedup is defined as the time it takes to run a simulator on a uniprocessor divided by the time it takes to run a parallel version of the simulator on a multiprocessor. The main problems related to this metric are: (i) It depends on implementation of the sequential simulator. For instance, if the sequential simulator is slow the speedup is higher! (ii) It is hardware dependent, i.e., it depends on speed of both uniprocessor and multiprocessor computer being used. As discussed by Ayani and Berkman [7], it would be more accurate to define speedup as the time it takes to run the *most efficient sequential simulator* on a single processor of a multiprocessor divided by the time it takes to execute the parallel simulator on n processors of the *same* multiprocessor.

3. Why Parallel simulation?

Parallel discret event simulation (PDES) refers to the execution of a single DES program on a parallel computer. PDES has attracted a considerable number of researchers in recent years, because:

(i) It has the potential to reduce the simulation time of a DES program. This interest is partly due to the fact that a single run of a sequential simulator may require several hours or even days.

(ii) Many real life systems contain substantial amounts of parallelism. For instance, in a communication network, different switches receive and redirect messages simultaneously. It is more natural to simulate a parallel phenomenon in parallel.

(iii) From an academic point of view, PDES represents a problem domain that requires solution to most of the problems encountered in parallel processing, e.g., synchronization, efficient message communication, deadlock management and load balancing.

One of the main difficulties in PDES is synchronization. It is difficult because the precedence constraints that dictate which event must be executed before each other is, in general, quite complex and data dependent. This contrasts sharply with other areas where much is known about the synchronization at compile time, e.g. in matrix algebra [24]

The common approach to PDES is to view the system being modeled, usually referred to as the *physical system*, as a set of *physical processes* (PPs) that interact at various points in simulated time. The simulator is then constructed as a set of *logical processes* (LPs) that communicate with each other by sending timestamped messages. In this scenario, each logical process simulates a physicaly process. Each LP maintains its own logical clock and its own event list. The logical process view requires that the state variables are statically partitioned into a set of *disjoint states* each belonging to an LP. This view of the simulation as a set of communicating LPs is used by all of the simulation methods reviewed in this paper.

It can be shown that no *causality* errors occur if each LP processes events in *non-decreasing* timestamp order [43]. This requirement is known as *local causality constraint*. The local causality constraint is sufficient, but not necessary. This is not necessary, because two events occurring within the same LP may be independent of each other and thus can be processed in any order. Ahmed et al. [2] suggest an approach where independent events belonging to the same LP may be identified and processed in parallel.

Two main paradigms have been proposed for asynchronous parallel simulation: *conservative* and *optimistic* methods. Conservative approaches strictly avoid the possibility of any causality error ever occurring. On the other hand, optimistic approaches make the optimistic assumption that messages arrive at different LPs in correct order. However, these approaches employ a detect and recovery mechanism to correct causality errors.

4. Conservative Approaches

Several conservative approaches to PDES have been proposed in the literature. These approaches are based on processing safe events. The main difference between these methods, as discussed in this section, lies in the way they identify safe events.

4.1 The Chandy-Misra Scheme

Chandy and Misra proposed one of the first conservative PDES algorithms [14]. In this method, as described by Misra [43], a physical system is modeled as a directed graph where arcs represent communication channels between nodes. Each node of the graph is called a logical process (LP). Each LP simulates a portion of the real system to be simulated and maintains a set of queues, one associated with each arc in the graph. Within each logical process, events are simulated strictly in the order of their simulated time. Interprocess communication is required whenever an event associated with one logical process wishes to schedule an event for another logical process. It is assumed that the communication medium preserves the order of messages, and that the timestamp of the messages sent along any particular arc are nondecreasing.

The method is conservative because a logical process is not allowed to process a message with timestamp t until it is certain that no messages will ever arrive with a timestamp less than t. To guarantee this, each node must select the message with the lowest timestamp that is now scheduled for the node or will be scheduled in future. If every input arc of a node has at least one unprocessed message, then the next message to be processed is simply the one with the lowest timestamp among all of the input arcs of the node. However, if any of the input arcs is empty, then the node will be *blocked* waiting for a message to arrive. The blocking mechanism is necessary, because if a node processes any message from one of its nonempty input queues, there is no guarantee that a message that arrives later to an empty input arc will have a timestamp equal or greater than the timestamp of the processed message.

There are two problems related to blocking a node: *memory overflow* and *deadlock*.

(i) Memory overflow: While a node is blocked because some of its input
queues are empty, the other queues may grow, leading to an unpredictable storage requirement. For instance, consider the system shown in Figure 1. If node 1
sends most of the messages to node 4 via node 2, there may be many messages
on arc (2,4) while node 4 is blocked waiting for a message on arc (3,4).

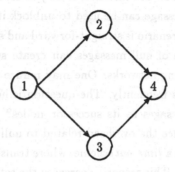

Figure 1. In this network, node 4 may cause memory overflow. For instance, node
4 may be blocked waiting for a message from node 3, while it receives lots of messages
from node 2.

(ii) Deadlock: If the directed graph representing the system contains a
cycle, as shown in Figure 2, then the Chandy-Misra paradigm is vulnerable to
deadlock. Several methods have been proposed in the literature to resolve the
deadlock problem. These methods are either based on deadlock avoidance or
deadlock detection and recovery.

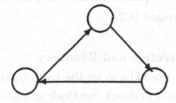

Figure 2. A circular network

4.2 Deadlock Avoidance Mechanisms

The original approach suggested by Chandy and Misra for avoiding deadlock, described in [43] is based on sending *null* messages. A null message is a dummy message used *only* for synchronoization purpose and does not correspond to any activity in the real system. A null message E_{null} with timestamp $T(E_{null})$ sent from LP_i to LP_j indicates that LP_i will not send any message to LP_j earlier than $T(E_{null})$. The receiver process may use this information to identify its next message to be processed. For instance, if LP_j is blocked waiting for a message from LP_i, this null message can be used to unblock it.

The null message scenario is straight-forward and simple to implement. However, the transmission of null messages can create substantial overhead, especially for high branching networks. One may reduce the overhead by transmitting null messages less frequently. The question is how frequently does a node need to send null messages to its successor nodes? Several mechanisms have been proposed to reduce the overhead related to null messages.

Misra [43] suggests a *time-out* scheme, where transmission of a null message is delayed for some time. This scenario decreases the total number of null messages required, because a real message with a higher timestamp may arrive or a null message with a higher timestamp may over-write the earlier null message during the time-out period. However, some processes might be delayed longer than in the original null message scheme.

Another approach is that a process sends null messages on each of its output arcs whenever it is *blocked*. It can be shown that this mechanism avoids deadlock if there is no cycle in which the collective timestamp increment of a message traversing the cycle could be zero [24].

Another approach would be to send null messages on *demand*. In this method, a process that is blocked sends a request to its predecessor asking for the earliest time the predecessor may send a message. Thus, a null message will be sent from LP_i to LP_j only when LP_j requests it. This scheme, however, may result in a cycle of requests. In this case, the message with the minimum timestamp can be processed [43].

4.3 Deadlock Detection and Recovery

Another possibility would be to let the basic Chandy-Misra schem deadlock, and provide a mechanism to detect deadlock and recover from it.

In an algorithm suggested by Misra [43], a marker circulates in a cycle of channels. The marker is a special type of message carrying some information. The cycle is constructed in such a way that the marker traverses every channel of the network sometimes during a cycle. If an LP receives the marker it will send it to the next channel within a *finite* time. An LP is said to be *white* if it has neither received nor sent a message since the last departure of the marker from it; the LP is *black* otherwise. The marker declares *deadlock* when it finds that the last N logical processes that it has visited were all white, where N is the number of nodes in the network. As discussed in [43], the algorithm is correct if the messages communicated between the LPs are received in the time order they are sent. As an example consider the network depicted by Figure 1. The network is deadlocked if the marker visits all the three nodes and finds that all of them are white, i.e., they have neither received nor sent a message since last visit.

The marker scheme may also be used to recover from deadlock. The marker may carry the *minimum* of the next-event-times for the white LPs it visits. When the marker detects deadlock, it knows the smallest event-time and the LP at which this event occurs. To recover from deadlock, the LP with the minimum next-event-time will be restarted.

Experimental results (e.g. [22], [53], [63]) suggest that the deadlock avoidance method is superior to the deadlock detection and recovery. Unfortunately, the deadlock avoidance presumes a nonzero minimum service time.

4.4 Conservative Time Window Schemes

Several researchers have proposed window based conservative parallel simulation schemes (e.g., see [9], [38], [47]). The main idea behind all these schemes is to identify a time window for each logical process such that events within these windows are safe and can thus be processed concurrently. The basic constraint on such schemes is that events occurring within each window are processed sequentially, but events within different windows are independent and can be processed concurrently.

Consider a system consisting of n logical processes LP1, LP2,...,LPn. Assume that the following Conservative Time Window (CTW) parallel simulation scheme is used.

The CTW-algorithm shown in Figure 3 works in the following way:

a) In the first phase, a window Wi is assigned to each LPi such that the events occurring within Wi are independent from the events occurring in Wj, $i \neq j$.

Repeat

1) Identification phase
Assign a window Wi to LPi such that events in Wi
can be processed concurrently with events in Wj,
$i \neq j$.
Barrier
2) Process phase
Process the events in W1, W2, ...,Wn.
Barrier

Until (End-of-Simulation)

Figure 3. A Conservative Time Window (CTW) parallel simulation scheme.

The way independent windows are identified has been discussed elsewhere, e.g.
see [9].

b) In phase 2 of the CTW-algorithm, the events occurring within each window
are processed sequentially, but events within different windows are independent
and can be processed concurrently.

c) Each phase of the algorithm may be executed by several processors in parallel. However, synchronization is required between the two consecutive phases.
Thus, the next iteration of the CTW-algorithm will be started after processing
all the time windows belonging to the current iteration.The algorithm produces
a Time Window, which may be empty, for each LP. The width of the windows is
calculated in each iteration of the algorithm. Figure 4 illustrates three iterations
of the CTW-algorithm for simulating a system consisting of three subsystems.

Generally, different windows have different sizes and contain different number of events. In other words, there will be n windows W1, W2, ..., Wn with
different widths to be assigned to m processors. The performance of the window
based schemes depends heavily on how the windows are assigned to the processors. Several scheduling schemes have been proposed and evaluated in [8]. As
discussed in [9], the number of non-empty windows produced in each iteration of
the algorithm and the size of each one depends on features of the system being
simulated, e.g. message population, network topology, and network size.

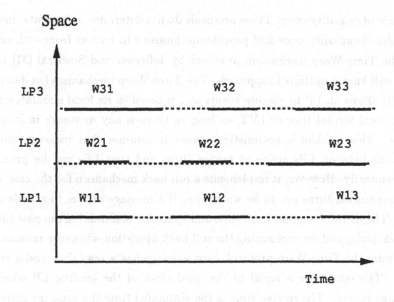

Figure 4. Results of performing 3 iterations of the CTW-algorithm on a system with three LPs, where Wij denotes the window generated for LPi in the jth iteration.

More information on the behavior of the window based parallel simulation algorithms can be found in [9].

4.5 Performance of the Conservative Schemes

Several researchers have studied the performance of the conservative schemes. The most extensive performance result has been reported by Richard Fujimoto [22], [24]. According to Fujimoto, performance of the conservative algorithms is critically related to the degree to which logical processes can look ahead into their future simulated time. Wagner and Lazowska [63] report on performance of a conservative scheme on a shared memory multiprocessor. Chandy and Sherman [16] report speedup in simulation of queueing networks. Ayani and Rajaei [9] present an intensive performance study of the conservative time window scheme on shared memory multiprocessors.

5. Optimistic Approaches

Optimistic approaches to PDES, as opposed to conservative ones, allow occurrence of causality error. These protocols do not determine *safe* events; instead they *detect* causality error and provide mechanisms to *recover* from such error.

The Time Warp mechanism proposed by Jefferson and Sowizral [31] is the most well known optimistic approach. The Time Warp mechanism (as described in [29]) allows an LP to execute events and proceed in its local simulated time, called local virtual time or LVT, as long as there is any messeage in its input queue. This method is optimistic because it assumes that message communications between LPs arrive at proper time, and thus LPs can be processed independently. However, it implements a roll back mechanism for the case when the assumption turns out to be wrong, i.e. if a message arrives to a node at its past. The method requires both time and space for maintaining the past history of each node, and for performing the roll back operation whenever necessary.

Under the Time Warp protocol, each message has a *send* time and a *receive* time. The send time is equal to the local clock of the sending LP when the message is sent. The receive time is the simulated time the message arrives at the receiving LP. The receive time is the same as the timestamp used in the conservative approaches. The send time concept is used to define GVT and to implement the Time Warp protocol correctly. Global virtual time (GVT) is the minimum of all LVTs and the send times of all messages that have been sent but not yet received.

If messages arrive to a process with receive times greater than the receiver's LVT, they are enqueued in the input queue of the receiver LP. However, if an LP receives an event message that "should" have been handled in its simulated past, i.e., its receive time is less than the receiver's LVT (such a message is called a *straggler*), then the receiving LP is rolled back to the simulation time before the timestamp of the straggler message. In addition to rolling back the receiving LP, however, the Time Warp mechanism must cancel all of the indirect side effects caused by any messages the receiving LP sent with timestamps greater than the time at which it is rolled back. This is done by sending *antimessages* to annihilate the corresponding *ordinary* messages.

In Time Warp, no event with timestamp smaller than GVT will ever be rolled back. Thus, all events with timestamp less than GVT can be committed and the memory space occupied by state variables up to GVT can be released. The process of committing events and reclaiming memory is referred to as *fossil collection* [23] and [24].

5.1 Lazy Cancellation

Several schemes for *undoing* side effects caused by erroneous messages have appeared in the literature. In the *aggressive cancellation* mechanism, when a process rolls back *antimessages* are sent immediately to cancel erroneous messages.

In *lazy cancellation* [23], antimessages are not sent immediately after rollback. Instead, the rolled back process resumes execution of events from its new LVT. If the reexecution of the events regenerates the *same* message, there is no need to cancel the message. Only messages that are different from the old messages are transmitted; after the process' clock passes time T, antimessages are sent only for those messages with timestamp less than T that are not regenerated. Under aggressive cancellation, a process may send unnecessary antimessages. Under lazy cancellation there are no unnecessary antimessages. However, lazy cancellation may allow erroneous computation to spread further because antimessages are sent later. 196z The lazy cancellation mechanism may improve or degrade performance of the time warp depending on features of the application. Most of the performance results reported in the literature suggest that lazy cancellation improves performance. However, one can construct cases where lazy cancellation is much slower than aggressive cancellation [23].

5.2 Performance of the Optimistic Schemes

Several researchers have report successes in using Time Warp to speedup simulation problems. Fujimoto has reported significant speedup for several queueing networks [23]. Some researchers have developed analytical models to evaluate performance of Time Warp. Analytical models for the case of two processors have been developed by Mitra and Mitrani [44], and Feldman and Kleinrock [20]. Models for multiprocesses have been developed by Akyildiz et al. [4] and Gupta et al. [26], among others.

6. Hybrid Approaches

The deadlock handling is the main cost factor in conservative methods. In optimistic approaches, the detection and recovery of causality errors require state saving and rollback . State saving may require a considerable amount of memory if system state consists of many variables that must be saved frequently. The memory requirement may be reduced if the GVT is more frequently computed and the unnecessary states are removed, i.e. the fossil collection procedure is done more frequently. However, this requires more CPU time.

It seems reasonable to combine the advantages of these two approaches in a hybrid protocol. The issue of combining the two approaches has received considerable attention in recent years, since the limitations of each paradigm are better understood. It is believed that the future PDES paradigm will be a hybrid one!

There are three general categories of hybrid approaches:

(i) To add optimism into a conservative approach. For instance, in the speculative simulation method proposed by Horst Meh [42] whenever an LP is to be blocked, it optimistically simulates the events in its event list, but keeps the result locally until it becomes committed. In the Filtered Rollback proposed by Lubachevsky [39], the upper-bound is set to a larger value than the one determined by the the conservative bounded-lag algorithm . These hybrid schemes are still conservative and thus cannot support *dynamic* configuration of LPs.

(ii) To add conservatism to an optimistic approach. One may try to bound the advancement of LVTs in Time Warp. This technique reduces rollback frequency and the rollback distance in general. However, it tends to reduce the degree of available parallelism as well.

The main problem with this category of schemes is how to determine a boundary for limiting the optimism. For instance, in MIMDIX [40] special processes, called Genie processes, are introduced to compute upper bounds for the advancement of LVTs. In Wolf [41], whenever a rollback occurs, special messages are broadcasted to limit propagation of the erroneous messages. The bounded time warp (BTW) proposed by Turner and Xu [61] divides the simulation duration time interval into a number of equal intervals and all events within an interval is processed before the next one is started. Reiher and Jefferson [55] propose a window-based throttling scheme, where LPs are prevented from executing events in the far future. The local time warp (LTW) proposed by Rajaei [52] partitions the system into a set of clusters each containing a number of LPs. The LPs within each cluster are synchronized by Time Warp, whereas the inter-cluster synchronization is based on the conservative time window scheme described in [9].

(iii) Switching between Optismism and Conservatism. Some researchers, e.g. [5], suggest to switch between the conservative and the optimistic schemes. This approach is attractive, especially when the behavior of the application changes dynamically.

7. Conclusions

The state of the art in PDES has advanced very rapidly in the recent years and much more is known about the potentials of the parallel simulation schemes. In particular, the extensive performance studies conducted by several researchers have identified strengths and weaknesses of the parallel simulation schemes. In this paper, we attempted to provide an insight into various strategies for executing discrete event simulation programs on parallel computers and highlight future research directions in this field. The implementation of the event-list and its impact on performance, though important, was not covered in this tutorial. Interested readers are referred to [57], [58], [32] and other articles given in the reference list.

Conservative methods offer good potentials for certain classes of problems where application specific knowledges can be applied to exploit look ahead. Optimistic methods have had a significant success on a wide range of applications, however, reducing the state saving costs is still a research problem. The issue of combining the two approaches has received considerable attention in the recent years. It is believed that the future PDES paradigm will be based on hybrid approaches.

Acknowledgments

I would like to thank Hassan Rajaei and Eric Lin for reading a draft of the tutorial and suggesting improvements. Our research project on parallel simulation (PARSIM) supported by the Swedish National Board for Industrial and Technical Development, NUTEK (contract no. 90-01773), was the driving force behind this study. I would like to thank NUTEK for the support we received during the past five years.

References

[1] M. Abrams. The object library for parallel simulation (olps). In *1988 Winter Simulation Conference Proceedings*, pages 210–219, December 1988.

[2] H. Ahmed, L. Barriga, and R. Ayani. Parallel discrete event simulation using space-time events. *Submitted for publication.*

[3] I. F. Akyildiz, L. Chen, S. Das, R. M. Fujimoto, and R. F. Serfozo. Performance analysis of "time warp" with limited memory. Technical Report

TR-GIT-91-46, College of Computing, Georgia Institute of Technology, Atlanta, GA, October 1991.

[4] I. F. Akyildiz, L. Chen, S. R. Das, R. M. Fujimoto, and R. Serfozo. Performance analysis of time warp with limited memory. In *Proceedings of the 1992 ACM SIGMETRICS Conference on Measuring and Modeling Computer Systems*, volume 20, pages 213–224, May 1992.

[5] K. Arvind and C. Smart. Hierarchical parallel discrete event simulation in composite elsa. In 6th *Workshop on Parallel and Distributed Simulation*, volume 24, pages 147–158. SCS Simulation Series, January 1992.

[6] R. Ayani. A parallel simulation scheme based on the distance between objects. In *Proceedings of the SCS Multiconference on Distributed Simulation*, volume 21, pages 113–118. SCS Simulation Series, March 1989.

[7] R. Ayani and B. Berkman. Parallel discrete event simulation on simd computers. *To appear in Journal of Parallel and Distributed Computing*, 18, 1993.

[8] R. Ayani and H. Rajaei. Event scheduling in window based parallel simulation schemes. In *Proceedings of the Fourth IEEE Symposium on Parallel and Distributed Computing*, Dec 1992.

[9] R. Ayani and H. Rajaei. Parallel simulation based on conservative time windows: A performance study. *To appear in Journal of Concurrency*, 1993.

[10] D. Baezner, G. Lomow, and B. Unger. Sim++: The transition to distributed simulation. In *Distributed Simulation*, volume 22, pages 211–218. SCS Simulation Series, January 1990.

[11] R. Bagrodia and W.-T. Liao. Maisie:A language and optimizing environment for distributed simulation. In *Distributed Simulation*, volume 22, pages 205–210. SCS Simulation Series, January 1990.

[12] B. Berkman and R. Ayani. Parallel simulation of multistage interconnection networks on a SIMD computer. In *Advances in Parallel and Distributed Simulation*, volume 23, pages 133–140. SCS Simulation Series, January 1991.

[13] A. Boukerche and C. Tropper. A performance analysis of distributed simulation with clustered processes. In *Advances in Parallel and Distributed Simulation*, volume 23, pages 112–124. SCS Simulation Series, January 1991.

[14] K. M. Chandy and J. Misra. Distributed simulation: A case study in design and verification of distributed programs. *IEEE Transactions on Software Engineering*, SE-5(5):440–452, Sept. 1979.

[15] K. M. Chandy and J. Misra. Asynchronous distributed simulation via a sequence of parallel computations. *Communications of the ACM*, 24(4):198–205, April 1981.

[16] K. M. Chandy and R. Sherman. Space, time, and simulation. In *Proceedings of the SCS Multiconference on Distributed Simulation*, volume 21, pages 53–57. SCS Simulation Series, March 1989.

[17] M. Chung and Y. Chung. An experimental analysis of simulation clock advancement in parallel logic simulation on an SIMD machine. In *Advances in Parallel and Distributed Simulation*, volume 23, pages 125–132. SCS Simulation Series, January 1991.

[18] B. Cota and R. Sargent. A framework for automatic lookahead computation in conservative distributed simulations. In *Distributed Simulation*, volume 22, pages 56–59. SCS Simulation Series, January 1990.

[19] R. W. Earnshaw and A. Hind. A parallel simulator for performance modelling of broadband telecommunication networks. In *1992 Winter Simulation Conference Proceedings*, pages 1365–1373, December 1992.

[20] R. Felderman and L. Kleinrock. Two processor Time Warp analysis: Some results on a unifying approach. In *Advances in Parallel and Distributed Simulation*, volume 23, pages 3–10. SCS Simulation Series, January 1991.

[21] R. Fujimoto. Performance of Time Warp under synthethic workloads. In *Distributed Simulation*, volume 22, pages 23–28. SCS Simulation Series, January 1990.

[22] R. M. Fujimoto. Performance measurements of distributed simulation strategies. *Transactions of the Society for Computer Simulation*, 6(2):89–132, April 1989.

[23] R. M. Fujimoto. Time Warp on a shared memory multiprocessor. *Transactions of the Society for Computer Simulation*, 6(3):211–239, July 1989.

[24] R. M. Fujimoto. Parallel discrete event simulation. *Communications of the ACM*, 33(10):30–53, October 1990.

[25] P. Goli, P. Heidelberger, D. Towsley, and Q. Yu. Processor assignment and synchronization in parallel simulation of multistage interconnection networks. In *Distributed Simulation*, volume 22, pages 181–187. SCS Simulation Series, January 1990.

[26] A. Gupta, I. F. Akyildiz, and R. M. Fujimoto. Performance analysis of Time Warp with multiple homogenous processors. *IEEE Transactions on Software Engineering*, 17(10):1013–1027, October 1991.

[27] P. Heidelberger and D. M. Nicol. Simultaneous parallel simulations of continuous time markov chains at multiple parameter settings. In *Proceedings of the 1991 Winter Simulation Conference*, pages 602–607, 1991.

[28] P. Heidelberger and H. S. Stone. Parallel trace–driven cache simulation by time partitioning. In *Proceedings of the 1990 Winter Simulation Conference*, pages 734–737, 1990.

[29] D. R. Jefferson. Virtual time. *ACM Transactions on Programming Languages and Systems*, 7(3):404–425, July 1985.

[30] D. R. Jefferson, B. Beckman, F. Wieland, L. Blume, M. DiLorento, P. Hontalas, P. Reiher, K. Sturdevant, J. Tupman, J. Wedel, and H. Younger. The Time Warp Operating System. *11th Symposium on Operating Systems Principles*, 21(5):77–93, November 1987.

[31] D. R. Jefferson and H. Sowizral. Fast concurrent simulation using the Time Warp mechanism, part I: Local control. Technical Report N-1906-AF, RAND Corporation, December 1982.

[32] D. W. Jones. An empirical comparison of priority-queue and event-set implementations. *Communications of the ACM*, 29(4):300–311, Apr. 1986.

[33] Y.-B. Lin and E. D. Lazowska. Exploiting lookahead in parallel simulation. *IEEE Transactions on Parallel and Distributed Systems*, 1(4):457–469, October 1990.

[34] Y.-B. Lin and E. D. Lazowska. Optimality considerations of "Time Warp" parallel simulation. In *Proceedings of the SCS Multiconference on Distributed Simulation*, volume 22, pages 29–34. SCS Simulation Series, January 1990.

[35] Y.-B. Lin and E. D. Lazowska. A study of Time Warp rollback mechanisms. *ACM Transactions on Modeling and Computer Simulation*, 1(1):51–72, January 1991.

[36] W. M. Loucks and B. R. Preiss. The role of knowledge in distributed simulation. In *Proceedings of the SCS Multiconference on Distributed Simulation*, volume 22, pages 9–16. SCS Simulation Series, January 1990.

[37] B. D. Lubachevsky. Bounded lag distributed discrete event simulation. In *Proceedings of the SCS Multiconference on Distributed Simulation*, volume 19, pages 183–191. SCS Simulation Series, July 1988.

[38] B. D. Lubachevsky. Efficient distributed event-driven simulations of multiple-loop networks. *Communications of the ACM*, 32(1):111–123, Jan. 1989.

[39] B. D. Lubachevsky, A. Shwartz, and A. Weiss. Rollback sometimes works ... if filtered. In *1989 Winter Simulation Conference Proceedings*, pages 630–639, December 1989.

[40] V. Madisetti, D. Hardaker, and R. Fujimoto. The mimdix operating system for parallel simulation. In 6th *Workshop on Parallel and Distributed Simulation*, volume 24, pages 65–74. SCS Simulation Series, January 1992.

[41] V. Madisetti, J. Walrand, and D. Messerschmitt. Wolf: A rollback algorithm for optimistic distributed simulation systems. In *1988 Winter Simulation Conference Proceedings*, pages 296–305, December 1988.

[42] H. Mehl. Speedup of conservative distributed discrete-event simulation methods by speculative computing. In *Advances in Parallel and Distributed Simulation*, volume 23, pages 163–166. SCS Simulation Series, January 1991.

[43] J. Misra. Distributed-discrete event simulation. *ACM Computing Surveys*, 18(1):39–65, March 1986.

[44] D. Mitra and I. Mitrani. Analysis and optimum performance of two message passing parallel processors synchronized by rollback. In *Performance '84*, pages 35–50, Elsevier Science Pub., (North Holland), 1984.

[45] D. Nicol, A. Greenberg, B. Lubachevsky, and S. Roy. Massively parallel algorithms for trace-driven cache simulation. In 6th *Workshop on Parallel and Distributed Simulation*, volume 24, pages 3–11. SCS Simulation Series, January 1992.

[46] D. M. Nicol. Parallel discrete-event simulation of FCFS stochastic queueing networks. *SIGPLAN Notices*, 23(9):124–137, September 1988.

[47] D. M. Nicol. Performance bounds on parallel self-initiating discrete-event simulations. *ACM Transactions on Modeling and Computer Simulation*, 1(1):24–50, January 1991.

[48] J. K. Peacock, J. W. Wong, and E. G. Manning. Distributed simulation using a network of processors. *Computer Networks*, 3(1):44–56, February 1979.

[49] B. R. Preiss. The Yaddes distributed discrete event simulation specification language and execution environments. In *Proceedings of the SCS Multiconference on Distributed Simulation*, volume 21, pages 139–144. SCS Simulation Series, March 1989.

[50] H. Rajaei and R. Ayani. Language support for parallel simulation. In 6th *Workshop on Parallel and Distributed Simulation*, volume 24, pages 191–192. SCS Simulation Series, January 1992.

[51] H. Rajaei and R. Ayani. Design issues in parallel simulation languages. *To appear in IEEE Design and Test of Computers*, Sep 1993.

[52] H. Rajaei, R. Ayani, and L.-E. Thorelli. The local time warp approach to parallel simulation. In 7th *Workshop on Parallel and Distributed Simulation*, January 1993.

[53] D. A. Reed, A. D. Malony, and B. D. McCredie. Parallel discrete event simulation using shared memory. *IEEE Transactions on Software Engineering*, 14(4):541–553, April 1988.

[54] P. L. Reiher and D. Jefferson. Dynamic load management in the Time Warp Operating System. *Transactions of the Society for Computer Simulation*, 7(2):91–120, June 1990.

[55] P. L. Reiher, F. Wieland, and D. R. Jefferson. Limitation of optimism in the Time Warp Operating System. In *1989 Winter Simulation Conference Proceedings*, pages 765–770, December 1989.

[56] R. Righter and J. C. Walrand. Distributed simulation of discrete event systems. *Proceedings of the IEEE*, 77(1):99–113, Jan. 1989.

[57] R. Ronngren, R. Ayani, R. Fujimoto, and S. Das. Efficient implementation of event sets in time warp. In *Workshop on Parallel and Distributed Simulation (PADS)*, volume 23, pages 101–108. SCS Simulation Series, May 1993.

[58] R. Ronngren, J. Riboe, and R. Ayani. Fast implementation of the pending event set. In *International Workshop on Modeling, Analysis and Simulation of Computer and Telecommunication Systems*. SCS Simulation Series, Jan 1993.

[59] L. Sokol and B. Stucky. MTW:experimental results for a constrained optimistic scheduling paradigm. In *Distributed Simulation*, volume 22, pages 169–173. SCS Simulation Series, January 1990.

[60] J. Steinman. Speedes:an approach to parallel simulation. In *6th Workshop on Parallel and Distributed Simulation*, volume 24, pages 75–84. SCS Simulation Series, January 1992.

[61] S. Turner and M. Xu. Performance evaluation of the bounded Time Warp algorithm. In *6th Workshop on Parallel and Distributed Simulation*, volume 24, pages 117–128. SCS Simulation Series, January 1992.

[62] D. B. Wagner and E. D. Lazowska. Parallel simulation of queueing networks: Limitations and potentials. In *Proceedings of 1989 ACM SIGMETRICS and PERFORMANCE '89*, volume 17, pages 146–155, May 1989.

[63] D. B. Wagner, E. D. Lazowska, and B. N. Bershad. Techniques for efficient shared-memory parallel simulation. In *Proceedings of the SCS Multiconference on Distributed Simulation*, volume 21, pages 29–37. SCS Simulation Series, March 1989.

Properties and analysis of queueing network models with finite capacities

S.Balsamo
Dipartimento di Informatica
University of Pisa, Italy

Abstract

Queueing network models with finite capacity queues and blocking are used to represent systems with finite capacity resources and with resource constraints, such as production, communication and computer systems. Various blocking mechanisms have been defined in literature to represent the various behaviours of real systems with limited resources. Queueing networks with finite capacity queues and blocking, their properties and the exact and approximate analytical solution methods for their analysis are surveyed.

The class of product-form networks with finite capacities is described, including both homogeneous and non-homogeneous models, i.e., models of systems in which different resources work under either the same or different blocking mechanisms. Non-homogeneous network models can be used to represent complex systems, such as integrated computer-communication systems.

Exact solution algorithms to evaluate the passage time distribution of queueing networks with finite capacity are discussed, as well as some recent results on the arrival time queue length distribution and its relation to the random time queue length distribution. This result provides an extension of the arrival theorem to a class of product-form networks with finite capacity.

Properties of queueing network models with blocking are presented. These include insensitivity properties and equivalencies between models with and without blocking, between models with both homogeneous and non-homogeneous blocking types, and relationships between open and closed queueing network models with blocking.

Although properties of queueing networks with blocking have been mainly derived for the queue length distribution and average performance indices, we shall also present some equivalence properties in terms of passage time distribution in closed models.

1 Introduction

Queueing network models have been extensively applied to represent and analyze resource sharing systems, such as production, communication and computer systems. Queueing networks with finite capacity queues and blocking are used to represent systems with finite capacity resources and with resource constraints. Various blocking mechanisms have been defined in the literature to represent the various behaviours of real systems with limited resources.

We consider queueing network models with finite capacity queues and blocking, their properties, and analytical solution methods for their analysis.

The performance of systems with limited resources can be evaluated by considering both average performance indices, such as system throughput and resource utilization, and more detailed measures, such as queue length distribution and passage time distribution.

Most of the solutions proposed in literature concern exact or approximate evaluation

---

This work was partially supported by MURST and CNR Project Research Funds, by grant N. 92.00009.CT12.

of average performance indices and of the joint queue length distribution of the system in stationary conditions. Under special constraints, a product-form solution of the joint queue length distribution can be derived.

Identifying a class of product-form queueing networks with finite capacity queues is an important issue which allows efficient solution algorithms to be defined.

This paper introduces the class of product-form networks with finite capacities is introduced and the main key properties that lead to the closed form solution are discussed. This class of models has recently been extended to include both homogeneous and non-homogeneous models, i.e., models of systems in which several resources work under either the same or different blocking mechanisms. Non-homogeneous network models can be used to represent complex systems, such as integrated computer-communication systems.

A few results have been obtained for the evaluation of more detailed performance measures, such as passage time distribution and arrival queue length distribution. We survey algorithms to evaluate the passage time distribution exactly in closed network models with blocking. Some recent related results on the arrival time queue length distribution in queueing networks with finite capacity and its relationship with the random time queue length distribution are presented. This result provides an extension of the arrival theorem for a class of product-form queueing networks with finite capacity.

We briefly discuss the main approaches to approximate solution methods to evaluate performance indices of non product-form networks with finite capacity. These methods are based on the decomposition principle which is applied either to the network or to underlying Markov process. Approximate solutions with knowledge of the introduced error and bounded methods are discussed.

Finally, properties of queueing network models with blocking are presented, including insensitivity properties and equivalences between models with and without blocking, between models with both homogeneous and non-homogeneous blocking types, and relationships between open and closed queueing network models with blocking.

By using these equivalence relationships, it is possible both to extend product-form solution and solution methods defined for a given model to the corresponding one and to extend or to relate insensitivity properties for queueing networks with different blocking mechanisms.

Although properties of queueing networks with blocking have been mainly derived for the stationary joint queue length distribution and for average performance indices, we shall also present some equivalence properties in terms of passage time distribution in closed models.

This paper is organized as follows. Section 1 introduces the model and blocking type definition. In Section 2 analytical solution methods are surveyed. Exact analytical solutions are presented both for Markovian non product-form networks and for product-form networks with finite capacity in terms of different performance indices. Moreover we present an extension of the arrival theorem to this class of models. Section 3 deals with insensitivity and equivalence properties of networks with finite capacity and blocking, including equivalencies between networks with and without blocking, and between models with different blocking types. Finally, Section 4 presents the conclusions and open issues.

1.1 Queueing networks with finite capacity queues

We consider open and closed queueing networks with finite capacity queues. For the sake of simplicity we introduce model assumptions and notations for the single class network. Multiclass queueing networks with finite capacities and their relationship with single class networks under different blocking types is discussed in [23].

Consider a queueing network formed by M finite capacity service centers (or nodes). The queueing network can be either open or closed. For a closed network, N denotes the number of customers in the network. For open networks an exogenous arrival process is defined at each node i, $1 \leq i \leq M$. The arrival rate can be either load independent or load dependent, denoted as λ and λ a(n), $n \geq 0$, respectively, where a(n) is an arbitrary non negative function of the total number of customers in the entire network. The arrival process is usually assumed to be Poisson.
An exogenous arrival tries to enter node i with probability p_{0i}, $1 \leq i \leq M$. In other words, the Poisson arrival process at node i has a parameter λ p_{0i} for load independent arrivals, and λ a(n) p_{0i} for load dependent arrivals.
The customers' behaviour between service centers of the network is described by the routing matrix $P = \|p_{ij}\|$, $1 \leq i,j \leq M$, where p_{ij} denotes the probability that a job leaving node i tries to enter node j. For open networks p_{i0}, $1 \leq i \leq M$ denotes the probability that a job which exits node i leaves the network. By definition, the following relation holds, for $1 \leq i \leq M$:

$$\sum_{j=1}^{M} p_{ij} + p_{i0} = 1$$

Let us introduce vector $x = (x_1, ..., x_M)$ which can be obtained by solving the following linear system:

$$x_i = \lambda p_{0i} + \sum_{j=1}^{M} x_i p_{ji} \tag{1}$$

For closed networks, by definition, $p_{0i} = p_{i0} = 0$ for $1 \leq i \leq M$, and system (1) does not provide a unique solution.
For queueing networks with infinite capacity queues, component x_i of the solution vector represents the throughput of node i for open networks, whereas it represents the relative throughput or mean number of visits of customers at node i for closed networks, $1 \leq i \leq M$ [16, 41, 47].
For queueing networks with finite capacity this meaning is not generally true.
Network routing matrix P is said to be reversible if $x_i p_{ij} = x_j p_{ji}$, and $\lambda p_{0i} = x_i p_{i0}$ for $1 \leq i,j \leq M$ [39].
Service center i, $1 \leq i \leq M$, is described by the number of servers, the service time distribution and the service discipline. Let S_i denote the state of node i, which includes the number of jobs in node i, denoted by n_i, and other components depending on both the node type (service discipline and service time distribution) and the blocking type.
The service time distribution of jobs at node i is denoted by $F_i(t)$, $t \geq 0$, $1 \leq i \leq M$, and its mean value by $1/\mu_i$ if it is load independent. The node i job service rate can be defined as dependent on the number of customers in node i, $n_i \geq 0$, and is denoted by $\mu_i f_i(n_i)$, where f_i is an arbitrary non-negative function, $1 \leq i \leq M$.
We consider a Markovian network, i.e., we assume that the queueing network model with finite capacity can be represented by a Markov process.
This is a common assumption in the performance analysis of computer and communication systems. From the modelling viewpoint, the queueing network model introduced above can be represented by a continuous time Markov process if service time distributions and inter-arrival time distribution in open networks have a

phase-type or coxian representation [41, 47]. This allows us to consider a large class of distributions and to represent, possibly by approximation, arbitrary distributions.

In queueing networks with finite capacity queues and blocking, additional constraints on the number of customers are included to represent different types of resource constraints in real systems, which correspond to definitions of different parameters. We consider two types of constraints, related to the capacity of a single resource and to a set of resources, respectively.

In the first case, let B_i denote the maximum number of customers admitted at node i (i.e., the maximum buffer size), $1 \leq i \leq M$. The total number of jobs in node i, n_i, is thus assumed to satisfy the constraint $n_i \leq B_i$, $1 \leq i \leq M$. When the number of customers in a node reaches the finite capacity ($n_i = B_i$) the node is said to be full. Note that in multichain and multiclass networks one can also define a chain or a class dependent maximum queue length at node i.

In the second case, let B_W denote the maximum population admitted in a subnetwork W of the whole network. In certain cases, in order to represent particular system behaviours, a minimum population value L_W for subnetwork W it is also introduced. In other words, the total population in subnetwork W, $n_W = \Sigma_{i \in W} n_i$, is assumed to satisfy constraints $L_W \leq n_W \leq B_W$.

Finally, let $b_i(n_i)$ denote the blocking function, i.e., the probability that a job arriving at node i, is accepted when n_i is the state of the node, $1 \leq i \leq M$. For multiclass queueing networks the blocking function may also depend on the total number of jobs in the node and in the class or in the chain.

An example of a simple blocking function for single class queueing networks which allows us to define the maximum queue length B_i for each node i, $1 \leq i \leq M$, is defined as follows [36] :

$$b_i(n_i) = 1 \qquad \text{for } 0 \leq n_i < B_i, \qquad b_i(B_i) = 0 \qquad 1 \leq i \leq M$$

More generally, one can define

$$0 < b_i(n_i) \leq 1 \qquad \text{for } 0 \leq n_i < B_i, \qquad b_i(B_i) = 0 \qquad 1 \leq i \leq M \qquad (2)$$

as an arbitrary non-negative load-dependent function which can be used to represent a flow control mechanism of node i input traffic.

1.2 Definition of blocking mechanisms

Various blocking mechanisms or types that describe different behaviours of customer arrivals at a full capacity node and the servers' activity in the network have been defined in literature. We now introduce the most commonly used five blocking mechanisms.

The first three blocking types, Blocking After Service, Blocking Before Service and Repetitive Service Blocking, have been named and classified in [5,51]. They are due to the finite capacity of service centres of the network [5,51].

The last two blocking mechanisms, Stop and Recirculate Blocking, which are very common in communication systems, have been named and compared in [64, 65]. They are due to the maximum queue length constraint for either a subnetwork or the total queueing network population.

Blocking After Service (BAS): if a job attempts to enter a full capacity queue j upon completion of a service at node i, it is forced to wait in node i server, until the destination node j can be entered. The server of source node i stops processing jobs (it is blocked) until destination node j releases a job. Node i service will be resumed as soon as a departure occurs from node j. At that time the job waiting in node i immediately moves to node j.

If more than one node is blocked by the same node j, then a scheduling discipline must be considered to define the unblocking order of the blocked nodes when a departure occurs from node j. First Blocked First Unblocked is a possible discipline [7, 51] which states that the first node to be unblocked is the one which was first blocked.

This blocking mechanism, also called classical, transfer, manufacturing and production blocking [1, 5, 7, 9, 12, 14, 17, 26, 33, 35, 45, 49-57, 62], has been used to model production systems and disk I/O subsystems.

Blocking Before Service (BBS): a job declares its destination node j before it starts receiving service at node i. If at that time node j is full, the service at node i does not start and the server is blocked. If a destination node j becomes full during the service of a job at node i whose destination is j, node i service is interrupted and the server is blocked. The service of node i will be resumed as soon as a departure occurs from node j. The destination node of a blocked customer does not change.

Two different subcategories can be introduced [51] depending on whether the server can be used as a service centre buffer when the node is blocked:

BBS-SO (server occupied) when the server of the blocked node is used to hold a customer;

BBS-SNO (server is not occupied) when the server of the blocked node cannot be used to hold a customer. However note that BBS-SNO can only be defined for special topology networks, i.e., when the finite capacity node has only one possible sending node, i.e., if $n_i < B_i$, then there exists only one node j such that $p_{ji} > 0$, and $p_{ki} = 0$ for $k \neq j$, $1 \leq i,j,k \leq M$.

A variant of the BBS type has been considered [9, 29, 33, 42] when the overall set of sending nodes is blocked. This variant is defined as follows :

BBS-O (Overall Blocking Before Service): when a destination node j becomes full, it blocks the service in each of its possible sending nodes i, regardless of the destination of the currently processed job. Note that a job which arrives at an empty node i cannot begin the service if one of the downstream nodes of i is full. Services will be resumed as soon as a departure occurs from node j. The destination node of a blocked customer does not change.

This blocking mechanism, also called service or immediate blocking [7, 9-11, 13-15, 17, 19, 28, 30-34, 50-56] has been used to model production, telecommunication, and computer systems.

Repetitive Service Blocking (RS): a job upon completion of its service at queue i attempts to enter destination queue j. If node j is full, the job is looped back into the sending queue i, where it receives a new independent service according to the service discipline.

Two different subcategories have been introduced depending on whether the job, after receiving a new service, chooses a new destination node independently of the one that it had selected previously:

RS-RD (random destination) if a job destination is randomly chosen at the end of each new service, whatever the previous choices;

RS-FD (fixed destination) if a job destination is determined after the first service and cannot be modified.
This blocking type, also called rejection, retransmission or repeat protocol [2-4, 8-10, 19, 27, 32, 36, 37, 40, 43, 50-56, 59, 64, 66, 68, 69] has been used to model telecommunication systems.

For the following two blocking types the population either of a subnetwork or of the total network is assumed to be in the range [L,U], where L and U are the minimum and maximum populations admitted, respectively. This constraint can be represented by an appropriate definition of both the load dependent arrival rate functions a(n) and of a (network) blocking function d(n), where $n \geq 0$ is the total network population. For multichain networks, arrival and blocking functions can also be defined for each chain, dependent on the total network population in the chain.

STOP Blocking: the service rate of each node is delayed by a factor $d(n) \geq 1$, when there is a network population $n \geq 0$. In other words, the actual job service rate of each node depends on the state n of the entire network according to function d(n). When d(n) = 0 then the service at each node in the network is stopped. Services will be resumed at each node as soon as an exogenous arrival occurs.
This blocking mechanism, also called delay blocking [64, 65, 67] has been used to model communication systems.

RECIRCULATE Blocking: a job upon completion of its service at queue i actually leaves the network with probability $p_{i0} d(n)$, when n is the total network population, whereas it is forced to stay in the network with probability $p_{i0} [1-d(n)]$, according to routing probabilities. Consequently, a job completing the service at node i actually enters node j with state dependent routing probability $p_{ij} + p_{i0} [1-d(n)] p_{0j}$, $1 \leq i,j \leq M$, $n \geq 0$.
This blocking type, also called triggering protocol [38, 46, 64, 65] has been used to model communication systems.

Closed queueing networks with finite capacity queues and blocking can deadlock, depending on the blocking type definition. If a deadlock occurs then either prevention techniques or detection and resolving techniques must be applied. Deadlock prevention for blocking types BAS, BBS and RS-FD is based on the condition that the overall network population N is less than the total buffer capacity of the nodes in each possible cycle in the network, whereas for RS-RD blocking it is sufficient that routing matrix P is irreducible and N less than the total buffer capacity of the nodes in the network. Deadlock in queueing networks with blocking has been discussed in [45, 51]. Moreover, note that in order to avoid deadlocks for BAS and BBS blocking types we assume $p_{ii}=0$, $1 \leq i \leq M$.

Below we shall consider deadlock-free queueing networks in steady-state conditions.

1.3 Performance indices

The analysis and properties of queueing network models with finite capacity queues refer to a set of figures of merit of the system performance. These indices can be related to a single resource, corresponding to a service center of the queueing network, or to the overall system.

Specifically, for each resource i, $1 \leq i \leq M$, we consider the following average performance indices:

U_i utilization
X_i throughput
L_i mean queue length
T_i mean response time

and the following random variables whose distribution can be evaluated:

n_i number of customers in the resource
t_i customer passage time through the resource.

Random variable n_i is considered both at arbitrary times and at arrival times of a customer at the resource. The latter distribution is usually required in the evaluation of job residence time and passage time distributions in queueing networks.

Let $\pi_i(n_i)$ denote the stationary (marginal) queue length distribution of resource i, i.e., the stationary probability of n_i customers in node i at arbitrary time, $n_i \geq 0$, $1 \leq i \leq M$.
Let $\xi_i(n_i)$ denote the stationary queue length distribution of resource i at arrival times of a customer at that node, $n_i \geq 0$, $1 \leq i \leq M$.
Let $PB_i(n_i)$ denote the blocking probability of resource i, i.e., the probability that resource i is not empty and blocked by a full destination node, when there are n_i customers in node i. Let $PB_i = \sum_{n_i} PB_i(n_i)$ denote the overall blocking probability of node i, $1 \leq i \leq M$. The definition of these probabilities depends on the blocking type, as discussed in [9].

For open queueing networks with finite capacity another performance index of interest is the job loss probability, which can be computed by the stationary queue length distribution at arrival times.

Resource utilization and throughput in queueing networks with finite capacity depend on the blocking probability. For single server nodes this can be defined as follows:

$$U_i = 1 - \pi_i(0) - PB_i$$
$$X_i = \sum_{n_i} [\pi_i(n_i) - PB_i(n_i)] \mu_i(n_i)$$

which for constant service rate, i.e., when $\mu_i(n_i) = \mu_i$ for $n_i > 0$, reduces to

$$X_i = U_i \mu_i .$$

Mean queue length and mean response time for resource i can be computed as for queueing network models with infinite capacity queues as follows:

$$L_i = \sum_{n_i} n_i \pi_i(n_i)$$
$$T_i = L_i / X_i .$$

Performance indices of queueing networks with finite capacity can be evaluated through the analytical solution methods discussed in the next section. Insensitivity and equivalence properties of these models are expressed in terms of the performance measures and are presented in Section 3.

2 Analytical solution methods

In this section we overview analytical methods to analyze queueing network models with finite capacity queues and blocking.

Solutions have been proposed to evaluate both average performance indices and probability distribution of the number of customers in the nodes and of the passage time.

Exact solutions for the evaluation of average performance indices and of the stationary joint queue length probability distribution at arbitrary times of queueing networks with blocking have been derived in literature for different blocking mechanisms [1-4, 23, 27, 33, 36-39, 46, 50, 51, 59, 65, 66, 68-68].

Product-form solutions of the joint stationary queue length distribution have been obtained, under special constraints, for different blocking mechanisms. A survey of product-form solutions of queueing networks with blocking and equivalence properties among different blocking network models is presented in [10].

The exact evaluation of the arrival time queue length distribution in closed networks with different blocking types has been derived [11, 14] and a few results have been obtained for the passage time distribution for closed cyclic networks [11, 13].

In Section 2.1 we overview analytical solutions of Markovian networks with finite capacity in terms of average performance indices and stationary joint queue length distribution both at arbitrary and arrival times. Section 2.2 deals with product-form networks with blocking.

As regards the joint queue length distribution at arrival times, we discuss the conditions under which it can be related to the state distribution at arbitrary times for a class of non product-form networks with blocking. For the special case of product-form closed networks this result provides an extension of the arrival theorem for queueing networks with infinite capacity queues to networks with finite capacity queues and blocking.

Algorithms to evaluate the passage time distribution exactly in queueing networks with blocking are considered.

Several approximate solutions have been proposed for queueing networks with blocking, mostly to derive mean performance measures. A survey of exact and approximate methods for closed queueing networks with blocking is presented in [51]. Open queueing networks with blocking and a bibliography on networks with finite capacity queues are presented in [55, 56].

Since most of the approximation methods proposed in literature are based on the decomposition principle, in Section 2.3 we discuss the main approaches related to the decomposition applied either to the network model or to the underlying Markov process. The problem of the knowledge of the approximation error is discussed and bounded solution methods to evaluate queueing networks with blocking are considered.

2.1 Exact analysis of Markovian networks

The exact analysis of queueing networks with finite capacity and blocking concerns the evaluation of

1) mean performance indices and joint queue length distribution at arbitrary times;
2) stationary joint queue length distribution at arrival times;
3) passage time distribution.

In this section we deal with analytical solutions of Markovian networks which generally do not have a product-form solution. Product-form networks with finite capacity are considered in Section 2.2.

1) Mean performance indices and joint queue length distribution at arbitrary times

In order to evaluate the stationary joint queue length distribution at arbitrary times and the average performance indices, the queueing network behaviour can be represented by a homogeneous continuous time Markov process M with discrete state space E.

The state of a queueing network with finite capacity can be defined as an M-vector $S=(S_1,...,S_M)$, where S_i is the state of node i which includes the number of customers in the node, n_i, $1 \leq i \leq M$. The state space E of the network is the set of all feasible states. Queueing network evolution can be represented by a continuous time ergodic Markov chain M with discrete state space E and transition rate matrix Q. The stationary and transient behaviour of the network can be analyzed by the underlying Markov process.

Under the hypothesis of an irreducible routing matrix P, there exists a unique steady-state queue length probability distribution $\pi = \{\pi(S), S \in E\}$, which can be obtained by solving the following homogeneous linear system of the global balance equations [41]:

$$\pi Q = 0 \qquad (3)$$

subject to the normalising condition $\sum_{S \in E} \pi(S) = 1$ and where 0 is the all zero vector.

The definition of state space E and transition rate matrix Q depends on the network characteristics and on the blocking type of each node.

For example, for an open exponential network with Poisson load independent arrivals, where each node i has finite capacity B_i and works under the RS-RD blocking type, the state of node i can be simply defined as $S_i = n_i$, $1 \leq i \leq M$, the state space is given by

$$E = \{(n_1, n_2, ..., n_M) \mid 0 \leq n_i \leq B_i, 1 \leq i \leq M\}$$

and the transition rate matrix is defined as follows:
$Q = \|q(S,S')\|$, for $S, S' \in E$ and

$$q(S,S') = \delta(n_j) \, \mu_j \, b_i(n_i) \, p_{ji} \qquad \text{if } S' = S + e_i - e_j$$
$$q(S,S') = \delta(n_j) \, \mu_j \, p_{j0} \qquad \text{if } S' = S - e_j$$
$$q(S,S') = \lambda \, p_{0j} \, b_j(n_j) \qquad \text{if } S' = S + e_j$$
$$q(S,S) = - \sum_{S' \in E, \, S' \neq S} q(S,S')$$

where blocking functions $b_i(n_i)$ are given by formula (2), $\delta(n_i)$ is the following function: $\delta(n_i)=0$ if $n_i=0$, $\delta(n_i)=1$ otherwise, $1 \leq i \leq M$, and e_i denotes the M-vector with all zero components except one in i-th position.

Note that system state S definition depends on the network characteristics and on the blocking type. Hence the state of node i definition may be more complex than the example above, including information such as the state of the server (whether it is active or blocked) and, for the BAS blocking type, the description of the set of nodes that are blocked by the finite capacity resource and the unblocking scheduling. A detailed definition of the system state for each blocking type is given in the Appendix.

An exact solution algorithm of queueing networks with finite capacity and blocking based on the Markov process approach can be summarised as follows:

1) Definition of the appropriate system state depending on the network characteristics (i.e., service time distributions, arrival distribution, service disciplines, network dimensions), and on the blocking type.
   Definition of the system state space E.

2) Definition of the transition rate matrix Q which describes the queueing network evolution, according to the blocking type of each node.

3) Solution of linear system (3) to derive the stationary state distribution π at arbitrary times.

4) Computation from the solution vector π of the joint and marginal queue length distributions and of the average performance indices, such as throughput, utilization and mean response time, for each resource i of the network, $1 \leq i \leq M$.

Note that state space E is finite for closed and open networks where all the nodes have finite capacity. For open networks which include at least one infinite capacity queue state space, E is infinite and the solution of the linear system (3) has to be approximated numerically.

Although the joint queue length distribution of the queueing network with finite capacity can be obtained by solving linear system (3) and the average performance measures can be derived from π, this approach becomes unfeasible as the state space E dimension grows, proportionally to the dimension of the model, i.e., the number of customers, nodes and chains.

Consequently for non product-form networks, approximation methods have to be considered.

Nevertheless, under certain constraints, which depend both on the network definition and the blocking mechanism, π has a product-form solution, as discussed in Section 2.2. Hence, steps 2 and 3 of the algorithm above can be substituted by the direct evaluation of the closed form solution for which computationally efficient exact solution algorithms can be defined.

Remark. A special case in which the computation step 3 can be drastically reduced concerns the so-called symmetrical networks. This class of networks was introduced in [29] and is defined as having the same blocking type, service rate and buffer capacity for each node. The routing probabilities out of each node are the same, and routing matrix P can be rewritten so that all rows are identical up to a rotation of the entries.

For symmetrical closed exponential networks with BBS-SO, BBS-O and BAS blocking types, a reduction technique has been introduced to efficiently compute solution π and average performance indices [29, 51]. Note that the reduction algorithm is related to the exact aggregation procedure applied to the Markov process, which can be easily computed due to the special characteristics of the network.

2) Arrival time distribution

When the performance index of interest is the joint queue length distribution at input times at a given node, a different solution method has to be applied, based on a new homogeneous discrete time Markov process M^e embedded in process M. Let A denote the discrete state space of M^e and S^e the system state as seen by an arriving job at input time at node i, where the state does not include the arriving job. Informally, each state S^e of the embedded process M^e is identical, except for one less job at node i, to a corresponding state of the process M just after the customer transition to node i denoted by S^a. As in process M, also the state space definition of process M^e depends on the blocking type.

If the embedded Markov chain M^e is irreducible and recurrent then there exists the stationary state distribution ξ at arrival instants at node i. The direct evaluation of this distribution is not trivial. However, for a class of networks with finite capacity one can derive an expression of ξ in terms of the stationary state distribution at arbitrary times, π. By applying this result to some special cases of product-form networks with blocking, an extension of the arrival theorem for queueing networks with infinite capacity queues to networks with finite capacity queues and blocking can be derived, as discussed in Section 2.2.

For Markovian non-product-form networks the following relationship between stationary distributions ξ and π for the same network holds. The following theorem has been proved for closed exponential networks with a general routing topology and blocking types BAS, BBS-SO and RS-RD [14].

Theorem 1
The stationary state probability distributions ξ and π of a closed exponential network with finite capacity queues and blocking of type BAS, BBS-SO or RS-RD, are related as follows:

$$\xi(S^e) = \frac{1}{\eta} \sum_{S \in I(S^a)} \pi(S)q(S,S^a)$$

where $S^e \in A$, $S^a \in E$ is the state corresponding to S^e and, according to the blocking type:

$I(S^a)$ is the set of initial states of process M which occur just before a customer transition which leads to state S^a,

$q(S,S^a)$ is the transition rate from state S to S^a of process M and

η is a normalising constant.

The proof of the theorem and the detailed definition of set $I(S^a)$ and transition rates $q(S,S^a)$ is given in [14]. When the finite capacity node i has only one upstream or sending node, say k (i.e., $p_{ki}>0$ and $p_{ji}=0$, $j \neq k$, $1 \leq j \leq M$) then the set $I(S^a)$ is formed by a single state $S = S^a + e_k - e_i$ and, for blocking type RS and BBS-SO, this relationship can be simplified as follows [14]:

Corollary 1
If the node has only one sending node, then

$$\xi(S^e) = \frac{1}{\eta} \pi(S) \tag{4}$$

where $S^e \in A$, $I(S^a) = \{S\}$ and η is a normalising constant.

This result is an extension of a similar relationship for queueing networks with infinite capacity to networks with finite capacity queues. As a consequence, the evaluation of the steady-state probability distribution at arrival times ξ can be reduced to the evaluation of the probability distribution at arbitrary times π. This arrival time distribution can be used in the analysis of job passage time distributions in the network. Moreover the theorem can be simplified for a class of product-form networks with finite capacity, leading to an extension of the arrival theorem for queueing networks with infinite capacity queues to networks with finite capacity and certain blocking types, as discussed in Section 2.2.

3) Passage time distribution

The time spent by a customer in the entire system or in a subsystem (the passage time) is an important performance measure which provides a more detailed performance evaluation of system behaviour than the average indices. The passage time distribution in queueing networks is generally difficult to obtain even for queueing networks with infinite capacity; a survey of sojourn time results in queueing networks is presented in [18]. For queueing networks with finite capacity queues and blocking, a few results have been obtained in terms of cycle time distribution for cyclic models [11-13] and for central server model or star topology networks [15].

A recursive algorithm to derive the cycle time distribution for cyclic closed exponential queueing networks with $M \geq 2$ finite capacity nodes and BBS-SO blocking is defined in [11, 13] and for $M=2$ nodes and BAS in [12]. The method is based on the definition of a transient Markov process which describes the evolution of a specific (tagged) customer in a complete walk through the network. Sets E_0 and F of the possible initial and final states of the network are defined, corresponding to the beginning and the end of the walk of the tagged customer, respectively.

The cycle time distribution is computed by evaluating the first hitting time probability distribution of the Markov process to the final states, starting from the initial states.

Let Z denote a state of the transient Markov process and let $T(Z,s)$ denote the Laplace-Stieltjes transform (LST) of the passage time distribution from Z to the final states F.

The LST of the cycle time distribution, denoted by $T(s)$ can be computed as follows:

$$T(s) = \sum_{Z \in E_0} Prob(Z) \, T(Z,s) \tag{5}$$

where $Prob(Z)$ is the probability of state Z at the cycle starting time and $T(Z,s)$ can be computed by a recursive scheme. This recursive scheme can be reduced by taking into account the process structure and the blocking type definition, as described in [11, 13].

Since each state Z corresponds to a system state $S^e \in A$ of the embedded process M^e, as previously introduced to define the joint queue length distribution, then $Prob(Z)$ can be evaluated as the stationary distribution at arrival times, $\xi(S^e)$ and, by applying Theorem 1, as a function of the stationary distribution at arbitrary times, $\pi(S)$, $S \in E$.

From the recursive scheme to evaluate the LST of the cycle time distribution one can derive an explicit expression for the cycle time distribution in the time domain, where coefficients are defined by recursion.

For a two-node exponential network with BBS-SO or BAS blocking this approach leads to the following closed-form expression in the time domain of the density function $f(t)$ of the cycle time:

$$f(t) = \sum_{j=1}^{3} e^{-\mu_j t} \sum_{i=1}^{k_j} c_{ji} \frac{t^{i-1}}{(i-1)!}$$

where $k_1=k_2=N$, $k_3=2N-3$, $\mu_3=\mu_1+\mu_2$ and coefficients c_{ij} are recursively computed for each i and j [11].

Note that for the special case of a two-node network with blocking, the stationary distribution π has a product-form solution and consequently ξ and $Prob(Z)$ have a product-form solution. In this case an extension of the arrival theorem holds, as proved in [11, 12] and discussed in Section 2.2.

However, note that the algorithm sketched above to evaluate the passage time distribution applies to any Markovian non product-form network. For the class of product-form networks with finite capacity, the advantage consists in a more efficient computation of distribution π and consequently of $Prob(Z)$ in formula (5).

In many practical applications it is sufficient to evaluate the first few moments of the cycle time. A recursive evaluation of the cycle time moments can be derived for cyclic closed exponential networks [11, 13] and for central server model networks [15].

For a two node exponential network with BBS-SO or BAS blocking, the k-th moment of the cycle time distribution, $E(k)$, for $k=1,2,...$, is given by [11, 12]:

$$E(k) = \sum_{j=1}^{3} \sum_{i=1}^{k_j+1} \frac{c_{ji}}{\mu_j^{i+k}} \frac{(i+k-1)!}{(i-1)!}$$

The evaluation of the passage time distribution in other classes of queueing network models with finite capacity, including different types of blocking and non-exponential service time distribution is an open issue.

2.2 Product-form networks

In this section we survey the class of product-form queueing networks with finite capacity and blocking. This class is a subset of the class of Markovian networks with finite capacity considered in the previous section, and hence the same analytical techniques can be applied to solve these networks.

However, an important consequence of the identification of the class of product-form networks is the definition or extension of efficient algorithms to evaluate performance indices. Specifically, one could extend basic algorithms for the class of product-form BCMP networks with infinite capacity queues [16], such as MVA and Convolution algorithms [47] to queueing networks with finite capacity queues.

First we summarise the cases of product-form networks with finite capacity and different blocking types. The extension of the arrival theorem to some cases of this class of network is then discussed.

• *Product-form solutions of the joint queue length distribution*

Product-form solutions of the joint queue length distribution π for single class open or closed networks under certain constraints, depending both on the network definition and the blocking mechanism, can be defined as follows:

$$\pi(S) = \frac{1}{G} V(n) \prod_{i=1}^{M} g_i(n_i) \qquad (6)$$

where G is a normalising constant, and n is the total network population. The functions V and g_i, $1 \leq i \leq M$, are defined in terms of network parameters which include vector **x** defined by system (1) and service rates μ_i, $1 \leq i \leq M$, and depend on the blocking type and additional constraints.

Similarly, for multichain open, closed or mixed queueing networks with blocking, formed by M nodes and R chains, product-form solutions can be defined as follows:

$$\pi(S) = \frac{1}{G} V_r(m_r) \prod_{i=1}^{M} g_i(n_i)$$

where G is a normalising constant, m_r is the total network population in chain r, $1 \leq r \leq R$, and the functions V_r, $1 \leq r \leq R$, and g_i, $1 \leq i \leq M$, are defined in terms of network parameters.

Table I summarises product-form networks with finite capacity and different blocking types.

Both homogeneous networks, where each node works under the same blocking type, and non-homogeneous ones, where different nodes work under different blocking mechanisms, are considered for five topologies.

The first three topologies concern closed networks and are the two-node network, the cyclic topology and the central server or star topology. For the central server topology networks, node 1 denotes the central node, i.e., routing matrix P is defined as follows: $p_{ij} > 0$ for i=1, $2 \leq j \leq N$, $p_{i1} = 1$ for $2 \leq i \leq N$ and $p_{ij} = 0$ otherwise, $1 \leq i,j \leq N$.

The fourth case refers to queueing networks with reversible routing matrix P, as defined in the Section 2.1. The latter is the arbitrary topology network.

Table I shows the cases of product-form solution together with additional constraints, for each combination of blocking type and network topology, where:

- PFi denotes the corresponding product-form formula, $1 \leq i \leq 8$, defined below for i=3 and 6 and in Table II for all the other cases;
- an arrow denotes that the case is included in the more general class of arbitrary topology networks and, as far as we are aware, there are no special results which only hold for that specific topology;
- 'NO' means that, as far as we are aware, no product-form has been proved;
- 'NA' means that the blocking type is not applicable to the network topology;
- for non-homogeneous networks the allowed combination of blocking types is also given.

Some additional conditions are required in some cases:

Let $B \cdot = \sum_{i=1}^{M} B_i$ denote the total capacity of the network and let $B_{min} = min \{ B_j$, $1 \leq j \leq M \}$.

The *non-empty condition* for closed networks requires that at most one node can be empty, i.e., $N \geq B - B_{min}$.

This condition is said to be strictly verified when each node can never be empty, i.e., if the inequality strictly holds.

The *condition* which requires *at most one blocked node* is satisfied if $N = B_{min} + 1$.

In other words, if a node is full then at most one of its sending nodes is not empty and can be blocked.

Condition (A) refers to a particular model introduced in [4] of multiclass networks with parallel queues with interdependent blocking functions and service rates, and which satisfy a so-called invariant condition. See [4] for further details.

Condition (B) requires that each node i with finite capacity is the only destination node for each upstream node, i.e., it satisfies the following constraint:

if $p_{ji} > 0$ then $p_{ji} = 1$, $1 \leq j \leq M$.

To keep the presentation simple we only present formulas of product-form solutions for single class networks; the detailed expression of functions V_r, $1 \leq r \leq R$, and g_i, $1 \leq i \leq M$, in product-form solutions for multiclass networks is given in [10].

Table II shows the definitions of product-forms PFi, for i=1,2,4,5,7 and 8, in terms of conditions on the network model and expressions for functions V and g_i, $1 \leq i \leq M$, in product-form (6) for single class networks. In Table II, for product-form PF4, A-type nodes are defined as follows:

Definition. A node is said to be A-type if it has an arbitrary service time distribution and a symmetric scheduling discipline or exponential service times distributions, which are the same for each class at the same node, when the scheduling is arbitrary.

We shall now define the product-form solutions PF3 and PF6.

PF3:
Conditions:
- multiclass central server networks with the class type of a job fixed in the system,
- state-dependent routing depending on the class type,
- blocking functions dependent on node and class,
- A-type nodes.

blocking type	network topology				
	two-node	cyclic	central server	reversible routing	arbitrary
BAS	PF1	→	→	→	PF7 at most one blocked node
BBS-SNO	PF1 if $N \le B_1 + B_2 - 2$	NO	NO	NO	NO
BBS-SO	PF1	PF2 non-empty condition	PF3 if only $B_1 < \infty$	→	PF2 strictly non-empty cond. and cond. (B)
RS-RD	PF1	PF2 non-empty condition	PF3	PF4 PF6 and cond. (A)	PF2 strictly non-empty cond.
RS-FD	PF1	PF2 non-empty condition	PF3 if only $B_1 < \infty$	→	PF2 strictly non-empty cond. and cond. (B)
Stop	PF5	NO	PF5	PF5	PF8
Recirculate	NA	NA	NA	→	PF8
Non-Homogeneous	BAS BBS-SO RS-RD RS-FD	BBS-SO RS-RD RS-FD non-empty condition	BBS-SO RS-RD RS-FD node 1 with RS	RS-RD Stop	BBS-SO RS-RD, RS-FD strictly non-empty cond. and cond. (B) for BBS-SO and RS-FD
	PF1	PF2	PF3	PF5	PF2

Table I - Product-form networks with blocking.

For single class exponential networks with load dependent service rates $\mu_i(n_i) = \mu_i f_i(n_i)$ and state-dependent routing $p_{1j}(n_j) = w_j(n_j) w(N - n_1) \forall n_j$, $p_{j1} = 1$ for $2 \le j \le N$, where N is the number of customers in the network, product form (6) holds with

$$V(N) = \prod_{l=1}^{N-n_1} w(l-1) \prod_{j=2}^{M} \prod_{l=1}^{n_j} w_j(l-1), \quad g_i(n_i) = \prod_{l=1}^{n_i} \frac{1}{\mu_i} \frac{b_i(l-1)}{f_i(l)}, \forall n_i, \ 1 \le i \le M$$

PF6:
Conditions:
• multiclass networks with the class type of a job fixed in the system,

	Conditions	$V(n)$	$g_i(n_i), \forall n_i, \ 1\le i\le M$
PF1	multiclass networks BCMP type nodes class independent capacities	1	$(x_i / \mu_i)^{n_i}$
PF5	like PF4, but single class		
PF7	multiclass networks FCFS-exponential nodes class independent capacities		
PF8	multiclass open Jackson networks with class type fixed		
PF4	multiclass networks with class type fixed blocking functions dep. on node, class and chain A-type nodes load dependent service rates $\mu_i(n_i)=\mu_i f_i(n_i),$	1	$(x_i / \mu_i)^{n_i} \displaystyle\prod_{l=1}^{n_i} \dfrac{b_i(l-1)}{f_i(l)}$
PF2	single class networks exponential nodes load independent service rates with $\varepsilon =(\varepsilon_1,...,\varepsilon_M)$ $\varepsilon = \varepsilon \ \mathbf{P'}$ $\mathbf{P'}= \| p'_{ij} \|, \ p'_{ij}=\mu_j p_{ji}, \ i\neq j,$ $p'_{ii}=1-\Sigma_{j\neq i}p'_{ji} , \ 1\le i,j\le M$	1	$1 / \varepsilon_i^{n_i}$

Table II - Product-form formulas and conditions.

- interdependent blocking probability and service rates [4],
- A-type nodes.

Product-form (6) holds with

$$V(n) = 1, \ n\ge 0, \ g_i(n_i) = (x_i)^{n_i} \ h_i(\mu_i, n_i), \ n_i\ge 0, \ 1\le i\le M,$$

where $h_i(\mu_i, n_i)$ is a product-form function dependent on the state and the service rate of node i and defined according to the scheduling of the interdependent parallel queues; for a complete definition see [4].

Product-form solutions can be proved by substituting the closed-form expression into the global balance equations of the underlying Markov process (linear system (3)).
Note that product-form expression (6) generalizes the closed-form expression for BCMP networks, and in certain cases, such as PFi, i=1,5,7 and 8, it corresponds to the same solution as the one for queueing networks with infinite capacity queues computed on the truncated state space of the network with finite capacities.
This relationship provides the basis for the equivalence between product-form networks with and without blocking discussed in Section 2.3.

Observations
Identification of necessary and sufficient conditions under which a queueing network model has a product-form solution is an open issue for networks with infinite capacity queues as well.
We observe that most of the product-form solutions for queueing networks with finite capacity queues have been derived by using the following properties:
- reversibility of the underlying Markov process,
- duality.

The first approach can be applied to networks with finite capacity whose underlying Markov process is shown to be obtained by truncating the reversible Markov process of the network with infinite capacity. Hence, a product-form solution immediately follows from the theorem for truncated Markov processes of reversible Markov processes. This theorem states that the truncated process shows the same equilibrium distribution as the whole process normalised on the truncated sub-space [39].
A product-form solution of both homogeneous and non-homogeneous two-node cyclic networks can be proved by using this property for exponential single class networks [1, 36, 40, 59] and for multiclass networks with BCMP nodes under additional constraints in [24, 50, 66].
Similarly, it has been proved that closed queueing networks with a reversible routing matrix P have a reversible underlying Markov process under RS-RD or Stop blocking and different types of nodes [36, 40, 59]. This class of product-form networks with RS-RD blocking for multiclass networks has been extended [3, 50, 68, 69] to include A-type nodes and more general blocking functions which may depend both on the total population, class population and routing chain population at the node.
The central server or star topology network is a special case of product-form networks with reversible routing. However, some product-form results have only been specifically proved for central server networks [2, 27, 44, 63, 68].

Remark. Although some of these results concern networks where routing probabilities are dependent on the state of the network, they are related to queueing networks with finite capacity and blocking. In fact, by using blocking functions, the actual routing probabilities of queueing networks with finite capacity can be interpreted as state dependent probabilities, and they are obtained by combining the routing probability matrix P with blocking functions $b_i(n_i)$, $1 \leq i \leq M$. Therefore, product-form solutions for networks with state dependent routing, such as the one proved in [63], can be interpreted in the same way as for blocking networks, as discussed and extended in [44] and [68] to multiclass networks. A generalization of these results obtained by combining state dependent routing and finite capacity queues is presented in [2].

Routing reversibility [36, 37, 39, 40, 59] which leads to the Markov process reversibility is related to the job-local-balance of the underlying Markov process introduced in [37]. This balance property, which is related to local balance and station balance for queueing networks with infinite capacity [16, 20, 21, 24, 40, 46], states that the rate outside a state due to any particular job in the system is equal to the rate inside that state which is due to that particular job [37]. Job-local-balance provides the basis for deriving equivalence and insensitivity properties, as discussed in Section 3.

The second approach to derive product-form solution of queueing networks with blocking is based on duality. Product-form PF2 has been obtained by adding the capacity constraint to the Gordon-Newell closed exponential networks and by defining a dual network which has the same stationary joint queue length distribution [33].

Consider a cyclic closed network with M nodes, N customers, node capacities B_i, $1 \leq i \leq M$ and BBS-SO or RS blocking. The dual network is obtained from the original one by reversing the connections between the nodes. It is formed by M centers and (B - N) customers which correspond to the 'holes' of the original (primal) network. When a customer moves from node i in the original network, a hole moves backward to node i in the dual one. When there are n_i customers in node i the original networks, the i-th center of the dual one contains $B_i - n_i$ holes, $1 \leq i \leq M$. It can be shown that the underlying Markov process which describes the evolution of customers in the network is equivalent to the one which describes the behaviour of holes in the dual network [33]. As a consequence, when the non-empty condition is satisfied, then the total number of holes in the dual network cannot exceed the minimum capacity, i.e., $(B - N) \leq B_{min}$, and the dual network has a product-form solution like a network without blocking. Hence the product-form solution for the primal network is given by formula (6) with $V(N)=1$ and $g_i(n_i) = (1/\mu_{i-1})^{n_i}$, $1 \leq i \leq M$, (where if $i=1$ then $i-1=M$) [33], which corresponds to expression PF2. This solution can be extended to arbitrary topology networks with load independent service rates for RS-RD blocking [36]. This result has been extended to homogeneous networks with BBS-O blocking under condition (B) and to heterogeneous networks [9].

The concept of duality introduced in [33] has been applied to closed cyclic networks with phase-type service distributions and BBS-SO blocking for which the throughput of the network is shown to be symmetric with respect to its population [28].

• *Arrival theorem for product-form queueing networks with blocking*

The arrival theorem for product-form networks with infinite capacity [48, 60] provides the basic principle for the MVA computational algorithm. It states that the stationary state distribution at arrival instants of a customer at a particular node is equal to the stationary state distribution at arbitrary times of the same network, for open networks, and of the network with one less job, for closed networks. This result can also be applied for an efficient computation of the stationary state distribution at arrival times in the evaluation of passage time distribution, as discussed in Section 2.1.

Since the proof of the arrival theorem [48, 60] is based on the BCMP product-form solution [16] which does not allow blocking due to the finite capacity of the queues, the direct application of the arrival theorem to queueing networks with finite capacities does not hold. For example, the direct application of the arrival theorem to a product-form network with Stop protocol is shown to fail, as discussed in [67].

An extension of the arrival theorem has been proved for a special class of networks in which a particular type of blocking can be defined by using the 'loss' and 'trigger' functions, which allow a constraint on the overall network population of a chain in multichain queueing networks with infinite capacity queues [60] and is related to Recirculate blocking. A similar case is considered in [67].

A recent result related to product-form queueing networks with blocking is the extension of the arrival theorem to some finite capacity networks with either BBS-SO, BAS and RS-RD blocking [11, 12, 14].

In fact, from corollary 1 one can derive a relationship between the joint queue length distribution at arrival and arbitrary times of networks with different parameters for some closed exponential networks under BBS-SO, BAS and RS-RD blocking [11, 13, 14].

Consider closed networks with either a cyclic or central server topology. Let W denote the network model introduced above and let W^* denote a new network identical to W except for one less customer, and modified finite capacities denoted by B_j^*,

$1 \leq j \leq M$. Let π^* denote the steady-state probability distribution at arbitrary times of network W^*. One can prove the following theorem [11, 14].

Theorem 2
The stationary state distribution at arrival instants at node i of network W is identical to the state distribution at arbitrary times of network W^*, i.e., $\forall S^e \in A$

$$\xi(S^e) = \pi^*(S^e)$$

i) for product-form networks with RS-RD or BBS-SO blocking and
    for a cyclic topology with $M \geq 2$ nodes and
        $B_j^* = B_j - 1$, for $j = i, i-1$ and $B_j^* = B_j$ for $j \neq i, i-1$, $1 \leq j \leq M$, $1 \leq i \leq M$,
    and for a central server topology with
        $B_j^* = B_j - 1$, for $j = 1, i$ and $B_j^* = B_j$ for $j \neq 1, i$, $1 \leq j \leq M$, $2 \leq i \leq M$,
    where 1 denotes the central node;
ii) for the two-node product-form network with BAS blocking and $B_j^* = B_j - 1$, for $j = 1, 2$.

The extension of the arrival theorem to queueing network models with a more general topology and different blocking types is an open issue.

2.3 Approximate analysis

Many approximate solution methods to analyze queueing network models with finite capacity queues have been proposed in literature both for open and closed networks.
In this section we consider approximate solution techniques to solve queueing networks with finite capacity. We discuss the basic ideas and principles on which the approximations are based and the main results.

Approximate solution techniques have been proposed to evaluate the joint queue length distribution at arbitrary times and average performance indices, such as resource throughput and utilization [5, 51, 55].
Most of the approximations do not provide any bound on the introduced error and they are validated by comparing numerical results against either simulation results or exact solutions if the state space is small enough.
These approximate techniques are heuristics which are mainly based on:
    • the decomposition principle applied to the underlying Markov process,
    • the decomposition principle applied to the network,
    • the forced solution of a non-blocking (product-form) network,
    • special structural properties of a specific class of networks.

The decomposition principle applied to the Markov process consists in the identification of a partition of the state space E into K subsets E_k, $1 \leq k \leq K$, which leads to a decomposition of the rate matrix Q into K^2 submatrices. By referring to a decomposition-aggregation procedure, the solution of the entire system (3) is reduced to the solution of K subsystems of smaller dimensions, each related to a subset of E. These solutions are then combined to obtain the solution of the overall system.
This approach is based on the following relationship between the stationary state probability $\pi(S)$, the conditional probability of state S in E_k, $Prob(S \mid E_k)$, and the aggregate probability of the subset E_k, $Prob(E_k)$, $\forall S \in E_k$, $1 \leq k \leq K$:
$$\pi(S) = Prob(S \mid E_k) \, Prob(E_k)$$
Instead of the direct computation of $\pi(S)$, the decomposition technique requires the computation of $Prob(S \mid E_k)$ and $Prob(E_k)$ for each S and E_k.

Unfortunately the exact computation of the decomposition-aggregation approach for Markov processes is comparable to the cost of solving the entire model and so soon becomes computationally intractable. However, exact aggregation can be performed efficiently for some classes of Markovian models such as symmetric networks.

Approximate solutions based on the decomposition of the Markov process provide an approximate evaluation of the conditional and aggregate probabilities $Prob(S \mid E_k)$ and $Prob(E_k)$. Heuristics are defined by taking into account both the network model characteristics and the blocking type [5, 7, 17, 26, 27, 29, 31, 33, 35, 42, 43, 51, 52, 55-58, 62, 68, 69].

An important issue is the identification of an appropriate state space partition which affect both the accuracy and the time computational complexity of the approximate algorithm.

When the state space partition is related to a network partition into subnetworks, then the decomposition principle is applied to the queueing network and the subsystems can be solved in terms of solving (possibly modified) subnetworks in the original network. Various approaches have been proposed to determine the parameters of each subnetwork [26, 30, 31, 33, 43, 57, 58, 62, 68, 69].

Approximation methods are often based on the forced application of the exact aggregation technique to queueing networks with blocking for product-form queueing networks with infinite capacity [22]. This approach has a low computational cost and the accuracy observed by experimental results makes such approximate aggregation techniques suitable for many practical cases. However, the error introduced by the approximation is unknown.

Many approximation methods based on the decomposition approach require the iterative solution of subsystems or subnetworks to derive the approximate solution. Hence for such techniques, conditions and the speed of convergence should also be considered, as in [26].

Although few approximate solution techniques with known accuracy have been proposed, this is still an important issue which should be considered in the definition of approximations.

Another issue concerns bound solutions which can be used as approximate solution methods with known accuracy. A bounded aggregation technique has been defined for Markov processes and applied to queueing networks with blocking in [25] by exploiting the special structure of the underlying Markov process. Extending this work to more general classes of networks with finite capacities and different blocking mechanisms are challenging issues which are still open.

3 Properties of queueing networks with blocking

In this section we discuss some properties of queueing networks with finite capacity and blocking, which arise from the comparison of different models.

We consider insensitivity and equivalence properties in queueing network with blocking.

Insensitivity concerns how the characteristics of the service requirements affect the network performance.

Equivalence properties are the basis of problem reducibility. Equivalencies include both identity and reducibility relationships and can be defined between networks with and without blocking, between both homogeneous and non-homogeneous networks with different blocking types, and between open and closed networks.

Note that identifying these equivalencies depends on the performance indices involved.

Insensitivity and equivalence properties provide the basis for comparing the performance of system models with different parameters and with different blocking mechanisms.

These results can be applied, for example, in the study of the impact of the blocking type on system performance, by referring to a given set of performance indices and network parameters.

Another important consequence of these properties is that solution methods and algorithms already defined for a certain class of networks could be extended to other classes of network models with different blocking types and/or network parameters. For example, equivalence between networks with and without blocking immediately leads to the extension of efficient computational solution algorithms defined for BCMP networks such as MVA and Convolution algorithm to queueing networks with finite capacity queues.

3.1 Insensitivity

Insensitivity is the property which states that stationary characteristics of the stochastic process underlying the queueing network depends on the service requirements only in terms of their averages. Product-form queueing networks without blocking have been proved to be insensitive [16], i.e., the stationary joint queue length has been proved to depend on the service time distributions only in terms of their means.

Insensitivity can be extended to a certain class of queueing networks with finite capacity and blocking.

Referring to product-form networks with finite capacity, Tables I and II and product-form definitions show the cases where the stationary state distribution at arbitrary times depends on the distribution of the service time only in terms of the mean value (or the service rate μ_i).

Specifically, this insensitivity property holds for product form solutions PF1 which allow BCMP nodes, and for product-form PFi, i=3,4,5 and 6 which allow A-type nodes, as defined in Section 2.2.

Insensitivity for a two-node network with multiple class and RS blocking has been shown both for the joint stationary state distribution and for the call congestion of a job, i.e., the stationary probability that a job is blocked when requesting service at the next node [66].

Insensitivity of the joint queue length distribution for the central server and for reversible routing networks with A-type nodes and RS-RD and Stop blocking types has been discussed in [2-4, 50, 64, 68, 69].

3.2 Equivalence properties

Equivalence can be defined by referring to different performance indices. Most of the equivalence properties have been defined in terms of identity of the underlying Markov process of the queueing networks, which leads to an identical solution of the state probability vector π obtained by system (3).

However, note that network state S definition depends on the blocking type, as discussed in Section 2. Therefore although a bijective function between two state spaces of two networks can be identified such that the Markov process are identical, the meaning of corresponding states may be different and hence performance measures may be not equivalent. Moreover the identity of the joint queue length distribution between two networks does not necessarily imply that mean performance indices are identical as well.

Network with RS-RD blocking	Relationship	Network without blocking: parameters
reversible routing, solution PF4	$\pi \propto \pi^*$	$\mu_i^* = \mu_i$ $f_i^*(k) = f_i(k) / b_i(k-1)$ $\qquad\qquad 1 \le k \le B_i$ $P^* = P$
arbitrary routing, solution PF2	$\pi \propto \pi^*$	$\mu_i^* = \mu_i h_i$ $f_i^*(k) = 1 / b_i(k-1)$ $\qquad\qquad 1 \le k \le B_i$ $P^* = P$
	$\pi \propto 1 / \pi^*$	$\mu_i^* = \max_j \mu_j$ $f_i^*(k) = b_i(k-1)$ $\qquad\qquad 1 \le k \le B_i$ $P^* = \| p^*_{ij} \|,\ p^*_{ij} = \mu_j p_{ji} / \mu_i^*$ $i \ne j,\ p^*_{ii} = 1 - \Sigma_{j \ne i} p^*_{ji},\ 1 \le i,j \le M$

Table III - Equivalence between networks with and without blocking.

We shall now survey equivalence relationships expressed in terms of state probability π. These equivalence in some cases can be extended to average performance indices such as throughput, utilization, mean queue length and mean response time.
Then, we consider some equivalence properties in terms of passage time distribution.

• *Mean performance indices and joint queue length distribution at arbitrary times*

Some equivalence properties can be defined between networks with and without blocking. They allow us to analyse queueing networks with finite capacity by applying standard computational algorithms for queueing networks with infinite capacity, e.g., MVA and Convolution.
By comparing product-form solutions of queueing networks with and without blocking one can define a non-blocking network with appropriate parameters such that the stationary state distributions of the two networks are identical.
Let W denote the network with finite capacity, and W* the network identical to W except for infinite capacity queues and with the following different parameters: load dependent service rate $\mu^*_i f^*_i(n_i)$, and routing matrix P*. Let π^* denote the stationary state distribution of network W*. Single class exponential networks with RS-RD blocking have been shown to be equivalent, in terms of stationary state distribution, to a corresponding network without blocking, as defined in Table III [8].
The two cases of product-form networks with blocking considered refer to solutions PF4 and PF2, respectively, defined in Section 2.2. Table III shows the type of relationship between the two state distributions and the definition of the parameters of the network without blocking. Note that load dependent function $f^*_i(k)$ can be any positive arbitrary function for $k > B_i$, and in the second case h_i is defined as follows: $h_i = \epsilon_i y_i$ where ϵ_i is given in PF2 definition in Table II and $y = (y_1, ..., y_M)$ is obtained by the solution of $y = y A$, where $A = \| a_{ij} \|$, $a_{ij} = p_{ji}$, $j \ne i$, $a_{ii} = 1 - \Sigma_{j \ne i} a_{ij}$, $1 \le i,j \le M$.

network topology	performance indices	blocking types	assumptions
two-node	π	BBS-SO=BBS-O RS-RD=RS-FD	
		BBS-SO=RS-RD= =RS-FD=BBS-O	(I) : multiclass networks BCMP type nodes class independent capacities
		BBS-SO=BBS-SNO	assumption (I) and if $N \leq B_1 + B_2 - 2$
		BBS-SO→BAS	assumption (I) and with $B_i BBS\text{-}SO = B_i BAS + 1$, $1 \leq i \leq M$
	π U_i, X_i, L_i, T_i	BBS-SO=BBS-SO= =RS-RD	(II) : single class networks exponential nodes load independent service rates
	π U_i, X_i	BBS-SO→BAS	assumption (II) and with $B_i BBS\text{-}SO = B_i BAS + 1$, $1 \leq i \leq M$
cyclic	π	BBS-SO=BBS-O RS-RD=RS-FD	
	π U_i, X_i, L_i, T_i	BBS-SO=RS-RD	assumption (II)
		BBS-SO=BBS-SNO	assumption (II), M>2 and $N \leq \min\{B_i + B_j : p_{ij} > 0\} - 1$
	π U_i, X_i	BBS-SO→BAS	assumption (II) and with $B_i BBS\text{-}SO = B_i BAS + 1$, $1 \leq i \leq M$
central server	π U_i, X_i, L_i, T_i	BBS-SO=BBS-SNO= =BBS-O= =RS-RD=RS-FD	assumption (II) and if only $B_1 < \infty$ and $B_i = \infty$, $2 \leq i \leq M$
	π	BBS-SO=RS-RD= =BBS-SNO	assumption (II) and if $B_1 = \infty$
		BBS-O→BAS	assumption (II) and if $B_1 = \infty$ and $B_i BBS\text{-}O = B_i BAS + 1$, $2 \leq i \leq M$

Table IV - Equivalence between closed networks with different blocking types.

Note that since the product-form for queueing networks with finite capacity has a similar structure to the product-form solution of networks with infinite capacity, this type of equivalence could be extended to other cases of product-form networks with blocking, including multiclass networks with different types of nodes. Equivalencies between networks with both homogeneous and non-homogeneous blocking types have been identified both for open and closed networks.

They include both identity relationship and reducibility. Identity states that the state distributions of the two networks are identical, while reducibility allows a correspondence between the two distributions to be defined. Most of the reducibility

network topology	performance indices	blocking types	assumptions
tandem	π	BBS-SO=BBS-O RS-RD=RS-FD	
		BBS-SO=RS-RD=RS-FD	assumption (II)
		BBS-SO=BBS-SNO	assumption (II), M=2 and if $B_1=\infty$
		BBS-SO$\rightarrow$BAS	assumption (II) and with B_iBBS-SO$=B_i$BAS+1, $2\leq i\leq M$
split	π	BBS-SO=RS-RD=RS-FD	assumption (II) and if only $B_1<\infty$ and $B_i=\infty$, $2\leq i\leq M$
		BBS-SO=BBS-SNO= =RS-FD	assumption (II) and if $B_1=\infty$
merge	π	BBS-SO=BBS-O RS-RD=RS-FD	
		BBS-SO=RS-RD=RS-FD	assumption (II) and if $B_1=\infty$
		BBS-SO=RS-RD= =RS-FD= =BBS-SNO=BBS-O	assumption (II) and if only $B_1<\infty$ and $B_i=\infty$, $2\leq i\leq M$

Table V - Equivalence between open networks with different blocking types.

network topology	performance indices	blocking types	assumptions
reversible routing	π	RS-RD=Stop	single class closed/open networks A-type nodes load independent service
arbitrary routing		BBS-SO=RS-FD	(II): single class networks exponential nodes load independent service rates
		Stop=Recirculate	multiclass open Jackson networks with class type fixed
		BBS-SO=RS-RD= =RS-FD=BBS-O	assumption (II) and condition (B)
	π	BBS-SO=BBS-SNO	assumption (II) and $N\leq\min\{B_i+B_j : p_{ij}>0\}$ - 1
		Stop$\rightarrow$BBS-O (open) (closed)	single class Jackson networks

Table VI - Equivalence between networks with different blocking types.

between networks can be defined by modifying the buffer capacities. A detailed definition of reducibility and of the definition of the correspondence function for equivalent exponential closed networks is given in [9]. Let $X=Y$ and $X \rightarrow Y$ respectively denote identity and reducibility of blocking types X and Y.

Let B_i^X denote the buffer capacity when node i works under blocking type X and π^X the stationary state distribution of the homogeneous network with blocking type X.

Tables IV, V and VI show equivalences of state distribution and, in some cases, of average performance indices between some blocking types for certain special topology networks.

Tables IV and V concern some closed and open networks, respectively, while Table VI refers to both open and closed networks.

Closed networks with two-node, cyclic and central server topologies are considered in Table IV. The central node in central server networks is denoted by 1.

Tandem open networks and two special cases of open networks denoted as split and merge topology are reported in Table V.

Split topology can be defined as follows: $p_{01}=1$, $p_{0i}=0$, $2 \leq i \leq M$, $p_{ij}>0$ for i=1 and $2 \leq j \leq M$, $p_{ij}=0$ otherwise, $p_{10}=0$, $p_{i0}=1$ for $2 \leq i \leq M$,

i.e., an external arrival enters the network only at node 1, from which it can go to nodes 2,...,M and from which it eventually exits from the network.

Merge topology can be defined as:

$p_{01}=0$, $p_{0i}>0$, $2 \leq i \leq M$, $p_{ij}>0$ for $2 \leq i \leq M$ and j=1, $p_{ij}=0$ otherwise, $p_{10}=1$, $p_{i0}=0$ for $2 \leq i \leq M$,

i.e., an external arrival enters in any of nodes 2,...,M and then it goes to node 1 from which it leaves the network.

Tables IV, V and VI show the conditions under which equivalence properties between networks with different blocking types hold, including network characteristics and special conditions on system parameters. More specifically, for reducible networks with different blocking types the relationships between finite capacities are shown.

Remark. Note that non-homogeneous networks where service centers work under different and equivalent blocking mechanisms are also equivalent to homogeneous networks with one of the considered blocking types.

The last equivalence reported in Table VI is a special case which relates an open network with M nodes and Stop blocking, which allows a total network population n in the range $L \leq n \leq U$, with a closed network, with an additional node with appropriate parameters and BBS-O blocking, as proved in [10]. Specifically, the closed network is defined by adding a node, denoted by 0, with service rate $\mu_0(n_0)=a(n)$, finite capacity $B_0=U-L$, blocking function $b_0(n_0)=d(n)$, where $n_0=U-n$, $0 \leq n_0 \leq B_0$ and a(n) and d(n) are the arrival rate and the network blocking functions of the open network with Stop blocking. Hence the following correspondence between state distributions holds: $\pi^{Stop}(S)=\pi^{BBS-O}(n_0,S)$ for each state S of the open network.

For the special class of symmetrical networks introduced in the previous section, some equivalence results have been obtained for BBS-SO blocking type in terms of throughput. Specifically, closed cyclic networks have the same throughput for N and N-B customers, as showed for exponential service times in [29] and generalised to phase-type distributions in [28]. Moreover, the relationship between this symmetry property and reversibility is discussed in [28]. Some monotonicity properties of the network throughput for this class of networks has been proved in [61] by considering increasing service rates or finite capacities or the overall network population.

• Passage time distribution

Equivalence between networks defined in terms of joint queue length distribution and average performance indices does not necessarily lead to equivalence in terms of passage time distributions.

Some equivalence results have been obtained in terms of cycle time distributions for cyclic networks with BAS and BBS-SO blocking types.

The extension of such results to other networks with different parameters including blocking type, service distribution and routing topology is an open issue.

Consider a two-node cyclic exponential network with N customers, finite capacities B_1 and B_2 and either BBS-SO or BAS blocking. Let f_{N,B_1,B_2} (t) denote the density function of the cycle time. The following equivalence property can be proved [11, 12]:

Theorem 3

Consider two cyclic networks with two exponential nodes, N customers, service rates μ_i, i=1,2, BBS-SO or BAS blocking and finite capacities B_i and B_i', respectively, for i=1,2. If

$$B_1 + B_2 = B_1' + B_2'$$

then the two networks are equivalent in terms of cycle time distribution, i.e.:

$$f_{N,B_1,B_2} (t) = f_{N,B'_1,B'_2} (t).$$

In other words this equivalence states that the distribution of the cycle time does not depend on the single buffer size of each node, but on the total buffer capacity of the network. The extension of these equivalencies to queueing networks with a more general topology and different blocking types is an open issue.

Remark. Note that since the two networks have the same number of customers but different capacities they are also equivalent in terms of throughput, but they are not equivalent in terms of joint queue length distribution and other average performance indices (mean response time, utilization and mean queue length).

4 Conclusions

Performance evaluation of systems with finite capacity resources represented by queueing network models with finite capacity queues and different blocking mechanisms has been discussed.

The main analytical solution methods have been presented, by considering both the analysis of average performance indices and more detailed measures such as passage time distribution.

Properties of queueing networks with blocking have been discussed including equivalence between networks with and without blocking, between models with both homogeneous and non-homogeneous blocking types, and relationships between open and closed queueing network models with blocking.

Although product-form solutions have been proved for queueing networks with blocking under certain constraints, research must to be done to define efficient solution algorithms for general multiclass networks, and in particular approximate solutions with knowledge of the error and bounded algorithms for non product-form networks.

Other open research issues include the analysis of discrete-time queueing networks with finite capacity queues and blocking which can be used to represent discrete time systems, such as for example ATM networks, and the performance comparison of queueing networks with different blocking types in order to identify optimal blocking mechanisms.

Acknowledgements

The author would like to thank Lorenzo Donatiello for helpful discussions and suggestions and Vittoria De Nitto for useful comments and careful reading of earlier draft of this paper.

Appendix

The system state definition of queueing networks with finite capacity and blocking depends both on network characteristics and on the blocking type. We shall now define system state for the single class network model introduced in Section 1.

For the sake of simplicity we consider exponential service time distribution and the First Come First Served discipline.

The extension to more general service time distributions and policies leads to the introduction of additional components to system states in a similar way as in queueing networks with infinite capacity queues. For this reason in order to define such additional state components which only depend on the node type and are independent of the blocking mechanism, it is sufficient to refer to state definitions introduced for networks with infinite capacity. For example, for queueing networks with BCMP-type nodes one can refer to the state definition introduced in [16] to complete the state definition of queueing networks with blocking defined below.

We consider the five blocking types introduced in Section 1.

$S=(S_1,...,S_M)$ denotes the system state, S_i the state of node i, and n_i the number of customers in node i, $1 \leq i \leq M$. Due to the finite capacity of the queues $n_i \leq B_i$, $1 \leq i \leq M$, and if the network is closed with N customers the following condition holds:

$$\max\left\{0, N - \sum_{j=1, j\neq i}^{M} B_j\right\} \leq n_i \qquad (A.1)$$

BAS

For BAS blocking, node i state can be defined as follows:

$S_i = (n_i, s_i, \mathbf{m}_i)$, $s_i = 0,1$, $\mathbf{m}_i = (m_i,...,m_{u(i)})$, $0 \leq u(i) \leq M-1$

where s_i denotes the server state and $\mathbf{m}_i$ is the vector of the nodes indices blocked by node i. The server state indicates whether the server is active ($s_i = 1$) or blocked ($s_i = 0$). Vector $\mathbf{m}_i$ is non-empty only if node i is full, i.e., if $n_i = B_i$. When $\mathbf{m}_i$ is not empty, it contains the indices of the nodes which have attempted to send a job to node i and which are still blocked by node i (i.e., $p_{ji}>0$ and $s_j =0$ for each $j=m_i,...,m_{u(i)}$). The number of components of vector $\mathbf{m}_i$, u(i), is at most equal to the number of possible sending (upstream) nodes of node i: $u(i) \leq \# \{ j : p_{ji}>0, 1 \leq j \leq M, j \neq i\} \leq M-1$.

Vector $\mathbf{m}_i$ is ordered according to the time at which the upstream nodes will be unblocked, that is according to the unblocking scheduling.

BBS-SO and BBS-SNO

In BBS blocking, node i state definition can be defined as follows:

$S_i = (n_i, d_i)$, $1 \leq d_i \leq M$

where d_i denotes the destination node of the next job that will exit from node i.

Note that d_i is the destination node of the next job currently in service if $n_i>0$, or of the next customer that will arrive at node i if $n_i=0$.

When node i is not empty and the destination node d_i is full, i.e., when $n_i>0$ and $n_{d_i}=B_{d_i}$, then by the blocking definition the server of node i is blocked and will be resumed as soon as a departure occurs from node d_i.

In addition to constraint (A.1) in BBS-SNO if node i is blocked ($n_{d_i}=B_{d_i}$) then $n_i<B_i$, because the server cannot be occupied by a job.

BBS-O

For BBS-O blocking, node i state can be defined as $S_i = n_i$. When at least one of the destination nodes of node i is full (i.e., there exists j : $p_{ij}>0$ and $n_j=B_j$), then the server of node i is blocked.

RS-RD

In RS-RD blocking node i state definition is simply $S_i = n_i$. Note that the server is always active and servicing a customer if $n_i>0$.

RS-FD

For RS-FD blocking the state of node i can be defined as for BBS blocking. Indeed in this case a customer that completes the service at node i and is not accepted by its destination node because of the full capacity does not change its destination as in RS-RD blocking. Hence the information on the destination node of the next customer that will exit from node i has to be included in state S_i.

However, note that when node i is not empty and the destination node d_i is full for RS-FD blocking the server of node i is not blocked as in BBS.

Like RS-RD the server of each node is always active and servicing a customer if $n_i>0$.

Stop and Recirculate

For Stop and Recirculate blocking node i state definition is $S_i = n_i$, like RS-RD and networks with infinite capacity.

Note that for Stop blocking all the servers are blocked when the total network population $n=n_1+...+n_M$ reaches its minimum value for which the (network) blocking function $d(n)=0$.

For Recirculate blocking the servers are always active and the routing probabilities are state dependent.

Note that even though the system state for RS-RD, BBS-O, Stop and Recirculate blocking types may have the same definition, the underlying Markov processes are different, i.e., the process transition rate matrices Q are defined differently according to the blocking type.

For example for RS-RD blocking matrix Q is defined as presented in Section 2.1, while for Stop blocking Q= ||q(S,S')|| can be defined as follows for each pair of states S,S' with S≠S':

$$q(S,S') = \delta(n_j) \mu_j d(n) p_{ji} \qquad \text{if } S'= S + e_i - e_j$$
$$q(S,S') = \delta(n_j) \mu_j d(n) p_{j0} \qquad \text{if } S'= S - e_j$$
$$q(S,S') = \lambda p_{0j} b_j(n_j) \qquad \text{if } S'= S + e_j$$

where $d(n)$ is the network blocking function and δ has been defined in Section 2.

References

[1] I.F. Akyildiz "Exact product form solution for queueing networks with blocking" IEEE Trans. Computer, C-36-1 (1987) 122-125.

[2] I.F. Akyildiz and H. von Brand "Central Server Models with Multiple Job Classes, State Dependent Routing, and Rejection Blocking" IEEE Trans. on Softw. Eng., SE-15-10 (1989) 1305-1312.

[3] I.F. Akyildiz and H. von Brand "Exact solutions for open, closed and mixed queueing networks with rejection blocking" J. Theor. Computer Science, 64 (1989) 203-219.

[4] I.F. Akyildiz and N. van Dijk "Exact Solution for Networks of Parallel Queues with Finite Buffers" in: Proc. Performance '90 (P.J.B. 40, I. Mitrani and R.J. Pooley Eds.) North-Holland (1990) 35-49.

[5] I.F. Akyildiz and H.G. Perros, Special Issue on Queueing Networks with Finite Capacity Queues, Performance Evaluation, Vol. 10, 3 (1989).

[6] T. Altiok, S.S. Stidham "A note on Transfer Line with Unreliable Machines, Random Processing Times, and Finite Buffers" IIE Trans., Vol.14, 4 (1982) 125-127.

[7] T. Altiok and H.G. Perros "Approximate analysis of arbitrary configurations of queueing networks with blocking" Ann. Oper. Res. 9 (1987) 481-509

[8] S.Balsamo, G.Iazeolla "Some Equivalence Properties for Queueing Networks with and without Blocking" in *Performance '83* (A.K.Agrawala, S.K.Tripathi Eds.) North Holland.

[9] S. Balsamo and V. De Nitto "Closed queueing networks with finite capacities: blocking types, product-form solution and performance indices" Performance Evaluation, Vol.12, 4 (1991) 85-102.

[10] S. Balsamo, V.De Nitto "A survey of Product-form Queueing Networks with Blocking and their Equivalences" to appear on Annals of Operations Research.

[11] S.Balsamo, L. Donatiello "On the Cycle Time Distribution in a Two-stage Queueing Network with Blocking" IEEE Transactions on Software Engineering, Vol.13, 10, Oct.1989.

[12] S.Balsamo, L. Donatiello "Two-stage Queueing Networks with Blocking: Cycle Time Distribution and Equivalence Properties", in *Modelling Techniques and Tools for Computer Performance Evaluation* (R. Puigjaner, D.Potier Eds.) Plenum Press, 1989.

[13] S.Balsamo, M.C. Clò, L. Donatiello "Cycle Time Distribution of Cyclic Queueing Network with Blocking", in *Queueing Networks with Finite Capacities* (R.O.Onvural and I.F.Akyidiz Eds.), Elsevier, 1993, and Performance Evaluation, Vol.14, 3 (1993).

[14] S. Balsamo, M.C. Clò "State distribution at arrival times for closed queueing networks with blocking" Technical Report TR-35/92, Dipartimento di Informatica, University of Pisa, 1992.

[15] S. Balsamo, M.C. Clò "Delay distribution in a central server model with blocking", Technical Report TR-14/93, Dipartimento di Informatica, University of Pisa, 1993.

[16] F. Baskett , K.M. Chandy, R.R.Muntz, G. Palacios "Open, closed, and mixed networks of queues with different classes of customers" J. of ACM, 22 (1985) 248-260.

[17] O. Boxma and A.G. Konheim "Approximate analysis of exponential queueing systems with blocking" Acta Informatica, 15 (1981) 19-66.

[18] O. Boxma and H. Daduna "Sojourn time distribution in queueing networks" in 'Stochastic Analysis of computer and Communication Systems' (H.Takagi Ed.) North Holland (1990).

[19] P. Caseau and G. Pujolle "Throughput capacity of a sequence of transfer lines with blocking due to finite waiting room" IEEE Trans. on Softw. Eng. 5 (1979) 631-642.

[20] K.M. Chandy, A.J. Martin "A characterization of product-form queueing networks" J. ACM, Vol.30, 2 (1983) 286-299.

[21] K.M. Chandy, J.H.Howard and D. Towsley "Product form and local balance in queueing networks"J. ACM, Vol.24, 2 (1977) 250-263.

[22] K.M. Chandy, U. Herzog and L. Woo "Parametric analysis of queueing networks" IBM J. Res. Dev., 1 (1975) 36-42.

[23] T. Choukri "Exact Analysis of Multiple Job Classes and Different Types of Blocking" in Queueing Networks with Finite Capacities (R.O.Onvural and I.F.Akyidiz Eds.), Elsevier (1993).

[24] J.W. Cohen "The multiple phase service network with generalized processor sharing" Acta Informatica, Vol.12 (1979) 245-284.

[25] P.J. Courtois and P.Semal "Computable bounds for conditional steady-state probabilities in large Markov chains and queueing models" IEEE Journal on SAC 4, 6 (1986) 920-936.

[26] Y. Dallery and Y. Frein, A decomposition method for the approximate analysis of closed queueing networks with blocking, Proc. First Int. Workshop on Queueing Networks with Blocking, (H.G. Perros and T. Altiok Eds.) North Holland (1989).

[27] Y. Dallery and D.D. Yao "Modelling a system of flexible manufacturing cells" in: Modeling and Design of Flexible Manufacturing Systems (Kusiak Ed.) North-Holland (1986) 289-300.

[28] Y. Dallery and D.F. Towsley "Symmetry property of the throughput in closed tandem queueing networks with finite buffers" Op. Res. Letters, 10 (1991) 541-547.

[29] V. De Nitto and D. Grillo "Managing Blocking in Finite Capacity Simmetrical Ring Networks" Third Int. Conf. on Data Comm. Systems and their Performance, Rio de Janeiro, Brazil, June 22-25 (1987) 225-240.

[30] Y. Frein and Y. Dallery , Analysis of Cyclic Queueing Networks with Finite Buffers and Blocking Before Service, Performance Evaluation, Vol. 10 (1989) 197-210.

[31] S. Gershwin "An efficient decomposition method for the approximate evaluation of tandem queues with finite storage space and blocking" Oper. Res., 35 (1987) 291-305.

[32] S. Gershwin and U. Berman "Analysis of transfer lines consisting of two unreliable machines with random processing times and finite storage buffers" AIIE Trans., 13, 1 (1981) 2-11.

[33] W.J. Gordon and G.F. Newell "Cyclic queueing systems with restricted queues" Oper. Res., 15 (1976) 286-302.

[34] L. Gün and A.M. Makowski "An approximation method for general tandem queueing systems subject to blocking" Proc. First Int. Workshop on Queueing Networks with Blocking, (H.G. Perros and T. Altiok Eds.) North Holland (1989) 147-171.

[35] F.S. Hillier and R.W. Boling "Finite queues in series with exponential or Erlang service times - a numerical approach" Oper.Res., 15 (1967) 286-303.

[36] A. Hordijk and N. van Dijk, Networks of queues with blocking, in: Performance '81 (K.J. Kylstra Ed.) North Holland (1981) 51-65.

[37] A. Hordijk and N. van Dijk, Networks of queues ; Part I: job-local-balance and the adjoint process; Part II : General routing and service characteristics, in: Lect. Notes in Control and Information Sciences (F.Baccelli and G.Fajolle Eds.) Springer-Verlag (1983) 158-205.

[38] J.R. Jackson "Jobshop-like queueing systems" Management Science, 10 (1963) 131-142.

[39] F.P. Kelly, Reversibility and Stochastic Networks, Wiley (1979).

[40] J.F.C. Kingman, Markovian population process, J. Appl. Prob., 6 (1969) 1-18.

[41] L. Kleinrock, Queueing Systems.Vol.1 :Theory, Wiley (1975).

[42] A.G. Konhein and M. Reiser "A queueing model with finite waiting room and blocking" SIAM J.Comput, 7 (1978) 210-229.

[43] D.Kouvatsos and N.P.Xenios "Maximum entropy analysis of general queueing networks with blocking" Proc. First Int. Workshop on Queueing Networks with Blocking, (H.G. Perros and T. Altiok Eds.) North Holland (1989).

[44] A.E. Krzesinski "Multiclass queueing networks with state-dependent routing" Performance Evaluation, Vol.7, 2 (1987) 125-145.

[45] S. Kundu and I.Akyildiz "Deadlock free buffer allocation in closed queueing networks" Queueing Systems Journal, 4, 47-56.

[46] S.S. Lam "Queueing networks with capacity constraints" IBM J. Res. Develop. 21 (1977) 370-378.

[47] S.S. Lavenberg, Computer Performance Modeling Handbook, (Prentice Hall, 1983).

[48] S. S. Lavenberg and M. Reiser "Stationary State Probabilities at Arrival Instants for Closed Queueing Networks with multiple Types of Customers" J. Appl. Prob., Vol. 17 (1980) 1048-1061.

[49] M.F. Neuts "Two queues in series with a finite intermediate waiting room" J.Appl. Prob., 5 (1986) 123-142.

[50] R.O. Onvural "A Note on the Product Form Solutions of Multiclass Closed Queueing Networks with Blocking" Performance Evaluation, Vol.10, 3 (1989) 247-253.

[51] R.O. Onvural "Survey of Closed Queueing Networks with Blocking" ACM Computing Surveys, Vol. 22, 2 (1990) 83-121.

[52] R.O. Onvural Special Issue on Queueing Networks with Finite Capacity, Performance Evaluation, Vol. 17, 3 (1993).

[53] R.O. Onvural and H.G. Perros "On equivalences of blocking mechanisms in queueing networks with blocking" Oper. Res. Letters (1986) 293-297.

[54] R.O. Onvural and H.G. Perros "Some equivalencies on closed exponential queueing networks with blocking" Performance Evaluation, Vol.9 (1989) 111-118.

[55] H.G. Perros "Open queueing networks with blocking" in : Stochastic Analysis of Computer and Communications Systems (Takagi Ed.) North Holland (1989).

[56] H.G. Perros "A bibliography of papers on queueing networks with finite capacity queues" Performance Evaluation, Vol. 10, 3 (1989) 225-260.

[57] H.G. Perros, A. Nilsson and Y.G. Liu "Approximate analysis of product form type queueing networks with blocking and deadlock" Performance Evaluation, Vol. 8 (1988) 19-39.

[58] H.G. Perros and P.M. Snyder "A computationally efficient approximation algorithm for analyzing queueing networks with blocking" Performance Evaluation, Vol. 9 (1988/89) 217-224.

[59] B. Pittel "Closed exponential networks of queues with saturation: the Jackson-type stationary distribution and its asymptotic analysis" Math. Oper. Res. 4 (1979) 367-378.

[60] K. S. Sevcik and I. Mitrani "The Distribution of Queueing Network States at Input and Output Instants" J. of ACM, Vol. 28, 2 (1981) 358-371.

[61] G.J. Shantikumar and D.D. Yao "Monotonicity properties in cyclic networks with finite buffers" Proc. First Int. Workshop on Queueing Networks with Blocking, (H.G. Perros and T. Altiok Eds.) North Holland (1989).

[62] R. Suri and G.W. Diehl "A variable buffer size model and its use in analytical closed queueing networks with blocking" Management Sci. Vol.32, 2 (1986) 206-225.

[63] D.F. Towsley "Queueing network models with state-dependent routing" J. ACM 27 (1980) 323-337.

[64] N. van Dijk "On 'stop = repeat' servicing for non-exponential queueing networks with blocking" J. Appl. Prob., 28 (1991) 159-173.

[65] N. van Dijk "'Stop = recirculate' for exponential product form queueing networks with departure blocking" Oper. Res. Lett., 10 (1991) 343-351.

[66] N. van Dijk and H.G. Tijms "Insensitivity in two node blocking models with applications" in: Proc. Teletraffic Analysis and Computer Performance Evaluation, Eds. Boxma, Cohen and Tijms (North Holland, 1986) 329-340.

[67] N. van Dijk "On the Arrival Theorem for communication networks" Computer Networks and ISDN Systems, 25 (1993) 1135-1142.

[68] D.D. Yao and J.A. Buzacott "Modeling a class of state-dependent routing in flexible manufacturing systems" Ann. Oper. Res., 3 (1985) 153-167.

[69] D.D. Yao and J.A. Buzacott "Modeling a class of flexible manufacturing systems with reversible routing" Oper. Res., 35 (1987) 87-93.

[70] P. Whittle "Partial balance and insensitivity" J. Appl. Prob. 22 (1985) 168-175.

Performance Analysis and Optimization with the Power-Series Algorithm

Hans (J.P.C.) Blanc [1]
Tilburg University, The Netherlands

Abstract

The power-series algorithm (PSA) is a flexible device for computing performance measures for systems which can be modeled as multi-queue/multi-server systems with a quasi-birth-and-death structure. An overview of this technique is provided, including a motivation of the principles of the PSA, the derivation of recursive computation schemes, discussions of efficient implementation of the PSA, of methods for improving the convergence of the power series, of the numerical complexity of the PSA, and of the computation of derivatives with respect to system parameters, and examples of application of the PSA.

1 Introduction

The performance analysis and control of many computer/communication systems lead to the formulation and study of multi-queue models. The stochastic processes underlying these systems are generally very hard to treat by analytical methods. Therefore, it is important to develop numerical methods for computing performance measures for such systems. The power-series algorithm (PSA) is one of the available methods. It requires a Markov representation of the queueing process, possibly with the aid of some supplementary variables. It is based on power-series expansions of the state probabilities in terms of the load of a system for (recursively) solving the global balance equations satisfied by these probabilities. It is a flexible method which is applicable to a wide class of multi-queue/multi-server models, with Markovian Arrival Processes (MAPs) and phase-type (PH) service time distributions. The PSA is also suitable for optimization purposes, since it allows the computation of derivatives of performance measures with respect to system parameters and control variables. For moderately sized systems, the PSA favourably compares with simulation and numerical methods based on truncation of the state space. This is mainly so because the PSA involves recursive schemes and allows the application of the so-called ϵ-algorithm which improves the convergence of the power series considerably. Since the memory requirements grow exponentially with the number of queues, the PSA can only produce accurate results for systems with a limited number of queues. Being an aid for studying the interaction between queues on a reduced scale and for developing and testing approximations of performance measures and optimal values of control variables for systems of a larger size is therefore the main contribution of the PSA.

---

[1] Postal address: Dept. of Econometrics, P.O. Box 90153, 5000 LE Tilburg; e-mail: blanc@kub.nl.

An important class of multi-queue models to which the PSA is applicable consists of polling models in which several users compete for service by a single server (e.g., a single communication channel in a computer network). The server switches from one queue to another in order to provide service. It is a very rich class of models which allows many visit-order rules and service disciplines, and may involve switch-over times, set-up times, etc.. Other examples of models to which the PSA can be applied are models with parallel servers, such as coupled-processor models, load-balancing models ("join the shortest queue" and variants) and parallel-processor models (fork systems in which jobs split into partial jobs which are to be processed on parallel machines), and networks of queues in which jobs move from one queue to another for sequential processing.

An s-dimensional state space is required to describe the joint queue-length process for a queueing system or network with s queues. For a large class of such systems, this process can be modeled as a multi-dimensional birth-and-death process (BDP), i.e., interarrival and service times are exponentially distributed and arrivals and departures occur one by one, or as a multi-dimensional quasi-birth-and-death process (QBDP), i.e., a BDP to which one or more finite-state supplementary variables are added to render the queue-length process Markovian. These supplementary variables can be used, e.g., to model MAPs or PH-distributions, or to indicate the position or the status of a moving server. Global balance equations can still be formulated for these processes, as in the one-dimensional case. But local balance equations often do not exist due to the multiple of paths which may exist between pairs of neighbouring states.

In section 2 the computation scheme of the PSA is derived for the case of BDPs. Section 3 contains discussions on the implementation of the PSA and on the improvement of the convergence of the power series by means of the ϵ-algorithm. Section 4 concerns the extension of the general principle of the PSA to QBDPs. The application of the PSA to parallel-server systems is discussed in section 5. Since the queue-length process in a fork system is not a birth-and-death process because of the grouped arrivals of partial jobs, the PSA has to be adapted for this model. Section 6 is devoted to the application of the PSA to polling systems. The PSA is extended to QBDPs with migration, with application to networks of queues, in section 7. Section 8 deals with the computation of derivatives of performance measures with respect to parameters of a system. The overview is concluded by an annotated bibliography on the PSA.

In order to keep the exposition as simple as possible Poisson arrival streams and exponential service times will be assumed in all models which will be discussed in some details, except for the tandem model in section 7. It should be kept in mind, however, that all these models can be generalized with MAPs and PH service time distributions. The increased complexity of the PSA will be indicated in terms of the number of stages of these processes and distributions. All systems are assumed to be in steady state, and each queue may contain an unbounded number of jobs.

At the end of this introduction some notations will follow which will be used throughout this overview. The number of queues in the system will be denoted by s; $n = (n_1, \ldots, n_s)$ will denote a vector with non-negative integer entries, i.e., in $\mathbb{N}^s$, the state space of the joint s-dimensional stationary queue-length process $N = (N_1, \ldots, N_s)$. The sum of the components of the vector n will be denoted by $| n |$, i.e., $| n | \doteq n_1 + \ldots + n_s$. Further, e_j will denote the unit vector consisting of all zero components except a component of 1 at the jth position, $j = 1, \ldots, s$, and $0 \doteq (0, 0, \ldots, 0)$ the empty state. Finally, $I\{E\}$ will denote the indicator function of an event or condition E.

2 The PSA for birth-and-death processes

Consider the class of multi-queue systems of which the underlying stochastic queue-length processes are multi-dimensional BDPs. Let $\rho a_j(\mathbf{n})$ be the arrival rate to queue j, and $d_j(\mathbf{n})$ the departure rate from queue j, $j = 1, \ldots, s$, in state $\mathbf{n} \in \mathbb{N}^s$. Of course, $d_j(\mathbf{n}) = 0$ if $n_j = 0$, for $\mathbf{n} \in \mathbb{N}^s$, $j = 1, \ldots, s$. The parameter ρ, the load of the system, will be used as variable in power-series expansions. The relative arrival rates $a_j(\mathbf{n})$, $\mathbf{n} \in \mathbb{N}^s$, $j = 1, \ldots, s$, are assumed to be normalized such that the system is stable for $0 \leq \rho < 1$. In section 2.1 it will be shown that the stationary state probabilities of a multi-dimensional BDP possess power-series expansions in terms of the load ρ at $\rho = 0$, and that the coefficients of these power-series expansions can be computed recursively. How other performance measures can be computed will be discussed in section 2.2.

2.1 A recursive computation scheme

Let $p(\mathbf{n})$ denote the probability that the process $\mathbf{N}$ is in state $\mathbf{n} \in \mathbb{N}^s$. A state $\mathbf{n} \in \mathbb{N}^s$ is left if either an arrival occurs at one of the queues or if a service at one of the queues is completed; it is entered if either an arrival occurs at queue j and the system was in state $\mathbf{n} - \mathbf{e_j}$ (only if $n_j \geq 1$) or if a service is completed at queue j and the system was in state $\mathbf{n} + \mathbf{e_j}$, $j = 1, \ldots, s$. Hence, the global balance equations for the flows out of and into state $\mathbf{n}$ read: for $\mathbf{n} \in \mathbb{N}^s$,

$$\left(\rho \sum_{j=1}^{s} a_j(\mathbf{n}) + \sum_{j=1}^{s} d_j(\mathbf{n}) \right) p(\mathbf{n}) = \rho \sum_{j=1}^{s} a_j(\mathbf{n} - \mathbf{e_j}) I\{n_j \geq 1\} p(\mathbf{n} - \mathbf{e_j})$$

$$+ \sum_{j=1}^{s} d_j(\mathbf{n} + \mathbf{e_j}) p(\mathbf{n} + \mathbf{e_j}). \qquad (2.1)$$

The state probabilities sum to 1. This can be written as

$$\sum_{n_1=0}^{\infty} \cdots \sum_{n_s=0}^{\infty} p(\mathbf{n}) = \sum_{m=0}^{\infty} \sum_{|\mathbf{n}|=m} p(\mathbf{n}) = 1. \qquad (2.2)$$

First, it will be shown that the following limits exist for all states $\mathbf{n} \in \mathbb{N}^s$:

$$b(0; \mathbf{n}) \doteq \lim_{\rho \downarrow 0} \rho^{-|\mathbf{n}|} p(\mathbf{n}), \qquad (2.3)$$

if the departure rates are such that not all servers are idle when jobs are present in the system, i.e., if for each state $\mathbf{n} \in \mathbb{N}^s$, $\mathbf{n} \neq \mathbf{0}$, the following condition holds:

$$\sum_{j=1}^{s} d_j(\mathbf{n}) > 0. \qquad (2.4)$$

For that purpose, introduce, for $m = 0, 1, 2, \ldots$,

$$A(\rho; m) \doteq \sum_{|\mathbf{n}|=m} p(\mathbf{n}) \sum_{j=1}^{s} a_j(\mathbf{n}), \quad D(\rho; m) \doteq \sum_{|\mathbf{n}|=m} p(\mathbf{n}) \sum_{j=1}^{s} d_j(\mathbf{n}). \qquad (2.5)$$

Summation of equations (2.1) over states $\mathbf{n} \in \mathbb{N}^s$ with $| \mathbf{n} | = m$ leads to:

$$\rho A(\rho;0) = D(\rho;1); \quad \rho A(\rho;m) + D(\rho;m) = \rho A(\rho;m-1) + D(\rho;m+1), \quad m = 1,2,\ldots. \tag{2.6}$$

By induction, balance relations between all states with $\mid n \mid = m$ and with $\mid n \mid = m+1$ follow:

$$\rho A(\rho;m) = D(\rho;m+1), \quad m = 0,1,2,\ldots. \tag{2.7}$$

It will be clear from (2.2) and (2.7) that the limit (2.3) exists for $n = 0$, and equals 1. Now, suppose that the limits (2.3) exist for all n with $\mid n \mid \le M$ for some $M \ge 0$. Then, because the coefficients $a_j(n)$ are non-negative, also the following limits exist:

$$\tilde{A}(m) \doteq \lim_{\rho \downarrow 0} \rho^{-m} A(\rho;m), \quad m = 0,1,\ldots,M. \tag{2.8}$$

A similar argument and equation (2.7) imply that the following limits exist:

$$\tilde{D}(m) \doteq \lim_{\rho \downarrow 0} \rho^{-m} D(\rho;m), \quad m = 0,1,\ldots,M+1. \tag{2.9}$$

Because all state probabilities and all departure rates are non-negative, assumption (2.4) implies that the limits (2.3) exist for all n with $\mid n \mid = M + 1$. By induction it follows that the limits (2.3) exist for all states $n \in \mathbb{N}^s$. Next, introduce the functions

$$q_0(n) \doteq \rho^{-|n|} p(n), \quad n \in \mathbb{N}^s. \tag{2.10}$$

Substitution of these functions into the balance equations (2.1) leads to the equations: for $n \in \mathbb{N}^s$,

$$\left(\rho \sum_{j=1}^{s} a_j(n) + \sum_{j=1}^{s} d_j(n) \right) q_0(n) = \sum_{j=1}^{s} a_j(n - e_j) I\{n_j \ge 1\} q_0(n - e_j)$$

$$+ \rho \sum_{j=1}^{s} d_j(n + e_j) q_0(n + e_j). \tag{2.11}$$

Notice the different position of the factor ρ in the righthand sides of (2.1) and (2.11). The law of total probability (2.2) can be rewritten as:

$$\sum_{m=0}^{\infty} \rho^m \sum_{|n|=m} q_0(n) = 1. \tag{2.12}$$

It has been shown above that the functions $q_0(n)$ possess finite limits as ρ vanishes. The foregoing equations imply that these limits satisfy:

$$b(0;0) = 1; \quad \sum_{j=1}^{s} d_j(n) b(0;n) = \sum_{j=1}^{s} a_j(n - e_j) I\{n_j \ge 1\} b(0;n - e_j), \quad \mid n \mid \ge 1. \tag{2.13}$$

Now, subtract the limits at $\rho = 0$ from the functions $q_0(n)$:

$$q_1(n) \doteq q_0(n) - b(0;n), \quad n \in \mathbb{N}^s. \tag{2.14}$$

Then, we obtain from (2.11) with (2.13) the relations: for $n \in \mathbb{N}^s$,

$$\left(\rho\sum_{j=1}^{s}a_j(\mathbf{n})+\sum_{j=1}^{s}d_j(\mathbf{n})\right)q_1(\mathbf{n})+\rho\sum_{j=1}^{s}a_j(\mathbf{n})b(0;\mathbf{n})$$

$$=\sum_{j=1}^{s}a_j(\mathbf{n}-\mathbf{e_j})I\{n_j\geq 1\}q_1(\mathbf{n}-\mathbf{e_j})$$

$$+\rho\sum_{j=1}^{s}d_j(\mathbf{n}+\mathbf{e_j})[q_1(\mathbf{n}+\mathbf{e_j})+b(0;\mathbf{n}+\mathbf{e_j})],\qquad(2.15)$$

and from (2.12) the relation

$$q_1(\mathbf{0})+\sum_{m=1}^{\infty}\rho^m\sum_{|\mathbf{n}|=m}[q_1(\mathbf{n})+b(0;\mathbf{n})]=0.\qquad(2.16)$$

Because the functions $q_1(\mathbf{n})$ vanish as $\rho\downarrow 0$ by (2.14), it follows readily by induction from the above relations that the limits

$$b(1;\mathbf{n})\doteq\lim_{\rho\downarrow 0}\rho^{-1}q_1(\mathbf{n}),\qquad(2.17)$$

exist for all states $\mathbf{n}\in\mathbb{N}^s$. In a similar way we can successively, for $k=2,3,\ldots$, define the functions

$$q_k(\mathbf{n})\doteq q_{k-1}(\mathbf{n})-\rho^{k-1}b(k-1;\mathbf{n}),\quad \mathbf{n}\in\mathbb{N}^s,\qquad(2.18)$$

and show that the limits

$$b(k;\mathbf{n})\doteq\lim_{\rho\downarrow 0}\rho^{-k}q_k(\mathbf{n}),\qquad(2.19)$$

exist for all states $\mathbf{n}\in\mathbb{N}^s$. By induction it follows that these limits satisfy: for $k=1,2,\ldots,$

$$b(k;\mathbf{0})=-\sum_{1\leq|\mathbf{n}|\leq k}b(k-|\mathbf{n}|;\mathbf{n});\qquad(2.20)$$

and for $k=1,2,\ldots$, for $\mathbf{n}\in\mathbb{N}^s$, $\mathbf{n}\neq\mathbf{0}$,

$$\sum_{j=1}^{s}d_j(\mathbf{n})b(k;\mathbf{n})=\sum_{j=1}^{s}a_j(\mathbf{n}-\mathbf{e_j})I\{n_j\geq 1\}b(k;\mathbf{n}-\mathbf{e_j})$$

$$-\sum_{j=1}^{s}a_j(\mathbf{n})b(k-1;\mathbf{n})+\sum_{j=1}^{s}d_j(\mathbf{n}+\mathbf{e_j})b(k-1;\mathbf{n}+\mathbf{e_j}).\qquad(2.21)$$

Consequently, we can formally expand the state probabilities as power series in terms of the load of the system, ρ:

$$p(\mathbf{n})=\rho^{|\mathbf{n}|}\sum_{k=0}^{\infty}\rho^k b(k;\mathbf{n}),\quad \mathbf{n}\in\mathbb{N}^s.\qquad(2.22)$$

The coefficients of these power-series expansions can be recursively computed from (2.13) and (2.20), (2.21). Notice that assumption (2.4) is necessary to allow the computation of the coefficients $b(k; \mathbf{n})$ according to this scheme. There is still quite some freedom in the order in which the coefficients can be computed. One convenient order is: compute $b(0; \mathbf{n})$ recursively for increasing value of $| \mathbf{n} |$ up to $| \mathbf{n} | = M$ for some value of M, then compute $b(1; \mathbf{n})$ recursively for increasing value of $| \mathbf{n} |$ up to $| \mathbf{n} | = M - 1$, and so on, until $b(M; \mathbf{0})$ is reached. Another approach is to compute the coefficients $b(k; \mathbf{n})$ according to increasing values of $m = k + | \mathbf{n} |$ for $m = 0, 1, \ldots, M$, where at each level m the coefficients have to be computed in increasing order of k, for $k = 0, 1, \ldots, m$. The latter approach implies that the coefficients are computed according to increasing power of ρ.

2.2 Computation of performance measures

For multi-queue systems, the (numerical) information of the individual state probabilities is usually too complex to be of much interest in itself. Of more interest are sometimes (aggregated) probabilities, such as the probabilities that a queue is empty, or that a queue exceeds some threshold. In most cases, however, one is interested in the first few moments of the queue length distribution, in particular, in the mean and the standard deviation of the queue lengths, and possibly in the correlation between the queue lengths. Let $g(\mathbf{n})$ be a function from $\mathbb{N}^s$ to $\mathbb{N}$. The expectation of the random variable $g(\mathbf{N})$ is defined as

$$E\{g(\mathbf{N})\} \doteq \sum_{n_1=0}^{\infty} \cdots \sum_{n_s=0}^{\infty} g(\mathbf{n}) p(\mathbf{n}) = \sum_{m=0}^{\infty} \sum_{|\mathbf{n}|=m} g(\mathbf{n}) p(\mathbf{n}). \tag{2.23}$$

By substituting the power-series expansions (2.22) of the state probabilities into this relation and by changing the order of summation this expectation can be written as

$$E\{g(\mathbf{N})\} = \sum_{m=0}^{\infty} \rho^m \sum_{|\mathbf{n}|=m} g(\mathbf{n}) \sum_{k=0}^{\infty} \rho^k b(k; \mathbf{n}) = \sum_{k=0}^{\infty} \rho^k \sum_{m=0}^{k} \sum_{|\mathbf{n}|=m} g(\mathbf{n}) b(k-m; \mathbf{n}). \tag{2.24}$$

This relation shows that $E\{g(\mathbf{N})\}$ possesses a power-series expansion at $\rho = 0$ of the form

$$E\{g(\mathbf{N})\} = \sum_{k=0}^{\infty} \rho^k f_g(k), \tag{2.25}$$

with coefficients given by

$$f_g(k) = \sum_{0 \leq |\mathbf{n}| \leq k} g(\mathbf{n}) b(k - | \mathbf{n} |; \mathbf{n}), \quad k = 0, 1, \ldots. \tag{2.26}$$

By appropriate choices of $g(\mathbf{n})$ various performance measures can be computed, e.g., $I\{n_j = i\}$ for the marginal probability that $N_j = i$, $g(\mathbf{n}) = n_j^i$ for the ith moment of N_j, $i = 0, 1, \ldots$, and $g(\mathbf{n}) = n_h n_j$ for the cross moment of N_h and N_j, $h, j = 1, \ldots, s$. It is more efficient for obtaining such performance measures to compute first their coefficients via (2.26) and then to use (2.25) than to compute first the state probabilities via (2.22) and then the performance measures directly from the state probabilities. In the first way, algorithms for accelerating the convergence can be applied directly to partial sums of the series (2.25) and the storage requirement for the coefficients can be reduced, cf. section 3. For many systems, characteristics of the waiting or response time distributions can be computed once the joint queue-length distribution has been determined, e.g., by Little's law for mean waiting or mean response times. These relations will not be discussed here.

3 On the implementation of the PSA

This section concerns some more technical issues of the PSA. Section 3.1 discusses a modification of the computation scheme by means of a conformal transformation in order to enlarge the radius of convergence of the power series. Further improvement of the convergence of these series can be obtained by applying the ϵ-algorithm; this matter is discussed in section 3.2. Section 3.3 is devoted to issues concerning the efficient storage of the coefficients of the power series.

3.1 Enlarging the radius of convergence of the power series

Experience has taught us that the power-series (2.22) and (2.25) usually do not converge for all values of ρ for which a system is stable (by definition for $\rho < 1$). One way to overcome this difficulty is to introduce the following bilinear mapping of the interval $[0,1]$ onto itself,

$$\theta = \Gamma_G(\rho) \doteq \frac{(1+G)\rho}{1+G\rho}, \qquad \rho = \Gamma_G^{-1}(\theta) = \frac{\theta}{1+G-G\theta}. \tag{3.1}$$

Any singularity outside the circle $\mid \rho - \frac{1}{2} \mid = \frac{1}{2}$ may be removed from the unit disk by this procedure with an appropriate choice of the parameter G. Another computation scheme is then obtained by introducing, instead of (2.22), the following power-series expansions of the state probabilities as functions of θ:

$$p(\mathbf{n}) = \theta^{|\mathbf{n}|} \sum_{k=0}^{\infty} \theta^k b_G(k;\mathbf{n}), \quad \mathbf{n} \in \mathbb{N}^s. \tag{3.2}$$

Replacing ρ by θ in the balance equations (2.1) according to (3.1), substituting the above power-series expansions in θ into these equations, and equating coefficients of corresponding powers of θ in the resulting equations leads to the following set of recursive relations: for $k = 0$, $\mathbf{n} \in \mathbb{N}^s$,

$$b_G(0;\mathbf{0}) = 1;$$

$$(1+G) \sum_{j=1}^{s} d_j(\mathbf{n}) b_G(0;\mathbf{n}) = \sum_{j=1}^{s} a_j(\mathbf{n} - \mathbf{e_j}) I\{n_j \geq 1\} b_G(0;\mathbf{n} - \mathbf{e_j}), \quad \mid \mathbf{n} \mid \geq 1; \tag{3.3}$$

for $k = 1, 2, \ldots$, for $\mathbf{n} = \mathbf{0}$,

$$b_G(k;\mathbf{0}) = - \sum_{1 \leq |\mathbf{n}| \leq k} b_G(k - \mid \mathbf{n} \mid; \mathbf{n}); \tag{3.4}$$

and for $\mathbf{n} \in \mathbb{N}^s$, $\mathbf{n} \neq \mathbf{0}$,

$$(1+G)\sum_{j=1}^{s} d_j(\mathbf{n})b_G(k;\mathbf{n}) = \sum_{j=1}^{s} a_j(\mathbf{n}-\mathbf{e_j})I\{n_j \geq 1\}$$

$$+ \sum_{j=1}^{s}\{Gd_j(\mathbf{n}) - a_j(\mathbf{n})\}b_G(k-1;\mathbf{n})b_G(k;\mathbf{n}-\mathbf{e_j})$$

$$+ \sum_{j=1}^{s} d_j(\mathbf{n}+\mathbf{e_j})\{(1+G)b_G(k-1;\mathbf{n}+\mathbf{e_j}) - GI\{k \geq 2\}b_G(k-2;\mathbf{n}+\mathbf{e_j})\}. \quad (3.5)$$

Relation (3.5) mainly differs from (2.21) through the occurrence of terms with coefficients of the form $b(k-2;\mathbf{n}+\mathbf{e_j})$, $j = 1,\ldots,s$. An appropriate choice of the parameter G depends on the radii of convergence of the power series. Since the latter usually are not known for models to which the PSA is applied, a good practical policy is the following. If only a few terms of the power series (say, 12-15) will or can be computed, take $G = 0$; otherwise, execute a test-run with $G = 0$ and 5-10 terms, estimate the smallest radius of convergence, and take a value of G such that the power series are not too strongly divergent for the highest value of the load ρ for which performance measures will be evaluated. The power series do not need to be convergent when the ϵ-algorithm, which will be discussed in the next section, is applied.

3.2 Improving the convergence of the power series

Another technique for removing singularities from inside the unit disk is application of the ϵ-algorithm. The ϵ-algorithm aims to accelerate the convergence of slowly convergent sequences or to determine a value for divergent sequences, cf. [17], [14]. It converts a polynomial into quotients of two polynomials. The ϵ-algorithm consists of the following recursive scheme:

$$\epsilon_{\kappa}^{(m)} = \epsilon_{\kappa-2}^{(m+1)} + [\epsilon_{\kappa-1}^{(m+1)} - \epsilon_{\kappa-1}^{(m)}]^{-1}, \quad m \geq -\kappa, \quad \kappa = 1,2,\ldots, \quad (3.6)$$

with initial conditions:

$$\epsilon_{2\kappa}^{-\kappa-1} \doteq 0, \quad \kappa = 0,1,\ldots; \qquad \epsilon_{-1}^{(m)} \doteq 0, \quad \epsilon_{0}^{(m)} \doteq \sum_{k=0}^{m} c_k\theta^k, \quad m = 0,1,\ldots; \quad (3.7)$$

here, the c_k, $k = 0,1,2,\ldots$, stand for coefficients of a series such as defined in (2.22), (2.25) or (3.2). Only the even sequences $\{\epsilon_{2\kappa}^{(m)}, m = 0,1,\ldots\}$, $\kappa = 1,2,\ldots$, may be sequences which converge faster to a limit than the initial sequence. The odd sequences are only intermediate steps in the calculation scheme. The ϵ-algorithm turns a divergent series into a convergent series if the analytic continuation of the function defined by the series at $\theta = 0$ possesses only a finite number of poles as singularities inside the unit circle $\mid \theta \mid \leq 1$. It transforms the initial sequence of polynomials into sequences of quotients of two polynomials. More precisely, $\epsilon_{2\kappa}^{(m-2\kappa)}$ will be a quotient of a polynomial of degree $m - \kappa$ over a polynomial of degree κ, and

$$\mid \epsilon_{0}^{(m)} - \epsilon_{2\kappa}^{(m-2\kappa)} \mid = O(\theta^{m+1}), \quad \theta \to 0, \quad \kappa = 1,2,\ldots,m, \quad m = 1,2,\ldots. \quad (3.8)$$

When the heavy traffic behaviour of the moments of the queue length distribution is known beforehand, the performance of the ϵ-algorithm can be improved by a modification of the initial values $\epsilon_0^{(m)}$, cf. [5]. Before application of the ϵ-algorithm the coefficients of the power series are extrapolated to take into account the pole at $\rho = 1$ ($\theta = 1$). It means that we take for first order poles

$$\epsilon_0^{(m)} = \sum_{k=0}^{m} c_k \theta^k + c_m \frac{\theta^{m+1}}{1-\theta}, \quad m = 0, 1, 2, \ldots, \tag{3.9}$$

and for second order poles

$$\epsilon_0^{(m)} = \sum_{k=0}^{m} c_k \theta^k + c_m \frac{\theta^{m+1}}{1-\theta} + [c_m - c_{m-1}] \frac{\theta^{m+1}}{(1-\theta)^2}, \quad m = 1, 2, \ldots, \tag{3.10}$$

instead of the last relation of (3.7). The pole at $\theta = 1$ is preserved in other even sequences produced by the ϵ-algorithm. It should be noted that not every queue grows without bound as $\rho \uparrow 1$ in some systems; modifications (3.9) and (3.10) should only be applied to those moments which do have a pole at $\theta = 1$ in order to accelerate the convergence, although the modified sequences will converge to the same limit as the original sequence if the latter is convergent. For probabilities which are known to vanish as $\rho \uparrow 1$ ($\theta \uparrow 1$), the initial sequence of the ϵ-algorithm can be replaced by

$$\epsilon_0^{(m)} = \sum_{k=0}^{m} c_k \theta^k - \theta^{m+1} \sum_{k=0}^{m} c_k = (1-\theta) \sum_{k=0}^{m} \theta^k \sum_{i=0}^{k} c_i, \quad m = 0, 1, 2, \ldots. \tag{3.11}$$

It may happen that the power series are so strongly divergent that numerical instabilities occur when a large number of terms is computed. In that case, a conformal mapping as discussed in section 3.1 should be used together with the ϵ-algorithm. Numerical instabilities of the PSA may also occur, because a large number of coefficients have to be summed to obtain the coefficients of the state 0, cf. (2.20), and the coefficients of aggregated performance measures, cf. (2.26). This problem can be impaired by splitting these large summations into smaller partial sums.

The number of terms M of the power-series expansions, and the number of steps κ in the ϵ-algorithm, cf. (3.6), which are needed to reach a certain accuracy, depend on various properties of the models. Generally, these quantities increase with increasing load, with increasing number of queues, with increasing coefficient of variation of distributions, and with increasing asymmetry between the parameters of the various queues. Numerical experience has taught us that application of the ϵ-algorithm strongly improves the performance of the PSA and that, in some cases, it even leads to good estimations of heavy traffic limits. For most systems it is very difficult to derive tight upper bounds on errors for the PSA together with the ϵ-algorithm. The order of magnitude of the errors usually has to be estimated from differences in performance measures computed on the basis of M and of $M - 1, M - 2, \ldots$ terms of their power-series expansions. Further, exact relations between performance measures, such as pseudo-conservation laws for polling systems, have proven helpful in estimating the order of magnitude of errors.

3.3 On the implementation of the PSA

For most models, limitations on storage capacity for the coefficients of the power-series expansions are more important restrictions on the applicability of the PSA than limitations on computing time. The evaluation of power-series expansions up to the Mth power of ρ (or θ, cf. (3.1)) requires the computation of

$$B_s(M) = \binom{M + s + 1}{s + 1} \tag{3.12}$$

coefficients $b(k; \mathbf{n})$, namely those with $k+ \mid \mathbf{n} \mid \leq M$. The complexity of the computation of a single coefficient $b(k; \mathbf{n})$ depends on the structure of the model, in particular on the number of non-zero transition rates. In order to make an efficient use of the available memory space we map the multi-dimensional region of lattice points $(k, \mathbf{n})$ with $k+ \mid \mathbf{n} \mid \leq M$ onto the set of integers $\{0, \ldots, B_s(M) - 1\}$ by means of the one-to-one mapping

$$C(k; \mathbf{n}) \doteq \binom{k + \mid \mathbf{n} \mid + s}{s + 1} + \sum_{j = \mid \mathbf{n} \mid + 1}^{\mid \mathbf{n} \mid + k} \binom{s + j - 1}{j} + \sum_{j=2}^{s} \binom{s - j + \sum_{i=j}^{s} n_i}{s - j + 1}. \tag{3.13}$$

This mapping has the property that points $(k - 1; \mathbf{n})$, $(k; \mathbf{n} - \mathbf{e_j})$, $(k - 1; \mathbf{n} + \mathbf{e_j})$, $(k - 2; \mathbf{n} + \mathbf{e_j})$, $j = 1, \ldots, s$, all have a lower value than the point $(k; \mathbf{n})$, $k = 0, 1, \ldots$, $\mathbf{n} \in \mathbb{N}^s$. Another mapping with this property has been discussed in [5], but the latter mapping has some disadvantages in more complicated models. The above procedure enlarges the number of terms of the power-series expansions which can be computed with a given storage capacity at the costs of increased computation time needed for the determination of the location of the coefficients in the array in which they are stored. A further reduction of storage requirement can be realized when only a limited number of performance measures has to be evaluated. In most cases, one is not interested in all individual state probabilities. Then, the coefficients of the power-series expansions of the important performance measures can be aggregated during the execution of the PSA, cf. (2.26), and stored in separate (relatively small) arrays, while the coefficients of the state probabilities can be deleted as soon as they are not needed anymore in further computations. This approach reduces storage requirement for calculating M terms of the power-series expansions from $B_s(M)$ to $D_s(M)$, where $D_s(M)$ is the largest distance (in terms of the mapping $C(k; \mathbf{n})$, cf. (3.13)) between coefficients occurring in a single equation of (2.21) or (3.5), cf. [5],

$$D_s(M) = \binom{M + s}{s}, \text{ if } G = 0, \quad D_s(M) = \binom{M + s}{s} + \binom{M + s - 2}{s - 1}, \text{ if } G > 0. \tag{3.14}$$

Notice that the PSA considers a parametrized set of systems with the same service rates and with the same proportions between their arrival rates, i.e., with arrival rates $\rho a_j(\mathbf{n})$ where ρ varies between 0 and 1. Hence, the fact that the PSA adds a dimension (of the power-series expansions) to the state space $\mathbb{N}^s$ is compensated for by the fact that once the coefficients of the power series have been computed, performance measures can be determined with relatively little effort for various values of the load ρ. Moreover, by deleting coefficients which are not needed anymore in further iterations the storage requirement is reduced to the original dimension.

4 Generalizations of the PSA

The concept of the PSA is generalized to QBDPs in section 4.1. Other generalizations of the PSA are briefly indicated in section 4.2.

4.1 The PSA for quasi-birth-and-death processes

In this section the PSA will be generalized to the class of multi-queue systems of which the underlying stochastic queue-length processes are multi-dimensional QBDPs. The finite supplementary space will be denoted by $\mathcal{V}$ and the supplementary variable by F. Let, in state $\mathbf{n} \in \mathbb{N}^s$ and phase $\phi \in \mathcal{V}$, $\rho a_j(\mathbf{n}, \phi, \psi)$ be the arrival rate to queue j causing a transition to phase ψ, $d_j(\mathbf{n}, \phi, \psi)$ the departure rate from queue j causing a transition to phase ψ, and $u(\mathbf{n}, \phi, \psi)$ the phase-transition rate to phase ψ, for $j = 1, \ldots, s$, $\psi \in \mathcal{V}$. Again, $d_j(\mathbf{n}, \phi, \psi) = 0$ if $n_j = 0$, for $\mathbf{n} \in \mathbb{N}^s$, $j = 1, \ldots, s$, $\phi, \psi \in \mathcal{V}$. Let $p(\mathbf{n}, \phi)$ denote the probability that the process $(\mathbf{N}, F)$ is in state $(\mathbf{n}, \phi)$, $\mathbf{n} \in \mathbb{N}^s$, $\phi \in \mathcal{V}$. The global balance equations for the flows out of and into state $(\mathbf{n}, \phi)$ read: for $\mathbf{n} \in \mathbb{N}^s$, $\phi \in \mathcal{V}$,

$$\sum_{\psi \in \mathcal{V}} \left(\sum_{j=1}^{s} [\rho a_j(\mathbf{n}, \phi, \psi) + d_j(\mathbf{n}, \phi, \psi)] + u(\mathbf{n}, \phi, \psi) \right) p(\mathbf{n}, \phi)$$

$$= \sum_{\psi \in \mathcal{V}} u(\mathbf{n}, \psi, \phi) p(\mathbf{n}, \psi) + \sum_{\psi \in \mathcal{V}} \sum_{j=1}^{s} \rho a_j(\mathbf{n} - \mathbf{e_j}, \psi, \phi) I\{n_j \geq 1\} p(\mathbf{n} - \mathbf{e_j}, \psi)$$

$$+ \sum_{\psi \in \mathcal{V}} \sum_{j=1}^{s} d_j(\mathbf{n} + \mathbf{e_j}, \psi, \phi) p(\mathbf{n} + \mathbf{e_j}, \psi). \qquad (4.1)$$

The state probabilities sum to 1. This can be written as

$$\sum_{m=0}^{\infty} \sum_{|\mathbf{n}|=m} \sum_{\phi \in \mathcal{V}} p(\mathbf{n}, \phi) = 1. \qquad (4.2)$$

In a similar way as in section 2 it can be shown that the state probabilities possess power-series expansions in terms of the load ρ: for $\mathbf{n} \in \mathbb{N}^s$, $\phi \in \mathcal{V}$,

$$p(\mathbf{n}, \phi) = \rho^{|\mathbf{n}|} \sum_{k=0}^{\infty} \rho^k b(k; \mathbf{n}, \phi). \qquad (4.3)$$

Substituting these power-series expansions into the global balance equations (4.1) and equating coefficients of corresponding powers of ρ leads to: for $k = 0, 1, 2, \ldots$, for $\mathbf{n} \in \mathbb{N}^s$, $\phi \in \mathcal{V}$,

$$\sum_{\psi \in \mathcal{V}} \left(\sum_{j=1}^{s} d_j(\mathbf{n}, \phi, \psi) + u(\mathbf{n}, \phi, \psi) \right) b(k; \mathbf{n}, \phi) = \sum_{\psi \in \mathcal{V}} u(\mathbf{n}, \psi, \phi) b(k; \mathbf{n}, \psi)$$

$$+ \sum_{\psi \in \mathcal{V}} \sum_{j=1}^{s} [a_j(\mathbf{n} - \mathbf{e_j}, \psi, \phi) I\{n_j \geq 1\} b(k; \mathbf{n} - \mathbf{e_j}, \psi)$$

$$-a_j(\mathbf{n}, \phi, \psi) I\{k \geq 1\} b(k-1; \mathbf{n}, \phi) + d_j(\mathbf{n} + \mathbf{e_j}, \psi, \phi) I\{k \geq 1\} b(k-1; \mathbf{n} + \mathbf{e_j}, \psi)]. \qquad (4.4)$$

These equations allow the computation of the sets of coefficients $\{b(k;\mathbf{n},\phi),\ \phi\in\mathcal{V}\}$ for vectors $(k;\mathbf{n})$ with $\mathbf{n}\neq\mathbf{0}$ in order of increasing value of $C(k;\mathbf{n})$, cf. (3.13), if for each $\mathbf{n}\in\mathbb{N}^s$, $\mathbf{n}\neq\mathbf{0}$, there is at least one $\phi_0\in\mathcal{V}$ with, cf. (2.4),

$$\sum_{j=1}^{s}\sum_{\psi\in\mathcal{V}}d_j(\mathbf{n},\phi_0,\psi)>0,\tag{4.5}$$

and if the set of transition rates $\{u(\mathbf{n},\phi,\psi),\ \phi,\psi\in\mathcal{V}\}$ is such that from any $\phi_1\in\mathcal{V}$ for which (4.5) does not hold there is a path to a $\phi_0\in\mathcal{V}$ for which (4.5) does hold. Then, the coefficients $\{b(k;\mathbf{n},\phi),\ \phi\in\mathcal{V}\}$ can be computed from (4.4), possibly by solving a set of at most $|\mathcal{V}|$ linear equations. That the state probabilities sum to 1 implies the following relations for the state $\mathbf{0}$:

$$\sum_{\phi\in\mathcal{V}}b(0;\mathbf{0},\phi)=1;\quad\sum_{\phi\in\mathcal{V}}b(k;\mathbf{0},\phi)=-\sum_{1\leq|\mathbf{n}|\leq k}\sum_{\phi\in\mathcal{V}}b(k-|\mathbf{n}|;\mathbf{n},\phi),\quad k=1,2,\ldots.$$

$$(4.6)$$

For QBDPs there does not need to be a unique empty state. The equations (4.4) become for $\mathbf{n}=\mathbf{0}$: for $k=0,1,2,\ldots$, for $\phi\in\mathcal{V}$,

$$\sum_{\psi\in\mathcal{V}}u(\mathbf{0},\phi,\psi)b(k;\mathbf{0},\phi)=\sum_{\psi\in\mathcal{V}}u(\mathbf{n},\psi,\phi)b(k;\mathbf{0},\psi)$$

$$+I\{k\geq 1\}\sum_{\psi\in\mathcal{V}}\sum_{j=1}^{s}[d_j(\mathbf{e_j},\psi,\phi)b(k-1;\mathbf{e_j},\psi)-a_j(\mathbf{0},\phi,\psi)b(k-1;\mathbf{0},\phi)].\tag{4.7}$$

For fixed k, $k=0,1,2,\ldots$, this is a dependent set of equations. Replacing one of these equations by (4.6) yields an independent set of equations if the Markov chain with transition probabilities $u(\mathbf{0},\phi,\psi)$, $\phi,\psi\in\mathcal{V}$, is irreducible. If one of the foregoing conditions is not satisfied then the order in which the coefficients of the power-series expansions are computed has to be modified. This rather technical issue will not be elaborated upon. The reader is referred to [13] for an example of how the PSA can be modified if one of these conditions is not satisfied. The complexity of the PSA mainly depends on the number of stations s and on the size of the supplementary space $\mathcal{V}$. If coefficients of the power-series expansions (4.3) are computed up to the Mth power of ρ, then the number of coefficients to be computed is at most $B_s(M)\times|\mathcal{V}|$, with $B_s(M)$ given by (3.12) and $|\mathcal{V}|$ the number of states in $\mathcal{V}$. For some states $\mathbf{n}\in\mathbb{N}^s$, the supplementary space may be smaller than $|\mathcal{V}|$, e.g., for the state $\mathbf{n}=\mathbf{0}$ if part of $\mathcal{V}$ is used to describe PH service time distributions.

4.2 Other generalizations of the PSA

Further generalizations of the PSA are possible to QBDPs with migration and with finite buffer sizes, and to Markovian models with batch arrivals. An example of a QBDP with migration is the tandem queueing system to be discussed in section 7.1. Finite buffers can be incorporated into the models by taking $a_j(\mathbf{n},\phi,\psi)=0$ for $\phi,\psi\in\mathcal{V}$ and for all $\mathbf{n}\in\mathbb{N}^s$ with $n_j\geq L_j$, L_j being the buffer size for queue j, $j=1,\ldots,s$. However, if all queues have finite capacity then the system is stable for all values of the offered load ρ, and this requires modification of the conformal mapping (3.1) and other aspects of the implementation of the PSA. It is still an open question if or under which circumstances the PSA in conjunction with the ϵ-algorithm is more efficient than solving the finite set of global balance equations for such systems directly. Admission of batch arrivals disturbs the birth-and-death structure, and thereby property (2.22). An example of a system with multiple arrivals is discussed in section 5.3; see further [16].

5   Parallel-server systems

The PSA will be applied in this section to models with several queues in parallel, and with a server assigned to each queue. The coupled-processor systems in section 5.1 and the load-balancing systems in section 5.2 are examples of BDPs. The fork systems in section 5.3 have multiple arrivals. It turns out that the leading terms in the power-series expansions of the state probabilities are different from those for BDPs. This leads to a different, but recursive, computation scheme for the coefficients of the power-series expansions.

5.1   Coupled processor systems

This section deals with a system consisting of s parallel servers (processors), each with its own queue. At queue j, jobs arrive according to a Poisson process with intensity $\lambda_j = \rho a_j$, $j = 1, \ldots, s$. Jobs arriving at queue j require an amount of service which is exponentially distributed with parameter μ_j, $j = 1, \ldots, s$. The service rate at queue j depends on the state of the system: it is equal to $r_j(\mathbf{n})$ if the system is in state $\mathbf{n}$, $\mathbf{n} \in \mathbb{N}^s$, $j = 1, \ldots, s$. The stationary state probabilities $p(\mathbf{n})$ satisfy the following set of global balance equations: for $\mathbf{n} \in \mathbb{N}^s$,

$$\left(\sum_{j=1}^{s} \lambda_j + \sum_{j=1}^{s} \mu_j r_j(\mathbf{n}) \right) p(\mathbf{n}) = \sum_{j=1}^{s} \lambda_j p(\mathbf{n} - \mathbf{e_j}) + \sum_{j=1}^{s} \mu_j r_j(\mathbf{n} + \mathbf{e_j}) p(\mathbf{n} + \mathbf{e_j}). \quad (5.1)$$

Further, the law of total probability (2.2) holds. The queue-length process is an s-dimensional BDP and, hence, the PSA can be applied directly, as in section 2.1. The only condition for the standard application of the PSA is that, cf. (2.4),

$$\sum_{j=1}^{s} r_j(\mathbf{n}) > 0, \quad \text{if } \mathbf{n} \neq \mathbf{0}, \quad \mathbf{n} \in \mathbb{N}^s. \quad (5.2)$$

If this condition which is not necessary for stability is not fulfilled, the computation scheme of the PSA has to be modified. This technical issue will not be discussed here. Finally, if the model is generalized with a MAP with Θ_j states at processor j and a PH service requirement distribution with Ψ_j stages for jobs at processor j, $j = 1, \ldots, s$, then the size of the supplementary space becomes

$$|\mathcal{V}| = \prod_{h=1}^{s} \Theta_h \times \prod_{j=1}^{s} \Psi_j. \quad (5.3)$$

5.2   Load-balancing systems

Consider a system consisting of s parallel servers, each with its own queue. There is one Poisson arrival stream with rate $\lambda = \rho a$. Jobs are routed to one of the queues upon arrival. The service rate of server j is μ_j, $j = 1, \ldots, s$. The balance equations for the state probabilities $p(\mathbf{n})$ read: for $\mathbf{n} \in \mathbb{N}^s$,

$$\left(\lambda + \sum_{j=1}^{s} \mu_j I\{n_j \geq 1\} \right) p(\mathbf{n}) = \sum_{j=1}^{s} \lambda \gamma_j (\mathbf{n} - \mathbf{e_j}) p(\mathbf{n} - \mathbf{e_j}) I\{n_j \geq 1\} + \sum_{j=1}^{s} \mu_j p(\mathbf{n} + \mathbf{e_j});$$

(5.4)

here, $\gamma_j(\mathbf{n})$ stands for the probability that an arriving job joins queue j when the system is in state $\mathbf{n}$ upon its arrival, $\mathbf{n} \in \mathbb{N}^s$, $j = 1, \ldots, s$. Further, the law of total probability (2.2) holds. For general allocation functions $\gamma_j(\mathbf{n})$ the queue-length process is a BDP so that it is possible to use the power-series expansions (2.22). If this function is such that $\gamma_j(\mathbf{n}) = 0$ if $n_j > \min\{n_i; i = 1, \ldots, s\}$, i.e., if every arriving job chooses one the shortest queues, then many coefficients $b(k; \mathbf{n})$ in (2.22) vanish. For this case, the following power-series expansions hold for the state probabilities:

$$p(\mathbf{n}) = \rho^{l(\mathbf{n})} \sum_{k=0}^{\infty} \rho^k b(k; \mathbf{n}); \quad l(\mathbf{n}) \doteq s \max_{j=1,\ldots,s} \{n_j\} - \#\{i; n_i < \max_{j=1,\ldots,s} \{n_j\}\}, \quad \mathbf{n} \in \mathbb{N}^s.$$

(5.5)

Notice that $l(\mathbf{n}) \geq \mid \mathbf{n} \mid$ for all $\mathbf{n} \in \mathbb{N}^s$, while $l(\mathbf{n}) = \mid \mathbf{n} \mid$ iff $\max\{n_i; i = 1, \ldots, s\} - \min\{n_i; i = 1, \ldots, s\} \leq 1$. By using (5.5) the PSA can handle systems with much more queues than that it can handle without this property, especially if all service rates are equal and the allocation function $\gamma_j(\mathbf{n})$ is symmetrical, and if also this symmetry is used to reduce the number of coefficients to be computed and stored. The number of coefficients to be computed if coefficients of the power-series expansions are computed up to the Mth power of ρ, is given in [10] for the asymmetrical as well as the symmetrical case. If the model is generalized with a MAP with Θ states and PH service time distributions, with Ψ_j stages for service at queue j, $j = 1, \ldots, s$, then the size of the supplementary space is

$$\mid \mathcal{V} \mid = \Theta \times \prod_{j=1}^{s} \Psi_j.$$

(5.6)

5.3 Fork systems

Fork systems are models for parallel computing devices. The system consists of s parallel processors, each with its own queue. There is one arrival stream of jobs. Jobs split upon arrival. Suppose for simplicity that every job sends a partial job to each queue. Let $\lambda = \rho a$ denote the arrival rate, and let μ_j be the service rate of processor j, $j = 1, \ldots, s$. The queue-length process of this model is a Markov process, but not a birth-and-death process, because an arrival leads to a transition in each component of the state space. The arrival process is a special kind of batch arrival process. The balance equations for the state probabilities $p(\mathbf{n})$ read: for $\mathbf{n} \in \mathbb{N}^s$,

$$\left(\lambda + \sum_{j=1}^{s} \mu_j I\{n_j > 0\} \right) p(\mathbf{n}) = \lambda p(\mathbf{n} - \mathbf{e}) I\{\forall j \ n_j \geq 1\} + \sum_{j=1}^{s} \mu_j p(\mathbf{n} + \mathbf{e_j}); \quad (5.7)$$

here, $\mathbf{e} \doteq (1, 1, \ldots, 1)$ denotes the s-dimensional unit vector. Further, the law of total probability (2.2) holds. For these systems, the following power-series expansions for the state probabilities hold:

$$p(\mathbf{n}) = \rho^{l(\mathbf{n})} \sum_{k=0}^{\infty} \rho^k b(k; \mathbf{n}); \quad l(\mathbf{n}) \doteq \max_{j=1,\ldots,s} \{n_j\}, \quad \mathbf{n} \in \mathbb{N}^s. \qquad (5.8)$$

Notice that $l(\mathbf{n} - \mathbf{e}) = l(\mathbf{n}) - 1$, and that $l(\mathbf{n} + \mathbf{e_j}) = l(\mathbf{n}) + 1$ if $n_j = l(\mathbf{n})$ while $l(\mathbf{n} + \mathbf{e_j}) = l(\mathbf{n})$ if $n_j < l(\mathbf{n})$, for $\mathbf{n} \in \mathbb{N}^s$, $j = 1, \ldots, s$. Hence, substituting (5.8) into (5.7) and equating coefficients of corresponding powers of ρ leads to: for $\mathbf{n} \in \mathbb{N}^s$,

$$\sum_{j=1}^{s} \mu_j I\{n_j \geq 1\} b(k; \mathbf{n}) = ab(k; \mathbf{n} - \mathbf{e}) I\{\forall j \; n_j \geq 1\} - aI\{k \geq 1\} b(k - 1; \mathbf{n})$$

$$+ \sum_{j=1}^{s} \mu_j I\{n_j < l(\mathbf{n})\} b(k; \mathbf{n} + \mathbf{e_j}) + \sum_{j=1}^{s} \mu_j I\{k \geq 1, n_j = l(\mathbf{n})\} b(k - 1; \mathbf{n} + \mathbf{e_j}). \qquad (5.9)$$

The fact that the state probabilities sum to 1 implies the following relations

$$b(0; \mathbf{0}) = 1; \qquad b(k; \mathbf{0}) = - \sum_{1 \leq l(\mathbf{n}) \leq k} b(k - l(\mathbf{n}); \mathbf{n}), \quad k = 1, 2, \ldots. \qquad (5.10)$$

The order of calculation has to be chosen such that coefficients $b(k; \mathbf{n} + \mathbf{e_j})$ for j with $n_j < l(\mathbf{n})$ are computed before $b(k; \mathbf{n})$, cf. (5.9). This means that for fixed k and $l(\mathbf{n})$, coefficients $b(k; \mathbf{n})$ have to be computed first for the vector $\mathbf{n}$ with $n_j = l(\mathbf{n})$ for all j, $j = 1, \ldots, s$, and then successively for vectors $\mathbf{n}$ with $min \{n_i; i = 1, \ldots, s\} = l(\mathbf{n}) - 1, l(\mathbf{n}) - 2, \ldots, 0$. In this way, the coefficients $b(k; \mathbf{n})$ can be recursively computed in order of increasing value of $m = k + l(\mathbf{n})$, and for fixed m in order of increasing value of k. The number of states $\mathbf{n} \in \mathbb{N}^s$ with $l(\mathbf{n}) = m$ for some m is equal to $(m+1)^s - m^s$. If coefficients of the power-series expansions (5.8) are computed up to the Mth power of ρ, then the number of coefficients to be computed is

$$B_s(M) = \sum_{m=0}^{M} (M + 1 - m)[(m + 1)^s - m^s] = \sum_{m=1}^{M+1} m^s. \qquad (5.11)$$

The coefficients of the power-series expansions of moments of the joint queue-length distribution can be computed in a similar way as in (2.26), but with $| \mathbf{n} |$ replaced by $l(\mathbf{n})$. If the model is generalized with a MAP with Θ states and PH service time distributions with Ψ_j stages for service at processor j, $j = 1, \ldots, s$, then the size of the supplementary space is given by (5.6).

6   Multi-queue systems with switching servers

An important class of models to which the PSA is applicable is the class of polling models. Polling systems are systems with several stations, each generating a stream of jobs or messages, and one or more servers which are not devoted to a specific class of jobs, but which alternately serve jobs from one of the stations. Usually, the times needed to switch service from one station to another are non-negligible. Polling systems form a very rich class of queueing systems due to the many priority or visit rules and service disciplines that they allow. Important areas for application of these models are computer-communication systems, in which several stations share a single communication channel and compete for access to this channel, e.g., local area networks. Section 6.1 contains a general introduction of the PSA for polling systems, the sections 6.2 and 6.3 are concerned with specific polling models.

6.1 The PSA for various polling strategies

The service strategies for polling systems can often be divided into three parts, which can be chosen independently of each other: a rule for the order in which the server visits the queues; rules for the number of services per visit to the various queues; and a rule for the behaviour of the server when the system is empty.

Examples of order-of-visit rules are: polling in a fixed periodic order (cyclic: $1, 2, \ldots, s$, $1, 2, \ldots$; star: $1, 2, 1, 3, \ldots, 1, s, 1, 2, 1, \ldots$; scanning: $1, 2, \ldots, s-1, s, s-1, \ldots, 2, 1, 2, \ldots$; or according to some general finite polling table); random or Markovian polling: the next queue to be visited is determined by a random mechanism which may depend on the current position of the server (Markovian polling) or not (random polling); polling according to fixed priorities attributed to the queues; or polling according to a dynamic (state-dependent) rule such as priority for the longest queue, priority for the queue with the most expected work, elevator-type polling, i.e., in principle as scanning above, but skipping queues which are empty, or a greedy strategy, choosing the closest non-empty queue. The choice of the order-of-visit rule will depend on the availability of information about the presence of jobs at the various stations. Further, this choice may depend on the configuration of the system, i.e., on whether or not direct connections between pairs of stations in the network exist, and on the distances between the stations, in terms of mean switching times. The PSA can handle all these rules, but in each case a supplementary variable is needed to indicate the position of the server. For the case of periodic polling this variable has to indicate the current entry of the table, for all other cases it has to indicate the station which is being visited by the server.

Examples of number-of-services rules are: exhaustive service (the server remains serving until a queue becomes empty); limited service (a fixed number of jobs is served, at most); Bernoulli service (after each service another service may be started with a fixed probability); gated-type service (only jobs present in a queue at the instant at which the server arrives at that queue are eligible for service); time-limited service (during a time interval of fixed length new services may start). The number-of-services rules may be different for the various queues or visits. The PSA can be applied to systems with Bernoulli service, including exhaustive and 1-limited service as special cases, without additional supplementary space. For general limited service an additional supplementary variable is needed to keep track of the number of services completed during the current visit. Time-limited service can only be approximated by Erlang distributed timers, and requires a supplementary variable to keep track of the stage of the timer. Gated-type disciplines cannot be modeled by an s-dimensional QBDP, because they require an unbounded supplementary space, but they can be modeled by an $(s+1)$-dimensional QBDP, where the additional queue contains the jobs which are eligible for service during the current visit.

Examples of empty-system rules are: the server keeps on switching according to the order-of-visit rule; the server remains at the last served queue; the server goes to a state of rest; the server goes to a specific queue (e.g., the queue with the highest arrival rate), or to one from a specific set of queues. The choice of the empty-system rule will also depend on the availability of information. The first rule requires only local information, the other rules require information from all stations. The PSA can be applied to systems in which the server keeps on switching or in which the server goes to one specific queue or state of rest in a straightforward manner. If the server may rest at several queues, then the computation scheme has to be modified, cf. [13].

In the next sections the PSA will be discussed in more detail for some specific polling strategies. The following notations will be used. A polling system will consist of s queues and a single server. Jobs arrive at queue j according to a Poisson process with rate $\lambda_j = \chi a_j$, $j = 1, \ldots, s$. The sum of the arrival processes at the various queues is a Poisson process with rate $\Lambda = \chi A = \chi \sum a_j$. Service times of jobs arriving at queue j are assumed to be exponentially distributed with rate μ_j, $j = 1, \ldots, s$. The load offered at queue j is $\rho_j \doteq \lambda_j / \mu_j$, $j = 1, \ldots, s$, and the total offered load to the system is $\rho \doteq \sum \rho_j$. The number-of-services rules are limited service, i.e., during a visit of the server to queue j at most K_j jobs will be served; if this number has been reached or queue j has been emptied, the server chooses the next queue according to the order-of-visit rule $(j = 1, \ldots, s)$. The times which the server needs for switching from queue i to queue j are assumed to be exponentially distributed with rates ν_{ij}, $i, j = 1, \ldots, s$. Two supplementary variables will be used to render the queue-length process into a QBDP. The supplementary variable H will indicate the position of the server, i.e., the queue to which the server is switching or to which the server is attending, and Z will indicate the status of the server; more specifically, $Z = -i$, $i = 1, \ldots, s$, indicates that the server is switching from queue i (to queue H) and $Z = \kappa$, $\kappa = 1, \ldots, K_H$, indicates that the server is performing the κth service during the current visit to queue H. If it is not necessary to keep track of the queue from which the server is switching, then $Z = 0$ will indicate the mere fact that the server is switching. The state probabilities of the QBDP (N, H, Z) will be denoted by $p(n, h, \kappa)$. In general, the condition for stability of a polling system depends, besides on the offered load ρ, also on the service strategy and the switching time distributions. Therefore, the PSA for polling systems will be based on power-series expansions of the state probabilities as functions of the *occupancy* χ of the system: for $n \in \mathbb{N}^s$, $h = 1, \ldots, s$, $\kappa = -s, \ldots, K_h$,

$$p(n, h, \kappa) = \chi^{|n|} \sum_{k=0}^{\infty} \chi^k b(k; n, h, \kappa); \qquad (6.1)$$

here, the occupance χ is defined in such a way that the system is stable for $0 \leq \chi < 1$. It is also possible to work with power-series expansions as functions of the offered load ρ, but then the conformal mapping (3.1) and the modifications (3.9), (3.10), (3.11) of the initial sequence of the ϵ-algorithm have to adapted.

6.2   Systems with cyclic polling strategies

This section is devoted to polling systems with limited service in which the order-of-visit rule is cyclic polling and in which the server continues to move along the queues when the system is empty. The condition for stability of these cyclic-polling systems reads:

$$\chi \doteq \rho + \delta_t \max_{j=1,\ldots,s} \{\lambda_j / K_j\} < 1; \qquad (6.2)$$

here, δ_t is the mean total switch-over time during one cycle of the server along the queues. For the case of cyclic polling it is not necessary to keep track of the queue from which the server is switching (this is queue $j - 1$ if the server is switching to queue

j, $j = 1, \ldots, s$; read here and below queue s for queue 0). Therefore, it is sufficient to have $Z = 0$ indicate that the server is switching. The switching rate from queue $j - 1$ to queue j will be denoted by ν_j, $j = 1, \ldots, s$. There is no unique empty state in this system, because the server continues to switch when the system is empty. The balance equations for the state probabilities $p(\mathbf{n}, h, \kappa)$ are: for $\mathbf{n} \in \mathbb{N}^s$, $h = 0, \ldots, s - 1$,

$$[\Lambda + \nu_{h+1}]p(\mathbf{n}, h+1, 0) = \sum_{j=1}^{s} \lambda_j I\{n_j \geq 1\}p(\mathbf{n} - \mathbf{e_j}, h+1, 0)$$

$$+\nu_h I\{n_h = 0\}p(\mathbf{n}, h, 0) + \mu_h \sum_{\kappa=1}^{K_h} I\{\kappa = K_h \vee n_h = 0\}p(\mathbf{n} + \mathbf{e_h}, h, \kappa); \qquad (6.3)$$

and for $\mathbf{n} \in \mathbb{N}^s$, $h = 1, \ldots, s$, $n_h \geq 1$, $\kappa = 1, \ldots, K_h$,

$$[\Lambda + \mu_h]p(\mathbf{n}, h, \kappa) = \sum_{j=1}^{s} \lambda_j I\{n_j \geq 1\}p(\mathbf{n} - \mathbf{e_j}, h, \kappa) + \nu_h I\{\kappa = 1\}p(\mathbf{n}, h, 0)$$

$$+\mu_h I\{\kappa \geq 2\}p(\mathbf{n} + \mathbf{e_h}, h, \kappa - 1). \qquad (6.4)$$

Further, it holds by the law of total probability that

$$\sum_{n_1=0}^{\infty} \cdots \sum_{n_s=0}^{\infty} \sum_{h=1}^{s} \sum_{\kappa=0}^{K_h} p(\mathbf{n}, h, \kappa) = 1. \qquad (6.5)$$

It should be noted that $p(\mathbf{n}, h, \kappa) = 0$ if $n_h = 0$, for all $\mathbf{n} \in \mathbb{N}^s$, $\kappa = 1, \ldots, K_h$, $h = 1, \ldots, s$. Substituting the power-series expansions (6.1) into the balance equations (6.3) and (6.4), and equating the coefficients of corresponding powers of χ in the resulting equations leads to the following set of equations for the coefficients in (6.1): for $k = 0, 1, 2, \ldots$, for $\mathbf{n} \in \mathbb{N}^s$, $h = 0, \ldots, s - 1$,

$$\nu_{h+1}b(k; \mathbf{n}, h+1, 0) = \sum_{j=1}^{s} a_j I\{n_j \geq 1\}b(k; \mathbf{n} - \mathbf{e_j}, h+1, 0)$$

$$-AI\{k \geq 1\}b(k-1; \mathbf{n}, h+1, 0) + \nu_h I\{n_h = 0\}b(k; \mathbf{n}, h, 0)$$

$$+\mu_h I\{k \geq 1\} \sum_{\kappa=1}^{K_h} I\{\kappa = K_h \vee n_h = 0\}b(k-1; \mathbf{n} + \mathbf{e_h}, h, \kappa); \qquad (6.6)$$

and for $k = 0, 1, 2, \ldots$, for $\mathbf{n} \in \mathbb{N}^s$, $h = 1, \ldots, s$, $n_h \geq 1$, $\kappa = 1, \ldots, K_h$,

$$\mu_h b(k; \mathbf{n}, h, \kappa) = \sum_{j=1}^{s} a_j I\{n_j \geq 1\}b(k; \mathbf{n} - \mathbf{e_j}, h, \kappa) - AI\{k \geq 1\}b(k-1; \mathbf{n}, h, \kappa)$$

$$+\nu_h I\{\kappa = 1\}b(k; \mathbf{n}, h, 0) + \mu_h I\{\kappa \geq 2, k \geq 1\}b(k-1; \mathbf{n} + \mathbf{e_h}, h, \kappa - 1). \quad (6.7)$$

It is readily verified that the set of equations (6.6) and (6.7) expresses coefficients $b(k; \mathbf{n}, h, \kappa)$ in terms of coefficients of lower order with respect to the mapping (3.13), or of the same order but with lower value of κ, $\kappa = 0, 1, \ldots, K_h$, with the exception of the term $b(k; \mathbf{n}, h, 0)$ in (6.6). The latter term only plays a role when $n_h = 0$ for some h, $h = 1, \ldots, s$. However, if $\mathbf{n} \neq \mathbf{0}$, the set of coefficients $b(k; \mathbf{n}, h, 0)$, for k and $\mathbf{n}$ fixed, can still be recursively computed by starting at a value $h = j$ with $n_j > 0$ and by proceeding the computations of the coefficients $b(k; \mathbf{n}, h, 0)$ then sequentially for $h = j + 1, \ldots, s, 1, \ldots, j - 1$. Hence, the only states which require further attention are those with $\mathbf{n} = \mathbf{0}$ and $\kappa = 0$. The equations (6.6) read for these states: for $k = 0, 1, 2, \ldots$, $h = 0, \ldots, s - 1$,

$$\nu_{h+1} b(k; \mathbf{0}, h+1, 0) = \nu_h b(k; \mathbf{0}, h, 0)$$
$$+ I\{k \geq 1\} \left(\mu_h \sum_{\kappa=1}^{K_h} b(k-1; \mathbf{e_h}, h, \kappa) - A b(k-1; \mathbf{0}, h+1, 0) \right). \tag{6.8}$$

It is readily seen, that these sets of equations are dependent for each k, $k = 0, 1, 2, \ldots$. Substituting the power-series expansions (6.1) into (6.5) and equating the coefficients of corresponding powers of χ in the resulting equation leads to the following equations:

$$\sum_{h=1}^{s} b(0; \mathbf{0}, h, 0) = 1;$$

$$\sum_{h=1}^{s} b(k; \mathbf{0}, h, 0) = - \sum_{1 \leq |\mathbf{n}| \leq k} \sum_{h=1}^{s} \sum_{\kappa=0}^{K_h} b(k - |\mathbf{n}|; \mathbf{n}, h, \kappa), \quad k = 1, 2, \ldots. \tag{6.9}$$

For each k, $k = 0, 1, 2, \ldots$, equation (6.9) and $s - 1$ equations of (6.8) form together a set of s linear equations by which the s coefficients $b(k; \mathbf{0}, h, 0)$, $h = 1, \ldots, s$, are uniquely determined.

If the model is generalized with a MAP with Θ_j states at station j, a PH service time distribution with Ψ_j stages for jobs at station j, and a PH switch-over time distribution with Ω_j stages for switches from station $j - 1$ to station j, $j = 1, \ldots, s$, then the size of the supplementary space is

$$| \mathcal{V} | = \prod_{h=1}^{s} \Theta_h \times \left(\sum_{j=1}^{s} \Omega_j + \sum_{j=1}^{s} K_j \Psi_j \right). \tag{6.10}$$

Systems with general periodic polling orders can be treated in a similar way as above, cf. [9]. It is rather straightforward to extend the PSA for cyclic-polling systems (as well as for polling systems with other order-of-visit rules) to systems with set-up times at the beginning of each visit to a station, cf. [1]. In particular, the sets of equations for the empty states remain similarly as above.

6.3 Systems with random polling strategies

This section is devoted to polling systems with limited service in which the order-of-visit rule is Markovian polling and in which the server continues to move along the queues when the system is empty. The probability that the server will switch to queue j after completion of a visit to queue i will be denoted by r_{ij}, $i, j = 1, \ldots, s$; these probabilities should be such that each queue is positive recurrent. The condition for stability of Markovian polling systems is

$$\chi \doteq \rho + \delta_a \max_{j=1,\dots,s} \{\lambda_j/(y_j K_j)\} < 1; \tag{6.11}$$

here, δ_a is the mean of an arbitrary switch-over time, and $\{y_j, \ j = 1,\dots,s\}$ is the stationary distribution of the Markov chain with transition probabilities $\{r_{ij}, \ i,j = 1,\dots,s\}$. The balance equations for the state probabilities $p(n,h,\kappa)$ of the QBDP (N,H,Z) are, for $n \in \mathbb{N}^s$, $h,\kappa = 1,\dots,s$,

$$[\Lambda + \nu_{\kappa h}]p(n,h,-\kappa) = \sum_{j=1}^{s} \lambda_j I\{n_j \geq 1\}p(n - e_j, h, -\kappa)$$

$$+ \sum_{j=1}^{s} \nu_{j\kappa}r_{\kappa h}I\{n_\kappa = 0\}p(n,\kappa,-j)$$

$$+\mu_\kappa r_{\kappa h}\sum_{i=1}^{K_\kappa} I\{i = K_\kappa \vee n_\kappa = 0\}p(n + e_\kappa, \kappa, i); \tag{6.12}$$

and for $n \in \mathbb{N}^s$, $h = 1,\dots,s$, $n_h \geq 1$, $\kappa = 1,\dots,K_h$,

$$[\Lambda + \mu_h]p(n,h,\kappa) = \sum_{j=1}^{s} \lambda_j I\{n_j \geq 1\}p(n - e_j, h, \kappa)$$

$$+\sum_{j=1}^{s} \nu_{jh}I\{\kappa = 1\}p(n,h,-j) + \mu_h I\{\kappa \geq 2\}p(n + e_h, h, \kappa - 1). \tag{6.13}$$

Further, it holds by the law of total probability that

$$\sum_{n_1=0}^{\infty} \cdots \sum_{n_s=0}^{\infty} \sum_{h=1}^{s} \left(\sum_{j=1}^{s} p(n,h,-j) + \sum_{\kappa=1}^{K_h} p(n,h,\kappa) \right) = 1. \tag{6.14}$$

As in section 6.2, $p(n,h,\kappa) = 0$ if $n_h = 0$, for all $n \in \mathbb{N}^s$, $\kappa = 1,\dots,K_h$, $h = 1,\dots,s$. Further, $p(n,h,-j) = 0$ if $r_{jh} = 0$, for all $n \in \mathbb{N}^s$, $j,h = 1,\dots,s$. Substituting the power-series expansions (6.1) into the balance equations (6.12) and (6.13), and equating the coefficients of corresponding powers of χ in the resulting equations leads to the following set of equations: for $k = 0,1,2,\dots$, for $n \in \mathbb{N}^s$, $h,\kappa = 1,\dots,s$,

$$\nu_{\kappa h}b(k;n,h,-\kappa) = \sum_{j=1}^{s} a_j I\{n_j \geq 1\}b(k;n - e_j, h, -\kappa)$$

$$-AI\{k \geq 1\}b(k - 1;n,h,-\kappa) + \sum_{j=1}^{s} \nu_{j\kappa}r_{\kappa h}I\{n_\kappa = 0\}b(k;n,\kappa,-j)$$

$$+\mu_\kappa r_{\kappa h}I\{k \geq 1\}\sum_{i=1}^{K_\kappa} I\{i = K_\kappa \vee n_\kappa = 0\}b(k - 1;n + e_h, \kappa, i); \tag{6.15}$$

and for $k = 0,1,2,\dots$, for $n \in \mathbb{N}^s$, $h = 1,\dots,s$, $n_h \geq 1$, $\kappa = 1,\dots,K_h$,

$$\mu_h b(k; \mathbf{n}, h, \kappa) = \sum_{j=1}^{s} a_j I\{n_j \geq 1\} b(k; \mathbf{n} - \mathbf{e_j}, h, \kappa) - AI\{k \geq 1\} b(k-1; \mathbf{n}, h, \kappa)$$

$$+ \sum_{j=1}^{s} \nu_{jh} I\{\kappa = 1\} b(k; \mathbf{n}, h, -j) + \mu_h I\{\kappa \geq 2, k \geq 1\} b(k-1; \mathbf{n} + \mathbf{e_h}, h, \kappa - 1). \quad (6.16)$$

As in section 6.2, the set of equations (6.15) and (6.16) expresses coefficients $b(k; \mathbf{n}, h, \kappa)$ in terms of coefficients of lower order with respect to the mapping (3.13), or of the same order but with lower value of κ, $\kappa = -s, \ldots, -1, 1, \ldots, K_h$, with the exception of the terms $b(k; \mathbf{n}, h, -j)$ in (6.15). In contrast with the cyclic-polling system, sets of linear equations may have to be solved for the present model also for states $\mathbf{n} \neq \mathbf{0}$, with size depending on the denseness of the transition matrix $\{r_{ij}, \; i, j = 1, \ldots, s\}$, but at most equal to $z^2(\mathbf{n})$; here, $z(\mathbf{n})$ stands for the number of zero components of a state $\mathbf{n}$. For $\mathbf{n} = \mathbf{0}$ the set of equations (6.15) is dependent, and has to be supplemented by an equation stemming from (6.14), cf. section 6.2: for $k = 0$

$$\sum_{h=1}^{s} \sum_{j=1}^{s} b(0; \mathbf{0}, h, -j) = 1; \quad (6.17)$$

respectively for $k = 1, 2, \ldots,$

$$\sum_{h=1}^{s} \sum_{j=1}^{s} b(k; \mathbf{0}, h, -j) = - \sum_{1 \leq |\mathbf{n}| \leq k} \sum_{h=1}^{s} \sum_{j=1}^{s} b(k- |\mathbf{n}|, \mathbf{n}, h, -j)$$

$$- \sum_{1 \leq |\mathbf{n}| \leq k} \sum_{h=1}^{s} \sum_{\kappa=1}^{K_h} b(k- |\mathbf{n}|; \mathbf{n}, h, \kappa). \quad (6.18)$$

Then, for each k, $k = 0, 1, 2, \ldots$, a set of at most s^2 independent linear equations is obtained for the same number of non-vanishing coefficients $b(k; \mathbf{0}, h, -j)$, $j, h = 1, \ldots, s$. If the model is generalized with a MAP with Θ_j states at station j, a PH service time distribution with Ψ_j stages for jobs at station j, and a PH switch-over time distribution with Ω_{ij} stages for switches from station i to station j, $i, j = 1, \ldots, s$, then the size of the supplementary space is given by

$$| \mathcal{V} | = \prod_{h=1}^{s} \Theta_h \times \left(\sum_{i=1}^{s} \sum_{j=1}^{s} I\{r_{ij} > 0\} \Omega_{ij} + \sum_{j=1}^{s} K_j \Psi_j \right). \quad (6.19)$$

7 Networks with job transitions

This section is devoted to open networks of queueing centres or stations in which the servers have been allocated permanently to one of the centres, and in which jobs may circulate through the network from centre to centre before they ultimately leave the network. The queue-length process for such a network is a (Q)BDP with migration. It will be shown that straightforward extension of the PSA to such processes leads to recursive computation schemes if migration occurs in one direction only. Section 7.1 deals with the extension of the PSA to tandem queueing systems, section 7.2 contains a discussion on more general networks.

7.1 The PSA for tandem queueing systems

The system consists of s single server centres in series. The queue-length process of the model with a Poisson arrival process and exponential service time distributions has a product form solution. To avoid discussion of this trivial model it is assumed that jobs arrive to the system at queue 1 according to a MAP. This MAP is defined as follows. It is governed by a Markov process with Θ stages. The transition rate from stage ω is $\rho \eta_\omega$, and when the process leaves stage ω it goes to stage ψ with probability $\xi_{\omega\psi}$, while an arrival is generated with probability $g_{\omega\psi}$, $\omega, \psi = 1, \ldots, \Theta$. It is assumed that the service times at centre j are exponentially distributed with rate μ_j, $j = 1, \ldots, s$. The state probabilities $p(n, \phi)$ of the process (N, Φ), where Φ indicates the actual stage of the MAP, satisfy the following global balance equations: for $n \in \mathbb{N}^s$, $\phi = 1, \ldots, \Theta$,

$$\left(\rho \eta_\phi + \sum_{j=1}^{s} \mu_j I\{n_j \geq 1\} \right) p(n, \phi) = \rho \sum_{\psi=1}^{\Theta} \eta_\psi \xi_{\psi\phi} g_{\psi\phi} I\{n_1 \geq 1\} p(n - e_1, \psi)$$

$$+ \rho \sum_{\psi=1}^{\Theta} \eta_\psi \xi_{\psi\phi}(1 - g_{\psi\phi}) p(n, \psi)$$

$$+ \mu_s p(n + e_s, \phi) + \sum_{j=1}^{s-1} \mu_j I\{n_{j+1} \geq 1\} p(n + e_j - e_{j+1}, \phi). \quad (7.1)$$

Further, the law of total probability holds. But a stronger property holds for models with MAPs which stems from the autonomy of the MAPs. For the present model this implies that

$$\sum_{n_1=0}^{\infty} \cdots \sum_{n_s=0}^{\infty} p(n, \omega) = v_\omega, \quad \omega = 1, \ldots, \Theta; \quad (7.2)$$

here, v_ω is the stationary probability that the MAP is in stage ω, $\omega = 1, \ldots, \Theta$; i.e., these probabilities are the solution of the set of equations

$$\sum_{\psi=1}^{\Theta} v_\psi \eta_\psi \xi_{\psi\omega} = v_\omega \eta_\omega, \quad \omega = 1, \ldots, \Theta; \quad \sum_{\omega=1}^{\Theta} v_\omega = 1. \quad (7.3)$$

Substitution of power-series expansions (4.3) into (7.1) yields: for $k = 0, 1, 2, \ldots$, $n \in \mathbb{N}^s$, $\phi = 1, \ldots, \Theta$,

$$\sum_{j=1}^{s} \mu_j I\{n_j \geq 1\} b(k; n, \phi) = \sum_{\psi=1}^{\Theta} \eta_\psi \xi_{\psi\phi} g_{\psi\phi} I\{n_1 \geq 1\} b(k; n - e_1, \psi)$$

$$+ I\{k \geq 1\} \sum_{\psi=1}^{\Theta} \eta_\psi \xi_{\psi\phi}(1 - g_{\psi\phi}) b(k - 1; n, \psi) - \eta_\phi I\{k \geq 1\} b(k - 1; n, \phi)$$

$$+ \mu_s I\{k \geq 1\} b(k - 1; n + e_s, \phi) + \sum_{j=1}^{s-1} \mu_j I\{n_{j+1} \geq 1\} b(k; n + e_j - e_{j+1}, \phi). \quad (7.4)$$

From (7.2) it follows in a similar way that for $\omega = 1, \ldots, \Theta$,

$$b(0; \mathbf{0}, \omega) = v_\omega; \qquad b(k; \mathbf{0}, \omega) = - \sum_{1 \le |\mathbf{n}| \le k} b(k - |\mathbf{n}|; \mathbf{n}, \omega), \quad k = 1, 2, \ldots . \qquad (7.5)$$

Because $C(k; \mathbf{n} + \mathbf{e_j} - \mathbf{e_{j+1}}) < C(k; \mathbf{n})$, cf. (3.13), for all $\mathbf{n} \in \mathbb{N}^s$ with $n_{j+1} \ge 1$, for $j = 1, \ldots, s - 1$, $k = 0, 1, 2, \ldots$, the set of equations (7.4), (7.5) allows recursive computation of the coefficients $b(k; \mathbf{n}, \omega)$, $\omega = 1, \ldots, \Theta$, in order of increasing value of $C(k; \mathbf{n})$. If the model is generalized with PH service time distributions with Ψ_j stages for service at centre j, $j = 1, \ldots, s$, then the size of the supplementary space is given by (5.6).

7.2   The PSA for networks of queues

In more general networks, arrivals from outside the network may occur at each centre. Suppose that when the service of a job has been completed at centre i, this job leaves the network with probability r_{i0} and moves to centre j with probability r_{ij}, $i, j = 1, \ldots, s$. Because for $k = 0, 1, 2, \ldots$, $C(k; \mathbf{n} + \mathbf{e_j} - \mathbf{e_i}) < C(k; \mathbf{n})$, cf. (3.13), for all $\mathbf{n} \in \mathbb{N}^s$ with $n_i \ge 1$, for $i = j + 1, \ldots, s$, $j = 1, \ldots, s - 1$, the recursive scheme for the tandem queueing model can be readily extended to acyclic networks, i.e., to networks with $r_{ij} = 0$ for $j = 1, \ldots, i$, $i = 1, \ldots, s$, with a MAP at each centre and with PH service time distributions. If a network is not acyclic then standard application of the PSA does not lead to a recursive computation scheme, but requires the solution of sets of linear equations of which the size increases strongly with s and $|\mathbf{n}|$.

8   Optimization and sensitivity analysis

For optimization of a performance measure with respect to real-valued parameters of a system it is useful to be able to compute derivatives of the performance measure as function of these parameters. Then, optimization techniques as the conjugate gradient method can be used to determine optimal values of these parameters with respect to some objective function. Computation of derivatives may also be useful to study the sensitivity of performance measures for changes in system parameters. The method of extension of the PSA towards the computation of derivatives is discussed in section 8.1 for cyclic-polling systems with Bernoulli service. Other possible applications of this extension are indicated in section 8.2.

8.1   Derivatives with the PSA

The computation of derivatives with the PSA is illustrated in this section for the case of polling systems with Bernoulli schedules in which the order-of-visit rule is cyclic polling and in which the server continues to move along the queues when the system is empty, cf. section 6.2. A Bernoulli schedule is a vector of s probabilities $(q_1, \ldots, q_s)$ which are used as follows. When the server arrives at a queue, at least one job is served, unless this queue is empty (in which case the server directly proceeds to the next queue). After the completion of a service at queue j the server starts serving another job at this queue with probability q_j if queue j has not yet been emptied; otherwise, the server proceeds to the next queue ($j = 1, \ldots, s$). Special cases are 1-limited ($q_j = 0$) and exhaustive service ($q_j = 1$). The notations are further the same as in section 6.2. The system is stable if (6.2) holds with K_j replaced by $1/(1 - q_j)$, $j = 1, \ldots, s$. For this model, $Z = 0$ indicates that the server is switching, and $Z = 1$ that the server is serving. The balance equations for the state probabilities $p(\mathbf{n}, h, \kappa)$ of the process $(\mathbf{N}, H, Z)$ are: for $\mathbf{n} \in \mathbb{N}^s$, $h = 0, \ldots, s-1$,

$$[\Lambda + \nu_{h+1}]p(\mathbf{n}, h+1, 0) = \sum_{j=1}^{s} \lambda_j I\{n_j \geq 1\}p(\mathbf{n} - \mathbf{e_j}, h+1, 0)$$

$$+\nu_h I\{n_h = 0\}p(\mathbf{n}, h, 0) + \mu_h[1 - q_h I\{n_h \geq 1\}]p(\mathbf{n} + \mathbf{e_h}, h, 1); \qquad (8.1)$$

and for $\mathbf{n} \in \mathbb{N}^s$, $h = 1, \ldots, s$, $n_h \geq 1$,

$$[\Lambda + \mu_h]p(\mathbf{n}, h, 1) = \sum_{j=1}^{s} \lambda_j I\{n_j \geq 1\}p(\mathbf{n} - \mathbf{e_j}, h, 1) + \nu_h p(\mathbf{n}, h, 0) + \mu_h q_h p(\mathbf{n} + \mathbf{e_h}, h, 1).$$

$$(8.2)$$

Further, the law of total probability holds, cf. (6.5), with $K_h = 1$, $h = 1, \ldots, s$. As in section 6.2, $p(\mathbf{n}, h, 1) = 0$ if $n_h = 0$, for all $\mathbf{n} \in \mathbb{N}^s$, $h = 1, \ldots, s$. The equations for the coefficients of the power-series expansions (6.1) are: for $k = 0, 1, 2, \ldots$, for $\mathbf{n} \in \mathbb{N}^s$, $h = 0, \ldots, s-1$,

$$\nu_{h+1}b(k; \mathbf{n}, h+1, 0) = \sum_{j=1}^{s} a_j I\{n_j \geq 1\}b(k; \mathbf{n} - \mathbf{e_j}, h+1, 0)$$

$$+\nu_h I\{n_h = 0\}b(k; \mathbf{n}, h, 0)$$

$$+I\{k \geq 1\}\mu_h[1 - q_h I\{n_h \geq 1\}]b(k-1; \mathbf{n} + \mathbf{e_h}, h, 1) - Ab(k-1; \mathbf{n}, h+1, 0); \qquad (8.3)$$

and for $k = 0, 1, 2, \ldots$, for $\mathbf{n} \in \mathbb{N}^s$, $h = 1, \ldots, s$, $n_h \geq 1$,

$$\mu_h b(k; \mathbf{n}, h, 1) = \sum_{j=1}^{s} a_j I\{n_j \geq 1\}b(k; \mathbf{n} - \mathbf{e_j}, h, 1) + \nu_h b(k; \mathbf{n}, h, 0)$$

$$+I\{k \geq 1\}\mu_h q_h b(k-1; \mathbf{n} + \mathbf{e_h}, h, 1) - Ab(k-1; \mathbf{n}, h, 1). \qquad (8.4)$$

The law of total probability leads to relations similar to (6.9), with $K_h = 1$, $h = 1, \ldots, s$. Next, consider derivatives of the state probabilities with respect to the Bernoulli parameters. It can be shown that these derivatives possess power-series expansions of the form: for $\mathbf{n} \in \mathbb{N}^s$, $r, h = 1, \ldots, s$, $\kappa = 0, 1$,

$$\frac{\partial}{\partial q_r}p(\mathbf{n}, h, \kappa) = \chi^{|\mathbf{n}|} \sum_{k=0}^{\infty} \chi^k b_r(k; \mathbf{n}, h, \kappa);$$

$$b_r(k; \mathbf{n}, h, \kappa) \doteq \frac{\partial}{\partial q_r}b(k; \mathbf{n}, h, \kappa), \quad k = 0, 1, 2, \ldots. \qquad (8.5)$$

Taking derivatives of both sides of equations (8.1) and (8.2), substituting power-series expansions (8.5) and equating corresponding powers of χ, or taking derivatives directly in relations (8.3) and (8.4), leads to the following set of equations: for $r = 1, \ldots, s$, $k = 0, 1, 2, \ldots$, for $\mathbf{n} \in \mathbb{N}^s$, $h = 0, \ldots, s-1$,

$$\nu_{h+1}b_r(k;n,h+1,0) = \sum_{j=1}^{s} a_j I\{n_j \geq 1\}b_r(k;n-e_j,h+1,0)$$

$$+\nu_h I\{n_h = 0\}b_r(k;n,h,0) + I\{k \geq 1\}\mu_h[1 - q_h I\{n_h \geq 1\}]b_r(k-1;n+e_h,h,1)$$
$$-\mu_h I\{r = h, n_h \geq 1\}b(k-1;n+e_h,h,1) - Ab_r(k-1;n,h+1,0); \quad (8.6)$$

and for $r = 1,\ldots,s$, $k = 0,1,2,\ldots$, for $n \in \mathbb{N}^s$, $h = 1,\ldots,s$, $n_h \geq 1$,

$$\mu_h b_r(k;n,h,1) = \sum_{j=1}^{s} a_j I\{n_j \geq 1\}b_r(k;n-e_j,h,1) + \nu_h b_r(k;n,h,0)$$

$$+I\{k \geq 1\}\mu_h q_h b_r(k-1;n+e_h,h,1) + \mu_h I\{r = h\}b(k-1;n+e_h,h,1)$$
$$-Ab_r(k-1;n,h,1). \quad (8.7)$$

The law of total probability leads in a similar way to: for $r = 1,\ldots,s$,

$$\sum_{h=1}^{s} b_r(0;0,h,0) = 0;$$

$$\sum_{h=1}^{s} b_r(k;0,h,0) = - \sum_{1 \leq |n| \leq k} \sum_{h=1}^{s} \sum_{\kappa=0}^{1} b_r(k-|n|;n,h,\kappa), \quad k = 1,2,\ldots. \quad (8.8)$$

By means of (8.6), (8.7) and (8.8) the coefficients $b_r(k;n,h,\kappa)$ can be computed recursively, but only in conjunction with the coefficients $b(k;n,h,\kappa)$. Derivatives of other performance measures with respect to the Bernoulli parameters can be computed by taking term by term derivatives in relations (2.25) and (2.26). It is readily verified that $b_r(0;n,h,\kappa) = 0$ for all $n \in \mathbb{N}^s$, $h = 1,\ldots,s$, $\kappa = 0,1$, and $r = 1,\ldots,s$. By this property, the evaluation of power-series expansions of the state probabilities and their derivatives with respect to d Bernoulli parameters up to the Mth power of χ requires the computation of $B_{s,d}(M) \times |\mathcal{V}|$ coefficients, with

$$B_{s,d}(M) = \binom{M+s+1}{s+1} + d\binom{M+s}{s+1}. \quad (8.9)$$

The above computation scheme is readily extended to the computation of second order derivatives but the latter require still more additional storage space.

8.2 Optimization with gradient methods

Derivatives of performance measures with respect to Bernoulli service parameters can be computed for polling systems with arbitrary order-of-visit rules. Alternatively, derivatives with respect to the (mean) time limit can be computed for polling systems with time-limited service. For systems with Markovian polling, cf. section 6.3, also derivatives with respect to routing probabilities can be determined. Other examples of models which lend themselves to optimization with respect to real-valued parameters are load-balancing systems (routing probabilities) and tandem queueing systems (service rates at subsequent stations). When using the PSA together with an optimization procedure it is often a good strategy for reducing computation time to start the search with a moderate number of terms of the power-series expansions, and then to improve the approximated optimum by using more terms. Generally, the evaluation of power-series expansions of the state probabilities and their derivatives with respect to d parameters up to the Mth power of ρ or χ requires the computation of $B_{s,d}(M) \times |\mathcal{V}|$ coefficients, with

$$B_{s,d}(M) = (d+1)\binom{M+s+1}{s+1}. \tag{8.10}$$

9 Annotated bibliography on the power-series algorithm

The basic idea of using power-series expansions of state probabilities as function of the load of a system to solve the global balance equations stems from Keane. About a decade ago, Keane and his co-workers did some preliminary studies concerning state probabilities for exponential coupled-processor and shortest-queue models. Their results were presented at a 1985 workshop at Delft University of Technology, The Netherlands. In [2] the concept of the PSA has been extended with a first order extrapolation of the coefficients of the power-series expansions of the moments of a queue-length distribution, cf. (3.9), (3.10), and applied to exponential shortest-queue models. General conditions for application of the PSA to birth-and-death models are derived in [3]. Coupled-processor models in which the total number of jobs in the system behaves as in an M/M/1 queue are considered in [15]; for these very special models it has been proven that the state probabilities are regular functions of the load on the interval (0,1), and it has been experimentally found that their power-series expansions converge inside the unit circle. The latter property does not hold for most other models. Two coupled processors with general service speeds and phase-type service requirement distributions are considered in [4]; moreover, a second order extrapolation for the computation of moments is proposed in this paper. The application of the PSA has been extended to exponential cyclic-polling systems with zero switching times and Bernoulli schedules as service disciplines in [5]. This paper also introduces the combination of the ϵ-algorithm with the PSA. Further, it proposes a linear ordering of the state space which leads to efficient implementation of the PSA. In [6] it has been described how the PSA can be used in a symbolic manner to derive light-traffic asymptotes for performance measures; further, this report contains a study of the differences and resemblances of Bernoulli schedules and limited-service disciplines for cyclic-polling systems. The PSA has been extended to exponential cyclic-polling systems with non-zero switching times in [7]. This concerns the first model which does not possess a unique empty state. Computations with the PSA are compared with simulations in [7] and [8]. It has turned out that (pseudo)conservation laws for mean waiting times are much better fulfilled by computations with the PSA than by estimations obtained by simulations of comparable duration as required by the PSA. The review paper [9] discusses the PSA in its generality for QBDPs, and in details for periodic-polling systems with Bernoulli schedules and with Coxian distributed service and switching times; moreover, it discusses the applicability and complexity of the PSA for polling systems with other visit rules and service disciplines. In [1] the PSA has been extended to cyclic-polling systems with switch-over and switch-in times. The special property (5.5) has been exploited in [10] to obtain numerical results with the PSA for exponential shortest-queue models with much more queues than the number that can be handled for models without this property. The problem of optimizing a cost function with respect to the Bernoulli schedules has been addressed in [11] and [12] for cyclic-polling systems. In [11] several properties of the optimal schedules have been found using the PSA together with the conjugate gradient method; the gradients of the cost function are determined on the basis of finite differences. The extension of the PSA towards the computation of derivatives of performance measures with respect to parameters of the system has been discussed in [12]. Cyclic-polling systems in which the server rests at one or more specific queues when the system is empty are considered in [13]; application of the PSA to such models requires a slight modification of the order in which coefficients of the power-series expansions are computed. In all above mentioned studies Poisson arrival processes are assumed. Generalization of the concept of the PSA to models with Batch Markovian Arrival Processes (BMAP) is the goal of [16]. The stationary distribution of the underlying Markov process of the BMAP is needed to determine the coefficients of the power-series expansions of the empty-state probabilities. Batch arrivals require an adaptation of the computation scheme similar to that for the fork system, cf. section 5.3. The discussions of the PSA for networks of queues and for fork systems have not been published previously.

References

[1] Altman, E., J.P.C. Blanc, A. Khamisy, U. Yechiali. Polling systems with walking and switch-in times, report INRIA, Sophia-Antipolis, France, 1992; submitted to *Stochastic Models*.

[2] Blanc, J.P.C. A note on waiting times in systems with queues in parallel, *J. Appl. Prob.* **24** (1987), 540-546.

[3] Blanc, J.P.C. On a numerical method for calculating state probabilities for queueing systems with more than one waiting line, *J. Comput. Appl. Math.* **20** (1987), 119-125.

[4] Blanc, J.P.C. A numerical study of a coupled processor model, in: *Computer Performance and Reliability*, eds. G. Iazeolla, P.J. Courtois, O.J. Boxma (North-Holland, Amsterdam, 1988), 289-303.

[5] Blanc, J.P.C. A numerical approach to cyclic-service queueing models, *Queueing Systems* **6** (1990), 173-188.

[6] Blanc, J.P.C. Cyclic polling systems: limited service versus Bernoulli schedules, Tilburg University, Report FEW 422, 1990.

[7] Blanc, J.P.C. The power-series algorithm applied to cyclic polling systems, *Commun. Statist.-Stochastic Models* **7** (1991), 527-545.

[8] Blanc, J.P.C. An algorithmic solution of polling models with limited service disciplines, *IEEE Trans. Commun.* **COM-40** (1992), 1152-1155.

[9] Blanc, J.P.C. Performance evaluation of polling systems by means of the power-series algorithm, *Annals Oper. Res.* **35** (1992), 155-186.

[10] Blanc, J.P.C. The power-series algorithm applied to the shortest-queue model, *Operat. Res.* **40** (1992), 157-167.

[11] Blanc, J.P.C., R.D. van der Mei. Optimization of polling systems with Bernoulli schedules, Tilburg University, Report FEW 563, 1992; submitted to *Performance Evaluation*.

[12] Blanc, J.P.C., R.D. van der Mei. Optimization of polling systems by means of gradient methods and the power-series algorithm, Tilburg University, Report FEW 575, 1992.

[13] Blanc, J.P.C., R.D. van der Mei. The power-series algorithm applied to polling systems with a dormant server, CentER discussion paper 9346, Tilburg University, 1993.

[14] Brezinski, C. *Padé-type Approximation and General Orthogonal Polynomials*. Birkhäuser, Basel, 1980.

[15] Hooghiemstra, G., M. Keane, S. van de Ree. Power series for stationary distributions of coupled processor models, *SIAM J. Appl. Math.* **48** (1988), 1159-1166.

[16] Van den Hout, W.B., J.P.C. Blanc. The power-series algorithm extended to the BMAP/PH/1 queue, Tilburg University, 1993.

[17] Wynn, P. On the convergence and stability of the epsilon algorithm, *SIAM J. Numer. Anal.* **3** (1966), 91-122.

Metropolitan Area Networks (MANs): Protocols, Modeling and Performance Evaluation

M. Conti, E. Gregori, L. Lenzini

CNR - Istituto CNUCE Via S. Maria, 36, 56100 Pisa Italy

Abstract

With the continuing success of Local Area Networks (LANs), there is an increasing demand to extend their capabilities towards higher data rates and wider areas. At high data rates and long distances the packet transmission time may become comparable or significantly less than the network propagation delay. For this reason Medium Access Control (MAC) protocols which were developed for LANs are no longer viable. Together with the progress in fiber optic technology, this has given rise to the so-called Metropolitan Area Networks, or MANs. These can span much greater distances than current LANs, and offer data rates in the region of hundreds of Megabit/sec (Mbps). This survey first sketches the problems encountered in using the MAC protocols defined for LANs on higher-speed and longer-distance networks; and then it focuses on two MAC protocols (FDDI and DQDB) developed for MANs by standardization bodies. These two MAC protocols represents two different approaches to overcome the limits of LAN MAC protocols. FDDI represents the evolution of the token passing class of MAC protocols, while the latter is a new brand of MAC protocol with a completely distributed control. This survey focuses on both MAC protocols with particular attention on their performance analysis.

1 Introduction

The success of MANs is strictly connected to the opportunity they give to develop new networking products capable of providing high-speed communications and interconnectivity between communicating applications at competitive prices which nonetheless give an adequate return on the manufacturers' investments. A major factor in achieving this goal is the availability of appropriate Networking Standards. FDDI and DQDB are the two standard technologies for MANs for which industrial products are already available.

The importance of FDDI and DQDB has meant that their performance has been analyzed by several groups. Most of the existing results have been obtained via simulation as it is extremely difficult to analytically solve detailed models of both MAC protocols. In fact, FDDI has a more complex behavior than a polling system with an exhaustive-limited service discipline [59], while DQDB behaves like a round-robin scheduling algorithm [36] for very short networks, but it deviates significantly when the length of the network increases. Due to the complexity of these protocols, exact models of the FDDI and DQDB MAC protocols have only been solved through simulative analysis, while models with analytical solutions have been developed to approximate each protocol's behavior under specific network configurations and workload conditions.

Research in this field is facing a wide range of performance-related problems, such as: 1) determining the relationship between bandwidth allocation schemes and throughput, delay distribution and packet loss rate 2) dimensioning the key network components (e.g., buffer size), and 3) tuning the network parameters.

The target of this tutorial is to present a structured view of the performance modeling activity related to FDDI and DQDB which has been published. For both MAC protocols we propose a taxonomy of the analytical models. Some relevant models of each class will be discussed by presenting the main simplifying assumptions, the technique used for solving the model and the performance indices analyzed. In the presentation the original notation is used and this sometimes results in a non uniform use of symbols.

To make reading easier, the most relevant features of the MAC protocols will be summarized before the performance modeling issues of the protocols are discussed.

This survey is divided into three parts. Section 2 discusses the main issues related to the evolution from LAN to MAN. Sections 3 and 4 are devoted to FDDI and DQDB, respectively.

2 From LANs to MANs

Since a LAN/MAN network relies on a common transmission media, MAC protocols have been designed to manage the sharing of the transmission media. The aim of a MAC protocol is to control the interference and competition among users while optimizing overall system performance and yet nevertheless avoiding pitfalls. The target of a MAC protocol is thus to share resources efficiently among several users. This efficiency can be expressed in terms of *fairness* and *capacity* ([37], [1]).

Fairness means that the network does not differentiate between stations in granting them access rights to the transmission bandwidth [28].

Capacity indicates to what extent the protocol utilizes the channel bandwidth. In fact, a MAC protocol is a distributed algorithm among several stations; some information must be, either implicitly or explicitly, exchanged among the stations. Since the transmission media is the only means of communication among the stations, it will not always be fully used to transmit user-messages. In the literature the MAC protocol *capacity* figure (ρ_{max}) is used to characterize this aspect. This is defined as the fraction of the medium bandwidth used by the nodes when each node tries to seize all the medium capacity.

MAC protocols intended for LANs are not suitable for high transmission speeds and long distances. This applies to all the popular IEEE standards for LANs: Ethernet, Token Ring, and Token Bus. In these protocols, the MAC protocol capacity decreases when the ratio between the length of the network and the length of a packet increases. In literature this ratio is often referred to as a. The ρ_{max} value depends on the specific MAC protocol. In the following we report the ρ_{max} value for Ethernet, Token Ring and Token Bus

- Ethernet: $\rho_{max} \leq \dfrac{1}{1 + \chi \cdot a}$,

  where χ depends upon the approximations made during the analysis; for example, $\chi = 6.44$ in [55], $\chi = 3.44$ [57] and $\chi = 7.34$ [30].

- Token Ring [57]: $\rho_{max} \leq \begin{cases} \dfrac{1}{1 + \dfrac{a}{N}} & \text{if } a < 1 \\[4mm] \dfrac{1}{\left(1 + \dfrac{1}{N}\right) \cdot a} & \text{if } a > 1 \end{cases}$,

  where N is the number of active stations in the network.

Token Bus [30][1]: $\rho_{max} \leq \dfrac{1}{1+\dfrac{a}{3 \cdot N}}$,

By assuming that there are packets of 1000 bits and a light speed in the fiber of 200,000 km/sec in Table 1 we report the a values for various configurations and transmission speed.

Table 1:
a values for different network configurations and transmission speeds

Capacity	Coverage		
	1 km	10 km	100 km
10Mbps	0.05	0.50	5
100 Mbps	0.50	5	50

For a network with 50 active stations the maximum network utilization which can be achieved, for various a values, are reported in Table 2.

Table 2:
ρ_{max} values

	CSMA/CD	Token Ring	Token Bus
$a=0.05$	76%	100%	100%
$a=0.50$	24%	100%	100%
$a=5$	3%	20%	96%
$a=50$	0.3%	2%	75%

Table 2 clearly shows that the CSMA/CD and the Token Ring perform poorly at speeds and coverages typical of a MAN. On the other hand, the performance of the Token Bus does not drop significantly; in fact, one of the standard for high-speed LAN/MAN, FDDI, inherits most of the Token Bus MAC protocol mechanisms; in [45] it is provided a general proof of the equivalence between Token Bus and FDDI networks.

Fairness and capacity are used to evaluate the MAC protocol algorithms, however from the user standpoint other performance figures are needed to measure the quality of service the user can rely upon. The most widely used performance measure is the delay, which can be defined in several forms, depending on the time instants considered when measuring the delay (access delay, queueing delay, propagation delay, etc.).

In LAN networks, whose main target is the support of EDP data applications, the quality of service is generally expressed in terms of average delay and throughput; while for MANs, which have the potentiality to support beyond EDP data applications time-constrained applications (e.g., voice and video) as well, the delay distribution would also be necessary. In fact, the most important aspect of a time-constrained application is that messages should be delivered to the destination within a given amount of time after their generation. The most relevant performance figure for these applications is therefore the percentage of messages which are delivered with a delay lower than the given constraint.

Extensive analyses of distributed and "centralized" token-passing MAC protocols for MANs have been carried out. For both classes, the pros and cons have been identified. In particular, the most interesting features of the DQDB MAC protocol is its ability to

---

[1] This bound is obtained by assuming that each node can only transmit a single packet whenever it receives the token.

guarantee a utilization of the medium capacity which does not depend on bus length, medium capacity or packet length, and the capability to provide access delays of only a few microseconds at light loads ([5], [11], [12]). On the other hand, the FDDI MAC protocol [2] behaves more predictably and fairly than DQDB, and this means there is guaranteed bandwidth for at least one class of traffic. Unfortunately, the FDDI MAC protocol capacity still depends on the a value and this makes the FDDI MAC protocol unsuitable for Gigabit MANs.

Below we focus on the relevant aspects, from the performance analysis standpoint, of the FDDI and DQDB MAC protocol. We present an updated survey of some significant analytical models for each protocol.

3 FDDI

Fiber Distributed Data Interface (FDDI), which employs an optical fiber medium, is a 100 Mbit/s LAN based on a Token Ring protocol [2].

The network topology, two contra-directional rings, allows very flexible configurations extending from a few metres of fibre path length supporting a few stations, up to 100 km supporting up to 500 stations. Adjacent ring stations can be up to 2 km apart with standard multimode optical transmission links, but optionally single mode optical links may be used where greater inter-station distances of up to 40 km are required ([51], [44]).

Distributed protocols are used for initialisation and management of the FDDI ring and also for error recovery purposes [2].

The FDDI standard specifies the building blocks of the functional architecture of an FDDI station. The MAC block is mainly responsible for the FDDI performance since it controls the token passing ring protocol which determines the behavior of the FDDI ring. In this tutorial we only focus on the MAC protocol which will be described in the next section.

3.1 Description of the MAC Protocol

The MAC protocol controls the transmissions onto the physical ring media. This control is exercised by means of a Timed Token protocol, in which a unique sequence of data called a token is passed around the ring from station to station. A station wishing to transmit information must first wait for the token to arrive; the token is then "captured" by stripping it from the ring. The station can then transmit its queued frame(s) of data, after which it issues a new token which provides other stations with the opportunity to access the medium.

The frames of data transmitted by the originating station are regenerated and repeated by the other active stations on the ring. While repeating incoming frames, a station also examines the Destination Address for a match with its own address. If a match occurs, the station copies the frame contents into its receive buffers as it transmits the frame onwards.

Each frame of data transmitted eventually comes back to the station that originated it, which is then responsible for stripping the frame from the ring. The originating station recognises the Source Address contained in the frame as its own address, after which stripping takes place. The decision to strip a frame is based on the recognition of the frame's Source Address, which cannot occur until the initial part of the frame has been repeated. This means that the stripping process leaves frame fragments circulating on the medium. Frame fragments are ultimately discarded when they arrive at a station that is transmitting its own frames onto the medium.

Timed Token Protocol. The Timed Token protocol supports two major classes of service: *synchronous* and *asynchronous*.

The synchronous traffic has a preallocated bandwidth while the bandwidth for asynchronous transmissions is instantaneously allocated to a station, when it captures a token, from the unused bandwidth.

Specifically, a Target Token Rotation Time *(TTRT)* is negotiated by a station during ring initialization (the negotiated value of TTRT is named *T_Opr*) and a synchronous bandwidth is allocated to each station as an *X%* of TTRT, i.e., a station can transmit every time it captures the token synchronous data for a time up to its *X%* of TTRT. In any case the aggregate synchronous bandwidth can never exceed TTRT-α where α is a constant term defined in the standard which takes into account the maximum ring latency, the maximum frame length, and the time it takes to transmit a token.

To compute the maximum time a station can transmit asynchronous data when it captures a token two timers are used: the Token Rotation Timer *(TRT)* and the Token Holding Timer *(THT)*. TRT measures the time between the receipt of two consecutive tokens while THT is used to limit the transmission of a station when a token is captured. If TRT reaches TTRT before the token returns to the station, a variable, named *Late_Ct*, is set to one and TRT is restarted. When the token arrives at a station with Late_Ct=1 the token is called a *late token*, only synchronous transmissions are enabled and Late_Ct is set to 0. On the other hand if the token arrives before TRT reaches TTRT, the token is named an *early token*. Whenever an early token is captured, the current value of TRT is stored in the THT, TRT is reset and synchronous transmissions (up to *X%* of TTRT) are carried out. After synchronous transmission, THT is enabled and asynchronous transmissions start. The difference between TTRT and THT is the maximum time available for asynchronous transmissions in this cycle. A station may initiate a transmission of an asynchronous frame if the timer THT has not reached the TTRT threshold. This may cause an additional delay in the release of the token (hereafter called *asynchronous overrun*) since the transmission of an asynchronous frame is always completed. The asynchronous overrun is bounded by the time for the transmission of a frame of maximum length. In the FDDI standard asynchronous overrun is 0.361 msec, which corresponds to the time required to transmit a maximum frame length.

Multiple levels of asynchronous priorities may be distinguished by a station. For each priority level *n*, a threshold value (T_Pri(n)) is defined.

T_Pri(n) are an ordered sequence of values in the range [0,TTRT], higher priorities have higher T_Pri values and the highest priority has a threshold which is equal to TTRT ([23], [54]).

Asynchronous transmissions start from the highest priority. Asynchronous frames of priority *n* may only be transmitted if THT is less then T_Pri(n). If multiple asynchronous priority levels are not implemented, all asynchronous frames have a threshold value which is equal to TTRT.

The protocol behavior was formally studied in ([56], [34]). In these papers it was formally proved that: (1) the average token rotation time does not exceed the TTRT, and (2) the maximum token rotation time does not exceed twice the TTRT.

3.2 MAC Protocol Modeling

Although many FDDI analytical studies have already been published, the majority contain simplifying assumptions. The main difficulty for the analysis of the FDDI MAC protocol is the high degree of complexity and interdependence of the various processes that describe the operations of the protocol itself. In fact, when a station has seized the token, synchronous frames (if any) are always transmitted, whereas asynchronous frames are only transmitted if the preceding token rotation time does not exceed TTRT. This implies that there are interdependencies between the total service time given at one station, the service time required at subsequent stations and the total cycle time. Therefore, exact analytically-tractable solutions for an FDDI network are very difficult to formulate. Simplifying assumptions thus have to be made in order to obtain analytically-tractable solutions. Furthermore, even when only synchronous traffic is transmitted, and hence the token holding time constraint and the feedback mechanism of cycle time have no influence, only approximate solutions are known for the resulting model (which reduces to a polling system with an *Exhaustive Time-limited discipline*).

Table 3
FDDI Models Taxonomy

		Buffer size	Traffic Type	Performance indices		
	Deterministic		Model 1	A	Th	-	-
Network		M=1	Model 2	A/S	E[D]	Pl	-
Wide	Stochastic	M>1	Model 3	A	E[D]	M-pdf	Pl
Models		M=∞	Model 4	S	E[D]	-	-
		M>1	Model 5	A	E[D]	M-pdf	Pl
Station	Stochastic		Model 6	A	E[D]	M-PGF	-
in Isolation		M=∞	Model 7	S	E[D]	M-pdf	D%
Models			Model 8	S	D-LST	M-PGF	-

Th: Throughput;
E[D]: Average Delay;
Pl: Packet loss rate;
M-pdf: Probability distribution function of the buffer occupancy;
M-PGF: Probability generating function of the buffer occupancy;
D-LST: Laplace-Stieltjes Transform of the delay distribution,
D%: Delay percentiles.

In order to provide a structured overview of the FDDI analytical studies we introduce the taxonomy shown in Table 3, which preliminarily classifies the FDDI models into two categories: the former (or first category) contains *Network-Wide Models* while the latter (or second category) contains *Station-in-Isolation Models*.

The models in the first category characterize the overall FDDI structure in terms of the ring and stations spaced along it. All the models in this category belong to the class of *multiqueue systems with cyclic service* [59]. In literature, these systems have frequently been investigated. They can be distinguished from each other in a number of ways [59] depending on the buffering at each station, the type of service, the polling order, and the assumptions of arrival processes at the various stations.

The analytical models in the second category tag the station under study. With respect to the tagged station, the FDDI network is partitioned into the tagged station itself, and the complementary part of the network (C_NET) which aggregates all the other stations. In this approach the tagged station is modelled as a *single server queueing system with server vacations* [61]. The server vacation time represents the period between the token's departure from the tagged station and its subsequent arrival at this station, i.e., the time it takes the token to cross C_NET.

Models belonging to both classes can be further subdivided (see Table 3) on the basis of buffer size (i.e., M=1, M finite and M infinite), traffic type (i.e., synchronous *(S)*, asynchronous *(A)* and a mixing of both *(A/S)*) for which performance indices are derived. For each leaf of the taxonomy, presented in Table 3, we identify a significant model for which we provide the model description, the solution technique and the performance indices obtained.

3.3 Network-Wide Models
This section outlines four special cases of the network-wide model. All the models falling in this category are derived from the following abstract model

- The system has N queues (stations) and a single server. The queues can have either one M $(M > 1)$ or infinite buffers.
- Synchronous and asynchronous frames arrive at the queues in accordance with Poisson arrival processes.
- The server (token) walks from queue to queue in a fixed order. The time needed to switch the server from queue i to queue $(i+1)$ is modelled by a delay (*switchover time*) r_i. The switchover time r_i corresponds to the propagation delay of the signals between stations i and $(i+1)$ plus the latency caused within station i.
- When the server reaches a queue, synchronous frames are always transmitted (if any) whereas asynchronous frames are only transmitted if the preceding token rotation time does not exceed TTRT. Once the server has served a queue it goes to the next queue. The server can take either a constant or a random amount of time to transmit a frame.

The first model (*Model 1* [23]), performs a throughput analysis of the network under the assumption that all nodes are saturated by frames to send, i.e., Asymptotic Analysis. Under this assumption the network behavior is deterministic and the authors derive an exact solution of the network model. The other three models assume Poisson arrivals and thus the system behavior is stochastic. More specifically, under the assumption of a single buffer, *Model 2* [60] exactly represents the network behavior for which an exact solution is provided. *Models 3* and *4* are approximate models for which approximate solutions are derived. The main differences between these models is in the buffer size (finite or infinite) and the solution technique (approximation based on an iterative scheme vs. approximation based on a pseudo-conservation law).

Model 1: Asymptotic Analysis. This model, proposed and analysed by Dikeman and Bux in [23], is used for evaluating the maximum total throughput γ_{max} for *FDDI* when only one asynchronous priority level is in use.

The expression for γ_{max} is derived by assuming that each actively transmitting station continuously has asynchronous frames queued for transmission. To simplify the analysis, frame transmission times are assumed to have constant length F. Asynchronous overrun are assumed to be of constant length R. On the basis of the above assumptions, the ring quickly converges to steady-state operation, so that on successive rotations the active stations cycle through a finite number of transmission states. A transmission state is the set of token rotation timer and frame transmission time values for each active station on the ring.

By examining two scenarios in which one and two stations are actively transmitting frames the authors derive, by performing a pure deterministic analysis, the sequence of transmission states for both steady-state cycles. For each scenario, the duration of the steady-state cycle can be easily computed by summing up the duration of each state within the steady-state cycle. Similarly, the total frame transmission time in these states can be derived by summing up the frame transmission times of each state within the steady-state cycle. The total (normalized) throughput is derived by simply forming the ratio between the total frame transmission time and the steady-state cycle time.

By examining additional scenarios (not reported in [23]) the authors obtain a generalized throughput expression for an *FDDI* with an arbitrary number N of active stations.

$$\gamma_{max} = \frac{(N \cdot tot\_tx\_time + N^2 \cdot tx\_window) \cdot v}{N \cdot tot\_tx\_time + N^2 \cdot tx\_window + (N^2 + 2N + 1) \cdot r\_l}$$

where $tx\_window = T\_Opr - r\_l$, $tot\_tx\_time = CEILING(tx\_window / F) \cdot F$,

v is the transmission speed, and $r\_I = \sum_{i=1}^{N} r_i$ is the total ring-latency time.

Taking the limit of γ_{max} as the number of active stations (N) goes to infinity, a bound for the maximum total throughput is obtained

$$\lim_{N \to \infty} \gamma_{max} = \frac{tx\_window \cdot v}{tx\_window + r\_I} = \frac{T\_Opr - r\_I}{T\_Opr} \cdot v$$

Equation for γ_{max} is then generalized to produce the maximum total throughput for FDDI when multiple asynchronous priority levels are being used.

In [23] the lowest priority message that will ever be transmitted it is shown to belong to the class "low", which is the lowest priority level satisfying

$$E = [N - n(low) + 1] \cdot T\_Pri(low) - \left[\sum_{i=low+1}^{m} n(i) \cdot T\_Pri(i) \right] > 0$$

where m is the number of asynchronous priority traffic in use in a given scenario $(1 \le m \le 8)$; $n(i)$ is the number of stations that have priority level i messages ready to transmit during each cycle; and $N = \sum_{i=low}^{m} n(i)$ is the total number of stations transmitting.

Under the assumption that stations immediately stop transmitting frames when THT has reached $T\_Pri(i)$, Dykeman and Bux show that the throughput $t(i)$ of priority i messages is given by

$$t(i) = \frac{r(i)}{(N+1) \cdot r\_I + \sum_{j=low}^{m} r(j)} \cdot v, \quad \text{where}$$

$$r(i) = \begin{cases} n(i)E & \text{if } i = low \\ n(i)[N(T\_Pri(i) - T\_Pri(low)) + (N - n(low))T\_Pri(low) & \\ \quad - \sum_{i=low+1}^{m} n(i)T\_Pri(i) + T\_Pri(i) - r\_I] & \text{if } i = low+1,..,m \end{cases}$$

The overall throughput is given by the sum of the throughputs for each priority level.

Model 2: Single Buffer Model. This model was proposed and analyzed by Takagi in [60]. This model assumes a single-message buffer for each station which can accommodate two classes of messages (frames): the priority message (synchronous frame) and the ordinary message (asynchronous frame). The throughput and the mean waiting times of priority and ordinary messages, the mean token rotation time, and the buffer utilization are computed numerically.

The load is equally shared among the network stations (i.e., symmetric system) and when the buffer is empty a message in the generic station i is generated with an interval which is exponentially distributed with mean $1/\lambda$ for priority messages or $1/\lambda'$ for ordinary messages. Those messages that arrive when the buffer is occupied are lost. The transmission time of both an ordinary and a priority message is assumed to be the same constant b. The TTRT is defined as $R + M \cdot b$ where R is the latency (ring plus stations) M is an integer $0 \le M \le N$ where N is the number of stations in the FDDI network.

An exact solution of this model is obtained by applying an embedded Markov chain technique. Before introducing the state of the system, further notation is required.

Stations are indexed from 1 to N; $\tau_i^{(k)}$ denotes the time at which the token arrives at station i in the kth cycle and a cycle is assumed to start when the token arrives at station 1. The system is observed at the token arrival instants at each network station and the state vector at time $\tau_i^{(k)}$ is $\left(u_1^{(k)},...,u_{i-1}^{(k)},u_i^{(k)},u_{i+1}^{(k-1)},...,u_N^{(k-1)}\right)$ where $u_j^{(k)}$ is the state of station j at time $\tau_j^{(k)}$ and

$$u_j^{(k)} = \begin{cases} 0 & \text{buffer empty} \\ 1 & \text{ordinary message that will not be transmitted} \\ 2 & \text{ordinary message that will be transmitted} \\ 3 & \text{priority message} \end{cases}$$

The cycle time for station i at time $\tau_i^{(k)}$ is $R+Q_i^{(k)}\cdot b$ where $Q_i^{(k)}$ is a function of $u_1^{(k)},...,u_{i-1}^{(k)},u_i^{(k)},u_{i+1}^{(k-1)},...,$ and $u_N^{(k-1)}$ given by

$$Q_i^{(k)} = \sum_{j=i+1}^{N} I\left(u_j^{(k-1)} \in [2,3]\right) + \sum_{j=1}^{i-1} I\left(u_j^{(k)} \in [2,3]\right)$$

where $I(\bullet)$ is the indicator function. We are interested in computing the steady state probabilities of our system

$$P_i\left(u_1,...,u_{i-1},u_i,u_{i+1},...,u_N\right) = \lim_{k\to\infty} P_i\left(u_1^{(k)},...,u_{i-1}^{(k)},u_i^{(k)},u_{i+1}^{(k-1)},...,u_N^{(k-1)}\right)$$

where $P_i\left(u_1^{(k)},...,u_{i-1}^{(k)},u_i^{(k)},u_{i+1}^{(k-1)},...,u_N^{(k-1)}\right)$ is the probability that the state of the system at time $\tau_i^{(k)}$ is $\left(u_1^{(k)},...,u_{i-1}^{(k)},u_i^{(k)},u_{i+1}^{(k-1)},...,u_N^{(k-1)}\right)$. In steady state we also have that $P_{i-1}\left(u_1,...,u_{i-1},u_i,u_{i+1},...,u_N\right) = P_i\left(u_N,u_1,...,u_{i-1},u_i,u_{i+1},...,u_{N-1}\right)$.

Since all stations are statistically identical we can focus on station 1 omitting the subscript 1. Now $Q = \sum_{j=2}^{N} I\left(u_j \in [2,3]\right)$ and a set of 4^N linear equation among the 4^N unknowns (i.e., $P(u_1,...,u_N)$) are presented in the paper.

From these steady state probabilities several performance measures are obtained. The distribution of the cycle length is given by $P(C = R + nb) = \sum_{U(2,3)} P(u_1,...,u_N)$ where

$$U(2,3) = \left\{(u_1,...,u_N)\middle| \sum_{i=1}^{N} I(u_i \in [2.3]) = n\right\}$$ The distributions of the number of ordinary and priority messages transmitted in a cycle are $P(Q_{ordinary} = n) = \sum_{U(2)} P(u_1,...,u_N)$ and

$P(Q_{priority} = n) = \sum_{U(3)} P(u_1,...,u_N)$ where $U(j) = \left\{(u_1,...,u_N)\middle| \sum_{i=1}^{N} I(u_i \in [j]) = n\right\}$.

The throughput of ordinary and priority messages are $\gamma_{ordinary} = E[Q_{ordinary}]/E[C]$ and $\gamma_{priority} = E[Q_{priority}]/E[C]$ respectively.

The computation of the mean waiting time is more complex. The paper first focuses on the priority messages, it computes this waiting time computing the Laplace-Stieltjes transform of the waiting time for priority messages $W_{priority}(s)$ from which the average waiting time is derived with routine calculations

$$E\left[W_{priority}\right] = \frac{\sum_{u_2=0}^{3} \cdots \sum_{u_N=0}^{3}\left[R+bQ-\frac{1-e^{-(\lambda+\lambda')(R+bQ)}}{\lambda+\lambda'}\right] \cdot \sum_{u_1 \in [0,2,3]} P\left(u_N,u_1,...,u_{N-1}\right)}{\sum_{u_2=0}^{3} \cdots \sum_{u_N=0}^{3}\left[1-e^{-(\lambda+\lambda')(R+bQ)}\right] \cdot \sum_{u_1 \in [0,2,3]} P\left(u_N,u_1,...,u_{N-1}\right)}$$

The mean waiting time for ordinary messages is obtained by applying Little's formula $\overline{N}_{ordinary} = \gamma_{ordinary}\left(E\left[W_{ordinary}\right]+b\right)$ where $\overline{N}_{ordinary}$ is the mean number of ordinary messages in all buffers at an arbitrary time. $\overline{N}_{ordinary}$ is computed by exploiting the following relationship $U = \left(\overline{N}_{ordinary} + \overline{N}_{priority}\right)/N = 1 - \gamma_{priority}/\lambda' \cdot N$; and in this formula the only unknown is $\overline{N}_{priority}$ which is easily derived from $\gamma_{priority}$ and $E\left[W_{priority}\right]$.

The symmetric traffic assumption in the model proposed by Takagi was removed by Nakumara et al. [48] who considered the corresponding asymmetric system.

Model 3: G-limited with Time-Limit Variation Polling Model. This model, proposed by Tangeman and Sauer [62], is used to analyze the performance figures of an FDDI network with N stations which only transmit asynchronous traffic subdivided into multiple-priority levels. Each station transmits traffic of only one priority level, and the priority level of a station i is characterized by its threshold $T_{Pri}(i)$. The number of packets which can be buffered in a station i is limited by the value m_i. Packets arrive in the buffer of station i according to a Poisson distribution with rate λ_i. The service time of a packet buffered in a station i $\left(T_H(i)\right)$ and the switchover time from station i to station $i+1$ $\left(T_U(i)\right)$ are random variables sampled from general distributions. To represent the timed token protocol behavior the service discipline is of *G-limited with time-limit variation* type (see also Section 3.4). In fact, when a station i captures the token it can use the transmission media for a maximum time of $\max\left\{0, T_{Pri}(i) - T_{TRT}(i)\right\}$, where $T_{TRT}(i)$ measures the length of the previous cycle (i.e., it is equal to the *TRT* of the station i when it captures the token). With this discipline, when station i holds the token it can only transmit the packets that were in its buffer at the token arrival (i.e., gated service). The transmission period of a station ends when there are no more packets to transmit or the maximum transmission time for this cycle is reached, whichever occurs first. In the latter case the transmission of the last packet may be completed. In [62] this service discipline is called *cycle-time-dependent timer-controlled gated service discipline*.

The analysis of this model is divided into two main parts. First, for each station i, the statistics of the cycle time observed by the station $\left(T_C(i)\right)$ are derived, i.e., the time between two consecutive arrivals of the token at station i. Then by analyzing each station in isolation, the packet loss probability and the average waiting time are derived. The analysis of the cycle time is performed by studying, for each station i the steady state statistics of the sequence $\left\{A_i^{(n)}, T_{TRT}^{(n)}(i)\right\}$ embedded at the time instants at which the server arrives at the station; where $A_i^{(n)}$ is the number of packets waiting in station i at the nth token arrival, and $T_{TRT}^{(n)}(i)$ is the value of the TRT counter at the same time instant. To simplify the analysis, it is assumed that a station always restarts the TRT timer and therefore $T_{TRT}^{(n)}(i)$ has the same distribution as $T_C^{(n)}(i)$ which measures the time since the previous token arrival (i.e., the length of the interval between the $(n-1)^{th}$ and n^{th} token arrival instants) at station i.

Due to the complexity of the problem, the authors could not find closed formulas for the steady-state distribution of $\{A_i^{(n)}, T_{TRT}^{(n)}(i)\}$, but by applying an iterative scheme they are able to approximate this distribution. The iterative scheme, applied in this paper, is an extension of the method used by Tran-Gia and Raith to study a finite capacity polling system with limited service discipline [63].

The iterative approach starts by assigning initial values for $\{A_i^{(0)}, T_{TRT}^{(0)}(i)\}$. Through a set of equations the statistics of $\{A_i^{(1)}, T_{TRT}^{(1)}(i)\}$ are derived. This recursive scheme is applied until the system is stable $\sum_{i=0}^{N} E[A_i^{(n)}] - E[A_i^{(n-1)}]/E[A_i^{(n-1)}] < \varepsilon$, where ε determines the accuracy of the results. When the iteration ends the statistics of $\{A_i^{(n)}, T_{TRT}^{(n)}(i)\}$ approximate the steady state distributions of $\{A_i, T_{TRT}(i)\}$, where $A_i = \lim_{n\to\infty} A_i^{(n)}$, $T_{TRT}(i) = \lim_{n\to\infty} T_{TRT}^{(n)}(i)$. Specifically, each iterative step, starting from the statistics of $\{A_i^{(n)}, T_{TRT}^{(n)}(i)\}$, firstly provides the statistics related to $T_{TRT}^{(n+1)}(i)$ and secondly those of $A_i^{(n+1)}$.

The authors also propose to improve the above analysis by taking into consideration the dependencies between consecutive stations. To this end, they propose, in computing the variance of the cycle length, to consider the covariance of each couple $\left(T_E^{(n)}(i), T_E^{(n)}(i+1)\right)$ of adjacent stations.

In the second part of the analysis each node is analyzed in isolation. Starting from the approximate distribution of the number of packets in the queue of a tagged node at the token arrival instant, first the steady-state distribution of the queue length at arbitrary times is derived. Then from the distribution at arbitrary times the packet loss rate and the average waiting time are obtained.

Model 4: Exhaustive Time-Limited Polling System. This approximate model was proposed by Chang and Sandhu in [7] for the delay analysis of a polling system with a time-limited discipline. The MAC protocol is modelled as a Cyclic-service system with an exhaustive time-limited discipline. The time limited policies limit the duration of transmission whenever a station possesses the token; this makes this model suitable for the FDDI and Token Bus delay analysis. The delay analysis is carried out assuming that all the traffic is at the highest priority level i.e., in FDDI only a synchronous service is used. The algorithm can be applied both to FDDI and to the Token Bus with small differences because in FDDI the time a station can hold the server can never exceed the station threshold (H_i), while in the Token Bus when the H_i threshold is reached no further services are permitted but the server will only leave station i if the ongoing service is completed.

The idea behind the approximate model is to use results obtained in [8] for the polling systems with exhaustive-limited discipline to the exhaustive time-limited discipline. Obviously these two disciplines only coincide when the service time distribution is deterministic.

To derive the mean delay a pseudo-conservation law is used and approximations for the unknowns in the pseudo conservation law formula are proposed.

3.4 Station-in-Isolation Models

This section outlines four special cases of the station in isolation model. All the models falling in this category are variants of M/G/1 queueing models with vacation times. From the modeling standpoint, the token is a server that provides a service during its visit to the tagged station and is on vacation (i.e., within C_NET) when it is away from it. Thus, with respect to the tagged node, C_NET can also be viewed as a generator of vacation periods. In some of the station in isolation models which will be described in this section, the queue has a finite capacity and this motivates the use of M/G/1/N queue with vacation, where the queue capacity equals N, to represent the behavior of the tagged station. Several service disciplines ([24], [25], [61]) have been proposed and analyzed in the literature. The service disciplines implemented by the models described in this section belong to the following classes

Limited. A fixed limit is placed either on the maximum number of frames that can be served, or on the amount of time the server serves the queue, before going on vacation. The term time-limited is normally used to distinguish the latter discipline from the former. When the "time" prefix is missing, the limit refers to the number of frames. In both cases, the server serves until either (i) the (time-)limit is reached, or (ii) all the frames eligible for service have been served. Both service disciplines can operate in an *exhaustive-limited* (*E-limited*) or *gated-limited* (*G-limited*) manner. In the former case, all the frames in the queue are eligible for service, whereas in the latter case, only the frames that were in the queue upon the server's arrival are eligible;

Limited with limit variation. This policy extends the previous one since a dynamic limit (randomly chosen upon server arrival) is placed either on the maximum number of frames that can be served, or on the amount of time the server serves the queue, before going on vacation.

The M/G/1 and M/G/1/N systems with vacation times and *limited* or *limited with limit variation* service discipline are analyzed with the embedded Markov chain technique. The state of the Markov chain includes a random variable to denote the number of frames in the system and other random variables whose semantics vary from model to model. If the tagged station is modelled with a G-limited (or G-limited with limit variation) service discipline the embedding points correspond to the vacation termination instant (i.e., the arrival instants of the server at the tagged node); otherwise, if the service discipline is E-limited (or E-limited with limit variation), apart from the vacation termination instant the service completion instants are also included among the embedding points.

Three techniques have been used to solve these models: z-transform, matrix-analytic and iteration.

z-Transform. According to this technique, formulas for the probability generating functions (PGFs) of the embedded queue size distribution are obtained. These formulas have the following general structure

$$Q(z) = \frac{N(z)}{z^{c \cdot K} - B(z)}, \quad c \in \mathbb{N}^+,$$

where $N(z)$ and $z^{c \cdot K} - B(z)$ are analytic functions in the unit disk. The unknowns in $Q(z)$ are a set of $L = c \cdot K$ boundary probabilities in $N(z)$ which express the probability that the tagged station transmits less than K packets when it receives the token.

To compute the boundary probabilities a standard technique is generally used. In fact, if the system satisfies the stability condition, from Rouche's theorem it is possible to prove that the denominator of $Q(z)$ has L zeros in $|z| \le 1 + \varepsilon$. Of these L zeros, it is easy to verify that one of them is unity. Let us denote the remaining $L-1$ zeros, none of which is equal to unity, by z_i, $i = 1, 2, .., L-1$. Lagrange's theorem can be used to find an infinite series representation for each of these zeros. Since $Q(z)$ is analytic in

$|z| \leq 1$, it is possible to conclude that these $L-1$ denominator zeros in $|z| \leq 1$ are also zeros of $N(z)$. By evaluating this numerator at the $L-1$ zeros, it is possible to write $L-1$ linear equations in terms of the L unknown boundary probabilities. The normalization condition, $Q(1) = 1$, is used to find another equation in the L unknowns and this solves the problem of computing the L unknown boundary probabilities.

Matrix-analytic. Chiarawongse *et al.* [9] use the matrix-analytic technique to analyze an M/G/1 queueing system with vacations and timer-controlled service. With this technique, the boundary probabilities are computed by matrix-geometric analysis which involves matrix inversions and successive iterations. The steady state distribution of the embedded Markov chain is then generated recursively from these boundary probabilities to conduct queue size and delay analysis.

Iteration. Finally in Rubin *et al.* [53] an iteration procedure is used to evaluate the steady state probability distribution of the embedded Markov chain. The authors claim that this approach has the following advantages over the z-transform method and matrix-analytic technique, respectively:
- *without tackling the multidimensional boundary value problem in the transform-domain, the potential high-order root-solving problem incurred by the numerous boundary states is avoided;*
- *by iteratively calculating the boundary probabilities based on balance equations, the numerical difficulties involved in inverting huge matrices are eliminated.*

Obviously all the models presented in this section are approximate. The first two models (*Model 5* [53] and *Model 6* [38]) perform a delay analysis of the asynchronous traffic. The performance figures of an FDDI tagged station are studied by solving, either, with an iterative approach, an M/G/1/N queueing system with E-limited and time-limit variation service discipline [53], or. with z-transform, an M/G/1 queueing system with E-limited and limit variation service discipline [38]. *Model 7* ([13], [18]) and *Model 8* [27] are proposed and solved for analyzing the quality of service achieved by the synchronous frames. Since the synchronous service of FDDI is designed to deliver time critical messages, the emphasis in both works is on the development of models which provide estimates of the probability distribution of the number of packets queued in the tagged station, and of the delay experienced by these packets in the buffer. In fact, the analysis of the relationship between the probability distribution figures and the negotiated network parameter values (T_opr value, quota of synchronous traffic for the tagged node, etc.) indicate for a given network configuration the likelihood that a given deadline and packet loss rate will be met. In both works, the system is analyzed under the heavy load assumption as it is the most important case for network designers and managers (for the tuning of the network configuration).

Model 5: M/G/1/N with Vacation and E-limited with Time-limit Variation Service Discipline. In [53] the tagged station is modelled as an M/G/1/N single server (token) queuing system with server vacations. The service policy is such that the server can provide contiguous service to the tagged station for a (dynamic) limited period of time (i.e., E-limited with time-limit variation service discipline).

The tagged station queue, which has a finite packet buffer capacity of size N, is fed with packets arriving according to the Poisson distribution with rate λ. The packets belong to a single asynchronous priority class. The timing threshold associated with it is denoted by T_{pri}. A token holding time limit $\text{THTL} = \left[T_{pri} - \text{TRT}\right]^+$ is set, upon the arrival of the token at the station. The station is allowed to initiate transmission of its queued packets (when it has seized the token) at any time, provided at this time $\text{THT} < \text{THTL}$.

Each packet consists of a random number of fixed-size segments, and the transmitting time of a segment is equal to a slot duration, Δ. In addition, the length of the vacation period is assumed to be a multiple of Δ. Therefore the dynamics of the system can be described by means of a discrete time queueing model with time units equal to one slot.

If B_n (slots) denotes the nth packet transmission time, then $\{B_n, n \geq 1\}$ forms a sequence of independently identically distributed random variables. The probability distribution of the packet transmission time is denoted by $b(i) = P\{B_n = i\}$, $i = 1,...,b_{max}$; $b_{max} < \infty$ (note that for FDDI, the maximum packet length·is set to 4500 bytes). The mean packet transmission time is denoted by μ. The nth vacation time relative to the station is denoted as V_n (slots). To simplify the analysis, in [53] it is assumed that the successive vacation times $\{V_n, n \geq 1\}$ form a sequence of independently identically distributed random variables. The probability distribution of the vacation time is thus denoted by $v(i) = P\{V_n = i\}$, $i = 1,...,V_{max}$; $V_{max} < \infty$ (note that for an FDDI network $V_n \leq 2 \times TTRT$). The mean vacation time is denoted by $\overline{V}$. Furthermore, let G_n (slots) represent the nth token dwell time at the station, measured from the instant of the nth token arrival at the station to the instant of the nth token departure from this station. The maximum value of G_n, denoted G_{max}, is equal to $T_{pri} + b_{max} - 1$; note that this dwell time may be longer than T_{pri} due to the occurrence of transmission overruns. The mean token dwell time is represented by $\overline{G}$.

The FDDI network is analyzed by means of an embedded Markov chain, defined at the token arrival and packet departure instants. Those (ordered) time instants are represented as $\{\tau_0, \tau_1, \tau_2, ...\}$. The state of the station at an embedded point $\tau \in \{\tau_0, \tau_1, \tau_2, ...\}$, is described by a triplet (S_τ, N_τ, T_τ), where S_τ is the time since the most recent token arrived, N_τ is the number of packets in the queue (queue size; $N_\tau = N_{\tau^+}$ if τ is a packet departure point), and T_τ is the token holding time limit.

Note that T_τ is computed at the instant that the token arrives at the station and does not change until the next token arrival instant.

Based on the model assumptions, the process $\left\{\left(S_{\tau_i}, N_{\tau_i}, T_{\tau_i}\right), i \geq 0\right\}$ is a discrete-time Markov chain over the following finite state space A

$$A = \left\{(s,n,t) \mid \left(t = 0,1,..,T_{pri}; s = 0; n = 0,1,..,N\right)\right.$$
$$\left. \cup \left(t = 1,..,T_{pri}; s = 1,..,t + b_{max} - 1; n = 0,1,..,N-1\right)\right\}$$

The Markov chain $\left\{\left(S_{\tau_i}, N_{\tau_i}, T_{\tau_i}\right), i \geq 0\right\}$ is irreducible and aperiodic. Therefore a unique limiting (steady-state) distribution $p_{s,n,t} = \lim_{i \to \infty} P\{S_{\tau_i} = s, N_{\tau_i} = n, T_{\tau_i} = t\}$, $(s,n,t) \in A$ exists. From $p_{s,n,t}$ the station's normalized throughput can easily be obtained through the following relation $\rho = \overline{G}/\overline{G} + \overline{V} = (1-a)\mu/(1-a)\mu + a\overline{V}$, where

a denotes the probability that an embedding point is a token arrival point which can be expressed as follows $a = \sum_{n=0}^{N} \sum_{t=0}^{T_{pri}} p_{0,n,t}$.

In [53], an iteration procedure is used to evaluate $p_{s,n,t}$. Once $p_{s,n,t}$ have been evaluated, by using supplementary variables and sample biasing techniques, the queue size distribution at an arbitrary instant of time u, the blocking probability and the mean packet delay are derived.

By using the above techniques the steady-state queue size distribution at an arbitrary instant of time, $P(m) = \lim_{u \to \infty} P\{X_u = m\}$, are derived. Hence, the blocking probability is given by $P_b = P(N) = 1 - \rho/\lambda\mu$.

Finally, the mean packet delay (i.e., the interval from the instant at which a packet arrives at the tagged station to the instant that this packet departs from the station), denoted as $\overline{D}$, can be obtained using Little's formula $\overline{D} = \sum_{m=1}^{N} mP(m) \Big/ \lambda(1 - P_b)$.

An empirical procedure is employed to construct an approximation of the vacation time distribution at each station.

Model 6: M/G/1 with Vacation and E-limited with Limit Variation Service Discipline. In [38] the tagged station, which is fed with only one asynchronous traffic class, is modelled as an M/G/1 single server queueing system with server vacations. The service discipline is such that the server provides service until either the system is emptied or a randomly chosen limit of l frames has been served (*E-limited with limit variation or ELV service discipline*). The server then goes on a vacation before returning to service the queue again.

In the analysis performed in [38], the limit l is a bounded random variable for which a mass function, p_l, $l \in \{0,1,...,L\}$, is assumed. The limit l for a service interval is determined at the preceding vacation termination instant. Due to the way FDDI works, the value of l will differ from one token arrival to the next, depending upon the state of the system (i.e., Late_Ct and the TRT) at the time the token is seized by the tagged station. Consequently, a major difficulty in the analysis of FDDI is the fact that this limit depends upon the length of time that the token spends at each of the stations (including the current one) during the previous token cycle. To permit analysis, the following simplifying assumption is made; i.e., the sequence of limits chosen at these vacation termination instants are independent, identically distributed random variables.

It is assumed that the frame arrival process is Poisson with arrival rate λ and that at each station, the incoming frames wait in queues of infinite length. The service times (i.e., the frame transmission times) are assumed to be independent of any process in the system. The probability density function (*pdf*) of the service time and the corresponding Laplace-Stieltjes transform (*LST*) are denoted by $\tilde{b}(t)$ and $B^*(s)$, respectively. The first and second moments of the service time are denoted by b and $b^{(2)}$, respectively. In the analysis, the vacation time is only allowed to be correlated with the limit l that was used for the preceding service interval. The conditional pdf of the vacation time, given that the limit l was used for the preceding service interval, is denoted by $\tilde{v}_l(t))$ with LST $V_l^*(s)$ and first and second moments of v_l and $v_l^{(2)}$, respectively. Similarly, the marginal pdf of the vacation time is denoted by $\tilde{v}(t)$ with LST $V^*(s)$ and the first and second moments of v and $v^{(2)}$, respectively. Estimates of the function $\tilde{v}_l(t)$ and the mass function p_l that are used in the theory to obtain the mean waiting times are determined from the simulation.

The M/G/1 vacation model described above is analyzed by using a similar approach to the one used by Lee for an E-limited (i.e., with a fixed limit) service [41] (also see Takagi [61]). Specifically, it is defined an embedded Markov chain at the vacation termination and service completion instants. The state of the system at an embedded point $t \in \{t_0, t_1, ...\}$, is described by a triplet, $\{\tilde{k}_t, \tilde{n}_t, \tilde{l}_t\}$. $k_t = 0$ indicates that an embedded point t is a vacation termination instant while $k_t = k$, $(k = 1, 2, ..., L)$ indicates that it is a service completion instant of the kth frame in the service interval. The random variable $\tilde{n}_t$, is the number of frames in the system at time instant t. Finally, $\tilde{l}_t$, is the limit on the number of frames that can be served during the (possibly zero length) visit of the server as determined by a random choice of limit at the vacation termination instant. Thus, the limit $\tilde{l}_t$, associated with a vacation termination instant t is the limit chosen at this point for the following service interval. The Markov chain that derives from these definitions is irreducible and aperiodic. By assuming that the system is stable, closed formulas for the PGFs of the number of frames in the system at the above embedding points are derived. The following steady-state joint probabilities are first defined

$$f_{n,l} = \lim_{i \to \infty} P\{\tilde{k}_{t_i} = 0, \tilde{n}_{t_i} = n, \tilde{l}_{t_i} = l\}, \quad n = 0, 1, ...; \quad l = 0, 1, ..., L$$

$$\pi_{n,l}^{[k]} = \lim_{i \to \infty} P\{\tilde{k}_{t_i} = k, \tilde{n}_{t_i} = n, \tilde{l}_{t_i} = l\}, \quad n = 0, 1, ...; \quad l = 0, 1, ..., L; \quad k = 1, 2, ..., l$$

The steady-state probability that an embedded point is a vacation termination instant and there are n frames in the system in denoted by f_n, $n = 0, 1, ...$ Starting from f_n and $\pi_{n,l}^{[k]}$ the following $F(z) = \sum_{n=0}^{\infty} f_n z^n$ and $Q(z) = \sum_{n=0}^{\infty} \sum_{l=1}^{L} \sum_{k=1}^{l} \pi_{n,l}^{[k]} z^n$. PGFs are defined

After extensive algebraic manipulation the following expressions for $F(z)$ and $Q(z)$ are derived.

$$F(z) = \frac{\sum_{l=1}^{L} p_l V_l^*(\lambda - \lambda z) \left\{1 - \left[\frac{B^*(\lambda - \lambda z)}{z}\right]^l\right\} f_0 + R_l(1) - R_l\left(\frac{B^*(\lambda - \lambda z)}{z}\right) z^L}{z^L - \sum_{l=0}^{L} p_l V_l^*(\lambda - \lambda z) [B^*(\lambda - \lambda z)]^l z^{L-1}}$$

$$Q(z) = \frac{B^*(\lambda - \lambda z) \sum_{l=1}^{L} p_l \left\{\{F(z) - f_0\}\left\{1 - \left[\frac{B^*(\lambda - \lambda z)}{z}\right]^l\right\} - R_l(1) + R_l\left(\frac{B^*(\lambda - \lambda z)}{z}\right)\right\}}{z - B^*(\lambda - \lambda z)}$$

where $R_l(z) = \begin{cases} 0, & l = 1, \\ \sum_{k=1}^{l-1} \pi_0^{[k]} z^{l-k}, & l = 2, 3, ..., L. \end{cases}$

What is noteworthy in $F(z)$ and $Q(z)$ is the presence of L unknown boundary probabilities f_0, and $\pi_0^{[1]}, \pi_0^{[2]}, ..., \pi_0^{[L-1]}$ which can be found by using Rouche's theorem and the normalization condition. From the $F(z)$ and $Q(z)$ expressions the derivation of the mean queueing time in terms of the L boundary probabilities is straightforward. The mean queue length at the service completion instants is given by the normalized z-transform derivative, $Q'(1)/Q(1)$.

Since the stochastic process of the queue length only makes discontinuous changes of unit size, the queue length distribution immediately before the arrival instants is the same as the distribution immediately after the service completion instants ([36],[61]). Furthermore, since Poisson arrivals see time averages (PASTA) [68], the steady-state mean queue length (at arbitrary times) is equal to the steady-state mean queue length at the service completion instants. Using this argument and Little's law, the mean waiting (i.e., queueing) time can be found $W = Q'(1)/\lambda Q(1) - b$. After extensive algebraic manipulation it can be shown that

$$W = \frac{v^{(2)}}{2v} + \frac{\lambda v^{(2)} + 2v + \bar{l}\lambda b^{(2)}}{2[\bar{l}(1-\rho) - \lambda v]} - \frac{\bar{l}(1-\rho)(1-\rho+\lambda v)}{\lambda v[\bar{l}(1-\rho) - \lambda v]} \cdot \left[\sum_{l=1}^{L} lp_l v_l [F(1) - f_0] - \sum_{l=2}^{L} p_l v_l R_l'(1) \right]$$
$$+ \frac{(1-\rho)(1-\rho+\lambda v)}{2\lambda[\bar{l}(1-\rho) - \lambda v]} \cdot \left[\sum_{l=2}^{L} l(l-1)p_l [F(1) - f_0] - \sum_{l=2}^{L} p_l R_l'(1) \right]$$

In a parallel paper, Leung [42] analyzed an asymmetric cyclic-service system, with infinite capacity queues, that uses the same service discipline. In [42], a numerical technique based on discrete Fourier transforms is used to obtain the waiting time distributions for the queue.

LaMaire extended this work in [38] to the case of an M/G/1/N queueing system [39] with the same service discipline (E-limited with limit variation). The queue length distribution and the Laplace-Stieltjes transforms of the waiting time, busy period and cycle time distributions are derived in [39]. In addition, an expression for the mean waiting time is developed.

Model 7: Worst Case Model for Synchronous Traffic. In ([13], [18]) an FDDI network with synchronous and asynchronous traffic is analyzed. The authors evaluate whether the quality of service guaranteed by FDDI is adequate to support real time applications when the level of network congestion is very high. The analysis is performed by using a model which is based on the assumption that the interactions among stations generate a "worst" case for the performance indices of a tagged station. The worst case proposed and analysed in [18] assumes that the length of the cycle of the FDDI network, as seen from the tagged station, has its maximum length. Furthermore, to simplify the analysis the tagged station is assumed to transmit synchronous frames of fixed length, and therefore the synchronous quota (maximum number of frames) for the tagged station corresponds to an integer number of synchronous frames, which will be denoted throughout by M.

The resulting stochastic model is an extension of the single server queuing system with vacation and *E-limited service discipline* ([41], [60]) with parameter M. The distribution of the service time is deterministic and is equal to a frame transmission time. The input traffic to the station is generated by the superposition of discrete time Markov processes. Furthermore, to model the behavior of the Timed Token protocol, it is assumed that the cycle length can be either *TTRT* or $2 \times TTRT$ in order to model the *normal* network behavior (i.e., Late_Ct=0) and the *delayed* network behavior (i.e., Late_Ct=1), respectively. When the Late_Ct=0, with probability P_L the next cycle has a length TTRT and Late_Ct remains equal to zero, while with probability $(1 - P_L)$ the next cycle has a length equal to $2 \times TTRT$ (to model the maximum token rotation time delay) and Late_Ct is set to one. Until Late_Ct=1, cycle lengths are equal to TTRT. Late_Ct returns to zero when the queue of the tagged station becomes empty. While in FDDI the memory of a late token is lost when the average token rotation time is again below T_Opr, this model loses the memory of a late token whenever its effect on the congestion of the queue of the tagged station is lost (i.e., the queue becomes empty). Therefore, the average length of the cycle is greater than *TTRT*. As the tagged station has a maximum fixed throughput for each cycle this model represents a worst case since in a real FDDI subnetwork the average cycle length is less than or equal to *TTRT*.

The distance between this worst case model and a real system is evaluated in [10].

In [18] two solution methods for this model are proposed. The first one, which was developed to analyze a tagged station with a finite buffer, is based on the periodic Markov chain theory and, due to its computational complexity, it is applicable for buffer sizes less than a given threshold (approximately 250 cells). The second one, which can be applied when the tagged station buffer is infinite is based on an aperiodic positive recurrent embedded Markov chain for which a closed formula for the PGFs of the number of frames in the buffer at the embedding points are derived. There are two groups of embedding points: one related to the normal behavior (Late_Ct=0) and the other related to the delayed behavior (Late_Ct=1).

The state of the system for any cycle i at the embedding points is described by a couple $\{t, N_t, \xi\}_i$ where $\xi = 0$ represents normal states, while $\xi = 1$ identifies delayed states. $t=0$ indicates the vacation termination instant, while $t = m$, $m = 1, 2, ..., M$ is the embedding point just after the mth transmission. The random variable N_t is the number of frames in the station at time t. The resulting Markov chain is irreducible and aperiodic only if $0 < P_L < 1$.

By assuming that the system is stable, the following steady-state joint probabilities can be defined $\pi_k^{(m)} = \lim_{i \to \infty} P\{t = m, N_t = k, \xi = 0\}_i$, $m = 1, 2, ..., M$ and $s_k^{(m)} = \lim_{i \to \infty} P\{t = m, N_t = k, \xi = 1\}_i$, $m = 0, 1, ..., M$ where $\pi_k^{(m)}$ ($s_k^{(m)}$) is the steady state probability that the system is in the normal (delayed) state, immediately after the mth packet transmission and there are k packets in the buffer.

By using stochastic arguments $\pi_k^{(1)}$ and $s_k^{(0)}$ are derived. Starting from them, the steady state probabilities, which there are k frames at an embedded point corresponding to the mth service completion instant in the normal state and in the delay state, are computed by applying the following recursive relations

$$\pi_k^{(m)} = \sum_{j=1}^{k+1} \pi_j^{(m-1)} \cdot a_{k-j+1}^{(m)} + I_{\{k=0\}} \cdot s_1^{(m-1)} \cdot a_0^{(m)}, \quad m = 2, 3, ..., M, \ k > 0 \text{ and}$$

$$s_k^{(m)} = \sum_{j=1}^{k+1} s_j^{(m-1)} \cdot a_{k-j+1}^{(m)}, \quad m = 2, 3, ..., M, \ k > 0$$

By defining $\Pi_m(z) = \sum_{k=0}^{\infty} \pi_k^{(m)} z^k$ and $S_m(z) = \sum_{k=0}^{\infty} s_k^{(m)} z^k$ it is possible to show that both sets of z-transforms are functions of $2M$ unknown boundary probabilities $\{\pi_0^{(1)}, \pi_0^{(2)}, ..., \pi_0^{(M)}, s_1^{(0)}, s_1^{(1)}, ..., s_1^{(M-1)}\}$. They appear in the following closed formula for $S_0(z)$ which can be derived after some lengthy algebraic manipulations

$$S_0(z) = \frac{\sum_{i=1}^{M} \pi_0^{(i)} \cdot \psi(z) + s_1^{(0)} \cdot \phi(z) + \sum_{i=1}^{M-1} s_1^{(i)} \cdot \vartheta(z)}{[z^M - C(z)] \cdot [z^M - C(z)(1 - P_L)]},$$

where: $C(z)$ is the PGF of the number of arrivals in a cycle of length $TTRT$, $\psi(z)$, $\phi(z)$ and $\vartheta(z)$ are functions of z which contain known parameters.

Hence, $\{\pi_0^{(1)}, \pi_0^{(2)}, ..., \pi_0^{(M)}, s_1^{(0)}, s_1^{(1)}, ..., s_1^{(M-1)}\}$ can be found according to the general methodology described above by considering the normalization condition $\Pi(1) + S(1) = 1$ where $\Pi(z) = \sum_{m=1}^{\infty} \Pi_m(z)$, $S(z) = \sum_{m=0}^{\infty} S_m(z)$.

For the special case $P_L = 1$ the average and the standard deviation of the average number of frames in the tagged station are directly computed from the closed formula of $S(z)$ while the percentiles are overestimated by applying Chebyshev's inequality, and approximated by using a two-moments approximation [67]. In [19] it is shown how, in this type of model, it is possible to derive the delay statistics from the PGF.

Model 8: Model for Synchronous Traffic Under Heavy Load. The major problem in the analysis of an FDDI system is the correlation between the service time at each station (i.e., the time the station holds the token) and the total cycle time. This difficulty is overcome in [27] by observing that this correlation is almost negligible during heavy load conditions, as in these conditions the transmission of asynchronous traffic is often deferred until traffic moderates. In fact, simulation results have estimated that the TRT value has a very low coefficient of variation under heavy load conditions (e.g., $0.9 \cdot T\_opr \leq TRT \leq 1.1 \cdot T\_opr$). Furthermore, simulative experiments indicate that there is a negligible correlation between the time a station holds the token to transmit synchronous traffic and the total cycle time. On the basis of these considerations, in [27] the network behavior observed by a tagged station is approximated by assuming that the value of the TRT of the station is independent of the station behavior (i.e., the length and number of synchronous transmissions and the number of packets queued in the station). With these hypotheses the tagged station is modelled via an M/G/1 queuing system with vacation and G-limited service discipline with parameter M. The service time of a packet, and the vacation time are r.v. with continuous distributions $U(t)$ and $V(t)$, respectively. $U^*(s)$ and $V^*(s)$ are the LSTs of $U(t)$ and $V(t)$, respectively. As the service time is stochastic, M is only an approximation of the synchronous quota of the station. The PGF of the number of packets in the station at the token arrival instants is therefore [61]

$$Q(z) = V^*(\lambda - \lambda z) \frac{\sum_{n=0}^{M-1} \pi_n \left\{ \left[U^*(\lambda - \lambda z) \right]^n z^M - \left[U^*(\lambda - \lambda z) \right]^M z^n \right\}}{z^M - \left[U^*(\lambda - \lambda z) \right]^M V^*(\lambda - \lambda z)}$$

where π_n, $n = 0,1,..,M-1$ are the unknown boundary probabilities.

After computing the boundary probabilities by using classical arguments in [27] an expression for the LST of the waiting time is derived. By inverting the LST the probability density function of the waiting time of the synchronous traffic is finally obtained.

4.0 DQDB

In this section, firstly the basic DQDB MAC protocol is described. Then by analyzing the unfairness problems, the Bandwidth Balancing mechanism, which was included in the standard to recover this problem, is introduced. Finally, performance modeling of a DQDB network is discussed. A classification of the analytical models is proposed, and for each class some relevant models are presented.

DQDB has been the subject of intensive research related both to performance modeling issues, and to enhancements and architectural variations of the protocol. In this tutorial we will only focus on the performance modeling related to the standard version of the protocol. A complete overview and bibliography of the DQDB research activities as of 1992 is reported [47].

4.1 DQDB MAC Protocol Description
The basic structure of a DQDB network is shown in Fig. 1. The network consists of

two high speed unidirectional buses carrying information in opposite directions. The network nodes[2] are distributed along the two buses and they can transmit information to and receive information from both buses, as shown in Fig. 1. The node in the leading edge of each bus is designated as the *head of* its corresponding *bus (HOB)*. Each HOB continuously generates slots of fixed length (53 octets) which propagate along their respective buses. The first byte in a slot constitutes the *Access Control Field (ACF)*, which is utilised by the nodes in the network to co-ordinate their transmissions. Each slot accommodates one segment which is 52 octets long; 4 of these octets are designated as the *header* of the segment and the remaining 48 octets are used for information transmission.

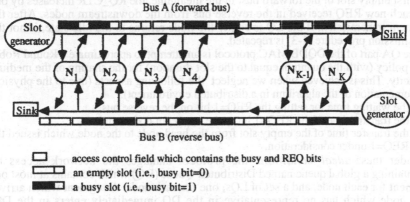

Fig. 1. DQDB Dual Bus Topology

The DQDB MAC protocol provides two modes of access control to the buses: *Queued Arbitrated (QA)* and *Pre-Arbitrated (PA)* which use QA and PA slots, respectively. The distinction between the two types of slots is made through the SL_TYPE bit in the ACF of a slot. PA access is reserved for *isochronous* services such as voice and video, while QA access is used typically to provide asynchronous services.

This tutorial will only deal with the QA mode of operation. The PA part of the protocol is analyzed in ([70], [71], [72]).

Without loss of generality, we name bus A the *forward* bus, and bus B the *reverse* bus. In each node, the segments, on arrival, are put in the proper *local node queue (LQ)*, as determined by the destination address (there are two local node queues, one for each bus). Below we will focus on segment transmission by using the QA slots in the forward bus, since the procedure for transmission in the reverse bus is the same.

To manage the QA mode of operation the ACF includes a *busy bit* and 3 *request (REQ) bits*. These four bits are set to "0" by the originating HOB. The busy bit indicates whether or not the corresponding slot has already been used for data transmission. The three REQ bits are provided to implement a three-level priority scheme to access the QA slots. For ease of presentation the tutorial focuses on one priority level.

The procedure for segment transmission on the forward bus utilizes the busy bits in the ACF of the slots of the forward bus and one request bit (the REQ bit below) in the ACF of the slots of the reverse bus.

Each node is either *idle*, when there is nothing to transmit, or *count_down*. When it is idle the node keeps count, via the *request counter (RQ_CTR)*, of the number of

---

2 In this survey the words node and station will be used interchangeably.

outstanding REQs from its downstream nodes. The RQ_CTR increases by one for each REQ received in the reverse bus and decreases by one for each empty slot in the forward bus. When a node in the idle state receives a segment, it enters the count_down state and starts the transmission procedure by taking the following actions: 1) the node transfers the content of the RQ_CTR to a second counter named the *count_down counter (CD_CTR)*, 2) resets the RQ_CTR to zero, and 3) generates a request which is inserted into the queue of the pending requests while waiting for transmission on the reverse bus (by setting REQ=1 in the first slot with REQ=0). In the count_down state the CD_CTR is decreased by one for every empty slot in the forward bus until it reaches zero. Immediately afterwards, the node transmits the segment into the first empty slot of the forward bus. In the meantime, the RQ_CTR increases by one for each new REQ received in the reverse bus from the downstream nodes. After the segment transmission, if the LQ is empty the node returns to the idle state, if not the transmission procedure (1-3) is repeated.

The QA part of the DQDB MAC protocol is an attempt to approximate a Round Robin [36] policy (with the quantum equal to the slot duration) for the sharing of the medium capacity. This is achieved when we neglect the following aspects (due to the physical implementation of the algorithm in a distributed environment):

1) the waiting time for setting the REQ=1 bit on the reverse bus,
2) the transfer time of the REQ=1 bit to the upstream nodes, and
3) the transfer time of the empty slot from the head node to the node which issued the REQ=1 under consideration.

Under these *ideal conditions* the protocol manages the network access by maintaining a global queue named Distributed Queue (DQ) which contains at most one segment for each node, and a set of LQs, one for each node. A segment which arrives in a node which has no representative in the DQ immediately enters in the DQ, otherwise it waits in the node LQ. Segments in the DQ are served on a FIFO basis (each segment gets a service quantum equal to the segment transmission time). After the transmission of one of its segments a node may insert a new segment (if any) at the end of the DQ.

Unfortunately, due to the propagation delays between the nodes, the information that a node receives is usually outdated. For this reason the DQDB MAC protocol deviates from the Round Robin schedule to a degree that depends on several parameters (e.g., the network physical size, the position of the nodes along the buses, the network load etc.) and this gives rise to the so called unfairness in DQDB.

4.2 DQDB Unfairness and the Bandwidth Balancing mechanism

DQDB provides quality of service, either in the form of access delays or bandwidth allocation, which is strongly dependent on the node position in the network ([65], [11], [5]).

The DQDB unfairness in bandwidth allocation was highlighted in [69] by analyzing the behavior of an earlier version of the DQDB MAC protocol (which however, under the configuration presented below, behaves exactly like the IEEE802.6 standard) in a simple network configuration with only two active stations and the propagation delay between the nodes equal to D slots. In [69] it is assumed that initially only the upstream node *(node{1})* sends data and that this node has enough traffic to fill all the slots travelling on the forward bus. This is allowed by the DQDB protocol as the upstream node, which is the only active node, does not see any request in the reverse bus. Let us now assume that the downstream node *(node{2})* becomes active at least D slot times after node{1} starts its transmission. When node{2} becomes active it immediately switches to the countdown state (with CD_CTR equal zero), issues a request on the reverse bus, and it stops to wait for an empty slot to appear on the forward bus. In this scenario, node{1} only leaves an empty slot in response to a node{2} request. Obviously, it takes D slots before the upstream node can observe a node{2} request.

When the upstream node reads the node{2} request, it allows a slot to remain idle. After a D slots propagation delay, the idle slot reaches the node{2} which transmits a segment, a new segment enters the distributed queue, and issues a new request on the reverse bus.

In this configuration the downstream node can only transmit one segment every $2D$ slots. With a separation of 30 Km between nodes, $2D \approx 100$, and consequently the downstream node receives about one slot out of a hundred.

DQDB unfairness in saturated conditions arises because the protocol enables a node to use every *unused slot* (i.e., an empty slot not reserved by downstream nodes) on the bus.

To overcome this problem the Bandwidth Balancing *(BWB)* mechanism [29] has been added to the DQDB standard [31].

The Bandwidth Balancing mechanism follows the basic DQDB protocol, except that a node can only take a fraction of the unused slots. Specifically, the Bandwidth Balancing mechanism limits the throughput of each node to some multiple M of the unused bus capacity (U); this limit is defined as *control rate*. Nodes with less demand than the control rate (not-rate-controlled nodes) get all the bandwidth they want.

Therefore, if $\rho(i)$ indicates the bandwidth requirements of node i the throughput $r(i)$ of node i satisfies the following relationship [29]

$$r(i) = \min\left[\rho(i), M \cdot U\right] = \min\left[\rho(i), M \cdot \left(1 - \sum_m r(m)\right)\right].$$

This scheme is fair, in fact if there are N rate-controlled nodes, and S is the utilization due to not rate-controlled nodes, all rate-controlled nodes get the same bandwidth $r(i) = M(1 - S)/(1 + M \cdot N)$.

The BWB mechanism achieves a fair bandwidth sharing by sparing a portion of the bus capacity. In fact, while in the basic DQDB (i.e., BWB mechanism disabled) a complete utilization of the transmission media can be always achieved, when the BWB mechanism is enabled, the network utilization depends on the number of active nodes. In [29] it is shown that the bandwidth wastage due to this mechanism is therefore $(1 - S)/1 + M \cdot N$; and the worst case bandwidth wastage is $1/(1 + M)$ which only occurs with one active node.

To implement this mechanism the protocol uses a counter *(BWB_CTR)* to keep track of the number of transmitted segments. Once *BWB_CTR* reaches the BWB_MOD value this counter is cleared and the RQ_CTR is increased by one. The value of BWB_MOD can vary from 0 to 63. The value 0 means that the BWB mechanism is disabled. For further details see [31].

The effectiveness of this mechanism has been extensively studied via simulation ([65], [11], [5]). Simulative analysis has shown that, with the BWB mechanism enabled, DQDB always reaches (after a transient time) a steady state condition where the bandwidth is equally shared among the nodes. During the transient time the network behavior remains unpredictable. The length of this transient interval depends significantly on the BWB_MOD value and initial state, while it is not significantly affected by medium capacity and bus length [11]. The relationship between the length of the transient period and the above parameters is still an open issue.

4.3 DQDB Analytical Modelling

Due to the discrete time nature of the DQDB network, it is natural to expect that Markov chains are natural modeling tools for the description of the network behavior. The problem in the use of a Markov chain model is the definition of an appropriate state space. In [46] a discrete time Markov chain which exactly describes a DQDB network with N nodes, constant internode distance of d slots, and K buffers per node is

proposed and the size of its state space is investigated. The state of the Markov chain includes
- the values of the RQ_CTR and CD_CTR in each of the nodes (excluding the most downstream one, since it never receives any requests);
- the number of segments queued at each of the nodes;
- the number of requests queued per node to be transmitted on the reverse bus (excluding the most upstream, since it never sends requests);
- the value of the busy bit for each slot in transit on Bus A;
- the value of the request bit for each slot in transit on Bus B.

However, not all the possible states can be reached. In order to study the relationship between the number of possible states and the number of the valid states (i.e., the reachable states) in [46][7] a network configuration with only two single buffer stations is analyzed. The relationship between the number of possible states and the number of valid states for this configuration is shown in Table 4.

Table 4
DQDB Modeling Complexity

d	Total possible states	Number of valid states
1	216	61
2	1536	305
4	38400	5642
6	884736	92604

It is easy to observe that the state space explodes quite rapidly and analysis is possible in a few simple cases. Thus a general solution for the DQDB network, i.e., one that encompasses any number of nodes and any internode distance, seems to be highly improbable. Simplifying assumptions therefore have to be made in order to obtain analytically-tractable solutions.

To the best of our knowledge, no exact solution of a general model of DQDB has been presented in literature. Approximate solutions have been proposed for general DQDB model, while exact solutions have been proposed for DQDB networks operating under specific conditions.

Table 5
DQDB Models Taxonomy

			Models	Performance indices
Network-Wide Models	Deterministic	Node-Spaced Models	1	Th
	Stochastic	Node-Concentrated Models	2	E[D]
		L_NET 1st-order	3	output process
Node In Isolation Models	Stochastic Models	n^{th}-order	4	output process
	Tagged node Models	Single buffer	5-6	E[D]
		Infinite buffer	7-8-9	E[D]

Th: Throughput; E[D]: Average Delay;

In order to provide a structured overview of the DQDB analytical studies we introduce the taxonomy shown in Table 5. Depending on whether the models consider explicitly all the network nodes or whether they focus on a tagged node, we preliminary identify two main classes of DQDB models: *Network-Wide Models* and *Node-in-Isolation Models* [47].

4.4 Network-Wide Models

Models of a DQDB network which explicitly represent the interdependencies among the network stations can be subdivided into two further classes: models which assume that the network nodes are spaced along the two buses *(Node-Spaced Models)* and models in which the nodes are concentrated in the same place *(Node-Concentrated Models)*.

Node-Spaced Models. Models of a DQDB network which represent few active stations spaced along the network buses are often used in literature to study the DQDB asymptotic behavior. By assuming that all network nodes, when active, always have segments to transmit, the resulting models have a deterministic behavior. These models are used to obtain expressions for throughput achieved by every node as a function of the network span and the nodes activation instants. The complexity of the interdependencies among stations make the analysis possible for only few active nodes.

As noted in the previous section, in [69] a model of this type was applied to an earlier version of the DQDB MAC protocol to highlight its unfairness. In [29] the model proposed by Wong was extended to the standard version of DQDB (with the BWB mechanism disabled)[3] by taking into consideration all the possible configurations of time instants at which nodes start to transmit.

As in [69], in this model, a simple network configuration with only two active nodes is assumed (hereafter the index 1 will be used to indicate the most upstream node) and the propagation delay between the nodes equal to D slots is analyzed. D (an integer number of slots) is used to indicate the difference in the starting times of the two nodes (i.e., node{2} starting time, t_2, minus the starting time of node{1}, t_1). When both nodes are active, node{1} leaves to node{2} an empty slot when it observes a request on the reverse bus. The rate at which node{2} can generate its requests is a function of the sum (X) of the number of requests travelling on the reverse bus, the empty slots on the forward bus, and the number of requests queued in the node{1} counters at the time instant at which both nodes are active. After this time, X becomes a constant and it causes the node{2} throughput. The value of X is determined by the following relationship $X = 1 + D - c(D)$, where

$$c(D) = \begin{cases} (t_2 - t_1) & \text{if } -D \leq (t_2 - t_1) \leq D \\ -D & \text{if } -D > (t_2 - t_1) \\ D & \text{if } D < (t_2 - t_1) \end{cases}.$$

Before continuing, the following definitions must be introduced.

- $r(1)$ and $r(2)$ are the throughputs of node{1} and node{2}, respectively;
- $Q(1)$ is the average length of the distributed queue observed by node{1} just after it inserts a segment in the distributed queue (i.e., 1+ the value of the CD_CTR of node{1});
- $Q(2)$ is the average length of the distributed queue observed at node{1} just after the insertion in the queue of a request from the downstream node;
- T is the average delay between the time node{2} issues a request and the time it receives the related empty slot.

The network behavior in steady state can be approximated by the following four equations [29]: $r(1) + r(2) = 1$, $r(1) = 1/Q(1)$, $r(2) = X/T$, and $T = 2D + Q(2)$.
Finally, by solving the system of linear equations, with the approximation

---

3 In [29] a model to analyze the transient behavior of the BWB mechanism in asymptotic conditions is also proposed. However the model assume that nodes follow the so called *deference scheduling* instead of the DQDB MAC protocol.

$T = 2D + Q(2) \approx 2D + Q(1)$, the nodes throughput are obtained

$$r(1) \approx \frac{2}{2 - D - c(D) + \sqrt{(D - c(D) + 2)^2 + 4Dc(D)}} \quad \text{and} \quad r(2) = 1 - r(1).$$

For a short network $(D \approx 0)$ the nodes get equal throughput. In a large network, the minimum throughput of node{2} $(\text{i.e., } c(D) = D)$ is $\approx 1/2D$, while in its most unfavourable scenario $(c(D) = -D)$ node{1} is less penalized as it gets $\approx 1/\sqrt{2D}$ of the network capacity.

Deterministic models to analyze the DQDB asymptotic behavior have also been presented in ([66], [21], [26], [43]).

Node-Concentrated Models. In [50] a DQDB network with N stations is analyzed. Packets arriving at a station for transmission on a bus are divided into fixed-length segments. Segments are then queued in the Local Queue, LQ, related to their priority level; four priority levels[4] are assumed for the transmission of the asynchronous traffic.

To make the analysis possible the following assumptions are made. Propagation and processing delays are zero. The request channel has an infinite capacity. The order in which packets arrive in the system is random, i.e., the order in which segments are transmitted does not depend on the position of the station.

It is then easy to observe that these hypotheses correspond to the *ideal conditions* (see Section 4.1) according to which DQDB provides a Round Robin *(RR)* sharing type of service to its nodes. Therefore, to analyze the DQDB behavior under these *ideal conditions* the authors propose a discrete time Multi-queue Processor Sharing *(MPS)* model which extends the classical RR model [36]. The classical RR model is based on a single server queue, in which newly arriving customers join the end of the queue. Customers are served on a FIFO basis. When a customer is served, it receives a quantum of service, and if it requires more service it rejoins the end of the queue. The MPS model extends the RR model by introducing multipriority levels, LQs and discrete time services.

In the MPS, arriving packets are queued in the LQ related to their priority level. There is a separate LQ for each priority class in each station. One representative (if any) for each LQ is inserted in the Processor Sharing (PS) queue. In the PS queue, packets of different priority levels are served on a strict priority discipline (HoL discipline). Packets of the same priority level are served on a RR basis: a packet in the PS queue recycles through the service facility, receiving (each time) a quantum of service equivalent to one segment transmission. The packet only leaves the PS queue after it has recycled enough times to service all the segments in the packet.

By assuming that the number of priority-p packets arriving in a slot time are independent and identically distributed (i.i.d.) and independent of the arrivals at the other LQs; and that the number of segments in the packets are discrete and i.i.d. (the distributions may differ for different priority levels), the authors derive a closed formula for the mean time $(D_p(n))$ that a priority-p packet made up of an n segments spends in the system (i.e., the time from its arrival until it is transmitted).

Hereafter $\bar{a}_p$ and $C_{a,p}^2$ will be used to denote the average and the squared coefficient of variation of the number of priority-p packet arrivals in a slot, respectively; while $\bar{b}_p$ and $C_{b,p}^2$ and $F_{b,p}(\cdot)$ will be used to denote the average, the squared

---

4   This model has been defined to analyze an older version of DQDB in which four priority levels for the asynchronous traffic were designed.

coefficient of variation, and the probability distribution function of the length (in segments) of a priority-p packets, respectively.

In the MPS model $D_p(n)$ includes the time a priority-p packet spends in the LQ (L_p) and the time it spends in the PS queue to serve all its n segments $(S_p(n))$.

As in the RR model, it can be proved that $S_p(n)$ linearly increases with n. In fact, in [50], by indicating with $N_p(n)$ the mean number of priority-p packets in the PS queue which have already obtained exactly n quantum of service (i.e., n segments transmission), it is shown that $S_p(n) = n(N_p(0)/\lambda_p)$, where λ_p is the total priority-p packet arrival rate to the system in a slot time. $N_p(0)$ is derived by measuring the delay of a *long test packet* as proposed by Kleinrock [36]. By considering a long test packet at priority-p made up of x segments, the time it spends in the PS queue tends towards the sum of 1) the service time x of the test packet, 2) the service times required by all the priority-p packets which join the PS queue during the service of the test packet (i.e., the priority-p packets representatives of the LQs except that related to the test packet), and 3) the service times of the packets with priority q higher than p $(q = p+1,..,H)$[5], which join the PS queue during the service of the test packet

$$S_p(x) \xrightarrow{x \to \infty} x + S_p(x)\left[\frac{M_p - 1}{M_p}\rho_p + \sum_{q=p+1}^{H}\rho_q\right],$$

where M_p is the number of priority-p LQs, and ρ_q is the priority-q bus utilization, $\rho_q = \lambda_q \cdot \bar{b}_q$, $q = 0,1,..,H$.

After some algebraic manipulations, it can be shown that

$$S_p(n) = \frac{n}{1 - \sigma_{p+1} - \dfrac{M_p - 1}{M_p}\rho_p}, \text{ where } \sigma_{p+1} = \sum_{q=p+1}^{H}\rho_q$$

To obtain L_p, the authors exploit the equivalence, in terms of average segment delay, between the MPS model and the discrete-time M/G/1 with preemptive resume priority queueing model (hereafter referred to as $D[M/G/1]_{PR}$) studied in [52].

Indicating with $R_p(k)$ the probability that a randomly selected priority-p segment is the kth in its own packet, in [50] it is shown that $R_p(k) = (1 - F_{b,p}(k-1))/\bar{b}_p$. Therefore the average segment delay in the MPS queueing system can be expressed as

$E[D_{seg(p)}] = \sum_{k=1}^{\infty}[L_p + S_p(k)] \cdot R_p(k)$. Finally, by equating the last expression with the expression of the average priority-p segment delay in the equivalent $D[M/G/1]_{PR}$ system a closed-form expression for L_p can be derived

$$L_p = \frac{v_p + \sum_{q=p}^{H}\dfrac{\rho_q v_q}{(1-\sigma_p)}}{2(1-\sigma_{p+1})} \cdot \frac{[\bar{b}_p(1+C_{b,p}^2)+1]}{2\left(1-\sigma_{p+1}-\dfrac{M_p-1}{M_p}\rho_p\right)} + \frac{1}{2},$$

---

5 The authors solve the model for a general number H of priority levels. Then they instantiate the model on DQDB by setting $H=4$.

where $v_q = \bar{b}_q\left(C_{b,q}^2 + \lambda_q C_{a,q}^2 / M_q\right)$

In [50] it is clearly shown, by using simulative results, that the performance indices obtained with the MPS provide an adequate estimation of the DQDB performance figures, given that the distance between stations is small.

4.5 Node-in-Isolation Models

The modeling and performance analysis of the DQDB network is very difficult problem due to the high degree of interactions among several processes. This implies that exact DQDB models must take into consideration all the details of the protocol (the values of the counters in each node, the status of the slots travelling in the network and the length of the local queues).

Exact models have a very large state space and this means that they can be analyzed in very specific scenarios. However, when DQDB operates in underload conditions the following observations indicate how DQDB modeling complexity can be reduced ([12], [14]):
1) in underload conditions the number of empty slots is greater than the number of segments to be transmitted;
2) the time it takes a REQ sent by node{j} to affect upstream nodes depends on the physical distance between the nodes. This time interval, in a MAN environment, may have a duration of several slots.

From 1) and 2) it follows that, when DQDB operates in underload conditions, a segment may often be transmitted in a slot ahead of the one corresponding to its REQ. Therefore, the correlation between the transmission of a segment and its REQ is almost negligible, and the only effect of the REQs is to widen the time interval between consecutive transmissions by a given node.

These observations indicate that a significant reduction in complexity is obtained by aggregating the influence of the downstream nodes, on a given node, in a process with the same average arrival rate of downstream REQs. In addition, the influence of the upstream nodes can be modelled via a stochastic process describing the status of the slots travelling on the forward bus observed by node{i}.

Knowledge of these processes reduces the complexity in DQDB modeling by looking at each *node-in-isolation*. Following this approximate approach [4] the node under study is tagged and, with respect to the *tagged node*, the network is partitioned into
*   an *L_NET* (for Left Network) which includes all the upstream nodes (from the tagged node);
*   the tagged node itself, and
*   the *R_NET* (for Right Network) which includes all the downstream nodes (from the tagged node).

With respect to the tagged node, the L_NET is a generator of Busy/Empty slots on Bus A *(L_NET process)*, while the R_NET is a generator of requests on Bus B *(R_NET process)*.

In all the existing analytical models R_NET generates requests according to a memoryless distribution (Poisson or Bernoulli process), while research on modeling DQDB nodes in isolation has concentrated on solving the following subproblems
1)   *L_NET* modeling;
2)   Tagged Node modeling.

L_NET Modeling. Results reported in ([11], [12], [5]) show that the number of consecutive busy slots observed by nodes close to the head node has a nearly geometric distribution, i.e. the number of the busy bit in consecutive slots is independent. On the other hand, while moving towards the end node the correlation among busy bit in consecutive slots sharply increases.

In literature, L_NET is frequently modelled by a Bernoulli process ([64], [4]).

Obviously, this model does not take into consideration the correlation between consecutive slots. To overcome this, in ([15], [16], [20]) models are presented which consider the correlation between consecutive slots.

In the previous section we pointed out that a node (e.g. node{i}) may often transmit a segment in an empty slot positioned ahead of the slot forced empty by the node's own REQ. This event can occur when:

a) no node upstream of the node{i} has a segment to transmit;

b) the empty slot (somewhere ahead of that requested by node{i}) has been forced by a REQ which has already been satisfied (henceforth referred to as a *worthless REQ*).[6]

If the L_NET process observed by a node were only due to point *a*), the L_NET process would correspond exactly to the busy period process of an M/D/1 system [TAKA91] where the input traffic is obtained by the superposition of the input streams of all the upstream nodes. However, in the light of point *b*), the busy periods of the M/D/1 system are subdivided into smaller units due to the worthless REQs.

It thus follows that L_NET can be studied by referring to a *Simplified DQDB* network which is characterized by the following assumptions.

The reverse bus is modelled by introducing, for each node, a Poisson process to characterize the arrival of REQs generated by downstream nodes; the forward bus is slotted and the status of the slots is modelled via the *L_NET process*; the MAC protocol is modelled by a queue where REQs and segments are stored on a FIFO basis. Consequently, for each node{i}, where $1 \leq i \leq K$, the input traffic is made up of segments and REQs. The arrival process is Poisson with $\lambda(i)$ parameters, where $\lambda(i) = \lambda_S(i) + \lambda_R(i)$; $\lambda_S(i)$ and $\lambda_R(i)$ are the segment and the REQ arrival rate, respectively. Obviously, $\lambda_S(i)$ depends on the workload characterization, whereas $\lambda_R(i) = \sum_{j=i+1}^{K} \lambda_S(j)$. The transmission time of both segments and REQs is constant and equal to the slot duration, and both can be transmitted in the first empty slot seen by a node. An empty slot used for a transmission remains empty if there is a REQ at the head of the queue, but becomes busy if there is a segment at the head of the queue. The probability that a queued packet is a REQ $\left(P_{REQ}\right)$ or a segment $\left(P_{SEG}\right)$ are $P_{REQ}(i) = \lambda_R(i)/(\lambda_R(i) + \lambda_S(i))$ and $P_{SEG}(i) = 1 - P_{REQ}(i)$, respectively.

Simulative results presented in [14] show that the Simplified DQDB behaves very similarly to DQDB at least from the slot-occupancy-pattern process standpoint.

In ([15], [16], [20]) the L_NET process of the Simplified DQDB is characterized by observing, for each node{i}, the L_NET process immediately ahead $\left(\left(S_{inp}(i) := \left\{S_j^{(i)}; \ j \in \mathbb{N}\right\}\right)\right)$ of and behind $\left(\left(S_{out}(i) := \left\{\left(S_j^{(i)}, A_j^{(i)}\right); \ j \in \mathbb{N}\right\}\right)\right)$ node{i} which are referred to as *input* and *output process* respectively. The random variable $S_j^{(i)}$ takes the value B if the jth slot is busy, and the value E if the jth slot is empty, while $A_j^{(i)}$ represents the action of node{i} on the jth slot. Thus the random vector $\left(S_j^{(i)}, A_j^{(i)}\right)$ takes the following values:

---

6 This can happen in two different scenarios. In the first the REQ has been generated by a node upstream of node{i} that, by the time it observes the requested empty slot, no longer has a segment to transmit. In the second, the REQ generated by a node downstream of node{i} has already been satisfied by the node{i} itself via a previous empty slot.

- (B0): if the slot is already busy in the input process;
- (E1): if the slot was empty and the node uses it for segment transmission;
- (E0): if the slot was empty, and the node queue is either empty or there is a REQ on top of it.

Obviously the states of consecutive slots are not independent and thus processes $S_{inp}(i)$ and $S_{out}(i)$ do not satisfy the Markov property. However, the correlation between the status of two slots separated by n slots tends to weaken as n increases. In [15] $S_{inp}(i)$ and $S_{out}(i)$ are therefore approximated with discrete time Markov processes $S_{inp}^{[n]}(i)$ and $S_{out}^{[n]}(i)$ which only capture the dependencies between n consecutive slots (n^{th}-order discrete-time Markov process).

The state space of $S_{inp}^{[n]}(i)$ is $\{(s_1, s_2, ..., s_n)|s_j \in \{B, E\}, 1 \le j \le n\}$, and its transition probabilities are $P_i\{S_{n+1} = s_{n+1}|(S_1 = s_1, S_2 = s_2, ..., S_n = s_n)\}$. Each n-tuple $(s_1, s_2, ..., s_n)$ describes the state of the last n consecutive slots observed on the forward bus by the tagged node. While the state space of $S_{out}^{[n]}(i)$ is $\{(s_1 a_1, s_2 a_2, ..., s_n a_n)|s_j a_j \in \{(B0), (E0), (E1)\}, 1 \le j \le n\}$, and its transition probabilities are $Q_i\{S_{n+1}A_{n+1} = s_{n+1}a_{n+1}|(S_1 A_1 = s_1 a_1, S_2 A_2 = s_2 a_2, ..., S_n A_n = s_n a_n)\}$.

By noting that $S_{inp}^{[n]}(1)$ is known (all slots observed by node{1} are empty), and that the $S_{inp}^{[n]}(i+1)$ can be easily constructed from $S_{out}^{[n]}(i)$ in ([16], [20]) the L_NET study is performed by defining algorithms to compute the nth-order Markov model of the output process of node{i} starting from the nth-order Markov model of the input process. All these algorithms first compute the joint probability distribution function of the status of $(n+1)$ consecutive slots in the output process $(j^{n+1} - pdf)$ and then define the transition probabilities in the output process by using the definition of the conditional probability density function and the $j^n - pdf$.

Following the methodologies used for deriving the output process model from the input process, below we divide the 1st-order models and the models which take into consideration higher orders of correlation.

1st-order Markov Models: for this class of models the computation is based on the result of the following theorem proved in [10].

Theorem: the first-order Markov model of the input process, and of the output process related to node{i} are regenerative processes with respect to the sequence $(T = \{T_j; \ j \in \mathbb{N}\})$, where T is a renewal process defined by the successive instants at which the queue of node{i} in the Simplified DQDB becomes empty (renewal times).

By using the regenerative property of the input and output processes we derive a closed formula for the $j^2 - pdf$. The paper focuses on the computation of $\Pr\{B, B\}$, as the transition probabilities of the output process can easily be determined from it; and $\Pr\{B, B\}$ is computed by applying renewal theoretical arguments [68]: $\Pr\{B, B\} = E[N_{BB}]/E[Cycle]$, where $E[N_{BB}]$ is the average number of (B,B) couples in a generic renewal period and $E[Cycle]$ is the average length of a generic renewal period. The computation of these unknown quantities is based on the fact that the renewal period has the same distribution as the delay period of an M/G/1 system with exceptional first service [61], [36].

Results presented in [15], show that even at light loads the interdependence between slots is significant, and that the Bernoulli hypothesis generally used for modeling the length of busy trains diverges from the real behavior at almost any load condition. On the other hand, by using a simulative analysis it is shown that the first-order Markov model is able to capture almost all the 1st-order dependencies in the output process of a DQDB network for a wide range of offered loads (up to OL=.70).

In [17] this model was extended to include the effect of the BWB mechanism on the L_NET process.

n^{th}-*order Markov Models*: the methodology developed for the 1st-order Markov Models (described in [15] and [17]) can be used only for approximating the slot-occupancy-pattern process via a 1st-order discrete-time Markov process, as it requires that the number of consecutive busy slots in the L_NET process be represented by i.i.d. random variables. On the other hand, the approach presented in ([16], [20]) can deal with all orders of correlation.

In ([16], [20]) the output process, immediately after a generic node{i}, is computed by studying the following auxiliary discrete-time Markov process $\{(S_1,A_1),(S_2,A_2),....,(S_n,A_n),L_n\}$, where $A_1,A_2,..,A_n$ are random variables which describe the actions performed by node {i} on the last n slots it observed and L_n $(L_n \in \mathbb{N})$ is the length of the node{i} queue immediately after the sequence of actions $A_1,A_2,..,A_n$.

Once the steady state probabilities of the auxiliary process are known the j^{n+1} − *pdf* and j^n − *pdf* of the output process are easily derived.

$$\Pr\{(S_1A_1),....,(S_nA_n)(S_{n+1}A_{n+1})\} =$$
$$\Pr\{(S_{n+1}A_{n+1}) \mid (S_1A_1),(S_2A_2),....,(S_nA_n)\} \cdot \Pr\{(S_1A_1),(S_2A_2),....,(S_nA_n)\} =$$
$$\Pr\{(S_{n+1}A_{n+1}) \mid (S_1A_1),(S_2A_2),....,(S_nA_n),L_n>0\} \cdot \Pr\{(S_1A_1),....,(S_nA_n),L_n>0\} +$$
$$\Pr\{(S_{n+1}A_{n+1}) \mid (S_1A_1),(S_2A_2),....,(S_nA_n),L_n=0\} \cdot \Pr\{(S_1A_1),....,(S_nA_n),L_n=0\}.$$

$\Pr\{(S_1A_1),....,(S_nA_n),L_n>0\}$ and $\Pr\{(S_1A_1),....,(S_nA_n),L_n=0\}$ are the steady state probabilities of the auxiliary process and

$$- \quad \Pr\{(S_{n+1}=s_{n+1}A_{n+1}=a_{n+1}) \mid (S_1A_1),(S_2A_2),....,(S_nA_n),L_n=0\} =$$
$$P\{S_{n+1}=s_{n+1} \mid S_1,S_2,...,S_n\} \cdot I_{\{a_{n+1}=0\}}$$

$$- \quad \Pr\{(S_{n+1}=s_{n+1}A_{n+1}=a_{n+1}) \mid (S_1A_1),(S_2A_2),....,(S_nA_n),L_n>0\} =$$

$$P\{S_{n+1}=s_{n+1} \mid S_1,S_2,...,S_n\} \cdot \{I_{\{s_{n+1}=B,a_{n+1}=0\}} + P_{SEG} \cdot I_{\{s_{n+1}=E,a_{n+1}=1\}} + P_{REQ} \cdot I_{\{s_{n+1}=E,a_{n+1}=0\}}\}$$

where $P\{\cdot\}$ are the transition probabilities of the input process and $I_{\{A\}}$ is the indicator function of the event A.

Two solution methods are proposed for computing the steady state probabilities of the auxiliary process required to compute the output process. In [16] a closed formula is derived for the probability generating functions of the number of users in the system (PGF), while in [20] steady state probabilities are numerically computed by solving an M/G/1-type system. The computation of the PGFs, requires a closed formula for the solution of a linear system of $3^{order\ of\ correlation}$ equations with $3^{order\ of\ correlation}$ unknowns and therefore it can only be applied for small orders of correlation (up to three). On the other hand, a numerical solution of the steady state probabilities is obtained by applying the theory developed by Neuts in [49] for M/G/1 type systems, where the size of the square blocks in the transition matrix is $3^{order\ of\ correlation}$.

By carrying out a simulative analysis in [20], it is shown that the nth-order Markov models can capture almost all the significant dependencies in the output process of a DQDB network for a wide range of offered loads (OL≤0.60). Furthermore, the nth-order-Markov-model characterization always outperforms the Bernoulli characterization.

Tagged Node Models. The exact queueing model of the DQDB MAC protocol in the tagged node is a discrete time single server queue with two classes of customers: the segments generated by a (tagged) node and the reservations from downstream nodes. The two classes are served according to a *two-state discipline* which reflects the different behaviors of DQDB depending on whether or not the segment queue is empty. When the segment queue is empty, *idle-discipline*, the server attends the reservation queue continuously. When a segment arrives the *busy-discipline* is applied. In this discipline the server serves the reservations queued according to a gated discipline, and then the segment queue according to a one limited discipline. After segment transmission, the busy-discipline is repeated over and over again until the segment queue becomes empty. This two state discipline is referred to as *quasi-gated* discipline in [6] or the consistent gated/limited priority policy with head of line service (*c-G/L/HoL*) in [40].

Several papers in literature have analyzed the tagged node in isolation with the quasi-gated discipline. A general solution has not yet been found. Exact solutions exist only when the tagged node has a single buffer for queueing its messages ([4], [33]). In the case of a tagged node with an infinite buffer, the works in this survey can be divided into two classes: 1) papers which reports solution methodologies which provides bounds on the average performance figures ([3], [40]); 2) papers which provide simple closed formulas which approximate the tagged node performance figures ([64], [14], [22]).

Single Buffer Models: an exact analysis of the node model which provides the generating function of the access delay is reported in [4]. The main simplifying hypothesis is that no more than one segment can be stored in a node (single buffer model); while the cumulative traffic generated by L_NET and R_NET are assumed to be Bernoulli processes with probabilities α, and β to observe a busy and a request, respectively.

The work computes the waiting time *(W)* experienced by a packet from the moment it enters the buffer until the time instant at which its transmission starts. To this end, the author first derives the probability generating function of the random variable F which is equal to the number of outstanding requests at the time a packet is ready for transmission ($G_F(z) = \sum_{i=0}^{\infty} \phi_i z^i$, where ϕ_i is the steady state probability that a packet finds i outstanding requests) and then, he easily computes the statistics of the packet waiting time by conditioning on the number of outstanding requests. In fact, by conditioning the waiting time on the event $\{F = i\}$ its probability generating function $(G_W(z;i))$ satisfies the following equation $G_W(z;i) = \left(\dfrac{(1-\alpha)z}{1-\alpha z}\right)^i$, $|z| \le 1$, $i = 0,1,2,\ldots,$

and then $G_W(z) = \sum_{i=0}^{\infty} G_W(z;i) \cdot \phi_i = G_F\left(\dfrac{(1-\alpha)z}{1-\alpha z}\right)$, $|z| \le 1$.

Finally, the statistics of the access delay *(D)* of a packet, which is equal to the waiting time in the buffer plus a slot time (which corresponds in this analysis to the time unit) to transmit the packet itself (i.e., $D=W+1$) are easily derived from its probability generating function, $G_D(z)$.

$$G_D(z) = zG_W(z) = zG_F\left(\frac{(1-\alpha)z}{1-\alpha z}\right), \ |z| \le 1.$$

From this probability generating function the average access delay is obtained

$$E[D] = \frac{1-\alpha}{1-\alpha-\beta}\left[\beta + \frac{e^{-\lambda}}{1-e^{-\lambda}}\{\alpha\beta - (1-\alpha)(1-\beta)(1-\theta)\} + 1 - \theta(1-\alpha)\right]$$

where $1-e^{-\lambda}$ represents the probability of a segment generation in a slot by the tagged node in the hypothesis of exponential segment interarrival times, and θ represents the probability that a segment finds no outstanding requests ahead of it when it is generated by the tagged node; θ can be numerically calculated from the analysis of the Markov chain.

The main part of this work is therefore devoted to deriving the steady state probabilities ϕ_i that an incoming packets finds i outstanding requests. To compute these statistics the author exploits, that, if we denote with F_n the number of outstanding requests at the arrival of the nth -packet, the sequence $\{F_n, n \ge 1\}$ is a Markov chain embedded at the packet's arrival instants. This Markov chain is homogeneous, irreducible, aperiodic and it is ergodic if $\beta < 1-\alpha$ (i.e., the request arrival rate is less then the rate of the empty slots observed by the tagged node).

The computation of the transition probabilities $\psi_{i,j} = \Pr\{F_{n+1} = j | F_n = i\}$ of the Markov chain is subdivided by applying the Chapman-Kolgomorov equation

$\psi_{i,j} = \sum_{k=0}^{\infty} \sigma_{i,k}\tau_{k,j}$; where $\sigma_{i,k}$ is the conditional probability that there are k outstanding requests after the transmission of a packet given that there were i outstanding requests when the packet arrived; and $\tau_{k,j}$ is the conditional probability that a packet finds j outstanding requests at its arrival given that there were k outstanding requests just after the transmission of the previous packet.

By denoting with $Y(i)$ a random variable such that $\Pr\{Y(i) = k\} = \sigma_{i,k}$, and with $G_Y(z;i)$ its generating function of Y(i) the paper shows that

$$G_Y(z;i) = (1-\beta+\beta z)\left(\frac{(1-\alpha)(1-\beta+\beta z)}{1-\alpha(1-\beta+\beta z)}\right)^i, \ |z| \le 1.$$

The conditional probabilities $\tau_{k,j}$ are studied by investigating the sequence of random variables $\{Z_n(k)\}$ which denote the conditional number of outstanding requests n time units after the last packet transmission, given that there were k outstanding requests just after the transmission. The analysis of the sequence $\{Z_n(k)\}$ is equivalent to studying of the transient behavior of a random walk with the barrier at level 0.

By using the following definition

- $R(k)$ is the value of the sequence $\{Z_n(k)\}$ at a packet arrival instant;
- $G_R(z;k)$ is the generating function of $R(k)$;
- $\pi_j(n; k) = \Pr\{Z_n(k) = j\}$
- $\hat{\pi}_j(k) = \Pr\{R(k) = j\} = (1-e^{-\lambda})\sum_{n=0}^{\infty} \pi_j(n; k)e^{-n\lambda}$;

with some elaborate manipulation

$$G_R(z;k) = \frac{\left(1-e^{-\lambda}\right)z^k + \varepsilon\left(1-z^{-1}\right)e^{-\lambda}\hat{\pi}_0(k)}{1-\left(\delta z+1-\delta-\varepsilon+\varepsilon z^{-1}\right)e^{-\lambda}}, \text{ where}$$

$\delta = \alpha\beta$, is the probability that there is a slot with Busy=1 on the forward bus and with REQ=1 on the reverse bus;

$\varepsilon = (1-\alpha)(1-\beta)$, is the probability that there is a slot with Busy=0 on the forward bus and with REQ=0 on the reverse bus;

$\hat{\pi}_0(k)$ is the probability that the sequence is at the barrier level at the arrival instant; it can be calculated numerically.

From $G_R(z;k)$ and $G_Y(z;i)$ the probability generating function $G_F(z)$ can eventually be derived. In fact, by utilizing the relationship $\phi_j = \sum_{i=0}^{\infty}\phi_i\psi_{i,j} = \sum_{i=0}^{\infty}\phi_i\sum_{k=0}^{\infty}\sigma_{i,k}\tau_{k,j}$ it can be verified that the following functional equation holds.

$$G_F(z) = \sum_{j=0}^{\infty}\phi_j\sum_{i=0}^{\infty}\psi_{j,i}z^i = (\Theta)^{-1}\left[\left(1-e^{-\lambda}\right)(1-\beta+\beta z)\cdot G_F\left(\frac{(1-\alpha)(1-\beta+\beta z)}{1-\alpha(1-\beta+\beta z)}\right) + \right.$$
$$\left.(1-\alpha)(1-\beta)\left(1-z^{-1}\right)e^{-\lambda}\theta\right]z + \theta(1-\alpha)(1-z)$$

where $\theta = \phi_0/(1-\alpha)$ is the probability that an arriving packet finds no outstanding requests; and $\Theta = 1-\left[\alpha\beta z + \alpha + \beta - 2\alpha\beta + (1-\alpha)(1-\beta)z^{-1}\right]e^{-\lambda}$.

The model in [4] has been extended in [33] to the case where each node can queue one message of fixed length (l) segments. Results obtained from this model show that for sufficiently large l the message delay behaves like a linear function of the message length which was also observed in the simulative study reported in [5].

Bounds on the Performance Figures for Infinite Buffer Models: in [3] a model for a tagged node which by following the *quasi-gated* discipline is analyzed. For Poisson processes with intensity λ_r for requests registered by a node and λ_s for segments generated by a node and general service requirements for each class of arrivals, the analysis of the priority queueing system (assisted by the conservation law for work conserving queues [36]) yields the following for the mean delay $\overline{D}_s$ experienced by the segments [3]

$$\overline{D}_s = \left(\overline{R} - (1-\rho)\frac{\rho_r}{\rho_s}\zeta\overline{S}_s\right)\bigg/\left((1-\rho_r)(1-\rho)\right) + \overline{S}_s \text{ where } \overline{R}, \text{ the residual service time}$$

of the customer in service, $\overline{R} = \frac{1}{2}\left[\lambda_r\overline{S_r^2} + \lambda_s\overline{S_s^2}\right]$, and $\overline{S_i^2}$ ($i \in \{1,2\}$) is the second moment of the service time, $\overline{S}_i$ is the average service time, ρ_i is the offered load to the queue due to class i customers, $\rho = \rho_r + \rho_s$, and ζ is the probability that the segment queue is empty and the server serves the request queue. An analysis of a dominant and dominated queue shows that $\left[1-(1-\rho_s)/S_s^*(\lambda_s)\right]\rho_r \leq \zeta \leq \min\left[\overline{R}\rho_s/\overline{S}_s(1-\rho), \rho_r\right]$.

A simulative analysis in [3] shows that these bounds are tight especially in light or heavy traffic conditions. In [6] the same queueing system is analyzed in the discrete time domain, but the derived bounds are not as tight as in the continuous case.

The discrete time version of the above model has been studied in [40]. Through an analysis of the model based on renewal/regenerative theory and a work conservation law the authors obtain upper and lower bounds on the average access delay in the tagged DQDB node. In this model three class of traffic are considered which represent the busy slots travelling on the forward bus (upstream traffic), the segment queue in the tagged node and the request traveling on the reverse bus. In this system the time is assumed to be slotted and the service time of all classes is deterministic and equal to one slot. The segment and request arrival processes are assumed to be Bernoulli, while the busy slot arrival process is modelled by 1st-order Markov model [15] with at most one packet per slot. The upstream traffic queue have the highest priority and is served in accordance with the HoL discipline [68] while the segment and request queue are served following to the consistent gated/limited discipline (c-G/L) [40]; where c-G/L discipline is exactly the two states discipline previously described whenever the service time is deterministic and equal to one slot. This discipline is a priority discipline which guarantees that high priority packets will be served before any low-priority packets which arrive on the same slot or at a future time but at the same time is not inconsiderate of low priority traffic such as HoL. The analysis is based on renewal/regenerative theory, a work conservation law and the theory for approximating the solution of infinite systems of equation [35].

Let $\{S_n : n \in N\}$ be the sequence of time instants in which the system is empty. This sequence S_n denotes renewal cycles and the length of the nth renewal cycle is $X_n = S_n - S_{n-1}$. Let C_n^i indicate the cumulative delay of the ith-priority packets that arrived during the nth cycle. $\{C_n^i : n \in N\}$ is a regenerative process with respect to the renewal process $\{S_n : n \in N\}$ and thus by applying classical renewal/regenerative arguments the mean delay of an ith priority packet D^i can be obtained from $D^i = \overline{C^i}/\lambda^i \cdot \overline{X}$, where $\overline{C^i}$ is the expected value of the cumulative delay of the ith-priority packets that arrived during a renewal cycle, λ^i is the arrival rate of the ith class, and $\overline{X}$ is the average length of a renewal cycle.

Since the c-G/L/HoL is a work conserving system a work conservation law can be used to define a relationship between the average access delay of the same system with the FIFO service discipline $\left(D_{FIFO}\right)$ and the weighted sum of the average access delay of each class in the c-G/L/HoL system: $\lambda \cdot D_{FIFO} = \sum_{i=1}^{3} \lambda_i \cdot D_i$.

By analyzing the system in a renewal cycle a set of linear equations among cumulative delays is obtained. The structure of the generic equation is

$$C^H(i,j) = a^H(i,j) + \sum_{i'=0}^{\infty} \sum_{j'=0}^{\infty} b^H(i,j,i',j') \cdot C^H(i',j'), \text{ where}$$

- $a^H(i,j)$ and $b^H(i,j,i',j')$ are constants;
- $C^H(i,j)$ is a r.v. describing the cumulative delay of all the H packets which arrived (and were served) over the time it takes the system to move from the state i,j (at time t_n) to empty;
- j is the amount of time that has elapsed since the gate was closed in High priority queue for the nth time;
- i is such that $i+j$ describes the time distance from t_n and the arrival of the packet at the head of the low priority queue.

By applying the theory of infinite dimensional linear equations for each class a lower bound of the average access delay $\left(D_i^{lo}\right)$ is computed. From the work conservation law and the lower bounds $\left(D_i^{lo}\right)$ the upper bound for a specific class can easily be

derived: $D_j^{up} = \dfrac{1}{\lambda_j}\left\{\lambda \cdot D_{FIFO} - \displaystyle\sum_{\substack{i=1, \\ i \neq j}}^{3} \lambda_i \cdot D_i^{lo}\right\}$.

Approximate Solutions for Infinite Buffer Models: in [64], simple closed-formulas for approximating the performance figures of a tagged node in a DQDB network are derived. The analyzed DQDB network has N stations transmitting asynchronous traffic of one priority level[7]. Incoming messages to the network stations are made up of single segments; segments arrive at each node$\{i\}$ according to a Poisson distribution with rate λ_i. The L_NET process of a node$\{i\}$ is modelled by a Bernoulli process with a

probability q_i $\left(q_i = \displaystyle\sum_{j=1}^{i-1} \lambda_j\right)$ to observe a busy slot, while the R_NET process of

node$\{i\}$ is modelled by a Poisson process with rate Λ_i $\left(\Lambda_i = \displaystyle\sum_{j=i+1}^{N} \lambda_j\right)$. By indicating

with τ the slot duration, it follows that the bus utilization of node$\{i\}$ is $\rho_i = \lambda_i \cdot \tau$, and

the total bus utilization is $\rho = \displaystyle\sum_{i=1}^{N} \rho_i$.

One of the key concepts in the analysis of this model is the decomposition of a tagged-segment access delay (the time a segment spends within a node) in intervals identified by the following time instants: 1) arrival epoch of the segment; 2) time instant, at which the observed segment is scheduled for transmission on bus A; 3.) the time instant at which the observed segment arrives at the top of the distributed queue; 4) end of the transmission of the tagged segment on the forward bus.

The segment access delay at a given node i is obviously the interval between instant 1 and 4 (T_{14}), and it can be decomposed into the following random variables.

- T_{12}: is the waiting time in the local queue in station i.
- T_{23}: is time that a segment spends in the distributed queue from its insertion in the distributed queue to the time instant at which it arrives at the head of the distributed queue.
- T_{34}: is the virtual transmission time, i.e., the time between successive empty slots (on Bus A) as seen by the (tagged) node i. According to the above hypothesis T_{34} has a geometric distribution and its LST is $\Phi_{34}(s) = \left[(1 - q_i)z\right]/(1 - q_i z)$, where $z = e^{-s\tau}$.
- T_{34} is the time to transmit a segment or to satisfy a downstream reservation. Therefore the waiting time T_{23} of segments in the scheduling position is studied with a standard M/G/1 system with arrival rate Γ_i $\left(\Gamma_i = \displaystyle\sum_{j=i}^{N} \lambda_j\right)$ and service time T_{34}.

---

[7] In the paper it is also proposed an approximation to study the effect of the isochronous traffic on the performance figures of the asynchronous traffic.

Thus the LST of T_{23} is $\Phi_{23}(s) = \dfrac{s(1 - \Gamma_i \cdot E[T_{34}])}{s - \Gamma_i(1 - \Phi_{34}(s))}$, where $E[T_{34}] = \dfrac{\tau}{1 - q_i}$ is the

average of T_{34}. $\Phi_{23}(s) \cdot \Phi_{34}(s)$ can be seen by the segments arriving at node$\{i\}$ as *the virtual service time* to be transmitted on the bus. Therefore T_{12} can be approximated with the waiting time experienced by the segments in an M/G/1 system with arrival rate λ_i with service time equal to the virtual service time. Hence,

$$\Phi_{12}(s) = \left[s(1 - \lambda_i \cdot E[T_{24}]) \right] / \left[s - \lambda_i(1 - \Phi_{24}(s)) \right].$$

Finally, the LST of the access delay (T_{14}) is approximated by $\Phi_{14}(s) = \Phi_{12}(s) \cdot \Phi_{23}(s) \cdot \Phi_{34}(s)$

Obviously, the main approximations introduced in this approach are related to the computation of the T_{23} distribution. In fact, both the possibility of having more than one segment per node in the distributed queue and the Poisson hypothesis on the REQs arrival are conservative. Despite these approximations, the model is able to capture the dependence of the performance figures either from the node position or from the traffic pattern.

The model proposed in [64] was extended in [14] to take into consideration a non memoryless distribution of the *length of the busy train* (T_{34}), i.e., the number of consecutive busy slots. In that paper the lengths of consecutive busy trains constitutes a renewal process and hence those messages which arrive when the queue is empty are considered separately (i.e., such messages experience an exceptional service). The waiting time of the messages (segments or requests) from the distributed queue (T_{23}) is therefore modelled by the waiting time in an M/G/1 system with an exceptional first service in a busy period [61].

In [22], an attempt to extend the nested M/G/1 queue model to the multi-segment messages was made. Unfortunately, even for small (5-segment) messages and moderate loads (0.60), the proposed approximation significantly deviates from simulative results.

Just recently, [58] reports an M/G/1-type model of the tagged node from which the statistics of the queue-length occupancy distribution are derived. To obtain an M/G/1-type model the authors assume that *a)* the maximum number of outstanding requests in the tagged node is bounded; and *b)* the L_NET process is modelled via a Bernoulli process.

Bibliography

[1] B. W. Abeysundara, A. E. Kamal, "High-Speed Local Area Networks and their Performance: a Survey", *ACM Computing Surveys*, 23, (2), pp. 221-264.

[2] FDDI Token Ring Media Access Control, ANSI X3.139, 1987, ANSI, New York.

[3] C. Bisdikian, "A Queueing Model with Applications to Bridges and the DQDB MAN", IBM Research Report, RC 15218, December 1989.

[4] C. Bisdikian, "Waiting time analysis in a single buffer DQDB (802.6) network", *IEEE Journal on Selected Areas in Communications*, Vol. 8, No. 8, October 1990, pp. 1565-1573.

[5] C. Bisdikian, "A Performance Analysis of the IEEE 802.6 (DQDB) Subnetwork with the Bandwidth Balancing Mechanism", *Computer Networks and ISDN Systems*, Vol. 24 (1992), pp. 367-385.

[6] C. Bisdikian, "A Queueing Model for a Data Station within the IEEE 802.6 MAN", Proceedings IEEE 17th Local Computer Networks Conference, Minneapolis, MN, USA, September 13-16, 1992.

[7] K. W. Chang and D. Sandhu, "Delay Analysis of Token-Passing Protocols with Limited Token Holding Times", Proceedings IEEE INFOCOM' 92 Conference, Florence, May 1992, pp. 2299-2305.

[8] K. W. Chang and D. Sandhu, "Mean Waiting Time Approximations in Cyclic-Service Systems with Exhaustive Limited Service Policy", *Performance Evaluation*, 15 (1992), pp. 21-40.

[9] J. Chiarawongse, M. M. Srinivasan, T. J. Teorey, "The M/G/1 Queueing System with Vacations and Timer Controlled Service", Technical Report, Center for Information Technology Integration, The University of Michigan, May 1991.

[10] M. Conti, E. Gregori, L. Lenzini, "On the Approximation of the Slot Occupancy Pattern in a DQDB Network", CNUCE Report C91, December 1991.

[11] M. Conti, E. Gregori, and L. Lenzini, "A Methodological Approach to an Extensive Analysis of DQDB Performance and Fairness", *IEEE Journal on Selected Areas in Communications*, Vol. 9, No. 1, January 1991, pp. 76-87.

[12] M. Conti, E. Gregori, L. Lenzini, "A Comprehensive Analysis of DQDB", *European Transactions on Telecommunications and Related Technologies* Vol. 2, No. 4, July/August 1991, pp. 403-413.

[13] M. Conti, E. Gregori, L. Lenzini, "A Vacation Model for Interconnected FDDI Networks", Proceedings ACM 1992 Computer Science Conference, March 3-5, 1992, Kansas City, pp. 9-16.

[14] M. Conti, E. Gregori, L. Lenzini, "DQDB Modeling: Reduction of the Complexity and a Solution via Markov Chains", *IFIP Transactions on Performance of Distributed Systems and Integrated Communication Networks*, C-5, 1992.

[15] M. Conti, E. Gregori, L. Lenzini, "On the Approximation of the Slot-occupancy Pattern in a DQDB Network", *Performance Evaluation*, Vol. 16 (1992) No. 1-3, November 1992, pp. 159-176.

[16] M. Conti, E. Gregori, L. Lenzini, " 2nd-order Markov Approximation of the Slot-Occupancy Pattern in a DQDB Network", Proceedings IEEE GLOBECOM'92, December 6-9, 1992, Orlando, Florida, pp. 1647-1651.

[17] M. Conti, E. Gregori, L. Lenzini, "A Model to Evaluate the Effects of the BWB Mechanism in a DQDB Network in Underload Conditions", Proceedings ACM 1992 Computer Science Conference, March 3-5, 1992, Kansas City, pp. 395-405.

[18] M. Conti, E. Gregori, L. Lenzini, "Analysis of a Medical Communication System Based on FDDI", to appear on the *International Journal of Microcomputer Applications*. See also Proceedings IC^{3}N, San Diego, CA, 8-10 June, 1992, pp.138-142.

[19] M. Conti, "Analysis of the Quality of Service in a MAN Environment", Proceedings IFIP WG10.3 International Conference on Decentralized and Distributed Systems, Palma de Mallorca, Spain 15-17 September, 1993.

[20] M. Conti, E. Gregori, L. Lenzini, M. F. Neuts, "An M/G/1 Type Approach to the Approximation of the Slot-occupancy Pattern in a DQDB Network", submitted for publication.

[21] P. Davids and P. Maini, "Performance analysis of DQDB," Proceedings IEEE 1990 Phoenix Conference, Phoenix, AZ, March 1990, pp. 548-555.

[22] L. F. M. de Moraes, "Simple Approximation for Frame Delays in DQDB Networks and Comparison with a Slotted Bus without Reservations", Proceedings 8th Annual EFOC/LAN Conference, Munich, Germany, June 27-29,1990, pp. 240-245.

[23] D. Dykeman and W. Bux, "Analysis and Tuning of the FDDI Media Access Control Protocol", *IEEE Journal on Selected Areas in Communications*, Vol. 6, No. 6, July 1988, pp. 997-1010.

[24] B.T. Doshi, "Queueing System with Vacations - a Survey", *Queueing Systems* 1(1986), pp. 29-66.

[25] B.T. Doshi, "Single Server Queues with Vacations", Stochastic Analysis of Computer and Communication Systems, Ed. H. Takagi (Elsevier/North-Holland, 1990), pp. 217-318.

[26] J. Ferguson, "Towards Formal Structures for IEEE 802.6", NATO Advanced Research Workshop, Sophia Antipolis, France, June 1990.

[27] W. L. Genter, K. S. Vastola, "Delay Analysis of the FDDI Synchronous Data Class", Proceedings IEEE INFOCOM'90, San Francisco, June 1990, pp. 766-773.

[28] M. Gerla, H. W. Chan, J. R. Boisson de Marca, "Fairness in Computer Networks", Proceedings ICC'85, pp. 1384-1389.

[29] E. L. Hahne, A. K. Choudhury, N. F. Maxemchuck, "DQDB Networks with and without Bandwidth Balancing", *IEEE Transactions on Communications* Vol. 40, N. 7, July 1992, pp. 1192-1204.

[30] J. L. Hammond, P. J. P. O'Reilly, "Performance Analysis of Local Computer Networks", Addison-Wedsley, 1988.

[31] IEEE802.6 Standard: Distributed Queue Dual Bus (DQDB) Metropolitan Area Network, 1990.

[32] N. K. Jaiswal. "Priority Queues", Academic Press, 1968.

[33] W. Jing and M. Paterakis, "Message Delay Analysis of the DQDB (IEEE 802.6) Network", Proceedings IEEE INFOCOM'92, Florence, May 6-8, 1992, pp. 527-535.

[34] M. J. Johnson, "Proof that Timing Requirements of the FDDI Token Ring Protocol are Satisfied", *IEEE Transactions Communications*, Vol. COM-35, June 1987, pp. 620-625.

[35] L. V. Kantorovich, V. I. Krylov "Approximate Methods of Higher Analysis", P. NoordHoff Ltd, Groningen, The Netherlands, 1958.

[36] L. Kleinrock *Queueing Systems*, Vol. 1 (1975), Vol. 2 (1976), Wiley, New York.

[37] J. F. Kurose, M. Schwartz, Y. Yemini, "Multiple Access Protocols and Time-constrained Communication", *ACM Computing Surveys*, 16, (1), pp. 43-70.

[38] R. O. LaMaire, "An M/G/1 Vacation Model of an FDDI Station", *IEEE Journal on Selected Areas in Communications*, Vol. 9, No. 2, February 1991, pp. 257-264.

[39] R. O. LaMaire, "M/G/1/N Vacation Model with Varying E-limited Service Discipline", *Queueing Systems* 11(1992)357-375.

[40] R. Landry, I. Stavrakakis, "A Three-Priority Queueing Policy with Applications to Communication Networks", Proceedings IEEE INFOCOM'93, San Francisco, 1993, pp. 1067-1074.

[41] T. T. Lee, "M/G/1/N Queue with Vacation Time and Limited Service Discipline", *Performance Evaluation*, Vol. 9, pp. 181-190, June 1989.

[42] K.K. Leung, "Cyclic-service Systems with Probabilistically-limited Service Discipline", *IEEE Journal on Selected Areas in Communications*, SAC-9(1991), pp. 185-193.

[43] P. Martini, "Fairness Issue of the DQDB Protocol", Proceedings IEEE 4th Conference on Local Computer Networks, Minneapolis, MN, Oct. 1989, pp. 160-170.

[44] S. Mirchandani, R. Khanna (editors), "FDDI Technology and Applications", Wiley, New York, 1993.

[45] P. Montuschi, A. Valenzano, L.Ciminiera, "On the Equivalence of IEEE 802.4

and FDDI Timed Token Protocols", Proceedings IEEE INFOCOM'91, Miami, 1991, pp. 435-440.

[46] B. Mukherjee and S. Banerjee, "Alternative Strategies for Improving the Fairness in and an Analytical Model of the DQDB Network", *IEEE Transactions on Computers*, Vol. 42, N. 2, February 1993, pp. 151-167.

[47] B. Mukherjee, C. Bisdikian, "A Journey Through the DQDB Network Literature", *Performance Evaluation*, Vol. 16, Nos. 1-3, 1992, pp. 159-176.

[48] K. Nakumara, T. Takine, Y. Takahashi, and T. Hasegawa, "An analysis of an Asymmetric Polling Model with Cycle-time Constraint", NATO Advanced Research Workshop, Sophia Antipolis, France, June 1990.

[49] M. F. Neuts, "Structured Stochastic Matrices of M/G/1 Type and their Applications", Marcel Dekker, Inc., 1989.

[50] P. G. Potter and M. Zukerman, "Analysis of a Discrete Multipriority Queuing System Involving a Central Shared Processor Serving Many Local Queues", *IEEE Journal on Selected Areas in Communications*, Vol. 9, No. 2, February 1991, pp. 194-202.

[51] R. Reardon (editor), "FDDI Networking", IBC Technical Services Ltd, 1992.

[52] I. Rubin, Z. H. Tsai, "Message delay Analysis of multiclass priority TDMA, FDMA, and discrete-time queueing systems", *IEEE Transactions Information Theory*, Vol. 25, No. 3, May 1989.

[53] I. Rubin, and J. C.-H. Wu, "Analysis of an M/G/1/N Queue with Vacations and its Application to FDDI Asynchronous Timed-Token Service System", Proceedings IEEE GLOBECOM'92, December 6-9, 1992, Orlando, Florida, pp. 1630-1634.

[54] A. Schill, M. Zieher, "Performance analysis of the FDDI 100 Mbit/s Optical Token Ring", Proceedings IFIPTC6/WG 6.4 High Speed Local Area Networks (HSLAN), Aachen,Germany, February 1987, pp. 53-74.

[55] M. Schwartz, "Telecommunication Networks", Addison-Wedsley, 1987.

[56] K. C. Sevcik and M. J. Johnson, "Cycle Time Properties of the FDDI Token Ring Protocol", *IEEE Transactions on Software Engineering*, Vol. SE-13, pp. 376-385, March 1987.

[57] W. Stallings, "Local Networks", Macmillian, 1984.

[58] I. Stavrakakis, S. Tsakiridou, "Occupancy Distribution for a DQDB Station based on a Queueing System with Markov-Structured Service Requirements", Proceedings IEEE INFOCOM'93, San Francisco, 1993, pp. 1083-1090.

[59] H. Takagi, "Analysis of Polling Systems", The MIT Press, 1986.

[60] H. Takagi, "Effects of the Target Token Rotation Time on the Performance of a Timed-Token Protocol", Proceeding Performance 90, Edinburgh, Scotland, September 1990, pp. 363-370.

[61] H. Takagi, "Queueing Analysis", Volume 1: Vacation and Priority Systems, Part 1, North-Holland, 1991.

[62] M. Tangemann, and K. Sauer, "Performance Analysis of the Timed Token Protocol of FDDI and FDDI-II", *IEEE Journal of Selected Areas in Communications*, Vol. 9, No. 2, February 1991, pp. 271-278.

[63] P. Tran-Gia, T. Raith, "Performance Analysis of Finite Capacity Polling Systems with Nonexhaustive Service", *Performance Evaluation* 9 (1988), pp. 1-16.

[64] P. Tran-Gia, Th. Stock, "Approximate Performance of the DQDB Access Protocol", *Computer Networks and ISDN Systems*, Vol. 20 (1990), No. 1-5, December 1990, pp. 231-240.

[65] H. R. van As, J. W. Wong, P. Zafiropulo: "Fairness, Priority and Predictability of the DQDB MAC Protocol Under Heavy Load", Proceeding 1990 International Zurich Seminar, Zurich, March 1990, pp. 410-417.

[66] M. Kabatepe, K. S. Vastola, "Exact and Approximate Analysis of DQDB Under Heavy Load", Proceedings INFOCOM'92, Florence, Italy, May 1992.

[67] W. Whitt, "The Queueing Network Analyzer", BSTJ, Vol. 62, No. 9, November 1983, pp. 2779-2847.

[68] R. W. Wolff, "Poisson Arrivals See Time Averages", *Operation Research*, Vol. 30, March 1982, pp. 223-231.

[69] J. W. Wong, "Throughput of DQDB Networks Under Heavy Load", Proceedings EFOC/LAN'89, Amsterdam, The Netherlands, June 1989.

[70] M. Zukerman, "QPSX - The Effect of Circuit Allocation on Segment Capacity Under Burst Switching", Proceedings IEEE ICC'88, Philadelphia, PA, June 1988, pp. 599-603.

[71] M. Zukerman, "Queueing Performance of QPSX," Proceedings 12th ITC, Torino, Italy, June 1988, paper 2.2B.6.

[72] M. Zukerman, "Overload Control of the Isochronous Traffic in QPSX", Proceedings IEEE GLOBECOM'88, Hollywood, FL, Nov. 1988, pp. 1241-1245.

Multiprocessor and Distributed System Design: The Integration of Functional Specification and Performance Analysis Using Stochastic Process Algebras*

Norbert Götz   Ulrich Herzog   Michael Rettelbach

Universität Erlangen-Nürnberg
Informatik VII, Martensstr. 3
91058 Erlangen, Germany

Abstract

We introduce *Stochastic Process Algebras* as a novel approach for the structured design and analysis of both the functional behaviour and performance characteristics of parallel and distributed systems. This is achieved by integrating performance modelling and analysis into the powerful and well investigated formal description technique of process algebras.

After advocating the use of stochastic process algebras as a modelling technique we recapitulate the foundations of classical process algebras. Then we present extensions of process algebras such that the requirements of performance analysis are taken into account. Examples illustrate the methodological advantages that are gained.

1 The Challenge: Constructive Performance Modelling and System Design

1.1 Motivation

There are three fundamental categories of attributes indispensable for the viability of any technical system: functionality, performance and economicity [Fer86]. However, it is not unusual for a system to be fully designed and functionally tested before an attempt is made to determine its performance characteristics [Har86]: Redesign of both hardware and software is usually the consequence; this is costly and may cause late system delivery. This is particularly true for real-time systems and a dramatic misdesign of mobile communication ground stations has occurred only recently.

---

*This research is supported in part by the German National Research Council *Deutsche Forschungsgemeinschaft* under *Sonderforschungsbereich 182* and by the Commission of the European Community as *ESPRIT basic research action QMIPS*, project no. 7269.

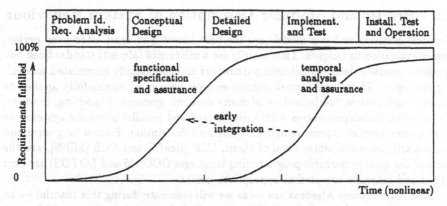

Figure 1: System Life Cycle and Quality Assurance

Figure 1 sketches the phases of any system life cycle and the irresponsible lag between functional and temporal quality specification and assurance. Usually, both functional specification and performance evaluation techniques are separated from each other. System designers use distinct hardware and software specification techniques, while performance assurance is the task of modelling specialists. Such a separation has several advantages, mainly simplicity and understandability. However, to prevent the problems discussed above, performance evaluation has to be intergrated fully into the design process from the very beginning: to eliminate competing approaches, to design and configure components properly, and, last not least, to convince management and customers in due time [Rei91]. Integration of performance analysis into the specification process allows a more accurate description, yields more information about the system behaviour and, again, assures efficient system design.

The need for combined specification methods was already recognized in the seventies. The most successful examples are Stochastic Petri Nets (SPN) [ABC86] and Stochastic Graph Models [ST87, Söt90]. We propose and recommend Stochastic Process Algebras [Her90a, Her90b, Ret91, GHR92, Hil93, SH93] mainly for two important reasons:

- Languages are the principal means of designing hardware and software components: Process algebras are *abstract languages* tailored to the description of parallel and distributed systems; they are well founded, allow a detailed formal specification and support the process of implementation and verification.

- Structuring is the only way to deal with complex systems: Process algebras offer a design methodology, called *constructivity*, that allows to build systematically complex systems from smaller ones. There are operators available for composition as well as mechanisms for abstraction. Finally, process algebras offer an algebraic characterization of equivalent system behaviour.

We emphasize these two important aspects in the next two subsections. Then, in section 2, we give a brief introduction to the basic concepts of process algebras. In section 3 we extend these concepts to Stochastic Process Algebras and present our approach TIPP, a language for *TI*med *P*rocesses for *P*erformance evaluation.

1.2 Precise and Modular Description of System Behaviour

Classical queueing and loss models are the best known and most often used performance evaluation techniques. They mainly use a mixture of (almost) standardized box symbols, precisely defined stochastic parameters and colloquially formulated scheduling strategies. These semi-formal techniques have been most successfully applied to describe and analyse the behaviour of many dynamic systems. Modelling, however, the complex interdependencies within distributed and parallel processor systems we need a more precise, expressive and unambiguous description. Formal languages and particularly process algebras (two of them, CSP [Hoa85] and CCS [Mil89], are the basis of the quite remarkable programming languages OCCAM and LOTOS) are best suited and generally accepted as appropriate means.

Stochastic Process Algebras are — as we will elaborate during this tutorial — an extension of these classical abstract languages including random time variables and operators for the description of probabilistic behaviour. Some examples are shown below to illustrate intuitively their expressive power. (Here we assume exponentially distributed time intervals, characterized by their rates; in general these rates just have to be replaced by an appropriate parameter set.)

- The sequential arrival of three different jobs is specified by a process *Jobstream* describing explicitly each arrival point before halting:

$$Jobstream := (job_1, \lambda_1).(job_2, \lambda_2).(job_3, \lambda_3).Stop$$

- Consequently, a Poisson-arrival process is defined by an infinite sequence of incoming requests, $(in, \lambda).(in, \lambda).(in, \lambda).(in, \lambda). \ldots$, which can be formulated recursively:

$$Poisson := (in, \lambda).Poisson$$

- A service process consisting of an Erlangian distribution of order two is given by:

$$Erl2 := (end_1, \mu).(end_2, \mu).Stop$$

- Using the probabilistic choice operator, hyperexponentially distributed arrivals are generated by the following process:

$$Hyp2 := Exp_1 \, [\pi] \, Exp_2 \quad where \quad Exp_i := (in_i, \lambda_i).Hyp2$$

- Both a precise and concise description of every service or arrival process is possible; this is illustrated by a so-called train-process, which is important for the modelling of file transfers in local area networks. Thereby the overlap and interleaving of different 'trains' is captured by the parallel operator ($\|$):

$$Train := (lok, \lambda).\{ \, ((wag_1, \mu).(wag_2, \mu). \, \ldots \, (wag_n, \mu).Stop) \, \| \, Train\}$$

Passive actions allow the description of receptive behaviour, i.e. the behaviour of components waiting for activities of some partner, for example:

- The behaviour of a queue, with i jobs already queued, is described by a choice (operator $+$) between waiting for a further job or delivering a job on request to a server:

$$Queue_0 := (in, -).Queue_1$$
$$Queue_i := (in, -).Queue_{i+1} + (dlv, -).Queue_{i-1} \quad i \geq 1$$

- An empty server is requesting the delivery of a job, then serves it, and requests again a new job:

$$Server := (dlv, \infty).(srv, \mu).Server$$

The synchronous execution of activities by two components, i.e. joint work or communication, is expressed, again, by the parallel operator, specifying now the synchronous actions explicitly ($\|_{\{...\}}$), for example:

- A queueing system with poisson arrivals and one server is given by

$$QSystem := Poisson \|_{\{in\}} Queue_0 \|_{\{dlv\}} Server$$

where all component processes are specified as above.

Having seen the expressive power of process algebras, this last example indicates already the second important property, outlined next.

1.3 Constructivity: the Basis for Systematic Modelling and System Design

From the very beginning a salient intention of process algebras has been to support a (functional) design methodology which systematically allows to build complex systems from smaller ones. Building blocks for this constructive procedure are *processes* describing the behaviour of the individual system components. Communication activities between these components are accomplished by (synchronous or asynchronous) message passing. There are three important features supporting constructivity:

1. **Composition operators**
   We have already seen several examples for the sequential, parallel or alternative composition of single activities and entire processes. More complex examples will be shown later. The resulting building block is in each case again a process.

2. **Abstraction mechanisms**
   In order to maintain the clearness and transparency of a system design there are operators hiding the internal behaviour of a component. Such a process then shows only its external communication activities to the outside world while internal actions are invisible. Therefore, hiding supports the systematic, clean-cut design and allows the hierarchical structuring of complex systems.

3. **Algebraic characterization of equivalent behaviour**
   Usually there are several possibilities to build a complex system with a specific, intended behaviour. Therefore, alternative designs have to be compared, and components may be interchanged or replaced by others. A major goal of process algebras is the algebraic treatment of system descriptions by means of a simple but powerful calculus. There is a set of transformation rules which allows to build and compare systems with the same behaviour.

Including temporal aspects into such a calculus raises our hope that there is a way to construct and evaluate complex performance models systematically from smaller ones. Nowadays, hierarchical modelling is still an art and only experienced specialists are successful. Stochastic process algebras can offer means for systematic, constructive modelling strategies.

2 Introduction to Process Algebras

Classical process algebras — e.g. CSP [Hoa85], CCS [Mil89], ACP [BW90] — have been developed as formal description techniques for systems of processes that run asynchronously in parallel and communicate with each other by synchronously exchanging messages. They showed to be well suited for the description and analysis of so-called 'reactive systems' like robot control systems, operating systems, communication protocols, etc.

The investigation of process algebras has led to comprehensive theories extending classical automata theory in several respects: They provide a *compositional description technique* by defining composition operators for building large and complex descriptions of smaller and simpler ones. Most important are the parallel composition operator for describing synchronized execution of concurrent processes and an operator for abstracting from actions that are considered irrelevant. Different descriptions of the same system can be compared by means of *equivalence relations*. Several notions of equivalence with different granularity have been formally defined and investigated. *Algebraic characterizations* of such equivalence relations yield equational laws that can be used for transforming system descriptions into equivalent ones.

2.1 Describing Systems

Modelling the behaviour of a real system means to find a *representation* of the system that covers the relevant aspects of the behaviour and is mechanically tractable. Usually such a representation is given in terms of *states* and *transitions*, where transitions represent state changes that are caused by the execution of system activities. Instead of directly finding such a state-transition based model, process algebras use a clearly defined two-step procedure. First, the system behaviour is described by an abstract language. Second, there is a formally defined semantics, i.e. for each language expression there is a unique interpretation as a state-transition based semantic model. The advantage of such a two-step procedure is obvious: While the first step is design-oriented and user-friendly, the transformation into a state-transition model and its evaluation can be performed automatically.

Within process algebras the basic elements of descriptions are actions and composition operators. Actions describe relevant activities of the system. They are considered to be atomic at the level of abstraction that was chosen for modelling. Descriptions can be composed in order to yield descriptions of more complex systems. Formally, the ways descriptions can be built are defined by a grammar. We assume a fixed set of *action names* $Act := Com \cup \{\tau\}$, where we use τ as a distinguished symbol for internal, invisible activities and let Com be the set of regular, visible activities (the communication actions).

Definition 2.1 The set $\mathcal{L}$ of terms of the language is given by the grammar

$$\mathcal{P} ::= 0 \mid X \mid a.\mathcal{P} \mid \mathcal{P} + \mathcal{P} \mid \mathcal{P} \|_S \mathcal{P} \mid \mathcal{P} \backslash L \mid recX : \mathcal{P},$$

where $a \in Act$, $S, L \subseteq Com$, and $X \in Var$ with Var being a set of process variables.

□

The intuitive meaning of the operators is as follows: 0 denotes a terminated process which cannot perform any actions. The process which performs the action a and then behaves like the process A is denoted by $a.A$. The process $A + B$ can behave either like A or like B. The decision is taken as soon as either A or B performs any action. In $A \|_S B$ the component processes A and B proceed concurrently and independently, except for actions in S, which must be performed as joint actions. With $A \backslash L$ a set of actions L of the process A is hidden, i.e. these actions become internal and invisible from the outside. Transitions of A due to actions in L will be presented to the environment of A only as anonymous τ-transitions, thus they cannot take part in joint transitions with the environment and can therfore be regarded as invisible. An infinite behaviour is described by a recursive term $recX : A$ with X occurring freely[1] in A. An alternative way of writing down a description of recursive behaviour is by using defining equations (cf. the examples of section 1.2). E.g. instead of the term $recX : tick.X$ we can name this process and use this name to indicate the recursion: $Clock := tick.Clock$.

For example consider the task of modelling a send-and-wait protocol. We can describe the protocol by composing three processes: a sender, a receiver, and a communication medium for reliable message transfer. These processes run in parallel but sychronize on actions which describe the handing over of messages from and to the medium.

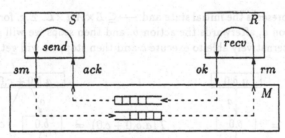

The sender S repeatedly assembles messages that are to be sent (action *send*). These messages are handed over to the medium (action *sm* - *send message*) and the sender waits for an acknowledge of successful transmission (action *ack*). The receiver R gets a message from the medium (action *rm* - *receive message*), processes it (action *recv*) and returns an acknowledge message (action *ok*).

$$S \;=\; recX : send.sm.ack.X \qquad R \;=\; recX : rm.recv.ok.X$$

The medium is modelled as two independent one-place-buffers, one for each direction:

$$M \;=\; (recX : sm.rm.X) \;\|_\emptyset\; (recY : ok.ack.Y)$$

---

[1]A variable X is called to occur *freely* in a term A if it occurs outside of all subprocesses of the form $recX : B$.

Finally, a desciption of the entire protocol is obtained by a parallel composition of the three processes with appropriate synchronizations:[2]

$$SaW\text{-}Prot \;=\; S \;\|_{\{sm,ack\}}\; M \;\|_{\{rm,ok\}}\; R$$

2.2 Operational Semantics

By giving a semantics to our language we define a formal way of creating a behavioural representation of a system from its description. Usually this is done by means of an *operational semantics* that associates a labelled transition system with a process description. Formally, a *transition system labelled over Lab* (the set of labels) is a structure

$$(\, S \, , \, s_0 \, , \, \longrightarrow \,)$$

where S is a set of states, s_0 is the initial state and $\longrightarrow \subseteq S \times Lab \times S$ is a transition relation. $(s, l, t) \in \longrightarrow$ means that there is a transition from state s to t with label l; this will be written $s \xrightarrow{\;l\;} t$.

For presenting a concrete semantics for our language we adopt the Structural Operational Semantics (SOS) style which was introduced by Plotkin [Plo81] and became the most prominent style for process algebra semantics.

With this style, process descriptions and their formal semantics, i.e. their associated labelled transition systems, are formally interweaved by using the set $\mathcal{L}$ of terms of our language as (names of) the states of the transition systems. With a process $P \in \mathcal{L}$ the semantics associates a transition system

$$\mathcal{T}(P) \;=\; (\, \mathcal{L} \, , \, P \, , \, \longrightarrow \,)$$

where P itself represents the initial state and $\longrightarrow \subseteq \mathcal{L} \times Act \times \mathcal{L}$. E.g. for a process that executes the action a, afterwards the action b, and then stops we will get $\mathcal{T}(a.b.0)$; if this process is alternatively able to execute c and then stop, we will get $\mathcal{T}(a.b.0 + c.0)$.

The main part that remains of the presentation of a semantics is the formal definition of the transition relation. In the SOS-style this is done by means of deduction rules: Every operator of the language constitutes a syntactic form, e.g. $A + B$, of building up descriptions. For every syntactic form we present operational rules defining the transitions that are possible for a process of this form, by referring to the transitions possible for the components of this process. E.g. the rule "If $A \xrightarrow{\;a\;} A'$

---

[2]In this case we can omit brackets, but in general brackets are necessary to fix the order of applying the composition operators.

$$\frac{}{a.A \xrightarrow{\ a\ } A} \ \langle . \rangle$$

$$\frac{A \xrightarrow{\ a\ } A'}{A + B \xrightarrow{\ a\ } A'} \ \langle +_l \rangle \qquad\qquad \frac{B \xrightarrow{\ a\ } B'}{A + B \xrightarrow{\ a\ } B'} \ \langle +_r \rangle$$

$$\frac{A \xrightarrow{\ a\ } A'}{A \parallel_S B \xrightarrow{\ a\ } A' \parallel_S B} \ \langle \parallel_l \rangle \ \ (a \notin S) \qquad\qquad \frac{B \xrightarrow{\ a\ } B'}{A \parallel_S B \xrightarrow{\ a\ } A \parallel_S B'} \ \langle \parallel_r \rangle \ \ (a \notin S)$$

$$\frac{A \xrightarrow{\ a\ } A' \quad B \xrightarrow{\ a\ } B'}{A \parallel_S B \xrightarrow{\ a\ } A' \parallel_S B'} \ \langle \parallel \rangle \ \ (a \in S)$$

$$\frac{A \xrightarrow{\ a\ } A'}{A \backslash L \xrightarrow{\ a\ } A' \backslash L} \ \langle \backslash_{no} \rangle \ \ (a \notin L) \qquad\qquad \frac{A \xrightarrow{\ a\ } A'}{A \backslash L \xrightarrow{\ \tau\ } A' \backslash L} \ \langle \backslash_{yes} \rangle \ \ (a \in L)$$

$$\frac{A\{recX : A/X\} \xrightarrow{\ a\ } A'}{recX : A \xrightarrow{\ a\ } A'} \ \langle rec \rangle$$

Figure 2: Operational Semantics Rules

then $A + B \xrightarrow{\ a\ } A'$ " defines that it is possible for a compound process $A + B$ to perform an action a and thereby change into A' if its subprocess A can do so. (A symmetric rule will capture the possible transitions of subprocess B.) The general way of writing such rules is

$$\frac{premise_1 \ \ldots \ premise_n}{conclusion} \ \langle name \rangle \ \ (condition)$$

and they are read:

> If *condition* is satisfied, the rule $\langle name \rangle$ can be applied and it can be deduced that *conclusion* holds in case all of the assumptions $premise_1 \ldots premise_n$ hold.

Now we can present a semantics for our language:

Definition 2.2 Let $P \in \mathcal{L}$ be a process description. The semantics of P is defined to be the labelled transition system

$$T(P) = (\ \mathcal{L}, \ P, \ \longrightarrow\ )$$

where $\longrightarrow \subseteq \mathcal{L} \times Act \times \mathcal{L}$ is the least relation that satisfies the rules of figure 2. $\quad\Box$

The rule for sequential expressions $\langle . \rangle$ is the simplest one. A process of the form $a.A$ can always perform the action a and then changes into A. This rule has no precondition and thus serves as an axiom of the deduction system.

A process of the form $A + B$ behaves either like A (according to rule $\langle +_l \rangle$) or like B (according to rule $\langle +_r \rangle$).

If we want to deduce a possible transition of the process $A \parallel_S B$ we can, according to rule $\langle \parallel_l \rangle$, try to deduce a possible transition for the left subprocess A. Let us assume that we can deduce e.g. $A \xrightarrow{\ a\ } A'$. In case $a \notin S$, i.e. a does not belong to the synchronization set S, the rule $\langle \parallel_l \rangle$ is applicable and thus we can deduce for $A \parallel_S B$ an a-transition to the state $A' \parallel_S B$ where A has changed into A' and B remained unchanged. In case $a \in S$, rule $\langle \parallel \rangle$ states that it is not sufficient to have just $A \xrightarrow{\ a\ } A'$ in order to deduce an a-transition for $A \parallel_S B$. There must also be a proof (deduction) that there is an a-transition for B, say $B \xrightarrow{\ a\ } B'$. In this case A and B will move simultaneously to $A' \parallel_S B'$ by executing a.

Hiding does not affect transitions due to actions not in L (rule $\langle \backslash_{no} \rangle$), otherwise the label of the transition is changed to the anonymous action τ denoting an invisible transition (rule $\langle \backslash_{yes} \rangle$). In both cases hiding remains in effect for the successor state. Finally rule $\langle rec \rangle$ states that a recursive term $recX : A$ behaves exactly like its body A, where all the process variables X in A are substituted by the entire recursive term itself.[3]

Note that there is no rule for the terminated process 0, since it does not have any transition that could be deduced.

To see how the operational rules work together and generate the labelled transition system, we deduce a possible transition for the medium of the send-and-wait protocol

$$M = (recX : sm.rm.X) \parallel_\emptyset (recY : ok.ack.Y) \ .$$

First we need to find applicable rules by following (top down) the structure of the process description, thereby reducing the term to a sequential form. When more than one rule is applicable we have to choose one of them (and can use the other(s) later for deducing other transitions).

$$\cfrac{\cfrac{sm.rm.(recX : sm.rm.X) \xrightarrow{\ ?\ } \qquad\qquad ?}{recX : sm.rm.X \xrightarrow{\ ?\ } \qquad\qquad\qquad ?} \ \langle rec \rangle}{recX : sm.rm.X \parallel_\emptyset recY : ok.ack.Y \xrightarrow{\ ?\ } \qquad\qquad ?} \ \langle \parallel_l \rangle$$

Here we chose to follow the left-hand term of the parallel composition (rule $\langle \parallel_l \rangle$), unfolded the recursion (rule $\langle rec \rangle$), and finally reached a term in sequential form. Now we apply axiom $\langle . \rangle$, the only rule without further premises, and complete the deduction (bottom up) by matching the single deduction steps with the patterns of the corresponding rules.

$$\cfrac{\cfrac{\cfrac{}{sm.rm.(recX : sm.rm.X) \xrightarrow{\ sm\ } rm.(recX : sm.rm.X)} \ \langle . \rangle}{recX : sm.rm.X \xrightarrow{\ sm\ } rm.(recX : sm.rm.X)} \ \langle rec \rangle}{recX : sm.rm.X \parallel_\emptyset recX : ok.ack.X \xrightarrow{\ sm\ } rm.(recX : sm.rm.X) \parallel_\emptyset recY : ok.ack.Y} \ \langle \parallel_l \rangle$$

This deduces a possible sm-transition for the medium (an ok-transition would also be possible and can be deduced starting with rule $\langle \parallel_r \rangle$ instead of $\langle \parallel_l \rangle$). The transitions that are possible in the new state, reached by performing sm, can be deduced in the same way (there is still the ok-transition possible for the right-hand side, and a rm-transition for the left-hand side, leading again to the initial state).

---

[3]The notation $A\{B/X\}$ denotes the *simultaneous* substitution of B for all *free* occurrences of X inside A.

This kind of reasoning by means of deduction rules, which are chosen according to the structure of the term, can be automated very easily. Furthermore, every state is represented by a process term containing all the necessary information about the possible transitions leaving this state. This allows to deduce transitions by need, and thus to avoid to create the whole state space in advance when it is not necessary.

2.3 Comparing Descriptions

When we model the behaviour of real systems *different representations* can be found, all of them capturing the *'same' behaviour*. E.g. consider the three transition systems (where * indicates the initial state):

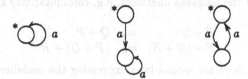

The first one executes a infinitely often, the second initially executes an a and then loops forever while executing a, and the third toggles between two states by executing a. All three transition systems (in fact we can find many more) represent the ability of a system to execute a infinitely often. An external observer watching the three systems and recording the actions they perform would not be able to tell the difference beween these systems from his observations. From the point of view of this observer these systems are considered *equivalent*.

This notion of equivalence of behavioural representations (transitition systems), which is expressed by the metaphor of an observer recording sequences of actions a system performs, can formally be captured as a relation between transition systems. All the possible sequences of actions a system $T = (S, s_0, \longrightarrow)$ can perform, starting from the initial state, are given by the set[4]

$$traces(T) = \{w \in Com^* \mid \exists n \in \mathbb{N}_0. \exists l_1, \ldots, l_n \in Com, s_1, \ldots, s_n \in S.$$
$$w = l_1 \ldots l_n \wedge s_0 \overset{l_1}{\Longrightarrow} s_1 \overset{l_2}{\Longrightarrow} \ldots \overset{l_n}{\Longrightarrow} s_n\}$$

where $s \overset{a}{\Longrightarrow} t := s \overset{\tau}{\longrightarrow} \ldots \overset{\tau}{\longrightarrow} s' \overset{a}{\longrightarrow} t' \overset{\tau}{\longrightarrow} \ldots \overset{\tau}{\longrightarrow} t$ is defined to disregard invisible transitions. We can now define

Definition 2.3 Two labelled transition sytems $T = (S, s_0, \longrightarrow)$ and $T' = (S', s_0', \longrightarrow')$ are *trace equivalent* ($\approx_{tr}$) iff they have the same set of traces:

$$T \approx_{tr} T' :\Longleftrightarrow traces(T) = traces(T')$$

□

Having a means of comparing behavioural representations we can use it to compare *descriptions* of them.

---

[4]Note that the empty trace is contained in every trace set.

Definition 2.4 Two process terms $P, P' \in \mathcal{L}$ are *trace equivalent* ($=_{tr}$) iff their associated transition systems are trace equivalent

$$P =_{tr} P' \;:\Longleftrightarrow\; \mathcal{T}(P) \approx_{tr} \mathcal{T}(P')$$

□

E.g. the three transition systems above can be described by the following equivalent terms

$$recX : a.X \quad =_{tr} \quad a.(recX : a.X) \quad =_{tr} \quad recX : a.a.X$$

In general we will look for patterns of process terms which are equivalent, thus establishing *equational laws*: There are rather obvious equational laws which reflect certain properties of the language operators, e.g. commutativity and associativity of the operator +:

$$
\begin{aligned}
P + Q &=_{tr} \; Q + P \\
P + (Q + R) &=_{tr} \; (P + Q) + R
\end{aligned}
$$

On the other hand there are special laws expressing the inability of an observer to distinguish between certain processes, e.g.

$$
\begin{aligned}
\tau.P &=_{tr} \; P \\
a.(P + Q) &=_{tr} \; a.P + a.Q \\
a.P \parallel_{\{\}} b.Q &=_{tr} \; a.(P \parallel_{\{\}} b.Q) + b.(a.P \parallel_{\{\}} Q)
\end{aligned}
$$

Such a collection of equational laws on processes turns our language into an *algebra*. Once a set of equational laws is presented, two properties of the algebra with respect to the given equivalence notion have to be shown. First, it must be proven that all of the laws are *sound*, i.e. only processes are equated which really have equal trace sets. Second, it must be proven that the set of laws is *complete*, i.e. whenever two processes have the same trace set, they can be shown to be equivalent by purely equational reasoning.

Apart from trace equivalence there is a variety of equivalence notions which have been investigated. In fact, trace equivalence is one of the simplest and coarsest equivalence relations. When we want to compare process descriptions, we must carefully choose an equivalence notion, such that it captures exactly the extent to which we want two processes to be considered equal.

2.4 Validation of System Descriptions

A crucial step of modelling real systems is to convince oneself and others that the presented description of a system really captures the system's important properties and represents the relevant aspects of its behaviour properly. To this end several techniques for validating process algebra descriptions have been investigated and are supported by a number of tools. A comprehensive overview of existing tools, their capabilities, and implementation aspects is presented in [IP91].

Validation techniques can be classified into three categories: simulation, equivalence checking, and model checking. They depend strongly on the type of model that is used to represent systems. For this presentation we will only consider validation techniques for systems being represented by transition systems.

Validation by Simulation Techniques in this category are based on examining the state space of the system.

Conducting a 'reachability analysis', the state space is searched for states indicating certain unwanted situations. Since with an SOS-style semantics states are represented by process terms, these terms can be checked to support the identification of such situations. As e.g. deadlock states must be distinguished from states representing a regular termination, it is not sufficient just to find states without transitions leaving them; by checking their names, deadlock states like $0 \parallel_{\{a\}} a.0$ can be detected and separated from termination states like $0 \parallel_{\{a\}} 0$.

Furthermore, it is also possible just to list the action sequences the system can perform (certainly almost never exhaustively), or to navigate through the state space, thereby 'testing' the system's ability to react to stimuli from the environment. For performing these kinds of investigations it is not necessary to create the whole state space, but it is sufficient to deduce from the operational semantics rules just the part of the state space needed.

Validation by Equivalence Checking Different descriptions of the same system can be proven equivalent. The chosen equivalence notion determines to what extent the behaviours coincide. Equivalence checking is useful in two common situations:

Consider a system consisting of individual subsystems composed by operators of our language, e.g. $A \parallel_S B$. If we want to replace one subsystem, say B, by a different, perhaps more efficient, implementation C, we expect the new system $A \parallel_S C$ to have the same behaviour as the former one. In case the used equivalence relation $(=_{eq})$ respects the composition operators of the language, i.e. $=_{eq}$ is in fact a congruence relation, we can make use of the following property

$$\forall A, B, C \in \mathcal{L}. \quad B =_{eq} C \implies A \parallel_S B =_{eq} A \parallel_S C.$$

Only the subsystem has to be proven equivalent to the new one replacing it, this is easier than comparing the whole system.

Another situation, where equivalence checking is often used, is the task of verifying that a detailed description of a complex system satisfies an abstract specification. Consider the example of the send-and-wait protocol of section 2.1. If we think of the visible behaviour of the sender and receiver working together being described abstractly by the 'service specification'

$$SaW\text{-}Serv = recX : send.recv.X$$

then we can prove that this is equivalent to the behaviour of the protocol if we disregard (hide) the internal communication of the sender and receiver with the medium

$$SaW\text{-}Serv =_{tr} (SaW\text{-}Prot) \backslash \{sm, ack, ok, rm\}$$

Validation by Model Checking A different approach is to use a *logical formalism* for the specification of a system. Relevant properties, which we expect the system to have, are stated one by one as logical expressions and specify conjunctively the system's behaviour. For this purpose temporal logics formalisms can usefully be applied. The task of proving that a behavioural representation (transition system) of a system satisfies its specification is called *model checking* and can be done mechanically.

In contrast to the approach with equivalence checking, where we start with a specification given in form of a process description, which already shows the entire expected behaviour of the final implementation abstractly, the logical approach is more appropriate when such a prototype description is difficult to find and not available from the beginning.

3 TIPP — a Language for Timed Processes and Performance Evaluation

3.1 Process Algebras and Time

In classical process algebras, only the relative ordering of events is modelled. In order to describe the temporal behaviour of systems, all standard process algebras have been recently extended to *real time process algebras*, which allow to model the *exact timing of events*, and thereby are able to represent time dependent behaviour properly (see [NS91] for an overview). These approaches differ in detail, but have in common the objective to model and analyse the influence of fixed time durations on the functional behaviour rather than to investigate quantitative aspects. Being interested in the analysis of performance characteristics, the concept of *random variables* and *stochastic processes* is still the only feasible way to capture the particulars of a complex system: In many situations there is no exact timing behaviour available because of the complexity of the problem, because of a randomly changing environment, or because of the indeterminacy inherent in any transmission system. Therefore we propose to develop *stochastic process algebras* by incorporating random variables into classical approaches. By doing this we are able to combine the potentials of performance modelling and analysis with the modelling power of standard process algebras.

To the best of our knowledge only two attempts have been made in the past in this direction [NY85, Zic87]. However, the fascinating properties of process algebras are attracting more people now [Hil93, SH93]. In the following sections we report on our research and experiences during the past [Her90b, Ret91, GHR92, GHR93] as well as on ongoing activities.

3.2 Stochastic Process Algebras

The Concept The basic ideas of our concept are summarized in figure 3. We strictly follow the concept of classical process algebras describing the system behaviour by an abstract language (*system description*) with an underlying state-transition graph representing the exact meaning of the process (*semantic model*). Rather than considering only the functional behaviour we also add temporal information: each activity is described as a pair consisting of its type and time. This additional information in the semantic model allows to evaluate various system aspects:

- *functional behaviour* (e.g. liveness or deadlocks)
- *temporal behaviour* (e.g. throughput or waiting times)

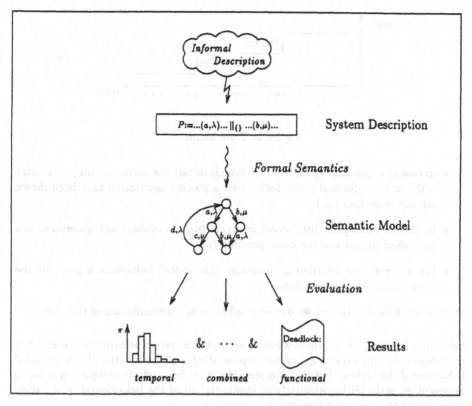

Figure 3: Modelling Procedure

- *combined properties* (such as the duration of certain event sequences, the probability of deadlocks or timeouts, etc.)

Dependent on the stochastic assumptions (e.g. Markovian, semi-Markovian, general) different timing parameters are necessary and the expenditure for evaluations may vary significantly; this is true also for the algebraic characterization of equivalent systems behaviour.

There is not a unique way of solution and there are many possiblities to specify operators, semantic models and equivalences. In principle, however, stochastic process algebras offer the same exciting possiblities as their purely functional forefathers.

System Description To incorporate a stochastic time description into process algebras and to guarantee compositional properties, we have chosen the standard concept of stochastic modelling and performance evaluation, a specification by (random) interarrival times: the execution instant of each event is specified by the time interval between the event and its immediate predecessor event; for an illustration cf. figure 4. The events, represented by pairs (a_i, p_i), describe both the functional and temporal behaviour of the process: a_i denotes the type of activities and p_i is a parameter (or parameter set) specifying uniquely the distribution function of the related time intervals:

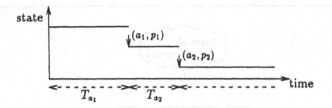

Figure 4: Time Model

- In case of exponentially distributed time intervals the corresponding parameter is the rate λ_i. (Several examples for such a process description have been shown already in section 1.2.)

- In case of Erlangian distributed intervals two parameters are necessary: the number of phases and the corresponding rate.

- For discrete time distribution functions the random behaviour is given by the appropriate step probabilities.

From a syntactic description we derive a behavioural representation of the system.

Semantic Model   By means of a formal semantics a system description is translated unambiguously into a transition system representing both the functional and temporal behaviour of the system. For that the semantic must be carefully designed in order to represent properly (either explicitly or implicitly) all of the behavioural information contained in the syntactic description.

- For generally distributed time intervals we preserve this information by so-called 'start-reference'; they allow to solve the problem of residual time intervals in the case of parallel and competing process execution [Ret91, GHR93].

- In case of exponentially distributed time intervals the Markovian property allows a drastic simplification. The structure of the semantic model corresponds to that of the standard Markov chain representation.

Note, however, that the system designer does not see this more or less complicated semantic model; he just formulates the problem to be investigated using the language elements.

In the following two sections we will restrict ourselves to exponentially distributed time intervals and present a stochastic process algebra called Markovian TIPP. Several examples will demonstrate the applicability of our constructive approach to system modelling. Finally, we will show that stochastic process algebras are not limited to the presented version. We briefly sketch how additional language elements like the probabilistic choice operator can be included, and how we can deal with residual execution times when allowing generally distributed time intervalls.

3.3 Formal Semantics of Markovian TIPP

In a stochastic process algebra we are dealing with activities which have (random) time duration (described by random variables with a certain time distribution function). Since we will be dealing only with exponential distributions, timed actions can be described by their name and the rate of the exponential distribution function, (a, λ). It is often useful to have not only timed actions but also timeless, immediate actions, denoted by (a, ∞). Similar to immediate transitions in Generalized Stochastic Petri Nets [ABC86] they are suitable for the proper modelling of a specific functional behaviour. From a temporal point of view they can be neglected and, by doing so, the number of states of the associated Markov chain model is reduced. Both kinds of actions are called *active*. A third kind of actions, the *passive* actions are introduced to describe subsystems, whose temporal behaviour is not completely determined by their own but by activities of other subsystems communicating with them; e.g. the interarrival time of customers in a queue is determined not by the queue but by the environment (which can be a complex system or be modelled simply by an arrival process) (cf. section 3.4.1). Passive actions, denoted by $(a, -)$, will prove to be very helpful for combining systems by means of synchronized parallel composition.

The formal definition of the language and its operational semantics is completely analogous to the basic process algebra presentation in section 2.2. We assume a fixed set of *action names* $Act := Com \cup \{\tau\}$ with Com being the set of visible actions and τ a distinguished symbol denoting invisible, internal activities. An action a can either be passive $(a, -)$, immediate (a, ∞), or timed (a, λ) with an exponentially distributed duration represented by the parameter λ.

Definition 3.1 The set $\mathcal{L}$ of terms of our language is given by the grammar

$$\mathcal{P} ::= 0 \mid X \mid \alpha.\mathcal{P} \mid \mathcal{P} + \mathcal{P} \mid \mathcal{P} \|_S \mathcal{P} \mid \mathcal{P} \backslash L \mid recX : \mathcal{P},$$

where $\alpha \in Act \times Rate$ with $Rate := \{-\} \cup \mathbb{R}^+ \cup \{\infty\}$, $S, L \subseteq Com$, and $X \in Var$ with Var being a set of process variables. □

Definition 3.2 Let $P \in \mathcal{L}$ be a process description. The semantics of P is defined to be the labelled transition system

$$\mathcal{T}(P) = (\mathcal{L}, P, \longrightarrow)$$

where $\longrightarrow \subseteq \mathcal{L} \times (Act \times Rate \times \{l, r\}^*) \times \mathcal{L}$ is the least relation that satisfies the rules of figure 5. □

The difference between the semantics presented here and that of the basic process algebra (figure 2) is twofold.

First, auxiliary labels $(\in \{l, r\}^*)$ are introduced as a technical means to distinguish identical transitions. This is necessary to represent the temporal behaviour correctly. E.g. consider in the basic process algebra the process description $A = b.0 + c.0$. It will yield (according to the rules of fig. 2) two transitions $(A, b, 0), (A, c, 0) \in \longrightarrow$. If we want to change the description to $A' = a.0 + a.0$ where we no longer want to distinguish the activities b and c and call them identically a, these two transitions will coincide such that we have only the single transition $(A', a, 0) \in \longrightarrow$. This is all right

$$\frac{}{(a,\lambda).A \xrightarrow{a,\lambda,\varepsilon} A} \ (.)$$

$$\frac{A \xrightarrow{a,\lambda,w} A'}{A+B \xrightarrow{a,\lambda,lw} A'} \ \langle +_l \rangle \qquad\qquad \frac{B \xrightarrow{a,\lambda,w} B'}{A+B \xrightarrow{a,\lambda,rw} B'} \ \langle +_r \rangle$$

$$\frac{A \xrightarrow{a,\lambda,w} A'}{A \parallel_S B \xrightarrow{a,\lambda,lw} A' \parallel_S B} \ \langle \parallel_l \rangle \ \ (a \notin S) \qquad \frac{B \xrightarrow{a,\lambda,w} B'}{A \parallel_S B \xrightarrow{a,\lambda,rw} A \parallel_S B'} \ \langle \parallel_r \rangle \ \ (a \notin S)$$

$$\frac{A \xrightarrow{a,\lambda,v} A' \quad B \xrightarrow{a,\mu,w} B'}{A \parallel_S B \xrightarrow{a,max(\lambda,\mu),v\cdot w} A' \parallel_S B'} \ \langle \parallel \rangle \ \ (a \in S)$$

$$\frac{A \xrightarrow{a,\lambda,w} A'}{A \backslash L \xrightarrow{a,\lambda,w} A' \backslash L} \ \langle \backslash_{no} \rangle \ \ (a \notin L) \qquad \frac{A \xrightarrow{a,\lambda,w} A'}{A \backslash L \xrightarrow{\tau,\lambda,w} A' \backslash L} \ \langle \backslash_{yes} \rangle \ \ (a \in L)$$

$$\frac{A\{recX : A/X\} \xrightarrow{a,\lambda,w} A'}{recX : A \xrightarrow{a,\lambda,w} A'} \ (rec)$$

Figure 5: Operational Semantics Rules

for the representation of the functional behaviour. For a stochastic process algebra, however, this coincidence in case of $A' = (a,\lambda).0 + (a,\lambda).0$ would lead to a wrong representation of the system's temporal behaviour since the transition rate changes from 2λ to λ. Among different possibilities to avoid this coincidence or to adapt the transition rate, we have chosen in TIPP the most tractable solution and use auxiliary labels, l (left) and r (right), to distinguish identical transitions.[5]

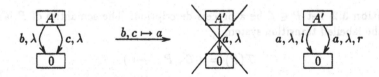

Second, and most important from a methodological point of view, the treatment of synchronization fits in the conception of the three kinds of actions we have. If two actions, (a,x) and (a,y), are to be synchronized, it must be considered whether they are active or passive. In order to treat different combinations uniformly, we choose, according to rule $\langle \parallel \rangle$, for the time parameter of the joint action the rate $max(x,y)$, where we extend the function max by defining for passive and immediate actions

$$\forall z \in \{-\} \cup \mathbb{R}^+ \cup \{\infty\}. \quad max(-,z) = z \ \land \ max(\infty,z) = \infty$$

---

[5]In general, in order to distinguish more than two transitions, we concatenate words $w \in \{l,r\}^*$, starting with the empty word ε in rule $(.)$.

This facilitates two important ways of using sychronization while composing descriptions (see also the examples in the next section): either a passive action is synchronized with an active one, $(a, -) \|_{\{a\}} (a, \lambda)$ or $(a, -) \|_{\{a\}} (a, \infty)$, or two identical actions are synchronized, $(a, x) \|_{\{a\}} (a, x)$.[6]

By *synchronizing active and passive actions*, waiting situations can be described. E.g. a processor waiting for a task to execute can be written.

$$Proc := (task, -). \ldots \qquad Workload := \ldots (task, \lambda). \ldots$$
$$System := Proc \|_{\{task\}} Workload$$

By *synchronizing identical actions*, system descriptions can be written in an elegant style, the so-called constraint-oriented specification style [V+91]. E.g. consider a workload consisting of three tasks (t_1, λ_1), (t_2, λ_2) and (t_3, λ_3) with the execution constraints 't_1 *has to be completed before* t_2 *can start*' and 't_2 *has to be completed before* t_3 *can start*'. We can describe this workload by following the structure of its informal specification, combining two constraints on the execution sequence of the three tasks:

$$Workload := (t_1, \lambda_1).(t_2, \lambda_2).0 \|_{\{t_2\}} (t_2, \lambda_2).(t_3, \lambda_3).0$$

In this description both subterms (constraints) refer to the *same* task t_2. Obviously this description is equivalent to $Workload := (t_1, \lambda_1).(t_2, \lambda_2).(t_3, \lambda_3).0$ but the first one explicitly represents the way it was composed from simpler descriptions. This specification style can usefully be applied not only to timed actions, but also to passive and immediate ones.

3.4 Examples

TIPP can be used for the specification and analysis of systems of various kinds. E.g. in [GHR93] we have modelled a *multiple send-and-wait protocol* (cf. section 2.1) using deterministic and exponential time distributions.[7] Here we want to demonstrate how to construct systematically queueing models from basic elements (queues, servers, jobs, etc.) and how the internal structure of the complex jobs can be taken into account.

3.4.1 Queueing Systems

We model a simple M/M/n queueing system (see figure 6). A formal description of this system, following the structure of its semi-formal graphical presentation, will be developed from a composition of three parts: an arrival process, a queue, and a number of servers.

The arrival process is modelled as a Poisson stream, creating jobs a (arrivals) with rate λ.

$$Arr := (a, \lambda).Arr$$

---

[6]Synchronizing timed actions with the same name but different rates, say (a, λ) and (a, μ), is not explicitly precluded, but we cannot think of any special use for this case; nevertheless the semantics for this case is uniquely defined.

[7]This was carried out with a version of TIPP capable of dealing with general distribution functions (see also section 3.5.2).

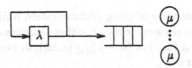

Figure 6: M/M/n queueing system

The queue waits for the arrival of a job, action $(a, -)$, or alternatively delivers a job to a server, if it is requested to do so and it is not empty, action $(d, -)$. In order to get finite models, the queue is bounded to a maximum number of jobs, $maxQ$.

$$Queue_0 := (a, -).Queue_1$$
$$Queue_i := (a, -).Queue_{i+1} + (d, -).Queue_{i-1} \quad 0 < i < maxQ$$
$$Queue_{maxQ} := (a, -).Queue_{maxQ} + (d, -).Queue_{maxQ-1}$$

The multiserver consists of n independent processing elements. Each processor repeatedly requests a job, being delivered from the queue, action (d, ∞), and processes it with rate μ, action (p, μ).

$$Proc := (d, \infty).(p, \mu).Proc$$
$$MultiS := \underbrace{Proc \parallel_{\{\}} Proc \parallel_{\{\}} \cdots \parallel_{\{\}} Proc}_{n\text{-times}}$$

The complete queueing system is then the synchronized parellel composition

$$M/M/n := (Arr \parallel_{\{a\}} Queue_0) \parallel_{\{d\}} MultiS$$

The underlying semantic model of this compact description is determined unambiguously by the semantics of TIPP. For $n = 2$ the model is depicted in figure 7, where the horizontal position of the nodes indicates the number of tasks in the system (0 – $maxQ+2$) and the vertical position represents the number of processors busy (0 – n). This model can be transformed quite easily into a Markov chain by eliminating

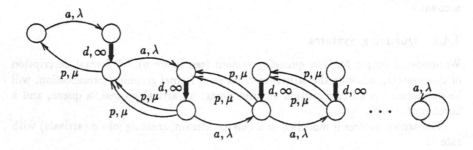

Figure 7: Semantic model of the system $M/M/n$

immediate transitions, dropping the action names, and joining multiple transitions by adding their rates.

3.4.2 Task Graphs

Jobs consisting of a number of interdependent tasks can be represented graphically by task graphs. E.g. consider a *Job* with tasks $t_1, \ldots, t_6$ and a precedence relation depicted in figure 8. The task graph can be assumed to be developed from the

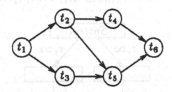

Figure 8: Task graph

combination of several precedence constraints, e.g.

$$
\begin{aligned}
C_1 &:= (t_1, \lambda_1).(t_2, \lambda_2).(t_4, \lambda_4).(t_6, \lambda_6).0 \\
C_2 &:= (t_1, \lambda_1).(t_3, \lambda_3).(t_5, \lambda_5).(t_6, \lambda_6).0 \\
C_3 &:= (t_2, \lambda_2).(t_5, \lambda_5).0 \\
Job &:= (C_1 \|_{\{t_1, t_6\}} C_2) \|_{\{t_2, t_5\}} C_3
\end{aligned}
$$

3.4.3 Mapping Workload onto a Multiserver

Now we want to present a more advanced example combining the two previous examples and describe the treatment of complex jobs with several tasks in a queueing network.

First we need to consider the effects of synchronization in some more detail. In general synchronization of system activities, modelled by timed actions, and system resources, modelled by passive actions, requires some care. Consider e.g. a system with a workload consisting of two independent tasks and a single processor, which, for the sake of this example, serves just one of the tasks and then stops.

$$Workload := (task, \lambda_1).0 \|_{\{\}} (task, \lambda_2).0 \qquad Proc := (task, -).0$$

$$System := Workload \|_{\{task\}} Proc$$

Unfortunately, describing the system in this way is incorrect, since the assigned behavioural representation contradicts our intuition about the system behaviour.

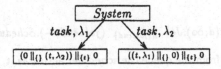

Here the overall transition rate from the initial state to a terminal state is $\lambda_1 + \lambda_2$. The reason is, that the *potential* parallelism of the workload is represented as *actual* parallelism rather than being eliminated.

A correct description would be to eliminate the parallelism of the workload by making first a decision, which of the tasks is to be started.

$$Workload := (start\_t, -).(task, \lambda_1).0 \parallel_{\{\}} (start\_t, -).(task, \lambda_2).0$$
$$Proc := (start\_t, \infty).(task, -).0$$

$$System := (Workload \parallel_{\{start\_t, task\}} Proc)\backslash\{start\_t\}$$

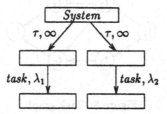

This leads to a branching structure in the transition system with two immediate transitions, representing a choice between the two alternative tasks with equal probability.

Now we can adapt the description of the task graph of the previous section for being included in the queueing network example (additionally, an immediate action *job_end* indicates the termination of the job).[8]

$$
\begin{aligned}
C_1 &:= (start\_t_1, -).(task_1, \lambda_1). (start\_t_2, -).(task_2, \lambda_2). \\
&\quad (start\_t_4, -).(task_4, \lambda_4). (start\_t_6, -).(task_6, \lambda_6). \\
&\quad (job\_end, \infty). 0 \\
C_2 &:= (start\_t_1, -).(task_1, \lambda_1). (start\_t_3, -).(task_3, \lambda_3). \\
&\quad (start\_t_5, -).(task_5, \lambda_5). (start\_t_6, -).(task_6, \lambda_6). 0 \\
C_3 &:= (task_2, \lambda_2). (start\_t_5, -). 0 \\
Job &:= (C_1 \parallel_{\{start\_t_1, task_1, start\_t_6, task_6\}} C_2) \parallel_{\{task_2, start\_t_5\}} C_3
\end{aligned}
$$

The queueing network is composed of the same parts as before: arrival process, queue and server. The arriving jobs are all of the same kind. As jobs consist of individual tasks, the processors of the server must be able to process any of these different tasks.[9]

$$Proc := \sum_{i=1}^{6}(start\_t_i, \infty).(task_i, -).Proc$$
$$MultiS := Proc \parallel_{\{\}} Proc \parallel_{\{\}} \dots \parallel_{\{\}} Proc$$

The complex structure of a job delivered from the queue makes it necessary to supplement the multiserver with a *scheduler* which mediates between the queue and the processors.

$$Scheduler := ((d, \infty).Job \parallel_{\{job\_end\}} (job\_end, -).Scheduler)\backslash\{job\_end\}$$

After requesting a job from the queue the scheduler activates it, so that the individual tasks of the job can be executed on the processors according to the precedence relation

---

[8] The description given in the previous section is all right if we want to analyse the task graph for its own, exploiting the full inherent parallelism.

[9] We will write $\sum_{i=1}^{n} P_i$ abbreviating the n-fold alternative composition $P_1 + \dots + P_n$.

specified in the description of *Job*. At the end of the job an internal (hidden) signal (*job_end*) (see description of C_1 above) reactivates the scheduler.

The complete system is then described by

$$(Arr \parallel_{\{a\}} Queue_0) \parallel_{\{d\}} (Scheduler \parallel_S MultiS)$$

with $S = \{start\_t_i, task_i \mid i = 1, \ldots, 6\}$.

This description can easily be modified such that certain tasks are only executed on certain processors. E.g. a server with two processors $Proc_1, Proc_2$, where $Proc_1$ executes only $task_1$ and $task_2$ and $Proc_2$ the others, is described by

$$
\begin{aligned}
Proc_1 &:= \sum_{i \in T_1} (start\_t_i, \infty).(task_i, -).Proc_1 & T_1 = \{1, 2\} \\
Proc_2 &:= \sum_{i \in T_2} (start\_t_i, \infty).(task_i, -).Proc_2 & T_2 = \{3, 4, 5, 6\} \\
MultiS &:= Proc_1 \parallel_{\{\}} Proc_2
\end{aligned}
$$

3.5 Extensions

3.5.1 Probabilistic Choice

For describing alternative behaviour with fixed branching probabilities we need to extend our language by a new operator, the probabilistic choice operator $A[\pi]B$. We will present here a rather staightforward way of incorporating it into the semantics.

A probabilistic choice $A[\pi]B$ is considered to be resolved instantaneously and completely internal. The decision is taken in favour of A with probability π and in favour of B with $1 - \pi$. This is represented in a transition system by branching off two immediate transitions which are labelled additionally with the corresponding probability.

Semantically, this requires to introduce new rules and to extend the labels of transitions. Labels are now quadrupels $Act \times Rate \times \mathbf{R}_{[0,1]} \times \{l, r\}^*$ with $\mathbf{R}_{[0,1]}$ being the closed interval of real numbers from 0 to 1. There are two new rules:

$$\frac{}{A[\pi]B \xrightarrow{\tau, \infty, \pi, l} A} (\pi_l) \qquad \frac{}{A[\pi]B \xrightarrow{\tau, \infty, 1-\pi, r} B} (\pi_r)$$

These rules have no preconditions, since the behaviour of a probabilistic choice does not depend on the behaviour of its constituent parts.

This treatment of probabilistic choice, however, interferes with the intuition of the competitive choice. E.g. in the system $A[\pi]B + (a, \lambda).C$

the a-transition competes with two immediate transitions and will therefore never be executed. Such situations can be ruled out in advance by syntactically demanding that a probabilistic choice must be *'guarded'*, i.e. a subterm $A[\pi]B$ can only occur inside a term if it is sequentially preceeded by an action. This can be expressed formally by distinguishing syntactic categories in the grammar of the syntax definition.

$$\mathcal{P} ::= \mathcal{Q} \mid \mathcal{P}[\pi]\mathcal{P} \mid recX : \mathcal{P}$$
$$\mathcal{Q} ::= 0 \mid X \mid \alpha.\mathcal{P} \mid \mathcal{Q} + \mathcal{Q} \mid \mathcal{Q} \|_S \mathcal{Q} \mid \mathcal{Q} \backslash L$$

3.5.2 General Distribution Functions

Dealing with time distribution functions other than exponential ones requires a careful semantic treatment of residual execution times. Consider a process $P = (a, p_a).0 \|_{\{\}}$ $(b, p_b).0$, where p_a, p_b are suitable parameters describing the time distributions of the associated random variables T_a, T_b (cf. figure 4). With the semantics of Markovian TIPP we would get the following transition system:

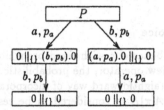

This representation would be incorrect, since the time distribution for the transition $0 \|_{\{\}} (b, p_b).0 \xrightarrow{b,p_b} 0 \|_{\{\}} 0$ is different from the one denoted by the parameter p_b: Action b was already enabled in state P, but action a, an action of a parallel and totally independent process, happened to be executed first. Thus the correct time distribution is $P(T_b \le t + T_a \mid T_b > T_a)$, with T_a, T_b being random variables recording the (total) execution time of a and b, respectively.

In order to represent residual execution times properly in the semantic model, there are two principal possiblities, it can be done either explicitly or implicitly. An explicit representation would adjust the time parameter of the transition, such that it denotes the correct residual time distribution. This treatment has several disadvantages; therefore we have chosen an implicit representation [GHR93]. We attach to every transition a so-called *start reference* that points to that state in the transition system where the corresponding action was enabled. Start references are represented by natural numbers, counting the number of actions that have happened since the considered action was ready to be performed. Thus it indicates the actual starting point of the time interval associated with the action.

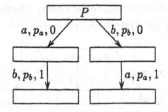

When it comes to analysing the performance of a system, the start references provide sufficient information to determine the actual time distribution. Thus it is avoided to determine residual time distributions unnecessarily.

4 Conclusions and Prospects

Usually both functional specification and performance modelling are separated from each other. Simplicity and understandability are strong arguments. However, in many situations an integrated approach is necessary and advantageous: to capture the particulars of parallel and distributed systems, to support hierarchical modelling, and to improve design productivity.

We introduced Stochastic Process Algebras as a novel approach for structured design and analysis, taking into consideration both the fuctional and temporal behaviour: The designer specifies the components of a system and their interactions by means of the language TIPP. Then this syntactic representation is (automatically) transformed into a semantic model which may be analysed in various directions: (1) functional characteristics, (2) performance characteristics, and (3) quality aspects influenced by both functional and temporal behaviour.

Combining performance modelling and analysis with the well investigated formal description technique of process algebras provides a rich source of further developments. A lot can be gained by exploiting the comprehensive theories of process algebras, which have been developed mainly during the last decade, and make their results and techniques available for performance modelling. Just to indicate a few ideas we are thinking of: The mapping of a workload onto a multiprocessor (cf. section 3.4.3) could be described more generally by parametrizing the parallel composition by a synchronization function [BW90]. Comparison of process descriptions can be done not only by equivalence relations; an order relation [Hen88] comparing e.g. the performance of processes would be very much desirable. Abstraction mechanisms, like the hiding operator, must be extended to include also the temporal behaviour; this could yield an approach to treat the problem of hierarchical modelling.

Our work is going on in three main directions: We are investigating the theoretical foundations ([Do93],[Her93]), we are searching for efficient evaluation algorithms, and, last not least, modelling the behaviour of real systems has a strong influence on the first two directions.

References

[ABC86] M. Ajmone Marsan, G. Balbo, and G. Conte. *Performance Models of Multiprocessor Systems*. MIT Press, 1986.

[BW90] Jos Baeten and Peter Weijland. *Process Algebra*. Cambridge University Press, 1990.

[Do93] Hu Trung Do. *Entwurf von Prozeßsprachen zur Leistungsbewertung*. Diplomarbeit, Universität Erlangen, 1993.

[Fer86] D. Ferrari. Considerations on the Insularity of Performance Evaluation. *IEEE Transactions on Software Engineering*, SE–12(6):678–683, June 1986.

[GHR92] Norbert Götz, Ulrich Herzog, and Michael Rettelbach. TIPP — a language for timed processes and performance evaluation. Interner Bericht IMMD7-4/92, Universität Erlangen, March 1992.

[GHR93] Norbert Götz, Ulrich Herzog, and Michael Rettelbach. TIPP — introduction and application to protocol performance analysis. In *Formale Beschreibungstechniken für verteilte Systeme*, Munich, to appear 1993. FOKUS series, Saur publishers.

[Har86] C. Harvey. Performance engineering as an integral part of system design. *British Telecom Technology Journal*, 4(3):143–147, July 1986.

[Hen88] Matthew Hennessy. *Algebraic Theory of Processes*. MIT Press, 1988.

[Her90a] Ulrich Herzog. EXL: Syntax, semantics and examples. Interner Bericht IMMD7-16/90, Universität Erlangen, November 1990.

[Her90b] Ulrich Herzog. Formal description, time and performance analysis — a framework. In *Entwurf und Betrieb verteilter Systeme*. Springer, 1990. Informatik Fachberichte 264.

[Her93] Holger Hermanns. *Semantik für Prozeßsprachen zur Leistungsbewertung*. Diplomarbeit, Universität Erlangen, to appear 1993.

[Hil93] J. Hillston. PEPA: Performance Enhanced Process Algebra. Technical Report CSR-24-93, University of Edinburgh, March 1993.

[Hoa85] Charles Hoare. *Communicating Sequential Processes*. Prentice-Hall, 1985.

[IP91] Paola Inverardi and Corrado Priami. Evaluation of tools for the analysis of communicating systems. *EATCS Bulletin*, 45:158–185, 1991.

[Mil89] Robin Milner. *Communication and Concurrency*. Prentice Hall, 1989.

[NS91] X. Nicollin and J. Sifakis. An overview and synthesis on timed process algebras. In *Real-Time: Theory in Practice*, pages 526–548. Springer LNCS 600, 1991.

[NY85] N. Nounou and Y. Yemini. Algebraic specification-based performance analysis of communication protocols. In *Protocol Specification, Testing and Verification*, pages 541–560. Elsevier Publishers, 1985.

[Plo81] Gordon Plotkin. A structural approach to operational semantics. Report DAIMI FN-19, Computer Science Department, Aarhus University, September 1981.

[Rei91] M. Reiser. A quarter century of performance evaluation — impact on science and engineering. In *Proceedings of the IEEE CompEuro '91*, pages 885–887. IEEE, May 1991.

[Ret91] Michael Rettelbach. *Leistungsbewertung mit Prozeßalgebren*. Diplomarbeit, Universität Erlangen, 1991.

[SH93]   Ben Strulo and Peter Harrison. Process algebra for discrete event simulation. Technical report, Imperial College, March 1993.

[Söt90]   F. Sötz. A method for performance prediction of parallel programs. In Burkhart, editor, *CONPAR 90-VAPP IV, Joint International Conference on Vector and Parallel Processing. Proceedings*, pages 98–107. Springer LNCS 457, 1990.

[ST87]   R. A. Sahner and K. S. Trivedi. Performance and reliability analysis using directed acyclic graphs. *IEEE Transactions on Software Engeneering*, SE-13(10):1105–1114, 1987.

[V+91]   Chris Vissers et al. Specification styles in distributed system design and verification. *Theoretical Computer Science*, 89:179–206, 1991.

[Zic87]   J. J. Zic. Extensions to communicating sequential processes to allow protocol performance specification. *ACM Computer Communication Review, Special Issue: SIGCOMM '87 Workshop on Frontiers in Computer Communications Technology*, 17(5):217–227, 1987.

Response time distributions in queueing network models

Peter G. Harrison

Department of Computing

Imperial College

180 Queen's Gate

London SW7 2BZ

England

Abstract Time delays in queueing networks are assuming increasing importance with the proliferation of transaction processing and time-critical real time systems. Mean values are insufficient and it is necessary to estimate time intervals that are not exceeded with a specified probability, i.e. *quantiles*. This paper presents results on time delay distributions in single server queues of various types and extends these to networks of queues. In particular, the class of Jackson networks that permit exact solution are analysed in both the open and closed cases, and approximation techniques for more general networks are proposed.

1   Introduction

The time delays experienced by tasks passing through a sequence of processing nodes define an important class of performance measures in computer-communication systems. Their mean values provide a good overall description of performance and are readily obtained by conventional techniques, but means alone are often insufficient. For example, we may wish to predict the variability of response time in a multi-access system or various reliability measures, such as the probability that a message transmission time will exceed a given value. The importance of obtaining quantiles of distributions—i.e. time intervals that are not exceeded with a specified probability—is becoming increasingly recognised, in particular in transaction-processing systems where quantiles are specified as minimal performance requirements in international standards, such as TPC.

Queueing network models which compute queue length distributions in a steady state network are well established and from the mean queue lengths, mean passage time along a given path can be determined directly. There is now, therefore, a need to consider the more difficult problem of finding the probability distribution of passage-times along a path in a queueing network. Mathematically, the simplest type of network to analyse is open, acyclic and Markovian, i.e. has external arrivals from independent Poisson processes and fixed-rate servers with exponentially distributed service times. The arrival process at every server is then independent and Poisson. Unfortunately, even these assumptions are too weak to allow the distribution of the passage-time along an arbitrary path to be obtained in a simple form. For paths on which a task cannot be overtaken, we can consider passage time as the sum of waiting times at independent single-server (M/M/1) queues and obtain a simple solution. If any of these assumptions is violated, e.g. for any closed network of servers, independence is lost and the above approach fails. However, a more complex result can be derived for overtake-free paths in Markovian closed networks. To derive time delay distributions in more general networks requires approximate methods.

Rather than the distributions themselves, it is generally easier to work with their Laplace transforms. This is because a time delay is a sum of sojourn times (i.e. times spent in some state or at some server) and, if these are independent, the required distribution is a mixture of convolutions of sojourn time distributions. But the Laplace transform of a convolution is the product of the Laplace transforms of the constituent distributions, which is much easier to manipulate than a convolution-integral. To obtain quantiles, of course, it is necessary to be able to invert the Laplace transform of the passage time distribution so as to recover the distribution itself. In general, inversion is by numerical methods which may be difficult to implement accurately. This may be especially so at high quantiles, i.e. in the tail of a distribution—often the most important region. However, analytic inversion is possible in the solvable networks referred to above, including closed, overtake-free, Markovian networks.

This paper is organised as follows. In the next section we consider the waiting time distribution at a single-server queue, beginning with first-come-first-served queueing discipline (i.e. an M/M/1 queue) and then examining the effect of non-exponential service times (i.e. M/G/1 queue), different queueing disciplines and, very briefly, negative customers (of the Gelenbe type, [3]). We then look at passage time distributions through an open, tandem network of M/M/1 queues in section 3; this result extends immediately to open tree-like networks. The Laplace transform of passage time distribution on overtake-free paths in closed Markovian networks is given in section 4 and its analytic inversion is considered in section 5. A case study—transmission time distribution in a packet-switched, multistage interconnection network—may be found in [6]. The paper concludes in section 6 which includes discussion of approximations for Laplace transforms in more general networks. The material is presented in more detail, including proofs of theorems, in Chapter 9 of the book "Performance Modelling of Communication Networks and Computer Architectures" by Harrison and Patel, published by Addison-Wesley (1993).

2 Time delays in the single server queue

There are many intervals of time that are of interest in queueing systems. We begin with the waiting and queueing times of a customer in M/M/1 and M/G/1 queues with FCFS discipline. Another important time interval is the busy period (or busy time) of the server, i.e. the interval between successive idle periods. In fact, the analysis of busy times will prove a powerful technique and lead, in particular, to the waiting time distribution of an M/G/1 queue with LCFS queueing discipline. PS queueing discipline will also be considered, but only for M/M/1 queues where we can make use of properties of the underlying continuous time Markov chain. In fact, we will see that the method used for PS can also be used for other queueing disciplines in an M/M/1 queue.

2.1 Waiting time distribution in the M/M/1 queue

In this section we investigate the time interval between the instants at which a given customer arrives at an M/M/1 queue and departs after completing service. This random variable is called the customer's **waiting time** and is denoted by T_W; it includes the time spent being served. The corresponding interval from the arrival instant to the instant at which the customer first enters service is called the **queueing time**, denoted T'; it excludes the service time. We consider the classical M/M/1 queue with arrival rate λ and service rate μ independent of the queue length. First, we can calculate the mean waiting time (and queueing time) quite easily using Little's result as follows. We know that the mean equilibrium queue length is $\rho/(1 - \rho)$, where $\rho = \lambda/\mu$, and that the mean arrival rate is λ. Hence, mean waiting time W is the ratio of these quantities, $1/(\mu - \lambda)$. For FCFS queueing discipline, we can now find the expected queueing time, Q, from the relation $T_W = T' + S$ where S is the service time random variable, i.e. exponential with parameter μ. Taking expectations gives

$$(\mu - \lambda)^{-1} = E[T_W] = E[T'] + E[S] = Q + \mu^{-1}$$

so that $Q = \rho/(\mu - \lambda)$.

Notice that the result for W holds regardless of the queueing discipline. However, we no longer have this invariance when we consider the probability distribution of waiting time. First, suppose the queueing discipline is FCFS and that immediately after a new arrival, the queue length is $n + 1$; i.e. the arrival "faces" a queue of length $n \geq 0$. The arriving customer's waiting time is now a sum of $n + 1$ random variables:

$$T_W = \begin{cases} U + S_1 + S_2 + \ldots + S_n & \text{if } n \geq 1 \\ S_1 & \text{if } n = 0 \end{cases}$$

Each S_i is independent and distributed as the service time, i.e. exponential with parameter μ, and U is the residual service time of the customer being served at the arrival instant. But, by the residual life (memoryless) property of exponential distributions, U has the same exponential distribution as service time. Thus, T_W is a sum of $n + 1$ independent exponential random variables with parameter μ when the queue length faced on arrival is $n \geq 0$. Similarly, T' is a sum of n such random variables. Since the arrival process is Poisson, by the Random Observer Property, the probability that the queue length faced by an arrival is n is the same as the equilibrium probability that the queue length is n, here $(1 - \rho)\rho^n$. Thus, by the law of total probability,

$$P(T_W \leq t) = \sum_{n=0}^{\infty} (1 - \rho)\rho^n F^{(n+1)*}(t)$$

where $F(t) = 1 - e^{-\mu t}$ is the service time distribution function and F^{k*} ($k \geq 1$) denotes the k-fold convolution of F with itself. But $F^{(n+1)*}$ is the Erlang-$(n + 1)$ distribution with parameter μ and so the waiting time density function f_W is defined by

$$
\begin{aligned}
f_W(t) &= \sum_{n=0}^{\infty}(1-\rho)\rho^n\mu\frac{(\mu t)^n}{n!}e^{-\mu t} \\
&= (1-\rho)\mu e^{-\mu t}\sum_{n=0}^{\infty}\frac{(\rho\mu t)^n}{n!} \\
&= (\mu-\lambda)e^{-(\mu-\lambda)t}
\end{aligned}
$$

Waiting time is therefore exponential with parameter $\mu - \lambda$, as expected from our derivation of the mean waiting time. The fact that waiting time is exponential can actually be deduced by a purely probabilistic argument, using the memoryless properties of both the geometric distribution (of the queue length) and the exponential distribution. We then need only the mean waiting time, which we have already determined, to characterise completely the waiting time random variable. This approach is taken by [11].

We can obtain waiting time distributions for variants of the M/M/1 queue, revealing the sensitivity to different queueing disciplines, for example. If we have a load dependent server, i.e. one with rate depending on the instantaneous queue length, waiting time distribution is much more difficult to obtain. In particular, the derivation of the result for PS discipline is lengthy, even when the arrival and (total) service rates are both constant; we consider this problem below. However, we can quite easily find the waiting time density for the multi-server queue, i.e. the M/M/m queue. In this case, a new arrival has to queue iff the queue length faced on arrival is at least m. Waiting time is now given by:

$$
T_W = \begin{cases} X_1 + X_2 + \ldots + X_{n-m+1} + S & \text{if } n \geq m \\ S & \text{if } n < m \end{cases}
$$

where X_i $(1 \leq i \leq n - m + 1)$ is distributed as the service time of a *single* exponential server with rate $m\mu$ and S is distributed as a single exponential server with rate μ. This follows because when the number of customers ahead of the customer being traced is $n, n - 1, \ldots, m$, there are m parallel servers active and the superposition of their departure processes is a Poisson process with rate $m\mu$ (i.e. the time to the next service completion is exponential with parameter $m\mu$). But this is exactly the situation with an M/M/1 queue with service rate $m\mu$. When there are fewer than m customers ahead of the customer being traced, including when the queue length faced on arrival is $n < m$, the remaining waiting time is just one service time, S. In this way we obtain (see [7, page 181]):

$$
F_Q(t) = \alpha + (1-\alpha)[1 - e^{-(m\mu-\lambda)t}] = 1 - (1-\alpha)e^{-(m\mu-\lambda)t}
$$

where α is the equilibrium probability that the queue length is less than m, i.e. the equilibrium probability of not having to queue (by the random observer property of the Poisson process).

Example 2.1.   A telephone exchange with holding facilities can be modelled as an M/M/m queue; calls arrive as Poisson processes with total rate λ and each has exponential duration with mean $1/\mu$. How many lines are necessary such that the probability of a caller being "on hold" for more than 1 minute is less than 0.1? We can simply use the above formula for $F_Q(t)$ since the probability of holding time exceeding 1 minute is $1 - F_Q(1)$. Thus we require

$$(1 - \alpha)e^{-(m\mu-\lambda)} < 0.1$$

i.e.

$$m\mu - \lambda > log_e 10(1 - \alpha)$$

i.e.

$$m > \frac{log_e 10(1 - \alpha) + \lambda}{\mu}$$

We already knew that m had to be bigger than λ/μ for stability—the above inequality says by how much in order to get the required performance. Of course, α is a non-trivial function of m, and numerical methods are needed to obtain particular solutions.

2.2   Waiting time distribution in the M/G/1 queue

The waiting time distribution for FCFS discipline is readily obtained from the following observation. For $n \geq 1$, the queue, of length X_n, existing on the departure of the nth customer, C_n, comprises precisely the customers that arrived during that customer's waiting time. In equilibrium, denoting the waiting time distribution of each customer C_n by F_W, the generating function for the queue length may be expressed as:

$$\Pi(z) = E[E[z^X|W]] = E[e^{-\lambda W(1-z)}] = W^*(\lambda(1 - z))$$

since X, conditional on W, has Poisson distribution. Writing $\theta = \lambda(1 - z)$ so that $z = (\lambda - \theta)/\lambda$, we now have

$$W^*(\theta) = \Pi((\lambda - \theta)/\lambda) = \frac{(1 - \rho)\theta B^*(\theta)}{\theta - \lambda[1 - B^*(\theta)]}$$

by substituting into the Pollacek-Khintchine formula for Π.

Note that we can now easily check Little's result for the M/G/1 queue since $-W^{*'}(0) = -\lambda^{-1}\Pi'(1)$. Notice too that we get the required exponential distribution in the case of an M/M/1 queue where Π is the generating function of the geometric random variable with parameter ρ.

Example 2.2.   A rotating disk can be modelled by an M/G/1 queue as follows. Suppose that read/write requests arrive at the head as a Poisson process with parameter λ, requiring blocks of data of fixed length 1 sector, beginning at a random sector boundary. The disk spins at rate r revolutions per second and has s sectors. We make the approximation that the next request to be served always finds the head at a boundary between two sectors—this will in general be violated by arrivals to an empty queue. We require the probability that a request takes more than t time units to complete. There are essentially two problems: to find the Laplace transform of the service time distribution, $B^*(\theta)$, and then to invert the resulting expression for $W^*(\theta)$. To obtain the solution requires numerical methods and we just give the analysis. First, the service time distribution function F_S is defined by

$$F_S(t) = \begin{cases} n/s & \text{if } n \leq rst < n + 1 \ (0 \leq n \leq s - 1) \\ 1 & \text{if } t \geq 1/r \end{cases}$$

so that the density function is

$$f_S(t) = \frac{1}{s} \sum_{n=1}^{s} \delta\left(t - \frac{n}{sr}\right)$$

The Laplace transform of this density is therefore

$$B^*(\theta) = \frac{1}{s} \sum_{n=1}^{s} e^{-n\theta/sr}$$

from which the Laplace transform of the required waiting time density is

$$W^*(\theta) = \frac{(1 - \rho)\theta \sum_{n=1}^{s} e^{-n\theta/sr}}{s\theta - \lambda\left(s - \sum_{n=1}^{s} e^{-n\theta/sr}\right)}$$

by substitution into the above formula.

2.3 Busy periods

To investigate the busy period, we first observe that its distribution is the same for all queueing disciplines that are work conserving and for which the server is never idle when the queue is non-empty. Suppose that, in equilibrium, whilst an initial customer C_1 is being served, customers $C_2, \ldots, C_{Z+1}$ arrive, where the random variable Z, conditional on service time S for C_1, is Poisson with mean λS. Without loss of generality, we assume a LCFS queueing discipline with no preemption so that, if $Z \neq 0$, the second customer to be served is C_{Z+1}. Any other customers that arrive while C_{Z+1} is being served will also be served before C_Z. Now let N be the random variable for the number of customers served during a busy period and let N_i be the number of customers served between the instants at which C_{i+1} commences service and C_i commences service ($1 \leq i \leq Z$). Then $N_1, \ldots, N_Z$ are independent and identically distributed as N. This is because the sets of customers counted by $N_Z, N_{Z-1}, \ldots, N_1$ are disjoint and (excluding $C_{Z+1}, C_Z, \ldots, C_2$ respectively) arrive consecutively after C_{Z+1}. Thus,

$$N \simeq \begin{cases} 1 + N_Z + N_{Z-1} + \ldots + N_1 & \text{if } Z \geq 1 \\ 1 & \text{if } Z = 0 \end{cases}$$

(The symbol $\simeq$ denotes "equal in distribution") Now, denoting the busy time random variable by T, its distribution function by H and the Laplace-Stieltjes transform of H by H^*, we have

$$T \simeq \begin{cases} S + T_Z + T_{Z-1} + \ldots + T_1 & \text{if } Z \geq 1 \\ S & \text{if } Z = 0 \end{cases}$$

where T_i is the length of the interval between the instants at which C_{i+1} commences service and C_i commences service ($1 \leq i \leq Z$). Moreover, the T_i are independent random variables, each distributed as T, and also independent of S. This is because the customers that arrive and complete service during the intervals T_i are disjoint Thus

$$
\begin{aligned}
H^*(q) &= E[E[E[e^{-\theta T}|Z, S]|S]] \\
&= E[E[E[e^{-\theta(S+T_1+\ldots+T_Z)}|Z, S]|S]] \\
&= E[E[e^{-\theta S} E[e^{-\theta T}]^Z|S]] \\
&= E[e^{-\theta S} E[H^*(\theta)^Z|S]] \\
&= E[e^{-\theta S} e^{-\lambda S(1 - H^*(\theta))}]
\end{aligned}
$$

since Z (conditioned on S) is Poisson with mean λS. Thus we obtain

$$H^*(\theta) = B^*(\theta + \lambda(1 - H^*(\theta)))$$

Although this equation cannot be solved in general for $H^*(\theta)$, we can obtain the moments of busy time by differentiating at $\theta = 0$. For example, the mean busy period, m say, is given by

$$-m = H^{*\prime}(0) = B^{*\prime}(0)\{1 + \lambda[-H^{*\prime}(0)]\} = -(1 + \lambda m)\mu^{-1}$$

since $H^*(0) = 1$, and so $m = (\mu - \lambda)^{-1}$, the M/M/1 queue result. The above technique, in which a time delay is defined in terms of independent, identically distributed time delays, is often called "delay cycle analysis" and is due to [13].

2.4   Waiting times in LCFS queues

Now let us consider waiting times under LCFS disciplines. For the preemptive-resume variant, we note that a task's waiting time is independent of the queue length it faces on arrival, since the whole of the queue already there is suspended until after this task completes service. Thus without loss of generality we may assume that the task arrives at an idle server. Waiting time then becomes identical to the busy period. We therefore conclude that the waiting time distribution in a LCFS-PR M/G/1 queue has Laplace-Stieltjes transform $H^*(\theta) = B^*(\theta + \lambda(1 - H^*(\theta)))$.

For LCFS without preemption we can modify the busy period analysis. First, if a task arrives at an empty queue, its waiting time is the same as a service time. Otherwise, its queueing time Q is the sum of the residual service time R of the customer in service and the service times of all other tasks that arrive before it commences service. This definition is almost the same as that of a busy period given above. The only differences are that the time spent in service by the initial customer C_1' (C_1 above) is not a service time but a residual service time and the random variable Z' (Z above) is the number of customers that arrive whilst C_1' is in (residual) service. Proceeding as before, we obtain

$$Q \simeq \begin{cases} R + T_Z + T_{Z-1} + \ldots + T_1 & \text{if } Z \geq 1 \\ R & \text{if } Z = 0 \end{cases}$$

We can now derive the Laplace-Stieltjes transform Q^* of the distribution function of Q similarly to obtain:

$$Q^*(\theta) = R^*(\theta + \lambda(1 - H^*(\theta)))$$

where R^* denotes the Laplace-Stieltjes transform of the probability distribution of R. But since R is a forward recurrence time, $R^*(\theta) = \mu[1 - B^*(\theta)]/\theta$. Thus,

$$Q^*(\theta) = \frac{\mu(1 - B^*(\theta + \lambda(1 - H^*(\theta))))}{\theta + \lambda(1 - H^*(\theta))} = \frac{\mu(1 - H^*(\theta))}{\theta + \lambda(1 - H^*(\theta))}$$

Finally, since a customer arrives at an empty queue with probability $1 - \rho$ in equilibrium, we obtain for the transform of the waiting time distribution

$$\begin{aligned} W^*(\theta) &= (1 - \rho)B^*(\theta) + \rho B^*(\theta)Q^*(\theta) \\ &= B^*(\theta)\left(1 - \rho + \frac{\lambda(1 - H^*(\theta))}{\theta + \lambda(1 - H^*(\theta))}\right) \end{aligned}$$

since waiting time is the sum of queueing time and service time and these two random variables are independent.

Example 2.3. Let us compare the response time variability in a computer system, modelled by an M/G/1 queue, with FCFS and LCFS scheduling policies. We can do this to a great extent by comparing the first two moments which are obtained by differentiating the respective formulae for $W^*(\theta)$ at $\theta = 0$. We obtain the same result for the mean waiting time, which is as expected from Little's result since the mean queue lengths are the same under each discipline. However, it turns out that the second moment of waiting time for FCFS discipline is $1 - \rho$ times that for LCFS. Thus, LCFS discipline suffers a much greater variability as ρ approaches 1, i.e. as the queue begins to saturate. The qualitative result is quite obvious, but the preceding analysis enables the load at which the effect becomes serious to be estimated quantitatively.

2.5 Waiting times with Processor-Sharing discipline

The problem with PS discipline is that the rate at which a customer receives service during his sojourn at a server varies as the queue length changes due to new arrivals and other departures. Thus, we begin by analysing the waiting time density (or rather its Laplace transform) in an M/M/1 queue of a customer with a given service time requirement.

Proposition 2.1 *In a PS M/M/1 queue with fixed arrival rate λ and fixed service rate μ, the Laplace transform of the waiting time density, conditional on a customer's service time being x is*

$$W^*(s|x) = \frac{(1 - \rho)(1 - \rho r^2)e^{-[\lambda(1-r)+s]x}}{(1 - \rho r)^2 - \rho(1 - r)^2 e^{-(\mu/r - \lambda r)x}}$$

where r is the smaller root of the equation $\lambda r^2 - (\lambda + \mu + s)r + \mu = 0$ and $\rho = \lambda/\mu$.

This result, proved in [7], was first derived by [1]. We can obtain the Laplace transform of the unconditional waiting time density as

$$W^*(s) = \int_0^\infty W^*(s|x)\mu e^{-\mu x} dx$$

The essential technique used in the proof of Proposition 1 splits the waiting time in an M/M/1 queue into an infinitesimal initial interval and the remaining waiting time. In fact the technique is quite general, applying to more disciplines than PS. In particular, it can be used to find the Laplace transform of the waiting time density in an M/M/1 queue with random discipline or FCFS discipline with certain queue length dependent service rates and in M/M/1 queues with "negative customers", [8].

3 Time delays in open networks of queues

Networks of queues present an entirely different kettle of fish to the case of a single server queue—even a stationary Markovian network. This is because, although we know the distribution of the queue lengths at the time of arrival of a given (tagged) customer at the first queue in his path (by the Random Observer Property or the Job Observer Property), we cannot assume this stationary distribution exists upon arrival at subsequent queues. The reason is that the arrival times at the subsequent queues are only finitely later than the arrival time at the first queue. Hence, the state existing at the subsequent arrival times must be conditioned on the state that existed at the time of arrival at the first queue. Effectively, a new time origin is set at the first arrival time, with known initial joint queue length probability distribution—the stationary distribution. Even in open networks with no feedback, where it is easy to see that all arrival processes are Poisson, this conditioning cannot be overlooked and we cannot assume all queues on a path are independent and in an equilibrium state at the arrival times of the tagged customer. The situation appears even more hopeless in open networks with feedback and closed networks.

However, things are not quite as bad as they seem when we have fixed arrival and service rates. First, we can prove that the FCFS queues in an **overtake-free** path in a Markovian open network behave as if they were independent and in equilibrium when observed at the successive arrival times of a tagged customer. By an overtake-free path, or a path with no overtaking, we mean that a customer following this path will depart from its last queue before any other customer that joins any queue in that path after the said custromer. Surprisingly, a similar result holds for overtake-free paths in closed networks, e.g. all paths in networks with a tree-like structure—see Figure 2. In the next subsection, we consider those open networks for which a solution for the time delay density along a given path can be derived. This is followed by a discussion of the problems that confront us when we attempt to generalise the network structure. Closed networks are considered in the next main section.

3.1   Tandem networks

The simplest open network we can consider is a pair of queues in series. However, it is almost as easy to analyse a tandem series of any number of queues, as shown in Figure 1. In fact, we can be more general than this, as we will see shortly.

Figure 1: A tandem series of queues

Now, the distribution of the time delay of a customer passing through a tandem series of queues is the convolution of the stationary waiting time distributions of each queue in the series considered in isolation. This follows from the following result.

Proposition 3.1 *In a series of stationary M/M/1 queues with FCFS discipline, the waiting times of a given customer in each queue are independent.*

Proof

First we claim that the waiting time of a tagged customer, C say, in a stationary M/M/1 queue is independent of the departure process before the departure of C. This is a direct consequence of reversibility since C's waiting time is clearly independent of the arrival process after C's arrival under FCFS discipline at a single server. Applying this property to the stochastically identical reversed process, a corresponding customer C' arrives at the negative time of departure of C and departs at the negative time of arrival of C. It therefore has the same waiting time as C and the claim follows in the original process by the duality between the processes.

To complete the proof, let A_i, T_i denote C's time of arrival and waiting time respectively at queue i in a series of m queues ($1 \leq i \leq m$). Certainly, by our claim, T_1 is independent of the arrival process at queue 2 before A_2 and so of the queue length faced by C on arrival at queue 2. Now, we can ignore customers that leave queue 1 after C since they cannot arrive at any queue in the series before C, again because all queues have single servers and FCFS discipline. Thus, T_2 is independent of T_1 and similarly T_1 is independent of the arrival process at queue i before A_i and so of T_i for $2 \leq i \leq m$. Similarly, T_j is independent of T_k for $2 \leq j < k \leq m$. ♣

From this proposition it follows that, since the waiting time probability density at the stationary queue i, considered in isolation ($1 \leq i \leq m$), has Laplace transform $(\mu_i - \lambda)/(s + \mu_i - \lambda)$, the density of the time to pass through the whole series of m queues is the convolution of these densities, with Laplace transform $\prod_{i=1}^{m}(\mu_i - \lambda)/(s + \mu_i - \lambda)$.

There is one obvious generalisation of this result: the final queue in the series need not be M/M/1 since we are not concerned with its output. Also, the same result holds, by the same reasoning, when the final queue is M/G/n for $n \geq 1$. Moreover, Proposition 3.1 generalises to **treelike networks** which are defined as follows, and illustrated in Figure 2. A treelike network consists of:

- a linear **trunk segment** containing one or more queues in tandem, the first being called the **root** queue;

- a number (greater than or equal to zero) of disjoint **subtrees**, i.e. treelike subnetworks, such that customers can pass to the roots of the subtrees from the last queue in the trunk segment or else leave the network with specified routing probabilities (which sum to 1).

The **leaf** queues (or **leaves**) are those from which customers leave the network.

The proof of Proposition 3.1, extended to treelike networks, carries through unchanged since every path in the network is overtake-free. Hence we can ignore the customers that leave any queue on the path after the tagged customer. Indeed, we can generalise further to overtake-free paths in any Markovian open network for the same reason. Conditional on the choice of path of queues, numbered, without loss of generality, $1, \ldots, m$, the Laplace transform of the passage time density is the same as for the tandem queue of m servers considered above.

To generalise the network structure further leads to serious problems and solutions have been obtained only for very special cases. The simplest case of a network with overtaking is the following three-queue network.

In this network, the path of queues numbered $\{1, 3\}$ is overtake-free and so the passage time density can be obtained as described above. However, overtaking is possible on the path $\{1, 2, 3\}$ since when the tagged customer C is at queue 2, any customers departing queue 1 (after C) can reach queue 3 first. The arrival processes to every queue

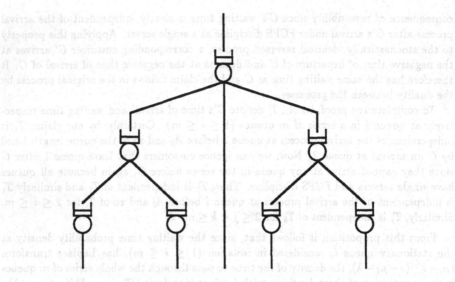

Figure 2: An open tree-like network

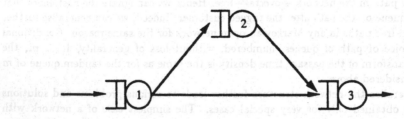

Figure 3: A three-node network with overtaking

in this network are independent Poisson, by Burke's theorem together with the decomposition and superposition properties of Poisson processes. However, this is not sufficient for the passage time distribution to be the convolution of the stationary sojourn time distributions at each queue on a path with overtaking: the proof of Proposition 3.1 breaks down. This particular problem has been solved, by considering the state of the system at the departure instant of the tagged customer from server 1 and using complex variable methods; see [10]. A similar analysis is required—for similar reasons—to analyse a tandem pair of queues with negative customers, [12]. In this case, negative arrivals at the second queue allow the first queue to influence the sojourn time of a tagged customer in the second; departures from the first queue offer a degree of "protection". More general networks appear intractable.

4 Time delays in closed networks

As for the case of open networks, we begin with the simplest case, a cyclic network that comprises a tandem network with departures from its last queue fed back into the first queue. There are no external arrivals and hence a constant population. Again, all service disciplines are FCFS and all service rates are constant.

We solve for the Laplace transform of the cycle time density by considering a dual network, viz. the tandem, open network consisting of the same servers $1, \ldots, m$ with no external arrivals. Eventually, therefore, the dual network has no customers, i.e. its state is $e = (0, 0, \ldots, 0)$, the empty state, with probability 1. All other states with one or more customers are transient. Now, given that the state immediately after the arrival of the tagged customer at queue 1 is i, the ensuing cycle time in the closed network is the same as the time interval between the dual network entering states i and e—the (first) passage time from i to e. This is so because there is no overtaking and service rates are constant. Thus the progress of the tagged customer in its cycle cannot be influenced by any customer behind it. We only need consider customers ahead of the tagged customer and can ignore those recycling after leaving the last queue. Observe that if service rates varied with queue length, we could not ignore customers behind the tagged customer, even though they could not overtake, because they would influence the service rate received by the tagged customer.

We therefore seek the density of the first passage time from state i to e in the dual network, $f(t|i)$, where i is a state of the form $(i_1, \ldots, i_m)$ with $i_1 > 0$, corresponding to the tagged customer having just arrived at server 1. We know the probability distribution of the state seen by the tagged customer on arrival at the first queue by the Job Observer Property and so can calculate the cycle time density by deconditioning f.

Given a cyclic network of population n, let the state space of the dual network be $S_n = \{(u_1, \ldots, u_m) | 0 \leq u_i \leq n, 1 \leq i \leq m; \sum_{i=1}^{m} u_i \leq n\}$ and define, for $u \in S_n$,

$$\lambda_u = \sum_{i=1}^{m} \mu_i \epsilon(u_i)$$

where μ_i is the service rate of server i, $\epsilon(n) = 1$ if $n > 0$ and $\epsilon(0) = 0$. Thus λ_u is the total service rate in state u, i.e. the instantaneous transition rate out of state u in the Markov process defining the queueing network. The holding time in state u is an exponential random variable with parameter λ_u and so has a density with Laplace transform $\lambda_u/(s + \lambda_u)$. Now, given that the network next enters state v after u, the passage time from u to e is the sum of the holding time in state u and the passage time from v to e. Thus, the density of the passage time from u to e has Laplace transform $L(s|u)$ given by the equations

$$L(s|u) = \sum_{v \in S_n} q_{uv} \frac{\lambda_u}{s + \lambda_u} L(s|v) \qquad u \neq e$$

$$L(s|e) = 1$$

where q_{uv} is the one-step transition probability from state u to v. Now let $\mu(u,v)$ denote the rate of the server from which a departure causes the state transition $u \to v$. Then $q_{uv} = \mu(u,v)/\lambda_u$. Thus, writing $q_{uv}^* = \mu(u,v)/(s + \lambda_u)$, we have the matrix equation

$$\mathbf{L} = \mathbf{Q}^* \mathbf{L} + \mathbf{1}_e$$

where $\mathbf{L} = (L(s|u)|u \in S_n)$, $\mathbf{Q}^* = (q_{uv}^*|u, v \in S_n)$ and $\mathbf{1}_e$ is the vector with component corresponding to state e equal to 1 and the rest 0.

Using this equation and deconditioning the state u seen on arrival via the Job Observer Property, we can obtain a product form for the Laplace transform of the cycle time probability density function. More generally, however, we consider cycle times in **closed tree-like** queueing networks. Such networks are defined in the same way as open tree-like networks except that customers departing from leaf-queues next visit the root queue. Clearly such networks have the no-overtaking property and if paths are restricted to start at one given server (here the root), they define the most general class for which it holds.

Now let Z denote the set of all paths through a closed tree-like network A, i.e. sequences of servers entered in passage through A. For all $z = (z_1, \ldots, z_k) \in Z$, $z_1 = 1$, z_k is a leaf-server and the order of Z is the number of leaf servers since there is only one path from the root to a given leaf in a tree. The probability of choosing path z is equal to the product of the routing probabilities between successive component centres in z. The Laplace transform of cycle time density is given by the following Proposition. The most general result, viz. the multidimensional Laplace transform of the joint density of the sojourn times spent by the tagged customer at each server on any overtake-free path in a network with multiple classes is given by [9]. The proof given in [7] is simpler, being based on the recursive properties of trees. At the same time the result is almost as general in that any overtake-free path must be tree-like (although several such intersecting paths could exist in the whole network) and the extension to multiple classes and joint sojourn times is straightforward.

Proposition 4.1 *For the closed tree-like network A of M servers, the Laplace transform of cycle time density, conditional on choice of path $z \in Z$ is*

$$L(s|z) = \frac{1}{G(n-1)} \sum_{u \in S(n-1)} \prod_{i=1}^{M} \left(\frac{e_i}{\mu_i}\right)^{u_i} \prod_{j=1}^{|z|} \left(\frac{\mu_{z_j}}{s + \mu_{z_j}}\right)^{u_{z_j}+1}$$

where $|z|$ is the number of servers in path z, $S(k)$ is the state space of the network when its population is $k \geq 1$, e_i and μ_i are the respective visitation rate and service rate of server i, and G is the network's normalising constant function.

In fact Proposition 4.1 holds for any overtake-free path in an arbitrary closed Jackson queueing network (recall the preceding discussion) and this form of the result is used in [6].

5 Inversion of the Laplace transforms

The majority of results on distributions of time delays in queueing networks and passage times in more general stochastic processes are given as Laplace (or Laplace-Stieltjes) transforms. The preceding is no exception. In general, numerical methods must be used to invert the Laplace transform which can be expensive to implement and are sometimes unreliable. However, in certain cases, analytical inversion is possible, typically when a stochastic model is based on exponential distributions. The result of Proposition 4.1 is a good example. First, we can simplify the summation giving $L(s|z)$ by partitioning the sum over $S(n-1)$ according to the total number of customers, p, at servers in the overtake-free path $1, 2, \ldots, m$ (say, without loss of generality). Now, the Laplace transforms in the inner sum are products of the Laplace transforms of Erlang densities. Moreover, their coefficients are geometric. Such transforms can be inverted analytically. In the simplest case, all the servers on the overtake-free path are identical, i.e. have the same rate, and the inversion can be done by inspection. In the case that the μ_i are all distinct $(1 \leq i \leq m)$, the density function is derived in [5] and the question of degenerate μ_i is addressed in [6]. These results are considered in the next two sections.

5.1 Overtake-free paths with identical servers

When all the rates μ_i in the path are the same, equal to μ say, the above Laplace transform is a mixed sum of terms of the form $[\mu/(s+\mu)]^{p+m}$ since in the inner summation $\sum_{i=1}^{m} u_i + 1 = p + m$. Each term can therefore be inverted by inspection to give a corresponding mixture of Erlangians for the passage time density. We therefore have:

Proposition 5.1 *If the centres in overtake-free path $1, 2, \ldots, m$ in the network of Proposition 4.1 all have service rate μ, the path's time delay density function is*

$$\frac{\mu^m e^{-\mu t}}{G(n-1)} \sum_{p=0}^{n-1} G_m(n-p-1) G^m(p) \mu^p \frac{t^{p+m-1}}{(p+m-1)!}$$

where $G^m(k)$ is the normalising constant for the subnetwork comprising servers $1, \ldots, m$ only, with population $k \geq 0$, and $G_m(k)$ is the normalising constant of the whole network with servers $1, \ldots, m$ removed and population $k \geq 0$.

From this result we can immediately obtain formulae for moments higher than the mean of a customer's transmission time.

Corollary

For a path of equal rate servers, message transmission time has kth moment equal to

$$\frac{1}{\mu^k G(n-1)} \sum_{p=0}^{n-1} G_m(n-p-1) G^m(p)(p+m) \ldots (p+m-k+1) \ .$$

5.2 Overtake-free paths with distinct servers

The case of paths with equal rate servers is easy, involving only some algebraic manipula-
ton of summations. However, even when the rates are different, the inversion can be done
analytically to give a closed form result. The analysis is now rather more difficult, however, and we just state the main result after giving a sketch of its derivation. The result
was first derived by the author, [5], for the case where all the service rates on the overtake-
free path are distinct, the opposite extreme to the previous section. The first step is to
invert the Laplace transform $L(n, s) = \prod_{i=1}^{m}[\mu_i/(s+\mu_i)]^{n_i}$ where $n = (n_1, \ldots, n_m)$, $n_i \geq 1$
and the μ_is are distinct. This yields the density function

$$f(n, t) = \prod_{i=1}^{m} \mu_i^{n_i} \sum_{j=1}^{m} D_j(n, t)$$

where the $D_j(n, t)$ are given by the following recurrence on n:

$$(n_j - 1)D_j(n, t) = tD_j(n_j, t) - \sum_{k \neq j} n_k D_j(n_j^k, t)$$

with boundary condition

$$D_j(n, t) = \frac{e^{-\mu_j t}}{\prod_{i \neq j}(\mu_i - \mu_j)^{n_i}} \qquad (n_i \geq 1, n_j = 1)$$

where $n_j = (n_1, \ldots, n_j - 1, \ldots, n_m)$ and $n_j^k = (n_1, \ldots, n_j - 1, \ldots, n_k + 1, \ldots, n_m)$.

Next, given real numbers $a_1, \ldots, a_M$ for integer $M \geq m$, define

$$H_{jm}(z) = \sum_{n \in S(M+m)} D_j(n, t) \prod_{i=1}^{M}(a_i z_i)^{n_i - 1}$$

so that passage time density is obtained from the $H_{jm}(1, \ldots, 1)$ with $a_i = e_i/\mu_i$. The
central result is an expression for $H_{jm}(z)$ from which follows:

Proposition 5.2 *If the servers in an overtake-free path $1, 2, \ldots, m$ have distinct service
rates $\mu_1, \mu_2, \ldots, \mu_m$, the passage time density function, conditional on the choice of path,
is*

$$\frac{\prod_{i=1}^{m} \mu_i}{G(n-1)} \sum_{p=0}^{n-1} G_m(n - p - 1) \sum_{j=1}^{m} \frac{e^{-\mu_j t}}{\prod_{i \neq j}(\mu_i - \mu_j)}$$

$$\times \sum_{i=0}^{p} \frac{(e_j t)^{p-i}}{(p-i)!} \sum_{n \in S_m(m+i), n_j=1} \prod_{1 \leq k \neq j \leq m} \left(\frac{e_k - e_j}{\mu_k - \mu_j}\right)^{n_k - 1}$$

*where $S_m(k)$ denotes the state space for the subnetwork of servers $1, \ldots, m$ with population
k.*

The summations over $S_m(m+i)$ are just normalising constants that may be computed
efficiently along with the $G_m(n - p - 1)$ and $G(n - 1)$ by Buzen's algorithm.

Example 5.1. For a *cyclic* network of M exponential servers and population N, cycle time distribution is

$$\frac{\left(\prod_{i=1}^{M} \mu_i\right) t^{N-1}}{(N-1)!G(N)} \sum_{j=1}^{M} \frac{e^{-\mu_j t}}{\prod_{i \neq j}(\mu_i - \mu_j)}$$

This follows by setting $e_1 = \ldots = e_M = 1$ in Proposition 5.2, so that all terms are zero in the rightmost sum except when $n_k = 1$ for all k, i.e. when $i = 0$. Finally, note there is only one partition of the state space, namely the one with all $N - 1$ customers at the servers $1, \ldots, M$. Thus we have $G_M(n) = 1$ if $n = 0$ and $G_M(n) = 0$ if $n > 0$, so that only terms with $p = N - 1$ give a non-zero contribution.

Proposition 5.2 can be generalised to allow arbitrary service rates at the nodes on an overtake-free path: not necessarily all the same nor all distinct. Essentially, we start with the case of distinct rates and successively combine any two servers with equal rates. The combination inolves manipulation of the summations and reduces the problem to two similar problems on networks with one less node in the overtake-free path. Thus, in each step, one degenerate server is removed until all the remaining problems are on paths with distinct rate servers. The details may be found in [6].

6 Conclusion

We have seen that finding time delay densities is a hard problem, often with complex and computationally expensive solutions when they can be found at all. Consequently, in most practical applications, the performance engineer requires approximate methods. There is no single established methodology for such approximation and most of the techniques used are *ad hoc*. In increasing order of sophistication, the following techniques have been used.

- A particular form is prescribed for the required distribution and its parameters are determined by matching moments. Moments may be predicted by an analytical model or estimated by simulation or actual measurement. Typical distributions include Coxian (with a small number of phases), Generalised Exponential and (mixtures of) Erlang. Although adequate for some purposes, involving probabilities near the median, for example, this approximation lacks a cause and effect relationship and is likely to be poor in the tail region in particular.

- A common simplifying assumption is that the queues in the path of a tagged customer in a queueing network behave as if independent, isolated and in equilibrium at the times of arrival of that customer; often called the **independence approximation**. The assumption is always true for the first queue in the path by the arrival theorem (with one less customer in the case of a closed network) but approximate for all the other queues, except in the case of simple open networks of the type we considered in section 3. The approximation is poorest when the ordering of customers in the network is most highly constrained, since then the independence assumption is clearly invalid. For example, in a 2-node cyclic network with FCFS queues and population N, it is known with probability one that if there are k customers at server 1 at any time, then there are $N - k$ at server 2. In particular, suppose server 1 is fast and its queue is empty on arrival of the tagged customer. Then it is very unlikely that queue 2 will be empty on arrival there and very likely that it will contain $N-1$ or $N-2$ customers. It does turn out that cyclic networks with FCFS queues give poor results under the independence approximation, but in networks where the ordering of customers has few constraints, for example richly connected networks or networks with PS discipline at many queues, it is usually quite accurate.

- An enhancement of the independence approximation admits limited dependence of the queue lengths faced by the tagged customer at successive servers. It is assumed that the queue length faced at any queue entered after the first in the path (which is independent by the arrival theorem) depends only on that faced at the previous node. This is called the **Paired Centre Approximation** and gives accurate results in a variety of queueing networks [4].

- Finally, it might be possible to use maximum entropy methods in continuous time to give the "least surprising" density function for a time delay subject to the constraints imposed by its moments. The maximum entropy method has been used mainly for discrete random variables in computer performance modelling and has produced accurate approximations for the state space distributions in a variety of networks. A continuous time analogue exists and appears well suited to predicting time delay distributions efficiently, given the expected values of certain functions of the state random variable. As usual, the most important step would be to identify and estimate the crucial constraints, but this is an open problem. The reader is referred to Kouvatsos's tutorial on this subject.

As with any approximate model, the above methods are subject to validation. The exact results described in the previous sections provide valuable benchmarks for this purpose. An approximation that passes these tests should be subjected to simulation testing and compared with real observations before being accepted as a performance engineering tool.

References

[1] E.G. Coffman Jnr, R.R. Muntz, H. Trotter
Waiting time distribution for processor-sharing systems
JACM 17, pp123—30, 1970

[2] H. Daduna
Passage times for overtake-free paths in Gordon-Newell networks
Adv. Appl. Prob. 14, pp672—86, 1982

[3] E. Gelenbe, P. Glynn, K. Sigman
Queues with negative arrivals
J. Appl. Prob. 28, pp245—50, 1991

[4] P.G. Harrison
An enhanced approximation by pair-wise analysis of servers for time delay distributions in queueing networks
IEEE Transactions on Computers C-35,1, pp54—61, 1986

[5] P.G. Harrison
Laplace transform inversion and passage time distributions in Markov processes
J. Appl. Prob. 27, pp74—87, 1990

[6] P.G. Harrison
On non-uniform packet switched delta networks and the hot-spot effect
IEE Proceedings E 138, 3, pp123—30, 1991

[7] P.G. Harrison, N.M. Patel
Performance Modelling of Communication Networks and Computer Architectures
Addison-Wesley, 1993

[8] P.G. Harrison, E. Pitel
Sojourn times in single server queues with negative customers
J. Appl. Prob., 1993 (to appear)

[9] F.P. Kelly, P.K. Pollett
Sojourn times in closed queueing networks
Adv. Appl. Prob. 15, 638—56, 1983

[10] I. Mitrani
Response time problems in communication networks
J. Roy. Stat. Soc. B-47, 3, pp396-406, 1985

[11] I. Mitrani
Modelling of Computer and Communication Systems
Cambridge University Press, 1987

[12] E. Pitel
Queues with negative customers and their applications
PhD Thesis, Department of Computing, Imperial College, University of London, 1994 (in preparation)

[13] L. Takacs
Introduction to the theory of queues
Oxford University Press, 1962

Fast Simulation of Rare Events in Queueing and Reliability Models

Philip Heidelberger

IBM T.J. Watson Research Center, Hawthorne
P.O. Box 704
Yorktown Heights, New York 10598

Abstract

This paper surveys efficient techniques for estimating, via simulation, the probabilities of certain rare events in queueing and reliability models. The rare events of interest are long waiting times or buffer overflows in queueing systems, and system failure events in reliability models of highly dependable computing systems. The general approach to speeding up such simulations is to accelerate the occurrence of the rare events by using importance sampling. In importance sampling, the system is simulated using a new set of input probability distributions, and unbiased estimates are recovered by multiplying the simulation output by a likelihood ratio. Our focus is on describing asymptotically optimal importance sampling techniques. Using asymptotically optimal importance sampling, only a fixed number of samples are required to get accurate estimates, no matter how rare the event of interest is. In practice, this means that the required run lengths can be reduced by many orders of magnitude, compared to standard simulation. The queueing systems studied include simple queues (e.g., GI/GI/1) and discrete time queues with multiple autocorrelated arrival processes that arise in the analysis of Asynchronous Transfer Mode communications switches. References for results on Jackson networks and and tree structured networks of ATM switches are given. Both Markovian and non-Markovian reliability models are treated.

1 Introduction

This survey paper is concerned with efficient simulation techniques for estimating the probability of certain rare, but important, events that arise in the analysis of queueing and reliability models. For example, consider a switch in a communications system that has a buffer capable of holding at most B packets. A switch designer is interested in the buffer sizing problem; namely determining a value of the buffer size so that the (steady state) packet loss probability is very small, say less than 10^{-9}. A designer of network session admittance and routing algorithms is faced with a related, but somewhat different problem; namely deciding whether or not to allow a new session to use the switch given the traffic already using the switch and the fixed buffer size B of the switch. For the session admittance problem, one criterion would be to admit the new session provided the packet loss probability remains acceptably low (again, say less than 10^{-9}). Depending on the stochastic characteristics of the sources and the service processes, exact (or numerical) solution of the relevant queueing model may be impossible and (discrete event) simulation may be the only feasible solution approach.

In the reliability context, consider the design of a fault tolerant computer system. The system designer wishes to select components (e.g., processors and disk drives) and configure the system so that it is very reliable, subject to some cost constraints. For example, the designer may wish to find a configuration so that, given a fixed time horizon t (say a month), the probability that the system fails (or operates at an unacceptably low level of performance) within the interval $(0, t)$ is very small. Even under Markovian assumptions on the failure and repair time distribution of the components, such models become difficult to solve using numerical techniques due to the problem of state space size explosion. For generally distributed failure and repair times, effective numerical techniques, for all practical purposes, do not exist. Thus simulation may be the only feasible solution approach.

But how practical is it to use simulation to estimate such small probabilities? For example, to estimate a packet loss probability of less than 10^{-9} would seem to require simulating at least 10^9 packets. As the probability of interest becomes smaller, the required simulation time grows ever larger and becomes excessive, except perhaps on highly parallel computers. *Somewhat remarkably, simple techniques exist that permit very accurate estimation of such small probabilities within a matter of minutes on even modest-sized workstations.* The basic approach is called *importance sampling* [46, 54]; the technique was first applied on computers for performing nuclear physics calculations done during the 1940's in collaborations between von Neumann, Ulam, Fermi, Kahn, Metropolis and their colleagues [53, 54, 63]. In the past several years importance sampling has also been applied to a variety of problems arising in the analysis of computer and communications systems.

The purpose of this paper is to describe how importance sampling can be used to speed up rare event simulations in queueing and reliability models. While analysis of the efficiency of importance sampling techniques can tend to be highly mathematical, this paper will emphasize basic concepts, thereby (hopefully) making the paper accessible to practitioners with a background in performance and/or reliability modeling, but with little or no background in simulation methodology. The rest of the paper is organized as follows. In Section 2, the problem of rare event simulation will be discussed in more detail and the technique of importance sampling introduced. This section will also describe the notion of optimal importance sampling, along with other preliminaries such as a brief description of regenerative simulation. Section 3 will describe the application of importance sampling in a variety of queueing systems, including the single server queue with independent interarrival and service time distributions (GI/GI/1), the multiple server queue (GI/GI/m), the single server queue with multiple correlated arrival processes. References for results on and some simple networks will be given. Section 4 will describe results for simulating models of highly dependable systems for the purpose of estimating reliability and availability characteristics. The paper is then summarized in Section 5, highlighting the similarities and differences of simulating queueing and reliability models.

2 Rare Event Simulation and Importance Sampling

2.1 The Problem of Rare Event Simulation

To further demonstrate the difficulty involved in simulating rare events, let us consider a simple example. Let X be a random variable that has a probability density function $p(x)$ and consider estimating the probability, γ, that X is in some set A;

$$\gamma = \int_{-\infty}^{\infty} 1_{\{x \in A\}} p(x) dx = E_p[1_{\{X \in A\}}] \tag{1}$$

where the subscript p denotes sampling from the density p and $1_{\{x \in A\}}$ is the indicator of the set A, i.e., $1_{\{x \in A\}} = 1$ if $x \in A$ and $1_{\{x \in A\}} = 0$ if $x \notin A$. Consider estimating γ by simulation. The standard approach would be to draw N samples, $X_1, \ldots, X_N$ from the density p, set $I_n = 1_{\{X_n \in A\}}$, and form the estimate $\hat{\gamma}_N = (1/N) \sum_{n=1}^{N} I_n$. Note that $E_p[\hat{\gamma}_N] = \gamma$ and that the variance of $\hat{\gamma}_N$ is $\gamma(1 - \gamma)/N$. By the central limit theorem, a $100(1 - \alpha)\%$ confidence interval for γ is (approximately) $\hat{\gamma}_N \pm z_{\alpha/2} \sqrt{\gamma(1 - \gamma)/N}$ where $z_{\alpha/2}$ is defined by the equation $\alpha/2 = P(N(0, 1) \geq z_{\alpha/2})$. ($N(0, 1)$ denotes a normally distributed random variable with mean zero and variance one.) Suppose we wish to estimate γ to within $\pm 10\%$ (about two significant digits of accuracy), i.e., we want the relative half-width of, say, a 99% confidence interval for γ to be less than 0.1 which implies that $2.576 \sqrt{\gamma(1 - \gamma)/N}/\hat{\gamma}_N \leq 0.1$. How large must N be in order to achieve this level of accuracy? Since $\gamma_N \to \gamma$ almost surely (a.s.) as $N \to \infty$, we see that $N \sim 100 \times 2.576^2 \times (1 - \gamma)/\gamma$, i.e., the required sample size is proportional to $1/\gamma$. The smaller γ is, the larger the sample size must be. For example, if $\gamma = 10^{-6}$, a sample size of 6.64×10^8 is required, while if $\gamma = 10^{-9}$, a sample size of 6.64×10^{11} (664 billion) is required. Note that these sample sizes must be increased by a factor of 100 in order to achieve one additional significant digit of accuracy ($\pm 1\%$ accuracy).

The relative error of the estimate $\hat{\gamma}_N$, $RE(\hat{\gamma}_N)$, is defined to be the standard deviation of the estimate divided by its expected value. Then $RE(\hat{\gamma}_N) \sim 1/\sqrt{\gamma N} \to \infty$ as $\gamma \to 0$. Thus, using standard simulation, the relative error is unbounded as the event becomes rarer.

As we will see, when importance sampling is properly applied, it is possible to construct (unbiased) estimates of γ whose relative error remains bounded even as $\gamma \to 0$. This implies that the required sample size to achieve a given relative error does not blow up as the event becomes rarer.

2.2 Importance Sampling

Importance sampling is based on the following simple observation. (Some of the discussion below basically follows that given in [54].) Consider the integral representation for γ in Equation 1. Multiplying and dividing the integrand by another density function $p'(x)$ we obtain (henceforth, we will suppress the limits of integration unless they are specifically required)

$$\gamma = \int 1_{\{x \in A\}} \frac{p(x)}{p'(x)} p'(x) dx = E_{p'}\left[1_{\{X \in A\}} \frac{p(x)}{p'(x)}\right] = E_{p'}[1_{\{X \in A\}} L(X)] \quad (2)$$

where $L(x) = p(x)/p'(x)$ is called the likelihood ratio and the subscript p' denotes sampling from the density p'. Equation 2 is valid for any density p' provided that $p'(x) > 0$ for all $x \in A$ such that $p(x) > 0$, i.e., a non-zero feasible sample under density p must also be a non-zero feasible sample under density p'. This equation suggests the following estimation scheme, which is called importance sampling. Draw N samples $X_1, \ldots, X_N$ using the density p' and define $Z_n = L(X_n)I_n$ (recall $I_n = 1_{\{X_n \in A\}}$). Then, by Equation 2, $E_{p'}[Z_n] = \gamma$. Thus an unbiased (and strongly consistent as $N \to \infty$) estimate of γ is given by

$$\hat{\gamma}_N(p') = \frac{1}{N} \sum_{n=1}^{N} Z_n = \frac{1}{N} \sum_{n=1}^{N} I_n L(X_n), \quad (3)$$

i.e., γ can be estimated by simulating a random variable with a different density and then unbiasing the output (I_n) by multiplying by the likelihood ratio. Sampling with a different density is sometimes called a change of measure and the density p' is sometimes called the importance sampling density (or if $p'(x) = dP'(x)/dx$, P' is called the importance sampling distribution).

Since essentially any density p' can be used for sampling, what is the optimal density, i.e., what is the density that minimizes the variance of $\hat{\gamma}_N(p')$? Selecting $p'(x) \equiv p^*(x) = p(x)/\gamma$ for $x \in A$ and $p^*(x) = 0$ otherwise has the property of making $Z_n = I_n p(X_n)/p^*(X_n) = \gamma$ with probability one. Since the variance of a constant is zero (and since the variance is always nonnegative), $p^*(x)$ is the optimal change of measure (and one sample from p^* gives you γ exactly). The optimal change of measure thus has the interpretation of being simply the ordinary distribution, conditioned that the rare event has occurred. However, there are several practical problems with trying to sample from this optimal density p^*. First, it explicitly depends upon γ, the unknown quantity that we are trying to estimate. If, in fact, γ were known, there would be no need to run the simulation experiment at all. Second, even if γ were known, it might be impractical to sample efficiently from p^*.

Since the optimal change of measure is not feasible, how should one go about choosing a good importance sampling change of measure? Since $E_{p'}[Z_n] = \gamma$ for any density p', reducing the variance of the estimator corresponds to selecting a density p' that reduces the second moment of Z_n;

$$E_{p'}[Z_n^2] = E_{p'}[((I_n L(X_n))^2] = \int 1_{\{x \in A\}} \left(\frac{p(x)}{p'(x)} \right)^2 p'(x) dx \qquad (4)$$

$$= \int 1_{\{x \in A\}} \frac{p(x)}{p'(x)} p(x) dx = E_p[I_n L(X_n)].$$

Thus to reduce the variance, we want to make the likelihood ratio $p(x)/p'(x)$ small on the set A. Since A is a rare event (under density p), roughly speaking, $p(x)$ is small on A. Thus to make the likelihood ratio small on A, we should pick p' so that $p'(x)$ is large on A, i.e., the change of measure should be chosen so as to make the event A likely to occur.

More formally, consider a sequence of rare event problems indexed by a "rarity" parameter ϵ so that $\gamma(\epsilon) \to 0$ as $\epsilon \to 0$. For example, in the buffer sizing problem, we could let $\epsilon = 1/B$ and $\gamma(\epsilon) = P(Q > B)$ where B is the buffer size and Q denotes a random variable having the steady state queue length distribution. In a reliability model, as is done in[57, 72, 88, 89], we could parameterize the failure rates of components by ϵ, e.g., the failure rate of component number i is given by $\lambda_i(\epsilon) = a_i \epsilon^{b_i}$ for some constants a_i and $b_i (b_i \geq 1)$. Then, defining $\gamma(\epsilon)$ to be the probability that the system fails before some fixed time horizon t fits into this framework. Suppose it is known that $\gamma(\epsilon) \sim c f(\epsilon)$ as $\epsilon \to 0$ for some constant c and function $f(\epsilon)$. (Thus $f(\epsilon) \to 0$ as $\epsilon \to 0$.) Now if a p' can be chosen so that $E_{p'}[Z_n^2] \sim d f(\epsilon)^2$ for some constant d, then $\sigma_{p'}(Z_n)$, the standard deviation of Z_n, $\sim k f(\epsilon)$ where $k = \sqrt{d - c^2}$. The relative error of the importance sampling estimate thus remains bounded as $\epsilon \to 0$:

$$\lim_{\epsilon \to 0} \frac{\sigma(\hat{\gamma}_N(p'))}{\gamma(\epsilon)} = \lim_{\epsilon \to 0} \frac{\sigma_{p'}(Z_n)}{\gamma(\epsilon)\sqrt{N}} = \frac{k}{\sqrt{N}} < \infty. \qquad (5)$$

In such a situation, we say that the importance sampling estimate has "bounded relative error" (see, e.g., [57, 72, 88, 89]). In practice, having bounded relative error is highly desirable, since it implies that only a fixed, bounded, number of samples N are required to estimate $\gamma(\epsilon)$ to within a certain relative precision, *no matter how rare the event of interest is*. For example, suppose $k \leq 10$, then two significant digit accuracy, i.e., making the relative half-width of a 99% confidence for $\gamma(\epsilon)$ less than 0.1, can be achieved in at most $N = 6.64 \times 10^4$ samples, regardless of how small ϵ (and thus $\gamma(\epsilon)$) is. Compared to the sample sizes of 6.64×10^8 and 6.64×10^{11} required by standard simulation to estimate $\gamma(\epsilon) = 10^{-6}$ and 10^{-9}, respectively, we see that orders of magnitude reduction in run lengths, or speedup, could thus be achieved using importance sampling. However, the variance reduction does necessarily not tell the whole story, since the cost of obtaining each sample may be so high as to effectively limit the number of samples that can be collected. It is usually somewhat more expensive to obtain a sample using importance sampling than standard simulation, however, the massive reduction in sample size generally more than makes up for the increase in the cost per sample. Such sampling costs are taken into account in a number of studies, e.g., [6, 86], and see [47] and the references therein for a theoretical treatment of this issue.

How can bounded relative error estimates be obtained? One way is to select p' so as to ensure that the likelihood ratio is always small on A. More specifically, suppose

$$L(X_n) \leq d_1 f(\epsilon) \qquad (6)$$

whenever $X_n \in A$, then

$$E_{p'}[Z_n^2] = E_{p'}[I_n L(X_n)^2] \leq d_1^2 f(\epsilon)^2 E_{p'}[I_n] \leq d_1^2 f(\epsilon)^2. \qquad (7)$$

Thus, sampling under such a p' produces an estimate with bounded relative error. How likely is the event A to occur under such a p'? The probability of A is given by

$$E_{p'}[I_n] = \int 1_{\{x \in A\}} p'(x) dx = \int 1_{\{x \in A\}} \frac{p'(x)}{p(x)} p(x) dx \qquad (8)$$

$$\geq \frac{1}{d_1 f(\epsilon)} \int 1_{\{x \in A\}} p(x) dx = \frac{\gamma(\epsilon)}{d_1 f(\epsilon)} \sim \frac{c}{d_1} > 0.$$

(The inequality in Equation 8 is true by Inequality 6.) Thus, asymptotically, the probability of A under p' does not depend on ϵ, i.e., A is not a rare event under p', and the problem has been transformed from a rare event simulation into a non-rare event simulation.

Note that bounded relative error is obtained by making the second moment, $E_{p'}[Z_n^2]$, approach zero at the same at the same rate, $f(\epsilon)^2$, that $\gamma(\epsilon)^2$ approaches zero. Is it possible to do any better? The answer is essentially no, since suppose $E_{p'}[Z_n^2] \sim dg(\epsilon)^2$ where $g(\epsilon) \to 0$ as $\epsilon \to 0$. Because importance sampling is unbiased and the variance is non-negative, we must have $E_{p'}[Z_n^2] \geq E_{p'}[Z_n]^2 = \gamma(\epsilon)^2$. Thus, $\underline{\lim}_{\epsilon \to 0} g(\epsilon)/f(\epsilon) \geq c/\sqrt{d}$, i.e., $g(\epsilon)$ can approach zero no faster than a constant times $f(\epsilon)$. When in fact, $g(\epsilon) \sim kf(\epsilon)$, some authors (e.g., [16, 17, 21, 26, 36, 85, 87, 95]) term the importance sampling scheme "asymptotically optimal" or "asymptotically efficient." These terms are thus seen to be equivalent to bounded relative error. (As seen from Equation 5, it is possible to obtain a relative error of zero as $\epsilon \to 0$ if one is lucky enough to have $d = c^2$, but, in practice, such situations are the exception rather than the rule.) Note that bounded relative error is also obtained if $\gamma(\epsilon) \geq cf(\epsilon)$ and if $L(X_n) \leq d_1 f(\epsilon)$ for $X_n \in A$. Also, in some applications, it may not be possible to find a constant d_1 such that $L(X_n) \leq d_1 f(\epsilon)$ but it is possible to find a random variable D such that $L(X_n) \leq Df(\epsilon)$ (on A). If $\overline{\lim}_{\epsilon \to 0} E_{p'}[D^2] < \infty$, then bounded relative error is still obtained. Juneja [61] shows that in order to obtain bounded likelihood ratios, one must make the likelihood ratio equal to one on every cycle of states. Although our focus is on asymptotic optimality, it is important to recognize that, for a fixed ϵ, there may be other changes of measure that, because of the (unknown) constants in the variance, result in a lower variance than that obtained by the asymptotically optimal change of measure; indeed the zero variance estimator is always better, but as mentioned above, it is usually impractical to sample from that distribution. In addition, there may be several different formulations for estimating the same quantity; asymptotic optimality refers only to a particular formulation of a problem. (For example, see Section 3.1 for several formulations to estimate large waiting times in the single server queue.)

As used in this context, the purpose of importance sampling is to reduce the variance of an estimator. Thus importance sampling is called a "variance reduction technique." (See [4, 46, 56, 84] for a different application of importance sampling; so-called "what if" simulations in which importance sampling is used to estimate the performance of a system at many different input parameter settings from a single simulation run.) Does importance sampling always lead to a reduction in variance? The answer is (an emphatic) *NO*, as the following simple example illustrates. Suppose $p(x) = \lambda e^{-\lambda x}$ and $A = \{x > t\}$, i.e., we are interested in estimating $\gamma = P_p(X > t)$ where X has an exponential distribution with rate λ. Suppose we employ importance sampling using an exponential distribution with rate λ', i.e., $p'(x) = \lambda' e^{-\lambda' x}$. From Equation 4, the second moment of the estimator is given by

$$E_{p'}[Z_n^2] = \int_{x=t}^{\infty} \frac{p(x)}{p'(x)} p(x) dx = \frac{\lambda^2}{\lambda'} \int_{x=t}^{\infty} e^{(\lambda' - 2\lambda)x} dx \qquad (9)$$

which is infinite if $\lambda' \geq 2\lambda$. Thus, not only can importance sampling result in a variance increase, but it can produce arbitrarily bad results if not applied carefully. (Conditions, and counter-examples, under which importance sampling of discrete time Markov chains over a random time horizon has a finite variance are given in [44, 46, 53].) So, essentially all work on using importance sampling in practical applications deals with choosing an importance sampling distribution (change of measure) that leads to actual variance reduction, with particular emphasis being placed on finding asymptotically optimal changes of measure. As we will see, selecting such asymptotically optimal changes of measure generally involves understanding quite a bit about the structure of the system being simulated. Fortunately, the understanding does not have to so thorough as to imply a complete solution of the problem; there is a rather large class of queueing and reliability models for which exact solutions do not exist (or numerical solutions are impractical) but for which asymptotically optimal importance sampling distributions can be explicitly given.

Note that importance sampling is well suited for parallelization by running independent replications (or replications with different input parameter settings) in parallel on multiple computers. (See [45, 55] and the references therein for a discussion of the statistical properties and efficiencies of a variety of parallel replications approaches.) If the cost of computing each sample is high, and the variance is relatively large, then such parallelization can be very effective; this is especially true if the asymptotically optimal importance sampling distribution is unknown. Several such examples, including the analysis of fault-tolerant routing algorithms on a hypercube, where parallelization is effective are considered in [77].

2.3 Likelihood Ratios

The discussion of the previous section dealt with a very special situation: using importance sampling for a single random variable that has a probability density function. However, importance sampling is true much more generally as we will describe briefly (without getting too technical). In particular suppose $\gamma = \int H(\omega)dP(\omega)$ for some arbitrary random variable H and arbitrary probability measure P. Then, as in Equation 2, $\gamma = \int H(\omega)L(\omega)dP'(\omega) = E_{P'}[HL]$ for another probability measure P' where $L(\omega) = dP/dP'(\omega)$ is again the likelihood ratio or, in measure-theoretic terms, the Radon-Nikodym derivative. (This requires that the measure P be "absolutely continuous" with respect to the measure P'.) The reason for this brief excursion into measure theory is to make the point that the probabilistic setting in which importance sampling applies is extremely general. For example, it can involve stochastic processes such as discrete or continuous time Markov chains, semi-Markov process, or more general stochastic processes such as generalized semi-Markov processes (see [43, 99] and the references therein). The (rare) event A can also be defined quite generally; typically it is defined in terms of "stopping times" [24]. For example, in a reliability model defined by a continuous time Markov chain (CTMC), suppose τ_F is the first time that the process enters a "bad" set of states F in which the system is considered unavailable. Then an event of interest (which is hopefully rare) is $A = \{\tau_F \leq t\}$ for some given value of t.

In order to apply importance sampling, it must be possible to compute the relevant likelihood ratio. We briefly give several examples; explicit formulas for a variety of stochastic processes are given in [46]. In the case of sampling from a single probability density function, as described above, the likelihood ratio $L(X) = p(X)/p'(X)$. This equation is also valid if X is drawn from a discrete distribution, i.e., if $P(X = a_i) = p(a_i), i = 1, \ldots, m$ and $P'(X = a_i) = p'(a_i), i = 1, \ldots, m$. We require that $p'(a_i) > 0$ if $p(a_i) > 0$, but note that we can have $p'(a_i) > 0$ even if $p(a_i) = 0$ since the likelihood ratio is zero in this case, i.e., no weight is given to an impossible (under p) sample path. Suppose $X = (X_1, \ldots, X_m)$ is a random vector, where X_i is drawn from density $p_i(x)$ and X_i is independent of $X_j(j \neq i)$. If, under importance sampling, X_i is drawn from density $p'_i(x)$, and again X_i is independent of $X_j(j \neq i)$, then

$$L(X) = \prod_{i=1}^{m} \frac{p(X_i)}{p'(X_i)}. \tag{10}$$

Suppose $\{X_i, i \geq 0\}$ is a discrete time Markov chain (DTMC), on the state space of nonnegative integers where X_0 has (the initial) distribution $p_0(i)$ and the one-step transition probabilities are given by $P(i,j) = P(X_n = j|X_{n-1} = i)$. Let $X_m = (X_0, X_1, \ldots, X_m)$. If, under importance sampling, X_0 is drawn from $p'_0(i)$, and the process is generated with the one-step transition probabilities

$P'(i, j)$, then

$$L(\mathbf{X}_m) = \frac{p_0(X_0)}{p_0'(X_0)} \prod_{i=1}^{m} \frac{P(X_{i-1}, X_i)}{P'(X_{i-1}, X_i)}. \tag{11}$$

We require that $p_0'(i) > 0$ if $p_0(i) > 0$ and $P'(i, j) > 0$ if $P(i, j) > 0$. In fact there is no requirement that the importance sampling distribution correspond to a time homogeneous DTMC; see [30, 50, 51] for examples in which it is advantageous to use a process other than a time homogeneous DTMC for importance sampling to estimate quantities associated with a DTMC. Identities for the variance of $L(\mathbf{X}_m)$ and $L(\mathbf{X}_m)Y_m$ where Y_m is a function of $\mathbf{X}_m$ may be found in [44, 46]; the relationship of such identities to the problems of rare event simulation covered here is beyond the scope of this paper.

For a CTMC, let $p_0(i)$ denote the initial distribution, $\lambda(i)$ denote the total rate out of state i and let $P(i, j) = Q(i, j)/\lambda(i)$ denote the transition probabilities of the embedded DTMC, where $Q(i, j)$ is the rate from state i to state j. If importance sampling is done using a CTMC with initial distribution $p'(i)$, holding rates $\lambda'(i)$, and embedded DTMC transition probabilities $P'(i, j)$, then the likelihood ratio after m transitions is

$$L(X) = \frac{p_0(X_0)}{p_0'(X_0)} \prod_{i=1}^{m} \frac{\lambda(X_{i-1})e^{-\lambda(X_{i-1})t_{i-1}}}{\lambda'(X_{i-1})e^{-\lambda'(X_{i-1})t_{i-1}}} \frac{P(X_{i-1}, X_i)}{P'(X_{i-1}, X_i)} \tag{12}$$

where the sequence of states of the embedded DTMC is $X_0, \ldots, X_m$ and t_i is the holding time in state X_i. (Note that this expression simplifies somewhat since $\lambda(X_{i-1})P(X_{i-1}, X_i) = Q(X_{i-1}, X_i)$.)

Another example, that will be of use in reliability models, concerns using uniformization, or thinning, [60, 71, 93] to sample points from a nonhomogeneous Poisson process (NHPP). Let $\{N(s), s \geq 0\}$ denote a NHPP with intensity rate $\lambda(s)$. Suppose there exists a finite constant β such that $\lambda(s) \leq \beta$ for all $s \geq 0$. Then points in the NHPP can be simulated (without importance sampling) as follows. Let $\{S_n, n \geq 1\}$ denote the points in an ordinary Poisson process $\{N_\beta(s), s \geq 0\}$ with (constant) rate β. Then, S_n is accepted as a point in the NHPP with probability $\lambda(S_n)/\beta$, otherwise it is rejected as a "pseudo event" (with probability $1 - \lambda(S_n)/\beta$). To implement importance sampling, we could simply thin the Poisson process $\{N_\beta(s), s \geq 0\}$ with different probabilities, in effect generating a NHPP with a different intensity rate, say $\lambda'(s)(\lambda'(s) \leq \beta)$. Let $N(t)$ denote the number of accepted (real) events and $P(t)$ denote the number of rejected (pseudo) events; then $N_\beta(t) = N(t) + P(t)$. Let T_n denote the time of the n-th real event $(n \leq N(t))$ and let P_n denote the time of the n-th pseudo event $(n \leq P(t))$. Then, the likelihood ratio (at time t) has a simple form:

$$L(t) = \prod_{n=1}^{N(t)} \frac{\lambda(T_n)}{\lambda'(T_n)} \times \prod_{n=1}^{P(t)} \frac{1 - \lambda(P_n)/\beta}{1 - \lambda'(P_n)/\beta}. \tag{13}$$

This requires that $\lambda'(s) > 0$ whenever $\lambda(s) > 0$ and $1 - \lambda'(s)/\beta > 0$ whenever $1 - \lambda(s)/\beta > 0$. In the reliability context, $\lambda(s)$ might represent the total component failure rate at time s which, because components are reliable, is very small. Therefore, to see system failure events, we need to accelerate the rate at which components fail, which can be accomplished simply by increasing the component failure rate, i.e., by sampling using failure rate $\lambda'(s)$ where $\lambda'(s) \gg \lambda(s)$.

2.4 Regenerative Simulation

In simulations of stochastic systems, one is often interested in steady state performance measures. For example, in queueing models one might be interested in $P(W > x)$ where W is the steady state waiting time distribution. In a reliability model, one might be interested in u the steady state unavailability of the system, i.e., the long run fraction of the time that system is in a state that is considered failed. In both these cases, one is interested in estimating a quantity associated with a rare event. If the system is regenerative [27, 96], then the "regenerative method" can be used to estimate steady state performance measures. Let X_s be the process at time s. We assume there is a particular state, call it 0, such that the process returns to state 0 infinitely often and that, upon hitting state 0, the stochastic evolution of the system is independent of the past and has the same distribution as if the process were started in state in 0. Arrivals to an empty GI/GI/1 queue constitute regeneration points, as do entrances to a fixed state in a CTMC. Let β_i denote the time of the i-th regeneration ($\beta_0 = 0$) and assume that $X_0 = 0$. Let $\alpha_i = \beta_i - \beta_{i-1}$ denote the length of the i-th regenerative cycle. If $E[\alpha_i] < \infty$, then (under certain regularity conditions) $X_s \Rightarrow X$ as $s \to \infty$ where $\Rightarrow$ denotes convergence in distribution and X has the steady state distribution. Let h be a function on the state space and define $Y_i = \int_{\beta_{i-1}}^{\beta_i} h(X_s)ds$. Then $\{(Y_i, \alpha_i), i \geq 1\}$ are i.i.d. and

$$r = E[h(X)] = \frac{E[Y_i]}{E[\alpha_i]} \tag{14}$$

(provided $E[Y_i]$ exists and is finite). Equation 14 and the i.i.d. structure of regenerative processes forms the basis of the regenerative method; simulate N cycles and estimate $E[h(X)]$ by $\hat{r}_N = \bar{Y}_N / \bar{\alpha}_N$ where $\bar{Y}_N$ and $\bar{\alpha}_N$ are the averages of the Y_i-s and α_i-s, respectively. It is possible to form confidence intervals for r by applying the central limit theorem. (See [27] for a discussion of estimating the variance in this central limit theorem.) For example, to estimate $P(W > x)$, the process is in discrete time, $h(w) = 1_{\{w > x\}}$, α_i is the number of customers to arrive in a busy period and $Y_i = \sum_{k=\beta_{i-1}}^{\beta_i} h(W_k)$. To estimate u, the steady state unavailability, $h(x) = 1_{\{x \in F\}}$ where F is the set of failed states. In both of these cases, $Y_i = 0$ with high probability so obtaining a non-zero Y_i is a rare event. Thus importance sampling can be applied to estimate the numerator, $E[Y_i]$, of Equation 14. Typically importance sampling is used until a non-zero value of Y_i occurs, and then it is "turned off" and the process is allowed to return naturally to the regenerative state. Note that the denominator, $E[\alpha_i]$ is simply the expected cycle time, so importance sampling need not be applied to estimating the denominator. Letting L_i denote the likelihood ratio of the process over cycle i, then $E[Y_i] = E_{P'}[L_i Y_i]$ where importance sampling is done using distribution P'. (See [11, 42, 46] for an alternative expression that uses partial likelihood ratios in regenerative simulation.)

To obtain variance reduction in estimating $E[Y_i]$, roughly speaking, we want to chose P' so as make the rare event likely to occur during a cycle, thus making the likelihood ratio small. But suppose one is interested in estimating the expected time (starting in state 0) until the rare event occurs, e.g., estimating $E_0[\tau_F]$ where τ_F is the first time the reliability model enters a failed state (in F). Using importance sampling to accelerate the occurrence of τ_F will result in unusually small values of τ_F, thereby increasing the variance. However, this problem can be avoided by exploiting a ratio formula for $E_0[\tau_F]$:

$$E_0[\tau_F] = \frac{E_0[\min(\tau_0, \tau_F)]}{P_0(\tau_F < \tau_0)} \tag{15}$$

where τ_0 is the first time to return to state 0 (see [51, 64, 92]). Equation 15 is valid because the number of cycles until hitting τ_F before τ_0 has a geometric distribution with success probability $\gamma = P_0(\tau_F < \tau_0)$. Now the problem becomes one of estimating γ, which is a rare event problem. Thus quantities such as the mean time to failure and the mean time until buffer overflow can be estimated by using importance sampling to estimate γ and standard simulation to estimate $E_0[\min(\tau_0, \tau_F)]$. The geometric distribution and Equation 15 also form the basis for showing that $\tau_F/E_0[\tau_F] \Rightarrow E$ as $\gamma \to 0$ where E is an exponential random variable with mean one [15, 64].

In some applications, the model may not be regenerative (e.g., a reliability model with non-exponential failure time distributions), yet a ratio formula similar to that of Equation 14 exists. For a subset, A, of the state space define A-cycles to begin whenever the process enters A. Then

$$r = E[h(X)] = \frac{E[Y_i(A)]}{E[\alpha_i(A)]} \tag{16}$$

where $Y_i(A)$ is the integral of the process over an A-cycle and $\alpha_i(A)$ is the length of an A-cycle [14, 25]. In Equation 16, the initial distribution is the stationary distribution conditioned on the process just entering A. Importance sampling can be used to estimate the numerator, while standard simulation can be used to estimate the denominator. A "splitting" technique can be used to obtain the proper initial distributions as follows. Simulate the process (without importance sampling) until it is approximately in steady state. Then whenever the process enters A, simulate two A-cycles; one using importance sampling and one without using importance sampling. These provide samples for the ratio estimate. Also, the A-cycle simulated without importance sampling provides a starting point (with approximately the steady state distribution on A) for the next pair of samples. The method of batch means can be used for variance estimation; see [21, 81] for a discussion of this approach, and see [1] for a similar idea applied to estimating bit error rates over certain communications channels.

3 Queueing Models

3.1 The Single Server Queue

We are now ready to apply importance sampling to some specific applications arising in queueing and reliability theory. We start with the waiting time process in the stable single server, GI/GI/1, queue. This queue has quite a lot of random walk related structure that can be exploited. Let W_n denote the waiting time of the n-th customer, $\{A_n\}$ denote the interarrival time sequence and $\{B_n\}$ denote the service time sequence. Then the waiting time sequence follows the well known Lindley's recursion (see, e.g., [7, 33]): $W_0 = 0$ and $W_{n+1} = (W_n + X_{n+1})^+$ for $n \geq 0$ where $X_{n+1} = B_n - A_{n+1}$ and $x^+ = \max(0, x)$. Let $A(x) = P(A_n \leq x)$ and $B(x) = P(B_n \leq x)$. Then, if $E[X_n] < 0$ (or equivalently $\rho = E[B_n]/E[A_n] < 1$), then the queue is stable and $W_n \Rightarrow W$ where W denotes the steady state waiting time. We will be interested in estimating $P(W > x)$ for large values of x. To do so we will exploit the equivalence between the distribution of W and the maximum of the (time-reversed) random walk. Define $\tilde{X}_1 = X_n, \tilde{X}_2 = X_{n-1}, \ldots, \tilde{X}_n = X_1$, $\tilde{S}_0 = 0$, and $\tilde{S}_k = \tilde{X}_1 + \cdots + \tilde{X}_k$ for $k \geq 1$. Then, it is well known that

$$W_n = \tilde{M}_n \equiv \max\{\tilde{S}_0, \tilde{S}_1, \ldots, \tilde{S}_n\} \qquad n \geq 0. \qquad (17)$$

Thus, letting $n \to \infty$, W has the same distribution as $\tilde{M}$, the maximum of the time-reversed random walk (assuming the distribution of $\{X_{n-k}, 0 \leq k \leq n\}$ converges as $n \to \infty$). For the GI/GI/1 queue, $\tilde{X}_n$ has the same distribution as X_n, so we can say that W has the same distribution as $M = \max\{S_k, k \geq 0\}$, the maximum of the random walk (which has negative drift).

We note that $P(W > x) = P(M > x) = P(\tau_x < \infty)$ where τ_x is the first time the random walk exceeds x. Using standard simulation, estimation of $P(\tau_x < \infty)$ is not efficient since, with high probability $\tau_x = \infty$. (Not only is the event rare, but it takes a potentially long time to determine that the rare event did not happen.) However, we will use importance sampling to transform the random walk into one with positive drift, so that $\tau_x < \infty$ with probability one. We follow the queueing oriented development in Asmussen [6, 7]. (Siegmund [95] considers this and related problems in the context of sequential analysis and sequential probability ratio tests. Asmussen also discusses the relevance of this problem to "risk theory" in insurance applications.) We will use a specific importance sampling change of measure known as "exponential twisting," "exponential tilting," or embedding within a "conjugate family." Define the moment generating function $M(\theta) = E[e^{\theta X_n}]$ which we will assume is finite for all $0 \leq \theta < \bar{\theta}$ where $\bar{\theta} > 0$. (For technical reasons, we also assume that $M(\theta) \to \infty$ as $\theta \uparrow \bar{\theta}$.) Note that $M(\theta) = E[e^{\theta(B_{n-1} - A_n)}] = M_B(\theta)M_A(-\theta)$ where $M_B(\theta) = E[e^{\theta B_n}]$ and $M_A(\theta) = E[e^{\theta A_n}]$. Let $F(x)$ denote the distribution function of X_n. Now define the exponentially twisted distribution $F_\theta(x)$ by $dF_\theta(x) = [e^{\theta x}/M(\theta)]dF(x)$; if $F(x)$ has a density function $f(x)$, then $dF_\theta(x) = f_\theta(x) = e^{\theta x}f(x)/M(\theta)$. If $X_1, \ldots, X_n$ are independently sampled from $F_\theta(x)$, then the likelihood ratio has a very simple form:

$$L_n(\theta) = \frac{M(\theta)^n}{e^{\theta(X_1+\ldots+X_n)}} = M(\theta)^n e^{-\theta S_n}. \tag{18}$$

Now if $\tau_x = n$, then by definition, $S_n > x$ and thus

$$L_n(\theta) = M(\theta)^n e^{-\theta x} e^{-\theta(S_n-x)} \leq M(\theta)^n e^{-\theta x}. \tag{19}$$

What value of θ should be chosen? Note that there exists a θ^* such that $M(\theta^*) = 1$. This is true since $M(0) = 1$, the derivative of $M(\theta)$ is negative at $\theta = 0$ (because $E[X_n] < 0$) and $M(\theta)$ is convex, continuous and approaches ∞ as $\theta \uparrow \bar{\theta}$.) By the above argument, at this value of θ^*, the titled random walk has strictly positive drift so $\tau_x < \infty$ with probability one. Thus, using Equations 2 and 19, we obtain

$$P(W > x) = P(\tau_x < \infty) = e^{-\theta^* x} E_{\theta^*}[e^{-\theta^* O_x}] \tag{20}$$

where O_x is the (random) "overshoot" $O_x = S_{\tau_x} - x$. Note that the decay rate, $-\theta^*$, is known; only $E_{\theta^*}[e^{-\theta^* O_x}]$ is unknown and requires estimation. Why is θ^* a good value with which to do importance sampling? It can be shown that, under suitable regularity conditions, $E_{\theta^*}[e^{-\theta^* O_x}]$ converges to a constant, say $a(\theta^*)$, as $x \to \infty$, thus $P(W > x) \sim a(\theta^*)e^{-\theta^* x}$. (This provides a very simple proof that the stationary waiting time distribution in the GI/GI/1 queue has an exponentially decaying tail, provided the moment generating function is finite.) In addition, by Equation 19, the likelihood ratio is also bounded by $e^{-\theta^* x}$. Thus, by the arguments of Section 2.2, importance sampling with this value of θ^* is asymptotically optimal. (Identify $\epsilon = 1/x$ and $f(\epsilon) = e^{-\theta^*/\epsilon}$.) In fact Siegmund [95] showed that θ^* is the unique asymptotically optimal value within the class of exponentially twisted distributions, while Lehtonen and Nyrhinen [68] showed that it is the unique asymptotically optimal change of measure within the class of (essentially) all distributions with i.i.d. increments. Asmussen [9] also suggests using the identity in Equation 20 for $P(W > x)$ to estimate $E[W] = \int P(W > x)dx$ using importance sampling (and quantities such as higher moments), although it needs to be combined with additional techniques in order to be effective.

For GI/GI/1, the equation $M(\theta^*) = 1$ is equivalent to $M_A(-\theta^*)M_B(\theta^*) = 1$. For the M/M/1 queue with arrival rate λ and service rate μ, $M_A(-\theta) = \lambda/(\lambda+\theta)$ and $M_B(\theta) = \mu/(\mu-\theta)$ for $\theta < \mu$. Solving for θ^* yields $\theta^* = \mu - \lambda$. At this value of θ^*, the interarrival time density $a_{\theta^*}(x) = \mu e^{-\mu x}$ and the service time density $b_{\theta^*}(x) = \lambda e^{-\lambda x}$, i.e., the process is simulated with arrival rate μ and service rate λ. Thus, with the asymptotically optimal importance sampling distribution, the simulated queue is indeed unstable. This flipping of arrival and service rates will also occur in other rare event problems as will be discussed later.

Further interpretation as to why exponential twisting with parameter θ^* is a good idea can be found in [2, 5]. Suppose one is told that $W_n > na$ for some constant a and large value of n. Then how did the queue come to be in such a (bad) state? Let $\mu^* > 0$ denote the mean of the tilted random walk, i.e., the random $S_k(\theta^*)$ with increment distribution $F_{\theta^*}(x)$. The titled random walk builds up linearly at rate μ^*, i.e., by the strong law of large numbers, $S_{[nt]}(\theta^*)/n \to t\mu^*$ a.s. as $n \to \infty$ for $0 \le t \le 1$. Now suppose $a \le \mu^*$. Then, the titled random walk is capable of reaching the level na by time n. In fact, the tilted random walk reaches level na at approximately time na/μ^*. Define $t(a) = 1 - a/\mu^*$. Anantharam [2] shows that in this case as $n \to \infty$, given $W_n > na$, with probability one, $W_{[nt]}/n \to 0$ for all $t \le (1 - t(a))$, and then $W_{[nt]}/n \to \mu^*(t - t(a))$ for all t such that $t(a) \le t \le 1$. In other words, W_k remains stable until a certain time, $t(a)n$, and then starts building up linearly at the same rate that the titled random walk builds up until reaching level na at time n. (If $a > \mu^*$, then the tilted random walk with parameter θ^* cannot reach level na by time n. In this case, the waiting times build up linearly at rate a, corresponding to exponential twisting with a parameter θ_a such that the drift at θ_a is a.) In fact, related conditional limit theorems for the GI/GI/1 queue (see [5] and the references therein) show that during such a buildup, the waiting time behavior is (asymptotically) identical to that of the tilted random walk. Recall that in Section 2.2 we stated that the zero variance estimator was obtained by sampling from the ordinary distribution given that the rare event has occurred. The above results show, roughly speaking, that given a large waiting time has occurred, the ordinary distribution *is* the twisted distribution. Thus it is very natural that exponential twisting with parameter θ^* should be very effective. Indeed, experimental results in [68], show that for the M/M/1 queue (a problem not requiring simulation but convenient as a simulation benchmark) with $\rho = 0.5$, $P(W > 20) \approx 10^{-9}$ can be estimated to within $\pm 5\%$ in only 129 replications. In fact, if a non-optimal value of $\theta \ne \theta^*$ is used, then good estimates are obtained within reasonable time even if θ is as much as 30% away from θ^*.

(Interestingly, if $M_B(\theta) = \infty$ for all $\theta > 0$, it is shown in [2] that large waiting times are essentially the result of a single customer experiencing a very large service time. The assumption that $M_B(\theta) < \infty$ for some $\theta > 0$ implies that the tail of the distribution $B()$ goes to zero exponentially fast. Thus if $M_B(\theta) = \infty$ for all $\theta > 0$, the tail of the distribution is "fat" and very large values are not that unlikely.)

The above analysis makes use of the fact that, in the GI/GI/1 queue, the stationary waiting time has the same distribution as the maximum of a random walk with negative drift. This relationship does not occur more generally, e.g., in multiserver queues, queues with finite buffers, or networks of queues. Therefore it is desirable to consider techniques that work directly with the queueing processes. The first such problem we consider is estimating the mean time until a GI/GI/1 queue reaches a queue length of n (not including the customer in service). Recalling the ratio formula of Equation 14, we see that we need to estimate $\gamma_n = P(\tau_n < \tau_0)$ where τ_n is the first time the queue length reaches n and τ_0 is the first time the queue empties. (This problem is related to determining the distribution of the maximum waiting time during a busy period in the GI/G/1 queue, see [59].) We assume that the initial conditions are that a customer (customer number 0) has just arrived to an empty queue. We basically follow the analysis in Sadowsky [85]. This analysis provides a rigorous justification for a heuristic developed by Parekh and Walrand [83], which will be described in Section 3.2. Let $S(k) = \{\tau_n = k, \tau_0 > k\}$. On $S(k)$, the arrival time of customer number k customer is less than the departure time of the $k - n$-th customer to depart the queue (customer number $k - n - 1$), i.e.,

$$\sum_{j=1}^{k} A_j < \sum_{j=1}^{k-n} B_{j-1}. \tag{21}$$

For $k \geq n$ define $Z_k(n) = \sum_{j=1}^{k} A_j - \sum_{j=1}^{k-n} B_{j-1}$. Consider using exponential twisting with parameter θ^*. Then, on $S(k)$, $Z_k(n) \leq 0$ by Equation 21 and the likelihood ratio $L(\theta^*)$ is bounded as follows:

$$L(\theta^*) = M_B(\theta^*)^{k-n} M_A(-\theta^*)^k e^{\theta^* Z_k(n)} \leq M_B(\theta^*)^{-n} = M_A(-\theta^*)^n \tag{22}$$

since $Z_k(n) \leq 0$ and the fact that θ^* satisfies $M_A(-\theta^*)M_B(\theta^*) = 1$. Since the likelihood ratio is bounded by $M_A(-\theta^*)^n$ whenever $\tau_n < \tau_0$, taking expectations we have $\gamma_n \leq M_A(-\theta^*)^n$. Asymptotic optimality will be established if we can show that $\gamma_n \geq c M_A(-\theta^*)^n$ for some constant c. To do so, we will make the simplifying assumption that the service times are bounded, i.e., $B_j \leq b$ for all j and some constant b. On $S(k)$,

$$Z_k(n) = Z_{k-1}(n) + A_k - B_{k-n-1} \geq Z_{k-1}(n) + A_k - b \geq -b \tag{23}$$

where the second inequality is true because, on $S_k(n)$, $Z_{k-1}(n) \geq 0$. Combining the equality part of Equation 22 with Inequality 23 we obtain

$$L(\theta^*) \geq M_A(-\theta^*)^n e^{-\theta^* b} \tag{24}$$

whenever $\tau_n > \tau_0$. Taking expectations yields

$$\gamma_n = E_{\theta^*}[L(\theta^*)1_{\{\tau_n < \tau_0\}}] \geq M_A(-\theta^*)^n e^{-\theta^* b} P_{\theta^*}(\tau_n < \tau_0). \tag{25}$$

But since, at θ^*, the queueing process is unstable, $P_{\theta^*}(\tau_n < \tau_0)$ is bounded away from 0 as $n \to \infty$, thereby establishing the result.

Note that $\lim_{n\to\infty}(1/n)\log(\gamma_n) = \log(M_A(-\theta^*))$. In addition, it is true that $\lim_{n\to\infty}(1/n)\log V_n(\theta^*) = 2\log(M_A(-\theta^*))$ where $V_n(\theta^*)$ is the variance of a single observation using importance sampling with parameter θ^*. For queueing models, asymptotic optimality is often stated in these terms.

Sadowsky shows that the bounded service time assumption can be removed. He furthermore shows that exponential twisting with parameter θ^* is the unique asymptotically optimal change of measure within the class of all simulations having i.i.d. interarrival and service time distributions. Further optimality results, concerning higher moments of the estimate (not just the variance), are established in [86].

3.2 A Large Deviations Approach to the Single Server Queue

The above results are in fact closely related to the theory of large deviations [16], which basically deals with estimating the probability that S_n/n is far from its mean. We will give an overly simplified, and somewhat heuristic, description of certain basic results and show how they can be applied to fast simulation of certain queues; see [16] for a rigorous (and readable) treatment of this topic in much greater detail. (There are a number of technical issues and difficulties which tend to obscure what's going on, so we will not deal with them here.) Consider a random walk, S_n, whose increments, X_k, have a distribution function F, finite moment generating function $M(\theta)$, and twisted distribution function $dF_\theta(x) = e^{\theta x} dF(x)/M(\theta)$ as described earlier. Cramér's theorem, which dates to 1937, roughly states that

$$P(S_n/n \approx y) \approx e^{-nI(y)} \qquad (26)$$

where $I(y)$ is the Cramér transform (or large deviation rate function):

$$I(y) = \sup_\theta [\theta y - \log(M(\theta))]. \qquad (27)$$

(More precisely, by Equation 26 we mean $\lim_{\delta \to 0} \lim_{n \to \infty} (1/n) \log[P(|S_n/n - y| < \delta)] = -I(y)$ provided $I(y)$ is finite and continuous in a neighborhood about y.) At first glance this result looks somewhat mysterious, but the intuition behind it is actually quite simple. Pick a small positive δ and consider estimating $P(\mathcal{S}(n, y)) = P(y - \delta \le S_n/n \le y + \delta)$ by simulating the random walk with exponential twisting. If $y \ne E[X_k]$, then $\mathcal{S}(n, y)$ is a rare event. It is natural to chose the twisting parameter $\theta = \theta_y$ so that $P_\theta(\mathcal{S}(n, y)) \to 1$, i.e., select θ_y so that $y = E_{\theta_y}[X_k] = \int x dF_{\theta_y}(x)$. Then

$$P(\mathcal{S}(n, y)) = E_{\theta_y}[L(\theta_y) 1_{\{\mathcal{S}(n,y)\}}] = M(\theta_y)^n E_{\theta_y}[e^{-\theta_y S_n} 1_{\{\mathcal{S}(n,y)\}}] \qquad (28)$$

$$\approx M(\theta_y)^n e^{-\theta_y n y} E_{\theta_y}[1_{\{\mathcal{S}(n,y)\}}] = e^{-n[\theta_y y - \log(M(\theta_y))]}$$

where the $\approx$ is (approximately) true because $S_n \approx ny$ on $\mathcal{S}(n, y)$. It thus remains to be shown that $I(y) = \theta_y y - \log(M(\theta_y))$ which is established by setting the derivative of the function $h(\theta) = \theta y - \log(M(\theta))$ equal to zero. (It can be shown that $I(y)$ is convex and nonnegative on its domain of finiteness.) Note that if $y = E[X_k](= E_0[X_k])$, then, by definition $\theta_y = 0$, $I(y) = 0$, and thus Equation 26 is equivalent to $P(S_n/n \approx E[X_k]) \approx 1$ as it should be.

Let us see how this result can be used (heuristically) in the GI/GI/1 queue. Following Parekh and Walrand [83], again consider estimating $\gamma_n = P(\tau_n < \tau_0)$ where τ_n is the first time the queue length reaches n and τ_0 is the first time the queue empties. Suppose this event happens at some time T and that during the interval $(0, T)$, the arrival rate is some constant λ' and the service rate is some constant μ'. Thus the number of arrivals is approximately $\lambda' T$, the number of departures is approximately $\mu'T$ and the queue builds up at rate $\lambda' - \mu'$. Now, by Equation 26, the probability of observing such rates λ' and μ' is approximately

$$p(\lambda', \mu') = \exp\left[-\lambda'TI_A(1/\lambda') - \mu'TI_B(1/\mu')\right] \tag{29}$$

where $I_A()$ and $I_B()$ are the Cramér transforms of the interarrival and service time distributions respectively. The values of λ' and μ' should be chosen so as to maximize the probability $p(\lambda', \mu')$ of this event. Since $\tau_n = T$, we have the (approximate) constraint

$$(\lambda' - \mu')T = n. \tag{30}$$

Substituting this into Equation 29, differentiating the exponent with respect to λ' and μ', setting the derivatives equal to 0 and solving yields the result that, as before, the optimal λ^* and μ^* correspond to twisting with rates $-\theta^*$ and θ^* such that $M_A(-\theta^*)M_B(\theta^*) = 1$. An extension of this heuristic approach to certain networks of queues was also described in [83] and will be discussed in Section 3.5.

Parekh and Walrand also relate this approach to the asymptotically optimal simulation of slow Markov walks as developed by Cottrell, Fort and Malgouyres [26]. These results are based on the Wentzell-Freidlin theory of large deviations for appropriately scaled diffusion processes (see [16] for a discussion), the details of which are beyond the scope of this paper. The basic model is

$$X_{n+1}^\epsilon = X_n^\epsilon + \epsilon V_n(X_n^\epsilon) \tag{31}$$

for some small ϵ (and $X_0^\epsilon = 0$). Thus $\{X_n^\epsilon, n \geq 0\}$ is a Markov chain (with a general state space) in discrete time with small increments. (The distribution of the increments can depend on the current value of chain.) Let $F^x(y) = P(V_n \leq y | X_n^\epsilon = x)$ and assume that $M^x(\theta) = \int e^{\theta y} dF^x(y) < \infty$. Under appropriate technical conditions, there is a large deviations result, similar in spirit to Equation 26, but in which the decay rate $I(y)$ is replaced by integral of an "action functional." Define the twisted increment distribution $dF_\theta^x(y) = e^{\theta y} dF^x(y)/M^x(\theta)$. Assume the process is one-dimensional and let $\gamma(\epsilon) = P(X_n^\epsilon$ hits 1 before 0). In [26], it is shown that the asymptotically optimal method for estimating $\gamma(\epsilon)$ is obtained by using exponential twisting with parameter θ_x whenever $X_n^\epsilon = x$ where $M^x(\theta_x) = 1$. Cottrell, Fort and Malgouyres apply their method to certain Aloha systems. Parekh and Walrand discuss how it can be applied to the M/M/1 queue, but point out difficulties in trying to use this approach for networks of queues. The application of this approach to certain other simple simple single server queues (e.g., M/D/1) is considered in [37].

3.3 The Multiple Server Queue

Sadowsky [85] also obtains asymptotic optimality results for the multiple server GI/GI/m queue ($m > 1$). In this case, the probability of interest is $\gamma_n = P(\text{queue length exceeds } n \text{ during a "cycle"})$ where a cycle is defined to start whenever a customer arrives to find all but one of the servers busy. (The initial distribution is assumed to be the stationary distribution at such instances.) Under similar conditions to those described in Section 3.1, it is shown that the unique asymptotically optimal change of measure is given by

$$dA_{\theta^*}(x) = \frac{e^{-m\theta^* x} dA(x)}{M_A(-m\theta^*)}, \qquad dB_{\theta^*}(x) = \frac{e^{\theta^* x} dB(x)}{M_B(\theta^*)} \qquad (32)$$

where θ^* satisfies $M_A(-m\theta^*)M_B(\theta^*) = 1$. Some experimental results are given in [85]; in one example with $m = 4$ servers and $n = 20$, γ_n, which is approximately 2.2×10^{-8}, could be estimated to within $\pm 10\%$ accuracy with only 602 samples using asymptotically optimal importance sampling, whereas over 10^9 samples would be required using standard simulation.

3.4 Discrete Time Queues With Correlated Arrival Processes

We next turn to analysis of queueing systems that arise in ATM (Asynchronous Transfer Mode) communications systems. In such systems, it is important to model bursty and/or correlated arrival processes, such as those that might occur in transmitting video data streams across a network. We begin by considering a particularly simple model of such a queueing system. The model is in discrete time. Let a_t denote the number of packets that arrive during time slot t and let $A_T = a_0 + \cdots + a_t$ denote the total number of arrivals by time T. We assume that the server has the capacity to serve up to c packets/time slot. Letting Q_t denote the queue length at time t, then Q_t obeys Lindley's recursion $Q_{t+1} = (Q_t + a_{t+1} - c)^+$. For simplicity, we assume that the arrival process is Markovian, i.e., $P(a_{t+1} = j | a_t = i) = P(i, j)$, which we assume is aperiodic, irreducible and has a finite state space ($0 \le i, j \le b$). We again consider $\gamma_n = P(\tau_n < \tau_0)$ given that the queue is empty at time 0. The appropriate change of measure can be inferred from large deviations results for Markov additive processes [16]. Define the matrix $A_\theta(i, j) = e^{\theta j} P(i, j)$. By the Perron-Frobenius theorem, there exists a real valued eigenvalue $\lambda(\theta)$ (the spectral radius) such that if λ is any other eigenvalue, then $|\lambda| < \lambda(\theta)$. Corresponding to $\lambda(\theta)$ is a positive (right) eigenvector $h(i, \theta)$ satisfying

$$\sum_{j=0}^{b} A_\theta(i, j) h(j, \theta) = \lambda(\theta) h(i, \theta). \qquad (33)$$

From Equation 33, we see that

$$P_\theta(i, j) = \frac{A_\theta(i, j) h(j, \theta)}{\lambda(\theta) h(i, \theta)} = \frac{e^{\theta j} P(i, j) h(j, \theta)}{\lambda(\theta) h(i, \theta)} \qquad (34)$$

defines the transition matrix of a Markov chain, which is called the conjugate process. Now apply importance sampling using the conjugate process. For simplicity assume the initial distribution using importance sampling is the same as in the original system. Thus by Equation 11, the likelihood ratio after T transitions is given by

$$L(\theta, T) = \prod_{t=1}^{T} \frac{P(a_{t-1}, a_t)}{P_\theta(a_{t-1}, a_t)} = \lambda(\theta)^T e^{-\theta A_T} H(\theta, T) \tag{35}$$

where $H(\theta, T) = h(a_0, \theta)/h(a_T, \theta)$. Let $S(T)$ denote the event that $Q_T \geq n$ and the queue has not emptied before time T. Then $A_T \geq Tc + n$ on $S(T)$, i.e., as in Equations 19 and 21, $A_T = Tc + n + O_T$ where O_T is the (nonnegative) overshoot at time T. Also, on $S(T)$, the likelihood ratio is given by

$$L(\theta, T) = \lambda(\theta)^T e^{-\theta(Tc+n+O_T)} H(\theta, T) = e^{-\theta n - \theta O_T + T[\log(\lambda(\theta)) - \theta c]} H(\theta, T). \tag{36}$$

Which value of θ should be chosen? Similar to the GI/GI/1 case in which we set $M(\theta^*) = 1$, by selecting $\theta = \theta^*$ so that $\log(\lambda(\theta^*)) - \theta^* c = 0$ (assuming it exists), we obtain the simplification that

$$L(\theta^*, T) = e^{-\theta^* n - \theta^* O_T} H(\theta^*, T). \tag{37}$$

Because the state space of the arrival process is finite, $O_T \leq b$ and there exist positive finite constants $\underline{H}$ and $\overline{H}$ such that $\underline{H} \leq H(\theta^*, T) \leq \overline{H}$. Thus, on $S(T)$ we have

$$e^{-\theta^*(n-b)} \underline{H} \leq L(\theta^*, T) \leq e^{-\theta^* n} \overline{H}. \tag{38}$$

Equation 38 implies both that $\lim_{n \to \infty} (1/n) \log(\gamma_n) = -\theta^*$ and that simulating the conjugate process with $\theta = \theta^*$ is asymptotically optimal. Thus finding the asymptotically optimal change of measure involves solving the nonlinear equation

$$\frac{\log(\lambda(\theta^*))}{\theta^*} = c. \tag{39}$$

If the source actually has independent arrivals, i.e., if $P(i, j) = p(j)$ for all i, then the model reduces to the waiting time in the GI/D/1 queue. In this case it can be shown that $\lambda(\theta) = M_A(\theta)$ and that Equation 39 is equivalent to $M(\theta^*) = 1$.

These results extend to the case when there are multiple independent arrival sources feeding the same queue. Suppose now that we have K independent Markovian sources defined by transition matrices $P_k(i, j)$ for $1 \leq k \leq K$. Note that a numerical solution of this model is typically infeasible. As above, let $\lambda_k(\theta)$ denote the spectral radius of the matrix defined by $A_{k,\theta}(i, j) = e^{\theta j} P_k(i, j)$ and let $h_k(i, \theta)$ denote the corresponding eigenvectors. If each source is twisted by the same parameter θ, i.e.,

$$P_{k,\theta}(i, j) = \frac{A_{k,\theta}(i, j) h_k(j, \theta)}{\lambda_k(\theta) h_k(i, \theta)}, \tag{40}$$

then as in Equation 36, on $S(T)$ the likelihood ratio at time T is given by

$$L(\theta, T) = \exp\left[-\theta n - \theta O_T + T\left(\sum_{k=1}^{K} \log(\lambda_k(\theta)) - \theta c\right)\right] H(\theta, T) \tag{41}$$

where now $H(\theta, T)$ is the (bounded) term involving the product of the eigenvector ratios as defined above. Thus, simulating each process with parameter θ^* where

$$\sum_{k=1}^{K} \frac{\log(\lambda_k(\theta^*))}{\theta^*} = c \qquad (42)$$

(assuming it exists) results in the likelihood ratio given by Equation 37. This again implies that $\lim_{n\to\infty}(1/n)\log(\gamma_n) = -\theta^*$ and yields an asymptotically optimal simulation scheme. Note that each source is still simulated independently, however the distributions of the sources are related by Equation 42.

More general types of arrival processes are also possible. For example, suppose source k is a Markov arrival process. In this model, there is an environment variable X_t^k and the distribution of arrivals is described by $P_k(a, j|i) = P(a_t^k = a, X_t^k = j|X_{t-1}^k = i)$. Let $\lambda_k(\theta)$ be the spectral radius of the matrix $A_{k,\theta}(i, j) = \sum_{a=0}^{b} e^{\theta a} P_k(a, j|i)$ and let $h_k(i, \theta)$ be the corresponding eigenvector. The twisted distribution is now given by

$$P_{k,\theta}(i, j) = P_\theta(a_t^k = a, X_t^k = j|X_{t-1}^k = i) = \frac{e^{\theta a} P_k(a, j|i)h_k(j, \theta)}{\lambda_k(\theta)h_k(i, \theta)}. \qquad (43)$$

Again, simulating each arrival process with twisting parameter θ^* where θ^* satisfies Equation 42 is asymptotically optimal.

The analysis above follows that described Chang, Heidelberger, Juneja and Shahabuddin [21, 22], however there are a number of related results and papers [8, 16, 17, 69, 87] that deal with large deviations of Markov additive processes. For example, Asmussen [8] considers the M/G/1 queue with Markov modulated arrivals. Although not primarily a simulation paper, Asmussen suggests using exponential twisting on the time reversed arrival process along with the maximum representation (in this case for the virtual waiting time) as described in Section 3.1. Descriptions of large deviations and asymptotically optimal simulation results for Markov additive process may be found [16, 17, 87]. Here the problem is estimating $P(S_n/n > a)$ $(a \geq 0)$ where $S_n = f(X_0)+\ldots+f(X_n)$ and $\{X_n\}$ is a Markov chain such that $\lim_{n\to\infty} S_n/n < 0$. These papers show that the twisted distribution is the unique asymptotically optimal change of measure within the class of all time-homogeneous Markov chains. Lehtonen and Nyrhinen [69] show that this is also the unique asymptotically optimal change of measure for estimating the distribution of the maximum of a Markov additive process with negative drift. Conditional limit theorems also exist for Markov additive processes (see [28]) showing that given a large value of S_n/n has occurred, the process got there according to the same distribution as the conjugate process. Similar results for a fluid model of a queue with a Markovian fluid-type arrival process are obtained in [10]. This provides additional interpretation as to why exponential twisting is asymptotically optimal.

These results are closely related to the theory of "effective bandwidths" in telecommunications; see [41, 52, 66] for early papers in this area. A comprehensive treatment of effective bandwidths is given in Chang [20]; see also Whitt

[100] for additional results and references. The effective bandwidth (also called the minimum envelope rate in [20]) of a source is given by

$$a^*(\theta) = \lim_{T \to \infty} \frac{\log\left(E[e^{\theta A_T}]\right)}{\theta T} \tag{44}$$

(assuming the limit exists). The existence of this limit (plus some technical assumptions) is sufficient to show that the stationary queue length distribution has an exponentially decreasing tail with rate θ^* where $a^*(\theta^*) = c$, i.e., $\lim_{n \to \infty}(1/n)\log(P(Q > n)) = -\theta^*$ where Q has the stationary queue length distribution. (If the limit in Equation 44 does not exist, but the lim sup is given by $a^*(\theta)$, then the tail of the stationary queue length distribution decreases at least as fast as an exponential with rate $-\theta^*$.)

The relationship between these effective bandwidth results and fast simulation is explored in [21, 22]. Consider, for example, the Markovian arrival process in which $P(a_t = j | a_{t-1} = i) = P(i, j)$. Then

$$E[e^{\theta A_T}] = E_\theta[L(\theta, T)e^{\theta A_T}] = \lambda(\theta)^T E_\theta[H(\theta, T)] \tag{45}$$

where the second equality follows from Equation 35. Thus,

$$\lim_{T \to \infty} \frac{\log\left(E[e^{\theta A_T}]\right)}{\theta T} = \frac{\log(\lambda(\theta))}{\theta} = a^*(\theta). \tag{46}$$

Thus the effective bandwidth equation $a^*(\theta^*) = c$ is identical to the asymptotically optimal fast simulation Equation 39. The key idea is found in Equation 35 which implies that

$$\underline{H}(\theta) \le \frac{L(\theta, T)e^{\theta A_T}}{e^{\theta a^*(\theta)T}} \le \overline{H}(\theta). \tag{47}$$

More generally, if a family of processes (called envelope processes in [21, 22]) can be found such that the likelihood ratio with respect to the original distribution satisfies the likelihood ratio bounds of Inequalities 47, then Equation 44 holds, simulation with parameter θ^* such that $a^*(\theta^*) = c$ is asymptotically optimal for estimating γ_n, and $\lim_{n \to \infty}(1/n)\log(\gamma_n) = -\theta^*$. For multiple independent arrival processes, the coupling equation is the same as Equation 42, i.e., $a_1^*(\theta^*) + \ldots + a_K^*(\theta^*) = c$ and simulation with this value of θ^* is asymptotically optimal. This is true for essentially any type of arrival process (e.g., autoregressive), provided 47 is true, in which case the conditions for the Gärtner-Ellis theorem (see [16, 32, 38]) relating to large deviations results for A_T/T are basically satisfied, where A_T is the sum of random variables that may have a very general dependency structure. Thus, the Gärtner-Ellis theorem, effective bandwidths, and fast simulation are all closely related.

It is observed in [22] that envelope processes can be constructed by minimizing the relative entropy rate, or Kullback-Leibler distance (subject to a drift constraint); see also [16, 26] for applications of the Kullback-Leibler distance in large deviations, and [67] in which a related fast simulation heuristic for on-off Markovian fluid sources is proposed. (This distance is defined as $K(P', P) = \int \log(dP'/dP)dP'$.) The splitting technique described in Section 2.4 can be used to estimate quantities such as the steady state buffer loss probability. Define an A-cycle to begin whenever the queue is empty. Note that the expected number of packets lost during an A-cycle is zero unless $\tau_n < \tau_0$ where n is the buffer size. Thus, (asymptotically optimal) importance sampling can be used to bring the queue up to level n at which point it can be turned off allowing the queue to empty again. This technique was shown to be very effective in [21, 22].

3.5 Networks of Queues

There are fewer papers on fast simulation of rare events in networks of queues, and the situation is currently not as well understood as in the single queue case. Rather than giving a detailed description of results for networks, a set of references will simply be given. Papers dealing with overflows in Jackson networks include [3, 34, 35, 36, 58, 83, 97]. In such networks, roughly speaking, a buildup to an overflow occurs along the same path that the corresponding time-reversed network (see [65]) empties from such an overflow, but in the opposite direction.

Large deviations results for the the way in which rare certain rare events happen in a class of multidimensional Markov jump processes are given in [94, 98]. Tree-structured networks of discrete time queues such as those considered in Section 3.4 have been studied in [21, 22].

Heuristics for simulating certain queueing networks that arise in high speed communications switches, such as a Clos switch, have been developed in Devetsikiotis and Townsend [29, 30, 31]. They consider a family of importance sampling change of measures parameterized by a (perhaps multidimensional) parameter θ; exponential twisting is one such example. Let $\sigma^2(\theta)$ denote the (unknown) variance of the estimator using importance sampling with parameter θ. The basic idea is to run relatively short pilot studies to obtain estimates of $\sigma^2(\theta)$ and then select the value of θ^* that optimizes the estimated variance for use in longer runs. This can be done dynamically within stochastic optimization procedures similar to simulated annealing, although some care has to be taken to discard values of θ with exceptionally small estimates of $\sigma^2(\theta)$, since in finite samples "overbiasing" the simulation can lead to small estimates of $\sigma^2(\theta)$ with high probability even though the actual value of $\sigma^2(\theta)$ is high. Other heuristics for some networks have been proposed in [12].

4 Reliability Models

We now turn to a discussion of fast simulation techniques for models of highly reliable systems. An additional overview of this material may be found in [82]. The general class of models that we will be interested in simulating are basically those that can be described by the SAVE (System AVailability Estimator) modeling language [49, 48] that has been developed at IBM Research (initially in cooperation with Kishor Trivedi of Duke University for modeling language and numerical algorithm development and subsequently in cooperation with Peter Glynn of Stanford University for development of importance sampling techniques). The models are a class of generalized machine repairmen models. A system consists of components and repairmen; components may fail and repairmen repair failed components. When a component fails, it may "affect" other components (with some probability), thereby causing the other components to fail simultaneously. Components may fail in a variety of failure modes (according to some probability distribution). Associated with each failure mode is a set of components (possibly empty) to be affected, a repairman, and a repair distribution; all of these may be different for different failure modes. The operation of a component may "depend upon" the operation of certain other components. For example, a disk drive may need a control unit in order to access data; if the control unit fails, the disk drive has not failed (thereby requiring repair) but rather is said to be "dormant" to reflect its inoperable state. Similarly, the repair of a component may depend upon other components, e.g., repairing (restarting) an operating system requires an operational processor. The modeler describes Boolean-type conditions involving the states of the components under which the system as a whole is considered to be operational, or operating at a reduced level of performance. Thus the system as a whole can tolerate the failure of certain combinations of component failures. In SAVE, all failure and repair distributions are assumed to be exponentially distributed, although we will consider importance sampling for systems with non-exponential distributions as well. For small models, the generator matrix of the underlying CTMC can be constructed and numerical algorithms can be used to solve for the relevant output measures, e.g., steady state availability, mean time to system failure, system failure time distribution, etc. However, for large models consisting of many components, numerical techniques are not feasible and simulation is used. Since system failure events are (hopefully) rare, importance sampling can be used, and SAVE automatically incorporates a provably good importance sampling heuristic called "balanced failure biasing," which will be described in this section.

While the general approach of importance sampling can be applied, it must be done somewhat differently for reliability models than for queueing models. The main reason is that the rare events of interest happen in very different ways in these two types of systems. In queueing models, events such as buffer overflows happen because many events, none of which are particularly rare (e.g., shorter interarrival times and longer service times), combine to produce an event that is extremely rare. In highly dependable computing systems, there is a limited amount of redundancy, so system failure events happen because a few events, each of which is relatively rare (e.g., component failures), combine to produce an event that is extremely rare. Since importance sampling is effective when the simulation follows typical failure paths, different importance sampling approaches are required for queueing and reliability models.

4.1 Markovian Models

We begin by describing results for Markovian reliability models. We assume that the system can be described by CTMC with a finite space; let i and j denote generic states in the system and let $Q(i, j)$ be the generator matrix. We assume there are two types of transitions possible: failures and repairs. For state i, let $\lambda(i) = -Q(i, i)$ denote the total rate out of state i, let $\lambda_F(i)$ denote the total failure rate out of state i and let $\mu_R(i)$ denote the total repair rate out of state i, i.e., $\lambda_F(i) = \sum_{j \in F(i)} Q(i, j)$ where $F(i)$ denotes the set of failure transitions from state i and $\mu_R(i) = \sum_{j \in R(i)} Q(i, j)$ where $R(i)$ denotes the set of repair transitions from state i. Note that $\lambda(i) = \lambda_F(i) + \mu_R(i)$. We assume that there is a single state, 0, in which all components are operational (and thus there are no repair transitions); all other states are assumed to have at least one repair transition. In order to analyze importance sampling approaches, Shahabuddin [88, 89] parameterizes the generator matrix by a rarity parameter ϵ as follows: $Q(i, j) = q(i, j)\epsilon^{d(i,j)}$ for failure transitions where $d(i, j) \geq 1$ and $q(i, j)$ does not depend on ϵ. Also, $Q(i, j)$ is assumed not to depend upon ϵ for repair transitions. Allowing different exponents $d(i, j)$ in the failure rate transitions permits modeling of systems in which either:

- some components are much more reliable than others, or

- some failure modes are very unlikely, e.g., when a component fails, with some small probability it also causes other components to fail with it.

If $d(i, j)$ is the same for all failure transitions the system is said to be balanced; otherwise it is unbalanced. With this parameterization, for small ϵ, failure transitions are unlikely (except out of state 0 from which all transitions are failure transitions). The transition matrix of the embedded DTMC, $P(i, j) = Q(i, j)/\lambda(i)$ then has a similar form to $Q(i, j)$ (for $i \neq 0$), i.e., $P(i, j) = p(i, j)\epsilon^{d(i,j)} + o(\epsilon^{d(i,j)})$ for failure transitions and $P(i, j) = p(i, j) + o(1)$ for repair transitions. Since all transitions from state 0 are failures, the above representation for $P(0, j)$ does not hold; for state 0, $P(0, j) = p(i, j)\epsilon^{d(j)} + o(\epsilon^{d(j)})$, where $d(j) = d(0, j) - \min_k\{d(0, k)\}$. For state 0, it is assumed that any transitions directly into a system failure state are unlikely, i.e., $d(j) \geq 1$ for $j \in F$ (otherwise system failure events are not rare).

Regenerative simulation, starting in state 0, can be used to estimate steady state measures and the mean time to failure using the ratio formula 15 to estimate $\gamma(\epsilon) = P_0(\tau_F < \tau_0)$, the probability, starting in state 0, of hitting a failure state before returning to 0. Shahabuddin shows that there exists an $r \geq 1$ such that $\gamma(\epsilon) = c\epsilon^r + o(\epsilon^r)$. This generalizes a result in [40], although the value of r is typically unknown. Thus we are faced with a rare event simulation. Note that without importance sampling, a typical cycle consists of a failure transition followed by one or more repair transitions until returning to state 0.

In general, we would like to apply importance sampling so as to sample most often from the most likely paths to failure. However, in complex systems, it may not be easy to identify these most likely paths. Thus, heuristics that are simple to implement need to be developed that search many different paths to failure, yet sample often enough from the most likely failure paths so as to obtain variance reduction. The basic class of techniques known as failure biasing is designed to do this. The first such technique, known as simple failure biasing, was introduced in [70]. In simple failure biasing, if $i \neq 0$, the probability of failure events is increased by selecting a failure transition with some fixed probability p that does not depend on ϵ. Note that in the original system (without importance sampling) the probability of this event is $\lambda_F(i)/\lambda(i)$ which is very small. If a failure transition is selected, then the failure transition to state j is selected proportionally to the original transition rates, i.e., with probability $Q(i,j)/\lambda_F(i)$. If a repair transition is selected, with probability $(1-p)$, then the repair transition to state j is selected with probability $Q(i,j)/\mu_R(i)$. In the original system, the probability of a repair event is very close to one. Note that to estimate $\gamma(\epsilon)$, only the embedded DTMC need be simulated; the likelihood ratio is obtained from Equation 11. Typically, p is chosen so that $0.25 \leq p \leq 0.9$.

Using simple failure biasing, the system ends up in a system failure state, at least some appreciable fraction of the time. However, it may not follow the most likely path to system failure, as the following simple example of an unbalanced system illustrates. Consider a system with two types of components. There is one component of type 1 that has failure rate ϵ^2 and three components of type 2 that each have failure rate ϵ. The system is considered operational if least one component of each type is operational. Under simple failure biasing, given that a failure event occurs, it is a type 1 failure with probability $\epsilon^2/(N_2\epsilon + \epsilon^2)$ where N_2 is the number of operational type 2 components; this probability is of order ϵ. Similarly, the (conditional) probability of a type 2 failure is $(1 - O(\epsilon))$. Thus, under simple failure biasing, when the system ends up in a failure state, most of the time it gets there by having three type 2 component failures. It only rarely (with probability of order ϵ) ends up in the state in which component 1 is failed. However, the path with a single component 1 failure is the most likely path to system failure; its probability is of order ϵ whereas any other system failure path has a much smaller probability of order ϵ^2. Thus while simple failure biasing takes the system to the set of failure states with reasonable probability, it does not push the system along the right failure path often enough. The result of this is that simple failure biasing applied to unbalanced systems may result in estimates having unbounded relative error. On the other hand, when simple failure biasing is applied to balanced systems, bounded relative error (asymptotically optimal as $\epsilon \to 0$) estimates are obtained [88, 89].

To overcome this problem, "balanced failure biasing" was introduced in [51, 88]; its asymptotic optimality for estimating $\gamma(\epsilon)$ was established in [88, 89] and experimental results are presented in [51]. In balanced failure biasing, a failure transition is again selected with probability p. Now however, given a failure event has occurred, the probabilities of all failure transitions are equalized, i.e., a failure transition from i to j is (conditionally) selected with probability $1/|F(i)|$ where $|F(i)|$ is the number of failure transitions from state i (or more generally selected from a distribution that is independent of ϵ). As in simple failure biasing, given a repair transition has been selected, the repair transition to state j is selected with probability $Q(i,j)/\mu_R(i)$. The proof technique in [88, 89] is matrix algebraic in nature, however a proof based on bounded likelihood ratios is also possible [61, 72, 74]; if $\tau_F < \tau_0$, then the likelihood ratio $L(X) \leq D[\epsilon^r + o(\epsilon^r)]$ for some random variable D that does not depend on ϵ. For estimating steady state unavailability, balanced failure biasing can be used until the set of system failure states is hit, and then importance sampling can be turned off until the start of the next cycle.

Note that in the example above, balanced failure biasing brings the system to the most likely failure state with probability 0.5 in one transition. Mathematically, balancing prevents the denominator of the likelihood ratio from getting too small, thereby producing stable estimates. Under balanced failure biasing, many unlikely paths to system failure may be generated, but enough of the most likely such paths are generated so as to guarantee good estimates. Nakayama [72, 73] formalizes the notion of most likely failure paths in this setting by showing that, given $\tau_F < \tau_0$, there exists a limiting (conditional) distribution on the set of paths. He also shows that balanced failure biasing results in asymptotically optimal estimates of the derivative of $\gamma(\epsilon)$ with respect to the failure rate of a component, as $\epsilon \to 0$. (See also [76] for empirical results.) Further analysis that characterizes when these and more general failure biasing schemes are efficient is given in Nakayama [74, 75].

For estimating transient quantities, such as the unreliability $U(t) = P(\tau_F \leq t)$, failure biasing needs to be augmented with a technique called "forcing" [70] which basically forces the first transition to occur before time t with high probability (perhaps 1). (For a fixed value of t, the probability that the first transition occurs before time t approaches zero as $\epsilon \to 0$.) If t is "small" (i.e., fixed), then balanced failure biasing and forcing produce bounded relative error estimates of $U(t)$ [91]. For "large" values of t, the empirical effectiveness of this technique decreases [51], and a somewhat different approach must be taken. This problem is analyzed in Shahabuddin and Nakayama [91]. Suppose $\lambda(0) = c\epsilon^{b_0} + o(\epsilon^{b_0})$, i.e., the mean holding time in state 0 is of order $1/\epsilon^{b_0}$. By the ratio formula Equation 15, $E_0[\tau_F]$ is of order $1/\epsilon^{r+b_0}$. Thus if $t_\epsilon = t/\epsilon^b$ where $b < b_0$, then both the first event occurring before time t_ϵ and the event $\tau_F < \tau_0$ are rare and balanced failure biasing with forcing is effective. However, if $t_\epsilon = t/\epsilon^b$ where $b_0 < b < r + b_0$, $\tau_F \leq t_\epsilon$ will still be a rare event, however the previous approach will be inefficient. In this case, importance sampling extends over a long time horizon and it is known that the variance of the likelihood ratio blows up in such cases [44]. In this case, the regenerative structure of the system can be exploited to estimate (tight) upper and lower bounds on $U(t)$, e.g.,

$$U(t) \leq \overline{U}(t) = 1 - e^{-\gamma(\epsilon)\lambda(0)t}. \tag{48}$$

This bound is true because $\tau_F \geq E_1 + \ldots E_N$ where N is geometric with success probability $\gamma(\epsilon)$ and the E_i's are i.i.d. exponentials with rate $\lambda(0)$, independent of N. For $t_\epsilon = t/\epsilon^b$ where $0 < b < r + b_0$, $U(t_\epsilon)/\overline{U}(t_\epsilon) \to 1$ and the upper bound $\overline{U}(t_\epsilon)$ is efficiently estimated by estimating $\gamma(\epsilon)$ using balanced failure biasing. If

$t_\epsilon = t/\epsilon^b$ where $b > r + b_0$, then the problem is no longer a rare event simulation. Conditions under which efficient large t estimates of the derivative of $U(t)$ (with respect to a failure rate) are obtained are also given in [91]. A similar approach to efficient estimation of another transient quantity, the expected fraction of time the system is unavailable during the interval $(0, t)$, is considered in Shahabuddin [90]. A different approach to estimating $U(t)$ is presented in Carrasco [19]. Instead of estimating $U(t)$, its Laplace transform $\hat{U}(s) = E[e^{-sT_F}]$ is estimated at a number of values of s. The regenerative structure is again exploited by deriving a renewal equation for $\hat{U}(s)$ in terms of quantities defined over a single cycle that can easily be estimated. Numerical inversion of the estimated Laplace transform is then used to recover estimates of $U(t)$.

Carrasco [18, 19] considers another failure biasing approach, termed failure distance biasing, that attempts to improve on the efficiency of balanced failure biasing by giving more weight to sample paths that are "closer" to the set of system failure states F. In this approach, failure transitions are grouped into classes based on their estimated distance to F and more weight is given to the classes corresponding to shorter distances. Once a class is chosen, if the probabilities given to individual transitions within the class are chosen proportionally to their original rates (as in simple failure biasing), then unbounded relative error may occur in an unbalanced system (see [75] for an example). However, if the probabilities given to individual transitions within the class are balanced, then a result in [88] implies that the resulting estimate has bounded relative error. In practice, the success of this approach depends on the ability to correctly (and efficiently) assign the distances; the class of systems for which this can be done is unclear. In some cases, significant improvements over balanced failure biasing have been obtained for systems with a large number of component types.

The above papers all assume that the repair rate is nonzero for all states, other than state 0. However, in some models this may not be the case, e.g., if repairs are deferred until a sufficient number of components are failed. Juneja and Shahabuddin [62] show that standard balanced failure biasing need not be asymptotically optimal in such situations. However, a generalization of balanced failure biasing is shown to be asymptotically optimal for balanced systems in [62].

4.2 Non-Markovian Reliability Models

We now turn to a discussion of importance sampling for highly reliable systems in which the failure and repair time distributions are not exponentially distributed. Although other techniques have been proposed (see, e.g., [39, 79, 80]), in this section we will concentrate on showing how balanced failure biasing can be generalized by appropriately applying importance sampling to a uniformization based simulation algorithm. This approach also produces bounded relative error estimates for estimating the unreliability $U(t)$ (under appropriate technical conditions). The discussion here follows that in [56, 57, 78, 81] and is based on the notion of hazard rates [13], e.g., if component i has failure density $f_i(x)$ and distribution function $F_i(x)$, then its failure hazard rate is $h_i(x) = f_i(x)/[1 - F_i(x)]$. For an exponential distribution, the hazard rate is constant. If component i is new at time 0, then the probability that it fails in the interval $(x, x + dx)$, given that it has not failed before time x, is approximately $h_i(x)dx$. Similarly, let $r_i(x)$ denote the hazard rate of component i's repair distribution. For simplicity, we assume that there are N components that can either be operational or failed (these assumptions can be relaxed). At simulation time s, let $O(s)$ denote the set of operational components and let $F(s)$ denote the set of failed components. Let $\lambda_i(s)$ denote the failure (hazard) rate of component i at time s, $\lambda_i(s) = h_i(A_i(s))$ where $A_i(s)$ is the age of component i at time s if $i \in O(s)$, and $\lambda_i(s) = 0$ if $i \notin O(s)$. Similarly, let $\mu_i(s)$ denote the repair rate of component i at time s, which is zero if i is not undergoing repair at time s. We assume that the component failure hazard rates are small and that repair distribution hazard rates are bounded from above and below, i.e., there exist positive, finite constants $\underline{\lambda}, \overline{\lambda}, \underline{\mu}, \overline{\mu}$ such that $\underline{\lambda}\epsilon^{b_i} \leq \lambda_i(s) \leq \overline{\lambda}\epsilon^{b_i}$ where $b_i \geq 1$ and $\underline{\mu} \leq \mu_i(s) \leq \overline{\mu}$. The total failure and repair rates at time s are given by $\lambda_F(s) \equiv \sum_i^N \lambda_i(s)$ and $\mu_R(s) \equiv \sum_i^N \mu_i(s)$, respectively. The total event rate at time s is $\lambda(s) \equiv \lambda_F(s) + \mu_R(s)$. Note the similarity between this situation and that in the Markovian case.

Consider a uniformization based simulation of this process. Generate a Poisson process $\{N_\beta(s)\}$ with rate β such that $\lambda(s) \leq \beta$ for all $0 \leq s \leq t$. Suppose an event in this process occurs at time S. Then the event is a component i failure with probability $\lambda_i(S)/\beta$, it is a component i repair with probability $\mu_i(S)/\beta$, and it is a pseudo-event (i.e., no event at all) with probability $1 - \lambda(S)/\beta$. Given that an event is real (i.e., failure or repair), it is a failure with probability $\lambda_F(S)/\lambda(S)$, which is small (provided $\mu_R(S) > 0$). The analog of balanced failure biasing is now apparent: given the event is real, increase the probability of a failure to p and decrease the probability of repair to $(1 - p)$. Then, if the event is a failure, pick component i to fail with probability $1/|O(S)|$, and if the event is a repair, repair component i with probability $\mu_i(S)/\mu_R(S)$. To be effective, the analog of forcing needs to be done in the transient case when no repairs are ongoing. We have also implicitly assumed that the components affected probabilities are not functions of ϵ and therefore do not require importance sampling, although this assumption can be relaxed. This approach can be described more generally by defining importance sampling failure and repair rates $\lambda_i'(s)$ and $\mu_i'(s)$ with which to do sampling such that $\lambda'(s) = \lambda_F'(s) + \mu_R'(s) \leq \beta$ for $(0 \leq s \leq t)$. Then the likelihood ratio at time t, $L(t) = L_F(t) \times L_R(t) \times L_P(t)$ where $L_F(t)$ is the failure event likelihood ratio, $L_R(t)$ is the repair event likelihood ratio, and $L_P(t)$ is the pseudo event likelihood ratio. For example, if component i fails $N_i(t)$ times in $(0, t)$ and T_{ij} denotes the j'th time that component i fails, then

$$L_F(t) = \prod_{i=1}^{N} \prod_{j=1}^{N_i(t)} \frac{\lambda_i(T_{ij})}{\lambda_i'(T_{ij})}. \tag{49}$$

If the importance sampling rates are chosen such that $\underline{\lambda'} \leq \lambda_i'(s) \leq \overline{\lambda'}$ whenever $\lambda_i(s) > 0$, $\underline{\mu'} \leq \mu_i'(s) \leq \overline{\mu'}$ whenever $\mu_i(s) > 0$, and $1 - \lambda'(s) \geq \underline{\beta'} > 0$ whenever $1 - \lambda(s) > 0$, then bounded relative error estimates are obtained for $U(t)$ [57].

The result is obtained by showing that $c(t)\epsilon^r \leq U(t)$ for some function $c(t)$ and $r \geq 1$, and then bounding the likelihood ratio when $\tau_f \leq t$: $L(t) \leq d^{N_\beta(t)}\epsilon^r$ for some constant $d \geq 1$. This establishes bounded relative error, but indicates that the method will only be effective for "small" values of t. "Large" t results for estimating $U(t)$, similar to the Markovian case, have not been obtained.

Since the hazard rate of some repair distributions may not be bounded (e.g., uniform and discrete distributions), the above importance sampling technique has been generalized so as to sample repairs from their given distributions, but to accelerate failure events with importance sampling. Under appropriate technical conditions, bounded relative error is still obtained when failure events are appropriately accelerated, e.g., either by using uniformization based importance sampling for failure events only as described above, or by sampling the time until the next failure event from an exponential distribution with rate bounded away from zero. These techniques can be adapted to steady state estimation using the ratio formula of Equation 16 and the splitting technique of Section 2.4, although bounded relative error has not been proven in this situation [81].

5 Summary

This paper has surveyed techniques for efficient simulation of rare events in queueing and reliability models. A number of common themes appear in both problem settings:

- Using importance sampling to accelerate the occurrence of the rare events.

- The notion of asymptotically optimal importance sampling.

- Obtaining asymptotically optimal importance sampling by bounding the likelihood ratio on the rare event of interest.

Among the differences between the two application settings are:

- In queueing models, the rare event happens because of a combination of a large number of events, none of which are particularly rare. In reliability models, rare events happen because of the occurrence of only a few events, each of which is itself rare. Thus different importance sampling approaches are required: exponential twisting in queueing models, failure biasing in reliability models. In addition, rare event probabilities in queueing models decrease exponentially at a known rate, whereas they decrease polynomially at an unknown rate in reliability models.

- Performing asymptotically optimal importance sampling of queueing models generally requires understanding quite a bit more about the structure of the problem, as compared to reliability models. Thus, the class of queueing models for which asymptotically optimal importance sampling algorithms are known is more limited.

- There is typically a unique asymptotically optimal change of measure for queueing models: exponential twisting with a certain parameter. Finding the optimal twisting parameter may be fairly complex, e.g., solving a nonlinear equation involving the largest eigenvalues of the sources as in the case of the discrete time queue with Markovian arrival processes. There is much more simplicity and flexibility in simulating reliability models: essentially any generalized form of balanced failure biasing is asymptotically optimal. Furthermore, there is flexibility in selecting the parameters of the failure biasing method, e.g., balanced failure biasing with any fixed p is asymptotically optimal, although the constant term in the variance can certainly be improved by, for example, selecting p appropriately.

- For the queueing models studied, the asymptotically optimal importance sampling distribution is equivalent to the (asymptotic) ordinary distribution, given that the rare event has occurred. For reliability models, it is harder to sample from the (asymptotic) ordinary distribution, given that the rare event has occurred. In practice, failure biasing techniques may devote a large fraction of the samples to highly unlikely sample paths.

- Thus, when the asymptotically optimal change of measure is known for a queueing model, better variance reduction is typically obtained than in reliability models (for estimating a probability of the same order of magnitude).

Acknowledgement

My understanding of importance sampling and rare event simulation has greatly benefited from interactions with my co-authors, whose names are listed in the bibliography. Special appreciation is due to Cheng-Shang Chang and Perwez Shahabuddin. Thanks also to Søren Asmussen for providing helpful comments on the manuscript.

References

[1] Al-Qaq, W.A., M. Devetsikiotis, and K.R. Townsend. 1993. Importance sampling methodologies for simulation of communication systems with adaptive equalizers and time-varying channels. *IEEE Journal on Selected Areas in Communications* 11: 317-327.

[2] Anantharam, V. 1988. How large delays build up in a GI/G/1 queue. *Queueing Systems* 5: 345-368.

[3] Anantharam, V., P. Heidelberger, and P. Tsoucas. 1990. Analysis of rare events in continuous time Markov chains via time reversal and fluid approximation. IBM Research Report RC 16280. Yorktown Heights, New York.

[4] Arsham, H., A. Fuerverger, D.L. McLeish, J. Kreimer, and R.Y. Rubinstein. 1989. Sensitivity analysis and the "what if" problem in simulation analysis. *Math. Comput. Modelling* 12: 193-219.

[5] Asmussen, S. 1982. Conditioned limit theorems relating a random walk to its associate. *Advances in Applied Probability* 14: 143-170.

[6] Asmussen, S. 1985. Conjugate processes and the simulation of ruin problems. *Stochastic Processes and their Applications* 20: 213-229.

[7] Asmussen, S. 1987 . *Applied Probability and Queues*. New York, NY: J. Wiley & Sons, Inc.

[8] Asmussen, S. 1989. Risk theory in a Markovian environment. *Scand. Actuarial J.*, 69-100.

[9] Asmussen, S. 1990. Exponential families and regression in the Monte Carlo study of queues and random walks. *The Annals of Statistics* 18: 1851-1867.

[10] Asmussen, S. 1993. Busy period analysis, rare events and transient behaviour in fluid models. To appear in *Journal of Applied Mathematics and Stochastic Analysis*.

[11] Asmussen, S., and R.Y. Rubinstein. 1992. The efficiency and heavy traffic properties of the score function method in sensitivity analysis of queueing models. *Advances in Applied Probability* 24: 172-201.

[12] Asmussen, S., R.Y. Rubinstein, and C.L. Wang. 1992. Efficient regenerative rare events simulation via the likelihood ratio method. Preprint.

[13] Barlow, R.E., and F. Proschan. 1981. *Statistical Theory of Reliability and Life Testing*. New York, NY: Holt, Reinhart and Winston, Inc.

[14] Breiman, L. 1968. *Probability*. Reading, MA: Addison-Wesley.

[15] Brown, M. 1990. Error bounds for exponential approximations of geometric convolutions. *The Annals of Probability* 18: 1388-1402.

[16] Bucklew, J. 1990. *Large Deviation Techniques in Decision, Simulation and Estimation*. New York, NY: J. Wiley & Sons, Inc.

[17] Bucklew, J.A., P. Ney, and J.S. Sadowsky. 1990. Monte Carlo simulation and large deviations theory for uniformly recurrent Markov chains. *J. Appl. Prob.* 27: 44-99.

[18] Carrasco, J.A. 1991. Failure distance-based simulation of repairable fault-tolerant systems. In *Proceedings of the Fifth International Conference on Modeling Techniques and Tools for Computer Performance Evaluation*, 337-351,

[19] Carrasco, J.A. 1991. Efficient transient simulation of failure/repair Markovian models. In *Proceedings of the Tenth Symposium on Reliable and Distributed Computing*, 152-161, IEEE Computer Society Press, Pisa, Italy.

[20] Chang, C.S. 1992. Stability, queue length and delay, Part II: Stochastic queueing networks. IBM Research Report RC 17709, Yorktown Heights, New York. Part of the report is published in *Proceedings of the IEEE CDC'92 Conference*, 1005-1010, IEEE Computer Society Press, Tucson, Arizona, 1992.

[21] Chang, C.S., P. Heidelberger, S. Juneja, and P. Shahabuddin. 1992. Effective bandwidth and fast simulation of ATM intree networks. IBM Research Report RC 18586, Yorktown Heights, New York. To appear in *Proceedings of the Performance '93 Conference*.

[22] Chang, C.S., P. Heidelberger, S. Juneja, and P. Shahabuddin. 1993. The application of effective bandwidth to fast simulation of communication networks. IBM Research Report RC 18877, Yorktown Heights, New York.

[23] Chen, H., and A. Mandelbaum. 1991. Discrete flow networks: bottleneck analysis and fluid approximations. *Mathematics of Operations Research* 16: 408-446.

[24] Çinlar, E. 1975. *Introduction to Stochastic Processes*. Englewood Cliffs, NJ: Prentice Hall, Inc.,

[25] Cogburn, R. 1975. A uniform theory for sums of Markov chain transition probabilities. *The Annals of Probability* 3: 191-214.

[26] Cottrell, M., J.C, Fort, and G. Malgouyres. 1983. Large deviations and rare events in the study of stochastic algorithms. *IEEE Transactions on Automatic Control* AC-28: 907-920.

[27] Crane, M.A., and D.L. Iglehart. 1975. Simulating stable stochastic systems III: regenerative processes and discrete event simulation. *Operations Research* 23: 33-45.

[28] Csiszár, I., T.M. Cover and B.-S. Choi. 1987. Conditional limit theorems under Markov conditioning. *IEEE Transactions on Information Theory* 33: 788-801.

[29] Devetsikiotis, M., and K.R. Townsend. 1992. On the efficient simulation of large communication networks using importance sampling. In *Proceedings of IEEE Globecom '92*, IEEE Computer Society Press.

[30] Devetsikiotis, M., and K.R. Townsend. 1992. A dynamic importance sampling methodology for the efficient estimation of rare event probabilities in regenerative simulations of queueing systems. In *Proceedings of the IEEE ICC '92 Conference*, 1290-1297, IEEE Computer Society Press.

[31] Devetsikiotis, M., and K.R. Townsend. 1993. Statistical optimization of dynamic importance sampling parameters for efficient simulation of communication networks. To appear in *IEEE/ACM Transactions on Networking*.

[32] Ellis, R. 1984. Large deviations for a general class of random vectors. *Annals of Probability* 12: 1-12.

[33] Feller, W. 1971. *An Introduction to Probability Theory and its Applications.* Vol. 2 (Second Edition). New York, NY: J. Wiley & Sons, Inc.

[34] Frater, M.R., and B.D.O. Anderson. 1989. Fast estimation of the statistics of excessive backlogs in tandem networks of queues. *Australian Telecommunications Research* 23: 49-55.

[35] Frater, M.R., R.R. Bitmead, R.A. Kennedy, and B.D.O. Anderson. 1989. Rare events and reverse time models. In *Proceedings of the 28th Conference on Decision and Control*, 1180-1183, IEEE Press.

[36] Frater, M.R., T.M. Lenon, and B.D.O. Anderson. 1991. Optimally efficient estimation of the statistics of rare events in queueing networks. *IEEE Transactions on Automatic Control* 36: 1395-1405.

[37] Frater, M.R., J. Walrand, and B.D.O. Anderson. 1990. Optimally efficient simulation of buffer overflows in queues with deterministic service times via importance sampling. *Australian Telecommunications Research* 24: 1-8.

[38] Gärtner, J. 1977. On large deviations from invariant measure. *Theory Probab. Appl.* 22: 24-39.

[39] Geist, R.M. and M.K. Smotherman. 1989. Ultrahigh reliability estimates through simulation. In *Proceedings of the Annual Reliability and Maintainability Symposium*, 350-355, IEEE Press.

[40] Gertsbakh, I.B. 1984. Asymptotic methods in reliability theory: A review. *Advances in Applied Probability* 16: 147-175.

[41] Gibbens, R.J., and P.J. Hunt. 1991. Effective bandwidths for the multi-type UAS channel. *Queueing Systems* 9: 17-28.

[42] Glasserman, P. 1993. Stochastic monotonicity and conditional Monte Carlo for likelihood ratios. *Advances in Applied Probability* 25: 103-115.

[43] Glynn, P.W. 1989. A GSMP formalism for discrete event systems. *Proceedings of the IEEE* 77: 14-23.

[44] Glynn, P.W. 1992. Importance sampling for Markov chains: asymptotics for the variance. Technical Report, Department of Operations Research, Stanford University, To appear in *Stochastic Models*.

[45] Glynn, P.W., and P. Heidelberger. 1992. Experiments with initial transient deletion for parallel, replicated steady-state simulations. *Management Science* 38: 400 - 418.

[46] Glynn, P.W., and D.L. Iglehart. 1989. Importance sampling for stochastic simulations. *Management Science* 35: 1367-1392.

[47] Glynn, P.W., and W. Whitt. 1992. The asymptotic efficiency of simulation estimators. *Operations Research* 40: 505-520.

[48] Goyal, A., W.C. Carter, E. de Souza e Silva, S.S. Lavenberg, and K.S. Trivedi. 1986. The System Availability Estimator. In *Proceedings of the Sixteenth International Symposium on Fault-Tolerant Computing*, 84-89, IEEE Computer Society Press.

[49] Goyal, A., and S.S. Lavenberg. 1987. Modeling and analysis of computer system availability. *IBM Journal of Research and Development* 31, 6: 651-664.

[50] Goyal, A., P. Heidelberger, and P. Shahabuddin. 1987. Measure specific dynamic importance sampling for availability simulations. In *1987 Winter Simulation Conference Proceedings*, 351-357, IEEE Press.

[51] Goyal, A., P. Shahabuddin, P. Heidelberger, V.F. Nicola, and P.W. Glynn. 1992. A unified framework for simulating Markovian models of highly reliable systems. *IEEE Transactions on Computers* C-41: 36-51.

[52] Guérin, R., H. Ahmadi and M. Naghshineh. 1991. Equivalent capacity and its application to bandwidth allocation in high-speed networks. *IEEE J. Select. Areas Commun.* 9: 968-981.

[53] Halton, J.H. 1970. A retrospective and prospective survey of the Monte Carlo method. *SIAM Review* 12: 1-60.

[54] Hammersley, J.M., and D.C. Handscomb, 1964. *Monte Carlo Methods*. London: Methuen and Co., Ltd.

[55] Heidelberger, P. 1988. Discrete event simulations and parallel processing: statistical properties. *SIAM Journal on Scientific and Statistical Computing* 9: 1114-1132.

[56] Heidelberger, P., Nicola, V.F., and Shahabuddin, P. 1992. Simultaneous and efficient simulation of highly dependable systems with different underlying distributions. In *Proceedings of the 1992 Winter Simulation Conference*, 458-465, IEEE Press.

[57] Heidelberger, P, P. Shahabuddin, and V.F. Nicola. 1993. Bounded relative error in estimating transient measures of highly dependable non-Markovian systems. IBM Research Report RC 18794, Yorktown Heights, New York.

[58] Heidelberger, P., and P. Tsoucas. 1991. Reverse time simulation of rare events. *IBM Technical Disclosures Bulletin* 34, No. 3: 163-165.

[59] Iglehart, D.L. 1972. Extreme values in the GI/G/1 queue. *Annals of Mathematical Statistics* 43: 627-635.

[60] Jensen, A. 1953. Markov chains as an aid in the study of Markov processes. *Skand. Aktuarietidskr.* 36: 87-91.

[61] Juneja, S. 1993. *Efficient Rare Event Simulation of Stochastic Systems.* Ph.D. Thesis, Department of Operations Research, Stanford University, California.

[62] Juneja, S., and P. Shahabuddin. 1992. Fast simulation of Markovian reliability/availability models with general repair policies. In *Proceedings of the Twenty-Second International Symposium on Fault-Tolerant Computing,* 150-159, IEEE Computer Society Press.

[63] Kalos, M.H., and P.A. Whitlock. 1986. *Monte Carlo Methods, Volume I: Basics.* New York, NY: John Wiley & Sons, Inc.

[64] Keilson, J. 1979. *Markov Chain Models - Rarity and Exponentiality,* New York, NY: Springer Verlag.

[65] Kelly, F.P. 1979. *Reversibility and Stochastic Networks.* New York, NY: John Wiley & Sons, Inc.

[66] Kelly, F.P. 1991. Effective bandwidths at multi-class queues. *Queueing Systems* 9: 5-16.

[67] Kesidis, G., and J. Walrand. 1993. Quick simulation of ATM buffers with on-off multiclass Markov fluid sources. To appear in *ACM Transactions on Modeling and Computer Simulation.*

[68] Lehtonen, T., and H. Nyrhinen. 1992. Simulating level-crossing probabilities by importance sampling. *Advances in Applied Probability* 24: 858-874.

[69] Lehtonen, T., and H. Nyrhinen. 1992. On asymptotically efficient simulation of ruin probabilities in a Markovian environment. *Scand. Actuarial. J.* 60-75.

[70] Lewis, E.E., and F. Bohm. 1984. Monte Carlo simulation of Markov unreliability models. *Nuclear Engineering and Design* 77: 49-62.

[71] Lewis, P.A.W., and G.S. Shedler. 1979. Simulation of nonhomogeneous Poisson processes by thinning. *Naval Research Logistics Quarterly* 26, 403-413.

[72] Nakayama, M.K. 1991. *Simulation of Highly Reliable Markovian and Non-Markovian Systems.* Ph.D. Thesis, Department of Operations Research, Stanford University, California.

[73] Nakayama, M.K. 1991. Asymptotics for likelihood ratio derivative estimators in simulations of highly reliable Markovian systems. IBM Research Report RC 17357, Yorktown Heights, NY.

[74] Nakayama, M.K. 1993. A characterization of the simple failure biasing method for simulations of highly reliable Markovian systems. IBM Research Report RC 18721, Yorktown Heights, New York.

[75] Nakayama, M.K. 1993. General conditions for bounded relative error in simulations of highly reliable Markovian systems. IBM Research Report RC 18993. Yorktown Heights, New York.

[76] Nakayama, M.K., A. Goyal and P.W. Glynn. 1990. Likelihood ratio sensitivity analysis for Markovian models of highly dependable systems. IBM Research Report RC 15400, Yorktown Heights, New York. To appear in *Operations Research*.

[77] Nicol, D.M., and D.L. Palumbo. 1993. Reliability analysis of complex models using SURE bounds. ICASE NASA Langley Research Center Technical Report 93-14.

[78] Nicola, V.F., P. Heidelberger and P. Shahabuddin. 1992. Uniformization and exponential transformation: techniques for fast simulation of highly dependable non-Markovian systems. In *Proceedings of the Twenty-Second International Symposium on Fault-Tolerant Computing*, 130-139, IEEE Computer Society Press.

[79] Nicola, V.F., M.K. Nakayama, P. Heidelberger and A. Goyal. 1990. Fast simulation of dependability models with general failure, repair and maintenance processes. In *Proceedings of the Twentieth International Symposium on Fault-Tolerant Computing*, 491-498, IEEE Computer Society Press.

[80] Nicola, V.F., M.K. Nakayama, P. Heidelberger, and A. Goyal. 1991. Fast simulation of highly dependable systems with general failure and repair processes. IBM Research Report RC 16993. Yorktown Heights, New York. To appear in *IEEE Transactions on Computers*.

[81] Nicola, V.F., P. Shahabuddin, P. Heidelberger and P.W. Glynn. 1993. Fast simulation of steady-state availability in non-Markovian highly dependable systems. In *Proceedings of the Twenty-Third International Symposium on Fault-Tolerant Computing*, 38-47, IEEE Computer Society Press.

[82] Nicola, V.F., P. Shahabuddin, and P. Heidelberger. 1993. Techniques for fast simulation of highly dependable systems. IBM Research Report RC 18956, Yorktown Heights, New York.

[83] Parekh, S., and J. Walrand. 1989. A quick simulation method for excessive backlogs in networks of queues. *IEEE Transactions on Automatic Control* 34: 54-56.

[84] Rubinstein, R.Y. 1991. How to optimize discrete-event systems from a single sample path by the score function method. *Annals of Operations Research* 27: 175-212.

[85] Sadowsky, J.S. 1991. Large deviations and efficient simulation of excessive backlogs in a GI/G/m queue. *IEEE Transactions on Automatic Control* 36: 1383-1394.

[86] Sadowsky, J.S. 1993. On the optimality and stability of exponential twisting in Monte Carlo estimation. *IEEE Transactions on Information Theory* 39: 119-128.

[87] Sadowsky, J.S., and J.A. Bucklew. 1990. On large deviations theory and asymptotically efficient Monte Carlo estimation. *IEEE Transactions on Information Theory* 36: 579-588.

[88] Shahabuddin, P. 1990. *Simulation and Analysis of Highly Reliable Systems.* Ph.D. Thesis, Department of Operations Research, Stanford University, California.

[89] Shahabuddin, P. 1991. Importance sampling for the simulation of highly reliable Markovian systems. IBM Research Report RC 16729, Yorktown Heights, New York. To appear in *Management Science.*

[90] Shahabuddin, P. 1993. Fast transient simulation of Markovian models of highly dependable systems. IBM Research Report RC 18587, Yorktown Heights, New York. To appear in *Proceedings of the Performance '93 Conference.*

[91] Shahabuddin, P., and M.K. Nakayama. 1993. Estimation of reliability and its derivatives for large time horizons in Markovian systems. IBM Research Report RC 18864, Yorktown Heights, New York. To appear in *Proceedings of 1993 Winter Simulation Conference.*

[92] Shahabuddin, P., V.F. Nicola, P. Heidelberger, A. Goyal, and P.W. Glynn. 1988. Variance Reduction in Mean Time to Failure Simulations. In *1988 Winter Simulation Conference Proceedings*, 491-499, IEEE Press.

[93] Shanthikumar, J.G. 1986. Uniformization and hybrid simulation/analytic models of renewal processes. *Operations Research* 34: 573-580.

[94] Shwartz, A., and A. Weiss. 1993. Induced rare events: analysis via time reversal and large deviations. To appear in *Advances in Applied Probability.*

[95] Siegmund, D. 1976. Importance sampling in the Monte Carlo study of sequential tests. *The Annals of Statistics* 4: 673-684.

[96] Smith, W.L. 1955. Regenerative stochastic processes. *Proc. Roy. Soc. Ser. A.* 232: 6-31.

[97] Tsoucas, P. 1989. Rare events in series of queues. IBM Research Report RC 15530, Yorktown Heights, New York.

[98] Weiss, A. 1986. A new technique for analyzing large traffic systems. *Advances in Applied Probability* 18: 506-532.

[99] Whitt, W. 1980. Continuity of generalized semi-Markov processes. *Mathematics of Operations Research* 5: 494-501.

[100] Whitt, W. 1993. Tail probability with statistical multiplexing and effective bandwidths in multi-class queues. To appear in *Telecommunication Systems*.

An Introduction to Modeling Dynamic Behavior With Time Series Analysis

Joseph L. Hellerstein

IBM Thomas J. Watson Research Center, Yorktown Heights, NY

Abstract. The need to model dynamic behavior in information systems arises in many contexts, such as characterizing the locality of file access patterns, evaluating the dynamic behavior of scheduling algorithms, and identifying performance problems by their time serial behavior. This paper provides an introduction to time series analysis (a statistical technique), and applies it to analyzing the performance of information systems. The autoregressive, moving average (ARMA) model is discussed in detail, with an emphasis on identifying time series models from measurement data using the autocorrelation and partial autocorrelation functions. The paper concludes with a case study in which time series analysis is used to diagnosis a performance problem in a large computer system.

1 Introduction

The need to model dynamic behavior in information systems arises in many contexts. Some examples include:

1. Designing a disk cache is facilitated by having a characterization of the time serial behavior of file access patterns.
2. Evaluating the dynamic behavior of a scheduling algorithm requires assessing its response to transients in arrival rates and service times.
3. Identifying performance problems in computer systems can often be accomplished by relating the dynamic behavior of the problem to the dynamic behavior of applications running on the computer system.

This paper describes time series analysis, a statistical approach to modeling dynamic behavior, and applies it to measurements of information systems. Considered are the autoregressive and moving average (ARMA) models, with an emphasis on model identification and evaluation. The paper concludes with a case study that applies time series analysis to diagnosing a performance problem in a large computer system.

A time series consists of serial measurements of a process, such as sequences of response times of computer system interactions. Herein, we assume that time is discrete (e.g., thirty second intervals) and that measurement values are continuous (i.e., we can, in theory, obtain an unlimited number of digits to the right of the decimal point). Throughout, t is used to denote the time index (or observation), and y_t denotes the value of the t-th observation. A time series can be displayed in either a tabular or a graphical manner. For example, Table 1 displays the first four observations of response times over a nine hour shift at a large computer installation, and Fig. 1 plots the response time data for the entire nine hour shift.

Table 1. Illustration of a Time Series

t	Time	Response Time
1	8:01:00	1.5
2	8:01:30	1.6
3	8:02:00	.75
4	8:02:30	1.8

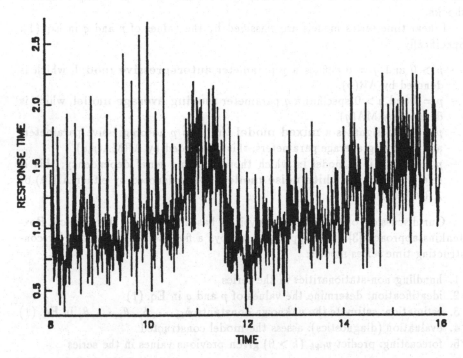

Fig. 1. Time Series Example

Constructing a time series model involves expressing y_t in terms of (i) previous observations (e.g., y_{t-1}, y_{t-2}) and (ii) shocks to the system, which are unobserved random variables that represent external events (e.g., changes in arrival rates and/or service times). In order to construct a time series model, y_t must be **stationary**. This means that (a) all terms in the series have the same mean and variance, (b) the covariance between terms in the series only depends on the number of time units between them (not their absolute position in the series), and (c) all of the foregoing are finite. The random shocks, which are denoted by a_t, are assumed to be independent and identically distributed (**i.i.d.**) with $E(a_t) = 0$ and $Var(a_t) = \sigma_a{}^2$.

A **time series model** specifies an algebraic relationship between random variables representing terms in the series; the t-th such random variable is denoted by $\tilde{y}_t$. (In contrast, the y_t are measured values, which are constants.) Since all terms in the series have the same mean, it is convenient to view $\tilde{y}_t$ as the deviation from the population mean; that is, $E(\tilde{y}_t) = 0$. Herein, we consider linear time series models that have the general form

$$\tilde{y}_t = \phi_1 \tilde{y}_{t-1} + \cdots + \phi_p \tilde{y}_{t-p} + a_t - \theta_1 a_{t-1} - \cdots - \theta_q a_{t-q}. \tag{1}$$

(It is a convention that a_{t-k} $(k > 0)$ be subtracted.) This equation states that the t-th term depends on the preceding p terms and on the preceding q random shocks.

Linear time series models are classified by the values of p and q in Eq. (1). Specifically,

- $p > 0$ and $q = 0$ defines a p parameter **autoregressive model**, which is denoted by AR(p).
- $p = 0$ and $q > 0$ specifies a q parameter **moving average model**, which is denoted by MA(q).
- $p, q > 0$ designates a **mixed model** that has p autoregressive parameters and q moving-average parameters; this is denoted by ARMA(p,q).
- $p = 0 = q$ is a model in which there no time serial dependency; this is referred to as the **white noise model**, and is denoted by either AR(0) or ARMA(0,0).

Our discussion of time series analysis is based largely on the classical Box-Jenkins approach [3]. This approach employs a five-step methodology for constructing time series models:

1. handling non-stationarities in the series
2. identification: determine the values of p and q in Eq. (1)
3. estimation: estimate the unknown constants $\phi_1, \cdots, \phi_p, \theta_1, \cdots, \theta_q$ in Eq. (1)
4. evaluation (diagnostics): assess the model constructed
5. forecasting: predict y_{t+k} $(k > 0)$ given previous values in the series

In practice, steps (1)-(4) are applied repeatedly before proceeding to step (5). Herein, we focus steps (1)-(4), with particular emphasis on the first two steps.

Applying time series analysis in practice requires that the analyst obtain values of a metric of interest (i.e., the y_t) and then apply the foregoing methodology to construct a time series model. How the model is used depends on the task at hand. In the case of workload characterization, y_t is a workload parameter, such as CPU consumption or input/output rates; the time series model can be used to generate a synthetic workload for a more complex system by using a random number generator to obtain the a_t. When evaluating the transient behavior of a scheduling algorithm, y_t is the performance of the system studied when the algorithm is employed; the time series model is used to evaluate the effect of transients by predicting y_{t+j} when the a_t are varied. For diagnosing performance problems, y_t is a metric that is used to detect performance problem; the cause of the problem can sometimes be deduced from the terms in the time series model.

Numerous books and articles have been written on the theory of time series analysis (e.g., [3], [12]). Unfortunately, it has been rare to apply time series analysis to information systems. One case in which it has been employed is forecasting the growth of workloads in computer systems (e.g., [6] and [8]), which is an important part of capacity planning. Another case in which time serial behavior is important is characterizing packet interarrival times in communications networks. Frequently, these interarrivals are not i.i.d. due to "train" effects induced by large transmissions (e.g., file transfers). For the most part, dependencies in interarrival times have been addressed using Markov modulated processes (e.g., [1], [4], [10], and [11]). However, time series techniques have been employed occasionally (e.g., [7]).

The remainder of this paper is organized as follows. Section 2 discusses how to identify and evaluate time series models given measurements of a stationary stochastic process. Section 3 addresses how to handle non-stationary data, which are common in information systems because of variations in workload. Section 4 contains a case study of applying time series analysis to diagnosing a performance problem. Our conclusions are contained in section 5.

2 Time Series Models

This section discusses how to construct ARMA(p,q) models, with an emphasis on AR(1) because of its importance in modeling dynamic behavior in queueing systems. We focus on the identification step in time series analysis, although the estimation and evaluation steps are considered as well. Throughout this section it is assumed that the underlying stochastic process is stationary. (Section 3 addresses non-stationary processes.)

A simple and very intuitive way to express time serial dependencies is to state that the current observation depends only on the previous observation and an i.i.d. random shock. This is the one parameter autoregressive model, or AR(1), which is expressed algebraically as

$$\tilde{y}_t = \phi \tilde{y}_{t-1} + a_t, \tag{2}$$

where $\phi = \phi_1$ in Eq. (1). (Readers familiar with the theory of stochastic processes will recognize the AR(1) model as a discrete-time, continuous-state Markov chain.) Key to this equation is the parameter ϕ, which determines how related successive observations are. If $|\phi| \approx 1$, we know much more about $\tilde{y}_t$ given $\tilde{y}_{t-1}$ than is the case if $|\phi| \approx 0$.

More insight into AR(1) processes can be obtained by expanding the recurrence relationship in Eq. (2).

$$\tilde{y}_t = \phi \tilde{y}_{t-1} + a_t$$
$$= \phi^2 \tilde{y}_{t-2} + \phi a_{t-1} + a_t$$
$$= \sum_{k=0}^{\infty} \phi^k a_{t-k}$$

This equation suggests that ϕ should be constrained so that $|\phi| < 1$. If this were not the case, shocks to the system that occurred in the distant past would have a larger effect on $\tilde{y}_t$ than shocks in the recent past (due to the exponent k of ϕ).

The importance of the $|\phi| < 1$ constraint can be demonstrated analytically by computing the variance of an AR(1) process. Since $E(\tilde{y}_t) = 0$, we have

$$
\begin{aligned}
Var(\tilde{y}_t) &= E(\tilde{y}_t \tilde{y}_t) \\
&= E[(\sum_{i=0}^{\infty} \phi^i a_{t-i})(\sum_{j=0}^{\infty} \phi^j a_{t-j})] \\
&= \sum_{k=0}^{\infty} \phi^{2k} E(a_{t-k} a_{t-k}) \\
&= \frac{\sigma_a^2}{1-\phi^2}
\end{aligned}
\tag{3}
$$

(The third equation follows from the a_t being i.i.d.) Thus, unless $|\phi| < 1$, the variance of $\tilde{y}_t$ is infinite, which means the process is nonstationary.

The AR(1) model is often effective at characterizing the dynamic behavior of queueing systems. To illustrate this, we develop an approximation for the dynamic behavior of a single server, first-come first-served (FCFS) queueing system. Let R_t, A_t, and S_t denote (respectively) the response time, interarrival time, and service time of the t-th customer arriving at the queueing system. For a lightly loaded system, we have

$$R_t = S_t,$$

and for a saturated system

$$R_t = R_{t-1} - A_t + S_t.$$

Thus, the general situation can be approximated by

$$R_t = \phi(R_{t-1} - A_t) + S_t,$$

where $0 \leq \phi < 1$ (to ensure finite response times). Put differently,

$$R_t - E[R_t] = \phi(R_{t-1} - E[R_t]) - \phi A_t + S_t + C, \tag{4}$$

where C is a constant. Letting $\tilde{y}_t = R_t - E(R_t)$ and $a_t = -\phi A_t + S_t + C$, Eq. (4) becomes $\tilde{y}_t = \phi \tilde{y}_t + a_t$, which is an AR(1) model.

How accurately does Eq. (4) model the dynamic behavior of a single server, FCFS queueing system? Commonly used statistics such as the sample mean, variance, and distribution do not answer this question since they provide no insight into time serial dependencies. An alternative is to compare plots of time serial FCFS response times with realizations of potential AR(1) models. Figure 2 contains such plots for an M/M/1, FCFS queueing system (with an arrival rate of .7 and a service time of 1) and three AR(1) processes with different values of ϕ; in all cases, initial transients have been deleted and so the values plotted constitute a stationary series. Unfortunately, it is unclear how these plots should be compared, and so it is unclear which AR(1) model (if any) adequately characterizes the dynamic behavior of the FCFS queueing system.

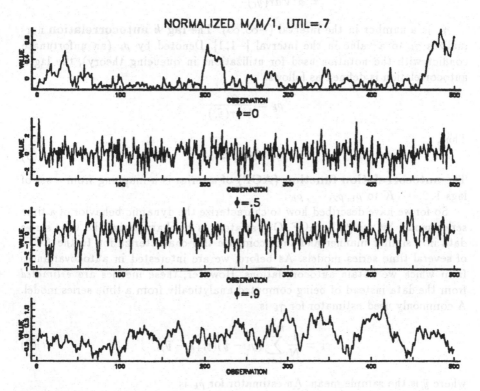

Fig. 2. Comparison of Several Time Series

The foregoing motivates the first step in time series analysis – model identification. The objective of this step is to use measurements of a stochastic process to determine a good choice for p and q in Eq. (1). Doing so requires having a way to characterize the time serial behavior of a stochastic process. One approach is to quantify the relationship between all observations separated by the same number of time units or **lags**. For example, lag 1 "relatedness" can be assessed from the pairs $(\tilde{y}_t, \tilde{y}_{t-1}), (\tilde{y}_{t-1}, \tilde{y}_{t-2}), \cdots$ and lag 2 "relatedness" from the pairs $(\tilde{y}_t, \tilde{y}_{t-2}), (\tilde{y}_{t-1}, \tilde{y}_{t-3}), \cdots$. Relatedness can be quantified by the covariance function; since this is applied to elements of the same series, it is referred to as autocovariance. The lag k **autocovariance** is denoted by γ_k, and is defined as

$$\gamma_k = E(\tilde{y}_t \tilde{y}_{t-k}).$$

(Since y_t is assumed to be stationary, γ_k does not depend on t.) γ_k can be computed directly from a time series model. For AR(1), this calculation is

$$\begin{aligned}
\gamma_k[AR(1)] &= E[\tilde{y}_t \tilde{y}_{t-k}] \\
&= E\left[\left(\sum_{j=0}^{k-1} \phi^j a_{t-j} + \phi^k \tilde{y}_{t-k}\right) \tilde{y}_{t-k}\right] \\
&= \phi^k Var(\tilde{y}_t)
\end{aligned}$$

γ_k is a number in the interval $(-\infty, \infty)$. The **lag k autocorrelation** normalizes γ_k to a value in the interval $[-1, 1]$. Denoted by ρ_k (an unfortunate conflict with the notation used for utilizations in queueing theory), the lag k autocorrelation is defined as follows:

$$\rho_k = \frac{\gamma_k}{Var(\tilde{y}_t)}$$

Thus,

$$\rho_k[AR(1)] = \phi^k \qquad (5)$$

The **autocorrelation function (ACF)** of a series is a mapping from a set of lags $1, 2, \cdots, K$ to $\rho_1, \rho_2, \cdots, \rho_K$.

So for we have described how to characterize the dynamic behavior of a time series model by using the ACF. Our strategy is to characterize the time series data in a similar manner and then compare this characterization to the ACFs of several time series models. As before, we are interested in autocovariances from which we obtain autocorrelations. However, these metrics are *estimated* from the data instead of being computed analytically from a time series model. A commonly used estimator for γ_k is

$$c_k = \frac{1}{N} \sum_{i=1}^{N-k} (y_k - \bar{y})(y_{i+k} - \bar{y}), \qquad (6)$$

where $\bar{y}$ is the sample mean. An estimator for ρ_k is

$$r_k = \frac{c_k}{c_0}.$$

(Note that c_0 is the sample variance.) Since r_k only *estimates* ρ_k for the stochastic process that produced the time series data, it is important to know when r_k values are truly significant and when, due to randomness in the measurements collected, an r_k is approximately 0. Such concerns are addressed by the Bartlett bound [3], which tests the hypothesis (at each lag) that $r_k = 0$ at a specified significance level. Figure 3 displays autocorrelations (vertical bars) versus lags for the time series data in Fig. 1. The Bartlett bounds (at the 5% significance level) are depicted by the dotted lines; bars that lie within the bounds are not considered different from 0. Note that the M/M/1 data have an ACF that has

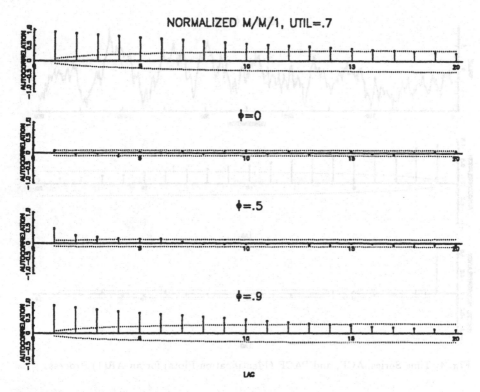

Fig. 3. Empirical ACFs with Bartlett Bounds

the form of a damped exponential, and all three AR(1) models have an ACF that decays in a similar manner (as suggested by Eq. (5) with $0 < \phi < 1$). However, none of the AR(1) models has a decay that is as long as that for the M/M/1 data, which suggests that $\phi > .9$.

One drawback of using the ACF for model identification is that terms in the ACF are highly correlated. For example, the AR(1) model expresses a *direct* relationship between $\bar{y}_t$ and $\bar{y}_{t-1}$. However, depending on ϕ, $\bar{y}_t$ may also have a large correlation with $\bar{y}_{t-2}$ $\bar{y}_{t-3}$, and so on. This situation can be remedied by using the **partial autocorrelation function (PACF)**, which computes the lag k autocorrelation after having removed autocorrelations for lags $1, 2, \cdots, k-1$. As with the ACF, bounds can be computed for the PACF; herein, a 5% significance level is used. The PACF is commonly displayed in combination with the original time series and the series' ACF; together, we refer to these as the **identification plots**. Figure 4 contains the identification plots for a realization of an AR(1) process with $\phi = .9$. Note that the PACF is a single spike; this follows from the fact that once the lag 1 autocorrelation is removed from $\bar{y}_t$, only a_t remains and the a_t are i.i.d..

After model identification, we proceed to the estimation step. Algorithms

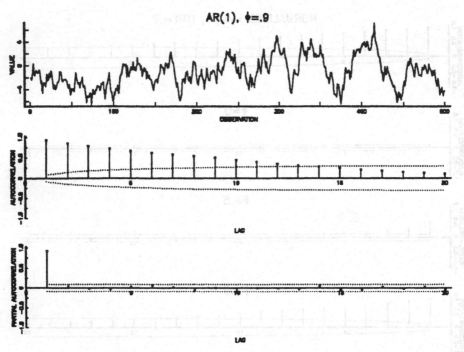

Fig. 4. Time Series, ACF, and PACF (Identification Plots) for an AR(1) Process

used for estimating model parameters are discussed in [3], although such details are typically not required in practice since many software packages implement these algorithms (e.g., [9], [13]). In the case of AR(1), there is only one parameter to estimate. The estimator, which is denoted by $\hat{\phi}$, is computed as follows:

$$\hat{\phi} = \frac{c_1}{c_0}.$$

Applying this calculation to the M/M/1 data in Fig. 2, we determine that $\hat{\phi} = .94$, which confirms our suspicion that $\phi > .9$.

Before proceeding to the evaluation step, we introduce a key concept: the model **residuals**. Denoted by e_t, the model residuals are the difference between the observed and estimated values of the y_t. For example, AR(1) residuals are computed as follows:

$$e_t = (y_t - \bar{y}) - \hat{\phi}(y_{t-1} - \bar{y})$$

The residuals provide a way to assess what is *not* explained by the model.

Model evaluation requires some negative logic. A good statistical model explains all patterns in the data. Thus, in a good model, the e_t should have no time serial dependencies since removing the effect of the time series model from

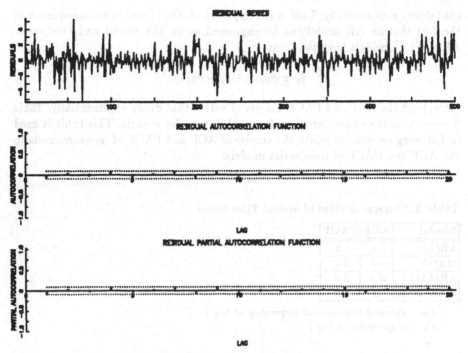

Fig. 5. Evaluation of the AR(1) Model of the M/M/1 Data

the data should leave no patterns in the residuals. Put differently, the residuals should be white noise, which means that both the ACF and the PACF should be 0 (since in a white noise model the terms are i.i.d.). A common way of assessing if the residuals are white noise is to display the identification plots for the e_t. For example, Fig. 5 contains the identification plots for the residuals of the M/M/1 data using an AR(1) model with $\hat{\phi} = .94$ (as obtained from model estimation). Note that both the ACF and the PACF are close to 0, which suggests that the residuals have no time serial dependency. Hence, we conclude that an AR(1) model with $\phi = .94$ provides a fairly good approximation to the dynamic behavior of the M/M/1 time series in Fig. 2. Had the residuals not been white noise, we would have revised the model to include the time serial behavior present in the residuals.

Our focus has been AR(1) models. Other models are often of interest as well. In particular, the one parameter moving average model, or MA(1), sometimes arises. The time series equation for MA(1) is

$$\tilde{y}_t = a_t - \theta a_{t-1}.$$

The ACF of an MA(1) model has a single spike at lag 1, and the PACF has values that decay exponentially. This is the opposite of AR(1) and is a consequence of the fact that an AR model can be expressed as an MA model and vice versa. ARMA(1,1) models have the form

$$\tilde{y}_t = \phi\tilde{y}_{t-1} + a_t - \theta a_{t-1}.$$

Here, both the ACF and PACF consist of values that decay exponentially. Table 2 summaries the characteristics of several time series models. This table is used in following sections to relate the empirical ACF and PACF of measurements to the ACF and PACF of time series models.

Table 2. Characterizations of Several Time Series

Model	ACF	PACF
AR(1)	d.e.	s.s.
MA(1)	s.s.	d.e.
ARMA(1,1)	d.e.	d.e.
White Noise	0	0

- d.e. - damped exponential beginning at lag 1
- s.s. - single spike at lag 1

To summarize, the key to model identification is characterizing the time series in terms of its autocorrelation function (ACF) and its partial autocorrelation function (PACF); these functions describe the relationship between terms in the series that are separated by the same number of time units (or lags). The identification step of time series analysis chooses a model whose theoretical ACF and PACF (as computed from the equation for the model) most closely matches the empirical ACF and PACF of the data. The evaluation step involves looking at the residuals obtained for the model chosen. A good model has residuals that show no evidence of time serial behavior; that is, the residuals are white noise. Time serial behavior in the residuals is detected by applying the identification step to the residuals.

3 Handling Non-Stationary Data

Constructing an ARMA model requires that the underlying process be stationary. Often, this is not the case, especially for measurements of information systems. For example, in time-shared computer systems, usage tends to peak in the mid-morning and just after lunch; as a result, the mean response time is larger at these times. A commonly used approach for handling non-stationary data is to develop two separate models. The first models the non-stationarity. The residuals from this model (i.e., what remains after the effects of the non-stationarity have been removed) should be stationary; otherwise the model is inadequate.

The second model applies the techniques described in section 2 to the residuals of the first model.

One approach to modelling non-stationary behavior is the **integrated (I)** model. To motivate this approach, consider an AR(1) process for which $\phi = 1$. That is, $\tilde{y}_t = \tilde{y}_{t-1} + a_t$. From Eq. (3), we see that this process has an infinite variance and so is non-stationary. However, the *difference* between successive terms in $\tilde{y}_t$ is stationary. Specifically, if $\tilde{w}_t = \tilde{y}_t - \tilde{y}_{t-1}$, then $\tilde{w}_t = a_t$. The $\tilde{w}_t$ series is called the first difference of the $\tilde{y}_t$ series. In theory, a series can be differenced an arbitrary number of times. Recovering the original series requires the inverse operation – summation or integration, which motivates the name integrated model.

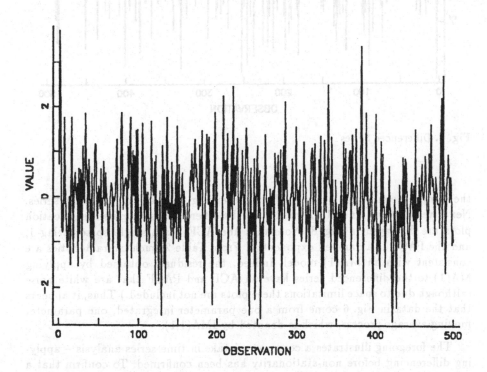

Fig. 6. Illustrative Data

How effective is differencing for handling non-stationarities? To answer this question, consider the data in Fig. 6. A cursory glance raises doubts about the stationarity of these data since there are several sequences that seem to be well above or well below the overall mean. Figure 7 plots the first difference of this data; the result lacks the long sequences of values that tend away from

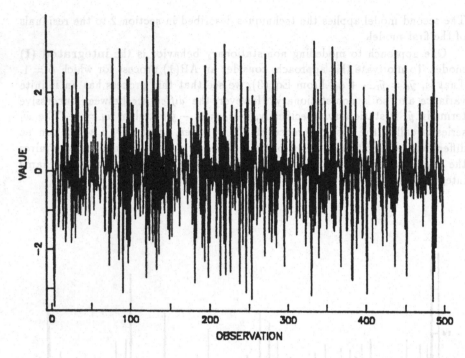

Fig. 7. Differenced Series

the sample mean, which suggests that differencing produced a stationary series. Next, we construct an ARMA model for the differenced series; its identification plots are displayed in Fig. 8. Note that the ACF has a single spike at lag 1, and the PACF is a damped exponential. From Table 2, such characteristics are consistent with an MA(1) model. Indeed, the residuals obtained by applying MA(1) to the differenced series have an ACF and PACF that are white noise (although due to space limitations these plots are not included.) Thus, it appears that the data in Fig. 6 come from a one parameter integrated, one parameter moving average process, which is denoted by IMA(1,1).

The foregoing illustrates a common mistake in time series analysis – applying differencing before non-stationarity has been confirmed. To confirm that a series is non-stationary, its ACF and PACF should be plotted; the data are non-stationary if the ACF and/or PACF do not stay within the significance bounds at large lags. Figure 9 contains the identification plots for the data in Fig. 6. We see that the original series is stationary; in fact, this series is white noise since both the ACF and PACF are in essence 0. In other words, differencing *created* an MA(1) process! To see why, let $\tilde{w}_t$ denote the differenced series. Since the

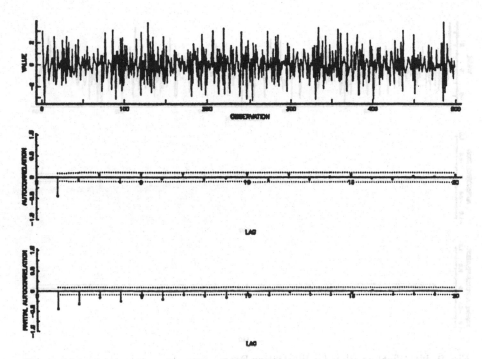

Fig. 8. Identification Plots For Differenced Series

original series is white noise, $y_t = a_t$, and so

$$\tilde{w}_t = \tilde{y}_t - \tilde{y}_{t-1}$$
$$= a_t - a_{t-1}$$
$$= a_t - \theta_1 a_{t-1}.$$

Considerable judgement is required when interpreting the ACF and PACF plots to determine if a series is stationary. Is there a way to eliminate non-stationarities without inadvertently creating an MA(1) model? One approach is to partition the series into multiple sub-series, each of which represents a different operating region. This too requires judgement, and so the ACF and PACF of each sub-series should be examined to confirm that the sub-series is stationary. This could be done by constructing identification plots for each sub-series. An alternative is to use least squares regression [5] to fit a moderate degree polynomial of time to the data. If this fit accounts for a small fraction of the variability in the data (say under 5%), no trend is present and so we feel more comfortable that the data are stationary. Both of these techniques are illustrated in the next section.

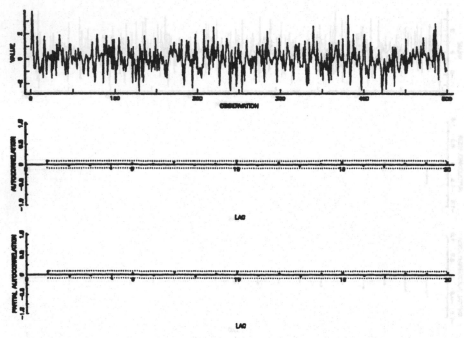

Fig. 9. Identification Plots for Illustrative Data

4 Case Study

This section illustrates time series analysis by applying it to the diagnosis of a performance problem in a large time sharing system at a major utility company. Users of this system complained of intermittently poor performance. In order to diagnosis the underlying problem, response times were measured every thirty seconds over a nine hour shift when there were performance complaints; Fig. 1 plots the measurements obtained. Herein is developed a time series model of these measurements with the objective of characterizing the cause of the performance problem.

The first step in developing a time series model is to detect and resolve non-stationarities in the data. Stationarity is an unreasonable assumption for the data in Fig. 1 in that there appear to be multiple operating regions: a relatively stationary (although highly variable) region from 8:00 AM until 10:30 AM, an abrupt increase in response time from 10:30 to 11:30, and an upward trend that starts at 12:00 PM and continues for the rest of the series. The identification plots in Fig. 10 confirm that these data are non-stationary since the ACF remains outside the significance bounds at large lags.

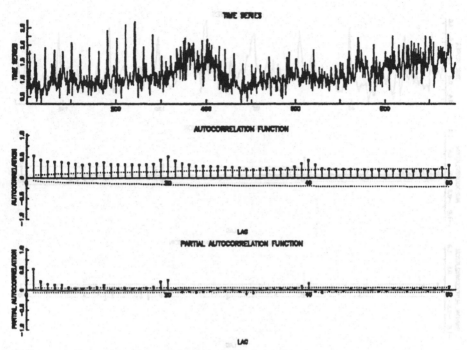

Fig. 10. Identification Plots for Full Time Series

One approach to resolving non-stationarities is to partition the data. This is particularly appropriate when there are multiple operating regions, as in Fig. 1 However, selecting a stationary sub-series requires some judgement. We focus on the sub-series from 8:00 AM to 10:30 AM (180 observations); Fig. 11 contains its identification plots. For the most part, the ACF and PACF lie within the significance bounds at larger lags. So, we could proceed with the identification step. Doing so might lead us to conclude that there is an AR(1) component in the time series since the first lag of the ACF is just above the significance bound. On the other hand, a lag 1 autocorrelation that is significant might be due to the sub-series being non-stationary.

To determine if the sub-series chosen is stationary, a second technique is applied: fitting a moderate degree polynomial of time to the data. Figure 12 displays a fifth degree polynomial of time (the dashed line) superimposed on the sub-series that we are modeling. The fitted curve, which we denote by $f(t)$, accounts for approximately 10% of the variation in the sub-series, which suggests that the sub-series is not stationary. If $f(t)$ adequately models the non-stationary behavior, the residuals of this model are stationary. Thus, our focus is these residuals. Denoted by w_t, the residuals are computed as $w_t = y_t - f(t)$.

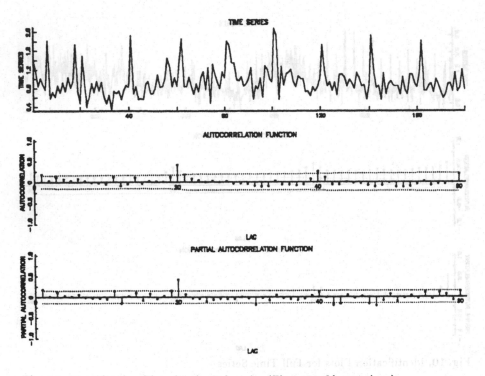

Fig. 11. Identification Plots for the Sub-series (First 180 Observations)

Figure 13 displays the identification plots for w_t. The lag one autocorrelation now lies within the Bartlett bounds, and so we conclude that there is no AR(1) component in w_t. However, there are several partial autocorrelations that lie just outside the significance bounds. Here some judgement is required. Since we have already taken several steps to eliminate non-stationary behavior and the offending values are just barely significant, we only consider the partial autocorrelation at lag twenty to be non-zero.

We now proceed to the identification step, which requires matching the ACF and PACF of the data with that of a time series model. The ACF plot in Fig. 13 has non-zero values at lags 20, 40, and 60; further, these autocorrelations show a gradual decline as the lag increases. The PACF consists of a single spike at lag 20. None of the models in table Fig. 2 have this kind of pattern. However, if we delete the non-zero lags from the ACF and PACF, the identification plots would look like an AR(1) model. In fact, what we have is an **AR(1) seasonal** model; seasonal models indicate the presence of a periodicity. Algebraically, this is expressed as:

$$\tilde{y}_t = \Phi \tilde{y}_{t-s} + a_t,$$

where s is the seasonality parameter that specifies the number of lags between a

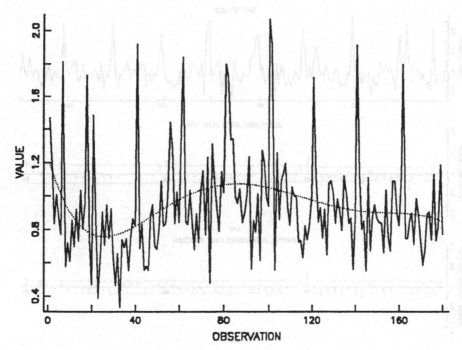

Fig. 12. Curve Fit (5-th degree polynomial) to Sub-series

periodic event. In our case, $s = 20$; that is, there is an event every twenty time units (or ten minutes) that has a significant effect on performance. Using the facilities of the AGSS statistical package [13], an estimate of .497 was obtained for Φ. Thus, we have the following model for the first 180 observations of the data in Fig. 1:

$$(\tilde{y}_t - f'(t)) = (.497)\,(\tilde{y}_{t-20} - f'(t-20)) + a_t, \qquad (7)$$

where $f'(t) = f(t) - \bar{y}$. We evaluate this model by using the identification plots for its residuals, where

$$e_t = (y_t - f(t)) - (.497)\,(y_{t-20} - f(t-20)).$$

From Fig. 14 we see that the residuals are white noise; so Eq. (7) seems to be a reasonable model.

Eq. (7) indicates that performance is degraded significantly by a process that executes every ten minutes. This information allowed the operations staff to focus on a small subset of their applications; relatively quickly they discovered an inefficiently written application that executed every ten minutes. After changing a search routine in this application, system performance improved substantially.

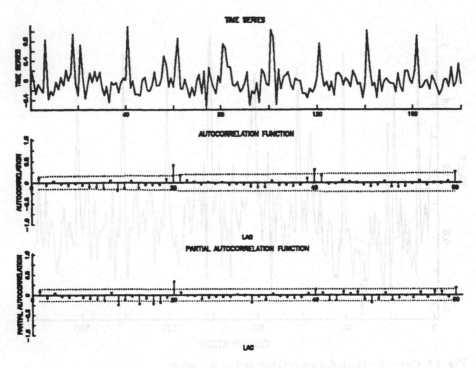

Fig. 13. Identification Plots for the Residuals of the Curve Fit

5 Summary

Modeling the dynamic behavior of information systems is of importance in many situations, such as characterizing the locality of disk accesses, evaluating the dynamic behavior of scheduling algorithms, and diagnosing intermittent performance problems. Time series analysis is a statistical approach to modeling dynamic behavior; a time series model is an algebraic expression that relates the t-th term to the proceeding p terms and to q random shocks (which represent random events that cannot be measured). Developing a time series model involves the following steps: (1) resolving non-stationarities in the data, (2) identifying the values for the parameters p and q, which determine the type of model such as autoregressive (AR) or moving average (MA), (3) estimating unknown constants, (4) evaluating the model constructed, and (5) forecasting future values. In general, model development is an iterative process in which steps (1) through (4) are applied repeatedly before proceeding to step (5).

Key to constructing a time series model is characterizing dynamic behavior. One commonly used approach employs the autocorrelation function (ACF) and partial autocorrelation function (PACF). For example, the second step in time

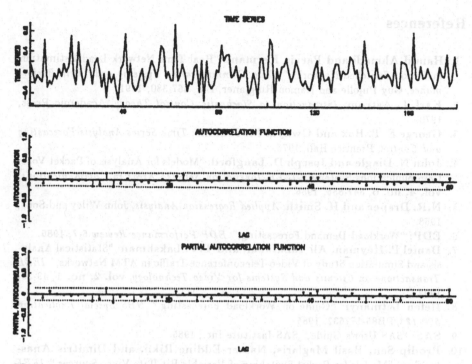

Fig. 14. Identification Plots for the Residuals of the Final Model

series analysis can be accomplished by comparing the empirical ACF and PACF of the time series data with the ACF and PACF of several time series models. (The latter are computed from the algebraic expression of the time series model).

There are several related topics that are worthwhile pursing. The case study in section 4 touched on AR(1) seasonal models. Seasonality can be incorporated into any ARMA model, and may appear in either (or both) the autoregressive or the moving average components. Another topic is transfer function models in which one time series is modelled in terms of one or more other time series (e.g., modelling response times in terms of interarrival and service times). Lastly, the area of stochastic control may be of particular interest to designers of information systems since it provides a formal approach to constructing optimal controls in the presence of random noise. The first two topics are discussed in depth in [3]; [3] touches on the third topic, but more details are contained in [2].

References

1. **Hamid Ahmadi and Parviz Kermani**: "Real Time Network Load Estimation in Packet Switched Networks," *Data Communication Systems and Their Performance*, Guy Pujolle and Ramon Ruigjaner, Ed., 367-380, 1991.

2. **Karl J. Astrom**: *Introduction to Stochastic Control Theory*, Academic Press, 1970.

3. **George E. P. Box and Gwilym M. Jenkins**: *Time Series Analysis Forecasting and Control*, Prentice Hall, 1976.

4. **John N. Diagle and Joseph D. Langford**: "Models for Analysis of Packet Voice Communications Systems," *IEEE Journal on Selected Areas in Communications*, **vol. 4, no. 6**, 847-855, 1986.

5. **N.R. Draper and H. Smith**: *Applied Regression Analysis*, John Wiley and Sons, 1968.

6. **EDP**: "Workload Demand Forecasting," *EDP Performance Review* 6-7, 1986.

7. **Daniel P. Heyman, Ali Tabatabai, and T.V. Lakshman**: "Statistical Analysis and Simulation Study of Video Teleconference Traffic in ATM Networks," *IEEE Transactions on Circuits and Systems for Video Technology*, **vol. 2, no. 1**, 49-59, 1992.

8. **Helen Letmanyi**: "Guide on Workload Forecasting," *NBS Special Publication 500-123*, PB85-177632, 1985.

9. **SAS**: "SAS User's Guide," SAS Institute Inc., 1985.

10. **Prodip Sen, Basil Maglaris, Nasser-Eddine Rikli, and Dimitris Anastassiou**: "Models for Packet Switching of Variable-Bit-Rate Video Sources," *IEEE Journal on Selected Areas in Communications*, 865-869, 1989.

11. **Ioannis Stavrakakis**: "An Analysis Approach to Multi Level Networking," *International Conference on Communications*, 274-301, 1990.

12. **Walter Vandaele**: *Applied Time Series and Box-Jenkins Models*, Academic Press, Inc., 1983.

13. **Peter Welch and Thomas Lane**: "The Integration of a Menu-Oriented Graphical Statistical System with its Underlying General Purpose Language," *Computer Science and Statistics: Proceedings of the 19th Symposium on the Interface*, 267-273, Philadelphia, February 1987.

Issues in Trace-Driven Simulation

David R. Kaeli

IBM T.J. Watson Research Center
P.O. Box 704
Yorktown Heights, N.Y. 10598

Abstract

Considerable effort has been devoted to the development of accurate trace-driven simulation models of today's computer systems. Unfortunately many modelers do not carefully inspect the input to their models. The fact is that the output of any model is only as good as the input to that model.

This paper discusses the many issues associated with the input traces used in trace-driven simulation. A description of the different types of traces is provided, followed by survey and discussion of the following trace issues: trace generation techniques, trace-length reduction techniques, trace selection and representativeness, and common trace misuse.

The aim of this tutorial paper is to equip modelers with enough information about the different trace types and tracing methodologies, so that they can be more critical of the quality of the input traces used in their trace-driven simulations. Keywords: *instruction traces, address traces, trace-driven simulation, representativeness.*

1. Introduction

Trace-driven simulation is a popular technique used to evaluate future computer designs [1, 2]. Many times the modeler is so focused on the problem being studied that the content of the input trace used in the evaluation is overlooked. If the modeler is not critical of the input traces chosen as input to his or her model, the output of the model may be of little value.

Many different types of traces can be used as input to models. The content of the input trace is dictated by the particular elements of a computer that the modeler chooses to study, and also by the level of detail that is of interest. Next, a review of the different trace types is provided.

1.1 Address Traces

Address traces are probably the most commonly used kind of trace. An address trace is a record of memory reference activity at some level of the memory hierarchy. An address trace typically contains the following information:

- virtual/physical address
- stride (the number of types transferred)
- type or identification (e.g., instruction vs. data, fetch vs. store, etc.)

The trace can contain all or a subset of the above fields. Other fields frequently captured in an address trace are updates to translation lookaside buffers, process identifiers, and program state indicators.

Typical uses of address traces include memory hierarchy studies, program pathlength analysis, and page size sensitivity studies. More papers have been published on trace-driven memory hierarchy studies (using address traces as input), than on any other topic in computer architecture [3, 4, 5, 6].

Address traces contain a snapshot of the memory reference activity during a time interval. One problem encountered when attempting to capture address traces on current microprocessors is the inability to collect memory references that are resolved on the on-chip cache [7]. Either the on-chip cache must be disabled (which will introduce some perturbation into the trace) or the input address lines to the cache must be surfaced to the external world (i.e., to I/O pins). The ability to capture traces on these microprocessors must be included in the design process.

1.2 Instruction Traces

Instruction traces contain the actual instructions executed during a snapshot of time. These traces contain similar information to that found in address traces, with the addition of instruction opcodes, interrupts, and exceptions. These traces, while being substantially "wider" than address traces, are also commonly used in memory hierarchy studies. Other common uses of instruction traces are:

- processor pipeline studies,
- branch prediction studies,
- floating-point unit evaluation, and
- instruction profiling

Instruction traces are considerably more difficult to collect, since instruction opcodes must be captured as well as memory reference addresses. This can pose a technological challenge on current superscalar microprocessors, where multiple instructions can be executed on a single processor clock cycle [8].

1.3 I/O Traces

A third type of trace used in trace-driven simulations is an I/O trace [9, 10, 11, 12]. This type of trace is a record of I/O events, capturing a variety of disk I/O activity. Other activity captured in I/O traces includes transfers between devices on an external bus (e.g., LAN, video adapter, etc).

A typical I/O disk trace contains the following information:

- disk address (e.g., sector #, track #, etc.),
- # of blocks transferred, and
- memory address.

Typical uses for I/O traces are for tuning paging algorithms, studying disk caches, and analyzing I/O subsystems. Many times, queuing models are used in favor of trace-driven simulation for studying I/O performance issues [13].

Trace Type Summary

While address traces are the most common type of trace, all three of the trace types just presented are frequently used to evaluate design trade-offs. The remainder of this paper will discuss the many issues related to traces. The organization is as follows. Section 2 reviews the many trace generation methodologies. Section 3 discusses trace-length reduction strategies. Section 4 discusses trace selection and trace representativeness. Section 5 provides some examples of common trace misuse. Section 6 summarizes this work and provides some rules-of-thumb for the trace-driven simulation modeler.

2. Trace Generation Methodologies

Many approaches have been proposed to obtain traces on computer systems. These approaches can be divided into two class: 1) software-based, and 2) hardware-based.

2.1 Software-based Trace Generation

A variety of software-based tools have been made available for obtaining traces on current computer systems [14, 15, 16]. These tools modify the source program at different stages of the compilation process. There are two compiler-based modification methodologies: 1) compile-time modification, and 2) link-time modification.

Compile-time Code Modification

:hp1Compile-time code modification is a commonly used method of generating traces of program execution [14, 15, 17, 18]. This methodology takes as input the assembly code of a program, and produces a modified version of the assembly code. The modified version contains additional code that will call trace library routines. Another feature allows a program map of the code to be generated. This provides for the generation of instruction traces. The modified code is then linked with the standard libraries, as well as with the additional tracing library routines (as provided by the tracing tool). When the program is run, a trace is generated which consists of an encoded stream of events. The encoded trace is then expanded using the program map generated previously. Eggers etal. provide a description of such a tool for generating traces on a multiprocessor system [14].

Link-time Code Modification

Another methodology commonly used is called *link-time code modification* [18, 19]. Using this methodology, code is added at link time for each memory reference. When the modified code is executed, memory reference information is stored in the trace buffer. Code is added at the entry and exit of every basic block in the program. When the code is executed, the basic block information is also stored in the buffer.

The major advantage of link-time tracing over compile-time tracing is that the former captures trace information for all code, including the code in link libraries. Compile-time tracing does not trace this code. One example of link-time code modification for a RISC-based machine can be found in [16].

Microcode-based Trace Generation

Microcode-based trace generation collects traces by modifying the processor microcode on the target machine. A detailed description of this approach can be found in [20, 21].

No changes are made to the source code when using microcode-based trace generation. Instead, the microcode of the microprocessor is modified. Routines are added to the microcode which store address information in a reserved memory area on each memory request. The major advantage of this approach is that both application and operating system code can be traced. Since the operating system can produce a significant number of memory references (Flanagan etal. report, that for their MACH 2.6 single-process traces, 12-24% of all references are due to the operating system [22], LaMaire and White report that in MVS workloads, up to 70% of the references are due to the operating system [23]), it is very important to capture these references.

Software Emulation

Another approach used to generate traces is called *software emulation*. Using this methodology, a software program is developed that emulates the instruction set architecture (ISA) of the system of interest [24]. Code compiled for this system will run on the emulator.

A translation takes place between the target system ISA and the ISA of the host machine (i.e., the system upon which the emulator runs). When a program is run on the emulator, a trace is generated. The speed of the software emulation system typically depends upon the efficiency of the translation between the two ISA's and the overhead associated with saving the trace data.

2.2 Hardware-based Trace Generation

An alternative approach to modifying code/microcode or writing an emulator is to use a hardware-based trace generation methodology. There are two types of hardware tracing mechanisms: 1) trap-bit tracing, and 2) real-time tracing.

Trap-bit Tracing

Trap-bit tracing is a commonly used technique to generate instruction traces on microprocessor-based systems. A bit is provided by the ISA of the microprocessor which, when set, causes an interrupt to occur on the machine being traced. An interrupt service routine is entered which inspects the current instruction and captures any desired information (e.g., addresses, instructions, etc.). The Intel 80386 microprocessor family provides such a facility [25], as does the VAX architecture [26].

The interrupt service routine, which is called when the microprocessor traps out, can be customized to gather the particular information of interest. The trap bit is reset during the time when the interrupt service routine runs, and is set upon the exit from the interrupt service routine (otherwise the interrupt service routine would be traced). When the next instruction is executed, a trap will occur, and the procedure is repeated.

Real-time Tracing

Real-time tracing captures traces from the target machine by electronically monitoring signals on pins and/or busses [22, 27, 28, 29] Traces are gathered while the machine is running, so the hardware used to capture the traces must match the fastest trace generation speed. Real-time tracing has the main advantage of not perturbing the system being traced. The traces are complete and accurate.

The two main challenges when designing a real-time tracing system are: 1) matching peak data rates, and 2) capturing long traces. Next, the trade-offs associated with the different mechanisms presented are discussed.

2.3 Trace Methodology Comparison

Figure 1 lists the six different tracing methodologies just presented. The table compares the six methodologies based on: 1) the amount of time dilation introduced into the trace, 2) whether the operating system is captured, 3) the typical sample size gathered, and 4) the typical cost.

Time Dilation

Time Dilation occurs because the trace methodology introduces some type of overhead into the system. The reason why this is a concern is that by slowing the system down, events that used to occur in real time (e.g., input/output, interrupts, and timers) now occur with non-realistic timings. These events may timeout or may occur, artificially, too soon due to the overhead of the tracing mechanism. This will affect the correctness of the trace.

Link-time and compile-time code modification suffer substantially from time dilation in that considerable time is spent storing information into the trace buffer on each memory reference or basic block entry/exit. Published results indicate that a 10x slowdown (1/10 as fast as real-time) is experienced when using these methods [20].

Similarly, microcode modification experiences considerable time dilation. Again, the overhead is associated with saving the trace information. It has been reported that microcode-based tracing produces slowdowns comparable in magnitude to those found in the compiler-based modification methodologies [20].

Software emulation suffers from at least two sources of inaccuracy: 1) emulation of an ISA typically does not emulate the I/O subsystem, and 2) the time to translate between the target ISA and the host ISA can be on the order of 10x. Either of these issues can substantially affect the correctness of a trace.

	Time Dilation	O/S Coverage	Sample Size
compile-time code modification	10X	NO	1GS
link-time code modification	10X	NO	1GS
microcode-based code modification	10X	YES	1GS
software emulation	10X	YES	UNLIMITED
trap-bit tracing	100X	YES	UNLIMITED
real-time tracing	1X	YES	100MS

GS - 1 billion samples
MS - 1 million samples

Figure 1. Trace Methodology Comparison

The overhead introduced into the system with trap-bit tracing is due to trapping out to an interrupt service routine, executing the code necessary to save the desired trace information, and then returning to the next instruction. This sequence is performed for every instruction executed, and thus more overhead is associated with using this methodology than with the code modification techniques. System execution is dilated on the order of 100x using trap-bit tracing.

Real-time tracing does not introduce time dilation into the system. Some real-time tracing implementations have suggested slowing down the system clock. This should not be considered real-time tracing. Some events (e.g., I/O, timers, etc.) will still execute at full speed, thus corrupting the integrity of the trace. Other reported implementations suggest stopping the system to unload the trace buffer [22]. If this approach is employed, it should be clearly understood what perturbations are caused by halting the system. It must be stressed that stopping the system at all will usually produce some perturbation.

Operating System Coverage

It is quite important to capture accesses made by the operating system. There are two reasons why: 1) a large percentage of all references on the system are due to the operating system (as reported earlier), and 2) the behavior of operating system code is very different from application code (e.g., operating system code is notorious for causing poor cache performance [20]).

Summarizing the second column in Figure 1, only the two compiler-based code modification methodologies are incapable of capturing the operating system code (unless, of course, the entire operating system has been instrumented and recompiled). The other three methodologies capture both the operating system and the user programs.

Sample Size

The appropriate length of a trace will be dictated by the problem being studied when using the trace. It has been stated that traces longer than 5 billion references in length are necessary for modeling current memory hierarchy designs [16]. This point is debatable, but having longer traces is always more desirable (i.e., we do not have to use the entire trace, but if we have it in hand, we can then determine what length is appropriate).

Figure 1 lists the longest possible trace lengths for the six tracing methodologies. We see that code modification techniques can generate very long traces. The limiting factor here is the size of the trace buffer allocated on the machine. Software emulation can generate traces of unlimited length. Tracing is under software control, such that the trace can be unloaded from the system at any time, and tracing can pick up from where it left off. The trap-bit tracing approach can also capture traces of unlimited length. This is true because the traced system is under the control of a interrupt service routine. The interrupt service routine can detect when the buffer is full and take the appropriate action. While this is not true for the code modification methodologies, a separate detection routine could be invoked when an addressing exception occurs.

Real-time tracing is the most severely restricted is this category, being limited by the amount of memory (random access memory or disk) supplied on the trace system implementation. One option is to allow the tracing system to detect when the trace buffer is full. The system being traced can be halted, the trace memory unloaded, and then tracing resumed. Even though this approach is feasible, it is undesirable to stop the system under test since some artifacts may be introduced.

Cost

The last column in Figure 1 shows the estimated cost of each of these six methodologies. The cost for the software-based code modification methodologies is low. Either the compiler or the linker needs to be modified. Some systems already provide such tools [30].

Microcode-based modification is quite expensive, unless one is fortunate enough to be a microprocessor manufacturer and have access to the microcode.

Development of a software emulation system can be a substantial software coding project. The emulation program has to be able to execute every instruction in the target ISA. This can be over 300 instructions for some ISA's [25].

The cost of implementing a trap-bit tracer is low, since many of the current microprocessors provide such a feature. The only development effort necessary is associated with the coding of the interrupt service routine that will save the trace information.

The cost of custom hardware to perform real-time tracing is quite high. The system must be able to capture traces at high clock frequencies (when full instruction traces are desired). The memory used to store the trace must be able to accept samples at very fast rates (typically faster than 100 MHz.). The cost of static and dynamic random access memory in this clock frequency range is quite high (see Figure 2 for a range of current prices for static random access memory).

One approach suggested to reducing the cost of a real-time tracing system is to interleave between banks of slower memory, buffering the data in high-speed registers, and multiplexing in a round-robin pattern through the slower memory arrays [31]. This can reduce the cost of a real-time tracing system by an order of magnitude, since a majority of the cost of the system is tied to the cost of the trace memory.

2.4 Summary of Trace Generation Methodologies

Comparing the many tracing methodologies just presented, there exist disadvantages in each of the approaches. If the goal is to acquire accurate and complete traces (i.e., containing no time dilation and containing all operating system execution,) the only choice is to use a real-time tracing methodology. The main problem with real-time tracing is the cost of the storage necessary for capturing the trace. The cost of the tracing system is directly proportional to the amount of storage necessary to hold the trace. By using the simple multiplexing scheme described above, the speed requirements on the trace memory can be relaxed.

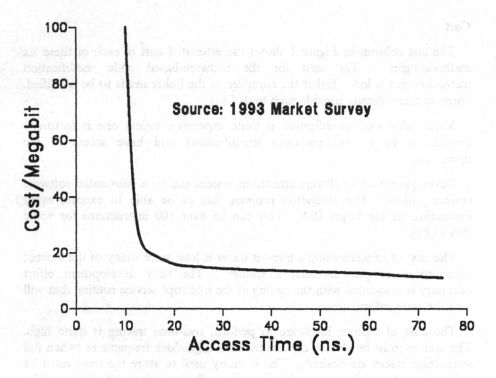

Source: 1993 Market Survey

Figure 2. Static RAM cost vs. Access Time

3. Trace Length Reduction

Assuming that the required trace has been obtained, we now need to explore how we can store and use the trace efficiently. Traces take up a considerable amount of space. Trace-driven simulation execution time is directly proportional to the length of the trace being processed. The next two topics covered describe how to minimize the amount of space occupied by a trace, as well as how to reduce the amount of time needed to process a full trace in a trace-driven simulation run.

3.1 Compacted Traces

Typically, traces consume a considerable amount of space (some traces are many gigabytes in size). Methods have been devised to reduce the physical space consumed by a trace. Some of the desirable attributes of a trace size reduction methodology are:

- the size reduction factor should be significant,
- the reduction/expansion algorithm should run efficiently, and
- no information should be lost.

One strategy that has proven to be successful in reducing the length of address traces is called *Mache* [32]. This technique combines a type of cache filter, emitting either a miss or hit record, and then uses the Lempel-Ziv compression algorithm [33] to compress the miss/hit records. The algorithm reduced address traces (containing both instruction and data references) by 91-97%.

While this methodology does reduce the size of the trace, it does not reduce the overall trace-driven simulation time. The trace record still needs to be expanded in order to be input to the model. The trade-off is that less disk I/O is taking place, while extra processing is occurring due to expansion.

3.2 Simulation Time Reduction

If the goal is to reduce the overall execution time of the trace-driven simulation, then another strategy besides compaction must be employed. It has been noted that memory references tend to display the property of temporal locality [34]. By taking advantage of this characteristic in address traces, significant reductions in simulation time can be realized.

Smith proposed a method called *stack deletion* [35]. Using this approach, all references that hit to the top N levels of an LRU stack are discarded from the trace. The assumption is that most memory management systems will typically retain these references in memory, and thus, a similar number of misses will occur when discarding the hits to the top of the stack. While the results presented indicate a substantial reduction in trace length (25-95% shorter), the method has only been applied in paging studies. The large variance in the reduction factor is due to a large variance in the locality of the page references contained in the traces used.

Another methodology, that produces exact results when using the reduced address trace, is called *trace stripping* [36]. A direct-mapped cache is modeled, and only misses to the model are kept in the reduced trace. Exact results are obtained when modeling caches with the same or less number of sets, provided that the cache line size remains the same. Traces are reduced by a factor of (90-95%) using trace stripping.

Other extensions to trace stripping have been proposed. Wang and Baer describe how to reduce traces using a modified version of trace stripping, that addresses simulation of write-back caches [37]. In addition to misses in a direct-mapped cache, first-time writes are also kept in the reduced trace.

Agarwal and Huffman propose a scheme called *trace blocking* [38], which takes advantage of both the temporal and spatial locality in programs to reduce the size of the trace. A cache filter with a block size of 1 is used to discard references within a temporal locality. Then a block filter is used to compact the trace to take advantage of spatial locality in the trace. Some errors are introduced using this method. The size of the resulting trace is reduced by 95-99% when using trace blocking.

Chame and Dubois introduce a new method for reducing the length of multiprocessor traces used in trace-driven simulation called *trace sampling* [39]. Their strategy first applies the Wang and Baer method, and then samples a number of processors. While this approach suffers from inaccuracies, the errors are typically small (less than 5%), while the overall simulation time is reduced by more than 97%.

While each of these methodologies reduces the overall simulation time, the accuracy of the methodology must be clearly understood. Errors as small as 5% can invalidate the modeling results.

4. Workload Selection and Representative Traces

In the preceding sections, the issues of how to capture traces and how to use them more efficiently were presented. The next question is: "What do we want to trace?" In this section we will discuss how to select an appropriate workload to trace and how to obtain representative traces.

4.1 Workload Selection

The selection of an appropriate workload to trace is typically driven by the particular problem under study (i.e., what type of work is typically performed on the machine we are designing). Workload types can be broken down into various categories:

- fixed-point vs. floating point,
- processor bound vs. memory bound vs. I/O bound,
- standardized benchmark vs. application vs. operating system, and
- scientific vs. transaction processing vs. database vs. general purpose.

The above list is not nearly complete, but it demonstrates the many different facets of selecting an appropriate workload.

To clearly understand the performance of the modeled system, the correct input must be selected. Besides tracing workload that is particular to the problem being studied, it is vital to use a range of workloads. Many of the new benchmark suites (e.g. SPEC 92 [40] and SDM [41]) attempt to provide this range of workloads. Gray provides a good reference covering the current state of benchmark programs [42].

While benchmarks are the most readily available, and easiest to trace, traces of real workload on customer machines are more interesting. In an attempt to create a more realistic transaction processing benchmark, the Transaction Processing Council was formed. Since its creation, the council has produced a number of benchmarks (TPCA, TPCB, TPCC). A very good description of each of these benchmarks can be found in [42].

Other workloads of interest include the SPLASH benchmark suite [43], commonly used in multiprocessor studies [44, 45], and the PERFECT Club benchmark set [46], used to study supercomputer performance issues [47].

4.2 Collecting Representative Traces

After the particular environment that needs to be traces has been selected, and after traces have been obtained, how do we know if our traces are of any value (i.e., did we capture the *important* part of the execution in our trace).

To help answer this question, we introduce the term *representativeness*, which describes how well the sample we have collected captures the certain characteristics (we are probably only focusing on a subset of the workload characteristics) of the entire execution that we are studying. To better judge the representativeness of a trace, workload characterization is commonly used [2].

Two approaches can be taken to perform characterization: 1) execution monitoring, and 2) trace sampling. Execution monitoring involves using either internal instrumentation provided with the system, or some external hardware to monitor particular events on the system. In [23], LaMaire and White provide a workload characterization study for the IBM System/370 system.

The second approach to characterizing the workload on the system is to obtain samples of execution. Two approaches can be taken here. One approach is to capture a set traces and then use statistics to evaluate the representativeness of any particular trace. A second approach captures short samples over the entire execution of the trace and then attempts to stitch them back together [48, 49]. The selection of the which method to use will

Instruction Opcode	% of all instr.
MOV rw,m	7.53
PUSH rw	5.77
POP rw	5.31
JNE disp	4.46
LOOP disp	4.40
JE disp	3.82
MOV m,rw	3.02
JMP disp	3.02
MOV rw,rw	2.81
CALL disp	2.76
RET	2.67
CMP rb,kk	2.23
Total	47.8

(Combined statistics for 96 traces)

Figure 3. Instruction Opcode Frequencies

depend upon the amount of transient behavior encountered in the entire execution. If the execution is predictable, then a single trace should prove to be sufficient. If the execution exhibits more random behavior, then the short sample technique may be more useful.

Figures 3, 4, and 5 show examples of workload characteristics commonly used to study representiveness in traces. Figure 3 shows the opcode frequencies contained in a set of 96 traces, taken from an Intel 80386-based personal computer workload [50]. Figure 4 shows the number of unique memory pages touched over the execution of a single trace. Figure 5 shows the frequency, over time, of the memory references across the memory address space (also called the basic block usage). Each of these characteristics helps the modeler to gain more insight into the contents of the captured trace.

5. Common Trace Misuse

Traces are commonly misused in trace-driven simulation studies. There are many reasons why. In this section we will discuss examples of trace misuse, and suggest how they can be avoided.

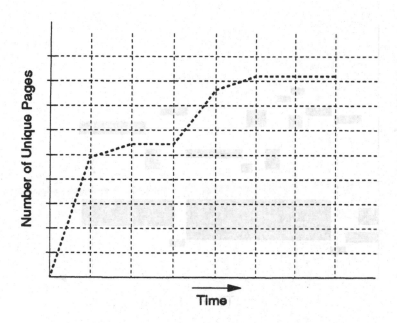

Figure 4. Cumulative Number of Unique Pages Touched

5.1 Appropriate Workload

Modelers often decide to use traces that are inappropriate for their purposes. One example of an inappropriate workload would be to use a compute-bound benchmark (e.g., matrix300 from SPEC '89 [48]) to study cache performance. The cache hit rate would be so high for any reasonably-sized cache, such that the results would be very misleading (i.e., this benchmark is compute-bound, and does not stress the memory subsystem).

To avoid this type of trace misuse, review the suggestions provided in section 4.1. Another important issue here is to learn as much about the benchmark or application that you can. Inspect source code if possible. Attempt to identify what parts of the application that you have captured in your trace (e.g., modules, functions, etc.).

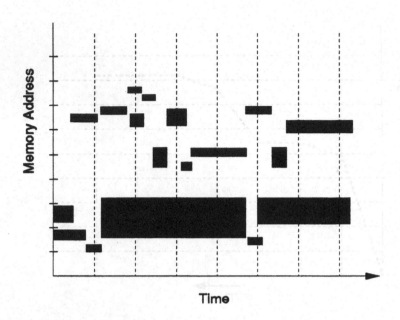

Figure 5. Address Space Traversal

5.2 Generality of Results

To be able to claim generality of a particular modeling result, a range of benchmarks or applications needs to be used. We often review papers that leave a particular application out of the results section. Sometimes this is done legitimately, but sometimes this is done in order to hide some less favorable results.

If a particular application does not perform as well as the rest of the benchmarks/applications in the set, find out why. Generality is a key quality that reviewers look for in papers. If the particular design issue has some shortcoming, as long as the reason why this occurs is understood and explained clearly, the merits of the design will still be evident.

5.3 Snapshot Selection

Besides selecting the appropriate workload to study, it is very important to understand, within the workload, what you have captured in the trace. One mistake that is often made is to begin tracing an application from the beginning of its execution. What happens is that the trace will contain a majority of the overhead of loading the code into memory, and the initialization of variables. If a majority of the execution is devoted to initialization, then capturing the startup of the execution is fine. But in most applications/benchmarks, execution is dominated by steady-state execution. Always attempt to determine the dominating behavior of the code being traced.

The next issue after deciding when to begin tracing is to decide when to stop tracing (i.e., what is the right trace length). One example of this is found when modeling caches. The miss rate in the cache will be quite high as the *working set* [34] is loaded. If the trace ends while the working set is still being loaded, unrealistic (i.e., very high) miss rates will be produced. For this reason, a study of the *cache footprint* [51] should be performed before deciding what the appropriate length of a trace should be.

5.4 Snapshot Length

Once the correct length is determined, a methodology should be selected that captures a representative sample. While there is not one methodology that can be applied to every trace, an evaluation using workload characteristics (as described in section 4.2) should be performed. One example of using the wrong trace sample is when a tight (small) timing loop is captured in a trace (timing loops are quite common in personal computer workloads). The performance evaluation will center around speeding up the timing loop. The net effect of increasing a timing loop's execution speed is to generate more iterations of the timing loop in the optimized design. Increasing the speed of timing loops does not generally improve the program execution time.

6. Conclusions

This paper has provided an overview of the issues related to the content of the traces used in trace-driven simulation. A review of the three types of traces was provided. The issues of trace generation, trace-length reductions, workload selection and representativeness, and trace misuse were covered. An extensive set of references is also provided, which should be used for further information on any particular trace-related issue.

The modeler should come away from this paper with a more critical view of input traces. Some important questions that should be raised when using traces are:

- What type of trace is required by the model?
- Is the trace complete, and does it contain any perturbations?
- What is an appropriate trace length?
- Can I reduce the size or length of my trace?
- Does the trace contain the appropriate workload?
- Does the trace contain the appropriate execution snapshot?
- Can I identify the portion of the application contained in the trace?

Increasing the emphasis on the quality of the input trace can only improve the quality of the modeling results.

References:

1. D. Ferrari, G. Serazzi, and A. Zeigner, *Measurement and Tuning Computer Systems,* Prentice Hall, 1983.
2. R. Jain, *The Art of Computer Systems Performance Analysis,* John Wiley and Sons, 1991.
3. A.J. Smith, "Cache Memories," *ACM Computing Surveys* , Vol. 14, No. 3, Sept. 1982, pp. 473-530.
4. J. Goodman, "Using Cache Memory to Reduce Processor-Memory Traffic," *Proc. of the 10th International Symposium on Computer Architecture,* June 1983, pp. 124-131.
5. J. Archibald and J.-L. Baer, "Cache Coherence Protocols: Evaluation Using a Multiprocessor Simulation Model," *ACM Transactions on Computers,* Vol. 4, No. 4, Nov. 1986, pp. 273-298.
6. J. Tsai and A. Agarwal, "Analyzing Multiprocessor Cache Behavior Through Data Reference Modeling," *Proc. of Sigmetrics '93,* May 1993, pp. 236-247.
7. *i486 Microprocessor Programmer's Reference Manual,* Intel Corporation, Santa Clara, CA, 1990.
8. *Alpha Architecture Reference Manual,* DEC, Burlington, MA, 1992.
9. J.T. Robinson and M.V. Devarakonda, "Data Cache Management Using Frequency-Based Replacement," *Proc. of Sigmetrics '90,* May 1990, pp. 134-142.
10. A.J. Smith, "Disk Cache - Miss Ratio and Design Considerations, " *ACM Transactions on Computer Systems,* No. 3, Aug. 1985, pp. 161-203.
11. J. Ousterhout , H. Da Costa, D. Harrison, J. Kunze, M. Kupfer, and J. Thompson, "A Trace-Driven Analysis of the UNIX 4.2 BSD File System," *Proc. of the 10th Symposium on Operating System Principles,* December 1985, pp.35-50.
12. A.J. Smith, "Analysis of Long Term File Reference Patterns for Application to File Migration Algorithms," *IEEE Transactions on Software Engineering,* Vol. SE-7, No. 4, July 1981, pp. 403-417.

13. S.S. Lavenberg, *Computer Performance Modeling Handbook*, Academic Press, New York, N.Y., 1983.

14. S.J. Eggers, D.R. Keppel, E.J. Koldinger, and H.M. Levy, " Techniques For Efficient Inline Tracing on a Shared-memory Multiprocessor," *Proc. of Sigmetrics '90,* May 1990, pp. 37-46.

15. C. Stephens, B. Cogswell, J. Heinlein, and G. Palmer, " Instruction Level Profiling and Evaluation of the IBM RS/6000," *Proc. of the 18th International Symposium on Computer Architecture,* May 1990, pp. 180-189.

16. A Borg., R. Kessler, and D.E. Wall, "Generation and Analysis of Very Long Address Traces," *Proc. of the 17th International Symposium on Computer Architecture,* May 1990, pp. 270-279.

17. E.J. Koldinger, S.J. Eggers, and H.M. Levy, "On the Validity of Trace-Driven Simulation for Multiprocessors," *Proc. of the 18th International Symposium on Computer Architecture,* May 1991, pp. 244-253.

18. C.B. Stunkel and W.K. Fuchs, "TRAPEDS: Producing Traces for Multicomputers Via Execution Driven Simulation," *Proc. of Sigmetrics '89,* May 1989, pp. 70-78.

19. D.W. Wall, "Experience with a Software-Defined Machine Architecture," *ACM Transactions on Programming Languages and System,* Vol. 14, No. 3, July 1992, pp. 299-338.

20. A. Agarwal, *Analysis of Cache Performance for Operating Systems and Multiprogramming,* Kluwer Academic Pub., Norwell, Mass., 1989.

21. A. Agarwal, R.L. Sites, and M. Horowitz, "ATUM: A Technique for Capturing Address Traces," *Proc. of the 17th International Symposium on Computer Architecture,* , May 1986, pp. 119-127.

22. J.K. Flanagan, B. Nelson, J. Archibald, and K. Drimsrud, "BACH: BYU Address Collection Hardware; The Collection of Complete Traces," *Proc. of the 6th International Conference on Modeling Techniques and Tools for Computer Performance Evaluation,* Sept. 1992.

23. O.R. LaMaire and W.W. White, "The Contribution to Performance of Instruction Set Usage in System/370," *Proc. of the Fall Joint Computer Conference,* Dallas, TX., Nov. 1986, pp. 665-674.

24. H. Davis, S.R. Goldschmidt, and J. Hennessy, "Tango: A Multiprocessor Simulation and Tracing System, " *Proc. of International Conference on Parallel Processing,* Aug. 1991, pp. 99-107.

25. *Intel 80386 Programmer's Reference Manual,* Intel Corporation, Santa Clara, CA, 1986.

26. *VAX-11 Architecture Reference Manual,* Digital Equipment Corporation, Bedford, MA, 1982, Form EK-VARAR-RM-001.

27. D.W. Clark, "Cache Performance in the VAX-11/780," *ACM Transactions on Computer Systems,* Vol. 1, Feb. 1983, pp. 24-37.

28. D.R. Kaeli, O.R. LaMaire, P.P. Hennet, W.W. White, W. Starke, "Real-Time Trace Generation," submitted to the *International Journal of Computer Simulation*, July 1993.

29. T. Horikawa, "TOPAZ: Hardware-Tracer Based Computer Performance Measurement and Evaluation System," *NEC Research and Development* Vol. 33, No. 4, Oct. 1992, pp. 638-647.

30. *MIPS Languages and Programmer's Manual*, MIPS Computer Systems, Inc., 1986.

31. P.P. Hennet, O.R. LaMaire, P.J. Manning, and W.J. Starke, "Self-Clocking SRAM Sequential Memory System," *IBM Technical Disclosure Bulletin*, Vol. 32, No. 2, July 1991, pp. 40-42.

32. A.D. Samples, "Mache: No-Loss Trace Compaction," *Proc. of Sigmetrics '89*, May 1989, pp. 89-97.

33. J. Ziv, and A. Lempel, "A Universal Algorithm for Sequential Data Compression," *IEEE Transactions on Information Theory*, Vol. 23, 1976, pp. 75-81.

34. P.J. Denning, "The Working Set Model for Program Behavior," *Communications of the ACM*, 11(5), May 1968, pp. 323-333.

35. A.J. Smith, "Two Methods for the Efficient Analysis of Memory Address Trace Data," *IEEE Transactions on Software Engineering*, Vol. SE-3, No. 1, January 1977, pp. 94-101.

36. T.R. Puzak, "Analysis of Cache Replacement-Algorithms," Doctoral Dissertation, Univ. of Massachusetts, Amherst, Mass., February 1985.

37. W.H. Wang, J.L. Baer, "Efficient Trace-Driven Simulation Methods for Cache Performance Analysis," *Proc. of Sigmetrics '90*, May 1990, pp. 27-36

38. A. Agarwal and M. Huffman, "Blocking: Exploiting Spatial Locality for Trace Compaction," *Proc. of Sigmetrics '90*, May 1990, pp. 48-57.

39. J. Chame, and M. Dubois, "Cache Inclusion and Processor Sampling in Multiprocessor Simulations," *Proc. of Sigmetrics '93*, May 1993, pp. 36-47.

40. K.M. Dixit, "CINT92 and CFP92 Benchmark Descriptions," *SPEC Newsletter*, 3(4), Dec. 1991.

41. S.K. Dronamraju. S. Balan, and T. Morgan, "System Analysis and Comparison Using SPEC SDM 1," *SPEC Newsletter*, 3(4), Dec. 1991.

42. J. Gray, *The Benchmark Handbook*, Morgan Kaufmann Pub., San Mateo, CA., 1993.

43. J.P. Singh, W.-D. Weber, and A. Gupta, "SPLASH: Stanford Parallel Applications for Shared-Memory," *Technical Report CSL-TR-91-469*, Stanford University, April 1991.

44. L.A. Barroso, and M. Dubois, "The Performance of Cache-Coherent Ring-based Multiprocessors," *Proc. of the 20th International Symposium on Computer Architecture*, May 1993, pp. 268-277.

45. A.L. Cox, and R.J. Fowler, "Adaptive Cache Coherency for Detecting Migratory Shared Data," *Proc. of the 20th International Symposium on Computer Architecture,* May 1993, pp. 98-108.
46. G. Cybenko, L. Kipp, L. Pointer, and D. Kuck, "Supercomputer Performance Evaluation and the Perfect Benchmarks," *CSRD Report No. 965,* Univ. of Illinois, March 1990.
47. S. Vajapenyam, G.S. Sohi, an W.-C. Hsu, "An Empirical Study of the CRAY Y-MP Processor using the PERFECT Club Benchmarks," *Proc. of the 18th International Symposium on Computer Architecture,* May 1991, pp. 170-179.
48. M. Martonosi, and A. Gupta, "Effectiveness of Trace Sampling for Performance Debugging Tools, " *Proc. of Sigmetrics '93,* May 1993, pp. 248-259.
49. S. Laha, J.H. Patel, and R.K. Iyer, "Accurate Low-Cost Methods for Performance Evaluation of Cache Memory Systems," *IEEE Transactions on Computers,* Vol. 37, No. 11, Nov. 1988, pp. 1325-1336.
50. *SPEC Benchmark Suite, Release 1, Supercomputing Review,* 3(9), Sept. 1990, pp. 48-57.
51. H.S. Stone, and D. Thiebaut, "Footprints in the Cache," *Proceedings of Performance '86,* May 1986, pp. 1-4.

Maximum Entropy Analysis of Queueing Network Models

Demetres Kouvatsos
Computer Systems Modelling Research Group
University of Bradford
Bradford, BD7 1DP
England

Abstract

The principle of Maximum Entropy (ME) provides a consistent method of inference for estimating the form of an unknown discrete-state probability distribution, based on information expressed in terms of true expected values. In this tutorial paper entropy maximisation is used to characterise product-form approximations and resolution algorithms for arbitrary continuous-time and discrete-time Queueing Network Models (QNMs) at equilibrium under Repetitive-Service (RS) blocking and Arrivals First (AF) or Departures First (DF) buffer management policies. An ME application to the performance modelling of a shared-buffer Asynchronous Transfer Mode (ATM) switch architecture is also presented. The ME solutions are implemented subject to Generalised Exponential (GE) and Generalised Geometric (GGeo) queueing theoretic mean value constraints, as appropriate. In this context, single server GE and GGeo type queues in conjunction with associated effective flow streams (departure, splitting, merging) are used as *building blocks* in the solution process. Physical interpretations of the results are given and extensions to the quantitative analysis of more complex queueing networks are discussed.

1. Introduction

Queueing network models (QNMs) are widely recognised as powerful tools for representing discrete flow systems (such as computer, communication and flexible manufacturing systems) as complex networks of queues and servers and analysing their performance. Within this framework the servers represent the active or passive resources of the system such as processors, memory and communication devices and the customers circulating through the servers stand for the jobs, messages or components being processed by and competing for these resources.

Classical queueing theory provides a conventional framework for formulating and solving the QNM. The variability of interarrival and service times of jobs can be modelled by continuous-time or discrete-time probability distributions. Exact and approximate analytical methods have been proposed in the literature for solving equations describing system performance. These techniques lead to efficient computational algorithms for analysing QNMs and over the years a vast amount of progress has been made worldwide (e.g., [1-19]). However, despite persistant attempts for generalisation some problems still remain without a satisfactory solution.

In the continuous-time domain the accuracy of analytic approximations for general QNMs, particularly those with finite capacity and multiple-job classes, may be adversely affected when based on intuitive heuristics, while very often gross assumptions are made in order to assure exact numerical solutions (e.g., [1-14]). Many theoretical advances on continuous-time queues have been extended to discrete-time queues (e.g., [15-19]). However, there are few standard and unique results that are known for discrete-time queues due to the inherent difficulties associated with the occurrence of simultaneous events at the boundary epochs of a slot including bulk arrivals and departures (c.f., [20]).

Since the mid-60s it has become increasingly evident that classical queueing theory cannot easily handle *by itself* complex queueing systems and networks with many interacting elements. As a consequence, alternative ideas and tools, analogous to those applied in the field of Statistical Mechanics, have been proposed in the literature (e.g., [21-28]). It can be argued that one of the most fundamental requirements in the analysis of complex queueing systems is the provision of a convincing interpretation for a probability assignment free from arbitrary assumptions. In a more general context, this was the motivation behind the principle of Maximum Entropy (ME), originally developed and thoroughly discussed by Jaynes [29-31] in Statistical Physics. The principle provides a self-consistent method of inference for estimating uniquely an unknown but true probability distribution, based on information expressed in terms of known true mean value constraints. It is based on the concept of the entropy functional introduced earlier in Information Theory by Shannon [32]. Over the recent years the principle of ME, subject to queueing theoretic constraints, has inspired a new and powerful analytic framework for the approximate analysis of complex queueing systems and arbitrary queueing networks (c.f., [22, 25-28, 33-64]).

This tutorial paper presents ME product-form approximations and resolution algorithms for both continuous-time and discrete-time First-Come-First-Served (FCFS) QNMs at equilibrium, subject to Repetitive-Service (RS) blocking mechanism with either Fixed (RS-FD) or Random (RS-RD) destination and Arrivals First (AF) or Departures First (DF) buffer management policies. An ME application to the performance analysis of a shared buffer Aynchronous Transfer Mode (ATM) switch architecture is also described. The ME solutions are implemented subject to queueing theoretic Generalised Exponential (GE) and Generalised Geometric (GGeo) mean value constraints. In this context, single server GE and GGeo-type queues in conjunction with associated flow streams (departure, splitting, merging) play the role of *building blocks* in the solution process.

The principle of ME is introduced in Section 2. The GE and GGeo distributions and related formulae for merging of flow streams are described in Section 3. The ME analysis of GE and GGeo type queues in conjunction with interdeparture-time flow formulae are presented in Section 4. The ME product form approximations and resolution algorithms for arbitrary QNMs are reviewed in Section 5. A ME application to a shared buffer ATM switch architecture is carried out in Section 6. Conclusions are given in the last Section, followed by an annotated bibliography.

Remarks: RS blocking occurs when a job upon service completion at queue i attempts to join a destination queue j whose capacity is full. Consequently, the job is rejected by queue j and immediately receives another service at queue i. In the case of RS-FD blocking this is repeated until the job completes service at a moment where the destination queue j is not full. In the RS-RD case each time the job completes service at queue i, a downstream queue is selected independently of the previously chosen destination queue j. Moreover, AF and DF policies for discrete-time queues stipulate how the buffer is filled or emplied in case of simultaneous arrivals and departures at a boundary epoch of a slot (or unit time interval). Under AF arrivals take precedence over departures while the reverse takes place under DF (c.f., Fig. 1).

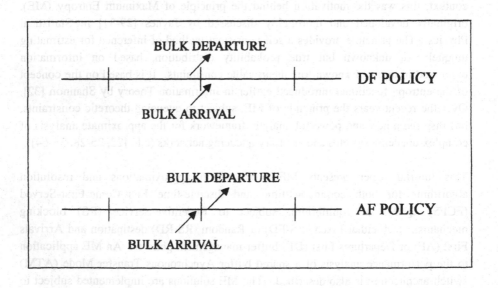

Fig. 1. AF and DF buffer management policies per slot

2. The Principle of ME
2.1 Formalism

Consider a system Q that has a set of possible discrete states $S = \{S_0, S_1, S_2, ...\}$ which may be finite or countable infinite and state S_n, n=0,1,2,... may be specified arbitrarily. Suppose the available information about Q places a number of constraints on $p(S_n)$, the probability distribution that the system Q is at state S_n. Without loss of generality, it is assumed that these take the form of mean values of several suitable functions $\{f_1(S_n), f_2(S_n), ..., f_m(S_n)\}$, where m is less than the number of possible states. The principle of maximum entropy (ME) [29-31] states that, of all distributions satisfying the constraints supplied by the given information, the minimally prejudiced distribution $p(S_n)$ is the one that maximises the system's entropy function

$$H(p) = - \sum_{S_n \in S} p(S_n) \, \ell n\{p(S_n)\}, \tag{2.1}$$

subject to the constraints

$$\sum_{S_n \in S} p(S_n) = 1, \tag{2.2}$$

$$\sum_{S_n \in S} f_k(S_n) p(S_n) = \langle f_k \rangle, \quad k=1,2,...,m, \tag{2.3}$$

where $\{\langle f_k \rangle\}$ are the prescribed mean values defined on the set of functions $\{f_k(S_n)\}$, k=1,2,...,m. Note that in a stochastic context, for example, these functions may be defined on the state space S of a Markov process with states $\{S_n\}$, n ≥ 0, and $p(S_n)$ can be interpreted as the asymptotic probability distribution of state S_n at equilibrium.

The maximisation of H(p), subject to constraints (2.2)-(2.3), can be carried out using Lagrange's Method of Undetermined Multipliers leading to the solution

$$p(S_n) = \frac{1}{Z} \exp\left\{ -\sum_{k=1}^{m} \beta_k f_k(S_n) \right\}, \tag{2.4}$$

where $\exp\{\beta_k\}$, k=1,2,...,m are the Lagrangian coefficients determined from the set of constraints $<f_k>$, and Z, known in statistical physics as the *partition function* (or normalising constant), is given by

$$Z = \exp\{\beta_0\} = \sum_{S_n \in S} \exp\left\{-\sum_{k=1}^{m} \beta_k f_k(S_n)\right\}, \qquad (2.5)$$

where β_0 is a Lagrangian multiplier specified by the normalisation constraint. It can be verified that the Lagrangian multipliers $\{\beta_k\}$, k=1,2,...,m satisfy relations:

$$-\frac{\partial \beta_0}{\partial \beta_k} = <f_k>, \quad k=1,2,...,m, \qquad (2.6)$$

while the ME functional can be expressed by

$$\max_{p} H(p) = \beta_0 + \sum_{k=1}^{m} \beta_k <f_k>. \qquad (2.7)$$

Although it is not generally possible to solve (2.6) for $\{\beta_k\}$ explicitly in terms of $\{<f_k>\}$, numerical methods for obtaining approximate solutions are available. When system Q has a countable infinite set of states, S, the entropy function H(p) is an infinite series having no upper limit, even under the normalisation constraint. However, the added expected values $\{<f_k>\}$ of (2.3) introduce the upper bound (2.7) and the ME solution $\{p(S_n)\}$ exists.

The characterisation of a closed-form ME solution requires the priori estimation of the above multipliers in terms of constraints $\{<f_k>\}$. Note that these constraints may not all be known a priori; but it may be known that these constraints exist. This information, therefore, can be incorporated into the ME formalism in order to characterise the form of the state probability (2.4). As a result, the mean value constraints may become explicit parameters of the ME solution. The analytic implementation of this solution, however, clearly requires the priori calculation of these constraints via queueing theoretic (or even operational) exact of approximate formulae expressed in terms of basic system parameters.

2.2 Justification of ME Principle

The principle of ME has its roots in Bernoulli's principle of *Insufficient Reason (IR)* implying that *the outcomes of an event should be considered initially equally probable unless there is evidence to make us think otherwise.* The entropy functional H(p) may be informally interpreted as the expected amount of uncertainty that exists prior to the system occupying anyone of its states. For a finite set of states $\{S_n\}$, H(p) reaches its maximum (2.7) when all outcomes of an event are equally probable (i.e., prior to the execution of an experiment one is faced with maximum uncertainty on which outcome will be realised). To this end, one should initially start with the distribution of *IF* (i.e., a uniform type distribution) and then *adjust* this distribution to maximise the entropy if prior constraint information is known. In this context, the principle of ME may be stated as *Given the propositions of an event and any information relating to them, the best estimate for the corresponding probabilities is the distribution that maximised the entropy subject to the available information.*

In an information theoretic context [29], the ME solution corresponds to the maximum disorder to system states, and thus is considered to be the least biased distribution estimate of all solutions that satisfy the system's constraints. In sampling terms, Jaynes [30] has shown that, given the imposed constraints, the ME solution can be experimentally realised in overwhelmingly more ways than any other distribution. Major discrepancies between the ME distribution and the experimentally observed distribution indicate that important physical constraints have been overlooked. Conversely, experimental agreement with the ME solution represents evidence that the constraints of the system have been properly identified.

More details on the principle of ME can be found in Tribus [65]. A generalisation to the principle of Minimum Relative Entropy (MRE) - requiring, in addition, a prior estimate of the unknown distribution - can be seen in Shore and Johnson [66].

2.3 ME Analysis in Systems Modelling

In the field of systems modelling expected values of various performance distributions of interest, such as the number of jobs in each resource queue concerned, are often known, or may be explicitly derived, in terms of moments of interarrival and service time distributions. Note that the determination of the distributions themselves, via classical queueing theory, may prove an infeasible task even for systems of queues with moderate complexity. Hence, the methodology of entropy maximisation may be applied to characterise useful information theoretic approximations of performance distributions of queueing systems and networks.

Focusing on a general QNM, the ME solution (2.4) may be interpreted as a product-form approximation, subject to the set of mean values $\{<f_k>\}$, k=1,2,...,m, viewed as marginal type constraints per queue. Thus, for an open QNM, entropy maximisation suggests a decomposition into individual queues with revised interarrival and service times. The marginal ME solutions of these queues, in conjunction with related formulae for the first two moments of the effective flow, can play the role of building blocks towards the computation of the performance metrics (c.f., [27]). For a closed QNM, the implementation of ME solution (2.4) clearly requires the a priori estimation of the Lagrangian coefficients $\exp\{\beta_k\}$, k=1,2,...,m. To this end, a modified algorithm of an open network satisfying the principles of flow and population conservation (*pseudo* open network) may be used in conjunction with a convolution type procedure for the estimation of the performance metrics (c.f., [28]).

3. The GE and GGeo Distributional Models
3.1 The GE Distribution

The GE distribution is of the form

$$F(t) = P(W \le t) = 1 - \tau\, e^{-\sigma t}, t \ge 0, \tag{3.1}$$

where

$$\tau = 2/(C^2 + 1), \tag{3.2}$$

$$\sigma = \tau v, \tag{3.3}$$

W is a mixed-time random variable (rv) of the interevent-time, while $1/v$ is the mean and C^2 is the squared coefficient of variation (SCV) of rv W(c.f., Fig 2).

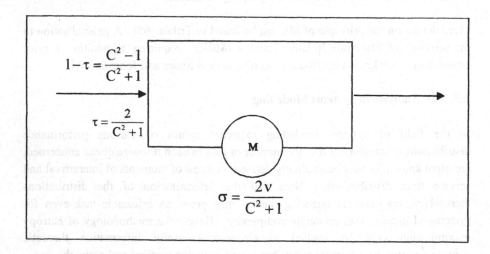

$$1 - \tau = \frac{C^2 - 1}{C^2 + 1}$$

$$\tau = \frac{2}{C^2 + 1}$$

M

$$\sigma = \frac{2v}{C^2 + 1}$$

Fig. 2. The GE distribution with parameters τ and σ.

For $C^2 > 1$, the GE model (3.1) is a mixed-time probability distribution and it can be interpreted as either

(i)   an extremal case of the family of two-phase exponential distributions (e.g., Hyperexponential-2 (H_2)) having the same v and C^2, where one of the two phases has zero service time; or

(ii)   a bulk type distribution with an underlying counting process equivalent to a Compound Poisson Process (CPP) with parameter $2v/C^2 + 1$) and geometrically destributed bulk sizes with mean $= (C^2 + 1)/2$ and SCV $= (C^2 - 1)/(C^2 + 1))$ given by

$$P(N_{cp} = n) = \begin{cases} \sum_{i=1}^{n} \dfrac{\sigma^i}{i!} \, e^{-\sigma} \begin{pmatrix} n-1 \\ i-1 \end{pmatrix} \tau^i (1-\tau)^{n-i}, & \text{if } n \geq 1, \\[2mm] e^{-\sigma}, & \text{if } n = 0, \end{cases} \tag{3.4}$$

where N_{cp} is a Compound Poisson (CP) rv of the number of events per unit time corresponding to a stationary GE-type intervent rv.

By using the bulk interpretation of the GE-type distribution and applying the Law of Total Probability it can be shown that merging M GE-type streams with parameters (v_i, C_i^2), i=1,2,...,M results in a GE-type overall stream. This stream, however, generally corresponds to a non-renewal CPP process (with non-geometric bulk sizes) - unless all C_i^2's are equal - with parameters (τ, C^2) determined by [27, 28].

$$v = \sum_{i=1}^{M} v_i, \tag{3.5}$$

$$C^2 = -1 + \left[\sum_{i=1}^{M} \dfrac{v_i}{v} (C_i^2 + 1)^{-1} \right]^{-1}. \tag{3.6}$$

3.2   The GGeo Distribution

The GGeo distribution is of the form

$$f_n = P(Y = n) = \begin{cases} 1 - \tau, & \text{if } n = 0, \\[2mm] \tau\sigma(1-\sigma)^{n-1}, & \text{if } n \geq 1, \end{cases} \tag{3.7}$$

where

$$\tau = 2/(C^2 + 1 + v),\qquad(3.8)$$

$$\sigma = \tau v,\qquad(3.9)$$

Y is a discrete-time rv of the interevent-time, while $1/v$ and C^2 are the mean and SCV of rv Y (c.f., Fig. 3).

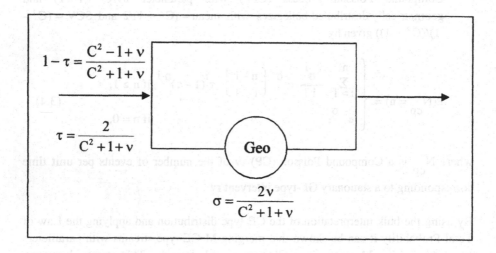

$$1 - \tau = \frac{C^2 - 1 + v}{C^2 + 1 + v}$$

$$\tau = \frac{2}{C^2 + 1 + v}$$

Geo

$$\sigma = \frac{2v}{C^2 + 1 + v}$$

Fig. 3. The GGeo distribution with parameters τ and σ.

For $C^2 \geq |1 - v|$, the GGeo model (3.7) is a discrete-time probability distribution implying a bulk intervent pattern according to a Bulk Bernoulli Process (BBP) with a rate σ, while the number of events (e.g, arrivals or departures) at the boundary epochs of a slot is geometrically distributed with parameter τ. Thus, the GGeo distribution is generated by a sequence of bulk Bernoulli independent and identically distributed non-negative integer valued rv.'s $\{Y_k\}$, where Y_k is the number of events in a slot, with a probability distribution given by

$$g_\ell = \begin{cases} P(Y_k = 0) = 1 - \sigma, & \text{if } \ell = 0, \\ P(Y_k = \ell) = \sigma\tau(1 - \tau)^{\ell - 1}, & \text{if } \ell \geq 1. \end{cases} \qquad (3.10)$$

It can be verified via the Law of Total Probability that merging M GGeo-type streams with parameters (v_i, C_i^2), i=1,2,...,M, the corresponding overall parameters (v, C^2) are given by (3.5) and

$$C^2 = -1 - v + \left[\sum_{i=1}^{M} \frac{v_i}{v} (C_i^2 + v_i + 1)^{-1} \right]^{-1}, \qquad (3.11)$$

respectively [60, 64]. Note, however, that the resulting distribution is not of GGeo-type.

Remarks: The GE and GGeo distributions are versatile, possessing pseudo-memoryless properties which make the solution of many queueing systems and networks analytically tractable. The GE and GGeo cannot be physically interpreted as stochastic models outside the ranges $C^2 \geq 1$ and $C^2 \geq | 1 - v |$, respectively. However, they can be meaningfully considered as pseudo-distributions of flow model approximations of stochastic models, in which negative branching pseudo-probabilities (or weights) are permitted. The utility of other pseudo-distributions in systems modelling has been pointed out in [67, 68].

4. The ME Building Blocks: GE and GGeo Type Single Server Queues

This Section determines the form of ME solutions for stable G/G/1 and G/G/1/N queues, subject to queueing theoretic GE and GGeo type constraints. Moreover, it presents closed-form expressions for the SCV of the interdeparture-time distribution of the GE/GE/1 and GGeo/GGeo/1 queues at equilibrium.

4.1 A Stable ME G/G/1 Queue

Consider a stable FCFS G/G/1 queue with infinite capacity where jobs belong to a single class and arrive according to an arbitrary interarrival-time distribution with mean $1/\lambda$ and SCV, Ca^2. Moreover, they are served by a single server having a general service-time distribution with mean $1/\mu$ and SCV, Cs^2. Let at any given time the state of the system be described by the number of jobs present (waiting or receiving service) and $p(n)$ be the steady-state probability that the G/G/1 queue is at state n, $n=0,1,2,\dots$.

The form of a universal ME solution, $p(n)$, for either a continuous-time or discrete-time G/G/1 queue at equilibrium can be obtained by maximising the entropy functional, $H(p)$, subject to the following constraints:

(a) Normalisation

$$\sum_{n=0}^{\infty} p(n) = 1 .$$

(b) Server utilisation (UTIL), $\rho\,(0 < \rho = \lambda/\mu < 1)$,

$$\sum_{n=1}^{\infty} h(n)\, p(n) = \rho,$$

where $h(n) = 0$, if $n = 0$, or 1, if $n \geq 1$.

(c) Mean Queue Length (MQL), $L\,(\rho < L < +\infty)$,

$$\sum_{n=1}^{\infty} n\, p(n) = L.$$

The maximisation of H(p), subject to constraints (a)-(c), can be obtained via Langrange's Method of Undetermined Mulitipliers leading to the following solution:

$$p(n) = \begin{cases} 1 - \rho, & \text{if } n = 0, \\[2mm] (1 - \rho)g\, x^n, & \text{if } n \geq 1, \end{cases} \tag{4.1}$$

where g and x are the Lagrangian coefficients corresponding to constraints ρ and L, respectively, and are given by

$$g = \frac{(1 - x)\,\rho}{(1 - \rho)\,x} = \frac{\rho^2}{(L - \rho)\,(1 - \rho)}, \tag{4.2}$$

and

$$x = \frac{L - \rho}{L}. \tag{4.3}$$

The ME solution (4.1) can be rewritten, via (4.2), as a GGeo state probability distribution with parameters ρ and $1 - x$, namely

$$p(n) = \begin{cases} 1 - \rho, & \text{if } n = 0, \\[2mm] \rho(1 - x)x^{n-1}, & \text{if } n \geq 1. \end{cases} \tag{4.4}$$

The implementation of the ME solution (4.4) depends on the analytic determination of the MQL, L. This is achieved in the next Section by focusing on the GE/G/1 and GGeo/G/1 queues at equilibrium.

4.1.1 The GE and GGeo Type Information Constraints

Consider GE/G/1 and GGeo/G/1 queues at equilibrium. By applying the generalised Laplace and z-transform equations, respectively, it can be shown [39, 60] that for either queue the random observer's MQL is given by the same formula, namely

$$L = \frac{\rho}{2} \left[1 + \frac{Ca^2 + \rho \ Cs^2}{1 - \rho} \right] , \tag{4.5}$$

where for $L \geq \rho$ it follows that $\rho \geq (1 - Ca^2)/(1 + Cs^2)$. It is, therefore, implied that the ME solution of a G/G/1 queue is insensitive with respect to GE and GGeo interarrival-time distributions. Moreover, it can be established, via the generalised embedded Markov chain approach for continuous-time and discrete-time queues, that the ME solution, $p(n)$ $n=0,1,2,...$ becomes exact if the underlying service time distributions of the GE/G/1 and GGeo/G/1 queues at equilibrium are also of $GE(\mu, Cs^2)$ and $GGeo(\mu, Cs^2)$ types, respectively (c.f., [39, 60]).

In the next Section closed-form expressions for the SCV of the interdeparture-time process are established.

4.1.2 The GE and GGeo Type Parameters of the Interdeparture Process

Consider the GE/GE/1 and GGeo/GGeo/1 queues at equilibrium. By applying the Laplace transform and z-transform equations of the interdeparture-time distribution (within continuous-time and discrete-time domains), respectively, it can be shown that the mean departure rate is given by λ, while the SCV, Cd^2, is determined by

(i) $Cd^2 = \rho(1 - \rho) + (1 - \rho) Ca^2 + \rho^2 Cs^2 ,$ \hfill (4.6)

for a stable GE/GE/1 queue [27] and

(ii) $Cd^2 = \rho^2 (Cs^2 + \mu - 1) - \rho(Ca^2 + \lambda - 1) + Ca^2 ,$ \hfill (4.7)

for a stable GGeo/GGeo/1 queue under both AF and DF buffer management policies [60].

4.2 A Stable ME G/G/1/N Queue

Consider a single class FCFS G/G/1/N censored queue at equilibrium with finite capacity, N and general interarrival and service time distributions with known first two moments. The notation of Section 4.1 applies, as appropriate. It is assumed that the arrival process is *censored*, i.e., arriving jobs are turned away when the buffer is full.

The form of a universal ME solution p(n), n=0,1,2,...,N, applicable to either a continuous-time or discrete-time G/G/1/N queue at equilibrium, can be established, subject to the constraints of

(a) Normalisation

$$\sum_{n=0}^{N} p(n) = 1 \,,$$

(b) UTIL, υ $(0 < \upsilon < 1)$,

$$\sum_{n=1}^{N} h(n)\, p(n) = \upsilon \,,$$

(c) MQL, Ω $(\upsilon \leq \Omega < N)$,

$$\sum_{n=1}^{N} n\, p(n) = \Omega$$

(d) Full buffer state probability, $\varphi = p(N)$ $(0 < \varphi < 1)$,

$$\sum_{n=0}^{N} f(n)\, p(n) = \varphi \,,$$

where $f(n) = 0$, if $0 \leq n \leq N\text{-}1$, or 1, if $n = N$, satisfying the flow-balance condition

$$\lambda(1 - \pi) = \mu\, \upsilon \,, \tag{4.8}$$

where π is the blocking probability that a tagged job within an arriving bulk will find a full buffer.

By applying the Method of Lagrange's Undetermined Mulitipliers the ME solution, p(n), subject to constraints (a)-(d), is expressed by

$$p(n) = \begin{cases} 1/Z , & \text{if } n=0 , \\ (1/Z)g\,x^{n}, & \text{if } n=1,2,...,N-1 , \\ (1/Z)g\,x^{n}\,y, & \text{if } n=N , \end{cases} \qquad (4.9)$$

where Z is the normalising constant given by

$$Z = 1 + g\,x\,\frac{1-x^{N-1}}{1-x} + g\,y\,x^{N} , \qquad (4.10)$$

and $\{g, x, y\}$ are the Lagrangian coefficients corresponding to constraints υ, Ω and φ, respectively. By making asymptotic connections to infinite capacity G/G/1 queues at equilibrium as $N \to +\infty$, the Lagrangian coefficients g and x are assumed invariant with respect to N and are given by (4.2) and (4.3), respectively, while Ω reduces to L and is given by (4.5). The determination of Lagrangian coefficient y, however, depends on the blocking probability of a tagged job, π and the probability of an arriving bulk to find a n jobs in the system, $p_{a}(n)$, n=1,2,...,N. These probabilities are determined in the next Section by considering GE/GE/1/N and GGeo/GGeo/1/N queues at equilibrium.

4.2.1 The Blocking Probability π

Consider a stable GE/GE/1/N queue or a GGEo/GGeo/1/N queue under AF or DF buffer management policy. An universal analytic expression for blocking probability π can be established in terms of Lagrangian coefficients $\{x, g, y\}$ by applying probabilistic arguments focusing on a tagged job within an arriving bulk. Clearly, the blocking probability π is conditioned on the position of a tagged job within the bulk and the number of jobs a bulk finds on arrival in the system. The following two distinct and exhaustive blocking cases are considered:

(i)   The arriving bulk finds the queue empty with probability $p_{a}(0)$ and the tagged job is blocked. This event occurs with probability

$$\pi(N_{a}=0, N_{t}=N)$$

$$= p_{a}(0) \sum_{j=N+1}^{\infty} j \left[\frac{\tau_{a}(1-\tau_{a})^{j-1}}{1/\tau_{a}} \right]^{j-(N+1)} \sum_{k=0}^{} \tau_{s}(1-\tau_{s})^{k}\,\frac{j-N-k}{j} , \qquad (4.11)$$

where N_a, N_t are rv.'s representing the number of jobs seen in the queue by an arriving bulk and its tagged job, respectively, $j \tau_a^2 (1 - \tau_a)^{j-1}$ is the probability that the bulk containing the tagged job has size j, $\tau_s (1 - \tau_s)^k$ is the probability that the first k jobs depart through the zero service branch of $GE(\tau_s, \sigma_s)$ or GGeo (τ_s, σ_s) distribution and (j-N-k)/j is the probability that the tagged job occupies one of the positions N+k+1, N+k+2, ..., j within the bulk (i.e., it is blocked). Expression (4.11) can be written simplified to the following compact form:

$$\pi(N_a = 0, N_t = N) = \delta \, p_a (0) (1 - \tau_a)^N, \tag{4.12}$$

where $\delta = \tau_s / (\tau_s (1 - \tau_a) + \tau_a)$.

(ii) An arriving bulk finds on arrival n jobs in the queue, n=1,2,...,N (including the one in the Exponential or Geo service branch of a $GE(\tau_s, \sigma_s)$ or GGeo (τ_s, σ_s) distribution, respectively) and the tagged job is blocked. By applying similar arguments to those of case (i), this event takes place with probability

$$\pi (N_a \geq 1, N_t = N) = \sum_{n=1}^{N} (1 - \tau_a)^{N-n} p_a (n), \tag{4.13}$$

where $p_a (n)$ is the probability that the arriving bulk finds n(≥ 1) jobs in the queue.

Thus, a general form of the blocking probability π of a GE/GE/1/N or GGeo/GGeo/1/N queue (under AF or DF policies) can be expressed as the sum of the probabilities (4.12) and (4.13), namely,

$$\pi = \delta \, p_a (0) (1 - \tau_a)^N + \sum_{n=1}^{N} (1 - \tau_a)^{N-n} p_a (n). \tag{4.14}$$

4.2.2 The Arriver's Probability, $p_a (n)$, $n \geq 1$

The arriving bulk of a GE/GE/1/N queue or GGeo/GGeo/1/N queue under AF policy has the same steady state probability as that of the random observer's ME solution

(4.4), i.e., $p_a(n) = p(n) \; \forall n$ (c.f., [20, 54]). However, for a censored GGeo/GGeo/1/N queue under DF buffer management policy, the following mutually exclusive events are distinguished:

(i) $\{N_a = 0\}$

An arriving bulk finds an empty system (with probability $p_a(0)$). Under DF policy the state of the queue before any departure(s) take place (i.e., outside observer's view point) can only be in one of the following cases:

(i₁)   The queue was idle with probability $p(0)$;

(i₂)   The queue was in state n $(1 \le n \le N)$ with probability $p(n)$, n = 1,2,...,N and, therefore, all cells of the queue departed at the end of the slot together with the one in Geo service. This even occurs with probability

$$\sigma_s (1 - \tau_s)^{n-1} \; .$$

Thus,

$$p_a(0) = p(0) + \sigma_s \sum_{n=1}^{N} (1 - \tau_s)^{n-1} p(n), \tag{4.15}$$

(ii) $\{N_a = n \ge 1\}$

An arriving bulk finds n(n = 1,2,...,N) jobs in the queue. In a similar fashion to case (i₂), just before any departure(s) take place (under DF policy) there were k(k $\ge$ n) cells in the queue with random observer's probability $p(k)$. Two mutually exclusive cases are encountered in this situation:

(ii₁) $\{k = n\}$

The cell in Geo service stays there for another service slot with probability

$$1 - \sigma_s$$

(ii₂) $\{k \ge n + 1\}$

The cell in Geo service departs (with probability σ_s) together with k - (n + 1) the cells who leave through the zero service branch of the GGeo distribution with probability

$$(1 - \tau_s)^{k-n-1} \tau_s.$$

Combining cases (ii$_1$) and (ii$_2$) - and applying the Law of Total Probability, it follows that

$$p_a(n) = (1 - \sigma_s)\, p(n) + \sigma_s \sum_{k=n+1}^{N} \tau_s (1 - \tau_s)^{k-n-1}\, p(k). \qquad (4.16)$$

Substituting (4.15) and (4.16) into (4.14) and after some algebraic manipulation, it follows that

$$\pi = \delta\, p(0)\, (1 - \tau_a)^N + (1 - \sigma_s) \sum_{k=1}^{N} p(k)\, (1 - \tau_a)^{N-\kappa}$$

$$+ \sigma_s\, \delta\, (1 - \tau_a) \sum_{k=1}^{N} p(k)\, (1 - \tau_a)^{N-k}. \qquad (4.17)$$

4.2.3 The Lagrangian Coefficient, y

The Lagrangian coefficient y corresponding to the full buffer state probability can be determined by substituting π into the flow balance condition (4.8) and solving with respect y. After some manipulation it can be verified that for a GE/GE/1/N queue and GGeo/GGeo/1/N queue under a DF policy, y is given by a universal form, namely,

$$y = \frac{1}{1 - (1 - \tau_s)x}. \qquad (4.18)$$

For a GGeo/GGeo/1/N queue under AF policy it can be shown that y is given by

$$y = \frac{1-\rho}{1-x} + (1-\tau_a) \left[\frac{\rho}{1-\tau_a-x} \right.$$

$$\left. - \left(\frac{1-\rho}{1-x}\, \delta + \frac{\rho}{1-\tau_a-x} \right) \left(\frac{1-\tau_a}{x} \right)^{N-1} \right]. \qquad (4.19)$$

Remarks: It can be shown that the ME solution (4.9) satisfies the global balance equations of the censored GE/GE/1/N and GGeo/GGeo/1/N queues at equilibrium (c.f., 53, 54]). Moreover, these ME solutions can be used as building blocks in the performance analysis of some multi-buffered ATM switch architectures (e.g., [63]).

5. Entropy Maximisation and Arbitrary QNMs
5.1 Open QNMs with RS Blocking

Consider an arbitrary open queueing network under RS-RD or RS-FD blocking mechanisms consisting of M FCFS single server queues with general external interarrival and service times. The notation of Section 4 is adopted with the incorporation of subscript i. At any given time the state of the network is described by a vector $\underline{n} = (n_1, n_2,...,n_M)$, where n_i denotes the number of jobs at queue i, i=1,2,...,M, such that $0 \le n_i \le N_i$. Let $p(\underline{n})$ be the equilibrium probability that the queueing network is in state $\underline{n}$.

It can be shown that the ME solution, $p(\underline{n})$, subject to normalisation and marginal constraints of the type (b)-(d), namely υ_i, Ω_i and φ_i (i=1,2,...,M), is given by the product-form approximation (c.f., [53, 54, 58])

$$p(\underline{n}) = \prod_{i=1}^{M} p_i(n_i), \qquad (5.1)$$

where $p_i(n_i)$ is the marginal ME solution of a censored G/G/1/N_i queue i, i=1,2,...,M (c.f., Section 4.2). Thus, entropy maximisation suggests a decomposition of the original open network into individual censored G/G/1/N_i queues with revised interarrival-time and service-time distributions.

Assuming that all flow processes (i.e., merge, split, departure) are renewal and their interevent-time distributions being of GE or GGeo type, each queue i, i=1,2,...,M, can be seen as a censored GE/GE/1/N_i or GGeo/GGeo/1/N_i queue with (a) GE or GGeo overall interarrival process (including *rejected* jobs), formed by the merging of departing streams towards queue i, generated by queues {j}, $\forall j \in A_i$, where A_i is the set of upstream queues of queue i (which may include outside world *queue 0*) and (b) an effective service-time distribution reflecting the total time during which a server of queue i is occupied by a particular job.

The rate and SCV of the effective service-time depend on (a) the type of RS blocking mechanism enforced, and (b) all blocking probabilities π_{ij}, $i \neq j$, $\forall j \in D_i$ (i.e., the probabilities that a completer from queue i is blocked by queue j ($\neq$ i)), where D_j is the set of all downstream queues of queue i. Using the properties of the GE or GGeo distribution it can be verified that the rate $\hat{\mu}_i$, and SCV, $\hat{C}s_i^2$, of the effective service time are determined for all i=1,2,...,M by [54].

$$
\hat{\mu}_i =
\begin{cases}
\mu_i (1 - \pi_{ci}) \,, & \text{if RS-RD,} \\[2em]
\mu_i \left(\displaystyle\sum_{j \in D_i} \frac{\alpha_{ij}}{1 - \pi_{ij}} \right)^{-1}, & \text{if RS-FD,}
\end{cases}
\tag{5.2}
$$

$$
\hat{C}s_i^2 =
\begin{cases}
\pi_{ci} + Cs_i^2 (1 - \pi_{ci}) \,, & \text{if RS-RD,} \\[2em]
-1 + \dfrac{Cs_i^2}{\displaystyle\sum_{j \in D_i} \frac{\alpha_{ij}}{(1 - \pi_{ij})}} + \dfrac{\displaystyle\sum_{j \in D_i} \frac{\alpha_{ij}(1 + \pi_{ij})}{(1 - \pi_{ij})^2}}{\left[\displaystyle\sum_{j \in D_i} \frac{\alpha_{ij}}{(1 - \pi_{ij})} \right]^2}, & \text{if RS-FD,}
\end{cases}
\tag{5.3}
$$

where π_{ci} is the blocking probability that a completer from queue i is blocked under RS-RD blocking mechanism, i.e., $\pi_{ci} = \sum_{j \in D_i} \alpha_{ij} \pi_{ij}$, with $\{\alpha_{ij}\}$, i=1,2,...,M (i$\neq$j) being the associated transition probabilities. Note that only in the case of RS-RD blocking the effective service-time is represented exactly by a GE or GGeo distribution with parameters $\hat{\mu}_i$ and $\hat{C}s_i^2$.

The effective arrival stream of jobs at the GE/GE/1/N_i or GGeo/GGeo/1/N_i queue can be seen as the result of a two-way splitting of overall merging stream with parameter π_i (i.e., the blocking probability of either an external arriver or a completer in the network is blocked by queue i). Denoting $\hat{\lambda}_i$ and $\hat{Ca}_i^2$ as the parameters of the effective interarrival process, it follows that the corresponding parameters of the overall interarrival process are given by

$$\lambda_i = \frac{\hat{\lambda}_i}{1 - \pi_i}, \quad Ca_i^2 = \frac{\hat{Ca}_i^2 - \pi_i}{1 - \pi_i}, \quad i=1,2,...,M. \tag{5.4}$$

Moreover, $\{\hat{\lambda}_i\}$, $i=1,2,...,M$, must satisfy the effective job flow rate equations, i.e.,

$$\hat{\lambda}_i = \hat{\lambda}_{0i} + \sum_{j=1}^{M} \hat{\alpha}_{ji} \hat{\lambda}_j, \quad i=1,2,...,M, \tag{5.5}$$

where $\hat{\lambda}_{0i}$ is the effective external arrival rate and $\hat{\alpha}_{ji}$ is the effective transition probability [58] given by

$$\hat{\alpha}_{ji} = \begin{cases} \dfrac{\alpha_{ji} (1 - \pi_{ji})}{(1 - \pi_{cj})}, & \text{if RS-RD}, \\[3mm] \alpha_{ji}, & \text{if RS-FD}, \end{cases} \tag{5.6}$$

$j=1,2,...,M, i \in D_j$ (n.b., $\pi_{j0} = 0$).

The SCV of the effective interarrival process of each queue i, $\hat{Ca}_i^2$, $i=1,2,...,M$, can be approximated within a continuous-time or a discrete-time domain by applying the merging GE-type or GGeo-type flow formulae (3.6) and (3.11), respectively and is given by

$$
\hat{Ca}_i^2 =
\begin{cases}
-1 + \left[\dfrac{\hat{\lambda}_{0i}}{\hat{\lambda}_i} \left(\hat{Cd}_{0i}^2 + 1 \right)^{-1} \right. \\
\qquad \left. + \sum_{j=1}^{M} \dfrac{\hat{\lambda}_j \, \hat{\alpha}_{ji}}{\hat{\lambda}_i} \left(\hat{Cd}_{j i}^2 + 1 \right)^{-1} \right]^{-1}, \quad \text{for GE streams,} \\[4em]
-1 - \hat{\lambda}_i + \left[\dfrac{\hat{\lambda}_{0i}}{\hat{\lambda}_i} \left(\hat{Cd}_{0i}^2 + 1 + \hat{\lambda}_{0i} \right)^{-1} \right. \\
\qquad \left. + \sum_{j=1}^{M} \dfrac{\hat{\lambda}_j \, \hat{\alpha}_{ji}}{\hat{\lambda}_i} \left(\hat{Cd}_{j i}^2 + 1 + \hat{\lambda}_j \hat{\alpha}_{ji} \right)^{-1} \right]^{-1}, \quad \text{for GGeo streams,}
\end{cases}
\tag{5.7}
$$

where for i=1,2,...,M

$$
\hat{\lambda}_{0i} = \lambda_{0i} (1 - \pi_{0i}),
\tag{5.8}
$$

$$
\hat{Cd}_{0i}^2 = \pi_{0i} + (1 - \pi_{0i}) Ca_{0i}^2, \quad 0 \in A_i,
\tag{5.9}
$$

$$
\hat{Cd}_{j i}^2 = 1 - \hat{\alpha}_{ji} + \hat{\alpha}_{ji} \hat{Cd}_j^2, \quad j \in A_i,
\tag{5.10}
$$

λ_{0i} and Ca_{0i}^2 are the overall rate and SCV of the external interarrival-times, while $\hat{Cd}_j^2$ is the SCV of the effective interdeparture time of queue j, j=1,2,...,M, represented by either a GE/GE/1/N$_j$ or GGeo/GGeo/1/N$_j$ queueing models, namely

$$
\hat{Cd}_j^2 =
\begin{cases}
\hat{\rho}_j (1 - \hat{\rho}_j) + (1 - \hat{\rho}_j) \hat{Ca}_j^2 + \hat{\rho}_j^2 \hat{Cs}_j^2, & \text{for GE/GE/ 1 /N}_j, \\[1em]
\hat{\rho}_j^2 (\hat{Cs}_j^2 + \hat{\mu}_i - 1) - \hat{\rho}_j (\hat{Ca}_j^2 + \hat{\lambda}_j - 1) + \hat{Ca}_j^2, & \text{for GGeo / GGeo /1/N}_j,
\end{cases}
\tag{5.11}
$$

with $\hat{\rho}_j = \hat{\lambda}_j / \hat{\mu}_j$. Moreover by applying the Law of Total Probability π_i is clearly given by

$$\pi_i = \sum_{j \in A_i} \lambda_{ji} \, \pi_{ji} \Big/ \sum_{j \in A_i} \lambda_{ji} \,, \tag{5.12}$$

where $\lambda_{ji} = \hat{\lambda}_j \, \hat{\alpha}_{ji}/(1 - \pi_{ji})$, $j \in A_i - \{0\}$. The behaviour of a single queueing station i as a building block within an open QNM can be observed in Fig. 4, while the revised GE/GE/1/N_i or GGeo/GGeo/1/N_i queue i in isolation can be seen in Fig. 5.

Finally, queue 0, $0 \in A_j$, and each queue i, $i \in A_j$, generate an overall arriving stream to queue j, j=1,2,...,M, seen as a censored GE/GE/1/N_j queue or GGeo/GGeo/1/N_j queue under AF or DF policies with rate $\hat{\lambda}_i \, \hat{\alpha}_{ij}/(1 - \pi_{ij})$ and SCV equal to $Cd_{ij}^2 = (\hat{Cd}_{ij}^2 - \pi_{ij})/(1 - \pi_{ij})$, $i \in A_j$. Thus, if each of these streams is considered in isolation to be the only arriving stream to queue j, then π_{ij} ($j \in D_i$ and $N_j < +\infty$) can be determined by an expressions analogous to (4.14) and (4.17), as appropriate. For example, for a GE/GE/1/N_i queue or GGeo/GGeo/1/N_i queue under AF policy, if clearly follows that

$$\pi_{ij} = (1 - \tau_{aij})^{N_j} \left[\frac{\hat{\tau}_{sj}}{\hat{\tau}_{sj}(1 - \tau_{aij}) + \tau_{aij}} \right] p_j(n_j)$$

$$\tag{5.13}$$

$$+ \sum_{n_j = 1}^{N_j} (1 - \tau_{aij})^{N_j - n_j} p_j(n_j), \quad i=0,1,...,M, \quad j=1,2,...,M \quad (i \neq j),$$

where

$$\tau_{aij} = \begin{cases} \dfrac{2}{Cd_{ij}^2 + 1} & , \text{ if } i \neq 0, \\[2ex] \dfrac{2}{Ca_{0i}^2 + 1} & , \text{ if } i = 0, \end{cases} \tag{5.14}$$

and

$$\hat{\tau}_{sj} = \frac{2}{\hat{Cs}_j^2 + 1} \quad , \quad j=1,2,...,M. \tag{5.15}$$

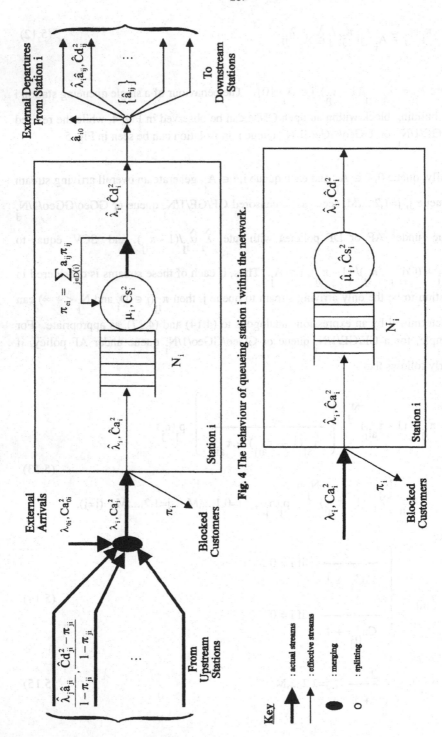

Fig. 4 The behaviour of queueing station i within the network.

Fig. 5 The revised censored queue i in isolation.

A similar expression to that of (4.17) holds for a GGeo/GGeo/1/N_j queue under DF policy.

The ME approximation algorithm involves the solution of the system of non-linear equations for the blocking probabilities $\{\pi_{ij}\}$. It starts with some initial value for $\hat{C}d_i^2$ and then an iterative procedure is applied involving all queues until a convergence for $\hat{C}d_i^2$, $i=1,2,...,R$, is achieved. A diagramatic representation of the solution process can be seen in Fig. 6. The main steps of a revised ME algorithm (c.f., [58]) are given below:

ME Algorithm
Begin
Inputs: M, N_i, μ_i, Cs_i^2, λ_{0i}, Ca_{0i}^2, $i=1,2,...,M$,

             $\{\alpha_{ij}\}$, $i=1,2,...,M$; $j=0,1,...,M$;

Step 1:   Feedback correction (if $\alpha_{ii} > 0$, $i=1,2,...,M$);

Step 2:   Initialisation: $\hat{C}d_i^2$, $i=1,2,...,M$;

             $\{\pi_{ij}\}$, $i=0,1,...,M$; $j=1,2,...,M$;

Step 3:   Solve the system of non-linear equations $\{\pi_{ij}\}$, $i=0,1,...,M$; $j=1,2,...,M$;

     *Step 3.1:*Calculate:

$$\{\hat{\alpha}_{ij}\}, i=1,2,...,M; j=0,1,...,M;$$

     *Step 3.2:*Compute:

$$\{\hat{\lambda}_i, \hat{\lambda}_{0i}, \pi_i, \hat{C}a_i^2, \lambda_i, Ca_i^2, \pi_{ci}, \hat{\mu}_i, \hat{C}s_i^2\}, i=1,2,...,M;$$

     *Step 3.3:*Use the Newton-Raphson method to find new values for $\{\pi_{ij}\}$, $i=0,1,...,M$; $j=1,2,...,M$;

     *Step 3.4:*Return to Step 3.1 until convergence of $\{\pi_{ij}\}$, $\forall$ i, j;

Step 4:   Fine new values for $\{\hat{C}d_i^2\}$, $i=1,2,...,M$;

Step 5:   Return to Step 3 until convergence of $\{\hat{C}d_i^2\}$, $\forall i$;

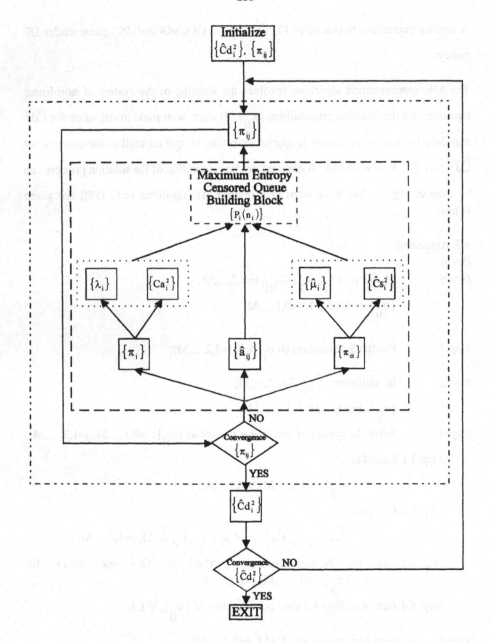

Fig. 6 A diagramatic representation of the two nested recursive schemes.

Step 6:   Apply entropy maximisation to evaluate each queue i, i=1,2,...,M, as a censored $GE(\lambda_i, Ca_i^2)/GE(\hat{\mu}_i, \hat{Cs}_i^2)/1/N_i$ queue or $GGeo(\lambda_i, Ca_i^2/GE(\hat{\mu}_i, \hat{Cs}_i^2)/1/N_i$ queue, if $N_i < +\infty$, and as corresponding infinite capacity queues at equilibrium, if $N_i \to +\infty$;

Step 7:   Obtain the performance metrics of interest;

End.

Remarks: The main computational effort of the ME algorithm is at every iteration between Steps 3 and 5. The non-linear system of equations $\{\pi_{ij}\}$, i=0,1,...,M, j=1,2,...,M, can be rewritten in the form $\pi = F(\pi)$, where π and F are column vectors of dimension Ψ, where Ψ is the cardinality of the set $\{\pi_{ij}\}$, $i \neq j$ and $N_j < +\infty$. It can be verified that the computational cost of the ME algorithm for open networks is $o(k\Psi^3)$, where k is the number of iterations between steps 3 and 5 and Ψ^3 is the number of manipulations for inverting the Jacobian matrix of F with respect to π.

Notably, the existence and unicity for the solution of the system of non-linear equations $\pi = F(\pi)$ cannot be proved analytically due to the complexity of the expression of the blocking probabilities $\{\pi_{ij}\}$. Furthermore, no strict mathematical justification can be given for the convergence of $\{\hat{Cd}_i^2\}$, i=1,2,...,M; nevertheless, numerical instabilities are very rarely observed in many experiments that have been carried out, even when the probabilities π_{ij} are relatively close to 1. Only in networks with high interarrival-time and service-time variability, in conjunction with high server utilisations and feedback streams, the solutions of the non-linear system $\pi = F(\pi)$ goes towards the trivial solution of $\pi_{ij} = 1$. This can be attributed to the fact that the effective utilisations $\{\hat{\lambda}_i/\hat{\mu}_i\}$ attain the value 1 and thus the system becomes unstable.

5.2 Closed QNMs with RS Blocking

Consider an arbitrary closed queueing network under RS-RD or RS-FD blocking mechanisms consisting of M FCFS single server queues with finite capacity N_i, i=1,2,...,M, general service-times and a fixed number of jobs K such that

$N_1 + N_2 + ... + N_M > K$. For each queue i, i=1,2,...,M the notation of the previous section apply and, in addition, let $\hat{N}_i$ be the virtual capacity of queue i, i.e., $\hat{N}_i = \min (N_i, K)$, κ_i be the minimum number of jobs always present, i.e., $\kappa_i = \max \{0, K - \sum_{i \neq j} \hat{N}_j\}$ and $\tilde{N}_i$ be the rv of the number of jobs in queue i as seen by a random observer.

By analogy to Sections 4 and 5.1, the form of the ME state probability, $p(\underline{n})$, $\underline{n} \in S(K, M)$, where $S(K, M) = \{\underline{n} ; \sum_i n_i = K, \kappa_i \leq n_i \leq \hat{N}_i, i=1,2,...,M\}$, can be determined subject to constraints of normalisation, *active* UTIL, $\upsilon_i(K)$, i.e., $\upsilon_i(K) = P(\tilde{N}_i > \kappa_i)$, *active* MQL, $\Omega_i(K)$, i.e., $\Omega_i(K) = \sum_{n_i > \kappa_i} (n_i - \kappa_i) p_i(n_i)$ and full buffer probability, $\varphi_i(K)$, $\varphi_i(K) = p_i(N_i)$, satisfying the job flow rate equations.

By applying Lagrange's Method of Undertermined Multipliers, a ME product-form aproximation is characterised, subject to the above constraints, and is given by

$$p(\underline{n}) = \frac{1}{Z(L, M)} \prod_{i=1}^{M} \hat{g}_i(n_i) x_i^{n_i - \kappa_i} y_i^{f(n_i)}, \qquad (5.16)$$

where $Z(L, M)$ is the normalising constant,

$$\hat{g}_i(n_i) = \begin{cases} 1 & , \text{ if } n_i = \kappa_i, \\ g_i & , \text{ if } \kappa_i < n_i \leq \hat{N}_i, \end{cases} \qquad (5.17)$$

$f(n_i) = \max \{0, n_i - \hat{N}_i + 1\}$, and g_i, x_i and y_i are the Lagrangian coefficients corresponding to constraints $\upsilon_i(K)$, $\Omega_i(K)$ and $\varphi_i(K)$, i=1,2,...,M respectively.

The implementation of ME solution (5.16) proceeds in two stages:

Stage 1: Determine the ME product-form approximation, $p(\underline{n})$, for a pseudo open network with RS blocking, subject to normalisation and constraints of the type υ_i, Ω_i and φ_i, i=1,2,...,M (c.f., Section 5.1). Incorporate the conservation of flow rate equations (i.e. $\hat{\lambda}_i = \sum_j \alpha_{ji} \hat{\lambda}_j$, i=1,2,...,M) and the fixed population mean constraints (i.e.,

$K = \sum_j \Omega_j$) within the ME algorithm for open QNMs with RS blocking (c.f., Section 5.1). Decompose the pseudo open network into individual censored $GE/GE/1/\kappa_i;N_i$ or $GGeo/GGeo/1/\kappa_i;N_i$ queues, if $N_i < K$ or stable $GE/GE/1/\kappa_i;+\infty$ or $GGeo/GGeo/1/\kappa_i;+\infty$ queues, if $N_i \geq K$, with modified arrival and service processes within a continuous-time or discrete-time domain, respectively (c.f., [53, 54]). (n.b., constraint $K = \sum_j \Omega_j(K)$ replaces, in a mathematical sense, the unknown external arrival process of the flow balance rate equations.)

Remarks: Focusing on state κ_i, $1 \leq \kappa_i \leq K - 1$, of $GE/GE/1/\kappa_i;N_i$ and $GGeo/GGeo/1/\kappa_i;N_i$ censored queues with $N_i<+\infty$ or $N_i \rightarrow +\infty$, a job on service completion is forced to repeat service so that there will always be a minimum number of κ_i jobs present. These queues can be analysed via entropy maximisation in a similar fashion to that of Section 4.2 (c.f., [53, 54]).

Stage 2: Associate the analytic estimates of Lagrangian coefficients g_i, x_i and y_i, i=1,2,...,M, from Stage 1 with the ME state probability $p(\underline{n})$ of the original closed network (c.f., (5.16)). For the general case $\{\kappa_i \geq 0$ and $N_i \leq K\}$, use an efficient convolution type technique to compute ME solution iteratively until the job flow rate equations as applied to the original closed network, are satisfied.

The overall computational requirements of the ME algorithm are of $o(\gamma_1 \Psi^3)$ for Stage 1 and of $o(\gamma_2 MK)$ for Stage 2, where γ_1, γ_2 are the numbers of the corresponding iterations at each stage, respectively. Note that the recursive calculation of the normalising constant $Z(M, K)$ in Stage 2 can be carried out under the most general type of product-form approximation.

As in the case of open networks (c.f., Section 5.1), no mathematical proof of convergence is given due to the complexity of the expressions involved in Stages 1 and 2. However, numerous experiments have always converged under stability conditions $(\hat{\lambda}_i/\hat{\mu}_i) < 1$, i=1,2,...,M.

Remarks: For the case of *reversible* networks with finite capacity, the ME algorithm captures their exact solution (c.f., [8]). However, the ME solutions for these networks may be viewed directly as the truncated ME solutions of the corresponding reversible networks with infinite capacity, reducing, clearly, to the exact solutions.

6. ME Application to a Queueing Model of a Shared Buffer ATM Switch

In the field of high speed networks the ATM switch architecture incorporating a single memory of fixed size which is shared by all output ports is of particular importance. An incoming cell (or packet) is stored in a shared buffer of finite capacity while its address is kept in the address buffer. The cells destined for the same output port can be linked by an address chain pointer or their addresses can be stored into a FCFS buffer which relates to a particular output port. A cell will be lost if on arrival it finds either the shared buffer or the address buffer full. An example of such a switch architecture is the Prelude architecture proposed by CNET, France [69]. Some specific types of queueing models and analytic approximations for a shared buffer ATM switch architecture can be seen in [70-72].

In this Section the principle of ME is applied to characterise product-form approximations for the performance analysis of a general FCFS queueing model of a shared buffer ATM switch architecture with bursty arrivals (c.f., Fig. 7). At the implementation stage of the ME solution the arrival process at each output port of the ATM switch is modelled by a CPP (c.f., continuous-time domain) or a BBP (c.f., discrete-time domain) with geometrically distributed bulk sizes. These processes are most appropriate to model simultaneous arrivals and departures at the output ports generated by different bursty sources under a given buffer management policy (c.f., AF or DF).

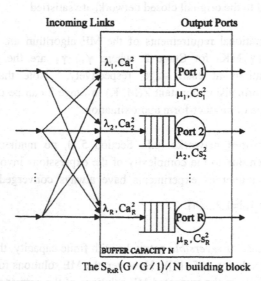

The $S_{RxR}(G/G/1)/N$ building block

Fig. 7 A queueing model of the shared buffer ATM switch

6.1 Shared Buffer Model Formulation and Notation

Consider a general queueing model of a shared buffer switch with bursty arrivals depicted in Fig. 7. The queueing model consists of R parallel single server queues, where R is the number of the input (or output) ports. Each server represents an output port, while each queue stands for the address queue of the shared buffer switch. There are R bursty and heterogeneous arrival streams of cells, belonging to a single class - one per input port - each of which is generally distributed. A cell upon arrival at the input port i joins the queue of the output port j with transition probability α_{ij}, i, j=1,2,...,R such that $\sum_j \alpha_{ij} = 1$, i=1,2,...,R. Assuming that a merging of the arrival streams at each output port queue j, j=1,2,...,R, has been applied, let $1/\lambda_j$, Ca_j^2, j=1,2,...,R be, respectively, the mean and SCV of the interarrival process. The transmission (or service)-time of a cell at each output port j follows a general distribution with mean and SCV $1/\mu_j$ and Cs_j^2, j=1,2,...,R, respectively.

Remark: For an ATM switch, due to the fixed cell size and the nature of the associated outgoing links, the transmission times are assumed to be Deterministic (D) (i.e., $Cs_j^2 = 0$, j=1,2,...,R).

The buffer management scheme adopted here is the so-called *complete sharing* with the buffer capacity of each queue, N_i being equal to N. In general, the queueing model of the shared buffer switch can be denoted by $S_{RxR}(G/G/1/)/N$ such that

(a) the interarrival and service times at an R x R switch are heterogeneous and generally distributed,
(b) each output port queue has a single server,
(c) shared buffer capacity of the switch is N.

Let at any given time the state of the system be represented by a state vector $\underline{n} = (n_1, n_2, ..., n_R)$, where n_i is the number of cells at each queue i, i=1,2,..,R. Moreover, let sets S(N, R) and A(η, R) be defined by

$$S(N, R) = \{\underline{n} = (n_1, n_2, ..., n_R) / \sum_{j=1}^{R} n_j \leq N, 0 \leq n_j \leq N, j=1,2,...,R\},$$

$$A(\eta, R) = \{\underline{n} = (n_1, n_2, ..., n_R) / \sum_{j=1}^{R} n_j \le \eta, 0 \le n_j \le \eta, j=1,2,...,R\}, \eta=0,1,...,N.$$

Moreover, let $\{p(\underline{n})\}$, $\underline{n} \in S(N, R)$, $\{p(\eta)\}$, $\eta=0,1,...,N$, and $p_i\{n_i\}$, $i=1,2,...,R$; $n_i=0,1,...,N$, be the joint, aggregate and marginal state probabilities, respectively. Finally, let $\{p_a(\underline{n})\}$, $\underline{n} \in S(N, R)$ and $\{p_a(n)\}$, $n=0,1,...,N$ be the joint and aggregate state probabilities of an arriving bulk, respectively.

6.2 A ME solution for an S_{RxR}(G/G/1)/N Queueing System

Consider a general S_{RxR}(G/G/1)/N queueing model of a shared buffer switch architecture depicted in Fig. 7. Motivated by earlier ME analysis of simpler types of queues and networks (c.f., Sections 4 and 5), it is assumed that the following constraints about the joint state probabilities $\{p(\underline{n}), \underline{n} \in S(N, R)\}$ are known to exist: The normalisation, and for all i=1,2,...,R, the UTIL, $U_i (0 < U_i < 1)$, MQL, $Q_i (U_i \le Q_i < N)$ and conditional state probability of an aggregate full buffer state with $n_i > 0$, ζ_i $(0 < \zeta_i < 1)$.

The form of the ME solution $p(\underline{n})$, $\underline{n} \in S(N, R)$, can be established by maximising the entropy function H(p), subject to normalisation, U_i, Q_i and φ_i, i=1,2,...,R, constraints.

The maximisation of H(p) can be carried out by using Lagrange's Method of Undetermined Multipliers leading to the product-form solution

$$p(\underline{n}) = \frac{1}{Z} \prod_{j=1}^{R} g_j^{s_j(\underline{n})} x_j^{n_j} y_j^{f_j(\underline{n})} , \quad \forall \underline{n} \in S(N, R), \tag{6.1}$$

where Z is the normalising constant,

$s_j(\underline{n}) = 1$, if $n_i > 0$ or 0, otherwise,

$f_j(\underline{n}) = 1$, if $\{\sum_i n_i = N$ and $s_j(\underline{n}) = 1\}$ or 0, otherwise,

and $\{g_j, x_j, y_j\}$ are the Lagrangian coefficients corresponding to constraints $\{U_j, Q_j, \zeta_j\}$, j=1,2,...,R, respectively.

Suitable formulae for computing the complex sums of Z and U_j, j=1,2,...,R can be determined by following the Generating Function Approach (c.f. [73]). By defining appropriate z-transforms involving the Lagrangian coefficients, the normalising constant can be expressed by

$$Z = \sum_{\eta=0}^{N-1} C_1(\eta) + C_2(N) , \qquad (6.2)$$

where $\{C_1(\eta), \eta=0,1,...,N-1\}$ and $C_2(N)$ are determined via the following recursive and refined formulae:

$$C_k(\eta) = \begin{cases} C_{1,R}(\eta) , & k = 1; \eta=0,1,...,N-1 , \\ C_{2,R}(N) , & k = 2; \eta = N , \end{cases} \qquad (6.3)$$

where

$$C_{k,r}(\eta) = C_{k,r-1}(\eta) - (1 - \beta_r) \times_r C_{k,r-1}(\eta - 1) + \times_r C_{k,r}(\eta - 1) , \qquad (6.4)$$

$$\eta=1,2,...,N-2+k; \quad k=1,2; \quad r=2,...,R,$$

with initial condition (for r = 1):

$$C_{k,1}(\eta) = \begin{cases} 1 , & \text{if } \eta=0 , \\ \beta_1 x_1^\eta , & \text{if } \eta=1,2,...,N-2+k, \end{cases}$$

$$C_{k,r}(0) = 1, \qquad k=1,2; \quad r=2,...,R,$$

where $\beta_r = g_r$, if k = 1, or $g_r y_r$, if k = 2.

Similarly, the utilisation U_i can be expressed as

$$U_i = \frac{1}{Z} \left\{ \sum_{\eta=1}^{N-1} C_1^{(i)}(\eta) + C_2^{(i)}(N) \right\}, \quad i=1,2,...,R , \qquad (6.5)$$

where

$$C_k^{(i)}(\eta) = (1 - \beta_i) x_i C_k^{(i)}(\eta - 1) + \beta_i x_i C_k(\eta - 1), \tag{6.6}$$

$$\eta = 2,3,...,N-2+k; \; k=1,2; \; i=1,2,...,R,$$

with initial condition (for $\eta = 1$): $C_k^{(i)}(1) = \beta_i x_i$.

The Lagrangian coefficients $\{g_i, x_i, i=1,2,...,R\}$ can be approximated by making asymptotic connections to infinite capacity queues. Assuming that x_i is invariant with respect to the capacity N, as $N \to +\infty$, it can be verified that (c.f., (4.2), (4.3))

$$g_i = \frac{\rho_i(1 - x_i)}{x_i(1 - \rho_i)}, \quad x_i = \frac{L_i - \rho_i}{L_i}, \quad i=1,2,...,R, \tag{6.7}$$

where L_i is the asymptotic MQL of queue i and $\rho_i = \lambda_i/\mu_i$. Moreover, the Lagrangian coefficients $\{y_i\}$, $i=1,2,...,R$, can be approximated by making use of the flow balance condition

$$\lambda_i(1 - \pi_i) = \mu_i U_i, \; i=1,2,...,R, \tag{6.8}$$

where π_i is the blocking probability (or cell-loss) that an arriving cell destined for queue i, $i=1,2,...,R$, finds the shared buffer of the switch full (i.e., $\Sigma_i n_i = N$).

6.3 Marginal State Probabilities $\{p_i(\ell_i), \ell_i=0,1,...,N; i=1,2,...,R\}$

Let $\tilde{N}^{(i)}$ be the rv of the number of cells seen by a random observer at queue i, $i=1,2,..,R$. Using ME solution (6.1) and recursive expressions (6.6), it follows that

$$p_i(\ell_i) = P_i[\tilde{N}^{(i)} \geq \ell_i] - P_i[\tilde{N}^{(i)} \geq \ell_i + 1], \tag{6.9}$$

with $P_i[\tilde{N}^{(i)} \geq N + 1] = 0$, where

$$P_i[\tilde{N}^{(i)} \geq \ell_i] = \frac{x_i^{\ell_i - 1}}{Z} \left\{ \sum_{\eta = \ell_i}^{N-1} C_1^{(i)}(\eta - \ell_i + 1) + C_2^{(i)}(N - \ell_i + 1) \right\}, \qquad (6.10)$$

$$\ell_i = 1, 2, \ldots, N; \quad i = 1, 2, \ldots, R.$$

Remarks: Appropriate recursive expressions can also be defined (c.f., [59]) for marginal MQLs $\{Q_i, i=1,2,\ldots,R\}$ and aggregate state probabilities $\{p(\eta), \eta=0,1,\ldots,N\}$, while the aggregate cell-loss probability, π_a, is expressed by $\pi_a = \sum_i (\lambda_i/\lambda)\pi_i$, where $\lambda = \sum_i \lambda_i$.

6.4 The GE and GGeo Type Blocking Probabilities

Analytic expressions for the blocking probabilities $\{\pi_i\}$, $i=1,2,\ldots,R$, can be established within a continuous-time or discrete-time domain by considering the $S_{RxR}(GE/GE/1)/N$ or $S_{RxR}(GGeo/GGeo/1)/N$ queueing models, respectively, and focusing on a tagged cell of an arriving bulk that is blocked. In this context, the blocking probability π_i is conditional on the position of a tagged cell within the bulk and also on the number of cells that its bulk finds in the system irrespective of its destination queue. Without loss of generality, it is assumed that the arriving bulk of the tagged cell is destined for output port queue i, $i=1,2,\ldots,R$.

The following distinct and exhaustive blocking cases of a tagged cell are considered:

(i)   The bulk on arrival finds the system in state $\{A(\eta, R)$ and $n_i = 0\}$, $\eta=0,1,\ldots,N-1$.

In this case the size of the arriving bulk must be at least $N - \eta + 1$ and the tagged cell is one of those members of the bulk that is blocked. By following the same probabilistic arguments as those used for a single queue with capacity $N - \eta$ (c.f., Section 4.2.1), it is implied that

Prob {A tagged cell is blocked and its bulk on arrival
finds the system at state $[A(\eta, R)$ and $n_i = 0]$}

$$= \delta_i \left[\sum_{\substack{\underline{n} \in A(\eta, R) \\ \wedge \ n_i = 0}} P_a(\underline{n}) \right] (1 - \tau_{ai})^{N-\eta}, \quad \eta = 0, 1, \ldots, N-1, \quad (6.11)$$

where
$$\delta_i = \tau_{si} / [\tau_{si}(1 - \tau_{ai}) + \tau_{ai}],$$

$$\tau_{ai} = \begin{cases} 2/(Ca_i^2 + 1), & \text{if GE}, \\ 2/(Ca_i^2 + \lambda_i + 1), & \text{if GGeo}, \end{cases} \quad \text{and,} \quad \tau_{si} = \begin{cases} 2/Cs_i^2 + 1), & \text{if GE}, \\ 2/(Cs_i^2 + \mu_i + 1), & \text{if GGeo}. \end{cases}$$

(ii)   The bulk on arrival finds the system in state $\{A(\eta, R) \text{ and } n_i > 0\}$, $\eta = 1, 2, \ldots, N-1$

In this case the bulk finds server i busy and there are in total η cells queueing or being transmitted in the entire system. Thus only $N - \eta$ buffer places are available and the tagged cell occupies any position within its bulk greater or equal to $N - \eta + 1$. It is therefore, implied that

Prob {A tagged cell is blocked and its bulk on arrival

finds the system at state $[A(\eta, R) \text{ and } n_i > 0]\}$

$$= \left[\sum_{\substack{\underline{n} \in A(\eta, R) \\ \wedge \ n_i > 0}} P_a(\underline{n}) \right] (1 - \tau_{ai})^{N-\eta}, \quad \eta = 1, 2, \ldots, N-1. \quad (6.12)$$

(iii)   The bulk on arrival finds the entire system full with aggregate probability $p_a(N)$.

Applying the Law of Total Probability it follows that

$$\pi_i = \delta_i \sum_{\eta=0}^{N-1} \left[\sum_{\substack{\underline{n} \in A(\eta, R) \\ \wedge \ n_i = 0}} P_a(\underline{n}) \right] (1 - \tau_{ai})^{N-\eta}$$

$$(6.13)$$

$$+ \sum_{\eta=1}^{N-1} \left[\sum_{\substack{\underline{n} \in A(\eta, R) \\ \wedge \ n_i > 0}} P_a(\underline{n}) \right] (1 - \tau_{ai})^{N-\eta} + p_a(N).$$

To determine a computational formula for π_i, the following two sets of queueing models are considered:

Case I: S_{RxR}(GE/GE/1)/N and S_{RxR}(GGeo/GGeo/1)/N Queueing Models under AF policy.

In this case, $p_a(\underline{n}) = p(\underline{n})$, $\forall$ $\underline{n} \in S(N, R)$ and $p_a(\eta) = p(\eta)$, $\eta = 0, 1, ..., N$ (c.f., [20, 53, 54]). Therefore, using z-transforms, ME solution $p(\underline{n})$, a corresponding expression for $p(\eta)$ (c.f., [59, 63]), $\eta = 0, 1, ..., N$ and coefficients $C_1(\eta)$, $\eta = 0, 1, ..., N-1$, $C_2(N)$ and $C_1^{(i)}(\eta)$, $\eta = 1, 2, ..., N-1$, it can be verified after some manipulation that

$$\pi_i = \frac{1}{Z} \{F_i(N) + C_2(N)\},$$ (6.14)

where

$$F_i(N) = \delta_i \sum_{\eta=0}^{N-1} C_1(\eta)(1 - \tau_{ai})^{N-\eta}$$

$$+ (1 - \delta_i) \sum_{\eta=1}^{N-1} C_1^{(i)}(\eta)(1 - \tau_{ai})^{N-\eta}.$$ (6.15)

Case II: S_{RxR}(GGeo/GGeo/1)/N Queueing Model under DF policy.

In this case $p_a(\underline{n})$, $\underline{n} \in S(N, R)$ can be determined analytically in a similar fashion to that of Section 4 under the assumption (made for mathematical tractability) that *only simultaneous arrivals and departures relating to the same queue i, i=1,2,...,R, can actually take place.*

To this end, the cell-loss probability, π_i, i=1,2,...,R can be expressed by [63]

$$\pi_i = \frac{1}{Z} \left\{ \hat{F}_i(N) + C_2(N) - \mu_i \tau_{ai} \delta_i C_2^{(i)}(N) \right\},$$ (6.16)

where

$$\hat{F}_i(N) = (1 - \sigma_{si}) \left\{ \delta_i \sum_{\eta=0}^{N-1} C_1(\eta) (1 - \tau_{ai})^{N-\eta} \right.$$

$$\left. + (1 - \delta_i) \sum_{\eta=1}^{N-1} C_1^{(i)}(\eta) (1 - \tau_{ai})^{N-\eta} \right\}$$

$$+ \sigma_{si} \delta_i \left\{ \sum_{\eta=0}^{N-1} C_1(\eta) (1 - \tau_{ai})^{N-\eta} - \tau_{ai} \sum_{\eta=1}^{N-1} C_1^{(i)}(\eta) (1 - \tau_{ai})^{N-\eta} \right\}, \quad (6.17)$$

and $\sigma_{si} = \mu_i \tau_{si}$.

Remark: In the case of $R = 1$, formulae (6.14) and (6.16) reduce to those of the corresponding GE/GE/1/N and GGeo/GGeo/1/N_i censored queues of Section 4 (c.f., (4.14) and (4.17)).

6.5 Estimating Lagrangian Coefficients $\{g_i, x_i, y_i, i=1,2,...,R\}$

The Lagrangian coefficients $\{g_i, x_i\}$, $i=1,2,...,R$ can be evaluated directly via expressions (6.7) by making use of the asymptotic MQL formula (4.5).

The Lagrangian coefficients $\{y_i\}$, $i=1,2,...,R$, can be determined numerically by substituting π_i of (6.14) or (6.16) and equations (6.2) and (6.5) into the flow-balance condition (6.8) and solving the resulting system of R non-linear equations with R unknowns $\{y_i, i=1,2,...,R\}$, namely

Case 1:

$$C_2^{(i)}(N) = \rho_i \left\{ \sum_{\eta=0}^{N-1} C_1(\eta) - F_i(N) \right\} - \sum_{\eta=1}^{N-1} C_1^{(i)}(\eta), \quad (6.18)$$

Case 2:

$$(1 - \mu_i \tau_{ai} \delta_i \rho_i) C_2^{(i)}(N) = \rho_i \left\{ \sum_{\eta=0}^{N-1} C_1(\eta) - F_i(N) \right\} - \sum_{\eta=1}^{N-1} C_1^{(i)}(\eta), \quad (6.19)$$

$i=1,2,...,R$ and $N \geq 2$.

Systems (6.18) and (6.19) can be solved by applying the numerical algorithm of Newton-Raphson in conjunction with an efficient recursive scheme (c.f., [59]).

Conclusions

The principle of ME, subject to queueing theoretic mean value constraints, provides a powerful methodology for the analysis of complex queueing systems and networks. In this tutorial paper, the ME principle is used to characterise product-form approximations and resolution algorithms for arbitrary FCFS continuous-time and discrete-time QNMs at equilibrium under RS-RD and RS-FD blocking mechanisms and AF or DF buffer management policies. An ME application to the performance modelling of a shared-buffer ATM switch architecture with bursty arrivals is also presented. The ME solutions are implemented computationally subject to GE and GGeo type mean value constraints, as appropriate. In this context, the ME state probabilities of the GE/GE/1, GE/GE/1/N, GGeo/GGeo/1 and GGeo/GGeo/1/N queues at equilibrium and associated formulae for the first two moments of the effective flow streams (departure, splitting, merging) are used as *building blocks* in the solution process.

The ME algorithms capture the exact solution of reversible QNMs. Moreover, extensive validation studies (c.f., [27, 28, 36, 39, 40, 42-64] indicate that the ME approximations for arbitrary GE and GGeo type QNMs are generally very comparable in accuracy to that obtained by simulation models. Moreover, it has been conjectured that typical performance measures (such as MQLs for open QNMs and system throughputs and mean response-times for closed QNMs) obtained by GE or GGeo type ME approximations, given the first two moments of the external interarrival-times and/or service-times, define optimistic or pessimistic performance bounds - depending on the parameterisation of the QNM (c.f., [51]) - on the same quantities derived from simulation models when representing corresponding interevent-times by a family of two-phase distributions, as appropriate (e.g., Hyperexponential-2), having the same given first two moments.

The analytic methodology of entropy maximisation and its generalisations are versatile and can be applied within both *queue-by-queue decomposition* and *hierarchical multilevel aggregation* schemes to study the performance of other types of queueing systems and networks, particularly in the discrete-time domain (e.g., Banyan interconnection networks with blocking), representing new and more complex digitised structures of high speed networks. Work of this kind is the subject of current studies.

Acknowledgements

The author wishes to thank the Science and Engineering Research Council (SERC), UK, for supporting research work on entropy maximisation and QNMs with grants GR/D/12422, GR/F/29271 and GR/H/18609. Thanks are also extended to Spiros Denazis for drawing diagrams of Figs. 1-7.

Bibliography

In the continuous-time domain exact solutions and efficient computational algorithms for arbitrary QNMs with or without blocking have been presented, subject to reversibility type conditions (e.g, [1, 2, 8, 12]. More general, and therefore more realistic, QNMs have been analysed via approximate methods (e.g, [3-7, 9-11]). These include diffusion approximations for general QNMs (e.g., [4, 5]) and heuristic MVA for Markovian QNMs with priority classes (e.g, [9]). The accuracy of approximate methods, however, may be adversely affected in certain cases when based on either gross assumptions or intuitive heuristics. Comprehensive surveys on open and closed QNMs with finite capacity can be seen in [13] and [14], respectively.

In the discrete-time domain analytical results are mainly based on reinterpretation of earlier theoretical advances on continuous-time queues (e.g., [15-19]). There are inherent difficulties and open issues associated with the analysis of discrete-time queues due to the occurrence of simultaneous events (e.g, arrivals and departures) at the boundary epochs of a slot.

To overcome some of the drawbacks of earlier techniques, alternative ideas and tools from Statistical Mechanics have been proposed in the literature (e.g., 21-28]. In this context, the principle of ME (c.f., Jaynes [29-31], based on the concept of entropy functional [32], has inspired over the recent years a novel analytic methodology for the approximate solution of complex queues and QNMs. Note that Tribus [65] used the principle to derive a number of probability distributions. The mathematical foundations of the method and its generalisation to the principle of Minimum Relative Entropy (MRE) can be found in Shore and Johnson [66].

Entropy maximisation was first applied to the analysis of Markovian queueing systems at equilibrium by Ferdinand [22] who determined the stationary ME queue length distribution (qld) of an M/M/1/N queue by analogy to Statistical Mechanics. It was also shown that the ME steady-state probability of an open QNM, subject to marginal MQL constraints, corresponds to the solution of an open Jacksonian queueing network. Shore [25, 33] applied the principle of ME to investigate the stationary qlds of the M/M/∞ and M/M/∞/N queues [33] and also to propose ME approximations for stable M/G/1 and G/G/1 queues, subject to mql and utilisation constraints, respectively [25]. The latter ME solution turns out to be identical to the qld of a stable M/M/1 queue. Independently, El-Affendi and Kouvatsos [26] derived a new ME qld for a stable M/G/1 queue, subject to both utilisation and MQL constraints. This ME solution becomes exact when the underlying service-time distribution is represented by the GE distribution. The ME principle was also applied to the analysis of a stable G/M/1 queue [26]. Cantor et al. [34] used the principle of MRE to characterise an equivalent stationary state probability to that of an M/M/c/N/K machine repair model and also to analyse two queues in tandem. Lutton et al. [35] applied the ME principle for solving under exponential assumptions queueing problems encountered in telephone exchanges. Guiasu [37] examined the ME condition for a stable M/M/1 queue. Rego and Szpankowski [38] investigated the presence of exponentiality in entropy maximised M/G/1 queues. Kouvatsos [39, 40] determined GE-type approximations for the ME qlds of the stable G/G/1 and G/G/1/N queues, respectively. Arizono et al. [41] analysed M/M/c queues at equilibrium, while Kouvatsos and Almond [42] and Wu and Chan [43] investigated stable G/G/c/N/K and G/M/c queues, respectively. Strelen [47] applied entropy maximisation to obtain a piecewise approximation for the waiting-time densities of G/G/1 queues. A new ME priority approximation for a stable G/G/1 queue was proposed by Kouvatsos and Tabet-Aouel [45]. This work was also extended to the ME analysis of a stable multiple server G/G/c/PR queue under preemptive-resume (PR) rule [46, 47]. Moreover, Kouvatsos and Georgatsos [48] presented an ME solution for a stable G/G/c/SQJ queueing system with c parallel serve queues operating under the shortest queue with jockeying (SQJ) routing criterion. A stable M/G/1 retrial queue was analysed via entropy maximisation by Falin et al. [49]. More recently, ME advances have been made towards the analysis of GGeo-type discrete-time queues (c.f., [60, 62, 73-74]).

The first ME approximation for arbitrary GE-type FCFS open closed QNMs with infinite capacity, subject to normalisation and marginal constraints of UTIL and MQL, was proposed in Kouvatsos [27]. Subsequent reformulation of the ME problem for closed QNMs incorporates the condition of flow conservation expressed by the job flow balance equations [28], or (equivalently) the work rate theorem [36]. Extensions of the ME methodology to the analysis of arbitrary GE-type QNMs with infinite capacity and mixed (priority/non-priority) service disciplines have been reported in [50, 51] (single server stations) and [52] (multiple server stations). ME has also been applied in the approximate analysis of arbitrary FCFS open and closed GE-type QNMs with finite capacity and RS-RD or RS-FD blocking mechanisms with single [53, 58] or multiple [54, 58] server stations. An ME extension to arbitrary open QNMs with RS-RD blocking and multiple-job classes with various non-priority based service disciplines has been recently presented by Kouvatsos and Denazis [56].

Furthermore, an ME analysis of arbitrary QNMs with GE-type stations and SQJ routing has appeared in [57]. The ME principle has also been used to study arbitrary FCFS open and closed discrete-time QNMs of GGeo-type with RS-RD blocking [64]. Finally, MRE applications, given fully decomposable subset and aggregate constraints, towards a hierarchical multilevel aggregation of arbitrary closed QNMs can be found in [74, 75].

In the performance modelling field of high speed networks entropy maximisation has been used in both continuous-time (GE-type) and discrete-time (GGeo-type) domains for the analysis of multi-buffered and shared buffer ATM switch architectures [59, 61, 63] as well as Distributed Queue Dual Bus (DQDB) networks with multiple-job classes [76-78].

A comprehensive review of entropy and relative entropy optimisation and arbitrary continuous-time QNMs with finite capacity, multiple-job classes, multiple-server stations and mixed service disciplines together with some computer and communication systems applications can be seen in Kouvatsos [79].

[1]   Baskett, F., K.M., Muntz, R.R. and Palacios, F.G., Open, Closed and Mixed Networks with Different Classes of Customers, JACM 22, 2 (1975) 248-260.

[2]   Reiser, M. and Kobayashi, H., Queueing Networks with Mulitple Closed Chains: Theory and Computational Algorithms, IBM J. Res. & Dev. 19 (1975) 283-294.

[3]   Marie, R., An Approximate Analytical Method for General Queueing Networks, IEEE Trans. on Software Eng. SE-5, No. 5 (1979) 530-538.

[4]   Reiser, M. and Kobayashi, H., Accuracy of the Diffusion Approximation for Some Queueing Systems, IBM J. Res. & Dev. 18 (1974) 110-124.

[5]   Gelenbe, E. and Pujolle, G., The Behaviour of a Single Queue in a General Queueing Network, Acta Info. 7 (1976) 123-160.

[6]   Courtois, P.J., Decomposability: Queueing and Computer Systems Applications, Academic Press Inc., New York (1977).

[7]   Chandy, K.M., Herzog, U. and Woo, L., Approximate Analysis of General Queueing Networks, IBM J. Res. & Dev. 19 (1975) 43-49.

[8]   Kelly, F.P., Reversibility and Stochastic networks, Wiley, New York (1979).

[9]   Bryant, R.M., Krzesinski, A.E., Lasmi, M.S. and Chandy, K.M., The MVA Priority Approximation, T.O.C.S. 2(4) (1984) 335-359.

[10] Altiok, T. and Perros, H.G., Approximate Analysis of Arbitrary Configurations of Queueing Networks with Blocking, Annals of OR (1987) 481-509.

[11] Van Dijk, N.M., A Simple Bounding Methodology for Non-Product-Form Queueing Networks with Blocking, Queueing Networks with Blocking, Perros, H.G. and Altiok, T. (Eds.), North-Holland (1980) 3-18.

[12] Akyildiz, I.F. and Von Brand, H., Exact Solutions for Open, Closed and Mixed Queueing Networks with Rejection Blocking, Theoret. Comput. Sci. 64 (1989) 203-219.

[13] Perros, H.G., Approximation Algorithms for Open Queueing Networks with Blocking, Stochastic Analysis of Computer and Communication Systems, Takagi (Ed.), North-Holland (1990) 451-494.

[14] Onvural, R.O., Survey of Closed Queueing Networks with Blocking, ACM Computing Surveys 22, 2 (1990), 83-121.

[15] Hsu, J. and Burke, P.J., Behaviour of Tandem Buffers with Geometric Input and Markovian Output, IEEE Trans. Commun. 25, (1976) 2-29.

[16] Bharath-Kumar, K., Discrete-Time Queueing Systems and their Networks, IEEE Trans. on Commun. 28, 2, (1980) 260-263.

[17] Hunter, J.J., Mathematical Techniques of Applied Probability, Vol. 2, Discrete-time Models: Techniques and Applications, Academic Press (1983).

[18] Kobayashi, H., Discrete-Time Queueing Systems, Chapter 4 of Probability Theory and Computer Science, Louchard, G. and Latouche, G. (Eds.), Academic Press (1983).

[19] Pujolle, G., Discrete-time Queueing Systems for Data Networks Performance Evaluation, Queueing, Performance and Control in ATM, Cohen, J.W. and Pack, C.D. (Eds.), North-Holland, (1991) 239-244.

[20] Gravey, A. and Hebuterne, G., Simultaneity in Discrete-time Single Server Queues with Bernoulli Inputs, Performance Evaluation, 14, (1992) 123-131.

[21] Benes, V.E., Mathematical Theory of Connecting Networks and Telephone Traffic, Academic Press, New York (1965).

[22] Ferdinand, A.E., A Statistical Mechanical Approach to Systems Analysis, IBM J. Res. Dev. 14 (1970) 539-547.

[23] Pinsky, E. and Yemini, Y., A Statistical Mechnics of Some Interconnection Networks, Performance '84, Gelenbe, E. (Ed.), North-Holland (1984) 147-158.

[24] Pinsky, E and Yemini, Y., The Canonical Approximation in Performance Analysis, Computer Networking and Performance Evaluation, Hasegawa, T. et al. (Eds.), North-Holland (1986) 125-137.

[25] Shore, J.E., Information Theoretic Approximations for M/G/1 and G/G/1 Queueing Systems, Acta Info. 17 (1982) 43-61.

[26] El-Effendi, M.A. and Kouvatsos, D.D., A Maximum Entropy Analysis of the M/G/1 and G/M/1 Queueing Systems at Equilibrium, Acta Info. 19 (1983) 339-355.

[27] Kouvatsos, D.D., Maximum Entropy Methods for General Queueing Networks, Modelling Techniques and Tools for Performance Analysis, Potier, D. (Ed.), North-Holland (1985) 589-609.

[28] Kouvatsos, D.D., A Universal Maximum Entropy Algorithm for the Analysis of General Closed Networks, Computing Networking and Performance Evaluation, Hasegawa, T. et al. (Eds.), North-Holland (1986) 113-124.

[29] Jaynes, E.T., Information Theory and Statistical Mechanics, Phys, Rev. 106, 4 (1957) 620-630.

[30] Jaynes, E.T., Information Theory and Statistical Mechanics II, Phys. Rev. 108, 2 (1957) 171-190.

[31] Jaynes, E.T., Prior Probabilities, IEEE Trans. Systems Sci. Cybern. SSC-4 (1968) 227-241.

[32] Shannon, C.E., A Mathematical Theory of Communication, Bell Syst. Tech. J. 27 (1948) 379-423, 623-656.

[33] Shore, J.E., Derivation of Equilibrium and Time-Dependent Solutions of M/M/∞/N and M/M/∞ Queueing Systems Using Entropy Maximisation, Proc. 1978 National Computer Conference, AFIPS (1978) 483-487.

[34] Cantor, J., Ephremides, A. and Horton, D., Information Theoretic Analysis for a General Queueing System at Equilibrium with Application to Queues in Tandem, Acta Info. 23 (1986) 657-678.

[35] Lutton, J.L., Bonomi, E. and Felix, M.R., Information Theory and Statistical Mechanics Approach to Solving a Queueing Problem Encountered in Telephone Exchanges, Research Report PA/1199, Division ATR - Centre National d'Etudes des Telecommunications, France (1984).

[36] Walsta, R., Iterative Analysis of Networks of Queues, PhD Thesis, Technical Report CSE1-166, University of Toronto, Canada (1984).

[37] Guiasu, S., Maximum Entropy Condition, in Queueing Theory, J. Opl. Res. Soc. 37, 3 (1986) 293-301.

[38] Rego, V. and Szpankowski, W., The Presence of Exponentiality in Entropy Maximised M/GI/1 Queues, Computers Opns. Res. 16, 5 (1989) 441-449.

[39] Kouvatsos, D.D., A Maximum Entropy Analysis of the G/G/1 Queue at Equilibrium, J. Opl. Res. Soc. 39, 2 (1989) 183-200.

[40] Kouvatsos, D.D., Maximum Entropy and the G/G/1/N Queue. Acta Info. 23 (1986) 545-565.

[41] Arizono, I., Cui, Y. and Ohta, H., An Analysis of M/M/s Queueing Systems Based on the Maximum Entropy Principle, J. Opl. Res. Soc. 42, 1 (1991) 69-73.

[42] Kouvatsos, D.D. and Almond, J., Maximum Entropy Two-Station Cyclic Queues with Multiple General Servers, Acta info. 26 (1988) 241-267.

[43] Wu, J.S. and Chan, W.C., Maximum Entropy Analysis of Multiple-Server Queueing Systems, J. Opl. Res. Soc. 40, 9 (1989) 815-825.

[44] Strelen, C., Piecewise Approximation of Densities Applying the Principle of Maximum Entropy: Waiting Time in G/G/1-Systems, Modelling Techniques and Tools for Computer Performance Evaluation, Puigjaner, R. and Potier, D. (Eds.), Plenum Press (1989) 421-438.

[45] Kouvatsos, D.D. and Tabet-Aouel, N.M., A Maximum Entropy Priority Approximation for a Stable G/G/1 Queue, Acta Info. 27 (1989) 247-286.

[46] Tabet-Aouel, N.M. and Kouvatsos, D.D., On an Approximation to the Mean Response Times of Priority Classes in a Stable G/G/c/PR Queue, J. Opl. Res. Soc., 43, 3 (1992) 227-239.

[47] Kouvatsos, D.D. and Tabet-Aouel, N.M., An ME-Based Approximation for Multi-Server Queues with Preemptive Priority, To appear in the European Journal of Operational Research (1993).

[48] Kouvatsos, D.D. and Georgatsos, P.H., General Queueing Networks with SQJ Routing, Proc. 5th UK Perf. Eng. Workshop, University of Edinburgh, September 1988.

[49] Falin, G., Martin, G.I. and Artaleo, J., Information Theoretic Approximations for the M/G/1 Retrial Queue, To appear in Acta Infomatica.

[50] Kouvatsos, D.D., Georgatsos, P.H. and Tabet-Aouel, N.M., A Universal Maximum Entropy Algorithm for General Multiple Class Open Networks with Mixed Service Disciplines, Modelling Techniques and Tools for Computer Performance Evaluation, Puigjaner, R. and Potier, D. (Eds.), Plenuum Publishing Corporation (1989) 397-419.

[51] Kouvatsos, D.D. and Tabet-Aouel, N.M., Product-Form Approximations for an Extended Class of General Closed Queueing Networks, Performance '90, King, P.J.B. et al. (Eds.), North-Holland (1990) 301-315.

[52] Kouvatsos, D.D. and Tabet-Aouel, N.M., Approximate Solutions for Networks of Queues with Multiple Server Stations under PR Discipline, Proc. 8th UK Perf. Eng. Workshop, Harrison, P. and Field, T. (Eds.), Imperial College, London, 1992.

[53] Kouvatsos, D.D. and Xenios, N.P., Maximum Entropy Analysis of General Queueing Networks with Blocking, Queueing Networks with Blocking, Perros, H.G. and Altiok, T. (Eds.), North-Holland, Amsterdam (1989) 281-309.

[54] Kouvatsos, D.D. and Xenios, N.P., MEM for Arbitrary Queueing Networks with Multiple General Servers and Repetitive-Service Blocking, Perf. Eval. 10 (1989) 169-195.

[55] Kouvatsos, D.D., Denazis, S.G. and Georgatsos, P.H., MEM for Arbitrary Exponential Open Networks with Blocking and Multiple Job Classes, Proc. 7th Perf. Eng. Workshop, Hillston, J. et al. (Eds.), Springer-Verlag (1991) 163-178.

[56] Kouvatsos, D.D. and Denazis, S.G., Entropy Maximised Queueing Networks with Blocking and Multiple Job Classes, Perf. Eval. 17 (1993) 189-205.

[57] Kouvatsos, D.D. and Georgatsos, P.H., Queueing Models of Packet-Switched Networks with Locally Adaptive Routing, Teletraffic and Datatraffic in Period of Change, ITC-13, Jensen, A. and Iversen, V.B. (Eds.), North-Holland (1991) 303-308.

[58] Kouvatsos, D.D. and Denazis, S.G., Comments on and Tuning to: MEM for Arbitrary Queueing Networks with Repetitive-Service Blocking under Random Routing, Technical Report CS-18-91, University of Bradford, (May 1991).

[59] Kouvatsos, D.D. and Denazis, S.G., A Universal Building Block for the Approximate Analysis of a Shared Buffer ATM Switch Architecture, Annals of Operations Research (to appear).

[60] Kouvatsos, D.D. and Tabet-Aouel, N.M., GGeo-type Approximations for General Discrete-Time Queueing Systems, Proc. IFIP Workshop TC6 on Modelling and Performance Evaluation of ATM Technology, Pujolle, G. et al. (Eds.), La Martinique, North-Holland (1993) (to appear).

[61] Kouvatsos, D.D., Tabet-Aouel, N.M. and Denazis, S.G., A Discrete-Time Queueing Model of a Shared Buffer ATM Switch Architecture with Bursty Arrivals, Proc. of 10th UK Teletraffic Symposium, IEE, BT Labs., Ipswich (1993) 19/1-19/9.

[62] Kouvatsos, D.D. and Tabet-Aouel, N.M., The GGeo/G/1 Queue under AF and DF Buffer Management Policies, Proc. of 1st UK Workshop on Performance Modelling and Evaluation of ATM Networks, Kouvatsos, D.D. (Ed.), University of Bradford (1993) 7/1-7/11.

[63] Kouvatsos, D.D., Tabet-Aouel, N.M. and Denazis, S.G., ME-Based Approximations for General Discrete-Time Queueing Models, Res. Rep. CS-11-93, Department of Computing, University of Bradford (1993).

[64] Kouvatsos, D.D., Tabet-Aouel, N.M. and Denazis, S.G., Approximate Analysis of Discrete-Time Networks with or without Blocking, Proc. of 5th International Conference on Data Communication Systems and their Performances, Viniotis, Y. and Perros, H. (Eds.), (to appear).

[65] Tribus, M., Rational Description, Decisions and Designs, Pergamon, New York (1969).

[66] Shore, J.E. and Johnson, R.W., Axiomatic Derivation of the Principle of ME and the Principle of Minimum Cross-Eentropy, IEEE Trans. Info. Theory TI-26 (1980) 26-37.

[67] Sauer, C., Configuration of Computing Systems: An Approach Using Queueing Network Models, PhD Thesis, University of Texas (1975).

[68] Nojo, S. and Watanabe, H., A New Stage Method Getting Arbitrary Coefficient of Variation by Two Stages, Trans. IEICE 70 (1987) 33-36.

[69] Devault, M., Cochennec, J.Y. and Servel, M., The *Prelude* ATD Experiment: Assessments and Future Prospects, IEEE J. Sac, 6(9) (1988) 1528-1537.

[70] Iliadis, I., Performance of a Packet Switch with Shared Buffer and Input Queueing, Teletraffic and Datatraffic in a Period of Change, ITC-13, Jensen, A. and Iversen, V.B. (Eds), North-Holland (1991), 911-916.

[71] Yamashita, H., Perros, H.G. and Hong, S., Performance Modelling of a Shared Buffer ATM Switch Architecture, Teletraffic and Datatraffic in a Period of Change, ITC-13, Jensen, A. and Iversen, V.B. (Eds), North-Holland (1991), 993-998.

[72] Hong, S., Perros, H.G. and Yamashita, H., A Discrete-Time Queueing Model of the Shared Buffer ATM Switch with Bursty Arrivals, Res. Rep., Computer Science Department, North Carolina State University (1992).

[73] Williams, A.C. and Bhandiwad, R.A., A Generating Function Approach to Queueing Network Analysis of Multiprogrammed Computers, Networks, 6 (1976) 1-22.

[74] Kouvatsos, D.D. and Tomaras, P.J., Multilevel Aggregation of Central Server Models: A Minimum Relative Entropy Approach, Int. J. Systems Science, 23, 5 (1992) 713-739.

[75] Tomaras, P.J. and Kouvatsos, D.D., MRE Hierarchical Decomposition of General Queueing Network Models, Acta Info. 28 (1991) 265-295.

[76] Tabet-Aouel, N.M. and Kouvatsos, D.D., A Discrete-Time Maximum Entropy Solution for the Performance Analysis of DQDB Architecture, Proc. of 9th UK Perf. Eng. Workshop, Woodward, M. (Ed.), Pentech Press (1993) (to appear).

[77] Tabet-Aouel, N.M. and Kouvatsos, D.D., Entropy Maximisation and Unfinished Work Analysis of the Logical DQDB Queue, Res. Rep. TAN/DDK 13, Department of Computing, University of Bradford (1993), 16/1-16/7.

[78] Tabet-Aouel, N.M. and Kouvatsos, D.D., Performance Analysis of a DQDB under a Priority MAC Protocol, Proc. of 1st UK Workshop on Performance Modelling and Evaluation of ATM Networks, Kouvatsos, D.D. (Ed.), University of Bradford (1993) 24/1-24/12.

[79] Kouvatsos, D.D., Entropy Maximisation and Queueing Network Models, Annals of Operations Research (to appear).

Performance Modeling using DSPNexpress*

Christoph Lindemann

Technische Universität Berlin
Institut für Technische Informatik
Franklinstr. 28/29
10587 Berlin, Germany

Abstract

This paper recalls the numerical solution method for Deterministic and Stochastic Petri Nets (DSPNs) and describes the graphical, interactive analysis tool DSPNexpress which has been developed at the Technische Universität Berlin since 1991. The software package DSPNexpress allows the employment of complex DSPNs for evaluating the performance and dependability of discrete-event dynamic systems such as computer systems, communication networks, or automated manufacturing systems. A DSPN of a memory consistency model for a multicomputer system with virtually shared memory is presented to illustrate the modeling power of DSPNs.

1 Introduction

Petri Nets in which transition firings can be augmented with a constant delay constitute an important tool for modeling various kinds of discrete-event dynamical systems, because such systems typically include activities with constant duration. Examples of activities which might have a constant duration are transfer times of data packets of fixed size in distributed computing systems, timeouts in real-time systems, and repair times of components in fault-tolerant systems. In Timed Petri Nets (TPNs) [20] all transitions have associated either constant delays (D-timed Petri Nets) or exponentially distributed delays (M-timed Petri Nets). Generalized Timed Petri Nets (GTPNs) have been introduced in [12] as an extension to TPNs. GTPNs contain immediate transitions firing without a delay and timed transitions firing after a deterministic delay. TPNs and GTPNs employ a discrete time scale for the underlying stochastic process. In TPN and GTPN timed transitions fire in three phases and the next transition to fire is chosen according to some probability distribution.

Deterministic and Stochastic Petri Nets (DSPNs) have been introduced in [2] as a continuous-time modeling tool which include both exponentially distributed and constant timing. In DSPNs, transition firing is atomic and the transition with the smallest firing delay is the next transition to fire. Under the restriction that in any marking at most one deterministic transition is enabled, a numerical solution method for calculating the steady state solution of DSPNs has been introduced. This method is based on the technique of the embedded Markov chain and requires the numerical calculation of transient quantities of continuous-time Markov chains defined by exponential transitions concurrently or competitively enabled with a deterministic

---
* This work was supported by the Federal Ministry for Research and Technology of Germany (BMFT) under grant ITR9003.

transition. Efficient computational formulas for the transient analysis of these Markov chains have been presented in [14]. DSPNs have been applied for modeling the performance of an Ethernet Bus LAN [3], and several fiber optic LAN architectures [5] as well as for deriving self-stability measures of a fault-tolerant clock synchronization system [18]. More recently, DSPNs have been employed for evaluating the performance of memory consistency models for multicomputer systems with virtually shared memory [17] and for an integrated performance/dependability analysis of an automated manufacturing system [15].

This paper recalls the numerical solution method for DSPNs and describes the graphical, interactive analysis tool DSPNexpress which which has recently become available [13]. The development of DSPNexpress has been motivated by the lack of a powerful software package for the numerical solution of DSPNs and the complexity requirements imposed by evaluating the performance and dependability of computer systems, communication networks, and automated manufacturing systems. The development of DSPNexpress has been motivated by the lack of a powerful software package for the numerical solution of DSPNs and the complexity requirements imposed by evaluating the performance and dependability of multicomputer systems, communication networks, and automated manufacturing systems. The remainder of this paper is organized as follows. Section 2 recalls the main steps of the numerical solution method for DSPNs. In Section 3 the software package DSPNexpress is described. A DSPN of a sequential memory consistency model for a multicomputer system with virtually shared memory is presented in Section 4. Finally, current research topics are outlined.

2 The Numerical Solution Algorithm for Deterministic and Stochastic Petri Nets

The numerical solution technique for computing steady-state marking probabilities of DSPN models introduced by Ajmone Marsan and Chiola [2] is based on the restriction that the DSPN does not contain markings in which two or more deterministic transitions are concurrently enabled. With this restriction they showed how to analyze the stochastic behavior of a DSPN using the technique of the *embedded Markov chain*. Sampling the stochastic behavior of the DSPN only at appropriately selected instants of time define regeneration points of a Markov regenerative stochastic process [9] in which the Markovian property holds. In case only exponential transitions are enabled the stochastic behavior of the DSPN is sampled at the instant of firing of an exponential transition. In case a deterministic transition is exclusively enabled the stochastic behavior of the DSPN is sampled at the instant of its firing. If a deterministic transition is competitively enabled with some exponential transitions, the stochastic behavior is sampled when either the deterministic or the exponential transition fires. If a deterministic transition is concurrently enabled with some exponential transitions, the stochastic behavior is sampled at the instant of time of firing the deterministic transition.

As a consequence, a change of marking in the DSPN due to firing of an exponential transition which is concurrently enabled with a deterministic transition is not represented in the embedded Markov chain by a corresponding state change. Thus, the embedded Markov chain typically contains fewer states than the number of tangible markings of the DSPN. The state space cardinalities of the DSPN and its embedded Markov chain are denoted by N and N', respectively. For example, the DSPN of the modified $E_r/D/1/K$ queue discussed below has $N = rK-1$ tangible markings, but its embedded Markov chain has only $N' = r(K-1)+1$ states. Assuming a DSPN contains markings in which a deterministic transition is competitively or concurrently enabled with some exponential transitions, the transition probabilities of its embedded Markov chain have to be derived by calculating transient quantities of the Markov chain defined by the firing rates of exponential transitions competitively or concurrently enabled with a deterministic transition and the firing probabilities of immediate transitions which are enabled directly after a firing of one of the exponential transitions. This continuous-time Markov chain has been referred to as the *subordinated Markov chain* (SMC) of a deterministic transition [14].

In the first step of the DSPN solution process the extended reachability graph consisting of tangible markings and directed arcs labelled with firing rates and weights causing the corresponding change of marking is generated. An efficient algorithm for generating the extended reachability graph for Generalized Stochastic Petri Nets has been introduced by Balbo, Chiola, Franceschinis and Molinar Roet [6].

The second step of the DSPN solution algorithm is the calculation of the transition probability matrix $\mathbf{P}$ of the embedded Markov chain and the conversion matrix $\mathbf{C}$. For markings which enable a deterministic transition T_k competitively or concurrently with some exponential transition the corresponding entries of these matrices are derived by calculating time-dependent quantities of the SMC. Transient state probabilities of the SMC of the deterministic transition T_k determine the corresponding transition probabilities of the embedded Markov chain. According to [2] the transition probability $P(S_i \rightarrow S_j)$ between two states S_i and S_j of the embedded Markov chain is given by:

$$P(S_i \rightarrow S_j) = u_i \cdot e^{\mathbf{Q}\tau_k} \cdot \Delta_k \cdot u_j^T \tag{1}$$

In formula (1) $\mathbf{Q}$ denotes the generator matrix of the Markov chain subordinated to the deterministic transition T_k with firing delay τ_k. The term u_i denotes the i-th row unity vector of dimension N_k ($u_i \in R^{I \times N_k}$) where N_k is equal to the dimension of the generator matrix $\mathbf{Q}$. The term u_j^T denotes the j-th column unity vector of dimension N' ($u_j^T \in R^{N' \times I}$). The matrix Δ_k denotes a transition probability matrix representing the feasible marking changes caused by a path of immediate transition firings which are enabled immediately after a firing of this deterministic transition. Nonzero entries of Δ_k are either "1" or given by the weights associated with conflicting immediate transitions. The matrix Δ_k is a rectangular matrix of dimension $N_k \times N'$.

In case the deterministic transition T_k is concurrently enabled with some exponential transitions, the sojourn times in tangible markings of the continuous-time stochastic behavior of the DSPN caused by firings of exponential transitions during the enabling interval of the deterministic transition are not taken into account in the discrete-time embedded Markov chain. Thus, *conversion factors* are employed to derive the steady-state probability vector of the DSPN of dimension N from the steady-state probability vector of the embedded Markov chain of dimension N'. These conversion factors are calculated as the average sojourn times in a state S_j during the enabling interval of the deterministic transition T_k assuming this transition has become enabled in state S_i. These conversion factors are given by:

$$C(i,j) = \int_0^{\tau_k} u_i \cdot e^{Qt} \cdot u_j^T \, dt \qquad (2)$$

As shown in [14] the time-dependent quantities of formula (1) and (2) can be efficiently computed using the randomization technique [11].

Subsequently, in the third step of the DSPN solution process the steady-state solution, $\pi(.)$ of the embedded Markov chain is calculated by solving the linear system of its global balance equations.

$$\pi \cdot P = \pi$$

$$\sum_{v=1}^{N'} \pi(v) = 1 \qquad (3)$$

In the final step of the DSPN solution algorithm the steady-state solution of the continuous-time DSPN, $p(.)$, is derived from the probability vector of the discrete-time embedded Markov chain, $\pi(.)$, and the conversion matrix C. Subsequently, the converted solution is normalized by Equation (5) in order to obtain the marking probability vector of the DSPN.

$$\tilde{p}(i) = \sum_{v=1}^{N'} C(v,i) \cdot \pi(v) \qquad 1 \le i \le N \qquad (4)$$

$$p(i) = \frac{\tilde{p}(i)}{\sum_{v=1}^{N} \tilde{p}(i)} \qquad 1 \le i \le N \qquad (5)$$

To illustrate the numerical DSPN solution algorithm an example of a for a single-server queueing system with constant service time and a finite capacity of K customers is considered. Figure 1 depicts a DSPN model of this queueing system. If free buffers are available, customers arrive according to an Erlang distribution with r phases. In case all buffers are occupied, the arrival process is blocked. Subsequently, this queueing system is referred to as the *modified $E_r/D/1/K$ queue*. The exponential transitions T2 and T3 are associated with a firing rate of $r\lambda$. The output arc from transition t1 to place P2 and the input arc from place P3 to transition T3 have the multiplicity $r-1$. Tokens contained in place P5 represent customers waiting in the queue or currently being served. The constant service requirement is modeled by the deterministic transition T4 with a firing delay of τ. The DSPN model has $rK+1$ tangible markings which can be classified as follows. One marking enables the deterministic transition exclusively, r markings enable only exponential transitions,

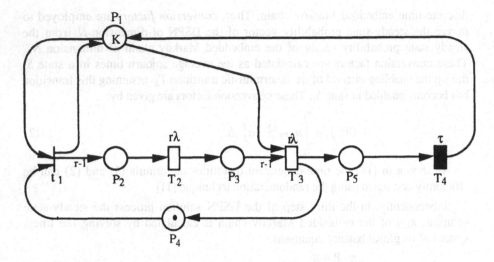

Figure 1. DSPN of the modified $E_r/D/1/K$ queue

and $r(K-1)$ markings enable one exponential transition concurrently with a deterministic transition. Observing the stochastic behavior of the modified $E_r/D/1/K$ queue only at departure points of customers defines an embedded Markov chain. Its state transition diagram is shown in Figure 2. The first index of a state $S_{i,j}$ denotes the number of customers in the system. The second index denotes the number of phases already completed by the next arriving customer. The states $S_{0,j} (1 \leq j \leq r-1)$ have a single state transition with probability 1. In case of $1 \leq i \leq K-1$, each state $S_{i,j}$ has nonzero transition probabilities to the states $S_{i-1,j} ... S_{K-1,0}$. Note, only for the states $S_{1,0}$ and $S_{K-1,0}$ of this class are all feasible state transitions included in Figure 2. Since the continuous-time behavior of the modified $E_r/D/1/K$ queue is observed only at departure points, the embedded Markov chain consists of $r(K-1)+1$ states rather than $rK+1$.

In case the deterministic transition T4 is enabled the corresponding transition probabilities of the EMC and the entries of the conversion matrix are derived by a transient analysis of the Markov chain subordinated to this deterministic transition. This Markov chain is shown in Figure 3. In the first r rows only diagonal elements of the matrix C have nonzero values, since in the corresponding markings only exponential transitions are enabled. For the remaining rows of the conversion matrix C the coefficients are determined by the mean sojourn times in states of the subordinated Markov chain of transition T4 during the time interval $[0, \tau]$.

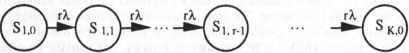

Figure 3. Subordinated Markov chain of the deterministic transition T4

296

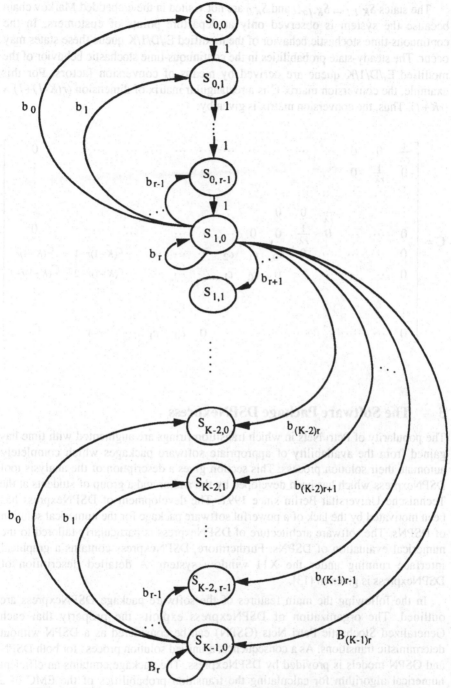

Figure 2. The embedded Markov chain of the modified $E_r/D/1/K$ queue

The states $S_{K-1,1}$ ... $S_{K-1,r-1}$ and $S_{K,0}$ are not visited in the embedded Markov chain because the system is observed only at departure points of customers. In the continuous-time stochastic behavior of the modified $E_r/D/1/K$ queue these states may occur. The steady-state probabilities in the continuous-time stochastic behavior of the modified $E_r/D/1/K$ queue are derived by means of conversion factors. For this example, the conversion matrix C is a rectangular matrix of dimension $(r(K-1)+1) \times (rK+1)$. Thus, the conversion matrix is given by:

$$
C = \begin{bmatrix}
\frac{1}{r\lambda} & 0 & 0 & \cdots & \cdots & \cdots & \cdots & \cdots & \cdots & \cdots & \cdots & \cdots & 0 \\
0 & \frac{1}{r\lambda} & 0 & \ddots & & & & & & & & & \vdots \\
\vdots & \ddots & \ddots & \ddots & \ddots & & & & & & & & \\
\vdots & & \ddots & \frac{1}{r\lambda} & 0 & 0 & & & & & & & \vdots \\
0 & \cdots & \cdots & 0 & \frac{1}{r\lambda} & 0 & 0 & \cdots & \cdots & \cdots & \cdots & \cdots & 0 \\
0 & \cdots & \cdots & 0 & c_0 & c_1 & c_2 & \cdots & \cdots & \cdots & \cdots c_{(K-1)r-1} & C_{(K-1)r} \\
0 & \cdots & \cdots & \cdots & 0 & c_0 & c_1 & \cdots & \cdots & \cdots & \cdots c_{(K-1)r-2} & C_{(K-1)r-1} \\
\vdots & & & & & \ddots & \ddots & \ddots & & & & \vdots \\
\vdots & & & & & & \ddots & \ddots & \ddots & & & \vdots \\
0 & \cdots & \cdots & \cdots & \cdots & \cdots & \cdots & 0 & c_0 & c_1 & \cdots & c_{r-1} & C_r
\end{bmatrix}
$$

3   The Software Package DSPNexpress

The popularity of Petri Nets in which transition firings are augmented with time has gained from the availability of appropriate software packages which completely automate their solution process. This section gives a description of the analysis tool DSPNexpress which has been developed by the author and a group of students at the Technische Universität Berlin since 1991. The development of DSPNexpress has been motivated by the lack of a powerful software package for the numerical solution of DSPNs. The software architecture of DSPNexpress is particularly tailored to the numerical evaluation of DSPNs. Furthermore, DSPNexpress contains a graphical interface running under the X11 window system. A detailed description of DSPNexpress is given in [13].

In the following the main features of the software package DSPNexpress are outlined. The organization of DSPNexpress exploits the property that each Generalized Stochastic Petri Nets (GSPN) can be considered as a DSPN without deterministic transitions. As a consequence, a unified solution process for both DSPN and GSPN models is provided by DSPNexpress. The package contains an efficient numerical algorithm for calculating the transition probabilities of the EMC of a DSPN and the corresponding conversion factors. A similar algorithm is employed for calculating transient solutions of a GSPN. The DSPN solution module of DSPNexpress considers each connected component of a Markov chain subordinated to a deterministic transition of a DSPN, separately, for calculating the corresponding transition probabilities of the EMC and the conversion factors. This leads to a considerable reduction of the computational effort and the memory requirements of the DSPN solution algorithm. The separate transient evaluation of each connected component of a SMC is related to the decomposition approach on the net level proposed by Ajmone Marsan, Chiola, and Fumagalli [4]. In their decomposition approach, *DSPN subnets with independent behavior* have to be identified by means of structural analysis on the net level. To obtain the transition probabilities of the EMC of a DSPN this approach requires a proper combination of the transient quantities calculated separately for each subnet. The algorithm implemented in DSPNexpress employs a depth-first-search algorithm for deriving the generator matrices of connected components of each SMC from the reachability graph of tangible markings of a DSPN. The transient analysis of a SMC yields immediately the corresponding transition probabilities of the EMC underlying the DSPN. The interaction between software modules of DSPNexpress is performed mostly by interprocess communication by means of sockets. As a consequence, the system overhead required by reading from or writing to files is substantially reduced. Moreover, this allows a parallel execution of the transient analysis of SMCs on a cluster of workstations. Due to this efficient numerical DSPN solution algorithm DSPNexpress is able to calculate steady-state solutions of complex DSPNs with reasonable computational effort on a modern workstation. To the best of the author´s knowledge DSPNexpress is the first software package with this feature.

The package DSPNexpress is organized as several sets of software modules which are stored in separate directories of a UNIX file system. We originally developed the package DSPNexpress for Sun™ workstations under SunOS.4.1, but the package has recently been ported to DEC™ and HP™ workstations under ULTRIX4.2 and HP-UX9.0, respectively. All software modules of DSPNexpress are implemented in the programming language C. To exploit the power of the numerical DSPN solution algorithm of DSPNexpress for solving complex DSPNs the package should run on machines with at least 16 MByte main memory. DSPNexpress allows a multi-user mode by including a link to the global directory DSPNexpress1.1 in the path expression in each user´s shell profile. Only the model descriptions and the user-defined settings for DSPNexpress are stored in a local directory at each user´s account.

The graphical interface of DSPNexpress runs under the release 5 of the X11 window system and is implemented using athena widgets of the X11 programming library. It allows a user-friendly definition, modification, and quantitative analysis of DSPN models. Places (*place*), immediate transitions (*imT*), exponential transitions (*expT*), deterministic transitions (*detT*), and arcs (*arc*) of a graphical description of a DSPN are processed by selecting the corresponding object and one of the commands *add*, *move*, *delete*, or *change* with the mouse. For example, in the setting depicted Figure 4 deterministic transitions may be inserted and the grid option is used to simplify the graphical editing. Marking parameters (*marking*), firing delays (*delay*), and tags (*tag*) associated with places and transitions are processed in a similar way. For each setting of the command line an online help is provided in the upper part of the graphical interface explaining the actions currently available. The message displayed in Figure 4 indicates that clicking the left mouse button inserts a deterministic transition. In Figure 4 a DSPN named *sequential* of the directory *VSM* is displayed. Each place and each transition of this DSPN is labeled with a tag (e.g. T1, t2,..., etc). Each timed transition is also labeled with a parameter specifying the mean value of its firing delay (e.g. write or d_locate_owner). The exponential transitions T1, T4, and T16 are also labeled with *inf.-serv.* to specify their enabling policy as infinite-server [1]. To illustrate the capabilities of DSPNexpress the DSPN solution popup is shown in Figure 5. In case the steady-state solution of a DSPN shall be computed the numerical method for solving the linear system of the global balance equations of its EMC may be chosen by the user by clicking in one of the toggles *automatic*, *iterative*, or *direct*. Moreover, a user may specify whether the transient analysis of the SMCs is performed sequentially on a single workstation (*sequential*) or in parallel on a cluster of workstations (*parallel*) and whether verbose output of the solution process is displayed and stored in a logfile. Transient solutions of GSPNs are computed by clicking in the toggle *transient* and specifying an instant of time. The design of the graphical interface has been influenced by the interface of the version 1.4 of the package GreatSPN [7]. Opposed to the graphical interface of GreatSPN

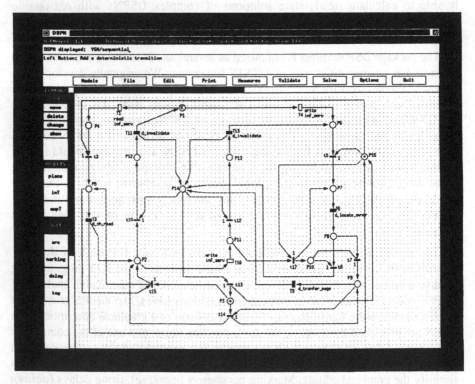

Figure 4. User Interface of DSPNexpress

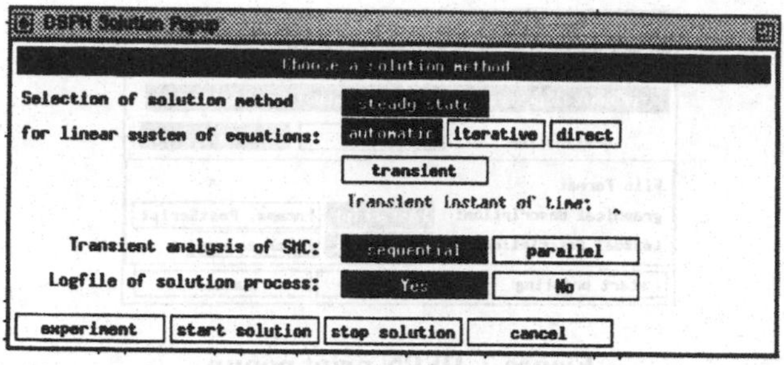

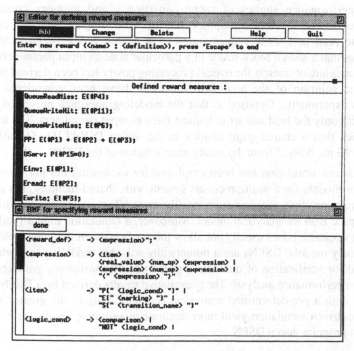

Figure 5. DSPN solution popup

special purpose editors are provided by DSPNexpress for defining steady-state reward measures and marking-dependent firing delays. The editor for specifying user-defined reward measures is shown in Figure 6. The definitions of eight reward measures (QueueReadMiss, QueueWriteMiss, etc.) of the DSPN *sequential* are displayed in the middle part. The Backus-Naur form of the specification language for reward measures is displayed in the lower part of this window by clicking the help button. The graphical interface provides popups for changing firing delays of timed transitions, changing the type of a transition and for changing the multiplicity or the direction of an arc. Similar popups are also provided for defining or modifying a delay or a marking parameter, changing the string of a tag, etc.

Figure 6. Reward measure editor

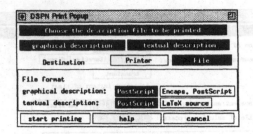

Figure 7. DSPN print popup

The print popup of DSPNexpress is shown in Figure 7. This popup allows the printing of the DSPN currently being displayed in the main window of DSPNexpress and/or its stochastic description such as delay and marking parameters and definitions and computed results of user-defined reward measures. These description may be either directly printed on a laser writer or stored in files named *<model>.graph* and *<model>.text*, respectively, by clicking the appropriate toggles with the left mouse button.

4   A DSPN of a Sequential Memory Consistency Protocol

Previous performance studies of cache consistency and memory consistency protocols of shared memory multiprocessors or multicomputer systems consider besides the read and write request rates to a shared block or page also the probabilities that a shared block reside in a particular state as input parameters of the model. As measure of interest the overall processing power has been derived from the steady-state solution of the analytical model or have been considered in the simulation experiments. Opposed to that the modeling approach presented in this section takes only the read and write request rates as input parameters. The long-run probabilities that a shared page resides in the states INVALID, SHARED, or EXCLUSIVE are derived from the steady-state solution of the DSPN.

Trace-driven simulation has been employed for evaluating the performance of consistency models for a multiprocessor system with shared-memory, but a trace-driven simulation study requires substantially more effort in computation time and memory space than an analytical model. Moreover, a simulation model (both trace-driven and stochastic) does usually not allow the verification of qualitative properties of consistency models. DSPNs are a numerically solvable modeling tool which are both suited for verification of qualitative properties of consistency paradigms and quantitative performance analysis. The quantitative results derived by a DSPN can be calculated with a pre-determined numerical accuracy. Due to the greater level of detail trace-driven simulation yield more accurate quantitative results for a specific application program than a DSPN.

A DSPN model of the behavior of a single shared page in a VSM system with sequential consistency and a write-invalidate protocol is depicted in Figure 8. A MIMD architecture is considered in which the nodes are connected by a low-latency scalable interconnection network (e.g. a crossbar interconnection network). The DSPN considers a subset of K+1 nodes of the multicomputer system which are competing for the same shared page. Each of the K tokens in place *INVALID* and the token in place *EXCLUSIVE* represent one of these nodes. The three main states of a shared page in the global address space, namely INVALID, SHARED and EXCLUSIVE are represented in the DSPN by places with corresponding labels. The token in place *Server available* represents the idle state of the server which maintains the data structures for managing the considered page. All other places and transitions of Figure 8 are also labeled according to their meaning. In the DSPN model requests causing a page status change from SHARED to EXCLUSIVE are given a higher priority than those from INVALID to EXCLUSIVE or from INVALID to SHARED. The latter ones are given the same priority. This is encoded in the DSPN model as follows. The immediate transition *Start process find owner* has associated a firing priority of 2 whereas the immediate transitions *Start process read miss* and *Start process write miss* have associated a firing priority of 1 and an equal weight. These assumptions can be easily modified by changing the appropriate firing priorities and weights of these immediate transitions. Since the delay required for a page status change is typically at least one order of magnitude smaller than a page transfer, this delay is neglected in the DSPN. In case of a read miss this approximation allows to represent a location of the owner and a page transfer by the single deterministic transition *Find owner and transfer page delay*.

The following explains the representation of the activities in the DSPN caused by a write miss to the shared page. Activities caused by the other types of requests are represented in a similar way. The firing of the exponential transition *Write miss* removes a token from the place INVALID and puts it to the place *Write miss queue*. In case the server is available (a token resides in place *Server available*) the immediate transition *Start process write miss* fires removing a token from the places *Server available* and *Write miss queue* and putting a token to the place *Process find owner*. The delay required by the system for this activity is represented by the deterministic transition *Find owner delay*. A firing of this transition puts the token in place *Decision*. Since the place *Write hit occurred* contains no token the immediate transition *Is write miss* fires and puts the token in the place *Process transfer page*. If the place *EXCLUSIVE* contains a token (the node owning the page has currently exclusive write permission), the immediate transition *Change access due to write miss* fires and puts this token in the place *SHARED*. This constitutes the first step of the invalidation of a former owner. The former owner is not stalled until a copy of the page has been transferred to the new owner, since residence times of tokens in the place *SHARED* contributes to the processing power. After the deterministic transition *Transfer page delay* has fired, the token residing in place *Process transfer page* is moved to the place *Process invalidations*. In case no further write request has occurred at the former owner (the exponential transition *Write hit* has not fired), the immediate transition *Start invalidating* fires and puts the token from place *SHARED* to the place *Invalidating*. This activity constitutes the second step of the invalidation

303

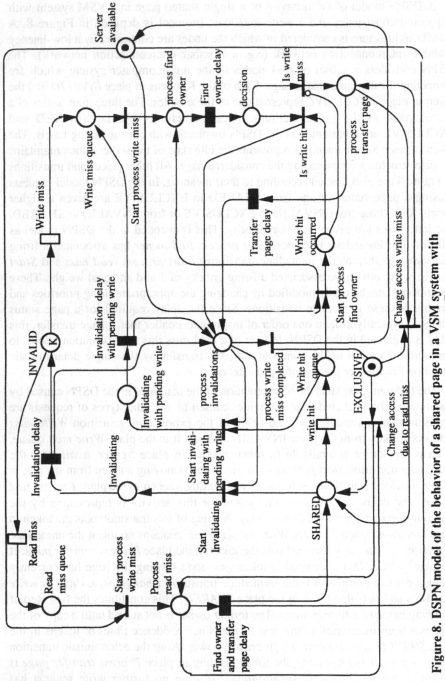

Figure 8. DSPN model of the behavior of a shared page in a VSM system with sequential consistency and a write-invalidate protocol [17]

which is equal to the invalidation of nodes with read permission. The firing of the deterministic transition *Invalidation delay* removes the token from place *Invalidating* and puts a token to the place *INVALID* and *Process Invalidations*.

Invalidations are modeled sequentially and represented by the subnet consisting of the places *Invalidating* and *Invalidating with pending write* together with the transitions *Start invalidation*, *Start invalidation with pending write*, *Invalidation delay*, and *Invalidation delay with pending write*. All nodes with SHARED access have to be invalidated before the new owner gets the access EXCLUSIVE. Thus, the immediate transitions *Start invalidation* and *Start invalidation with pending write* have associated the higher firing priority 2 than the immediate transition *Process write miss completed* which has priority 1. All other immediate transition have also associated the firing priority 1. The firing of the immediate transition *Process write request completed* removes the token from place *Process invalidations* and puts a token to each of the places *EXCLUSIVE* and *Server available*. Curves of the processing power achieved by a multicomputer system in which virtually shared memory is implemented by the sequential memory consistency model can be directly obtained from the steady state solution of the DSPN of Figure 8 and were presented in [17].

This DSPN model contains 5 deterministic transitions and its state space grows rather fast for increasing the number of tokens. Thus, for increasing marking parameter K the calculation of the solution of this DSPN is severely hampered due to state space explosion. For example, in case of $K = 20$ the DSPN has 59,101 tangible markings and its EMC consists of 6,004,585 nonzero state transitions. As shown in [14], DSPNs of this complexity could not be solved in practice with the adaptive matrix exponentiation method implemented in GreatSPN1.4. The experimental results presented in [13] show that this DSPN can be solved by DSPNexpress with reasonable computational effort on a modern workstation.

Recent Results

To summarize, the current state-of-the-art is that steady-state solutions of quite complex DSPNs can be calculated using DSPNexpress with reasonable computational effort on a workstation [13], [14]. This progress in the analysis of DSPNs has triggered other methodological work on DSPNs. Trivedi, Choi, and Mainkar introduced a technique for sensitivity analysis of DSPN [19]. In another recent work, extensions to the numerical solution method of DSPNs were introduced in order to cope with deterministic transitions with marking-dependent firing delays [16]. However, the numerical solution method for DSPNs which is currently implemented in the package DSPNexpress is still based on the restriction that in no marking two or more deterministic transitions are concurrently enabled. This structural restriction of DSPNs severely hampers their applicability for a wide gamut of problems. In order to fully establish DSPNs in the research community numerical methods for transient analysis and steady-state analysis of DSPNs with concurrently enabled deterministic transitions have to be developed. Recently, Choi, Kulkarni, and

Trivedi showed how transient solutions of DSPNs can be computed using numerical inversion of a Laplace-Stieltjes transform [8]. The same authors showed that the stochastic process underlying a DSPN is a Markov regerative stochastic process and introduced an approach for dealing with non-exponentially distributed firing delays other than the deterministic distribution [9]. However, in all of their work the structural restriction that in no marking of the DSPN two or more deterministic transitions are concurrently enabled is still assumed.

To relax this restriction the employment of the method of supplementary variables has been proposed for analyzing DSPNs [10]. In this paper it has been shown that the computation of steady-state solutions of DSPNs with concurrently enabled deterministic transitions by the proposed solution approach requires the solution of a partial system of differential equations. Furthermore, DSPNs in which the firing delay of timed transitions is either exponentially or non-exponentially distributed, but no concurrent firings of transitions with nonexponential delay have been considered. Employing the proposed solution approach for such DSPNs leads to a system of ordinary differential equations and integral equations. In case the non-exponential distributions belong to the class of polynomial distributions efficient computational formulas for solving this system of integro-differential system have been introduced by extending Jensen´s method, also called randomization or uniformization [11].

References

[1]   M. Ajmone Marsan, G. Balbo, A. Bobbio, G. Chiola, G. Conte, and A. Cumani. The Effect of Execution Policies on the Semantics of Stochastic Petri Nets. *IEEE Trans. Softw. Engin.*, 15, pages 832-846, 1989.

[2]   M. Ajmone Marsan and G. Chiola. On Petri Nets with Deterministic and Exponentially Distributed Firing Times", in: *G. Rozenberg (Ed.) Advances in Petri Nets 1986, Lecture Notes in Computer Science 266*, pages 132-145, Springer 1987.

[3]   M. Ajmone Marsan, G. Chiola, and A. Fumagalli. An Accurate Performance Model of CSMA/CD Bus LAN, in: *G. Rozenberg (Ed.) Advances in Petri Nets 1986, Lecture Notes in Computer Science 266* pages 146-161, Springer 1987.

[4]   M. Ajmone Marsan, G. Chiola, and A. Fumagalli. Improving the Efficiency of the Analysis of DSPN Models. in: *G. Rozenberg (Ed.) Advances in Petri Nets 1989, Lecture Notes in Computer Science 424*, pages 30-50, Springer 1990.

[5]   M. Ajmone Marsan and V. Signore. Timed Petri Net Performance Models for Fiber Optic LAN Architectures, *Proc. 2nd Int. Workshop on Petri Nets and Performance Models, Madison Wisconsin*, pages 66-74, 1987.

[6]   G. Balbo, G. Chiola, G. Franceschinis, and G. Molinar Roet. On the Efficient Construction of the Tangible Reachability Graph of Generalized Stochastic Petri Nets. *Proc. 2nd Int. Workshop on Petri Nets and Performance Models, Madison Wisconsin* , pages 85-92, 1987.

[7]   G. Chiola. A Graphical Petri Net Tool for Performance Analysis. *Proc. 3rd Int. Workshop on Modelling Techniques and Performance Evaluation, Paris France*, pages 323-333, 1987.

[8]   H. Choi, V. Kulkarni, and K.S. Trivedi. Transient Analysis of Deterministic and Stochastic Petri Nets, *Proc. 14th Int. Conf. on Applications and Theory of Petri Nets, Chicago Illinois, June 1993* (to appear).

[9]   H. Choi, V. Kulkarni, and K.S. Trivedi. Markov Regenerative Stochastic Petri Nets, *Proc. 16th Int. Symposium on Computer Performance Modeling, Measurement, and Evaluation (PERFORMANCE '93), Roma Italy October 1993*, (to appear).

[10]   R. German and C. Lindemann. Analysis of Stochastic Petri Nets by the Method of Supplementary Variables, *Proc. 16th Int. Symposium on Computer Performance Modeling, Measurement, and Evaluation (PERFORMANCE '93), Roma Italy October 1993*, (to appear).

[11]   D. Gross and D.R. Miller. The Randomization Technique as a Modeling Tool and Solution Procedure for Transient Markov Processes, *Operations Research, 32*, pages 345-361, 1984.

[12]   M.A. Holliday and M.K. Vernon. A Generalized Timed Petri Net Model for Performance Analysis, *IEEE Trans. Softw. Engin., 12*, pages 1297-1310, 1987.

[13]   C. Lindemann. DSPNexpress: A Software Package for the Efficient Solution of Deterministic and Stochastic Petri Nets, *Proc. 6th Int. Conf. on Modeling Techniques and Tools for Computer Performance Evaluation, Edinburgh Scotland*, pages 15-29, 1992.

[14]   C. Lindemann. An Improved Numerical Algorithm for Calculating Steady-state Solutions of Deterministic and Stochastic Petri Net Models, *Performance Evaluation, 18*, 1993 (in press).

[15]   C. Lindemann, G. Ciardo, R. German, and G. Hommel. Performability Evaluation of an Automated Manufacturing System with Deterministic and Stochastic Petri Nets, *Proc. Int. Conf on Robotics and Automation, Atlanta Georgia*, pages 576-581, 1993.

[16]   C. Lindemann and R. German. Modeling Discrete Event Systems with State-dependent Deterministic Service Times, *Discrete Event Dynamic Systems: Theory and Applications, 3*, pages 249-270, 1993.

[17]   C. Lindemann and F. Schön. Evaluating Sequential Consistency in a Virtually Shared Memory System with Deterministic and Stochastic Petri Nets, *Proc. Int. Workshop on Modeling, Analysis, and Simulation of Computer and Telecommunication Systems, San Diego California*, pages 63-68, 1993.

[18]   M. Lu, D. Zhang, and T. Murata. Analysis of Self-Stabilizing Clock Synchronization by Means of Stochastic Petri Nets, *IEEE Trans. on Computers, 39*, pages 597-604, 1990.

[19]   K.S. Trivedi, H. Choi, and V. Mainkar. Sensitivity Analysis of Deterministic and Stochastic Petri Nets, *Proc. Int. Workshop on Modeling, Analysis, and Simulation of Computer and Telecommunication Systems, San Diego California*, pages 271-276, 1993.

[20]   W.M. Zuberek. Timed Petri Nets: Definitions, Properties, and Applications, *Microelectronics & Reliability, 31*, pages 627-644, 1991.

RELAXATION FOR MASSIVELY PARALLEL DISCRETE EVENT SIMULATION

Boris D. Lubachevsky

AT&T Bell Laboratories
Murray Hill, NJ 07974, USA

ABSTRACT

The discussion in this tutorial is centered around a new space-time relaxation paradigm which appears to be a good candidate for rendering efficient a wide class of massively parallel discrete event simulations.

1 Discrete event simulation: what it is and why we consider it

Several forms of computer rendering, such as computer graphics or computer games, are sometimes called "simulations." Here, we focus attention on simulating a *dynamic system*. Simulation will be understood to be the process of generating the trajectory or sample path for such a system.

Typically, the user "pushes the limits" and simulates as large a model as computer memory permits and for as long as it is tolerable. Hence it is not surprising that a substantial fraction of the non-idle CPU time of many computers, perhaps, as large as 50%, is occupied with simulations. It might seem somewhat unexpected, though, to find a substantial fraction of all simulations to be dealing with *discrete event* models.

After all, most of us think of the world in Newtonian terms: a global clock with objects continuously changing their states governed by, say, differential equations that express the advancement of time. However, this intuitive and clear time-driven concept often generates inefficient computer algorithms. Specifically, each component of the system under study typically changes its state rarely and such changes are asynchronous among the components. If we make a snapshot of the model at a random time instance, we will see no or few changes that are taking place. The changes are sparsely "sprinkled" over the space-time. If the computer simulates such a system in a time-driven fashion by continuously monitoring each component, the processing power of the machine is wasted. Using a less intuitive but more efficient discrete event model we can simulate the same system orders of magnitude faster on the same computer.

In a discrete event model, the system and its components change their states instantaneously at discrete times; those changes are called *events*. The state remains constant on the intervals between the events. Time advancement is represented not in a time-driven form, like differential or difference equations, but in an event-driven form. In the latter form, the trajectory of the system is a directed acyclic *event dependency graph*. The nodes of it are the events, and the links represent cause-effect relations in pairs of events.

This graph can be also viewed as a data-flow diagram. To each node-event corresponds the event *descriptor*, which consists of the time of the event and the specification of the state change represented by the event. If events $e_1, e_2, \ldots, e_k$ are all the immediate causes of event e, then the descriptor of event e is a function of descriptors of $e_1, e_2, \ldots, e_k$. Computing the descriptor of e given the descriptors of e's causes is called *processing* of event e.

Not only the event descriptors but also the topology of the event dependency graph is unknown in advance. The discrete event simulation algorithm must both construct the event dependency graph and process the events on it. The former activity, also referred to as event *scheduling*, typically is the most calculation intensive and difficult for programming.

An example is helpful. Consider a gutter, bounded from both ends. The gutter contains $N = 4$ balls of equal mass and size. Assume the balls and the gutter walls are ideally rigid and elastic, the gutter is very massive, and its width is just enough to assure motions of the balls along its length in the absence of gravitation and friction. Figure 1 represents the initial segment of the system trajectory beginning with the positions and velocities of the balls at time t_0.

The depiction can be viewed both as a space-time diagram of the system trajectory and as an event dependency graph where the events e_i, $i = 1, 2 \ldots$ are ball-ball or ball-wall collisions. (The gutter and the four balls are depicted at the bottom of the diagram.) An event descriptor here consists of: the collision time, the positions and velocities of the involved balls immediately after the collision. One can check, for instance, that (the descriptor of) event e_5, which is a collision of balls 3 and 4, is a function of (the descriptors of) events e_4, a collision of 2 and 3, and e_2, a reflection of 4 from the wall. Specifically, we can compute time t_5 of collision e_5, if we know the times, positions, and velocities of balls 3 and 4 immediately after their previous events e_4 and e_2, respectively.

It was said above that the state of a discrete event system remains *constant* on the intervals between events. However, in this example positions of the balls are continuously *changing* between collisions. Is there a contradiction? No, there isn't. We simulate the given continuous time system *as if* the state remained constant between collisions. The "trick" is that although we do not consider trajectories of balls between collisions, no information is lost. This "trick" is exactly the reason why simulating the billiards in the discrete event format is much more efficient than in the continuous time format. In the latter, time-driven method, the computer updates the state of the system by scanning all balls at each small interval Δt. In most such intervals, like in the one indicated in Figure 1, there is simply no events, in others there are few events. By contrast, in an event-driven method, the computer updates the state of the system from collision to collision, i.e., from t_i to t_{i+1}. For example, immediately after processing collision e_4 of balls 2 and 3 the computer processes collision e_5 of 3 and 4.

To process event e_5 we must first make sure that e_5 takes place. This is the task of *scheduling*. This task is not trivial even in our simple example. Here is a "naive" way to schedule event e_5: First, we calculate the state of all balls at time t_4 of the last processed event; then from this state we try to match any

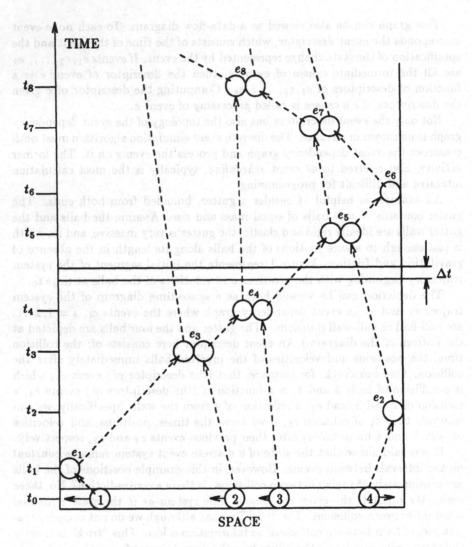

Figure 1: Billiards in one dimension

ball-ball or ball-wall pair in a next collision; lastly, we find the minimum of all these next potential collision times which delivers for us the time of event e_5 and also identifies the participating balls, 3 and 4. After the schedule for event e_5 is completed, we process the event by recomputing positions of balls 3 and 4 and by determining their new velocities after collision e_5. We use known formulas of elastic collision in recomputation of velocities.

The described method of scheduling is "naive" not only because it does not take advantage of 1D (balls can not "overtake" each other, hence only balls i and $i + 1$ can collide and only balls 1 and N can collide with the walls), but also because it examines all N balls in order to schedule only one event which involves at most two balls.

The task of designing an efficient scheduling usually constitutes the main difficulty of recasting a continuous time model in a discrete event format. Discussions of efficiency of discrete event simulations, are usually reduced to efficiency of implementing *queues of events*. One should realize, though, that handling such a queue, even if it is done efficiently, does not cover the entire task. Simulationist also has to design an efficient data manipulation, to figure out what *are* the events, which events to keep and which to forget and when during computations.

Say, in the billiards example, which data should be kept for each ball at each stage of computing? Should the entire prehistory of a ball be retained or only a part of it? How to avoid the order of N overhead of the "naive" method? There seems to be no general recipe for answering questions of this type and we are not going to discuss them in this tutorial. (In the specific example of simulating billiards, several methods equivalent in its results to the "naive" method, but which are much more efficient, are mentioned in Bibliography.) It will be assumed here that the discrete event model of a system subject to simulation is defined and is provided with the required mechanism for scheduling future events.

2 Parallel discrete event simulation: its intent and its caveats

The parallel discrete event simulation has the same objective as the serial one. It is supposed to generate the simulated system trajectory in the form of the event dependency graph. An obvious, but sometimes forgotten requirement is that the trajectory, including the topology of the graph and the descriptors of events in it, does not depend on the method of computation, whether serial or parallel. As the programmers know, writing a parallel code is always more difficult than writing a serial code for the same task. Then why do we get involved in parallelization? For one reason only: a promise of shorter running time.

To reduce the running time by parallel execution, a simulation task has to be split into a number of subtasks which can be carried concurrently by different processing elements (PEs) of the parallel computer. Three methods of splitting are commonly used with different PEs carrying:

1) independent simulation runs. This is called the *replication* method

2) different tasks in the serial processing of one simulation run. This is the method of *functional parallelism*

3) different components of the simulated system for one simulation run. This is the *space-parallel* method.

Recently a fourth method has been discussed, where different PEs concurrently carry simulation for different time segments of the same simulated component for one simulation run. It is natural to call it the *time-parallel* method.

The replication method is simple and efficient and should be exercised whenever possible, specifically, when we have to run many independent trajectories with initial conditions known in advance and when one PE is able to accommodate one run. Unfortunately, these conditions are satisfied rarely. Usually we need to speed up a single run or each run in a *sequence*.

The functional parallelism allows one to speed up a single run. In our billiards example in Section 1, the functions that can be executed concurrently may be: solving an equation to find the time of next collision of two given balls, computing the ball velocities after the collision, various data manipulations involved in scheduling the next event, such as the minimization. In addition to being to some extent independent in handling one event, these functions are somewhat independent when executed for successive events. Hence their execution can be pipelined, i.e., we may begin scheduling next collision while still processing the previous one.

The drawback in a functional parallelization is that the degree of parallelism does not scale with the size of the simulated system, e.g., with the number of balls. In scheduling the next event, there is always a serial section of the code. Even if simulation is pipelined, only a limited number of events are taken for processing at a time. Hence, functional parallelism as such is not appropriate for massively parallel execution (but can perhaps be used in combinations with other methods discussed below).

Only the third and the forth methods seem appropriate for massively parallel execution and we will discuss them in detail. Consider the third method, when different components or subsystems are hosted by concurrently running PEs. Recall that our concern is to simulate event dependencies correctly.

Let us first consider the space-parallel method in the application to the (notably inefficient) time-driven simulation. In this setting, at each step the PEs, based on the information about the events processed for times before t, process events for slot $[t, t + \Delta t)$. Because Δt is assumed to be very small it is not probable for both cause and effect events to fall into the same slot. Hence violations of causality almost never occur: between the steps the PEs will inform each other about the causes to correctly schedule the effects.

One source of inefficiency here is *statically fixed* Δt which thereby must be very small. We can improve efficiency by letting Δt *change dynamically* from iteration to iteration. We can choose Δt as large as possible at each new iteration with the restriction that no violation of causality occurs. Specifically, causality

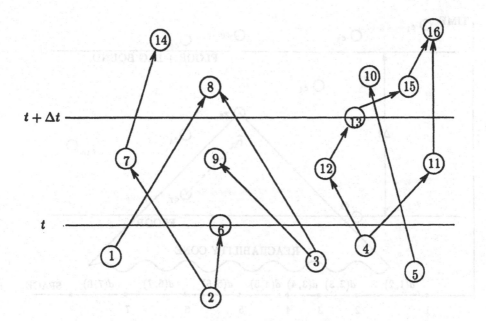

Figure 2: Adjustable time stepping algorithm

is preserved, if given that the smallest event time scheduled but not processed at previous iterations is t, any other such event (which is scheduled but not processed at previous iterations) whose time is smaller than $t + \Delta t$ is itself not an effect of such an event. We choose Δt to be the largest value that satisfies this condition.

This idea is illustrated in the fragment of the event dependency graph in Figure 2. It is assumed in this depiction that all dependency links among the shown events are also shown, and that no shown event will be canceled or rescheduled. (These assumptions are made for all the other pictures in this tutorial unless stated otherwise.) Here the events that are indexed 1, ...5 have been processed, the rest, events 6, ...16, have been scheduled but not processed. Of the latter set, event 6 has the smallest time t, all events in set $S = \{6, 7, 8, 9, 10, 11, 12\}$ are scheduled and unprocessed, and in addition are not effects of events in S. The key observation is that the events in S can be processed concurrently without violating causality. Event 13 has the smallest time among those that are *not* safe to process in parallel with events in S; indeed, 13 is an effect of event $12 \in S$. Events 13,14,15,16 will be processed at future iterations. Moreover, because of the time stepping restriction, events 8 and 10 will be processed at future iterations too, despite that it is safe to process them now. The next Δt is the maximum width of the strip that does not contain events which do not belong to S. The next iteration will begin with $t + \Delta t$ replacing t.

This idea was successfully implemented in several massively parallel simulations. Its use is hinged on finding a convenient method to generate non-trivial (i.e., not very small) estimates for cause-effect delays at least two cause-effect

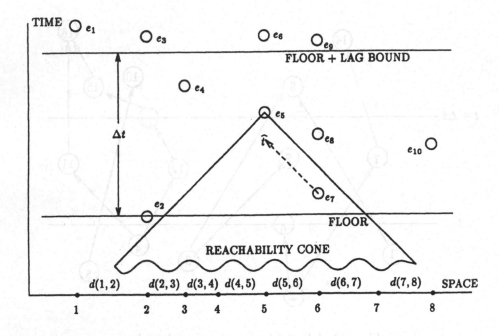

Figure 3: Bounded lag algorithm

links in advance. A success in this, of course, depends on an application (see Bibliography).

Another application-dependent method to preserve causality is based on estimates of *minimum propagation delays*. Here we also advance time by time stepping. However, the width Δt of the strip in the space-time diagram is not thought of as "small." On the other hand, an iteration does not necessarily exhaust all the events that fall within the strip. This is the *bounded-lag* algorithm. An instance of event scheduling and processing is shown in the space-time diagram in Figure 3. Eight sites indexed 1, ...8, are depicted along the space axis. It is assumed that events can not propagate from site i to site $i+1$ in time smaller than $d(i, i+1)$. Quantity $d(i, j)$ is induced for any pair of sites i and j so as to satisfy the triangle inequality $d(i, j) + d(j, k) \geq d(i, k)$. Quantity $d(i, j)$ is also non-negative, but unlike the standard definition of the *distance*, $d(i, j)$ is not necessarily equal to $d(j, i)$. To simplify the drawing, equality $d(i, j) = d(j, i)$ is also assumed to hold in the example of Figure 3, and it is also assumed that $d(i, j)$ is the Euclidean distance between the corresponding sites.

Suppose we want to test, whether or not event e_5 is safe to process at the current step. In the simplest version of the algorithm, we check all event-causes, whose effects might potentially affect site 5 in the past of event e_5. Space-time coordinates of those events have to belong to the *incoming reachability cone* constructed with respect to event e_5. The condition that an event with time t_1 that occurs at site s_1 belongs to the incoming reachability cone of an event with time t_0 that occurs at site s_0 can be expressed as: $t_0 - t_1 \geq d(s_1, s_0)$. For $s_0 = 5$, $s_1 = 6$, $t_0 = \text{time}(e_5)$, and $t_1 = \text{time}(e_7)$ this condition holds and we see that e_7 may cause an event at site 5 in the past of event e_5. This hypothetical trouble event would have time $\hat{t}$.

The events that are safe to process at the current iteration according to this test are e_2, e_7, and e_{10}. For the next iteration, the floor will be moved to $time(e_8)$.

Event propagation delays are easy to think of as physical delays of propagating signals. That may be the case, but more often *procedural* delays qualify as the event propagation delays. For example, the service time in a queuing system simulation can be translated into an event propagation delay. This might seem counter-intuitive, because both the cause, "service start" and the effect, "service end" occur at the same site (at the server node).

The two discussed above algorithms are examples of safe, causality preserving simulations, also called *conservative*. Without further discussing other safe parallel algorithms, we note that a successful realization in parallel for such an algorithm needs non-trivial (i.e., not equal to zero), a priori estimates of cause-effect delays. The "a priori" means that the estimate must be known before the corresponding events are simulated. One way to see how this is possible is to imagine that a cause and the corresponding effect mark the beginning and the end of a certain "activity." Without simulating this activity we should be able to say that the activity would take longer than a certain positive bound.

Simulations of *stochastic* models by the nature of the assumptions usually made in such models open an avenue for such an estimation. For example, if a job enters the service, the service time is usually assumed to be stochastically independent of the state of the system when service begins. Thus, we can pre-sample the service time several steps in advance, even when the corresponding job is not yet arrived for service. Another example: Ising spin simulations. Here we have an array of atoms and the state of each atom is changed at unpredictable random times which we model as a Poisson point process associated with this atom. The rate of arrivals is fixed for all atoms and arrivals for different atoms are independent. The state change depends on the states of the neighboring atoms, but the *time* of the change is independent of the state.

Paradoxically, whereas the times of state changes are random and hence conceptually unpredictable, in the simulation we can predict them. We sample these times any number of steps in advance using algorithmically generated random sequences. The fact that these sequences are fully deterministic (and reproducible once started with the same seeds) is an advantage! It is not appropriate for our purposes in pursuit of the "real" randomness to use physically generated and hence irreproducible random sequences instead. (Practitioners of simulation may not recognize this simple but important observation.)

However, presampling is not always possible. In some examples, in order to know a non-trivial estimate of the cause-effect delay we must, at the least, simulate both cause and effect events. This is a fundamental problems with the conservative parallel simulation algorithms, which thus can not always be successfully applied. An example of such impossibility for delay prediction is the simulation of billiards discussed in Section 1. Some may consider the simulation of billiards to be a "toy" example. In fact, this "toy" model is in many respects more difficult to simulate in parallel, than some "serious" models, e.g., queuing networks.

3   Space-time paradigm: everyone was skeptical at first

Figure 4 illustrates the space-time relaxation concept for parallel discrete event simulations. According to this concept, space-time is to be split (arbitrarily or as convenient) into regions and each region is to be assigned to a PE which is responsible for filling this region with events.

The computations are iterative. A synchronous version of such computations can be described as follows. Let $X^{(k)}$ denote a trajectory (event dependency graph) as known at iteration k. This $X^{(k)}$ is composed of segments of trajectories known to each PE. For the next iteration $k+1$ each PE updates its segment of trajectory, i.e., reprocesses its events after receiving relevant information from the neighboring PEs about events as they were known to them at the previous iteration. This reprocessing can be expressed as $X^{(k+1)} = F(X^{(k)})$ where function F symbolizes the cause-effect relation among the events.

The recomputation terminates at the iteration at which each PE detects that its events are the same as they were at the previous iteration. The termination is equivalent to finding X such that $F(X) = X$. This X is a *fixed-point* of the cause-effect relation map F.

Reducing problems to solving fixed-point equations is not unusual in mathematics. For example, we may try to solve equation $x = sin(2x)$ with respect to unknown x by iterating: beginning with $x^{(0)}$ we find $x^{(1)} = sin(2x^{(0)})$, then $x^{(2)} = sin(2x^{(1)})$, then $x^{(3)} = sin(2x^{(2)})$, and so on. The standard questions here are: Is the solution unique? If so, will the iterations converge to this solution? If so, how fast? In the $x = sin(2x)$ problem the solution is not unique and the convergence depends on the choice of the initial guess $x^{(0)}$.

On the other hand, in the discrete event simulation problem, the iterations *always converge* and the found fixed-point is *unique*. This can be seen by comparing the iterative fixed-point method to standard serial simulation. In the latter at each step we uniquely determine one more event using event dependency. Beginning with the same initial events as in the serial simulation, at each iteration of the parallel fixed-point method we settle at least one additional event. And since in the parallel fixed-point method we use the same event dependency (represented in F) the settled events must be the same as the ones in the serial simulation.

TIME

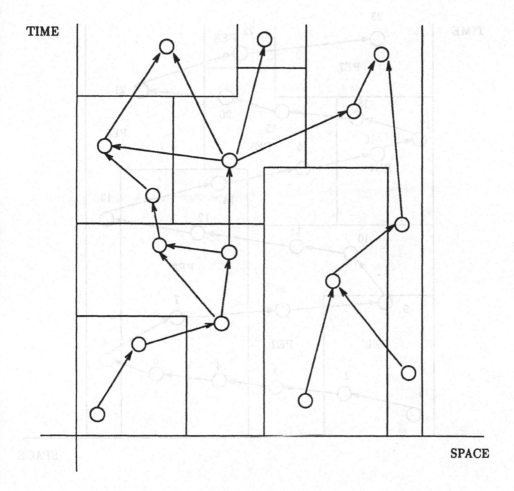

SPACE

Figure 4: Space-time simulation concept

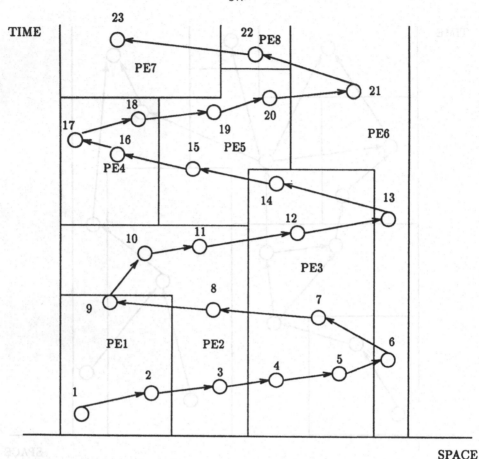

Figure 5: Non-parallelizable event dependency graph

Slow convergence may be an obstacle on the way to a practical realization of this idea. Indeed, for the event dependency graph depicted in Figure 5, no matter how we split the space-time among the PEs, serial event settling (in the shown order: 1,2,3...) is guaranteed: PE6 has to wait for PE3 to correctly determine event 5 before processing event 6 and then wait for PE3 again to correctly determine event 12 before processing event 13 and finally wait for PE5 to correctly process event 20 before processing event 21; similarly, PE 7 can not perform any useful work before events 1,...27 are correctly processed by the other processors, and so on.

During the first public presentation of this space-time relaxation paradigm in

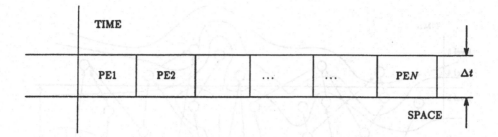

Figure 6: Partitioning of a one-time-step strip

1989 (see Bibliography) the audience seemed very skeptical for this very reason: questionable performance. In 1990 and later the question of performance was addressed as discussed in the following sections.

4 Space-parallel relaxation can be efficient

Here we discuss a specialization of the space-time relaxation idea of Section 3 for a space-parallel simulation. We consider a time-stepping algorithm, where "space" in the space-time diagram represents a large simulated system, like a large queuing network, or a large billiards table with many balls, whereas, the "time" is restricted to a relatively small Δt window. As in the time-stepping algorithms discussed in Section 2, the simulation is advanced by serially processing these strips, one after another. We are now discussing processing events in one specific strip at one step of such an algorithm. Each PE is assigned a subsystem, e.g., a subnetwork, or a region on the billiards table, with the task to process all events on the specified time interval Δt.

This would correspond to a partition of the Δt strip by vertical lines into rectangles as shown in Figure 6. Now if we apply the general iterative procedure described in Section 3 for this specific partition, how many iteration will there be until convergence? This, of course, depends on the event dependency subgraph that fits in the strip. For the event chains like the one in Figure 5 there will be many iterations. However, Figure 5 depicts an artificially difficult, worst case example.

In Figure 7, on the other hand, we do not assume an adversary simulation problem. Depicted here is an "average" example obtained (without thinking of a particular application) by "randomly" sprinkling the events-circles and possible event dependency arrows. How many iterations will be required for the shown event-dependency graph?

It turns out that a good upper bound on the number of iterations can be supplied by counting *levels*. Because the levels can be identified without knowing how the space-time strip is partitioned among the PEs, no partitioning is shown in Figure 7. Level 0 in Figure 7 consists of already processed events that are

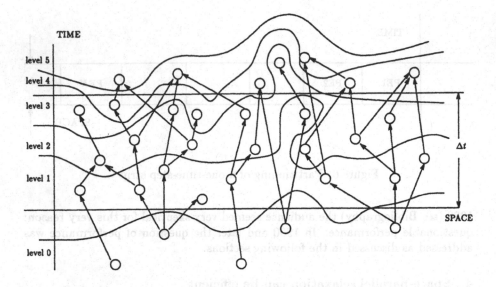

Figure 7: Event dependency levels

positioned below the strip. Level 1 consists of those events at or above the floor of the strip which are direct effects of only level 0 events. By induction, for $k = 1, 2, 3\ldots$, level k consists of the events at or above the floor of the strip, whose direct causes are level $k - 1$ events or lower. For a level k event there must be at least one level $k - 1$ event among its direct causes.

At the outset, all level 0 events are correct. After all the PEs process their subsystems once, more events will be correct and all level 1 events at least will be among the correctly settled events. It can be seen by induction that after iteration k of the relaxation procedure all events at level k or lower are determined correctly. Thus, the number of levels (for those events of the event dependency graph that fit within the considered Δt-strip) is the upper bound on the number of iterations needed for correctly determining all events for this strip. One more iteration with the exchange of information may be needed to detect convergence. Actual number of iterations can be smaller than this upper bound for two reasons:

1) initial guesses of events are correct by accident

2) the event dependency subgraph hosted by a processing element contains a

complete set of cause-effects for several levels without need to know events in the neighboring processing elements.

Situation 1 is not always negligibly rare: in the applications in which there are not many choices for an event (e.g., only two choices) reasonable initial guessing might save iterations.

An extreme case of situation 2 is completely independent subsystems hosted by different PEs, or, for that matter, just a single PE which hosts the entire system. In these conditions, all events are determined correctly at the first iteration.

The question remained is: How many event levels fits in the Δt-strip on an "average"? Let N be the size of the simulated system (examples: the number of nodes in the network, the number of billiards balls). We propose a conjecture which says, that, in a "generic" example, if Δt is fixed and N tends to infinity, the "average" number of levels increases not faster than $\log N$.

To investigate this conjecture rigorously one must supply a measure in the space of realizations, thereby assigning an exact meaning to "generic" and "average." Such a measure should express characteristics of the application. This exercise has been performed with some applications (see Bibliography) and, while proving to be not an easy one, confirmed the conjecture.

We will now attempt a superficial but short and easy "proof" of this conjecture irrespective of the application. An *event dependency chain* is a directed path $e_1 \to e_2 \to \ldots \to e_k$ on the event dependency graph. It can be easily seen that the number of levels in a subgraph of the event dependency graph is the length of the longest event dependency chain in this subgraph. (The length of an event dependency chain is the number of events on it.)

Let us assume that

(a) as N increases the number of event dependency chains increases not faster than proportionally to N

(b) the length of each chain is random and is bounded by distribution from the above with a fixed exponentially distributed random variable

With these assumptions, it can be proven rigorously, that even as different chains are interdependent, the mean value of the maximum of the lengths grows not faster than $\log N$ (see Bibliography).

Assumptions (a) and (b) together bound from the above the amount of the simulated event activity and its spatial non-uniformity. Singular very nonuniform activities, like a fast propagation of a signal through the entire simulated system, e.g., like in Figure 5, are allowed but they must be exponentially rare, as specified in (b).

5 Even time-parallel relaxation may be efficient, when augmented by certain other techniques

Consider the space-time diagram in Figure 8 which is "orthogonal" to that in Figure 6. Here the space interval is thought of as "small," e.g., the simulated

321

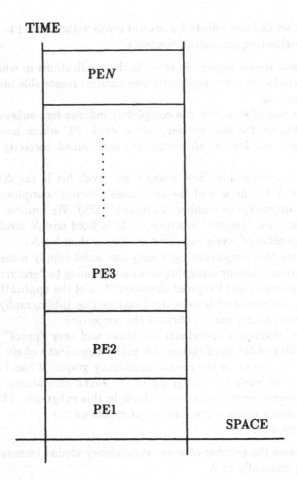

Figure 8: Time-parallel partitioning in a relaxation

system is of a fixed size, but the time interval is "large," e.g., unbounded. One would not expect quick convergence in this case for the same reason as in the case in Figure 5: PE2 is not expected to do useful work until PE1 sends to it the correct information about its events; this needs one iteration; PE3 is not expected to do useful work until PE2 sends to it correct information about its events; this needs at least one more iteration; and so on up to PEN which could only determine its event correctly after iteration N.

One expects the relaxation to converge not faster than in N iterations unless the event dependency graph can be decoupled, as it extends over time, into several independent "regenerative" components. With such an expectation, the following example comes as a surprise.

We simulate a single FIFO queue with feedback as depicted in Figure 9. We assume that each job makes two service demands. Specifically, job i arrives, say, at time A_i, joining the end of the queue, eventually receives its first service, which

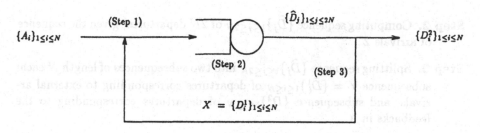

Figure 9: A FIFO queue with a feedback

terminates, say, at time D_i^1, then immediately at the same time D_i^1 reenters the end of the queue, eventually receives its second service, and then finally departs at time D_i^2. (If a job feeds back at the same time that new jobs arrive then, by convention, the new jobs enter the queue ahead of the job feeding back.) Three simulated durations correspond to each job i: time between consecutive arrivals $a_i = A_i - A_{i-1}$ (assuming $A_0 = 0$), first service S_i^1, and second service S_i^2, where $i = 1, 2, ...N$. It is assumed that there are also three corresponding distributions and that each duration is an independent (from system state or other durations) random sample drawn from the corresponding distribution. Thus, the system subject to simulation is a G/G/1 queue with a feedback.

This system fits our assumptions of "small" space interval and "large" time interval as stated above. We assign its simulation to N PEs, so that PEi carries simulation of the time interval that covers the arrival of job i. Exact boundaries between the intervals are not essential; also note that, in the beginning, the assignment of simulated time to PEs is known only implicitly, conditioned to finding the correct events. This distinguishes the presented example from the general scheme in Section 3.

First, the computer samples all random durations. Specifically, PEi obtains a_i, S_i^1, and S_i^2 using its individually seeded random number generator. Second, N values $\{A_i\}_{1 \leq i \leq N}$ are computed, so that PEi obtains $A_i = a_1 + a_2 + ... + a_i$. It takes only one application of the fast *parallel scan* (also called *parallel prefix*) operation. The scan is "felt" like a single programming step. Internally it takes $\log N$ steps of recursive doubling and pointer jumping (see Bibliography).

The final, most involved phase is computing the sequences of departures on the first and second visit, $\{D_i^1\}_{1 \leq i \leq N}$ and $\{D_i^2\}_{1 \leq i \leq N}$. This is done by an iterative relaxation, as discussed in Section 3. Specifically, let X denote the sequence $\{D_i^1\}_{1 \leq i \leq N}$ of first visit departures for the considered N jobs. Function F here can be expressed as a transformation of this sequence into a similar sequence $Y = \{\tilde{D}_i^1\}_{1 \leq i \leq N}$, thus $Y = F(X)$. F consists of three steps along the circular path in Figure 9, namely

Step 1. Merging sequence X with sequence $\{A_i\}_{1 \leq i \leq N}$ of original arrivals. Let Z be the obtained merged sequence of length $2N$.

Step 2. Computing sequence $\{\widehat{D}_j\}_{1 \leq j \leq 2N}$ of $2N$ departures, given the sequence of arrivals Z.

Step 3. Splitting sequence $\{\widehat{D}_j\}_{1 \leq j \leq 2N}$ into two subsequences of length N each: subsequence $Y = \{\tilde{D}_i^1\}_{1 \leq i \leq N}$ of departures corresponding to external arrivals, and subsequence $\{\tilde{D}_i^2\}_{1 \leq i \leq N}$ of departures corresponding to the feedbacks in X.

If we find this X, we can compute the sequence of second visit departures $\{D_i^2\}_{1 \leq i \leq N}$ by applying steps 1 and 2 of the procedure used to define F above and yielding in step 3 sequence $\{D_i^2\}_{1 \leq i \leq N}$, instead of Y.

Each iteration $X^{k+1} = F(X^k)$ of the relaxation is fast. It employs fast parallel merge at step 1 and fast scan (parallel prefix) for computing at step 2 the departures of the FIFO queues given the arrivals as discussed in the literature (see Bibliography). Step 3 is obviously fast too. It turns out that the number of iterations needed for convergence is also small.

Figure 10 represents an experiment where we fix the termination time $T = 20,000$ and the arrival rate $\lambda = 0.5$ so that the number of original arrivals N is about $T\lambda = 10,000$. The service rate for first and second visit is taken the same, and we vary this common rate μ. Several typical interarrival time and service duration distributions are tried such as singular (constant value), uniform, discrete, and exponential. Figure 10 shows the convergence for exponential distributions (the results for other distributions are similar). Here for each μ we simulate 10 differently seeded random samples; the average value of the number of iterations as a function of μ is represented by a solid line, the upper and lower 99.99% Student's confidence bounds are shown by vertical bars. The convergence is the worst around $\mu = 2\lambda$. Yet it takes less than 30 iterations for $N = 10,000$ arrivals (20,000 events).

This fast convergence is not only experimentally observed but can also be theoretically explained (see Bibliography). The most counter-intuitive case is when $2\lambda > \mu$, that is, of an unstable system. In this case a permanent queue is formed which eliminates the possibility of forming several regenerative subgraphs in the event dependency graph. This method works for a general queuing network also (see Bibliography).

6 Time Warp simulation: where it fits in our scheme of things

The Time Warp algorithm for parallel discrete event simulations has been widely popularized since 1985 (See Bibliography). The TW is a rollback-based algorithm (such algorithms are also called *optimistic*), that is, it allows each PE to process as many scheduled events as it can even without full assurance that these events are correct, thus avoiding the difficulties of event scheduling as discussed in Sections 1 and 2. Incorrectly processed events are corrected later by rolling the simulation time back and reprocessing.

The novelty of TW is its way of making these rollbacks: each PE maintains a queue of events (or "messages" in the original TW formulation) and tries

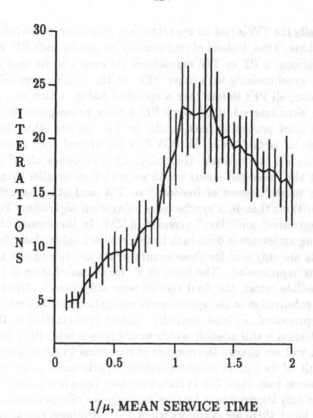

ITERATIONS

$1/\mu$, MEAN SERVICE TIME

Figure 10: Convergence for the simulation of a queue with a feedback

to process them in the time increasing order thereby scheduling future events for itself and other PEs. Events can be "positive," i.e., normal events, and "negative." Negative events are the instrument of rollback. A negative event $-e$ is generated by a PE in the process of un-doing the corresponding positive event e. This $-e$ is generated when the PE receives an evidence that previously sent out event e was incorrect. Event $-e$ is being sent out in the same way and to the same PEs to which event e was sent. The hope is that $-e$ catches up with e. Specifically, it may happen that this $-e$ finds its counterpart e not yet processed. When such a match of two unprocessed events $-e$ and e is detected, it means that $-e$ catches up with its positive counterpart e. Then both are erased from the event queue ("annihilated"), thereby terminating the "lineage" of wrong events. If $-e$ fails to catch up with e, because the PE has already processed e and sent its effects, then the "lineage" continues. Say, events e_1 and e_2 were generated as the effects of event e and were sent to other PEs. In this case, the PE that did this erroneous processing of e must similarly process $-e$ and must similarly send its effects $-e_1$ and $-e_2$ to the corresponding other PEs in the hope that they in turn would catch up with their positive counterparts.

Programmers see in the TW an ingenuous cancellation strategy. However, computationally the TW is just an *asynchronous relaxation* as the other rollback-based algorithms. Thus, instead of reprocessing events by each PE, maintaining common iterations, a PE in TW reprocesses its events at its own pace, without explicitly synchronizing with other PEs. In the synchronous relaxation, as described above, all PEs iterate over a specified batch, which may be a set of events or the time interval, until every PE detects convergence for this batch. Then all PEs start processing next batch. In TW, on the other hand, there is a notion of *global virtual time*. The GVT is the virtual (i.e., simulated) time below which no PE can rollback. Generally, a PE processes ahead of the GVT mark, so that the converged events are those with time smaller than GVT.

There are more "degrees of freedom" in TW and other asynchronous relaxation algorithms than in a synchronous relaxation algorithm. For example, there are "aggressive" and "lazy" versions in TW. In the former, the cancellation by sending antievents is done each time a rollback takes place. In the latter, the antievents are only sent for those events which are turned out to be wrong as seen during reprocessing. The hope in a "lazy" cancellation is that despite some intermediate errors, the final results were still correct. Obviously, there is no similar subdivision in the synchronous relaxation and at each iteration all events are reprocessed, at least virtually. (Some optimization in the flavor of "lazy" cancellation is still possible which would reduce inter-PE communication traffic, but it will not change the number of iterations to convergence.)

As a result of its tighter synchronization, synchronous relaxation behaves better in its worst case, than TW in its worst case. Long non-parallelizable event chains are the only known reason for slow convergence of synchronous relaxation. On the other hand, there are examples when TW introduces cascading and slows down unduly even for well parallelizable models.

Load disbalance, when some PEs have many more events to process than the other PEs can slow down each iteration of synchronous relaxation. Superficially, load disbalance seems not to be a problem for TW, as a lightly loaded PE is not explicitly restricted in advancing its local time. However, this would lead to a large discrepancy in local "virtual" times among the PEs which, as practice shows, slows down the computations significantly. Thus, the load disbalance is as much a problem for TW as for synchronous relaxation.

Synchronous relaxations is especially well suited for SIMD processing and since such machines with thousands of PEs are available, the synchronous relaxation algorithms have been implemented in examples. On the other hand, TW needs a MIMD parallel machine and since massively parallel MIMD computers are lagging in their commercialization as compared with SIMD computers, there has been no report yet of an efficient TW implementation for a computer with thousands of PEs. There are some reasons to suspect that in certain cases for thousands of PEs, the TW, if unprotected by additional mechanisms, may fail in performance due to cascading and echoing phenomena (see Bibliography).

326

7 Conclusion

The discussion of massively parallel discrete event simulation in this tutorial has been centered around the task of designing its computational engine. It is recognized here that by simply adapting the existing computation engine of serial simulation, which is an event list, no substantial progress can be achieved in the task of efficient massively parallel simulation. There is more to a vehicle than just an engine. For example, the *object oriented paradigm* of programming has recently become fashionable among simulationists. One should realize though that these techniques as well as recent advances in the *graphical user interface*, no matter how useful, can not improve performance of processing in simulation, when massive parallelism is concerned. Whether or not the task is performed efficiently is mostly determined by the mathematical properties of the underlying computational technique. Mostly, this tutorial discussed these algorithmic techniques. Among them relaxation appears the most promising one for the task. It is also amenable to implementations on currently available SIMD and SPMD massively parallel computers. In applications for such machines, speed improvement ratios in the hundreds have been obtained (in comparisons to fast work stations), while self-speedups (speed improvements with respect to a single PE of the same computer) have been in thousands.

Bibliography

Section 1

R.E. Shannon, "Introduction to Simulation," in *Proceedings, 1992 Winter Simulation Conference*, 65-73.

Presents a wider view on the simulation activity than the one accepted in this tutorial (constructing a dynamic system trajectory). One of many treatises on the subject.

D.C.Rapaport, "The Event Scheduling Problem in Molecular Dynamic Simulation," *Journal of Computational Physics*, Vol. 34, No.2, 1980.

Describes an algorithm for a serial billiards simulation. Uses a complex list structure to maintain all feasible scheduled collisions for a ball.

B.D. Lubachevsky, "How to Simulate Billiards and Similar Systems," *Journal of Computational Physics*, Vol. 94, No.2, 1991.

Introduces an alternative serial billiards simulation algorithm. Uses a simplified data structure: only two events per ball, one past event and one future event. This appears not less efficient that Rapaport's algorithm.

D.C.Rapaport, "A Note on Algorithms for Billiard-Ball Dynamics," *Journal of Computational Physics*, Vol. 105, No.2, 1993.

The note compares the algorithms by Rapaport and Lubachevsky for simulation of the billiards.

B.D.Lubachevsky, "Which Algorithm is Better?" *Journal of Computational Physics*, Vol. 105, No.2, 1993.

A comment on the note by Rapaport.

Section 2

P. Hontales, B. Beckman, et al., "Performance of the Colliding Pucks simulation on the Time Warp Operating systems" in *Proceedings, 1989 SCS Multiconference on Distributed Simulation, Simulation Series* (Society for Comput. Simulation, San Diego, CA, 1989), Vol. 21, No.2.

Presents serial and parallel billiards simulation based on Time Warp message queues paradigm.

B.D. Lubachevsky, "Simulating Billiards: Serially and in Parallel," *International Journal in Computer Simulation*, Vol. 2, 1992

Copes with unavoidable errors in parallel billiards simulations using a method different from Time Warp.

D. Nicol, "Conservative Parallel Simulation of Priority Class Queuing Networks," *IEEE Trans. on Parallel and Distributed Systems*, Vol. 3, No. 3, May 1992, 294-303.

Introduces the adjustable time-stepping algorithm as applied to parallel queuing networks simulation.

B. Gaujal, A. Greenberg, D. Nicol, "A Sweep Algorithm for Massively Parallel Simulation of Circuit-Switched Networks," *Journal of Parallel and Distributed Computing*, August 1993 (to appear).

Applies the adjustable time stepping paradigm to simulating long-distance telephone networks.

D. Nicol, A. Greenberg, B. Lubachevsky, "MIMD Parallel Simulation of Circuit-Switched Communication Networks," in *Proceedings, 1992 Winter Simulation Conference*, p. 629-636.

Reports implementations of the long-distance telephone network simulations on the Intel Touchstone Delta MIMD parallel computer. Utilizing up to 256 PEs the processing speed of up to 8 million telephone calls per minute is achieved.

B.D. Lubachevsky, "Bounded Lag Distributed Discrete Event Simulation," in *Proceedings, 1988 SCS Multiconference on Distributed Simulation, Simulation Series* (Society for Comput. Simulation, San Diego, CA, 1988), Vol. 19, No.3.

Introduces the bounded lag algorithm.

B.D. Lubachevsky, "Efficient Distributed Event-Driven Simulations of Multiple-Loop Networks," *Communications of the ACMΦ*, Vol. 32, No.1, 1989.

A more extended discussion of the bounded lag algorithm.

Section 3

M. Chandy and R. Sherman, "Space, Time, and Simulation," in *Proceedings, 1989 SCS Multiconference on Distributed Simulations, Simulation Series* (Society for Comput. Simulation, San Diego, CA, 1989), Vol. 21, No.2.

The original presentation of the space-time relaxation paradigm in parallel discrete event simulation.

Section 4

A.G. Eick, A.G. Greenberg, B.D. Lubachevsky, and A. Weiss, "Synchronous Relaxation For Parallel Simulations With Applications to Circuit-Switched Networks," in *Proceedings, 1991 SCS Multiconference on Distributed Simulations, Simulation Series* (Society for Comput. Simulation, San Diego, CA, 1991), Vol. 23, No.1.

The original presentation of the space-parallel synchronous relaxation. For the specified example (long-distance circuit-switched telephone networks), performance is analyzed mathematically, in particular, it is proven that the number of iterations to convergence for simulating a Δt-strip grows as $\log N$ where N is the number of links in the networks.

T.L. Lai and H. Robbins, "Maximally Dependent Random Variables" *Proc. Nat. Acad. Sci. USA*, Vol. 73, No. 2, 286-288 (Statistics).

Proves, in particular, that the mean value of the maximum of N dependent random variables grows not faster than $\log N$. The result is cited in the tutorial to explain a $\log N$ convergence of the space-parallel relaxation.

Section 5

A.G. Greenberg, B.D. Lubachevsky, and I. Mitrani, "Unboundedly Parallel Simulations Via Recurrence Relations," in *Proceedings, Conference on Measurement and Modelling of Computer Systems* (SIGMETRICS, Boulder, CO, 1990), Vol.18, No.1.

The first demonstration that time-parallel simulation can be efficient. Introduces fast algorithms for solving recurrence relations and relaxation for discrete event simulation on massively parallel processors. The latter algorithms are discussed in the following three papers

R.E. Ladner, and M.J Fisher, "Parallel Prefix Computation," *Journal of the ACM*, Vol. 27, 1980, pp 831-838.

C.P. Kruskal, "Searching, Merging, and Sorting in Parallel Computation," *IEEE Trans. Comput.*, TC-32 (1983), 942-946

Discusses, among others, a fast parallel merging which is used in the algorithm for simulating a queue with a feedback.

A.G. Greenberg and B.D. Lubachevsky, "A Simple Efficient Asynchronous Parallel Prefix Algorithm," in *Proceedings, 1987 International Conference on Parallel Processing* (Penn State Univ., 1987), pp. 66-69.

A.G. Greenberg, B.D. Lubachevsky, and I. Mitrani, "Algorithms for Unboundedly Parallel Simulations," *ACM Trans. on Computer Systems*, Vol. 9, No. 3, 1991

Extended version of the SIGMETRICS' paper of the same authors. Additionally shows that in simulating an unstable queue with a feedback the number of iterations to convergence grows as $\log N$ where N is the number of jobs.

A.G. Greenberg, B.D. Lubachevsky, and I. Mitrani, "Superfast Parallel Discrete Event Simulations," unpublished.

More discussion is provided on the reasons for fast convergence of time-parallel queuing network simulations. More examples of application of the relaxation techniques to parallel discrete event simulation are given (priority FIFO queues, slotted ALOHA protocol).

Section 6

D.R. Jefferson, "Virtual Time," *ACM Transactions on Programming Languages and Systems*, Vol. 7, No. 3, 1985.

The original presentation of the Time Warp algorithm. The system of distributed simulation that include message queues with messages and antimessages is described.

J.D. Biggins, B.D. Lubachevsky, A. Shwartz, and A. Weiss, "A Branching Random Walk with a Barrier," *The Annals of Applied Probability*, Vol. 1, No. 4, 1991.

Studies a mathematical model used in the analysis of the rollback-based algorithms.

B.Lubachevsky, A.Shwartz, and A. Weiss, "Rollback Sometimes Works ... if Filtered" in *Proceedings, 1989 Winter Simulation Conference*, 630-639.

Introduces possible failures modes of rollback algorithms (cascading and echoing) and describes the means to counter these modes.

B.Lubachevsky, A.Shwartz, and A. Weiss, "An Analysis of Rollback-Based Simulation" *ACM Trans. on Modelling and Computer Simulation*, Vol. 1, No. 2, 1991.

An extended version of the previous paper. Contains full mathematical proofs and discussion, including examples on each mode of rollback failure.

The BMAP/G/1 QUEUE: A Tutorial

David M. Lucantoni

AT&T Bell Laboratories, Room 3K-601, 101 Crawfords Corner Rd, Holmdel, New Jersey 07733-3030, USA, email:dave@buckaroo.att.com

Abstract. We present an overview of recent results related to the single server queue with general independent and identically distributed service times and a batch Markovian arrival process (*BMAP*). The *BMAP* encompasses a wide range of arrival processes and yet, mathematically, the *BMAP/G/*1 model is a relatively simple matrix generalization of the *M/G/*1 queue. Stationary and transient distributions for the queue length and waiting time distributions are presented. We discuss numerical algorithms for computing these quantities, which exploit both matrix analytic results and numerical transform inversion. Two-dimensional transform inversion is used for the transient results.

1 Introduction

It is well known that the basic $M/G/1$ and $GI/M/1$ queueing models can be analyzed via embedded Markov chains. As shown in Neuts [1] [2], a large class of interesting queueing models can be analyzed via matrix generalizations of these embedded Markov chains. These are called $M/G/1$-type and $GI/M/1$-type Markov chains, respectively.

Within the class of models that can be analyzed by $M/G/1$-type Markov chains is the $BMAP/G/1$ queue; it is the generalization of the $M/G/1$ model in which the Poisson arrival process is replaced by a *batch Markovian arrival process* (*BMAP*). Not only is the embedded Markov chain at departure epochs in a $BMAP/G/1$ queue an $M/G/1$-type Markov chain, but the entire model tends to be a matrix generalization of the $M/G/1$ queue (or, more exactly, its batch arrival generalization).

This paper is a tutorial on the *BMAP* and the $BMAP/G/1$ queue. The *BMAP* was first introduced with alternative notation as the versatile Markovian point process in Neuts [3], and the $BMAP/G/1$ queue was first analyzed (under the name $N/G/1$) by Ramaswami [4]. A major focus here is on exact and efficient numerical algorithms for both the steady-state and transient distributions for the $BMAP/G/1$ queue. This paper is largely based on the author's (mostly joint) work [5]–[12] but we give a general history in §4.

The idea of a *BMAP* is to keep the tractability of the Poisson arrival process but significantly generalize it in ways that allow the inclusion of dependent interarrival times, non-exponential interarrival-time distributions, and correlated batch sizes. The *BMAP* includes as special cases both phase type renewal processes (which include the Erlang, E_k, and hyperexponential, H_k, renewal processes) and non-renewal processes such as the Markov modulated Poisson process

($MMPP$) and many other processes in the applied probability literature. These are reviewed in §3. The class also allows correlated batch size distributions and is closed under superpositions, thinning, etc..

Matrix analytic solutions to the $BMAP/G/1$ queue have been available for some time now (see Ramaswami [4]) but the expressions were not in a form that allowed feasible numerical implementation in their full generality. Recent results (reviewed in §4) have resulted in much more transparent solutions that show that this model is indeed a simple generalization of the ordinary $M/G/1$ queue. In fact, many expressions for the performance measures of interest are natural matrix analogues of the corresponding expressions for the $M/G/1$ queue. The purpose of this review is to demonstrate the simplicity of the results which may occasionally have been obscured by the technicalities governing their derivations. This is accomplished by displaying the relevant results next to the corresponding $M/G/1$ formulas. There are no proofs in this paper; we refer the reader to referenced papers for proofs.

The rest of the paper is organized as follows. In §2 we define the $BMAP$, and in §3 we describe a number of special cases. A brief history of the $BMAP$ and $BMAP/G/1$ queue is presented in §4. This section may serve as an annotated bibliography of recent work related to this model. Expressions for the transforms of the stationary and transient queue length and waiting time distributions are presented in §5. Actual algorithmic procedures for obtaining numerical results for the performance measures of interest are discussed in §6. In particular, we discuss some of the standard matrix analytic algorithms as well as new transform inversion algorithms. Several examples are discussed in §7. A small list of current and future extensions to this model is discussed in §8.

2 The Batch Markovian Arrival Process

We motivate the $BMAP$ by starting with a constructive definition of the Poisson process. Start with a continuous-time Markov process with one state where the same state is visited successively. Since sojourn times in a Markov process are exponential, a sojourn time in this state expires after an exponentially distributed interval with some rate, say λ, but since there is only one state, it is immediately revisited and another sojourn begins. If we construct a point process by associating an arrival with each transition in the above Markov process then the resulting process is Poisson.

One way to generalize the Poisson process is to relax the assumption that interarrival times are exponentially distributed. In the context of the Markov process representation above, we can do this by adding additional (auxiliary) states to the Markov process and associating arrivals in the point process with certain transitions in the underlying Markov process. Let the underlying Markov process be irreducible and have infinitesimal generator D. The sojourn time in state i is thus exponentially distributed with parameter $\lambda_i \geq -D_{ii}$. At the end of a sojourn time in state i, there occurs a transition to another (or possibly the same) state and that transition may or may not correspond to an arrival epoch.

With probability $p_i(0,j)$, $1 \leq j \leq m$, $j \neq i$, there will be a transition to state j *without* an arrival. With probability $p_i(k,j)$, $k \geq 1$, $1 \leq j \leq m$, there will be a transition to state j with a batch arrival of size k. We therefore have, for $1 \leq i \leq m$,

$$\sum_{\substack{j=1 \\ j \neq i}}^{m} p_i(0,j) + \sum_{k=1}^{\infty} \sum_{j=1}^{m} p_i(k,j) = 1 .$$

It is convenient to represent the evolution of the system in terms of a sequence of matrices $\{D_k, k \geq 0\}$, by letting $(D_0)_{ii} = -\lambda_i$, $1 \leq i \leq m$, $(D_0)_{ij} = \lambda_i p_i(0,j)$, $1 \leq i,j \leq m$, $j \neq i$, and $(D_k)_{ij} = \lambda_i p_i(k,j)$, $k \geq 1$, $1 \leq i,j \leq m$. This definition implies that $\sum_{k=0}^{\infty} D_k = D$, the infinitesimal generator of the underlying Markov process. Intuitively, we think of D_0 as governing transitions in the phase process that do not generate arrivals and D_k as the rate of arrivals of size k (with the appropriate phase change).

The matrix D_0 has strictly negative diagonal elements, nonnegative off-diagonal elements, row sums less than or equal to zero and we assume it is nonsingular. In other words D_0 is a stable matrix (i.e., all of its eigenvalues have negative real parts; see e.g., p. 251 of Bellman [13]). This implies that the inter-arrival times are finite with probability one (see Lemma 2.2.1 of Neuts [1]) and that the arrival process does not terminate.

Let π be the stationary probability vector of the Markov process with generator D, i.e., π satisfies

$$\pi D = \mathbf{0}, \qquad \pi \mathbf{e} = 1 , \tag{1}$$

where $\mathbf{e}$ is a column vector of 1's. Then the component π_j is the stationary probability that the arrival process is in state j. The stationary arrival rate of the process is

$$\lambda = \pi \sum_{k=1}^{\infty} k D_k \mathbf{e} = \pi \boldsymbol{\eta} , \tag{2}$$

where $\boldsymbol{\eta} \equiv \sum k D_k \mathbf{e}$.

A key quantity for analyzing the $BMAP/G/1$ queue is the matrix generating function

$$D(z) = \sum_{k=0}^{\infty} D_k z^k, \qquad D(z) = -\lambda + \lambda z, \qquad \text{for } |z| \leq 1 . \tag{3}$$

$$(BMAP) \qquad\qquad (Poisson)$$

Here, and throughout this paper, we display certain results for the Poisson process or $M/G/1$ queue alongside the corresponding results for the $BMAP$ or $BMAP/G/1$ queue, respectively, to highlight the similarity of these expressions.

Let $N(t)$ count the number of arrivals in $(0,t]$ and $J(t)$ represent the auxiliary state or phase at time $t+$. It is significant that the pair $(N(t), J(t))$ is a continuous-time Markov chain on the state space $\{(i,j) : i \geq 0, 1 \leq j \leq m\}$ with infinitesimal generator

$$
Q = \begin{bmatrix}
D_0 & D_1 & D_2 & D_3 & \cdot & \cdot \\
 & D_0 & D_1 & D_2 & \cdot & \cdot \\
 & & D_0 & D_1 & \cdot & \cdot \\
 & & & \cdot & \cdot & \\
 & & & & \cdot & \cdot
\end{bmatrix} .
$$

where the states are listed in lexicographic order.

Let $P_{ij}(n,t) = P(N(t) = n, J(t) = j \mid N(0) = 0, J(0) = i)$ be the (i,j) element of a matrix $P(n,t)$. That is, $P(n,t)$ represents the probability of n arrivals in $(0,t]$ plus the phase transition. Let the matrix generating function $P^*(z,t)$ be defined by

$$
P^*(z,t) = \sum_{n=0}^{\infty} P(n,t)z^n , \quad \text{for } |z| \leq 1,\, t \geq 0 .
$$

By a routine argument conditioning on the first transition, one can get

$$
P^*(z,t) = e^{D(z)t} , \quad P^*(z,t) = e^{(-\lambda + \lambda z)t} , \quad \text{for } |z| \leq 1,\, t \geq 0 , \qquad (4)
$$
$$
(BMAP) \qquad\qquad (Poisson)
$$

where $e^{D(z)t}$ is an exponential matrix (see e.g., p. 169 of Bellman, [13]). By differentiating with respect to z and setting $z = 1$ in (4) we get the expected number of arrivals in $(0,t]$ given that the phase at time $t = 0$ is i as the ith element of the vector $\lambda t e + (I - e^{Dt})(e\pi - D)^{-1}\eta$. See Narayana and Neuts [14] for higher moment formulas, asymptotic expansions and the correlation of the number of arrivals in nonoverlapping intervals.

3 Special Cases

Many familiar arrival processes can be obtained as special cases of the $BMAP$. Here is a selected sample of some of the more useful examples.

3.1 Single Arrivals

(A $BMAP$ with all batch sizes equal to one is called a *Markovian arrival process* (*MAP*).)

a) *Poisson process.* As described above; in this case $D_0 = -\lambda$, $D_1 = \lambda$ and $D_k = 0$, for $k \geq 2$.

b) *PH-renewal process.* The phase type (PH) renewal process introduced in Neuts [15] (see Neuts [1], chapter 2) contains Erlang, E_k, and hyperexponential, H_k, as well as common renewal processes with interarrival time distributions distributed as finite mixtures of these. A phase type renewal process with representation (α, T), is a *BMAP* with $D_0 = T$, $D_1 = -Te\alpha$, and $D_k = 0$, for $k \geq 2$.

c) *Markov-modulated Poisson process (MMPP).* The *MMPP* is the doubly stochastic Poisson process whose arrival rate is given by $\hat{\lambda}[J(t)] \geq 0$, where $J(t)$, $t \geq 0$, is an m-state irreducible Markov process. The arrival rate therefore takes on only m values $\lambda_1, \ldots, \lambda_m$, and is equal to λ_j whenever the Markov process is in the state j. If the underlying Markov process has infinitesimal generator R and if $\Lambda = diag(\lambda_1, \ldots, \lambda_m)$, then we have $D_0 = R - \Lambda$, $D_1 = \Lambda$, and $D_k = 0$, for $k \geq 2$. (See Heffes and Lucantoni [16] for an application of this process to the superposition of packetized voice.)

d) *A sequence of PH interarrival times selected via a Markov chain.* For example, assume we have three PH distributions with representations (α, T), (β, S), (γ, L) labeled 1, 2, and 3, respectively, and that successive interarrival times are chosen from these according to a Markov chain with transition matrix P. The resulting semi-Markov process is the *MAP* defined by

$$
D_0 = \begin{bmatrix} T & 0 & 0 \\ 0 & S & 0 \\ 0 & 0 & L \end{bmatrix}, \quad D_1 = \begin{bmatrix} p_{11}\mathbf{T}^\circ\alpha & p_{12}\mathbf{T}^\circ\beta & p_{13}\mathbf{T}^\circ\gamma \\ p_{21}\mathbf{S}^\circ\alpha & p_{22}\mathbf{S}^\circ\beta & p_{23}\mathbf{S}^\circ\gamma \\ p_{31}\mathbf{L}^\circ\alpha & p_{32}\mathbf{L}^\circ\beta & p_{33}\mathbf{L}^\circ\gamma \end{bmatrix},
$$

and $D_k = 0$, for $k \geq 2$, where $\mathbf{T}^\circ = -Te$, $\mathbf{S}^\circ = -Se$ and $\mathbf{L}^\circ = -Le$. This process was originally studied in Latouche [17]. As an interesting special case of this, we could have an arrival stream consisting of a sequence of Erlang interarrival times where the orders of successive Erlang random variables form a Markov chain. Also, a trivial special case is the alternating PH-renewal process.

e) *Output and overflows from finite Markovian networks.* Since the *MAP* is defined as point process where arrivals are associated with transitions of an underlying Markov process, it is clear that the overflows and/or outputs of any finite state Markovian network can be modeled as a *MAP*. From a practical viewpoint the size of the network could, however, become a limiting factor.

3.2 Batch Arrivals

a) *Batch Poisson.* Let the arrival rate of batches be γ and the successive batch sizes have probability mass function $\{p_k, \ k \geq 1\}$ and probability generating function $p(z)$. In this case, $m = 1$, and the sequence $\{D_k\}$ are scalars with $D_0 = -\gamma$, and $D_k = \gamma p_k$, for $k \geq 1$. Note that $D(z) = -\gamma + \gamma p(z)$.

b) *A MAP with i.i.d. batch arrivals.* Consider a *MAP* defined by the pair (D_0, D_1) where each arrival epoch corresponds to a batch arrival. If successive batch sizes are independent and identically distributed (i.i.d.) with probability mass function $\{p_j, \ j \geq 1\}$ then this process is a $BMAP$ with $D_j = p_j D_1, \ j \geq 1$.

c) *A batch Poisson process with correlated batch arrivals.* Consider a batch Poisson process where the batch size distribution of successive batch arrivals is chosen according to a Markov chain. For example, let $\{q_i(k), \ k \geq 1\}$, $1 \leq i \leq m$, be a set of m discrete probability mass functions and let P be the transition probability matrix of an m-state, irreducible Markov chain. Let the rate of the Poisson process be λ and assume that successive batch size distributions are chosen from the set $\{q_i(\cdot), \ 1 \leq i \leq m\}$ according to P. This process is then a $BMAP$ with $D_0 = -\lambda I$ and $(D_k)_{ij} = \lambda P_{ij} q_j(k)$. A simple example is the overflow process of a $M^X/M/1/N$ system. This example is easily extended to a MAP with correlated batch sizes.

d) *Neuts' versatile Markovian point process.* This process, introduced in Neuts [3], is constructively defined by starting with a PH-renewal process as a substratum. There are three types of arrival epochs which are related to the evolution of the PH-renewal process as follows. There are Poisson arrivals with arbitrary batch size distributions during sojourns in the states of the Markov process governing the renewal process. The arrival rates of the Poisson process and the batch size distributions may depend on the state of the Markov process. The underlying Markov process can change states either with or without a corresponding renewal. Each time the process changes states there is a batch arrival (the batch size may be 0) where the batch size distribution can depend on the states before and after the change and whether a renewal occurred. The construction of this process allows easy incorporation of certain qualitative features into a model of a traffic stream. For example, background arrivals could be inhibited or stimulated by upcoming batch arrivals, etc. It can be shown that this process is equivalent to the $BMAP$. In Lucantoni [7] it was shown how an N-process could be represented as a $BMAP$. To go the other way is less obvious but the idea is to pick a state j for which $(D_n)_{jk}$ is nonzero for some n and k. Whenever a batch arrival of size n occurs at a transition from j to k assume that it happened through an artificial absorbing state. It is then easy to construct the parameters of the N-process in terms of the sequence $\{D_k\}$. An advantage of viewing the process in the framework of the $BMAP$ is that the notation is much simplified.

e) *A Markov-compound Poisson arrival process.* The class of processes discussed in Pacheco and Prabhu [18] is equivalent to the $BMAP$ except that their general formulation allows the auxiliary phase variable to have an infinite state space and also allows D to be reducible and D_0 to be singular. If D is reducible then the stationary version of the process might not be unique; moreover, when D_0 is singular there are two further possibilities. Either the auxiliary phase will enter an irreducible subset from which point the process is a $BMAP$ or the process will terminate (see Lemma 2.2.1 of Neuts [1]). When D is irreducible and D_0 is singular then the process is trivial and has no arrivals, i.e., $P(N(t) = 0) = 1$ for all t (see Lemma 5.4.1 and the following remark on pg. 289 of Neuts [2]).

f) *A superposition of BMAP's.* The class of *BMAP*'s is closed under superposition. That is, the superposition of n independent *BMAP*'s with representations $\{D_k(i)\}$, $1 \leq i \leq n$, is also a *BMAP* with

$$D_k = D_k(1) \oplus \cdots \oplus D_k(n), \qquad k \geq 0,$$

where "$\oplus$" denotes the matrix Kronecker sum (see, e.g., Bellman [13] or Graham [19]). This formulation has been useful in establishing certain asymptotic results; see Abate, Choudhury, and Whitt [20] and Choudhury and Whitt [21]. These extend results for the models of the $GI/M/1$ paradigm in Neuts [22]. This superposition property has recently been exploited by Choudhury, Lucantoni and Whitt [23]–[25] to study the effect of multiplexing bursty traffic streams in an ATM (asynchronous transfer mode) network.

Other examples of incorporating qualitative features of a traffic stream into a model by using a *BMAP* are presented in Neuts [26]. Although the *BMAP* is a special case of a semi-Markov process (SMP), its relationship to continuous time Markov processes leads to far more tractable expressions than would be afforded by a general SMP.

We also note that stationary *BMAP*'s are dense in the family of all stationary point processes; see Asmussen and Koole [27]. This shows that the *BMAP* can represent a wide range of behavior although, from a practical point of view, the dimension of the matrices may be a limiting factor. A negative result for the applicability of *MAP*'s is obtained in Olivier and Walrand [28] where it is shown that the output of an $MMPP/M/1$ queue is not a MAP unless the input is Poisson. This has implications for modeling networks of $MAP/M/1$ queues.

Finally, we point out that there is a completely analogous discrete time version of the *BMAP*; see Blondia [29] [30], Blondia and Theimer [31], Blondia and Casals [32], Briem and Theimer [33], Herrmann [34], Ohta, et al., [35], Alfa and Neuts [36], Berger [37], Garcia and Casals [38] [39], Ramaswami and Latouche [40] [41], and Neuts [26] [42]. The discrete model is often referred to as the $DMAP$ or $DBMAP$ for the single and batch arrival versions, respectively. In this case D_k is nonnegative for $k \geq 0$ and the sum of these matrices, D, is irreducible and stochastic. Many results related to the counting function, and moments of the number of arrivals in $(0,t]$, etc., can be derived in an analogous fashion. These involve matrix geometric expressions instead of the matrix exponential expressions in the continuous case. The results for the corresponding discrete time queue, however, are not as explicit as the ones for the continuous time $BMAP/G/1$ queue.

4 A Brief History of the BMAP and BMAP/G/1 Queue

In this section, we provide a brief history of the $BMAP/G/1$ queue. Since it is impractical to review the numerous papers written on special cases, we restrict attention to papers that are directly applicable to the model in its general formulation. We also recommend the annotated bibliography on phase-type distributions by Neuts [43]. There are several hundred papers cited there, many of which are related to special cases of the $BMAP/G/1$ queue.

The $BMAP$ is subclass of stochastic point processes on the real line; see Daley and Vere-Jones [44]. A distinguishing feature of the $BMAP$ is the underlying Markovian structure. An early point process exploiting Markov structure is the Wold process; see Wold [45] and p. 89 of Daley and Vere-Jones [44]. In a Wold process the successive interarrival times form a Markov chain.

A process very similar to the MAP was introduced by Rudemo [46] where arrivals occur at a subset of transitions of a finite Markov process. In that model the probability of an arrival at a transition from i to j was either zero or one. A number of interesting quantities for that process were derived but it was not used as the arrival process to a queue. In the current context of matrix analytic solutions to queues, the earliest cases of the MAP and $BMAP$ were constructed by Marcel Neuts, as follows.

In the mid-seventies, Neuts generalized the Erlang and hyperexponential distributions to the class of *phase type* distributions which are distributions that can be represented as those of the time till absorption in finite state absorbing Markov processes with one absorbing state [15]. Using matrix formalism it was shown that many quantities of interest such as the distribution and density functions, moments, the random modification, etc., could be written in a compact form which bore a striking similarity to the ordinary exponential distribution. Neuts [57] then defined the corresponding renewal process of phase type for which the inter-renewal times have a phase type distribution. This then formed the basis for the construction of Neuts' versatile Markovian point process [3]; see Example (d) in §3.2 above. Although the notation was fairly complex (to distinguish between all of the different types of arrivals) the matrix formalism showed that the process was indeed a natural generalization of the ordinary Poisson process.

During this same time, Neuts was developing a matrix-analytic methodology for analyzing complex queueing models which used purely probabilistic arguments to derive expressions and algorithms for computing the performance measures of interest; see, e.g., Neuts [1] [2]. One of the motivations for this effort was to provide an alternative solution technique which avoided the sometimes difficult problem of numerically searching for the roots of a (usually) transcendental equation. Neuts distinguished between two different paradigms: Markov chains of $GI/M/1$-type and $M/G/1$-type, respectively. Solutions to the models of $GI/M/1$-type tend to have a very elegant *matrix geometric solution*, which is a matrix generalization of the geometric distribution, (see Theorem 1.2.1 in Neuts [1]). The solution to the models of $M/G/1$ type are usually more complicated.

The key ingredient to the matrix analytic solution to models of $M/G/1$-type is the solution, G, of a matrix functional equation. In the general $M/G/1$ paradigm, G is related to the fundamental period of the queue; see §2.2 of Neuts [2]. In the context of the $BMAP/G/1$ queue, G is related to the busy period of the queue and indirectly, to the behavior of the arrival process during successive idle periods of the queue; see §5.2 below. The relationship between the matrix analytic approach and the traditional approach is that the roots in the traditional analysis are the eigenvalues of the matrix G. It has been shown in some cases that when some roots are close or identical, thus causing problems in the root finding algorithms, the matrix G can still be easily computed.

The matrix analytic methodology was applied by Ramaswami [4] to analyze the single server queue with general service times and Neuts' versatile Markovian point process (or N-process) as the arrival stream. Ramaswami derived expressions for the stationary queue length and waiting time distributions which generalized those for the $M/G/1$ queue. In particular, a matrix generalization of the familiar Pollaczek-Khinchin formula for the waiting time transform was obtained. The resulting algorithms were in principle computable, however, developing a program to solve the model in its full generality was a formidable task. The algorithms at that time required the explicit calculation of the parameters of the transition probability matrix of the Markov chain embedded at departures; see Lucantoni [7] for a full description of the algorithm needed to compute performance measures using the results in [4]. Subsequently, several other queues with this arrival process were analyzed. In particular, the $N/G/\infty$, $N/D/c$, finite $N/G/1$ models and the $N/G/1$ departure process were analyzed by Ramaswami [59], Neuts [60], Blondia [61], and Saito [62], respectively. The special case of a Markov modulated Poisson process ($MMPP$) (see Example (c) in §3.1 above) has been extensively studied; see e.g., Kuczura [47], Neuts [48] [49], Heffes [50], van Hoorn and Seelen [51], Heffes and Lucantoni [16], Burman and Smith [52], Rossiter [53], Ide [54], Baiocchi, et al., [55], Asmussen [56], Zhu and Prabhu [58], etc. It is a doubly stochastic Poisson process or Cox process directed by a Markov chain; see p. 532 of Daley and Vere-Jones [44].

Using uniformization, Lucantoni and Ramaswami [5] developed an algorithm for computing the matrix G without having to compute the parameters of the transition matrix of the embedded Markov chain. This drastically reduced the computational effort required for computing the waiting time distributions and other performance measures and lead to feasible implementations of special cases of the $N/G/1$ queue. In particular, using this result, Heffes and Lucantoni [16] outlined the general procedure for computing the waiting time in the $MMPP/G/1$ queue. Also, a recursive scheme for the queue length distribution eliminating the previous Gauss-Seidel iterations was obtained by Ramaswami [89] for general M/G/1-type models.

The Markovian arrival process (MAP) in its current formulation was introduced in Lucantoni, Meier-Hellstern, and Neuts [6] as a generalization of the phase type renewal process and the Markov modulated Poisson process. In studying a single server queue with server vacations, it was convenient to have a simple process which contained both renewal and non-renewal processes as special cases. This process was then easily generalized to the $BMAP$ by allowing batch arrivals [7]. It was immediately obvious that this process included many processes described in the applied probability literature and that the streamlined notation used for this process was a very natural generalization of that used for the Poisson process. In fact, all of the expressions derived for this process were direct matrix analogues of the simpler expressions for the Poisson process. It was also clear that the N-process was a special case of the $BMAP$ but we had originally conjectured that the class of $BMAP$'s was larger than the class of N-processes. Later we observed that these processes are in fact equivalent (see Example (d) in §3.2 above). Once you realize they are the same, it is not difficult to show this equivalence, although our notes on this were never published. By the time the equivalence was observed, there were already a number of papers referring to the $BMAP$. We therefore decided to keep the new name to distinguish the simplified notation and the results using it from the original more complex notation. It should be noted that all of the results for the models involving the N-process mentioned above could be put into simpler forms using the new notation.

The next major result in the solution to the $BMAP/G/1$ queue came about indirectly. Sengupta [63] showed that the functional equation arising in the solution to the $GI/PH/1$ queue could be written in a matrix exponential form. It was immediately clear that a similar situation occurred in the $PH/G/1$ queue and, consequently, also for the $BMAP/G/1$ queue for the matrix G. Neuts [64] proved the result for the $MMPP/G/1$ queue and the result for the $BMAP/G/1$ queue was derived simultaneously by Lucantoni [7] and Ramaswami [65]. Machihara [66] obtained the exponential form using a last-in-first-out (LIFO) argument and Asmussen [67] later obtained it using ladder heights. Recently, simple proofs of this result along with other key relationships were obtained in Lucantoni and Neuts [10]. Some key quantities were obtained explicitly by exploiting certain commutative properties unobserved earlier. That resulted in major algorithmic simplifications in [7]. Ramaswami [65] also contains detailed results for the $GI/BMAP/1$ queue where the $BMAP$ is used as a model for the service process; that model is a substantial generalization of the $GI/PH/1$ queue.

A goal in the development of the matrix analytic methods was to develop stable numerical algorithms for computing quantities of interest without resorting to numerical transform inversion. However, with the recent availability of improved transform inversion methods, it has become evident that numerical transform inversion can contribute significantly to the numerical solution of these models. Indeed, numerical transform inversion can provide extremely accurate results (see, e.g., Abate and Whitt [68] and Choudhury, Lucantoni and Whitt [12]). Hence, a good strategy for solving the $BMAP/G/1$ queue is to combine the standard matrix-analytic techniques with transform inversion routines. We discuss this more in §6.

Very recent results related to the $BMAP/G/1$ queue are the solutions for the transient queue length and waiting time distributions presented in Lucantoni, Choudhury and Whitt [8]; this involves two-dimensional transform inversion. An algorithm for inverting multi-dimensional transforms is presented in Choudhury, Lucantoni and Whitt [12].

5 The BMAP/G/1 Queue

Consider a single-server queue with a *BMAP* arrival process specified by the sequence of matrices $\{D_k, \ k \geq 0\}$. Let the service times be i.i.d. and independent of the arrival process; let the service time have an arbitrary distribution function H with Laplace-Stieltjes transform (*LST*) h and n^{th} moment α_n. We assume that the mean $\alpha \equiv \alpha_1$ is finite and define the *traffic intensity* to be $\rho \equiv \lambda \alpha$.

5.1 The Embedded Markov Renewal Process at Departures

The embedded Markov renewal process at departure epochs is defined as follows. Define $X(t)$ and $J(t)$ to be the number of customers in the system (including in service, if any) and the phase of the arrival process at time t, respectively. Let τ_k be the epoch of the kth departure from the queue, with $\tau_0 = 0$. (We understand that the sample paths of these processes are right continuous and that there is a departure at $\tau_0 = 0$.) Then $(X(\tau_k), \ J(\tau_k), \ \tau_{k+1} - \tau_k)$, for $k \geq 0$, is a semi-Markov process on the state space $\{(i, j) : \ i \geq 0, \ 1 \leq j \leq m\}$ and is *positive recurrent* when $\rho < 1$; see, e.g., Ramaswami [4].

The matrices of mass functions, $\widetilde{A}_n(x)$, have elements defined by

$[\widetilde{A}_n(x)]_{ij} = P$ (Given a departure at time 0 which left at least one customer in the system and the arrival process in phase i, the next departure occurs no later than time x with the arrival process in phase j, and during that service there were n arrivals).

We introduce the transform matrix

$$A(z, s) = \sum_{n=0}^{\infty} \int_0^{\infty} e^{-sx} d\widetilde{A}_n(x) z^n , \tag{5}$$

where $\text{Re}(s) \geq 0$ and $|z| \leq 1$. Then

$$A(z, s) = \int_0^{\infty} e^{-sx} e^{D(z)x} dH(x) \qquad A(z, s) = \int_0^{\infty} e^{-(s+\lambda-\lambda z)x} dH(x)$$

$$\equiv h(sI - D(z)), \qquad\qquad = h(s + \lambda - \lambda z) . \tag{6}$$

$$(BMAP/G/1) \qquad\qquad\qquad (M/G/1)$$

The definition in (6) above is consistent with the usual definition of a scalar function evaluated at a matrix argument (see Theorem 2, p. 113 of Gantmacher, [69]). In particular, since h is analytic in the right half-plane, the above function is defined by using the matrix argument in the power series expansion of h. This is well defined as long as the spectrum of the matrix argument also lies in the right half plane, which can be shown to hold. Note that from (6) we see that $A(z, s)$ is a power series in $D(z) - sI$. Thus, $A(z, s)$ and $D(z)$ commute. This important property is used repeatedly in the proofs. For later use, we define $A(z) \equiv A(z, 0)$.

5.2   The Busy Period

Define $\widetilde{G}_{jj'}^{[r]}(k;x)$, $k \geq 1$, $x \geq 0$, as the probability that the first passage from the state $(i+r, j)$ to the state (i,j'), $i \geq 1$, $1 \leq j$, $j' \leq m$, $r \geq 1$, occurs in exactly k transitions and no later than time x, and that (i,j') is the first state visited in level i, where level $i \equiv \{(i,1), \ldots, (i,m)\}$. The matrix with elements $\widetilde{G}_{jj'}^{[r]}(k;x)$ is $\widetilde{G}^{[r]}(k;x)$.

The joint transform matrix, $G(z,s)$, is defined by

$$G(z,s) = \sum_{k=1}^{\infty} \int_0^{\infty} e^{-sx} d\widetilde{G}^{[1]}(k;x) z^k, \quad \text{for } |z| \leq 1, \; \mathrm{Re}(s) \geq 0 .$$

In the context of the $BMAP/G/1$ queue, $G(z,s)$ is the two-dimensional transform of the number served during, and the duration of, the busy period (with the appropriate phase change information). It can be shown that the joint transform matrix governing the number served during and the duration of a busy period starting with r customers, is given by $G(z,s)^r$ (see, e.g., Neuts [70] [2]).

It was shown in Lucantoni [7] and Ramaswami [65] that $G(z,s)$ is the solution to

$$G(z,s) = z\int_0^{\infty} e^{-sx} e^{D[G(z,s)]x} dH(x) \qquad G(z,s) = z\int_0^{\infty} e^{-(s+\lambda-\lambda G(z,s))x} dH(x)$$

$$\equiv zh(sI - D[G(z,s)]), \qquad\qquad = zh(s+\lambda - \lambda G(z,s)) ,$$

$$(BMAP/G/1) \qquad\qquad\qquad (M/G/1)$$

$$\tag{7}$$

for $|z| \leq 1$, $\mathrm{Re}(s) \geq 0$, where $D[G(z,s)] \equiv \sum_{k=0}^{\infty} D_k G(z,s)^k$. Equation (7) is the matrix analogue of Takács' equation for the busy period in the ordinary $M/G/1$ queue [71]. Equation (7) with $z = 1$ is the matrix analogue of the Kendall functional equation, (see (59) in Kendall [72], and the discussion of I. J. Good on p. 182 there). Note from (7) that $G(z,s)$ commutes with $D[G(z,s)]$. The exponential form of the matrix $G(z,s)$ results in substantial reduction in the computational complexity of the implementation of the matrix analytic solution (see [7]).

Next define the matrices $G(s) \equiv G(1,s)$ and $G \equiv G(0)$ and note that G satisfies

$$G = \int_0^{\infty} e^{D[G]x} dH(x) . \tag{8}$$

The matrix G is stochastic when $\rho \leq 1$ (see, e.g., Theorem 2.3.1 in Neuts [2]) and is the key ingredient in the solution of the stationary version of this system. Efficient algorithms for computing this matrix are discussed in §6. For $\rho \leq 1$, the invariant probability vector $\mathbf{g}$, of the positive stochastic matrix G, satisfies

$$\mathbf{g}G = \mathbf{g}, \quad \mathbf{g}\mathbf{e} = 1 . \tag{9}$$

The matrix $D[G] \equiv D[G(1,0)]$ has a nice probabilistic interpretation which was originally pointed out in Lucantoni, Meier-Hellstern and Neuts [6]. Since G is strictly positive, it follows that the off-diagonal entries of $D[G]$ are nonnegative. When the queue is stable, G is stochastic so that $D[G]e = 0$; that is, $D[G]$ is the infinitesimal generator of a finite-state, irreducible Markov process. From the structure of the matrix we see that starting in some state i, there will be an exponential sojourn time with rate $|(D_0)_{ii}|$. Then there will either be a transition to state j, $j \neq i$, with rate $(D_0)_{ij}$ (i.e., without an arrival), or a transition to state j with rate $(\sum_{k=1}^{\infty} D_k G^k)_{ij}$. That is, a batch of size k arrives followed by k busy periods which end in phase j, corresponding to a phase change from i to j in this process. It is clear that this process is the phase of the arrival process observed only during idle periods, i.e., the time during the busy periods are *excised*. In the unstable case, i.e., $\rho > 1$, G is strictly substochastic so that $D[G]$ is a stable matrix. In other words, in this case the total amount of idle time observed before the last busy period (that never ends) is phase type (see, e.g., [1]) with representation $(\mathbf{a}, D[G])$, where $\mathbf{a}$ is the vector of initial phase probabilities at time 0 Note that Equation (8) implies that $\mathbf{g}$ is also the stationary vector of the matrix $D[G]$ and therefore its jth component is the stationary probability that the arrival process is in state j given that the server is idle. This has major implications in the computational algorithm.

5.3 The Stationary Distributions

For proofs of the results in this section, see Ramaswami [4], Lucantoni [7], and Lucantoni and Neuts [9]. Exponential asymptotics for the steady-state distributions below appear in Abate, Choudhury and Whitt [20], Choudhury and Whitt [21], and Baiocchi [73]; we will not discuss them here.

The Queue Length Distribution at Departures Let

$$x_{ij} = \lim_{k \to \infty} P(X(\tau_k) = i, J(\tau_k) = j),$$

(recalling that the sample paths are assumed to be right continuous), and define the vectors $\mathbf{x}_i = (x_{i1}, \ldots, x_{im})$, for $i \geq 0$. Then the vector generating function $\mathbf{X}(z) \equiv \sum_{i=0}^{\infty} \mathbf{x}_i z^i$, is given by

$$\mathbf{X}(z) = (1 - \rho)\lambda^{-1}\mathbf{g}D(z)A(z)[zI - A(z)]^{-1}, \quad X(z) = \frac{(1 - \rho)(z - 1)A(z)}{z - A(z)},$$

$$(BMAP/G/1) \qquad \qquad (M/G/1)$$

$$(10)$$

for $|z| \leq 1$. Note that $(z - 1)$ in the numerator for $M/G/1$ plays the role of $\lambda^{-1}\mathbf{g}D(z)$ for $BMAP/G/1$; see Equation (3). The general form of the generating function $\mathbf{X}(z)$ in (10) was proved in Ramaswami [4], however, the simplicity of the constant vector $(1 - \rho)\mathbf{g}$ went unnoticed until Lucantoni [7].

The Queue Length Distribution at an Arbitrary Time We first consider the continuous parameter process $\{[X(t), J(t)], t \geq 0\}$. The time-dependent joint distribution of the queue length and the arrival phase is given by the conditional probabilities

$$Y_{i_0i}^{jk}(t) = P(X(t) = i, \ J(t) = k \mid X(0) = i_0, \ J(0) = j, \ \tau_0 = 0) \, , \quad (11)$$

for $i_0, i \geq 0, 1 \leq j, k \leq m, t \geq 0$. We can show that the limits

$$y_{ik} \equiv \lim_{t \to \infty} Y_{i_0i}^{jk}(t) \, , \ \text{for } i \geq 0, \ 1 \leq k \leq m \, ,$$

exist and are independent of i_0 and j. For $i \geq 0$ let $\mathbf{y}_i = (y_{i1}, y_{i2}, \ldots, y_{im})$ and define the vector generating function, $\mathbf{Y}(z) = \sum_{i=0}^{\infty} \mathbf{y}_i z^i$. Then

$$\mathbf{Y}(z) = (1 - \rho)\mathbf{g}(z - 1)A(z)[zI - A(z)]^{-1} \quad , Y(z) = \frac{(1 - \rho)(z - 1)A(z)}{z - A(z)} \, ,$$

$$(BMAP/G/1) \qquad\qquad\qquad (M/G/1)$$

$$(12)$$

for $|z| \leq 1$. Note that $\mathbf{y}_0 = (1 - \rho)\mathbf{g}$ which is consistent with the probabilistic interpretation of $\mathbf{g}$ as the stationary phase probabilities given that the system is empty (see §5.2). Although (12) shows the similarity between solutions to the $BMAP/G/1$ and $M/G/1$ queues, a more convenient representation of $\mathbf{Y}(z)$ in the $BMAP/G/1$ queue is

$$\mathbf{Y}(z)D(z) = \lambda(z - 1)\mathbf{X}(z).$$

Therefore, numerically inverting $\mathbf{X}(z)$ and $\mathbf{Y}(z)$ can be done simultaneously. Alternatively, a recursion for $\mathbf{y}_i$ in terms of $\mathbf{x}_i$ can be derived by equating coefficients of z^i (see (38) in Lucantoni [7]; note that this recursion is much simpler than (3.3.16) in Ramaswami [4]).

The Queue Length Distribution at an Arrival Let $L(z)$ be the generating function of the number of customers in the system at an arbitrary arrival (not including the customers in the arriving batch). Then

$$L(z) = (1 - \rho)(\pi D_0 e)^{-1}\mathbf{g}(z - 1)A(z)[zI - A(z)]^{-1}D_0 e, \quad (BMAP/G/1)$$

$$L(z) = \frac{(1 - \rho)(z - 1)A(z)}{z - A(z)} \, , \quad (M/G/1)$$

$$(13)$$

for $|z| \leq 1$.

The Virtual Waiting Time Distribution In this section, we state results for the virtual waiting time or workload distribution. First, we define the following quantities $\widetilde{\mathbf{W}}_V(x) = (\widetilde{W}_{V,1}(x), \ldots, \widetilde{W}_{V,m}(x))$, where $\widetilde{W}_{V,j}(x)$ is the joint probability that at an arbitrary time the arrival process is in phase j and that a *virtual* customer who arrives at that time waits at most a time x before entering service. The Laplace-Stieltjes transform of $\widetilde{\mathbf{W}}_V(x)$ is $\mathbf{W}_V(s) = \int_0^\infty e^{-sx} d\widetilde{\mathbf{W}}_V(x)$. Then

$$\mathbf{W}_V(s) = s(1-\rho)\mathbf{g}[sI + D(h(s))]^{-1}, \quad \mathbf{W}_V(0) = \boldsymbol{\pi}, \quad W_V(s) = \frac{s(1-\rho)}{s - \lambda + \lambda h(s)},$$

$$(BMAP/G/1) \qquad\qquad\qquad (M/G/1)$$

$$(14)$$

for $\text{Re}(s) \geq 0$. The waiting time transform in (14) is a matrix generalization of the Pollaczek-Khinchin formula for the $M/G/1$ queue and was obtained using Markov renewal arguments in Ramaswami [4] along with the associated system of Volterra integral equations. An alternative derivation was obtained by Ide [54]. The simplified expression for the constant vector $(1-\rho)\mathbf{g}$ is due to Lucantoni [7].

The Waiting Time Distribution of the First Customer in a Batch Let $W_B(s)$ be the LST of the delay of the first customer in a batch. Then

$$W_B(s) = s(1-\rho)(\boldsymbol{\pi} D_0 \mathbf{e})^{-1}\mathbf{g}[sI + D(h(s))]^{-1}D_0\mathbf{e}, \quad W_B(s) = \frac{s(1-\rho)}{s - \lambda + \lambda h(s)},$$

$$(BMAP/G/1) \qquad\qquad\qquad (M^X/G/1)$$

$$(15)$$

for $\text{Re}(s) \geq 0$.

The Waiting Time Distribution of an Arbitrary Customer Let

$$\widetilde{\mathbf{W}}_A(x) = (\widetilde{W}_{A,1}(x), \ldots, \widetilde{W}_{A,m}(x)),$$

where $\widetilde{W}_{A,j}(x)$ is the joint probability that the arrival process is in phase j and the delay of an arbitrary arrival is at most x, and let $\mathbf{W}_A(s)$ be the LST of $\widetilde{\mathbf{W}}_A(x)$. Note that this delay includes the delay due to customers in the arriving batch who are ahead of the arbitrarily chosen customer. Then

$$\mathbf{W}_A(s) = \frac{1}{\lambda(1 - h(s))}\mathbf{W}(s)[D - D(h(s))] \qquad W_A(s) = W(s)\frac{1 - p(h(s))}{\bar{p}(1 - h(s))}$$

$$= \frac{1}{\lambda(h(s) - 1)}[\mathbf{W}(s)(sI + D) - s(1 - \rho)\mathbf{g}], \qquad = \frac{s(W(s) - (1 - \rho))}{\lambda(h(s) - 1)},$$

$$(BMAP/G/1) \qquad\qquad\qquad (M^X/G/1)$$

$$(16)$$

for $\text{Re}(s) \geq 0$, where, for the $M^X/G/1$ queue, $p(z)$ is the probability generating function of the batch size distribution and $\bar{p}$ is the mean batch size. Note that the first expression (for the $M^X/G/1$ queue) in (16) is Equation (2) in Burke [74]. This shows that the total delay is factored into the delay of the first customer in a batch plus the delay due to customers in the batch ahead of the tagged customer. That number of customers is distributed as the forward recurrence time in a discrete-time renewal process where the inter-renewal times are distributed as the batch size distribution. The second expressions in (16) are more convenient for deriving moment formulas since they do not involve the batch size distribution; see Lucantoni and Neuts [9].

5.4 The Transient Distributions

For proofs of the results in this section see Lucantoni, Choudhury and Whitt [8]. The $M/G/1$ counterparts appear in Takács [71].

The Emptiness Functions In this section we characterize the probability that the system is empty at time t. The key role of this function for general systems was demonstrated by Beneš [75]. Let $V(t)$ be the amount of work in the system at time t; for $1 \le i, j \le m$, $x \ge 0$ and $t \ge 0$, let

$$P_{x0}^{ij}(t) = P(V(t) = 0, J(t) = j \mid V(0) = x, J(0) = i), \qquad (17)$$

and let the $m \times m$ matrix $P_{x0}(t)$ have (i, j)-entry $P_{x0}^{ij}(t)$. The unconditional emptiness function, starting with initial workload distributed according to cdf F, defined by

$$P_0(t) \equiv \int_0^\infty P_{x0}(t)dF(x), \qquad \text{for } t \ge 0, \qquad (18)$$

has Laplace transform $p_0(s) \equiv \int_0^\infty e^{-st}P_0(t)dt$ given by

$$p_0(s) = f(sI - D[G(s)])(sI - D[G(s)])^{-1}, \quad p_0(s) = \frac{f(s + \lambda - \lambda G(s))}{s + \lambda - \lambda G(s)}, \qquad (19)$$

$$(BMAP/G/1) \qquad\qquad (M/G/1)$$

for $\text{Re}(s) > 0$, where f is the LST of F. The expression for $M/G/1$ in (19) is Equation (9) on p. 52 of Takács [71]. Since the components of the vector $G(s)e$ are Laplace-Stieltjes transforms and $|G(s)e| < 1$, for $\text{Re}(s) > 0$, the eigenvalues of $D[G(s)]$ are in the left half-plane. Therefore, for $\text{Re}(s) > 0$, the eigenvalues of $sI - D[G(s)]$ are in the right half-plane and the inverse appearing in (19) is well defined.

We can show from (19) that

$$\lim_{t \to \infty} P_0(t) = \begin{cases} (1 - \rho)\mathbf{eg} & \text{for } \rho \le 1, \\ 0 & \text{for } \rho > 1, \end{cases} \qquad (20)$$

as expected.

The Transient Workload In this section we present the transform of the workload (work in the system in uncompleted service time) at time t. Let $W(t, x)$ be the matrix whose $(i, j)^{\text{th}}$ element is the probability that the work in the system is less than or equal to x and the phase is j at time t, given that at time 0 the phase was i and the initial workload (including the customer in service, if any) was distributed according to F; let the Laplace-Stieltjes transform of F be f. Let $w(t, s)$ and $\widetilde{w}(\xi, s)$ be the transforms

$$w(t, s) = \int_0^\infty e^{-sx} d_x W(t, x) \quad \text{and} \quad \widetilde{w}(\xi, s) = \int_0^\infty e^{-\xi t} w(t, s) dt .$$

Then the matrix $\widetilde{w}(\xi, s)$ is given by

$$\widetilde{w}(\xi, s) = (f(s)I - sp_0(\xi))[\xi I - sI - D(h(s))]^{-1}, \quad \widetilde{w}(\xi, s) = \frac{f(s) - sp_0(\xi)}{\xi - s + \lambda - \lambda h(s)} ,$$

$$(BMAP/G/1) \qquad\qquad\qquad (M/G/1)$$

$$(21)$$

and the matrix $w(t, s)$ is given by

$$w(t, s) = \left(f(s)I - s \int_0^t P_0(u) e^{-[sI + D(h(s))]u} du \right) e^{[sI + D(h(s))]t},$$

$$(BMAP/G/1) \qquad\qquad (22)$$

$$w(t, s) = \left(f(s) - s \int_0^t P_0(u) e^{-(s - \lambda + \lambda h(s))u} du \right) e^{(s - \lambda + \lambda h(s))t},$$

$$(M/G/1) \qquad\qquad (23)$$

for $\text{Re}(s) \geq 0$, $\text{Re}(\xi) > 0$, where $P_0(u)$ and $p_0(\xi)$ are given in (18) and (19), respectively. The equations in (21) are formulas (28) in Lucantoni, Choudhury and Whitt [8] and (15) on p. 53 of Takács [71], respectively. Equation (23) for the $M/G/1$ queue is given on pg. 53 of Takács [71].

Although we are able to express the transform of the delay explicitly in terms of t in (22), we note that this expression is not trivial to evaluate numerically. It involves numerically inverting a Laplace transform where the evaluation of the transform at a value of s requires the numerical integration of the emptiness function times an exponential matrix. The values of the emptiness function are themselves obtained by inverting a Laplace transform. The corresponding expression in (23) for the ordinary $M/G/1$ queue also suffers from the same difficulty. This may partly explain why the known formulas for that case have not been widely used for practical computations.

In contrast, however, the transform expressions in (21) are relatively simple to evaluate, so that with an inversion algorithm for 2-dimensional Laplace transforms, we have a practical method for obtaining numerical results. An efficient and accurate multi-dimensional transform inversion algorithm is presented in Choudhury, Lucantoni and Whitt [12] and is briefly discussed in §6.

It can be shown using Rouché's theorem that for each s, $\text{Re}(s) \geq 0$, the determinant of the matrix $\xi I - sI - D(h(s))$ appearing in the inverse in (21) has exactly m roots in the region $\text{Re}(\xi) > 0$. (For similar arguments see Çinlar [76] and Neuts [77] [78].) Since $\tilde{w}$ is a Laplace-Stieltjes transform and is therefore analytic in the interior of the above region, these pairs of (ξ, s) must also be zeros of the first matrix on the right in (21). That is, they are removable singularities. The classical approach to this type of problem would then assume that the roots are distinct to obtain m independent linear equations for each row of the unknown matrix $p_0(\xi)$. In practice, the roots may not be distinct, or if they are close, there may be numerical difficulties in locating these roots. These technical problems are circumvented in the present case since we have an explicit expression for $p_0(\xi)$ (see Equation 19).

We see from (21) that the transform of the limiting distribution of the workload is given by

$$w(s) \equiv \lim_{\xi \to 0} \xi \tilde{w}(\xi, s) = \begin{cases} s(1 - \rho)\text{eg}[sI + D(h(s))]^{-1}, & \text{for } \rho \le 1, \\ 0, & \text{for } \rho > 1, \end{cases}$$

which agrees with (14).

The Transient Queue Length In this section, we present the transient queue length distribution at time t given an initial number of customers present immediately after a departure at time $t = 0$. Let $Y_{i_0 i}^{jk}(t)$ be as defined in (11) and let $Y_{i_0 i}(t)$ have (j, k)-entry $Y_{i_0 i}^{jk}(t)$. Recall that $\tau_0 = 0$ means that there is a departure at time 0. Let $y_{i_0 i}(s)$ be the Laplace transform of $Y_{i_0 i}(t)$. Then $y_{i_0 0}(s) = G(s)^{i_0}(sI - D[G(s)])^{-1}$ and the probability generating function of the queue length at time t, defined by $\tilde{y}_{i_0}(z, s) \equiv \sum_{i=0}^{\infty} y_{i_0 i}(s) z^i$, is given by

$$\tilde{y}_{i_0}(z, s) = [z^{i_0+1}(I - A(z, s))(sI - D(z))^{-1}$$
$$+ (z - 1)G(s)^{i_0}(sI - D[G(s)])^{-1} A(z, s)][zI - A(z, s)]^{-1},$$
$$(BMAP/G/1) \tag{24}$$

$$\tilde{y}_{i_0}(z, s) = \frac{1}{z - A(z, s)} \left(\frac{z^{i_0+1}(1 - A(z, s))}{s + \lambda - \lambda z} + \frac{(z - 1)G(s)^{i_0} A(z, s)}{s + \lambda - \lambda G(s)} \right),$$
$$(M/G/1) \tag{25}$$

for $\text{Re}(s) > 0$, $|z| < 1$ and $A(z, s)$ is given in (6).

Let the Laplace transform of the complementary queue length distribution be defined by

$$y_{i_0 i}^*(s) = \int_0^\infty e^{-st} \sum_{n=i+1}^{\infty} Y_{i_0 n}(t) dt,$$

with the corresponding generating function $\tilde{y}_{i_0}^*(z, s) \equiv \sum_{i=0}^{\infty} y_{i_0 i}^*(s) z^i$. Then since $\tilde{y}_{i_0}(1, s) = (sI - D)^{-1}$, the transform of the complementary queue length distribution, $\tilde{y}_{i_0}^*(z, s)$, is given by

$$\tilde{y}_{i_0}^*(z, s) = \frac{1}{1 - z} \left[(sI - D)^{-1} - \tilde{y}_{i_0}(z, s) \right], \quad \tilde{y}_{i_0}^*(z, s) = \frac{1}{1 - z} \left[\frac{1}{s} - \tilde{y}_{i_0}(z, s) \right],$$

$$(BMAP/G/1) \qquad\qquad (M/G/1)$$

for $\text{Re}(s) > 0$ and $|z| < 1$.
$$(26)$$

Transient Results at Arrivals and Departures Further transient results for the $BMAP/G/1$ queue have recently been derived and will be reported in Lucantoni [79]. In particular, we derived explicit expressions for the transform of the queue length at the n-th departure, assuming a departure at time $t = 0$, and the workload at the n-th arrival (keeping track of the appropriate phase changes). The departure process is characterized by the double transform of the probability that the n-th departure occurs at time less than or equal to time x (similar to that derived by Saito [62]). This leads to an explicit expression for the LST of the expected number of departures up to time t. All of these expressions are direct matrix analogues of the corresponding $M/G/1$ results in Takács [71].

6 Numerical Algorithms

It is evident from the results in §5 that the transforms for the stationary queue length and delay distributions are completely specified in terms of the vector **g**, the stationary probability vector of the matrix G. We discuss below several algorithms for computing this matrix. The transient distributions require evaluation of the matrix $G(s)$ for complex s. Computing the queue length distributions themselves can be done either by transform inversion or by other probabilistic algorithms. In the former case, typically the matrix $A(z)$ needs to be evaluated for complex z. In the latter case, the matrices $A_n \equiv \tilde{A}_n(\infty)$, $n \geq 0$, need to be evaluated. Both of these require additional overhead. Detailed comparisons of these methods have not yet been performed, however, it is our opinion that a full package for analyzing the $BMAP/G/1$ queue should include several alternatives for computing the desired results. Every numerical algorithm has limitations either in accuracy or in processing requirements and storage so it is useful to compute the results several different ways in order to check for consistency.

Due to space limitations, we do not present the explicit algorithms for computing the quantities of interest but instead, refer to appropriate references for the details and clear demonstrations of implementability.

6.1 Computing the Matrices G, G(s), and A(z)

The matrix G is the unique solution, in the class of substochastic matrices, to the matrix equation (8). It has been shown (see Neuts [2]) that Equation (8) can be solved by successive substitutions. Although early proofs of this result required an initial iterate of $G_0 = 0$, this is not a good starting solution for computations. It has been observed that convergence is slower with this initial solution as the traffic intensity, ρ, increases. By starting with G_0 equal to a stochastic matrix, each iterate will itself be stochastic and we have observed that in many cases the speed of convergence is insensitive to ρ. An efficient technique for evaluating the right hand side of Equation (8) based on uniformization is presented in

Lucantoni [7]. This requires the computation of a scalar sequence $\{\gamma_n, \ n \geq 0\}$ where $\gamma_n = \int_0^\infty (e^{-\theta x}(\theta x)^n / n!) dH(x)$, and $\theta = \max_i (-(D_0)_{ii})$. If H is phase type then the γ_n's can be computed recursively without any numerical integrations; see Theorem 2.2.8 in Neuts [1]. If H is arbitrary then the γ_n's can be computed by numerically inverting the probability generating function $h(\theta - \theta z)$; we have had much success with the transform inversion algorithm presented in Abate and Whitt [80] (see Choudhury, Lucantoni and Whitt [81]).

If H is Coxian (i.e., H has a rational Laplace-Stieltjes transform) then there is an efficient algorithm for evaluating the integral on the right hand side of (8) which is presented below (see Lucantoni, Choudhury and Whitt [8]). This algorithm is also directly applicable to computing $A(z)$ and $G(s)$, for complex z and s, from Equations (6) and (7), respectively.

Let

$$M' = \int_0^\infty e^{-Mx} dH(x) , \qquad (27)$$

where M and M' are, in general, complex matrices. If H has a Coxian distribution with the Laplace-Stieltjes transform

$$h(s) = \int_0^\infty e^{-sx} dH(x) = \frac{\sum_{k=0}^i a_k s^k}{\sum_{k=0}^j b_k s^k}, \qquad i \leq j, \qquad (28)$$

then (27) may be evaluated as

$$M' = \left(\sum_{k=0}^j b_k M^k \right)^{-1} \left(\sum_{k=0}^i a_k M^k \right) . \qquad (29)$$

Note that (29) only requires the computation of two matrix polynomials and one matrix inversion. Often the matrix polynomials may be computed with just a few matrix multiplications. As an example, note that when H is an Erlang distribution of order n, i.e., E_n, with mean μ, then $h(s) = (1 + \mu s/n)^{-n}$ and (27) is evaluated as

$$M' = \left(I + \frac{\mu}{n} M \right)^{-n} . \qquad (30)$$

If $n = 2^m$, for an integer m, then only m matrix multiplications are needed. For example, evaluating (27) when H is E_{1024} requires one matrix inverse and ten matrix multiplications. This example also shows that we can approach very close to the practically important, non-Coxian, deterministic distribution with relatively few matrix operations. (Of course, the results in this paper apply directly to general service-time distributions, but computing integrals like (27) even in the deterministic case is more computationally intensive than in the E_n case, for large n. Moreover, it is harder to get high accuracy in the transform inversion algorithms for deterministic service due to discontinuities in the derivative of the waiting time cdf in that case).

Application of the inversion formulas in Choudhury, Lucantoni and Whitt [12] to the transient workload (21) and the transient queue length (24) respectively, requires numerous evaluations of the matrix $G(s)$ for complex s. It was first proved in Lucantoni [82] that $G(s)$ can be computed by successively iterating in (7) starting with $G_0(s) \equiv 0$. That proof exploited the fact (which apparently was not well known even for the $M/G/1$ queue) that the successive iterates were in fact Laplace-Stieltjes transforms of first passage times along restricted sets of sample paths. (Similar arguments were later used in Latouche [83] to study various iterative algorithms in the general matrix paradigms.) Neuts [2] later proved convergence of the iterations using arguments from functional analysis. It was also shown in Choudhury, Lucantoni, and Whitt [11] that starting the iterations with $G_0(s) \equiv 0$ and $G_0(s) \equiv G$, respectively, produce the sequences of iterates, $\underline{G}_k(s)$ and $\overline{G}_k(s)$ where the matrices $\underline{G}_k(s)$ and $\overline{G}_k(s)$ are themselves Laplace-Stieltjes transforms of distribution functions $\underline{F}_k(x)$ and $\overline{F}_k(x)$. These distributions bound the true distribution in the sense that

$$\underline{F}_k(x) \le \widehat{G}(x) \le \overline{F}_k(x) ,$$

for all x, where $\widehat{G}(x)$ is the distribution function with LST $G(s)$. (This extends results for the $M/G/1$ queue in Abate and Whitt [84].) Thus, stopping the iteration at any point will give useful bounds on the true distributions. We usually carry out the computations until the bounds are within 10^{-12}. It is clear that the numerous evaluations of $G(s)$ may constitute a significant component of the total computational cost of evaluating the transient distributions; see §6.6. In the examples we have run so far, in order to get successive iterates to within 10^{-13}, the number of iterations has ranged from several tens to a few hundreds.

6.2 Computing Moments and Asymptotics of the Distributions

Explicit formulas for the moments of the distributions discussed in this paper can be derived from the corresponding transform expressions. The first two moments for the number served during and the duration of the busy period in the general $M/G/1$ paradigm were first derived in Neuts [70] [85]. Simpler expressions in the case of the $BMAP/G/1$ queue were derived in Choudhury, Lucantoni and Whitt [11]. The explosion in complexity of the expressions precludes explicit formulas for higher moments of the busy period.

A recursive algorithm for computing the moments of the queue length distribution is given in 3.3.11–13 of Neuts [2]. These require the evaluation of successive derivatives of $A(z)$ at $z = 1$. Recursive expressions for the moments of the virtual and actual delay distributions are given in Lucantoni and Neuts [9]. (We note that these correct several typos in the first two moments given in Equations (47) and (48) of Lucantoni [7]). These recursive expressions are efficient for the low order moments but lose precision if higher moments are required.

A recent algorithm by Choudhury and Lucantoni [86] has been found to be very effective in computing a large number of moments from a probability transform. Also, the high order moments can be used to compute the exact asymptotic parameters of the distributions; see [86] and Choudhury, Lucantoni and Whitt [87]. The asymptotic parameters can be used in approximating high percentiles or as a stopping criterion for the numerical inversion of the distributions; see

[87] for more details. We also note that an alternative technique for computing the asymptotic parameters for the delay and queue length distributions is given in Abate, Choudhury and Whitt [20].

6.3 Numerical Transform Inversion

The distributions presented in this paper can be computed by numerically inverting the corresponding transforms. We recommend first computing the asymptotic parameters as discussed above to be used as a stopping criteria for an inversion algorithm such as the one presented in Abate and Whitt [68] for the inversion; see [8], [11], [12], [81] and [88] for applications and discussions of this.

6.4 Computing the Stationary Queue Length Densities

We discuss two procedures for computing the queue length density. The first is a recursive scheme due to Ramaswami [89] and is a generalization of a device by P. J. Burke that eliminates the loss of precision in computing the queue length density in the $M/G/1$ queue; see p. 186 of Neuts [90]. This algorithm requires the explicit computation and storage of the matrices A_n, $n \geq 0$. An efficient algorithm for computing these is given in Lucantoni [7]. We have implemented Ramaswami's algorithm and generally find it very effective. However, cases where it loses precision for small tail probabilities have been reported by Wang and Silvester [91] [92]. One possibility for this loss of significance is that for very bursty arrival processes it may not be possible to compute a sufficient number of A_n matrices (with enough precision) in order to compute the queue length density to a high degree of accuracy. These problems were avoided by first computing the asymptotic tail by the methods mentioned in §6.2.

The second technique is to invert the transform directly using the algorithms mentioned in §6.3. These do not require the computation of the sequence $\{A_n\}$ but instead need the evaluation of $A(z)$ for several complex values of z, as discussed in §6.1. The inversion is most effectively done by first computing the asymptotic parameters discussed in §6.2 and using these as a stopping rule for the direct inversion of the queue length.

6.5 Computing Waiting Time Distributions

The waiting time distributions given by the transforms (14)–(16) can be computed by numerically solving the associated Volterra integral equations (see, e.g., Neuts [93] [2]) or by numerically inverting the transforms directly (see e.g., Abate and Whitt [68] and Choudhury, Lucantoni and Whitt [81]).

6.6 Computing Transient Distributions

We compute the transient queue length and waiting time distributions by numerically inverting the double transforms in (24) and (21), respectively, using new multi-dimensional transform inversion algorithms presented in Choudhury, Lucantoni and Whitt [12]. Note that $G(s)$ needs to be computed a large number of times (particularly if the inversion is needed for several values of queue length/waiting time and for several time points). However, upon closer examination of the inversion algorithms it is apparent that not all of the evaluations of $G(s)$ are at distinct s values. For a particular example in [8], $G(s)$ is needed 250,000 times but only at 500 distinct s values. By precomputing and storing these matrices for later use, the computational burden is greatly reduced. In fact, the computational effort for evaluating $G(\cdot)$ becomes an insignificant fraction of the overall computation. This allows feasible numerical computations for more complicated models such as the $BMAP_t/G_t/1$ discussed in §8 below.

7 Numerical Results

The computability of the results in this paper has been demonstrated recently in Choudhury, Lucantoni and Whitt [23] [8] and already put to practical uses. For example, in [23] we study the effectiveness of recently proposed "effective bandwidth" measures to be used for call admission algorithms in ATM networks. In particular, we compute the stationary delay and queue length distributions for a superposition of up to sixty identical bursty sources (modeled as $MMPP$'s). We found that effective bandwidth could lead to extremely conservative or extremely optimistic predictions depending on whether the individual streams were more or less bursty then Poisson, respectively. See [23] for more discussion of this and for references on effective bandwidth.

The transient delay and queue length distributions are computed in [8]. There we consider a $BMAP$ corresponding to the superposition of four i.i.d. $MMPP$'s, each having two environment states, and a gamma service-time distribution. As should be anticipated, these examples show, that the transient distributions can be very different from the steady-state distributions. We also compute the transient distributions when $\rho > 1$. This has applications to studying overloads in situations that cannot be studied by stationary models.

8 Current and Future Work

The $MAP/G/1$ queue with server vacations was analyzed in Lucantoni, Meier-Hellstern and Neuts [6], where it was shown that known factorization theorems in the $M/G/1$ queue with vacations carry over to the MAP case. Several new factorizations were also derived there. It is easy to generalize the expressions in [6] to the $BMAP/G/1$ queue with server vacations. The $BMAP/G/1$ queue with a more general vacation discipline than in [6] is analyzed in Ferrandiz [95].

All of the results for the $BMAP/G/1$ queue generalize to the $BMAP/SM/1$ queue; that is a single server queue with a $BMAP$ arrival process where successive service times form a semi-Markov process; see Lucantoni and Neuts [95] for the analogous stationary results.

Recently, results have been obtained for the $MMPP/G/1$ queue where the service time depends on the phase at arrivals (Asmussen [56], Zhu and Prabhu [58] [100]) and also for the corresponding $BMAP/G/1$ queue in He [96] and Takine and Hasegawa [97]. These papers allow a superposition of traffic streams each with its own service time distribution. Note that the latter paper also contains the transform expression for the transient workload and an application to priority queues with $BMAP$ arrivals.

Application of the transient results in [8] to the $M_t/G_t/1$ and $BMAP_t/G_t/1$ queues where the arrival processes and service time distributions are fixed on nonoverlapping intervals is currently in progress; see Choudhury, Lucantoni and Whitt [98] [99]. Here a novel use of the double transform inversion routines reduces the enormous amount of information that needs to be carried along at successive intervals.

From this tutorial it should be clear that successful algorithms for the $BMAP/G/1$ queue have benefitted from several different approaches. The combination of matrix analytic methods, transform inversion, embedded Markov chain analysis, techniques based on workload processes, etc., has yielded the possibility of carrying the algorithmic approach to these classes of queues to much greater levels than imagined possible.

Acknowledgements: The author thanks Gagan Choudhury, V. Ramaswami and Ward Whitt for many useful comments on this manuscript, Pat Wirth for her encouragement and support of this work and Susan Pope for converting the original TROFF manuscript to LaTeX.

References

1. Neuts, M. F., *Matrix-Geometric Solutions in Stochastic Models: An Algorithmic Approach.* Baltimore: The Johns Hopkins University Press, 1981.

2. Neuts, M. F., *Structured stochastic matrices of $M/G/1$ type and their applications.* New York: Marcel Dekker, 1989.

3. Neuts, M. F., A versatile Markovian point process. *J. Appl. Prob.*, **16**, (1979) 764–79.

4. Ramaswami, V., The $N/G/1$ queue and its detailed analysis, *Adv. Appl. Prob.*, **12**, (1980) 222–61.

5. Lucantoni, D. M. and Ramaswami, V., Efficient algorithms for solving the nonlinear matrix equations arising in phase type queues, *Stoch. Models*, **1**, (1985) 29–52.

6. Lucantoni, D. M., Meier-Hellstern, K. S, Neuts, M. F., A single server queue with server vacations and a class of non-renewal arrival processes, *Adv. Appl. Prob.*, **22**, (1990) 676–705.

7. Lucantoni, D. M., New results for the single server queue with a batch Markovian arrival process, *Stoch. Mod.*, **7**, (1991) 1–46.

8. Lucantoni, D. M., Choudhury, G. L., and Whitt, W., The transient $BMAP/G/1$ queue, submitted to *Stoch. Models*, 1993.

9. Lucantoni, D. M., and Neuts, M. F., The customer delay in the single server queue with a batch Markovian arrival process, submitted for publication, 1993.

10. Lucantoni, D. M., and Neuts, M. F., Simpler proofs of some properties of the fundamental period of the $MAP/G/1$ queue, *J. Appl. Prob.*, to appear in April, 1994.

11. Choudhury, G. L., Lucantoni, D. M., Whitt, W., The distribution of the duration and number served during a busy period in the $BMAP/G/1$ queue, in preparation.

12. Choudhury, G. L., Lucantoni, D. M., Whitt, W., Multi-dimensional transform inversion with applications to the transient $M/G/1$ queue, submitted for publication, 1993.

13. Bellman, R., *Introduction to Matrix Analysis*, New York: McGraw Hill, 1960.

14. Narayana, S. and Neuts, M. F., The First Two Moment Matrices of the Counts for the Markovian Arrival Process, *Stoch. Models*, **8**, (1992) 459–477.

15. Neuts, M. F., Probability distributions of phase type. In *Liber Amicorum Prof. Emeritus H. Florin*, Department of Mathematics. Belgium: University of Louvain, (1975) 173–206.

16. Heffes, H. and Lucantoni, D. M., A Markov modulated characterization of packetized voice and data traffic and related statistical multiplexer performance. *IEEE J. on Selected Areas in Communication, Special Issue on Network Performance Evaluation*, **6**, (1986) 856–868.

17. Latouche, G., A phase-type semi-Markov point process. *SIAM J. Alg. Disc. Meth.*, **3**, (1982) 77–90.

18. Pacheco, A. and Prabhu, N. U., Markov-compound Poisson arrival processes, Tech. Rept. No. 1059, School of Operations Research and Industrial Engineering, Cornell University, Ithaca, NY 14853, 1993.

19. Graham, A., *Kronecker Products and Matrix Calculus With Applications*. Chichester: Ellis Horwood Limited, 1981.

20. Abate, J., Choudhury, G. L. and Whitt, W., Asymptotics for steady-state tail probabilities in structured Markov queueing models, *Stoch. Models*, to appear 1994.

21. Choudhury, G. L. and Whitt, W., Heavy-traffic approximations for the asymptotic decay rates in $BMAP/GI/1$ queues, submitted to *Stoch. Models*, 1992.

22. Neuts, M. F. The caudal characteristic curve of queues. *Adv. Appl. Prob.*, **18**, (1986) 221-54.

23. Choudhury, G. L., Lucantoni, D. M., and Whitt, W., Squeezing the most out of ATM, submitted for publication, 1993.

24. Choudhury, G. L., Lucantoni, D. M., and Whitt, W., Tail probabilities in queues with many independent sources, in preparation.

25. Choudhury, G. L., Lucantoni, D. M., and Whitt, W., On the effectiveness of effective bandwidths for admission control in ATM networks, submitted to the *14th International Teletrtaffic Congress*, 1994.

26. Neuts, M. F., Models based on the Markovian arrival process, *IEICE Trans. Commun.* Vol. E75-B, No. 12, (1992) 1255-65.

27. Asmussen, S., and Koole, G., Marked point processes as limits of Markovian arrival streams, *J. Appl. Prob.*, to appear.

28. Olivier, C. and Walrand, J., On the existence of finite dimensional filters for Markov modulated traffic, *J. Appl. Prob.*, to appear.

29. Blondia, C., A discrete-time Markovian arrival process, *RACE Document* PRLB-123-0015-CD-CC, August 1989.

30. Blondia, C., A discrete time batch Markovian arrival process as B-ISDN traffic model, to appear in *JORBEL*, 1993.

31. Blondia, C. and Theimer, T., A discrete-time model for ATM traffic, *RACE Document* PRLB-123-0018-CD-CC/UST-123-0022-CD-CC, October 1989.

32. Blondia, C. and Casals, O., Statistical multiplexing of VBR sources: a matrix analytic approach, *Perf. Eval.*, **16**, (1992) 5–20.

33. Briem, U., Theimer, T. H. and Kröner, H., A general discrete-time queueing model: analysis and applications, *TELETRAFFIC AND DATATRAFFIC in a period of change*, ITC-13, A.Jensen and V. B. Iversen (Eds.), Elsevier Science Publishers B.V. (North-Holland) 1991.

34. Herrmann, C., Analysis of the discrete-time $SMP/D/1/s$ finite buffer queue with applications in ATM, *Proc. of IEEE Infocom '93*, San Francisco, March 28–29, (1993) 160–7.

35. Ohta, C., Tode, H., Yamamoto, M., Okada, H. and Tezuka, Y., Peak rate regulation scheme for ATM networks and its performance, *Proc. of IEEE Infocom '93*, San Francisco, March 28-29, (1993) 680–9.

36. Alfa, A. S. and Neuts, M. F., Modelling vehicular traffic using the discrete time Markovian arrival process, submitted for publication, 1991.

37. Berger, A., Performance analysis of a rate-control throttle where tokens and jobs queue, *J. of Selected Areas in Communications*, **9**, (1991) 165–170.

38. Garcia J. and Casals O., Priorities in ATM Networks, *High-capacity local and metropolitan area networks. Architecture and performance issues* G. Pujolle (Ed.) NATO ASI Series, Springer-Verlag, (1990) 527–1536.

39. Garcia J. and Casals O., Space priority mechanisms with bursty traffic, *Proc. Internat. Conf. of Distributed Systems and Integrated Communication Networks*, Kyoto, (1991) 363–82.

40. Ramaswami, V. and Latouche. G., Modeling packet arrivals from asynchronous input lines, In *"Teletraffic Science for New Cost-Effective Systems, Networks and Services,"* ITC-12, M. Bonatti Ed., North-Holland, Amsterdam, (1989) 721–27.

41. Latouche, G. and Ramaswami, V., A unified stochastic model for the packet stream from periodic sources, *Perf. Eval.*, **14**, (1992) 103-21.

42. Neuts, M. F., Modelling data traffic streams, *TELETRAFFIC AND DATATRAF-FIC in a period of change*, ITC-13, A.Jensen and V. B. Iversen (Eds.), Elsevier Science Publishers B.V. (North-Holland) 1991.

43. Neuts, M. F., Phase-type distributions: a bibliography, (1989) Working Paper.

44. Daley, D. J. and Vere-Jones, D., *An Introduction to the Theory of Point Processes*, Springer-Verlag, 1988.

45. Wold, H., On stationary point processes and Markov chains. *Skand. Aktuar.*, **31**, (1948) 229–240.

46. Rudemo, M, Point processes generated by transitions of Markov chains, *Adv. Appl. Prob.*, **5**, (1973) 262–286.

47. Kuczura, A., The interrupted Poisson process as an overflow process, *Bell. Syst. Tech. J.*, **52**, (1973) 437–48.

48. Neuts, M. F., The $M/M/1$ queue with randomly varying arrival and service rates, *Opsearch*, **15**, (1978) 139-57.

49. Neuts, M. F., Further results on the $M/M/1$ queue with randomly varying rates, *Opsearch*, **15**, (1978) 158-68.

50. Heffes, H. A class of data traffic processes — Covariance function characterization and related queueing results, *Bell Syst. Tech. J.*, **59**, (1980) 897–929.

51. van Hoorn, M. H., and Seelen, L. P., The $SPP/G/1$ queue: a single server queue with a switched Poisson process as input process. *O. R. Spektrum*, **5**, (1983) 207–218.

52. Burman, D. Y. and Smith, D. R., An asymptotic analysis of a queueing system with Markov-modulated arrivals, *Oper. Res.*, **34**, (1986) 105–119.

53. Rossiter, M., The switched Poisson process and the $SPP/G/1$ queue. *Proceedings of the 12th International Teletraffic Congress*, 3.1B.3.1-3.1B.3.7, Torino, 1988.

54. Ide, I., Superposition of interrupted Poisson processes and its application to packetized voice multiplexers, *Proceedings of the 12th International Teletraffic Congress*, 3.1B.2.1-3.1B.2.7, Torino, 1988. Torino, 1988.

55. Baiocchi, A., Blefari Melazzi, N., Listanti, M., Roveri, A. and Winkler, R., Loss performance analysis of an ATM multiplexer, *IEEE J. on Selected Areas in Communication, Special Issue on Teletraffic Analysis of ATM Systems*, **9**, (1991) 388–93.

56. Asmussen, S., Ladder heights and the Markov-modulated $M/G/1$ queue, submitted for publication, 1993,

57. Neuts, M. F., Renewal processes of phase type, *Nav. Res. Logist. Quart.*, **25**, (1978) 445–54.

58. Zhu, Y. and Prabhu, N. U., Markov-modulated queueing systems, *Queueing Systems*, **5**, (1989) 215–46.

59. Ramaswami, V., The $N/G/\infty$ queue, Tech. Rept., Dept. of Math., Drexel Univ., Phila., Pa., October, 1978.

60. Neuts, M. F., The c-server queue with constant service times and a versatile Markovian arrival process. In *"Applied probability - Computer science: The Interface,"* Proc. of the Conference at Boca Raton, Florida, Jan. 1981, R. L. Disney and T. J. Ott, eds, Boston: Birkhüser, Vol I, 31–70, 1982.

61. Blondia, C. The $N/G/1$ finite capacity queue, *Stoch. Models*, **5**, (1989) 273–94.

62. Saito, H., The departure process of an $N/G/1$ queue, *Perf. Eval.*, **11**, (1990) 241–251.

63. Sengupta, B., Markov processes whose steady state distribution is matrix-exponential with an application to the $GI/PH/1$ queue. *Adv. Appl. Prob.*, **21**, (1989) 159–80.

64. Neuts, M. F., The fundamental period of the queue with Markov-modulated arrivals, In *Probability, Statistics and Mathematics, in Honor of Professor Samuel Karlin*, J. W. Anderson, K. B. Athreya and D. L. Iglehart (eds.) Academic Press, NY 1989, pp. 187–200.

65. Ramaswami, V., From the matrix-geometric to the matrix-exponential, *Queueing Systems*, **6**, (1990) 229–60.

66. Machihara, F., A new approach to the fundamental period of a queue with phase-type Markov renewal arrivals, *Stoch. Models*, **6**, (1990) 551–60.

67. Asmussen, S., Phase-type representations in random walk and queueing problems, *The Annals of Probability*, **20**, (1992) 772–789.

68. Abate, J. and Whitt, W., The Fourier-series method for inverting transforms of probability distributions, *Queueing Systems*, **10**, (1992) 5–88.

69. Gantmacher, F. R., *The Theory of Matrices, Vol. 1*, New York: Chelsea, 1977.

70. Neuts, M. F., Moment formulas for the Markov renewal branching process. *Adv. Appl. Prob.*, **8**, (1976) 690–711.

71. Takács, L., *Introduction to the Theory of Queues*, New York: Oxford University Press, 1962.

72. Kendall, D. G., Some problems in the theory of queues, *J. Roy. Statist. Soc.*, Ser. B **13**, (1951) 151–185.

73. Baiocchi, A., Asymptotic behaviour of the loss probability of the $MAP/G/1/K$ queue, Part I: Theory, submitted for publication, 1992.

74. Burke, P. J., Delays in single-server queues with batch input, *Oper. Res.*, **23**, (1975) 830–833.
75. Beneš, V., *General Stochastic Processes in the Theory of Queues*, Reading, MA: Addison-Wesley, 1963.
76. Çinlar, E., The time dependence of queues with semi-Markovian service times. *J. Appl. Prob.*, **4**, (1967) 356–64.
77. Neuts, M. F., The single server queue with Poisson input and semi-Markov service times, *J. Appl. Prob.*, **3**, (1996) 202–230.
78. Neuts, M. F., Two queues in series with a finite, intermediate waitingroom, *J. Appl. Prob.*, **5**, (1968) 123–42.
79. Lucantoni, D. M., Further transient analysis of the $BMAP/G/1$ queue, in preparation.
80. Abate, J. and W. Whitt, Numerical Inversion Of Probability Generating Functions. *OR letters.* 12/4, (1992) 2450–251.
81. Choudhury, G. L., Lucantoni, D. M., and Whitt, W., An algorithm for a large class of $G/G/1$ queues, in preparation.
82. Lucantoni, D. M., *An Algorithmic Analysis of a Communication Model with Retransmission of Flawed Messages*. London: Pitman, 1983.
83. Latouche, G., Algorithms for infinite Markov chains with repeating columns, *IMA Workshop on Linear Algebra, Markov Chains and Queueing Models*, January, 1992.
84. Abate, J., and Whitt, W., Solving probability transform functional equations for numerical inversion, *OR Letters*, **12**, (1992) 275–281.
85. Neuts, M. F., The second moments of the absorption times in the Markov renewal branching process, *J. Appl. Prob.*, **15**, (1978) 707–714.
86. Choudhury, G. L. and Lucantoni, D. M., Numerical computation of the moments of a probability distribution from its transform, *Oper. Res.*, to appear, 1994.
87. Choudhury, G. L., Lucantoni, D. M. and Whitt, W., Asymptotic analysis based on the numerical computation of a large number of moments of a probability distribution, in preparation.
88. Choudhury, G. L., Lucantoni, D. M. and Whitt, W., Numerical transform inversion to analyze teletraffic models, submitted to the *14th International Teletrtaffic Congress*, 1994.
89. Ramaswami, V., Stable recursion for the steady state vector for Markov chains of $M/G/1$ type, *Stoch. Models*, **4**, (1988) 183–88.
90. Neuts, M. F., Algorithms for the waiting time distributions under various queue disciplines in the $M/G/1$ queue with service time distribution of phase type, in *"Algorithmic Methods in Probability,"* TIMS Studies in Management Sciences, No. 7, London: North Holland Publishing Co. (1977) 177–97.
91. Wang S. S. and Silvester, J. A., A discrete-time performance model for integrated service ATM multiplexers, submitted for publication, 1993.
92. Wang S. S. and Silvester, J. A., A fast performance model for real-time multimedia communications, submitted for publication, 1993.
93. Neuts, M. F., Generalizations of the Pollaczek-Khinchin integral equation in the theory of queues, *Adv. Appl. Prob.*, **18**, (1986) 952–90.
94. Ferrandiz, J. M., The $BMAP/G/1$ queue with server set-up times and server vacations, *Adv. Appl. Prob.*, **25**, (1993) 235–54.
95. Lucantoni, D. M. and Neuts, M. F., Some steady-state distributions for the $MAP/SM/1$ queue, submitted for publication, 1993.
96. He, Q-M., Queues with marked customers, submitted for publication, 1993.

97. Takine, T., and Hasegawa, T., The workload process of the $MAP/G/1$ queue with state-dependent service time distributions and its application to a preemptive resume priority queue, submitted for publication, 1993.

98. Choudhury, G. L., Lucantoni, D. M. and Whitt, W., Numerical solution of the $M_t/G_t/1$ queue, submitted for publication.

99. Choudhury, G. L., Lucantoni, D. M. and Whitt, W., Numerical solution of the $BMAP_t/G_t/1$ queue, in preparation.

100. Zhu, Y. and Prabhu, N. U., Markov-modulated $PH/G/1$ queueing systems, *Queueing Systems*, 9, (1991) 313–22.

AN OVERVIEW OF TES PROCESSES
AND MODELING METHODOLOGY

BENJAMIN MELAMED

NEC USA, Inc.
C&C Research Laboratories
4 Independence Way
Princeton, New Jersey 08540

Abstract

TES (Transform-Expand-Sample) is a versatile methodology for modeling stationary time series with general marginal distributions and a broad range of dependence structures. From the viewpoint of Monte Carlo simulation, TES constitutes a new and flexible input analysis approach whose principal merit is its potential ability to simultaneously capture first-order and second-order statistics of empirical time series. That is, TES is designed to fit an arbitrary empirical marginal distribution (histogram), and to simultaneously approximate the leading empirical autocorrelations. This paper is a tutorial introduction to the theory of TES processes and to the modeling methodology based on it. It employs a didactic approach which relies heavily on visual intuition as a means of conveying key ideas and an aid in building deep understanding of TES. This approach is in line with practical TES modeling which itself is based on visual interaction under software support. The interaction takes on the form of a heuristic search in a large parameter space, and it currently relies on visual feedback supplied by computer graphics. The tutorial is structured around an illustrative example both to clarify the modeling methodology and to exemplify its efficacy.

1 INTRODUCTION

TES (Transform-Expand-Sample) is a recent approach to modeling stationary time series [15, 7, 8, 9]. The TES approach is non-parametric in the sense that it makes no assumptions on marginal distributions, though the underlying temporal dependence structure is postulated to be Markovian, with a continuous state space. Nevertheless, its modeling scope is quite broad: Additional transformations may be applied, leading to non-Markovian processes; and stationary TES processes may be combined into new ones, e.g., via modulation of TES processes by another process, often a discrete-state Markov process. The main application of TES to date has been to create source models (of incoming traffic or workload), in order to drive Monte Carlo simulations [2, 10].

What is new about TES is its potential ability to capture (fit) both the marginal distribution (a first-order statistic) and the autocorrelation function (a second-order statistic) of empirical data. Most importantly, TES aims to fit both marginals and autocorrelations *simultaneously*. This goal is not new; in fact, engineers have attempted such simultaneous fitting, mainly in the context of signal processing (see, e.g., [13] and references therein). The TES variation on this theme is to precisely fit the empirical marginal distribution (typically an empirical histogram), and at the same time capture *temporal dependence* proxied by the autocorrelation function (a measure of linear dependence). Being able to do this is no small feat. In fact, other modeling approaches to time series are able to do either one or the other but not both. For example, autoregression can fit a variety of autocorrelation functions, but not arbitrary marginal distributions. Conversely, the minification/maxification approach [12] can fit general marginal distributions, but has a relatively limited repertoire of autocorrelation functions. And approaches that use Gaussian processes as in [20] are difficult to implement in practice. All modeling approaches which try to capture marginals and autocorrelations simultaneously (TES included) appear to lack an effective algorithmic modeling procedure. TES itself employs a heuristic search over a large parameter space; nevertheless, experience shows that this is actually a viable approach which utilizes human visual perception to guide the search process.

Why should one insist on modeling both first-order and second-order properties simultaneously? From a purely philosophic viewpoint, it is clear that fitting more statistical aspects of empirical data is a priori desirable, as it can only increase one's confidence in a model. From a more practical vantage point, ignoring temporal dependence in data can often carry serious modeling risks. The perils inherent in failing to capture temporal dependence will be illustrated in the sequel. In recognition of these perils, the TES approach stipulates that fitting both first-order and second-order statistics is a minimal modeling requirement.

1.1 Temporal Dependence and Autocorrelations

Dependence, temporal and spatial, pervades many real-world random phenomena. Temporal dependence is a major cause of burstiness in telecommunications traffic, especially in emerging high-speed communications networks; typical examples are file transfers and compressed VBR (variable bit rate) video. Spatial dependence underpins reference of locality in caches and data bases. The combined effect of temporal and spatial dependencies underlies fault cascades observed in network management.

The autocorrelation function is a convenient measure of linear temporal dependence in real-valued stochastic processes, frequently used by engineers [1]. For a discrete-time, real-valued stationary stochastic process $\{X_n\}_{n=0}^{\infty}$, the autocorrelation function $\rho_X(\tau)$ consists of the lagged correlation coefficients

$$\rho_X(\tau) = \frac{E[X_n X_{n+\tau}] - \mu_X^2}{\sigma_X^2}, \quad \tau = 1, 2, \ldots \tag{1.1}$$

where $\mu_X < \infty$ and $\sigma_X^2 < \infty$ are the common mean and variance, respectively, of the X_n. While autocorrelation is a measure of linear dependence, it is often used to proxy for general dependence, and this is satisfactory in most cases.

1.2 The Importance of Modeling Temporal Dependence

Many systems, encountered in practice, have both deterministic and stochastic components. The deterministic components are usually easy to capture faithfully in a simulation model. However, the stochastic components tend to be the weak link in the chain of modeling assumptions in both simulation models and analytic ones. This tendency is most pronounced in analytical models, where oversimplified assumptions are routinely made to facilitate tractability. A typical case in point is renewal queueing, namely, GI/GI/m queues. Here dependence is eliminated or overlooked for the sake of analytical or numerical tractabilty, or because it is not clear how to model temporal dependence in arrivals or services. Occasionally, this attitude is justified, for example, when no additional knowledge is available, and one seeks qualitative insights and does not insist on quantitative accuracy. Analytical models often trade quantitative accuracy for analytical or numerical tractability. But where more accurate predictions are needed (often in the context of a Monte Carlo simulation model), this attitude cannot be routinely justified.

Since dependence is frequently ignored by modelers, even when it is clearly present, it is important to understand the modeling risk of inadequately capturing dependence or ignoring it altogether; we refer to this aspect as *undermodeling*. We note, in passing, that *overmodeling* is also undesirable; one is merely interested in the simplest possible model that would yield adequate predictions (the Principle of Parsimony). Queueing systems, so prevalent in computer and communications modeling, illustrate the risk of this kind of undermodeling. Consider a queueing system with bursty arrivals. Note that burstiness occurs because short interarrival intervals tend to follow in succession, until interrupted by a lull. Burstiness can be due either to the shape of the marginal interarrival distribution (say, due to a high coefficient of variation), or more commonly, because significant positive autocorrelations are present in the interarrival time process. A little reflection reveals that burstiness can make waiting times arbitrarily high, without increasing the arrival rate. For illustration, consider the effect of merely increasing the average number of customers that arrive in a single burst (think of batch arrivals), while spacing the bursts farther and farther apart on the average. Clearly, we can keep the arrival rate constant, this way, but the effect on mean waiting times will be disastrous: customers arriving in larger and larger bursts will experience increasing waiting times, while the longer and longer lulls separating bursts just waste the server's work potential. While this simple thought experiment should convince the reader that temporal dependence is important, the magnitude of its effect in queueing systems can be quantitatively startling. Indeed, various studies [5, 14, 18] have shown that when autocorrelated traffic is offered to a queueing system, the resulting performance measures are considerably worse than those corresponding to renewal traffic. In fact, mean waiting times can differ by orders of magnitude!

A growing realization of the impact of temporal dependence in traffic streams on queueing system performance has provided a prime motivation for devising input analysis methods that can capture such dependence. In general, prudent modelers ought to conclude that temporal dependence cannot be ignored! They should heed the cautionary admonition in the closing sentence of [21]: *"Would you rather be elegant and precisely wrong, or messy and vaguely right?"*

1.3 Goodness Criteria for Modeling Empirical Time Series

The TES modeling approach stipulates a number of requirements — precise requirements as well as heuristic ones — for the goodness of a candidate time series model based on empirical sample paths (see also [13, 12, 20] for related views):

Requirement 1: The marginal distribution of the model should match its empirical counterpart.

Requirement 2: The autocorrelation function of the model should approximate its empirical counterpart. Because the empirical data is finite, the model need only approximate the significant leading autocorrelations. For an empirical sample size of N, a rule of thumb for the maximal lag is the rounded value of $\sqrt{N}$; see [3], Chapter 5.

Requirement 3: Sample paths generated by a Monte Carlo simulation of the model should "resemble" the empirical data.

Note that these requirements are arranged in decreasing stringency. Requirements 1 and 2 constitute quantitative goodness-of-fit criteria, requiring that first-order and second-order properties of the empirical data be adequately captured. These are precise and well-defined requirements, although the particular metric of goodness is left up to the analyst. Requirement 3, however, is a heuristic qualitative requirement which cannot be defined with mathematical rigor. It is simply too subjective, and is better left to human cognitive judgment. Nevertheless, human cognition excells at pattern recognition; we are routinely called to judge for visual similarity, without having to be precise or even able to verbalize how we reached that judgment. Furthermore, the same judgment is often shared by different observers. Recall that it does not make sense to reproduce the empirical sample paths; one merely wishes to approximate their statistical signature. If a model can imitate the qualitative character of the empirical data, so much the better, as this would increase a practitioner's confidence in the model. It is important to realize that qualitative similarity *should not* substitute for the two preceding quantitative requirements. Rather, it is *in addition*, not *instead*. In short, Requirement 3 is merely the qualitative icing on the quantitative cake.

To get a more concrete idea regarding the three modeling requirements above, examine Figure 1. It displays a graphics screen produced by a TES modeling tool, called TEStool

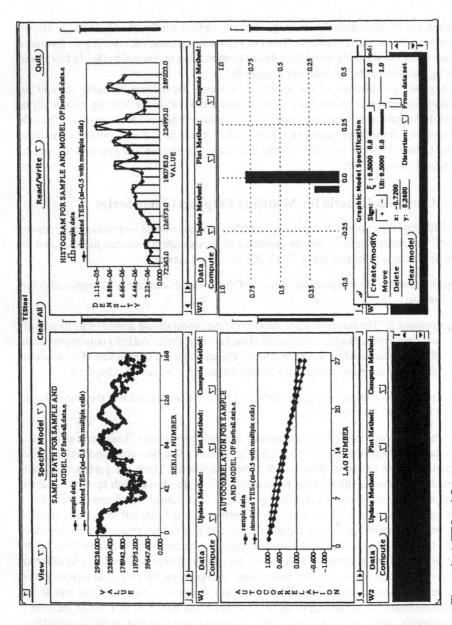

Figure 1: A TEStool Screen

[6, 16], to be described in Section 4.2. The screen consists of four tiled canvases (sub-windows). The lower-right canvas contains a visual specification of a TES model, to be explained in Section 4.2. The remaining three canvases display various statistics, illustrating the modeling requirements above. In each of them, the corresponding statistics are superimposed on each other for comparison; the empirical statistics are marked with bullets, and their TES counterparts by diamonds (see the legend at the top of each canvas). The upper-left canvas displays an empirical sample path against a TES model sample path generated by Monte Carlo simulation; the TES model was constructed from the emprical sample path data, so as to approximate the empirical statistics. The upper-right canvas displays two histograms, corresponding to the two sample paths in the upper-left canvas. Finally, the lower-left canvas displays the empirical autocorrelation function against its TES model counterpart; the latter was numerically computed from an analytical formula, to be presented in Section 3.3. Note, that Requirements 1 and 2 are apparently satisfied, as evidenced by the excellent agreement of the curves in the upper-right and lower-left canvases. It is also interesting to note that the upper-left canvas exhibits considerable "similarity" between corresponding sample paths, in apparent compliance with Requirement 3. Altogether, Figure 1 displays the results of a successful TES modeling effort, when judged against the three modeling requirements above.

1.4 The Merits of the TES Modeling Methodology

It appears that TES is the only modeling method that is designed to simultaneously meet the three goodness-of-fit requirements above in a systematic way. First, TES guarantees an exact fit to arbitrary marginals. More accurately, we are assured of an arbitrarily close fit, provided the simulation run of any of its sample paths is long enough. In particular, TES can match any empirical density (histogram). Second, TES possesses a large degree of freedom in approximating empirical autocorrelations, even as it maintains an exact match to the empirical marginal. TES autocorrelation functions have diverse functional forms including monotone, oscillatory, alternating and others. And third, TES processes span a wide qualitative range of sample paths, including cyclical as well as non-cyclical paths. Altogether, TES defines a very large class of models, encompassing both Markovian and non-Markovian processes.

TES processes enjoy two important computational advantages. To begin with, TES sequences are easily generated on a computer, and their periods are much longer than the underlying pseudo-random number stream. Their generation time complexity is small compared to that of the underlying pseudo-random number generator, and its space complexity is negligible. Furthermore, TES autocorrelations (and spectral densities) can be computed from accurate and fast (near real-time) analytical formulas without requiring simulation.

Because TES autocorrelations can be calculated in near real time on a modern work-station, TES modeling of empirical data can be carried out interactively, with guidance from visual feedback provided by a Graphical User Interface. This observation motivated the implementation of the TEStool modeling software package [6, 16] (recall Figure 1). TEStool makes heavy use of visualization in order to provide a pleasant interactive environment for TES modeling of general autocorrelated stationary time series. It supports visual modeling in the sense that the user can immediately see the statistics for each TES model (obtained by incremental modifications), superimposed on their empirical counterparts, and thereby judge the goodness of the current model. The environment speeds up the modeling search process, cuts down on modeling errors, and relieves the tedium of repetitive search. Modeling interactions are easy to grasp by experts and non-experts alike, since the search problem and search activities are cast in intuitive visual terms.

While TES is very versatile and its statistics exhibit rich behavior, the definition of TES processes is surprisingly simple. In essence, a TES process is a modulo-1 reduction of a simple linear autoregressive scheme, followed by additional transformations. The basic TES formulation is Markovian; however, the aforementioned transformations usually result in non-Markovian processes. Thus, TES is a non-linear autogressive scheme, encompassing Markovian and non-Markovian processes, which may explain in part its diversity and versatility.

1.5 Organization

This paper is a tutorial introduction to TES processes and the TES modeling methodology. As such it contains a certain amount of redundancy to facilitate the presentation.

The rest of the paper is organized as follows. Section 2 puts together the technical preliminaries required in the sequel. Section 3 contains a tutorial overview of TES processes. Section 4 explains the TES modeling methodology and overviews the TEStool modeling environment. Finally, Section 5 contains the conclusion of this paper.

2 TECHNICAL PRELIMINARIES

Several key technical concepts are essential to the understanding of TES processes and the TES modeling methodology. These will be intuitively explained in this section.

2.1 The Inversion Method

The *inversion method* is a standard technique of long standing for transforming a uniform random variable to one with an arbitrary prescribed distribution F. It has been used by Monte Carlo simulation analysts from its earliest days [2, 10].

For a random variable X and distribution F, let $X \sim F$ denote the fact that F is the distribution of X. In particular, $X \sim \text{Uniform}(c, d)$ means that X is uniformly distributed over the interval $[c, d)$.

Lemma 1 (Inversion Method) *Let F be any distribution function and* $U \sim \text{Uniform}(0, 1)$. *Then the random variable* $X = F^{-1}(U)$ *satisfies* $X \sim F$.

For a proof, see *ibid*. Lemma 1 provides a very simple method of converting a marginally uniform sequence $\{U_n\}$ into a sequence $\{X_n\}$ with an arbitrary marginal distribution F. Simply set for each n,

$$X_n = F^{-1}(U_n). \tag{2.1}$$

A transformation of the form (2.1) is called an *inversion*. It always exists because F, being a cumulative distribution function (cdf), is non-decreasing, and therefore can always be inverted; although the inversion is not unique (unless F is strictly increasing), all choices of an inverse produce the same effect when applying the inversion method.

2.2 Histogram Inversions

In practical modeling, one usually estimates the empirical marginal density of an empirical sample by an empirical histogram statistic of the form $\hat{\mathcal{H}} = \{(l_j, r_j, \hat{p}_j) : 1 \leq j \leq J\}$, where J is the number of histogram cells, $[l_j, r_j)$ is the interval of cell j with width $w_j = r_j - l_j > 0$, and $\hat{p}_j$ is the probability estimator of cell j (the relative frequency of observations that fell into that cell). Note that hats signify that the corresponding quantity is a sample-based estimate, whereas the others are user-specified parameters. The empirical probability density function (pdf) is estimated as

$$\hat{h}(y) = \sum_{j=1}^{J} 1_{[l_j, r_j)}(y) \frac{\hat{p}_j}{w_j}, \quad -\infty < y < \infty, \tag{2.2}$$

where $1_A(x)$ denotes the indicator function of set A. Observe that, mathematically, Eq. (2.2) is just the density of a probabilistic mixture of uniform variates, where component j in the mixture is Uniform(l_j, r_j) and occurs with probability $\hat{p}_j$. The corresponding cumulative distribution function (cdf) is the piecewise linear function

$$\hat{H}(y) = \sum_{j=1}^{J} 1_{[l_j, r_j)}(y) [\hat{C}_{j-1} + (y - l_j) \frac{\hat{p}_j}{w_j}], \quad -\infty < y < \infty, \tag{2.3}$$

where $\{\hat{C}_i\}_{i=0}^{J}$ is the cdf of $\{p_j\}_{j=1}^{J}$, i.e., $\hat{C}_j = \sum_{i=1}^{j} \hat{p}_i, 1 \leq j \leq J$ ($\hat{C}_0 = 0$ and $\hat{C}_J = 1$).

The *histogram inversion* corrsponding to $\hat{H}$ is the piecewise linear function

$$D_H(x) = \hat{H}^{-1}(x) = \sum_{j=1}^{J} 1_{[\hat{C}_{j-1}, \hat{C}_j)}(x) [l_j + (x - \hat{C}_{j-1}) \frac{w_j}{\hat{p}_j}], \quad 0 \leq x \leq 1. \tag{2.4}$$

The TES modeling methodology uses histogram inversions of the form (2.4) to construct random variables with prescribed histogram densities (estimated from empirical data) via the inversion method. However, the TEStool environment admits other distributions as well.

Finally, a philosophical remark on the inversion approach is in order at this junction. Analysts often try to fit an analytically-known density to empirical histograms. This approach has merit if it leads to tractable analytical models, or if it speeds up the inversion method on a computer. However, "smoothing" empirical histograms by analytic fitting may introduce inaccuracies instead of purportedly removing "noise" from the empirical data. Unless prior knowledge is availabele to justify this removal, it is best to stick with the empirical histogram. Not only do we save the labor of the fitting stage, but we work with a representation which contains more information than its fitted counterpart. Furthermore, the price paid for the fidelity of histogram inversions is low, since implementing the inversion method on a computer for a moderate-size histogram (20-25 cells) involves a very modest computational cost.

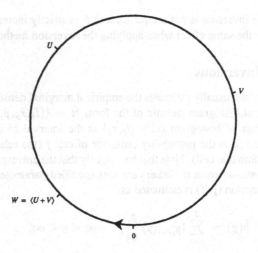

Figure 2: A Geometric Representation of Modulo-1 Addition

2.3 Modulo-1 Arithmetic

Modulo-1 arithmetic is simply the operation of taking the fractional part, after ordinary arithmetic is performed on real numbers. In order to extend the fractional part notion from its familiar form for positive numbers to negative ones, we need a bit of notation.

For any real x, let the *floor operator* $\lfloor \cdot \rfloor$ be defined as $\lfloor x \rfloor = \max\{\text{integer } n : n \leq x\}$, i.e., the integral part of x. Note that the floor operator always truncates downwards. Thus, $\lfloor 1.2 \rfloor = 1$, but $\lfloor -1.2 \rfloor = -2$. The *modulo-1* (fractional part) operator $\langle \cdot \rangle$ can now be defined for any real x by $\langle x \rangle = x - \lfloor x \rfloor$. Thus, $\langle 1.2 \rangle = 0.2$, but $\langle -1.2 \rangle = 0.8$. Note, that a fractional part always lies in the interval $[0, 1)$, even for negative numbers.

An intuitive understanding of modulo-1 arithmetic can be gained from the geometric representation of Figure 2. Here, the interval $[0, 1)$ (the range of fractional parts) has been topologically transformed into a circle in a distance-preserving manner; the origin was arbitrarily selected at the bottom, and represents the fractional part 0. Henceforth, this circle will be referred to as the *unit circle* (note that it is the circumference which is unity, not the radius). A number $0 < y < 1$ is represented by a point on the unit circle at distance y from the origin (the distance is measured by the length of the arc connecting the origin clockwise to y). Two such numbers, U and V, are marked on the unit circle in Figure 2. Suppose $0 < n \leq x < n+1$, for some positive integer n. To find $y = \langle x \rangle$ on the unit circle, perform the following thought experiment. Think of x as a virtual inelastic string of length x and zero width; the string can be bent, but cannot be stretched or compressed in length. Now, anchor one end of the string at the origin and proceed to overlay it precisely over the circle in a clockwise direction. You may have to wrap it around the circle several times (actually, $\lfloor x \rfloor = n$ times) before running out of slack, but wherever the string end comes to rest on the unit circle marks the required y. Pictorially, the wrapping action around the origin corresponds to discarding the integral part of x, so this procedure automatically yields the fractional part. For negative x, use a virtual string of length $|x|$, anchor at the origin as before, but overlay the unit circle in the counter-clockwise direction. It is now easy to see that for negative numbers $-1 < x < 0$, we have $\langle x \rangle = 1 - |x|$. Figure 2 illustrates the modulo-1 addition $\langle U + V \rangle$. First, sum $U + V$ in the ordinary way, and then perform the modulo-1 reduction as described before.

Just as modulo-1 arithmetic is an adaptation of ordinary arithmetic to the unit circle, the notion of *circular intervals* is an adaptation of ordinary intervals to the unit circle. The circular (modulo-1) interval $\langle a, b \rangle$ is defined for all $a, b \in [0, 1)$ by

$$\langle a, b \rangle = \begin{cases} [a, b), & a < b \\ [0, 1) \setminus [b, a), & b < a \\ \{a\}, & a = b \end{cases} \tag{2.5}$$

Intuitively, for $a \neq b$, the circular interval $\langle a, b \rangle$ consists of all the points on the unit circle from a and clockwise on the circle to b (including a but excluding b). If $a < b$, the result is the ordinary interval $[a, b)$; but if $b < a$, the resulting circular interval straddles point 0, and becomes in effect a union $[0, 1) \setminus [b, a) = [0, b) \cup [a, 1)$ of two intervals. This situation is depicted in Figure 2, with $a = V$ and $b = U$. The case $a = b$ is defined (somewhat inconsistently) as the singleton set rather than the empty set, for reasons of notational convenience.

2.4 Iterated Uniformity

Iterated uniformity refers to the ability to create sequences of variates, say $\{U_n\}_{n=0}^{\infty}$, where each U_n is distributed uniformly on $[0, 1)$. Modulo-1 arithmetic is intimately connected to iterated uniformity. Specifically, it can be shown that uniformity is closed under modulo-1 addition of independent random variables. While this result is not new (see, e.g., [4], p. 64), it plays such a central role in TES modeling that it merits rigorous quoting.

Lemma 2 (General Iterated Uniformity) *Let $U \sim Uniform(0, 1)$, and let V be any random variable, independent of U. Define $W = \langle U + V \rangle$. Then $W \sim Uniform(0, 1)$.*

Figure 2 illustrates how W is generated via modulo-1 addition on the unit circle, in accordance with Lemma 2. A plausibility argument goes as follows. Start by sampling U (independently) many times on the unit circle. Then any region of the unit circle is equally likely to have the same (uniform) density of points. Next, add a constant c modulo-1 to each point. This simply translates every point by the same amount on the unit circle either clockwise or counter-clockwise, depending on the sign of c. But the symmetry of the unit circle leaves the translated points still uniformly distributed on it. Since the argument holds for every c, it will also hold for any random variable V, as long as V is independent of U. A rigorous proof may be found in [7].

The significance of the Lemma stems from the fact that it gives us a simple prescription for generating a wide variety of marginally uniform sequences: Let $U_0 \sim Uniform(0, 1)$, and let further $\{V_n\}_{n=1}^{\infty}$ be a sequence of iid (independent identically distributed) random variables with arbitrary marginal density f_V, and independent of U_0. The random variables V_n are referred to as *innovations*. Then the recursive scheme

$$U_n = \langle U_{n-1} + V_n \rangle, \quad n > 0, \tag{2.6}$$

is marginally uniform on $[0, 1)$ by Lemma 2. Note carefully the surprising fact that the distribution of the V_n is entirely irrelevant! Any sequence of mutually independent innovations (even non-stationary ones) will do, as long as its members are independent of U_0. In fact, the V_n may be random, deterministic and even assume negative values. Thus, the space of all innovations constitutes a huge degree of freedom for creating marginally uniform sequences! Notice carefully, that every choice of an innovation density f_V gives rise to a different *dependence structure* in $\{U_n\}$, as defined by Eq. (2.6). This flexibility is a major reason for the modeling versatility of TES, and will be revisited in Section 3.

2.5 Step-Function Innovation Densities

While the class of all innovation densities affords broad freedom in defining TES sequences, that class is simply too large to handle operationally. What is needed is a suitable restriction which attains sufficient manageability without sacrificing too much generality.

The class of *step-function* innovation densities on the unit circle (represented by the interval $[-0.5, 0.5)$ for reasons to be explained later) is a natural choice. First and foremost, step-function densities can approximate any density arbitrarily closely, so considerable generality is retained. The second reason is mathematical and conceptual simplicity. Step-function densities, being piecewise constant, correspond to probabilistic mixtures of uniform densities. Mathematically, these densities can be characterized by simply specifying their steps as triplet sets of the form $\{(L_k, R_k, P_k)\}_{k=1}^K$, where K is the number of steps, $[L_k, R_k)$ is the support of step k ($-0.5 \leq L_k < R_k < 0.5$), and $0 < P_k \leq 1$ is the mixing probability of step k ($\sum_{k=1}^K P_k = 1$). It is convenient to require that steps do not overlap (i.e., $R_k \leq L_{k+1}$, $k = 1, \ldots, K-1$). Since the density value over step k is fixed at $P_k / (R_k - L_k)$, we formally have

$$f_V(x) = \sum_{k=1}^K 1_{[L_k, R_k)}(x) \frac{P_k}{R_k - L_k}, \quad -0.5 \leq x \leq 0.5. \tag{2.7}$$

The conceptual simplicity of step functions is immensely valuable in facilitating their visual (graphic) specification and manipulation on a computer screen. This point will be explained in detail in Section 4.2.

Notice the similarity between Eqs. (2.7) and (2.2). In fact, both are step-function densities, but the former is theoretical and the latter is empirical. We use similar but distinct notation to emphasize this point.

2.6 Foreground / Background Schemes

The reader can now see how the previous subsections on modulo-1 arithmetic and iterated uniformity combine with Lemma 1 to provide a generic scheme for generating stationary sequences with arbitrary marginal distribution F.

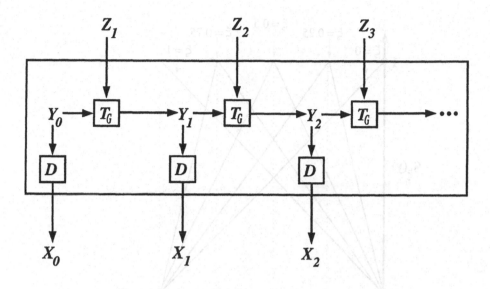

Figure 3: The Generic Foreground/Background Scheme

Figure 3 sketches the overall structure of such schemes, referred to as *foreground / background schemes*. The $\{Z_n\}$ sequence is a pseudo-random number stream (iid Uniform(0, 1) variates), available on most computers. The sequence $\{Y_n\}$ is the *background sequence*, obtained as a general autoregression T_G (that is, Y_n is a function of Y_{n-1} and Z_n, where the latter plays the role of innovation), in such a way that the resulting sequence is stationary with some marginal distribution G. A deterministic transformation D, called *distortion*, transforms each Y_n to a corresponding X_n, and the resulting sequence $\{X_n\}$ is the *foreground sequence*. Intuitively, the background sequence is an auxiliary one which runs "unobserved in the background". Its foreground counterpart is the real target, since the goal is to endow it with the desired statistical properties (a prescribed marginal distribution F is one of them). The tranformation D has the curious name distortion, because in a sense, uniform variates are "ideal" (being so very simple...), and any deviation from uniformity constitutes a "distortion". This connotation not withstanding, distortions are extremely useful, operationally.

As we shall later see, TES generation methods fall within the class of foreground / uniform background schemes.

2.7 Stitching Transformations

Imagine a random walk on the unit circle as depicted in Figure 2. Such random walks will have inherent sample path "discontinuities" due to modulo-1 "crossings" of point 0 in the clockwise or counter-clockwise direction. The term "discontinuities" is used here figuratively; it actually refers to transitions from large fractions to small ones and vice versa, when the random walk wraps around point 0 modulo-1 in each direction.

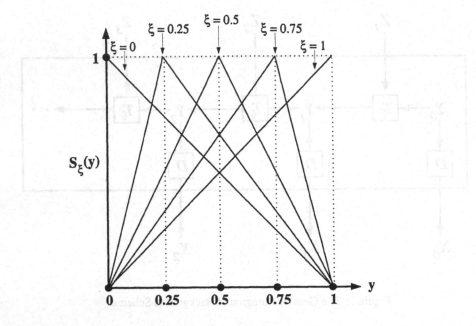

Figure 4: Select Stitching Transformations

In some select situations, such sample path "discontinuities" could be endowed with a valid modeling interpretation. For example, crossing point 0, properly defined, could model a catastrophe — perhaps in a cyclical economic model. But in most cases, such "discontinuities" in the sample path are undesirable, as they have no qualitative counterparts in empirical data. Their presence may violate Requirement 3 in Section 1.3, even though Requirements 1 and 2 may well be complied with. What is needed are "smoothing" transformations to achieve compliance with the former, but without sacrificing compliance with the latter. Most desirable are "smoothing" transformations which are uniformity-preserving, in order to fit arbitrary marginal distributions via the inversion method. The so-called *stitching transformations* [7] precisely fit the bill.

Formally, a stitching transformation S_ξ maps the interval $[0, 1)$ to itself, and is determined by a *stitching parameter* ξ in the range $0 \leq \xi \leq 1$. For a given ξ, S_ξ is defined by

$$S_\xi(y) = \begin{cases} y/\xi, & 0 \leq y \leq \xi \\ (1-y)/(1-\xi), & \xi \leq y < 1 \end{cases} \tag{2.8}$$

Figure 4 depicts select stitching transformations plotted for various values of ξ. The sobriquet "stitching" is motivated by the fact that for $0 < \xi < 1$, S_ξ is continuous on the unit circle. To see that, notice that all S_ξ are continuous in the ordinary sense in the interior of the unit interval. However, as the unit interval is closed into a unit circle by "stitching" together the edge points 0 and 1, the images of S_ξ at the edge points will be similarly stitched, in the sense that $S_\xi(0) = S_\xi(1) = S_\xi(1-)$, $0 < \xi < 1$. Now imagine that a highly autocorrelated, marginally uniform sequence $\{U_n\}$, is represented by points on the abcissa of the graph in Figure 4. Intuitively, this means that successive points of $\{U_n\}$ are not too far apart on the abcissa, except when they wrap around 0. But even then, S_ξ ensures that for $0 < \xi < 1$, successive images of $\{S_\xi(U_n)\}$ are similarly spaced on the ordinate. Thus, $\{S_\xi(U_n)\}$ is "smoother" than the original sequence $\{U_n\}$. Note that no "smoothing" takes place for $S_1(x) = x$ (the identity) and $S_0(x) = 1 - x$ (the antithetic transformation); indeed, Figure 4 shows that these are not "continuous" at the edges of the unit circle.

The primary utility of stitching transformations is that they all preserve uniformity, in addition to their "smoothing" effect.

Lemma 3 *If* $U \sim Uniform(0, 1)$, *then* $S_\xi(U) \sim Uniform(0, 1)$, *for all* $0 \leq \xi \leq 1$.

A simple proof may be found in [15]. It follows that a compound distortion of the form

$$D(x) = F^{-1}(S_\xi(x)), \quad x \in [0, 1], \tag{2.9}$$

employing stitching and inversion in succession, will allow us to to fit arbitrary marginal distributions, and simultaneously attain sample path "smoothing". The empirical TES modeling methodology, to be described in Section 4.1, employs compound distortions of the form (2.9).

An example of the "smoothing" effect of stitching on TES sequences is deferred until Section 3.3.

2.8 The TES Modeling Approach

We can now gather the strands of the foregoing discussion and sketch the main elements of the TES modeling approach.

Consider again Figure 3, and make the following specializations. Let $Y_0 = U_0$ be uniform on $[0, 1)$, and let T_G implement the iterated uniformity scheme (2.6), where each V_n is a function of the corresponding Z_n (the V_n could be possibly generated via the inversion method). The background sequence $\{Y_n\} = \{U_n\}$ will then be marginally uniform on $[0, 1)$, and so each U_n could be transformed by a distortion D to yield a foreground sequence $\{X_n\}$ with prescribed marginal distribution F. To this end, one may use an inversion distortion or a compound one of the form (2.9).

The TEStool modeling environment makes two additional specializations. It uses histogram inversions $\hat{H}^{-1}$ of the form (2.4) in constructing compound distortions of the form (2.9), and it restricts the range of innovation densities to the class of step functions (2.7) whose support is contained in the interval $[-0.5, 0.5]$. A detailed description of TES sequences will be presented in Section 3.

Note carefully, again, that for any distortion $D = F^{-1}$, we have $X_n \sim F$ *regardless* of the innovation sequence selected! Thus, the TES approach guarantees that Requirement 1 in Section 1.3 is always satisfied. How then should one approximate a prescribed autocorrelation function? Here, we take advantage of the fact, that the choice of an innovation density, completely determines the temporal dependence structure of the corresponding background sequence (for the foreground sequence, the distortion also participates in this determination). A choice of innovations (and to a lesser extent, of a stitching parameter) can then allow us to satisfy Requirement 2 in Section 1.3. Experience shows that these choices also have a strong impact on the qualitative nature of TES Monte Carlo sample paths, in line with Requirement 3 in Section 1.3.

All in all, the TES approach allows us to decompose the selection of the marginal distribution and autocorrelation function, rendering them largely orthogonal choices. Therein lie both the novelty of TES and its modeling power.

3 OVERVIEW OF TES SEQUENCES

Throughout the remainder of this paper we assume the following setup, over a common probability space:

1. $U_0 \sim \text{Uniform}(0, 1)$ is the initial variate in a background TES sequence.

2. $\{V_n\}_{n=1}^{\infty}$ is a sequence of innovations (iid random variables) with common density f_V, independent of U_0. Without loss of generality, we assume that the support of f_V is the interval $[-0.5, 0.5)$, representing the unit circle. In fact, any interval of length 1 can serve as an equivalent support for f_V, because of the modulo-1 arithmetic involved. The reason for this particular choice will become evident later.

3. D is a distortion (a measurable function from $[0, 1]$ to the real line). As in Eq. (2.9), we assume that D is composed of a stitching transformation S_ξ (for some stitching parameter $\xi \in [0, 1]$), followed by an inversion F_X^{-1} of a distribution function F_X.

These are the determining parameters for a TES process.

3.1 Basic Background TES Sequences

We start out by introducing two classes of the simplest TES background sequences: $\text{TES}^+(L, R)$ and $\text{TES}^-(L, R)$. Collectively called *basic* TES sequences, these were first studied in [15], and their construction motivated the TES (*Transform-Expand-Sample*) acronym. The superscripts (plus and minus) are suggestive of the fact that basic TES sequences cover all lag-1 autocorrelation; TES^+ sequences cover the positive range $[0, 1]$, while TES^- sequences cover the negative range $[-1, 0]$ (see below). Hereafter, we shall consistently append the proper superscript (plus or minus) to distinguish between similar mathematical objects associated with TES^+ and TES^-, respectively; the superscript is deleted in objects common to TES^+ and TES^-, or those for which the distinction is immaterial. For example, TES^+ and TES^- sequences are denoted $\{U_n^+\}$ and $\{U_n^-\}$, respectively, but U_0 is the common initial variate for all TES classes.

Basic TES sequences are parameterized by pairs (L, R), $-0.5 \leq L < R < 0.5$. These are used, in fact, to parameterize uniform innovation variates of the form

$$V_n = L + (R - L)Z_n, \tag{3.1}$$

where $\{Z_n\}$ is a sequence of iid $\text{Uniform}(0, 1)$ variates. The (L, R) parameterization is equivalent to the (α, ϕ) parameterization given by

$$\alpha = R - L, \quad \phi = \frac{R + L}{\alpha}, \tag{3.2}$$

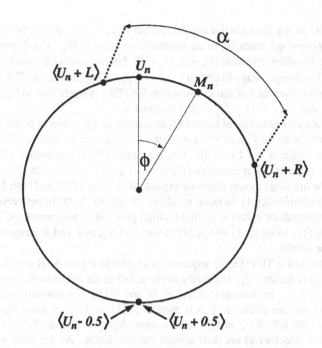

Figure 5: Geometric Interpretation of Basic Background TES Sequences

and the corresponding TES classes are denoted $TES^+(\alpha, \phi)$ and $TES^-(\alpha, \phi)$, respectively. As will be presently seen, the (α, ϕ) parameterization is analoguous to polar coordinates, whereas its (L, R) counterpart is analoguous to Cartesian coordinates. More importantly, the (α, ϕ) parameterization simplifies the representation of the autocorrelation function of TES sequences [7].

Figure 5 ascribes a simple geometric interpretation to $TES^+(\alpha, \phi)$. Here, $\langle U_n + L \rangle$ and $\langle U_n + R \rangle$ are translates of the current TES iterate $U_n = U_n^+$ by offsets $L < 0$ and $R > 0$ on the unit circle; $\alpha = R - L$ is the length of the circular interval $\langle U_n + L, U_n + R \rangle$; and ϕ is an indication of the rotation of that interval away from symmetric straddle of U_n (the angle between U_n and the interval midpoint M_n). The analogy of the (α, ϕ) parameterization to polar coordinates is now evident.

The construction of basic TES sequences is recursive, each resulting in a stationary Markovian sequence whose marginal distribution is uniform on $[0, 1)$; see [15] for formulas of the respective transition densities. Start with $U_0 \sim \text{Uniform}(0, 1)$ as the recursion basis. Next, assume that $U_n \sim \text{Uniform}(0, 1)$ has already been constructed in the recursion step. The next TES iterate U_{n+1} is constructed as follows (refer to Figure 5).

For $TES^+(\alpha, \phi)$, first construct the circular interval $\langle U_n + L, U_n + R \rangle$ about $U_n = U_n^+$, (the *Expand* stage of TES), and then sample U_{n+1} uniformly in $\langle U_n + L, U_n + R \rangle$, independently of the past (the *Sample* stage of TES). The *Transform* stage in TES^+ is the identity. Notice that this is just the geometrical interpretation of the iterated uniformity relation $U_{n+1}^+ = \langle U_n^+ + V_n \rangle$ from Eq. (2.6), for V_n of the form (3.1).

For TES$^-$ (α, ϕ), the recursive construction of $U_{n+1} = U_{n+1}^-$ is a bit more involved (*ibid.*) The *Transform* stage maps U_n to its antithetic variate $1 - U_n$. The *Expand* stage is step dependent: for odd n construct $\langle U_n + L, U_n + R \rangle$, but for even n construct $\langle 1 - U_n + R, 1 - U_n + L \rangle$. The *Sample* stage to obtain $U_{n+1} = U_{n+1}^-$ is the same as in TES$^+$$(\alpha, \phi)$. A little reflection should reveal that this construction for TES$^-$ is equivalent to $U_{n+1}^- = \langle U_n^- + V_n \rangle$ for odd n, and $U_{n+1}^- = \langle 1 - U_n^- - V_n \rangle$ for even n.

The qualitative behavior of basic TES sequences as a function of α and ϕ can be readily grasped with the aid of Figure 5. As $\alpha \downarrow 0$, the limiting circular intervals $\langle U_n + L, U_n + R \rangle$ shrink to a singleton set by (2.5). Consequently, $\{U_n^+\}$ approaches $\{U_0, U_0, \ldots\}$ with $\rho_U^+(\tau) \equiv 1$, while $\{U_n^-\}$ approaches $\{U_0, 1 - U_0, U_0, 1 - U_0, \ldots\}$, with $\rho_U^-(\tau) = -1$, $\tau \geq 1$. As $\alpha \uparrow 1$, the limiting circular intervals expand to $[0, 1)$ by (2.5), and both $\{U_n^+\}$ and $\{U_n^-\}$ approach iid Uniform(0,1) variates, so $\rho_U^+(\tau) \equiv \rho_U^-(\tau) \equiv 0$. In between these extremal cases lie intermediate values $\alpha \in (0, 1)$ which give rise to autocorrelated TES sequences, such that $\rho_U^+(1)$ covers $(0, 1)$ and $\rho_U^-(1)$ covers $(-1, 0)$, as L and R range over $[-0.5, 0.5)$; see [15] for details.

Consider now a TES$^+$$(\alpha, \phi)$ sequence, and refer to Figure 5. If $\phi = 0$, then $R = -L$, so that the next iterate U_{n+1}^+ is equally likely to fall to the left or to the right of the current iterate $U_n = U_n^+$. In this case, $E[V_n] = 0$, and $\{U_n^+\}$ is a random walk with zero net drift around the unit circle. If $\phi > 0$, then $R > |L|$, so U_{n+1}^+ is more likely to fall to the right than to the left of $U_n = U_n^+$. In this case, $E[V_n] > 0$, and $\{U_n^+\}$ is a random walk with positive (clockwise) net drift around the unit circle. As we shall see later on, this results in sawtooth-shaped cyclical sample paths. The case $\phi < 0$ is analogous but with counter-clockwise net drift, resulting from $E[V_n] < 0$. Clearly, the innovation variates V_n serve as differences between successive iterates U_n and U_{n+1}, and the average difference determines whether the TES sequence is driftless or directional as well as the drift direction. However, note carefully that these are no ordinary differences; rather, these are *differences on the unit circle*. In fact, one cannot deduce the innovation variates V_n from $\{U_n^+\}$ in a unique way, because the rules of modulo-1 arithmetic allow us to write $U_{n+1}^+ = \langle U_n^+ + V_n \rangle$ as well as $U_{n+1}^+ = \langle U_n^+ + V_n - 1 \rangle$. It follows that both V_n and $V_n - 1$ qualify as innovation variates. This is just a reflection of the fact that to get from one point to another on a circle, one can either go to the right or to the left with equal effect.

Although basic TES sequences have just two parameters, they already possess a considerable range of sample path behavior, and a variety of functional forms of associated autocorrelation functions. This variety is demonstrated in Figures 6–13 which depict four fundamental behavioral modes of basic TES(α, ϕ) background sequences.

An examination of the sample paths (Figures 6, 8, 10 and 12) reveals a qualitative difference between TES$^+$ and TES$^-$ sample paths. The latter are characterized by a visual "shadow" appearance (Figures 10, 12), due to the alternation of large and small values, which in turn gives rise to an alternating autocorrelation function with negative lag-1 autocorrelation. Another fundamental qualitative difference can be discerned between sequences without drift ($\phi = 0$), as in Figures 6 and 10, and those with drift ($\phi = 0.5$), as in Figures 8 and 12. The latter exhibit a distinct cyclical structure resulting from periodic drifting across the "origin" on the unit circle. This cyclical structure is absent for $\phi = 0$, because the resulting random walk is not directional. Subsequently, the behavior of the corresponding autocorrelation functions (Figures 7, 9, 11 and 13) displays four functional

376

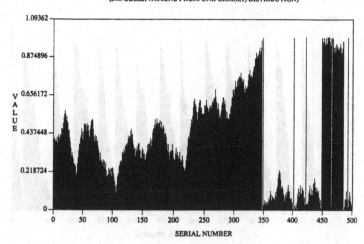

Figure 6: Sample Path of a Uniform TES$^+(\alpha, \phi)$ Process Without Drift

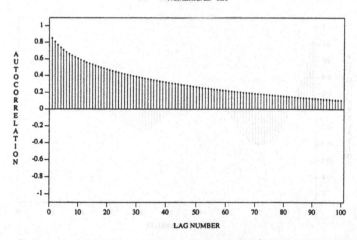

Figure 7: Autocorrelation Functions of a Uniform TES$^+$ Process Without Drift

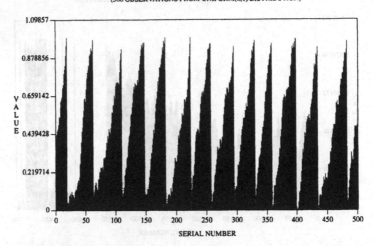

Figure 8: Sample Path of a Uniform TES$^+(\alpha, \phi)$ Process With Drift

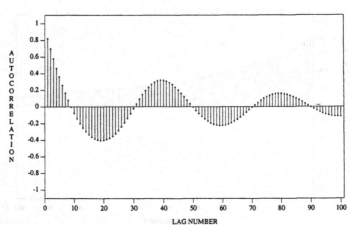

Figure 9: Autocorrelation Functions of a Uniform TES$^+(\alpha, \phi)$ Process With Drift

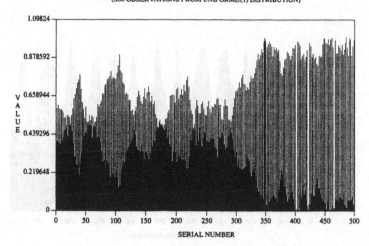

Figure 10: Sample Path of a Uniform TES$^-(\alpha, \phi)$ Process Without Drift

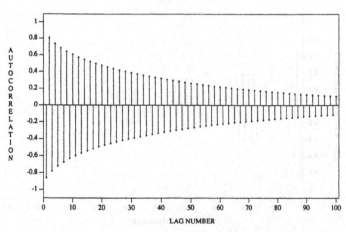

Figure 11: Autocorrelation Functions of a Uniform TES$^-(\alpha, \phi)$ Process Without Drift

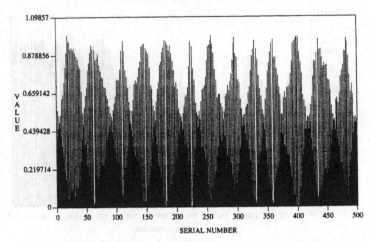

Figure 12: Sample Path of a Uniform TES$^-(\alpha, \phi)$ Process With Drift

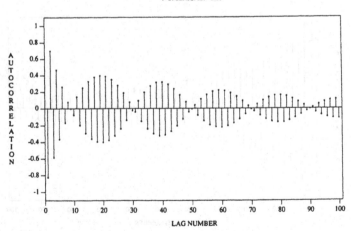

Figure 13: Autocorrelation Functions of a Uniform TES$^-(\alpha, \phi)$ Process With Drift

forms. The driftless TES$^+$ case in Figure 7 is monotone decreasing, whereas the driftless TES$^-$ case in Figure 11 is alternating with monotone decreasing envelope. The TES$^+$ case with drift in Figure 9 is oscillatory, whereas its TES$^-$ counterpart in Figure 13 is simultaneously alternating and oscillatory. All autocorrelation functions are bounded by envelopes with monotone decreasing magnitude. The effect of increasing the magnitude of ϕ on sample path behavior is to decrease the mean "cycle time" of the directional random walk around the unit circle, with the corresponding autocorrelation function oscillating more rapidly. As expected, an increase in α causes a decrease in the magnitude of the resultant autocorrelation functions for all lags.

When the full generality of TES sequences (general innovations and distortions) is invoked, the repertoire of TES sequences and their behavioral range is enhanced far more. This flexibility explains in a nutshell why one can hope a priori to define TES sequences which simultaneously approximate first-order and second-order properties of empirical sequences.

3.2 General TES Background Sequences

This section generalizes the scope of innovations of background TES sequences from uniform innovation densities to general ones.

General TES background sequences fall into two classes, denoted TES$^+$ and TES$^-$. Class TES$^+$ consists of random sequences $\{U_n^+\}$ of the form

$$U_n^+ = \begin{cases} U_0, & n = 0 \\ \langle U_{n-1}^+ + V_n \rangle, & n > 0 \end{cases} \tag{3.3}$$

and class TES$^-$ consists of random sequences $\{U_n^-\}$ of the form

$$U_n^- = \begin{cases} U_n^+, & n \text{ even} \\ 1 - U_n^+, & n \text{ odd} \end{cases} \tag{3.4}$$

It immediately follows that both $\{U_n^+\}$ and $\{U_n^-\}$ are Markovian sequences. Their transition densities were derived in [7], in terms of Fourier expansions, but these are beyond the scope of this paper and will not be reproduced here. By iterated uniformity (see Section 2.4), it further follows that both TES$^+$ and TES$^-$ processes are stationary sequences with Uniform$(0, 1)$ marginals. Eq. (3.4) readily implies that for any given innovation sequence $\{V_n\}$, the autocorrelation functions of the corresponding $\{U_n^+\}$ and $\{U_n^-\}$ sequences satisfy the relation

$$\rho_U^-(\tau) = (-1)^\tau \rho_U^+(\tau), \quad \tau = 0, 1, \ldots \tag{3.5}$$

It is clear from Eq. (3.5) that if TES$^+$ sequences cover the positive range $[0, 1]$ of lag-1 autocorrelations, then TES$^-$ sequences cover the negative range $[-1, 0]$.

Figure 14 provides a 3-dimensional geometric interpretation of the construction of background TES sequences with step-function innovation densities. Here the unit circle lies at the bottom, in the 2-dimensional plane, with the current TES variate U_n in the north/north-easterly sector. A step-function innovation density f_V was erected over the unit circle, with values in the third dimension (the "up" direction). The origin for the

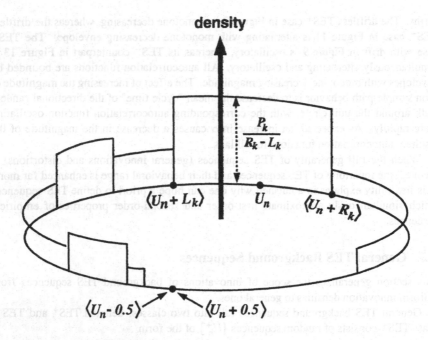

Figure 14: Geometric Interpretation of Background TES Sequences With Step-Function Innovations

support of f_V was set at the current TES variate U_n, implying that the support of f_V is the interval $[-0.5, 0.5)$. To obtain the next TES$^+$ variate U_{n+1}, just sample a value on the unit circle from the innovation density f_V. Indeed, because the origin of f_V was set at U_n, this procedure implies $U_{n+1} = \langle U_N + V_n \rangle$, in agreement with Eq. (3.3). To map a TES$^-$ method into a geometrical interpretation in Figure 14, simply use alternately f_V for even indices n, and its antithetic counterpart (corresponding to sampling $U_{n+1}^- = 1 - U_n^+$) for odd indices n, as prescribed by Eq. (3.4).

Figure 14 clarifies the reason for selecting the interval $[-0.5, 0.5)$ as the support set of f_V. Note carefully, that any interval of lenght 1 will do, due to the modulo-1 reduction perfomed in Eqs. (3.3)–(3.4). But Eq. (3.3) implies (and Figure 14 illustrates graphically) that we can think about general innovation variates V_n as *modulo-1 differences* between successive TES$^+$ variates, that is, *differences on the unit circle*. This interpretation is only valid for the choice of the natural support $[-0.5, 0.5)$ for f_V.

Although Figure 14 does not exhaust the full generality of TES processes, it embodies the level of generality of background TES sequences, adopted by the TES modeling methodology, and implemented in TEStool. For all practical purposes, we may, henceforth, adopt Figure 14 as the mental image characterizing the construction of general background TES sequences.

3.3 General TES Foreground Sequences

Recall that the background TES sequences, $\{U_n^+\}$ and $\{U_n^-\}$ from Eqs. (3.3)–(3.4), play an auxiliary, albeit important, role in TES modeling. The real modeling interest lies in general foreground TES sequences $\{X_n^+\}$ and $\{X_n^-\}$, obtained from Eq. (3.3) and Eq. (3.4), respectively, via a general distortion, as

$$X_n^+ = D(U_n^+), \tag{3.6}$$
$$X_n^- = D(U_n^-). \tag{3.7}$$

Figures 15 and 16 summarize the generation scheme of TES$^+$ and TES$^-$ sequences, respectively, in a self-explanatory manner.

Recall that a compound distortion D of the form (2.9) serves a dual goal: It "smoothes" sample paths of TES sequences, and it guarantees their marginal distribution to match, in principle, any prescribed one. We still need, though, to approximate a prescribed autocorrelation function; consequently, we need a way to calculate or estimate TES autocorrelations.

Naturally, a Monte Carlo simulation of the foreground TES sequences (3.6) and (3.7) can always provide a good estimate of the corresponding autocorrelation function, provided a sufficient sample size is generated. Unfortunately, this approach can be costly in terms of time complexity, especially when high autocorrelations necessitate large sample sizes for adequate statistical reliability (it takes some 10-15 minutes of elapsed time to estimate 100 lags of the autocorrelation function for a million-observation sample on a standard workstation). This pretty much precludes the use of simulation-based estimators in interactive heuristic searches for suitable TES models. Fortunately, fast and accurate numerical algorithms are available for general foreground TES processes $\{X_n^+\}$ and $\{X_n^-\}$, with general distortions and innovations.

Let $\tilde{f}(s) = \int_{-\infty}^{\infty} \exp(-sx) f(x)\, dx$ denote the Laplace Transform of a function $f(x)$. For a given lag τ, the corresponding autocorrelation functions are given, respectively, by

$$\rho_X^+(\tau) = \frac{2}{\sigma_X^2} \sum_{\nu=1}^{\infty} Re[\tilde{f}_V^{\tau}(i2\pi\nu)]\,|\tilde{D}(i2\pi\nu)|^2 \tag{3.8}$$

and

$$\rho_X^-(\tau) = \begin{cases} \rho_X^+(\tau), & \tau \text{ even} \\[2mm] \dfrac{2}{\sigma_X^2} \sum_{\nu=1}^{\infty} Re[\tilde{f}_V^{\tau}(i2\pi\nu)]\, Re[\tilde{D}(i2\pi\nu)^2], & \tau \text{ odd} \end{cases} \tag{3.9}$$

See [7] for the mathematical derivations. These formulas are given in terms of the Fourier coefficients $\tilde{f}_V(i2\pi\nu)$ and $\tilde{D}(i2\pi\nu)$, and so the effect of innovations and distortions on the autocorrelation function is conveniently separated. On the other hand, these infinite expansions do not constitute closed-form representations. In order to gain insight into the effect of innovations and distortions on the corresponding autocorrelation functions, one must perform a numerical summation for a sufficiently large number of terms. Fortunately, Eqs. (3.8) and (3.9) are eminently computable, and the sums converge rather rapidly for all popular and useful innovations and distortions, including compound distortions of the form (2.9) and step-function innovation densities of the form (2.7), both of which are utilized

383

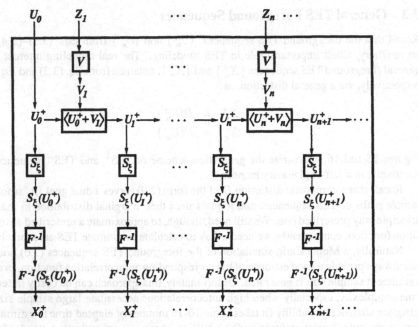

Figure 15: The General TES$^+$ Generation Scheme

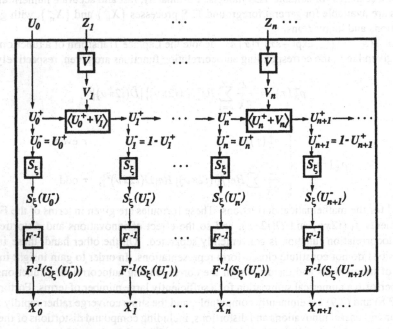

Figure 16: The General TES$^-$ Generation Scheme

in TEStool for empirical TES modeling. Formulas for these and other innovations and distortions were explicitly calculated in [8], and will not be reproduced here.

Figures 6–13 and 17–22 serve two purposes. They exhibit the efficacy of the numerical algorithms for calculating TES autocorrelations, and simultaneously demonstrate their range of functional forms, as well as the variety of the associated sample paths. The figures are arranged in pairs, where the first member displays a sample path obtained from a simulation run, and the next member displays the corresponding pair of TES autocorrelation functions of which one is estimated statistically from a simulation run of 10^6 observations (bullets), and the other is computed numerically from specializations of Eqs. (3.8)–(3.9). As evidenced by the graphs, the agreement is excellent (tabulated printouts confirm the accuracy of the algorithms for a large variety of additional cases). Recall that Figures 6–13 have already been discussed in Section 3.1.

The "smoothing" effect of stitching on basic TES sequences is demonstrated in Figures 6 and 17. Figure 17 is a stitched version ($\xi = 0.5$) of the sample path shown in Figure 6. Notice how the "discontinuities" in the sample path of Figure 6 (the two spikes around serial numbers 400 and 420, and the dip around serial number 470) have been eliminated in Figure 17; the latter has an overall "continuous" appearance. The effect of stitching on the corresponding autocorrelation functions is demonstrated in Figures 7–18. They clearly show that stitching has the effect of increasing the magnitude of the autocorrelation function. This phenomenon stems from the fact, that crossing point 0 in either direction (from large values to small ones or vice versa) introduces a negative component into the autocorrelations of unstitched sequences, and this negative component is eliminated in stitched ones. Refer to Figure 5 as a pictorial aid.

The effect of inversions (see Section 2.1) on sample paths and autocorrelation functions of background TES sequences is exemplified in Figures 19–22. Figures 19–20 correspond to exponential marginals (rate 1), while Figures 21–22 correspond to geometric marginals (parameter 0.5). These particular examples were selected to emphasize that TES can model discrete-valued sequences in addition to continuous-valued ones. A comparison of each distorted foreground sample path with its background counterpart reveals that certain visual features are preserved under unstitched inversions; this is due to the fact that inversion transformations (of a cdf) are monotonic; furthermore, the inversions in the aforementioned figures were applied to the same background sequence. For example, comparing Figures 19 and 21 to Figure 6 reveals that the general appearance of the sample path envelopes is quite similar, though the scales are different. In particular, the sample path "discontinuities" alluded to before are easily identifiable at the same serial numbers. An examination of the corresponding autocorrelation functions (Figures 20, 22, and 7) show that the functional form is largely preserved under inversion (up to scaling), though more complicated effects are described in [8].

The reader is referred to [8] for more information on TES sample paths and autocorrelations, and to [9] for the corresponding information on TES spectral densities.

385

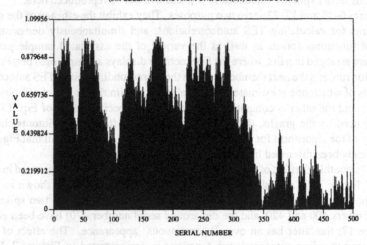

SIMULATED SAMPLE PATH REALIZATION
FOR TES⁺ (α= 0.10, φ= 0.00, ξ= 0.50)
(500 OBSERVATIONS FROM UNIFORM(0,1) DISTRIBUTION)

Figure 17: Sample Path of a Uniform Stitched Driftless $TES^+(\alpha, \phi)$ Process

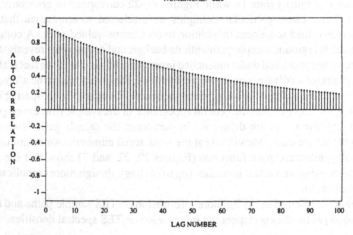

SIMULATED AND NUMERICAL AUTOCORRELATION FUNCTION
FOR TES⁺ (α= 0.10, φ= 0.00, ξ= 0.50)
(100 LAGS FROM UNIFORM(0,1) DISTRIBUTION)

SIMULATED: bullets
NUMERICAL: bars

Figure 18: Autocorrelation Functions of a Uniform Stitched Driftless $TES^+(\alpha, \phi)$ Process

386

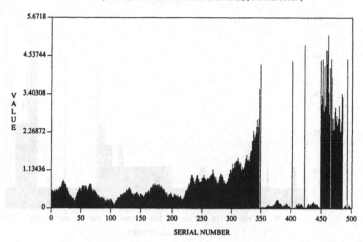

Figure 19: Sample Path of an Exponential TES$^+$ (α, ϕ) Process Without Drift

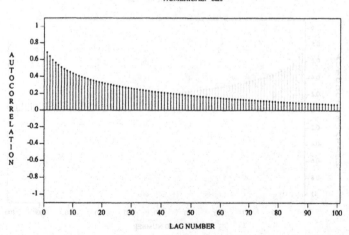

Figure 20: Autocorrelation Functions of an Exponential TES$^+$ (α, ϕ) Process Without Drift

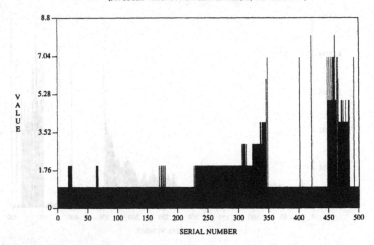

Figure 21: Sample Path of a Geometric TES$^+$(α, ϕ) Process Without Drift

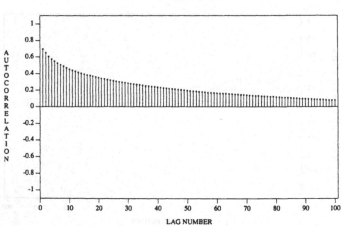

Figure 22: Autocorrelation Functions of a Geometric TES$^+$(α, ϕ) Process Without Drift

4 TES MODELING AND SOFTWARE SUPPORT

The TES modeling methodology, as currently implemented in TEStool, uses specialized innovation and distortions. Unless otherwise stated, all innovation densities are assumed to be step functions (see Section 2.5), and all distortions are restricted to stitched or unstitched histogram inversions (see Section 2.2).

Recall that Section 2.2 covers continuous empirical histograms. If the empirical histogram is known to contain discrete components (that is, discrete values occur with non-zero probabilities), then a simple modification of Eqs. (2.2)–(2.4) yields analoguous formulas; the corresponding transforms required to calculate autocorrelations in Eqs. (3.8) and (3.9) can be found in [8]. We shall not elaborate on the discrete histogram case, because it occurs relatively rarely and does not introduce significant new wrinkles.

4.1 The Empirical TES Modeling Methodology

Modeling empirical time series is the most common and useful application of the TES modeling methodology. Assume that we have at our disposal some empirical sample path, representing a partial time series history, to which we wish to fit a TES model. Assume further that an empirical histogram and autocorrelation function statistics have been computed from the empirical sample path. A complete specification of a TES sequence requires the modeler to specify a flavor of TES process (TES$^+$ or TES$^-$), a distortion D composed of a stitching parameter ξ and histogram inversion H^{-1}, and a step-function innovation density f_V. An outline of a typical modeling scenario is sketched below.

Selecting the TES Process sign: The selection of the TES process sign is based on the modeler's experience and knowledge of TES sequences.

Selecting the inversion: The natural inversion is the histogram distortion D_H, given in Eq. (2.4). Since this is completely determined by the empirical data, no additional choices are required on the modeler's part. Using a histogram inversion ensures that the TES sequence will match the empirical marginal distribution, regardless of other parameter selections.

Selecting the stitching parameter and innovation density: The core activity of empirical TES modeling is a heuristic search for a suitable stitching parameter and innovation density. The modeler searches through stitching parameters in the range $[0, 1]$ and innovation densities in the space of step-function densities whose support is contained in $[-0.5, 0.5)$. These selections fix the autocorrelation structure of a TES sequence.

Reference [8] provides the ingredients for a numerical calculation of TES$^+$ and TES$^-$ autocorrelation functions from the Fourier representations of Eqs. (3.8) and (3.9). Specifically, it contains the formulas for the Laplace transform of the histogram inversion (2.4), as well as stitched histogram inversions of the form $D(x) = H^{-1}(S_\xi(x))$ (a special case of Eq. (2.9)). It also contains formulas for stitched and unstitched inversions corresponding to a host of other distributions, such as uniform, exponential and geometric. Similarly, [8] also provides formulas for the Laplace transform of step-function densities, as well as other innovation densities.

We stress that the modeling outline above is highly heuristic. The modeler may loop back to any step, based on the quantitative fit of the current model's autocorrelation function and the qualitative fit of Monte Carlo sample paths to the respective empirical counterparts. Nevertheless, several rules of thumb have been gleaned from experimentation with various modeling applications in TEStool. Some important ones are summarized below.

Effect of the sign of a TES sequence: Experience shows that TES$^+$ models are the most common choice, in practice. Consequently, the rest of the comments below address this case. TES$^-$ sequences should be considered, however, when empirical sample paths or autocorrelation functions have an alternating (zigzag) appearance.

Effect of the width of an innovation density support: The width of the innovation density support affects the amplitude of the autocorrelation function. The larger the support, the smaller the amplitude. The intuitive reason is that a larger support permits larger distances between successive TES iterates, resulting in a reduced autocorrelation magnitude.

Effect of the location of an innovation density support: The location of the innovation density support controls the frequency of oscillation of the autocorrelation function. The farther the support from the origin, the higher the frequency of oscillation. This is more easily seen for basic TES$^+(\alpha, \phi)$ sequences (see Section 3.1). When $\phi = 0$, the random walk is driftless. The autocorrelation function is monotone decreasing, and a spectral analysis reveals no periodicities. When $\phi \neq 0$, the random walk is directional, and the autocorrelation function is oscillatory. Consequently, the sample paths have a cyclical appearance, and the presence of periodicities can be confirmed by spectral analysis.

Effect of the stitching parameter: The fundamental effect of $0 < \xi < 1$ is to "smooth" the sample paths of TES sequences, whereas for $\xi = 1$ or $\xi = 0$, no "smoothing" takes place. In cyclical TES processes, ξ can be used to skew sample paths in accordance with the corresponding stitching transformation. Applying S_ξ for ξ ranging in $[0,1]$ will shift the cycle peaks in the corresponding $\{S_\xi(U_n^+)\}$ in proportion to ξ. In particular, S_0 corresponds to the antithetic transformation ($S_0(y) = 1 - y$); S_1 is the identity ($S_1(y) = y$); and $S_{0.5}$ gives rise to stitched TES$^+$ processes with symmetrical cycles. Recall that a stitching transformation increases the magnitude of the autocorrelation function of a background sequence as ξ increases or decreases towards 0.5 (see Section 3.3). This effect is strictly monotonic. It can also be shown that for any background TES sequence $\{U_n\}$, the autocorrelation function of any compound distortion (2.9) has the symmetry property that the autocorrelation functions of $\{F^{-1}(S_\xi(U_n))\}$ and $\{F^{-1}(S_{1-\xi}(U_n))\}$ are identical [7].

Effect of inversion distortions: An inversion distortion affects the background sample paths through a "scaling" effect. Interestingly, it has a similar quantitative effect on the corresponding autocorrelation function. However, it does not affect it qualitatively, in the sense that it leaves the functional form of the background autocorrelation function unchanged. These effects can be attributed to the monotonic nature of inversion distortions.

4.2 The TEStool Modeling Support Environment

Undirected heuristic searches for a TES model can be both time-consuming and mentally tedious. In the absence of an algorithmic fitting method, a human modeler requires computerized support with visual interactive facilities. Because the TEStool software environment, developed for this purpose, is such an integral part of the TES modeling activities, it will be briefly overviewed in this section.

TEStool is a visual interactive software environment for fitting TES models to empirical data [6, 16]. It provides services to generate and modify TES models, and to examine their statistics, in the context of the heuristic search scenario outlined in Section 4.1.

TEStool distinguishes between three types of statistics. *Empirical* statistics are those associated with the empirical data (sample paths, histogram, autocorrelation function or spectral density). *Simulated* statistics are similarly calculated (estimated) from Monte Carlo simulations of TES sequences. *Analytical* statistics consist of numerical computations of autocorrelation functions and spectral densities of TES models, based on analytical formulas developed in [8].

Figure 1 displays the now familiar TEStool screen comprised of four tiled subwindows (canvases). The upper-left subwindow contains sample paths, the upper-right subwindow contains histograms, the lower-left subwindow contains autocorrelation functions, and the lower-right subwindow contains a graphical specification of a TES model. The latter consists of a joint specification of a TES sign (plus or minus), stitching parameter ξ, an innovation density f_V, and an initial value U_0 for the backgroundTES sequence. An inverse distribution distortion can be selected from a menu, including the histogram distortion (2.4) constructed from the empirical histogram. A TES model can also be specified in TEStool in standard text mode, by filling out text fields in a form. The buttons in the top border of the display and at the bottom of each subwindow control various modeling services. These include reading and writing datasets, subdividing the screen real estate, opening a TES specification window or menu, performing various computations and quitting the system.

The most important service is the visual specification of a TES model and the interactive computations associated with it. The advantage of a graphical specification is that it can be grasped intuitively; more importantly, it enables the user to interact flexibly with the modeling environment, significantly increasing modeling efficiency and substantially decreasing modeling tedium. In the visual specification mode, the user operates the mouse to draw non-overlapping rectangles; each rectangle represents the support and probability of a step, and together they define a step-function density. In the interactive mode, changes in model specification trigger an immediate recomputation and redisplay of model statistics. The modeler may then compare the new statisics to their empirical counterparts for goodness of fit, and decide whether the fit is satisfactory or whether another iteration is required. The heuristic search can then proceed efficiently, and the visual feedback has the additional advantage of aiding the modeler in learning from experience. Finally, since the search is cast in a visual-interactive mold, it can be carried out by experts and non-experts alike in the same way that a player of an arcade game can concentrate on the task at hand without having to understand the underlying software details.

The lower-right subwindow in Figure 1 serves to clarify the advantage of dealing with step-function densities, from a user interface vantage point. A step-function is particularly easy to specify on a compuer screen, as each step is visually represented as an ordinary rectangle — an exceptionally simple geomertical form. Contemporary computer graphics enable intuitive modifications of rectangles in a natural way with the aid of a mouse. It is a simple matter to change the size of a rectangle, by "stretching" a side or a corner. In a similar vein, translating a rectangle on the horizontal axis is accomplished by the familiar operation of "dragging" an icon. The same subwindow also clarifies the choice of the interval $[-0.5, 0.5)$ as the support set for innovation densities. Any such support set represents the unraveling of the unit circle into a linear interval, so any interval of length one is an equivalent choice due to the modulo-1 arithmetic employed in the definition of TES sequences. However, among all such support sets, the interval $[-0.5, 0.5)$ is most compatible with the intuitive interpretation of innovation variates as modulo-1 increments (decrements) of a TES$^+$ sequence, as explained in Sections 3.1 and 3.2. Because the origin represents the relative location of the current TES iterate on the unit circle, the innovation density·steps have an obvious interpretation: Step (L_k, R_k, P_k) simply means that the next increment (decrement) of the sequence is uniform on $[L_k, R_k)$ with probability P_k.

4.3 Example: A TES Model of Compressed Video Traffic

Figure 1 is reproduced from an actual workstation display screen to illustrate an example in which TEStool has been used to model real-world data. Here the empirical data is a (random) sequence of encoded (compressed) video frames [11, 19]. Video information is rarely transmitted over a network in its raw form. Rather, engineers take advantage of the considerable visual redundancy inherent in digitized pictures to compress each frame into a fraction of its original size. The compressed frames have random sizes (bit rates) which are then transported over the network and decoded at their destination. The term VBR (variable bit rate) video is used to refer to this kind of video traffic. The VBR video frames modeled in Figure 1 were generated by a video sequence from a football scene, whose raw frames were compressed by a variant of DCT (discrete cosine transform) [19]. See [17] for a review of compressed video modeling, using the TES methodology.

Recall that the upper-left subwindow in Figure 1 displays the empirical data (bullets); superimposed on it is a typical sample path (diamonds), generated by a Monte Carlo simulation of the TES model exhibited in the lower-right subwindow. The histogram and autocorrelation function of the TES model are similarly plotted against their empirical counterparts in the upper-right and lower-left subwindows, respectively. Recall that while the TES model histogram was computed from the TES Monte Carlo sample path, the TES model autocorrelations were calculated numerically with the aid of Eq. (3.8). The lower-right subwindow contains a visual specification of a TES$^+$ model with a stitching parameter $\xi = 0.5$ and a step-function density consisting of two steps.

Observe how the modeling results in Figure 1 satisfy the modeling requirements of Section 1.3. Indeed, the TES model closely matches the empirical histogram and approximates the leading autocorrelations quite well (there is no point here in trying to approximate more than about 10 lags, as there are only some 210 data points in the empirical time series). In addition, note that the qualitative "resemblance" of the TES model sample path to the empirical path is remarkable. Thus, the empirical TES modeling summarized in Figure 1 represents a successful modeling effort, by the criteria of Section 1.3.

5 CONCLUSION

This paper presented a fairly comprehensive tutorial on TES models, an outline of the empirical TES modeling methodology, and a brief overview of the TEStool visual interactive softare environment, designed to support TES modeling.

The TES modeling methodology is a novel input analysis approach which aims to provide more faithful models of temporally-dependent empirical time series; it strives to fit *simultaneously* both marginal distributions and the leading autocorrelations of empirical samples, and to imitate their qualitative character. Its primary purpose is to generate realistic synthetic source models to drive Monte Carlo simulations. Its approach to capturing first-order and second-order empirical statistics also qualifies it for "black-box" forecasting applications.

Practical TES modeling currently relies on software support to carry out heuristic searches for adequate models. The TEStool visual interactive software was created with this goal in mind. Its Graphical User Interface casts the heuristic search into an intuitive interactive activity of modifying a visual parametric representation of a TES model in small incremental stages; it, further, provides visual feedback to guide the search process. The TEStool modeling environment has been shown to yield remarkably accurate TES models in a reasonable amount of time. It also alleviates the tedium of repetitive search, transforming the modeling process into a pleasant activity.

Further information on TES-related topics may be found in the reference list enclosed. The reader is referred to [15, 7, 8, 9] for TES theory; to [11, 17, 14] for TES modeling applications; and to [6, 16] for the TEStool modeling environment.

Acknowledgments

I am indebted to David Jagerman and Jon Hill for carefully reading and commenting on the manuscript.

References

[1] J.S. Bendat and A.G. Piersol. *Random Data*. Wiley, 1986.

[2] P. Bratley, B.L. Fox and L.E. Schrage. *A Guide to Simulation*. Springer-Verlag, New York, NY, 1987.

[3] D.R. Cox and P.A.W. Lewis. *The Statistical Analysis of Series of Events*. Methuen, 1968.

[4] W. Feller. *An Introduction to Probability Theory and Its Applications*. Vol. 2, 2nd edition, Wiley, 1971.

[5] K.W. Fendick, V.R. Saksena and W. Whitt. Dependence in Packet Queues. *IEEE Trans. on Comm.*, Vol. 37, 1173–1183, 1989.

[6] D. Geist and B. Melamed, "TEStool: An Environment for Visual Interactive Modeling of Autocorrelated Traffic", *Proceedings of the 1992 IEEE International Conference on Communications*, Chicago Illinois, 1285–1289, 1992.

[7] D. Jagerman and B. Melamed. The Transition and Autocorrelation Structure of TES Processes Part I: General Theory. *Stochastic Models*, Vol. 8, No. 2, 193–219, 1992.

[8] D. Jagerman and B. Melamed. The Transition and Autocorrelation Structure of TES Processes Part II: Special Cases. *Stochastic Models*, Vol. 8, No. 3, 499–527, 1992.

[9] D. Jagerman and B. Melamed. Spectral Analysis of Basic TES Processes. *Preprint*, NEC USA, Inc., Princeton, New Jersey, 1992.

[10] A.M. Law and W.D. Kelton. *Simulation Modeling & Analysis*, (second edition). McGraw-Hill, 1991.

[11] D.-S. Lee, B. Melamed, A. Reibman and B. Sengupta. TES Modeling for Analysis of a Video Multiplexor. *Performance Evaluation*, Vol. 16, 21–34, 1992.

[12] P.A.W. Lewis and E. McKenzie. Minification Processes and Their Transformations. *J. Appl. Prob.*, Vol. 28, 45–57, 1991.

[13] B. Liu and D.C. Munson. "Generation of a Random Sequence Having a Jointly Specified Marginal Distribution and Autocovariance". *IEEE Transactions on Acoustics, Speech and Signal Processing* Vol. 30, No. 6, 973–983, 1982.

[14] M. Livny, B. Melamed and A.K. Tsiolis. The Impact of Autocorrelation on Queuing Systems. *Management Science*, Vol. 39, No. 3, 322–339, 1993.

[15] B. Melamed. TES: A Class of Methods for Generating Autocorrelated Uniform Variates. *ORSA J. on Computing*, Vol 3, 317–329, 1991.

[16] B. Melamed, D. Goldsman and J.R. Hill. The TES Methodology: Nonparametric Modeling of Stationary Time Series. *Proceedings of the 1992 Winter Simulation Conference*, Arlington, Virginia, 135–144, 1992.

[17] B. Melamed and B. Sengupta. "TES Modeling of Video Traffic". *IEICE Transactions on Communications*, Vol. E75-B, No. 12, 1291–1300, 1992.

[18] B.E. Patuwo, R.L. Disney and D.C. McNickle. The Effects of Correlated Arrivals on Queues. *IIE Tranactions*, Vol. 25, No. 3, 105–110, 1993.

[19] A.R. Reibman, "DCT-based Embedded Coding for Packet Video,", *Signal Processing: Image Communication*, Vol. 3, 231–237, 1991.

[20] B.W. Schmeiser. Simulation Experiments. In *Handbook of Operations Research and Management Science: Vol. 2* (D. Heyman and M. Sobel, editors). North Holland, New York, 1990.

[21] R.H. Thaler. *The Winner's Curse*. The Free Press, 1992.

Performance Engineering of Client-Server Systems

C. Murray Woodside
Real-Time and Distributed Systems Group
Carleton University
Ottawa K1S 5B6, Canada
email: cmw@sce.carleton.ca

Abstract

A great many distributed applications have a client-server architecture, and many more are being planned, including transaction processing systems, network services, and computational services. Almost all systems based on remote procedure calls (RPC) have a client-server structure and distributed processing architecture such as DCE (Distributed Computing Environment) from the open System Foundation do too. The performance of these systems has an unsettling characteristic because of the blocking nature of almost all RPC, that the service times of the software server tasks are not constant, but increase with load. This makes it more necessary than normal to model the performance of the system, using a model that incorporates this effect. Further, this effect also can modify the location of bottlenecks, and create "software bottlenecks" which are difficult to diagnose in advance.

1.0 Introduction

Client-server architectures are suitable for a wide variety of distributed systems. For this reason several proposals for standards for open distributed computing are based on a client-server architectures, with remote procedure calls (RPC) to servers. The DCE "Distributed Computing Environment" of the Open System Foundation is an example [1]. Also, operating systems such as SUN-OS, Mach and V which support distribution often provide many standard services through RPC to servers outside the kernel. Because of the many different potential sources of delay (in communications delays and overheads, in the server themselves, and in queues of requests at congested servers), performance must be carefully engineered.

This tutorial describes the performance aspects of client server (CS) systems. It begins with a canonical CS notation describing the relationship of the various processes, with examples. The notation includes parameters which summarize the workload in a simple way. A feature of the CS notation is that it treats resources of all kinds - software and hardware - uniformly. Once a system has been described with structure and parameters it can be solved by simulation, by well-established techniques, or by analytic calculations. The basis of the analytic methods is described.

A special phenomenon in CS systems is the *software bottleneck*, in which a software process can be effectively saturated by time it spends blocked waiting for responses from other servers. This may cause a system to saturate even though its processors are substantially under-utilized. The phenomenon of software bottlenecks is explained and their removal by *cloning* is studied in the final section.

2.0 The CS Notation for Client-Server Systems

The basic relationships in a Client Server system are illustrated in Figure 1. Requests are indicated by an arrow from the client (which sends the request in a message) to the server (which serves it and sends a reply). A "pure client" task only sends requests, as at the top of the figure; a pure server only receives them, and some tasks like the one in the middle do both.

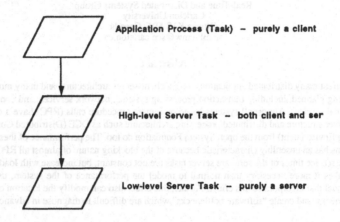

Application Process (Task) — purely a client

High-level Server Task — both client and ser

Low-level Server Task — purely a server

Figure 1. Clients and Servers: Architectural Relationships

The oval indicates a processor used by the middle server; in the CS notation a processor is also regarded as a server to the software task. For simplicity the processor servers may be omitted in some diagrams. Figure 2 shows the parts of a generic distributed database system. Figure 3 shows a frequently-discussed client-server configuration, in which the users and their terminals are also represented by "tasks" for the purposes of modelling, as are the disk controller and disk devices. The Client task typically does presentation management (screens and some verification) and the Server does the rest.

Notice that the CS architectural model is a *graph* with nodes for tasks and arcs for requests. The model assumes there are *no cycles* in the graph - that is, no closed path formed by following the arrows. Then the model has a set of topmost clients, representing human users or autonomous "demon" processes that generate work, and some pure servers at the bottom representing devices and processors.

In CS notation the service given by a server task may have two parts called "phases" as indicated in Figure 4. *Phase 1* is that part executed between receiving the request and sending the reply. For server i, phase 1 can be described by the parameters

s_{i1} = execution time on the processor for server i

y_{ij1} = the mean number of requests to another server j.

After sending the reply, *phase 2* is what is executed until the next message is received. It may be just necessary overhead, including buffer cleanup and task re-initialization or control code and in some cases a context switch (if there is no message waiting to be processed immediately). It may also include substantial work which is deliberately kept until after the reply to avoid delaying the client. A typical example is delayed writes to disk to update data, or to log the transaction. The second phase has the parameters s_{i2} and y_{ij2}, corresponding to those for phase 1. This model is defined more fully in [2] and [3].

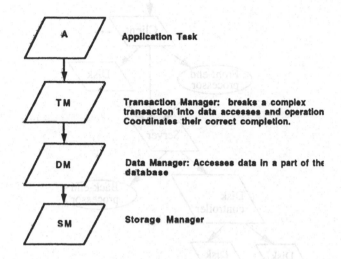

Figure 2. Example: On-Line Transaction Processing and Distributed Database Generic Architecture

The "service time" of a software server, as seen by its clients, is the total length of its first phase. The second phase cannot however be ignored, because it can delay the next client in the queue. The delay effect must be found by solving a performance model, for it depends on the probability that the next client arrives before the second phase is finished.

A Behavioral Model

The structural CS model with its parameters s and y (as defined above) is shown in its basic form in Figure 5(a). Figure 5(b) shows a flow graph for the CS view of the execution of one phase of task i, labelled phase p. In this view the execution is divided into "slices" of equal average length and the choice of whether to end the phase or to make a nested service request to another server is random. Defining $Y = 1 + \Sigma_j y_{ijp}$,

- The mean slice length is s_{ip}/Y

- the probability of ending the the slice with a request to server j is y_{ijp}/Y,

- the probability of ending the phase is $1/Y$.

The random choice models a data-dependent choice. Other behavioral models are possible. A particularly useful one is the "deterministic choice" model with exactly y_{ijp} requests to server j.

The random choice models a data-dependent choice. Other behavioral models are possible. A particularly useful one is the "deterministic choice" model with exactly y_{ijp} requests to server j.

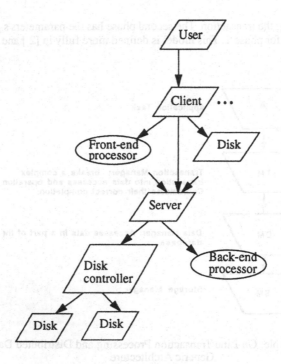

Figure 3. Client Front-end and Server Back-end

The topmost clients do not receive requests. In the CS model these clients *constantly cycle*. The cycle may include an average "think and type" time representing time before a user enters the next request. Seen as a "task" therefore the topmost clients are always busy. Since they never respond to requests or send replies their execution is modelled as *phase 2 only.*

3.0 Performance Factors in Client-Server Systems.

The service time of a software server is strongly load-dependent. This is the key property which makes client-server systems difficult to understand, and which makes performance modelling pay off. Figure 6 shows why. The service time x_{il} is made up of execution intervals (shaded) alternating with gaps for nested requests to another server, say server j.

Both the gaps and the execution intervals, when closely examined, include a waiting time which is load-dependent, and a service time. If the lower level queueing delays increase, the server i service time increases, even though much of this time is just "gaps". In this way server i could be saturated, meaning it is never idle, even though it is not executing for most of the time. This is a "software bottleneck"

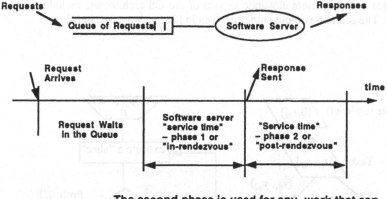

The second phase is used for any work that can be done after the response to the client:, such as buffer clean-up, logging, or data commitment. Pipelined work is also done in phase 2.

Figure 4. Synchronous Client-Server Interaction - A Template

Software bottlenecks tend to propagate upwards because they cause delays in higher level tasks in the CS diagram. This is illustrated in Figure 7. The left side shows a client task which makes infrequent requests from lightly loaded servers, which are therefore not very busy. The topmost client tasks in the CS model however are assumed to loop for ever and to never be "idle". This means that by convention the topmost client is always saturated, and it is shown shaded to indicate this. When only the topmost clients are saturated, as on the left, the system is lightly loaded.

The middle and right-hand sides of Figure 7 show saturated servers. In the middle, the 2nd level is heavily loaded, perhaps by having more clients. This has a push-up effect and the client cycle times are now longer, due to waiting. On the right side, the bottom server is saturated by requests from many clients. It now has long waiting, which saturates the middle server even if, by itself, it would not be saturated; this then affects the topmost client response time and throughput.

The system *capacity* is the throughput (or set of throughputs) which saturates the system. Typically saturation has a focus at a *bottleneck point* like the middle server in the middle case of Figure 7, which in turn saturates tasks above it in the CS architecture. Because service times are load dependent, they must be found by analyzing contention - they cannot be found from an examination of static parameters in the model.

4.0 Solving for Performance in Client-Server Systems

The previous section showed that an estimate of the mean waiting time at some servers is necessary in order to compute the system capacity. Simulation can be used to get these estimates, or an analytic model can be used. This section shows some relation ships between quantities in the system, and briefly describes analytic modelling. It also describes a slightly more elaborate version of the CS architecture including distinct task *entries*. The solution without entries is given in [2]; with entries, in [3].

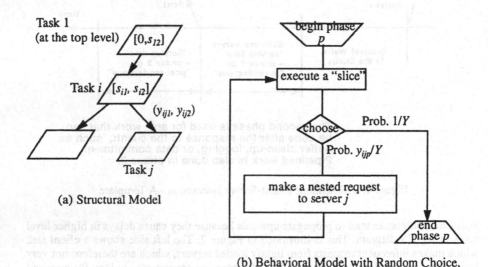

(a) Structural Model

(b) Behavioral Model with Random Choice,
for task *i*, phase *p*.

Figure 5. Structural and Behavioral Model of a Server

Components of Delay at a Server

The service time of server i is determined as follows:

- x_{i1} = phase 1 service time, between "begin service", and "send reply"

- x_{i2} = phase 2 service time, between send reply and next "receive request"

Supposing the server has a private processor, so it does not wait to execute:

$x_{ip} = s_{ip} + \Sigma_j y_{ijp} (w_{ij} + x_{j1})$

s_{ip} = execution time of server *i* in phase *p*

y_{ijp} = mean number of requests to server *j* in phase *p*

w_{ij} = mean queue wait at server *j*

x_{j1} = phase 1 service time at the nested server *j*

To include processor contention, let the processor also be a server. The parameters for requests from server i to its own processor are:

$y_{i,processor,p} = 1 + \Sigma_j y_{ijp}$

$x_{processor,p} = s_{processor,p} = s_{ip} / y_{i,processor,p}$

Then the service time of phase p is:

$x_{jp} = \Sigma_j y_{ijp} (w_{ij} + x_{j1})$ (where the sum over j includes the processor)

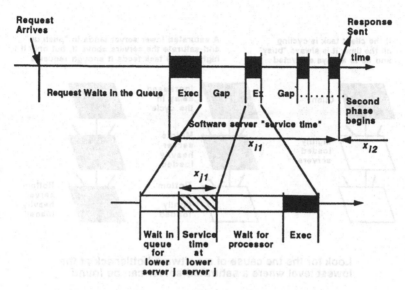

Figure 6. Recursive Expansion of Delays at Server i

Modifications for Separate Services ("Entries")

A server may offer several services, each with a separate address, or port, or (in a term used in the Ada language) "entry". We assume a single common queue with a FIFO discipline, or a priority queue in which priority is given to different entries.

Examples of different services are: *create record, read record, update record*. Figure 8 shows the modification made to the CS structure diagram for entries. The task node is divided and separate s and y parameters are attached to each entry. Figure 8 also shows an entry introduced to represent the processor execution of entry e, along the lines just described. The resulting equations are:

x_{ep} = service time of entry e, phase p. The entry belongs to task i.

$x_{ep} = \Sigma_d y_{edp} (w_{ed} + x_{d1})$

y_{edp} = mean number of requests to entry d, in phase p

w_{ed} = mean queue wait at server j, entry d

x_{d1} = phase 1 service time at the nested server j, entry d

As before, y and x for the processor of server j are found from s_{ep}.

To solve for the performance of a CS model:

* the *inputs* are the s and y parameters

the *outputs* are the *w* and *x* parameters, particularly the x_{i2} values for the topmost clients. These clients then have throughputs $1/x_{i2}$, for client *i*.

The only difficulty is in estimating w_{ab} between entries *a* and *b*.

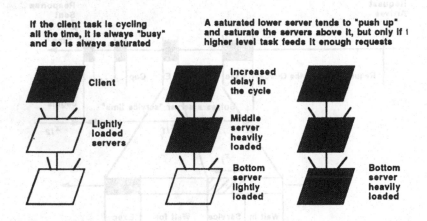

Look for the the cause of a software bottleneck at the
lowest level where a saturated server can be found

Figure 7. Vertical Dependency of Bottlenecks

Solving for waiting: Heuristic MVA [2]

An heuristic "mean value analysis" method has been developed. It finds w_{ab} as a sum of contributions from other tasks requesting service at *b*. Suppose a request from entry *a* of task *i* arrives to entry *b* of task *j*. It may find the server busy in various states, and it may find various competitor requests queued ahead of it. Its mean wait before starting service is:

$$w_{ab} = \Sigma_{c,d,p} \, V(a,b,d,p) \, \text{Prob}\{InService(a,b,c,d,p)\} + \Sigma_{c,d} \, x_{dp} \, \text{Prob}\{InQueue(a,b,c,d)\}$$

InService(a,b,c,d,p) signifies that the server is executing a request from entry *c* to entry *d*, and the server is in phase *p* of entry *d*. Then $V(a,b,d,p)$ is the "mean residual time" for the entry *d*.

InQueue(a,b,c,d) signifies that a request from entry *c* to entry *d* is in the queue ahead of it, when a request from entry *a* of task *i* arrives to entry *b* of task *j*.

Figure 9 illustrates the arrival states.

The notation $V(a,b,d,p)$ in the first term stands for the mean residual time of the service being executed at the arrival instant, if any.

Mean Residual Time $V(a,b,d,p)$ = (mean residual time of entry *d*, phase *p*) + (phases beyond *p*)

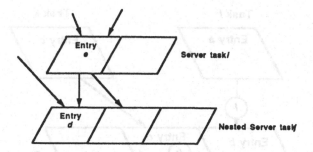

Figure 8. CS "Entry" Notation for Separate Services

The mean residual time of a phase depends on

- the mean and variance of the execution "slices" by the server task itself, in this phase
- the mean and variance of the gaps (nested services)
- the number of each of these (slices = gaps + 1).

The computation of V depends on the internal structure of a phase. Examples of phase structure for which V has been computed are:

- "stochastic" phase, with random number of each nested service (geometric distribution)
- "deterministic" phase, with a fixed number of each kind of nested service.

Standard techniques give the calculation.

Tools

Solution tools are available for these models. A heuristic MVA solver combines these equations in an iterative process. Petriu has improved the probability estimates by a detached Markovian analysis called "Task-Directed Aggregation" (TDA) (Aug. 91). Rolia has adapted standard queueing analysis techniques to solve one layer at a time, for systems with a strict layering [4].

The assumptions made by the analytic solvers are

- exponential "slice" execution times
- random or deterministic choice within a phase.

They are also capable of dealing with arrivals from outside at a stated rate, and with multiple copies of a task representing a set of identical clients, making up a server pool. In the "deterministic choice" model the service times can have general distributions.

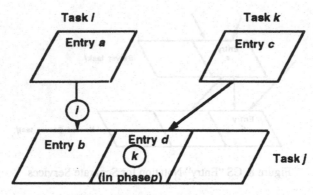

Figure 9. (a) An illustration of the arrival state InService(a,b,c,d,p)

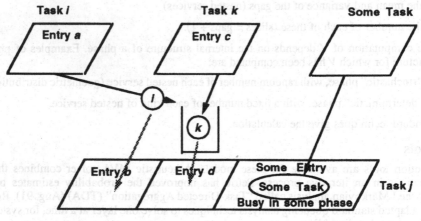

Figure 9. (b) An illustration of the arrival state InQueue(a,b,c,d)

404

Client I makes requests to Entry I of the server. Client I has one phase of length and entry I of the server has two phases of length t_{i1} and s_{i2}.

Figure 10(a). Basic Clients and One Server

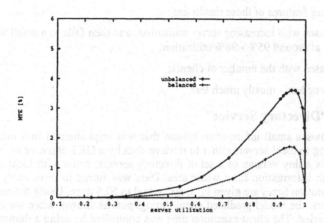

Figure 10(b). Errors for Various Server Utilizations

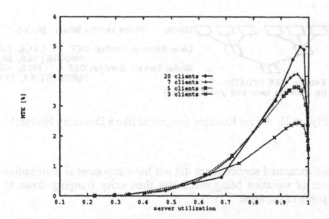

Figure 10(c). Errors for Various Numbers of Clients

Figure 10. Clients with separate service parameters (Entries)

Example: Basic Clients and One Server

A basic system with N clients and one server is shown in Figure 10(a), a separate entry for each client. The error of analytic modelling depends on the server utilization as shown in Figure 10(b). The Figure shows the magnitude of the largest throughput error among the N clients - the average error was much smaller. The results were found using TDA, which is exact for 2 clients. Figure 10(b) is for 5 clients, and for "balanced" service (all entries equal) and "unbalanced" (with service parameters varying over a range of an order of magnitude). Figure 10(c) is for various numbers of "unbalanced" clients, up to 20.

The outstanding features of these results are

- error increases with increasing server utilization, and then falls to a small value, with a peak value at around 95% - 98% utilization;

- error increases with the number of clients;

- error is 5% or less - mostly much less.

Example: "Directory Service"

Figure 11 shows a small information system that was implemented in a multiprocessor testbed running to local servers either to retrieve data by a GET entry, or to enter data by UPDATE. It is a tiny version of a set of directory servers, some with local information, and some with information for a wider area. Data was stored in in-memory tables, and measured execution times are given in "ticks" equal to 50.5 μsec. Using the measured service parameters, the model predicted client throughputs as shown, when the client "think time" x was varied. The client execution time was controlled by using a dummy loop. The error against the measured values again increased with load, since the load on the server is greater when x is smaller.

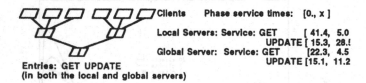

Clients   Phase service times: [0., x]

Local Servers: Service: GET   [41.4, 5.0
                            UPDATE [15.3, 28.!
Global Server: Service: GET   [22.3,   4.5
                            UPDATE [15.1,   11.2

Entries: GET UPDATE
(In both the local and global servers)

Figure 11. A Tiny Example Structured like a Directory Hierarchy

Notice that the measured service times did not have exponential distributions, shown by the coefficients of variation being much less than unity (ranging down to 0.04). This accounts for some of the error.

5.0 The Nature of Software Bottlenecks

Section 3 described how server saturation "pushes up" on higher-level processes, producing bottlenecks above them. A software server can be saturated even when its processor is not saturated, by dividing its service periods among requests for a variety of lower servers.

This section studies this effect through an example, beginning with a database server shown in Figure 14. It takes 20 time units to serve a request. Each of its 10 clients takes only 10 units to prepare the next request, so the database server is saturated. As it has its own processor that too is saturated (at least as the model is shown in Figure 14) it is a main-memory database with no secondary storage.

To relieve the bottleneck, the parts requiring mutual exclusion were factored out and re-allocated to three separate server tasks, each with a processor of its own, showin in Figure 15. The request goes to a dispatcher task which routes the parts to the servers, in order. There is shown no additional overhead for controlling the more complex execution path, and messaging; there is still 20 units of work per request, 2 units at the dispatcher and 6 at each server, in various combinations of first and second phases. Now the dispatcher can be run in multiple copiesl or clones, allowing requests to run in parallel.

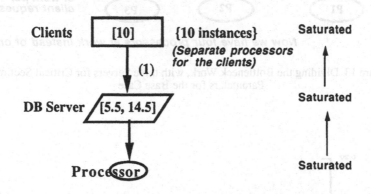

Figure 12. Original Case: Saturated DB Server

Figure 16 shows the effect of varying the number of clones. Perfect speedup with 4 processors and 20 sec of work per response would be 4x0.05, or 0.2 responses/sec; 50 clones give 0.156/sec. As there are 10 clients, it might be supposed that 10 clones would give all the available benefit, but the various second phases in the software make further gains possible up to 50 clones.

407

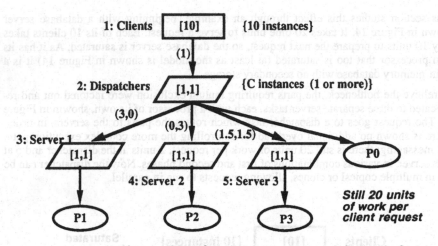

Figure 13. Dividing the Bottleneck Work, with three Servers for Critical Sections
Parameters for the Base Case

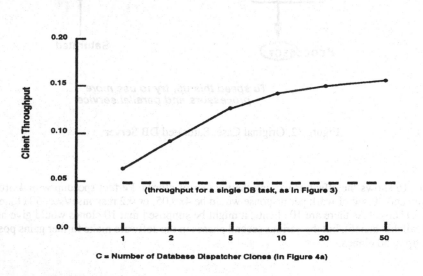

C = Number of Database Dispatcher Clones (in Figure 4a)

Figure 4c Base Case Client Throughput against Cloning Level

Figure 14. Results of Cloning the Dispatcher in the Base Case

Table 1. Full Results for the Base Case

Cloning Level	1	2	5	10	20	50
Client Throughput	0.065	0.093	0.126	0.143	0.152	0.156
Dispatcher Cycle	15.2	21.4	39.6	69.9	109.4	153.4
Dispatcher Queueing	135	86.6	49.4	25.8	7.9	0.74
Server 1 Queueing	0.54	1.23	3.27	6.38	8.35	8.85
Server 2 Queueing	0.54	1.22	3.25	6.73	13.0	24.3
Server 3 Queueing	0.36	1.00	2.93	6.13	11.3	14.2
Dispatcher Utilization:						
Task (each clone)	1.0	0.999	0.999	0.990	0.836	0.478
Processor	0.128	0.182	0.247	0.280	0.298	0.307
Server 1 Utilization	0.393	0.560	0.755	0.854	0.915	0.937
Server 2 Utilization	0.393	0.556	0.755	0.862	0.912	0.935
Server 3 Utilization	0.394	0.558	0.756	0.860	0.916	0.936
Bottleneck Strength	2.54	1.78	1.32	1.15	0.91	0.51
Actual ratio	2.40	1.68	1.23	1.09	1.03	1.03

Table 1 shows detailed results, including the task queueing delays and server utilization, found by simulation.

Software Bottleneck Strengh

We will now provide an operational definition of a software bottleneck:

A software bottleneck occurs when a task or its clone set exhibits a high utilization which is also high relative to the utilizations of all of its servers, either direct or indirect.

The second clause is necessary to differentiate between those tasks which may show high utilizations because of lower level bottlenecks and those which are at the root of the problem. It will be shown later that significant performance gains are possible only if the true bottleneck is identified and cloned.

In the Base Case with C = 1 the bottleneck is at the dispatcher because all three bottom level servers and its processor have lower utilizations. The bottleneck stays at the dispatcher up to C = 10.

The "bottleneck strength" of a task or its clone set is the ratio of its utilization to that of its most highly utilized server, direct or indirect.

If the bottleneck is somehow removed, and the limit is then determined by that most highly utilized server, then the bottleneck strength is also the ratio of the later throughput to the earlier one. To this extent the strength predicts the gain in performance through cloning. Let task b be the candidate bottleneck and U_i be the utilization of task i, for each task i which is a direct or indirect server of task b (including its processor). Then the bottleneck strength at task b is B_b defined by:

$$B_b = U_b / (\max_i U_i)$$

and the throughput after cloning task b cannot be greater than B_b times the value before cloning.

In the Base Case with $C = 1$, $B = 2..54$ and thru $= 0.65$; this predicts a potential throughput of 1.65, while the actual potential is 1.56. This is quite a close prediction.

Now returning to Table 1 we can calculate the bottleneck strength of the dispatches in the first column as BA=1.0/0.394=2.54. This is intended to predict the available gain due to cloning the administrator; if we examine the gain at 50 clones we find the throughput increase is a ratio of 0.156/0.065=2.40. More clones would perhaps give a little more gain, closer to 2.54; in any case it is close.

If we begin at 10 clones the measured bottleneck strength is only 1.15 and the experimentally obtained gain is 1.09 - again close.

Just in case this close agreement was due to the particular pattern of first and second phases the entire experiment was repeated for several other cases including all phase-1 - with similar results.

Table 2. The Nature of Software Bottlenecks

For the familiar bottleneck in a queueing network:	For a "Software Bottleneck":
• typically one saturated resource	• several, due to pushback
• relief by	
- speeding it up	- less effective
- adding resources	- YES
• throughput increase is locally proportional to	
- speedup at the sat. point	- less than proportional
- added resources	- YES, proportional
• bottleneck location is determined by a simple analysis of the parameters	• NO, requires a contention analysis

Table 2 summarizes the differences we see between the familiar "hardware" bottleneck, such as a processor or i/o device, and a software bottleneck as defined here. The reason that code speeding gives less than proportional system speedup is that the saturated server spends only part of the time executing its own code; the rest is spent blocked. Speedups which result in fewer requests will also be helpful but are not in the Table.

6.0 Conclusions

In this tutorial

- Service times in software servers were characterized in terms of nested services.
- "Rendezvous Networks" notation provides a compact view of the workload and communications relationships of client-server systems.
- Solution techniques were described based on queueing analysis.
- Locating *Software Bottlenecks* often requires a contention analysis.

7.0 Bibliography

[1]   W. Rosenberry and D. Kenney, "Understanding DCE", published by O'Reilly & Associates, Inc.,103 Morris Street, Suite A, Sebastopol, CA 95472, U.S.A.

[2]   C. M. Woodside, "Throughput Calculation for Basic Stochastic Rendezvous Networks", *Performance Evaluation*, vol. 9, n. 2, pp. 143-160, April 1989.

[3]   C. M. Woodside, J. E. Neilson, D. C. Petriu and S. Majumdar, "The Stochastic Rendezvous Network Model for Performance of Synchronous Multi-Tasking Distributed Software, *IEEE Transactions on Computer*, under review.

[4]   J. A. Rolia, "Predicting the Performance of Software Systems", PhD thesis, University of Toronto, January 1992.

QUEUEING NETWORKS WITH FINITE CAPACITIES

Raif O. Onvural, IBM, Research Triangle Park, NC 27709

1. INTRODUCTION

Queueing theory has been developed to predict the performance characteristics of computer systems, production systems, communications systems, and flexible manufacturing systems. A queueing system consists of a number of nodes connected according to the topology of the system being modeled. Each node consists of a service facility and a queue for customers to wait when the service facility can not provide service to these customers.

Queueing networks may be classified as open and closed. In an open model, customers arrive at the network from outside, receive service at one or more nodes, and eventually leave the network. In closed queueing networks, there is a fixed population of customers circulating in the network at all times. Both types of networks have been frequently used in the literature as models of complex service systems.

Queueing networks have been studied in the literature under a multiplicity of assumptions. Most performance metrics of interest can be obtained from the joint steady state queue length distribution of the model. Almost all queueing networks of practical importance can, in theory, be solved numerically. However, in practice, obtaining the solution may not always be possible. In particular, the number of equations can easily reach millions, even for simple models, making it infeasible to solve the linear system of equations. Other two methods developed to analyze such networks are simulation and heuristics. Two major problems with simulations are determining how close the simulation results are to the exact values and how long to run a simulation to obtain accurate estimates. Heuristics have been developed to obtain the performance metrics of interest approximately when it is expensive to use the other methods. The main problem with heuristics is to bound the error in the solution. Perhaps, one of the most pioneering results in queueing networks is that under certain assumptions on the system parameters, it has been shown that the joint steady state queue length distribution of a class of queueing networks is the product of some particular functions of nodes. Product form networks are relatively easier to study and various algorithms have been developed in the literature to obtain the exact values of their performance metrics of interest.

Almost all queueing networks with product form queue length distributions require infinite queues, that is, it is assumed that there is always a space in the queue for arriving customers. In real systems, the storage space is always finite. Hence, a more realistic model of such systems requires modeling finite node capacities. An important feature of queueing networks with finite queues is that the flow of customers through a node may be momentarily stopped when another node in the network reaches its capacity. That is, a phenomenon called *blocking* occurs. In particular, consider a simplistic view of a computer communications system. The individual queues represent the finite space which is available for intermediate storage and servers correspond to communication channels. A message may not be transmitted until the destination node has space available to store the message, thus, sometimes causing the blocking of communication to that node. Similarly, in production systems, intermediate storage areas have finite capacities. A unit completing its service at a station may be forced to occupy the machine until there is a space available in the next station. While the unit blocks the machine, it may not be possible for the machine to process other units waiting in its queue.

In addition to the problem of blocking, *deadlocks* may occur in queueing networks with finite queues. A set of nodes is in a deadlock state when every node in the set is waiting for a space to become available at another node in the set. In this case, corresponding servers are blocked, and they can never get unblocked because the required space required will never be available.

Queueing networks with blocking are difficult to solve: in general, their steady state queue length distributions could not be shown to have product form solutions. Hence, most of the techniques that are employed to analyze these networks are in the form of approximations, simulation, and numerical techniques. In recent years, there has been a growing interest in the development of computational methods for the analysis of both open and closed queueing networks with blocking. A comprehensive survey of the literature on open queuing networks with blocking was compiled by Perros [1989] and on closed queueing networks with blocking by Onvural [1989] in addition to the two workshops and two special issues in this area (cf. Perros and Altiok [1988], Akyildiz and Perros [1989], and Onvural and Akyildiz [1992a] and [1992b]).

1.1. Blocking Mechanisms

The effect of a full node on its downstream nodes depends on the type of the system being modeled. To model different characteristics of various real life systems with finite resources, various blocking mechanisms that define distinct models of blocking have been reported in the literature. In particular, each blocking mechanism defines when a node is blocked, what happens during the blocking period, and how a node becomes unblocked. The most commonly used blocking mechanisms are classified as follows:

1.1.1. Blocked After Service (BAS)

A customer upon completion of its service at node i attempts to enter destination node j. If node j at that moment is full, the customer is forced to occupy server i until it enters destination node j, and node i is blocked. Node i remains blocked for this period of time, and server i can not serve any other customer which might be waiting in its queue. In queueing networks with arbitrary topologies, it is possible that a number of nodes may be blocked by the same node simultaneously. This necessitates imposing an ordering on the blocked nodes to determine which node will be unblocked first when a departure occurs from the blocking node. This problem has not been elaborated on in the literature. We are only aware of the *First-Blocked-First-Unblocked* rule (FBFU), which states that the node which was blocked first will be unblocked first. It is possible that deadlocks might occur in queueing networks under BAS blocking. It was assumed in the literature that deadlocks in networks under BAS blocking can be detected immediately and resolved by instantaneously exchanging blocked customers. Lemma 1 below gives the necessary and sufficient condition for a network under BAS blocking to be deadlock free, where a *cycle* in a network is defined as a directed path that starts and ends at the same node.

Lemma 1: A closed queueing network with K customers under BAS blocking is deadlock free if and only if for each cycle, C, in the network $K < \sum_{j \in C} B_j$ where B_j is the capacity of node j.

Simply stated, the total number of customers in the network must be smaller than the sum of node capacities in each cycle.

The BAS blocking (also referred to as type 1 blocking, manufacturing blocking, classical blocking, and transfer blocking) has been used to model systems such as production systems and disk I/O subsystems. In particular, consider a simplistic view of a production system consisting of a sequence stations. The availability of a storage space in the next station has no effect on the operation of a machine until it completes its service. Upon service completion, if there is no space available in the destination station then there are two possibilities: the unit which completed its service at node i is 1) moved back from the i-th machine to the storage area of machine i (i.e. its queue) allowing a unit to enter service, or 2) allowed to occupy the machine, blocking the operation for other units waiting in the storage space (i.e. BAS blocking). In most cases, it may not be possible to move the unit from the machine back to the storage area due to the physical constraints of the unit, the system, or both. Hence, the operation of the machine is blocked until there is a space available at the destination station. An exception to this is considered in Mitra and Mitrani [1988] where a blocked customer is moved back to its queue in the context of open networks to model the Japanese Kenban scheme, used for cell coordination in production lines.

1.1.2. Blocked Before Service (BBS)

A customer at node i declares its destination node j before it starts receiving its service. If node j is full, the i-th node becomes blocked. When a departure occurs from the destination node j, node i is unblocked and its server starts serving the customer. If the destination node j becomes full during the service of a customer at node i, then the service is interrupted and node i is blocked. The service is resumed from the interruption point as soon as a space becomes available at the destination node. Depending upon whether the customer is allowed to occupy the service area when the server is blocked, the following sub-categories are distinguished.

BBS-SNO (Server is Not Occupied): Service facility of a blocked node can not be used to hold a customer.

BBS-SO (Server is Occupied): Service facility of a blocked node is used to hold a customer.

In BBS blocking mechanism, a full node j blocks all nodes i that are connected to it (i.e. $p_{ij} > 0$). When a departure occurs from node j, all blocked nodes become unblocked simultaneously and start serving their customers. Hence, there is no need to impose any ordering on the blocked nodes, unlike BAS blocking.

The BBS blocking mechanism (also called type 2 blocking, immediate blocking, service blocking, communications blocking) is motivated by considering servers which only move customers between stations and do no other work on them. In this case, the lack of downstream space must force the server to shut down.

The distinction between BBS-SO and BBS-SNO blocking mechanisms is meaningful when modeling different types of systems. For example, in communication networks, a server correspond to a communication channel. If there is no space in the downstream node then messages can not be transmitted. Furthermore, the channel itself can not be used to store messages due to physical constraints of the channel, i.e. BBS-SNO blocking. On the other hand BBS-SO blocking results if the service facility can be used to hold the blocked customer which, in this case, would be an approximate modeling of the system.

BBS-SO blocking has been used to model manufacturing systems, terminal concentrators, mass storage systems, disk to tape back up systems, window flow control mechanisms, and communication systems. Modeling these systems with BBS-SO blocking assumes that when its destination buffer is full the device is forced to stop its operation and the service facility can be used to hold a customer. A disk to tape back up model illustrated in figure 1 comprised of three servers, and two finite buffers between servers. The first server is the disk and channel which transfers blocks of data from from the disk to the main memory. The second server, the Central Processing Unit (CPU), transfer data from the main memory to the tape drive. The last server represents the tape drive. One of the performance objectives of interest is the tape back up rate (i.e. the throughput of the system). Blocking occurs due to finite spaces available for intermediate storage.

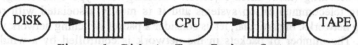

Figure 1: Disk to Tape Backup System

A simple terminal concentrator consists of a number of terminals, a concentrator, and a channel to transfer data to the main memory. The system configuration is the same as the disk to tape backup system illustrated above in figure 1 with the concentrator, the channel and the CPU replacing the disk, the CPU and the tape respectively. The two buffers in this terminal concentrator system have finite capacities which cause blocking of respective nodes. We note that the above examples are only sub-systems of larger configurations of computer systems, used only to illustrate the possibility of blocking due to finite storage capacities between the devices of such systems.

Queueing networks under BBS blocking are not always well defined for arbitrary topologies with an arbitrary number of customers in the network. This is because deadlocks in this blocking mechanism can not be resolved without violating its rules. As an example, let us assume that node i is blocked by node j and node j is blocked by node i. Then, the services at both nodes are suspended. Furthermore, the service can not start unless the blocking mechanism is temporarily switched to, for example, BAS blocking. In view of this, this blocking mechanism can only be used in deadlock free networks. Similar to lemma 1, it can be shown that a closed queueing network with BBS blocking is deadlock free if and only if for each cycle C in the network, i) $K< \sum_{j \in C} \{B_j - 1\}$ in BBS-SNO blocking, and ii) $K< \sum_{j \in C} B_j$ in BBS-SO blocking. That is,

a closed network under BBS-SO blocking is deadlock free if the number of customers in the network is less than the sum of node capacities in each cycle in the network, while in BBS-SNO, a network is deadlock free if the number of customers in the network is less than the sum of queue capacities (node capacity minus one for the server facility) in each cycle.

1.1.3. Repetitive Service (RS)

A customer upon service completion at node i attempts to join destination node j. If node j at that moment is full, the customer receives another service at node i. This is repeated until the customer completes a service at node i at a moment that the destination node is not full. Within this category of blocking mechanisms, the following two sub-categories are distinguished:

RS-FD (Fixed Destination): Once the customer's destination is determined it can not be altered.

RS-RD (Random Destination): A destination node is chosen at each service completion independently of the destination node chosen the previous time.

Similar to BBS-SO blocking, a network under RS-FD blocking is deadlock free if and only if $K< \sum_{j \in C} B_j$ for each cycle in the network, i.e. the number of customers in the network is less than the capacity of each cycle in the network. On the other hand, it can be shown that a network under RS-RD blocking is deadlock free if there is a path from every node to every other node in the network and, in case of closed networks, if there is at least one free space in the network, i.e. not for each cycle. This is because the existence of a free space in the network guarantees that all blocked customers will eventually depart, unblocking their servers.

The RS blocking (also called rejection blocking and type 3 blocking) arise in modeling telecommunication systems and it is mostly associated with reversible queueing networks. In particular, let us consider a packet switching network with fixed routing. The number of packets in the network is controlled by a window flow mechanism. A node transmits a packet to a destination node and waits for an acknowledgement. If the destination node does not accept the packet due to the fact that there is a lack of space, it will not send an acknowledgement. In this case, the packet may be retransmitted (RS-FD blocking) until it is accepted by the destination node (i.e.until an acknowledgement is received by the sender). Similarly, consider a manufacturing system consisting of a network of automated work stations (WS) linked by a computer controlled material handling device (MHD) to transport work-pieces that are to be processed from one station to another as illustrated in figure 2.

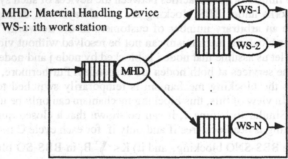

MHD: Material Handling Device
WS-i: ith work station

Figure 2: A Queueing Model of a Flexible Manufacturing System

In these systems, if a work-piece finds the next station full, then it has to wait for the next turn of the MHD. At the next turn, there are two possibilities: i) the work-piece can only be processed by one station, therefore, the next attempt can only be made to the previously chosen station (i.e. RS-FD blocking), or ii) the unit may be processed by all stations, hence, the next station is chosen independent of the previous choice(s) (i.e. RS-RD blocking). If the service time of the MHD is assumed to be exponentially distributed, the RS-RD blocking is equivalent to the following: The work-piece attempts to enter station 1, if station 1 is full, then it tries station 2, and so on, until a space is found in one of the stations.

1.2. Equivalencies of Blocking Mechanisms

Comparisons between these distinct types of blocking mechanisms have been carried out to obtain an equivalence between different blocking mechanisms applied to the same network. Two blocking mechanisms are said to be equivalent if the network under consideration has the same rate matrix under the both types of blocking mechanisms. We note that, all of the equivalences obtained in the literature assume that the service times are exponentially distributed. Furthermore, these equivalences are most often true only for specific topologies: cyclic networks and the central server model shown in figure 3 (Onvural (1987) and Balsamo, et al. (1986)).

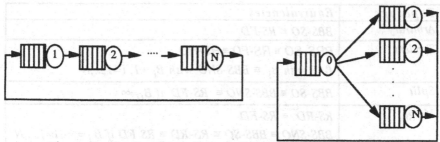

Figure 3: Cyclic Network and the Central Server Model

In the following two tables, the notation A ≡ B is used to denote that blocking mechanism A is equivalent to blocking mechanism B.

Topology	Equivalencies
Arbitrary	*BBS-SO ≡ RS-FD* *BBS-SO ≡ BBS-SNO for K≤min{B_i+B_j; i,j=1,...,N s.t.* *P_{ij}>0}-1*
Cyclic	*RS-FD ≡ RS-RD* *BBS-SNO with B_i ≡ BAS with B_i -1, i=1,...,N*
Central Server	*BBS-SO ≡ BBS-SNO if B_1=∞* *BBS-SO ≡ BBS-SNO if B_i = ∞, i=2,...,N* *RS-FD ≡ RS-RD if B_i = ∞, i=2,...,N*
Two node cyclic	*BBS-SNO ≡ BBS-SO ≡ RS-FD ≡ RS-RD* *BBS-SNO with B_1 and B_2 ≡ BAS with B_1 -1 and B_2 -1*

Table 1: Equivalencies of blocking mechanisms in closed networks

Similarly, equivalencies between different blocking mechanisms in open networks with finite capacity queues are given in table 2 for tandem, split, and merge configurations illustrated respectively in figure 4.

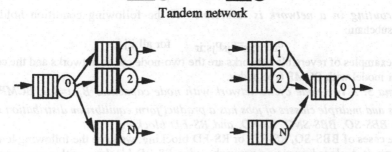

Tandem network

Split configuration   Merge configuration

Figure 4:Tandem, Split and Merge Configurations

Topology	Equivalencies
Arbitrary	BBS-SO ≡ RS-FD
Tandem	BBS-SO ≡ RS-FD ≡ RS-RD BAS with B_i ≡ BBS-SNO with B_i +1, i=1,...,N
Split	BBS-SO ≡ BBS-SNO ≡ RS-FD if $B_0 = \infty$
Merge	RS-RD ≡ RS-FD BBS-SNO ≡ BBS-SO ≡ RS-RD ≡ RS-FD if $B_i = \infty$, i=1,...,N
Two node tandem	BBS-SNO ≡ BBS-SO ≡ RS-FD ≡ RS-RD BBS-SNO with $B_1 = \infty$ and B_2 ≡ BAS with $B_1 = \infty$ and B_2 -1

Table 2: Equivalencies of blocking mechanisms in open networks

2. EXACT RESULTS

In special cases, networks with finite capacities are shown to have product form solutions. Furthermore, various exact results are obtained on the behavior of various performance measures of interest. These results are reviewed next.

2.1. Closed Networks

In this section, we present various exact results obtained in the literature for closed queueing networks with blocking.

2.1.1. Reversible Networks

A stochastic process $X(t)$ defined on the state space S is *reversible* if $\{X(t_1),...,X(t_n)\}$ has the same distribution as $\{X(t_0-t_1),...,X(t_0-t_n)\}$ for all $t_0, t_1,...,t_n$ $\in$T. All results in this sub-section can be explained as a consequence of the following lemma given in Kelly [1979].

Lemma 2: Consider a reversible Markov process with state space S and equilibrium distribution $\pi(j)$. If S is truncated to a sub-space A, then the Markov process is still reversible in equilibrium and it has distribution $\pi(j)/ \sum_{k \in A} \pi(k)$, k $\in$A.

A Markov process T(t) is called a *truncated process* of X(t) if it is irreducible and the state space of T(t) is a subset of the state space of X(t), i.e. the states of T(t) is a subset of X(t), and the transitions between the states of T(t) are the same as they are in X(t).

The *routing in a network is reversible* if the following condition holds for each subchain:

$$e_{ir}P_{ir;js} = e_{js}P_{js;ir} \quad \text{for all } i,j,r,s$$

Two examples of reversible networks are the two-node cyclic networks and the central server model with BCMP type nodes.

Lemma 3: A two-node cyclic network with node capacities B_i, i=1,2, BCMP type nodes and multiple classes of jobs has a product form equilibrium distribution under BAS, BBS-SO, BBS-SNO, RS-RD, and RS-FD blocking.

In the cases of BBS-SO, RS-RD, or RS-FD blocking, we have the following lemma.

Lemma 4: A closed queueing network under RS-RD blocking with node capacities B_i, multiple classes of jobs, BCMP type nodes, and state space A is a truncated process of the same network with infinite buffer capacities in which no more than B_i

jobs are allowed at node i. Furthermore, if the underlined Markov process of the network with infinite buffer capacities is reversible then the blocking network has a product form equilibrium distribution.

A closed queueing network under BAS blocking has a product form equilibrium distribution if the number of jobs in the network is equal to the minimum buffer capacity plus one. If this condition is met, then there can be at most one node in the network blocked at any time, and, the blocked node has exactly one job, i.e. the server's operation is not blocked. In this case, the server of a blocked node behaves like an additional buffer capacity to the blocking node.

Lemma 5: Consider a multi-class closed queueing network under BAS blocking. If

$$\sum_{i=1}^{R} K_r = min\{B_i, i=1,...,N\}+1 \text{ then the network has a product form equilibrium}$$

distribution.

2.1.2. Self Dual Networks

Closed queueing networks under BBS-SO blocking were first studied by Gordon and Newell [1967] in the context of cyclic networks. The service time at each node is assumed to be exponentially distributed. First, we will discuss the concept of holes as introduced by Gordon and Newell. Since the capacity of node j is B_j, let us imagine that this node consists of B_j cells. If there are i_j customers at node j, then i_j of these cells are occupied and B_j- i_j cells are empty. We may say that these empty cells are occupied by holes. Then, the total number of holes in the network is equal to $\sum_{j=1}^{N} B_j$-

K. As the customers move sequentially through the cyclic network, the holes execute a counter sequential motion since each movement of a customer from the j-th node to the (j+1)st node corresponds to the movement of a hole in the opposite direction (i.e. from the j+1st node to the j-th node). It is then shown that these two systems are *duals*. That is, if a customer (hole) at node j is blocked in one system then node j+1 has no holes (customers) in its dual. Let (B_i,μ_i) be the capacity and the service rate of node i and $\{ (B_1,\mu_1), (B_2,\mu_2),...., (B_N,\mu_N) \}$ be a cyclic network with K customers.

Then, its dual is $\{ (B_1,\mu_N, (B_N,\mu_{N-1}),...., (B_2,\mu_1) \}$ with $\sum_{j=1}^{N} B_j$-K customers. Let,

$p(\underline{n})$ and $p^D(\underline{n})$ be the steady state queue length probabilities of a cyclic network and its dual, respectively, where $\underline{n}=(i_1,i_2,...,i_N)$ is the state of the network with i_j being the number of customers at node j. Then, for all feasible states, we have:

$$p(i_1,i_2,....,i_N) = p^D(B_1-i_1, B_N-i_N,...,B_2-i_2)$$

We note that, if the number of customers in the network is such that no node can be empty, then the dual network is a non-blocking network (i.e. the number of holes is less than or equal to the minimum node capacity) and it has a product form queue length distribution. But then, from the concept of duality, the original network has a product form queue length distribution. Hence, we have the following lemma:

Lemma 6: Consider a cyclic network under BBS-SO blocking. The service time at each node is assumed to be exponentially distributed. The network has a product form based on the following three conjectures:

Conjecture 1: *The throughput of a closed queueing network with finite node capacities is less than or equal to the throughput of the same network with infinite node capacities, i.e. $\lambda(K) \leq \beta(K)$; $K=1,...,M$*

Conjecture 2: *Probability that a node is empty does not increase as the number of customers in the network increases, i.e. $p_i^K(0) \geq p_i^{K+1}(0)$, $K=1,...,M-1$, where $p_i^J(0)$ is the probability that node i is empty when there are J customers in the network.*

Conjecture 3: *Probability that a node is blocked does not decrease as the number of customers in the network increases, i.e. $p_i^{K+1}(b) \geq p_i^K(b)$, $K=1,...,M-1$, where $p_i^J(b)$ is the probability that node i is blocked when there are J customers in the network.*

Lemma 11: *Consider a closed exponential queueing network under BAS blocking, and let $M = \sum_{i=1}^N B_i$, $n=min\{B_i, i=1,...,N\}$, and $\lambda^* = \{\lambda(K), K=1,...,M\}$. For a moment, assume that the network has infinite queue capacities and let $\beta(K)$ be its throughput when there are K customers in it. Then: $\beta(n+1) \leq \lambda^* \leq \beta(M-min\{B_i, i=1,...,N\}+1)$. Now, let K^* be such that $\lambda^* = \lambda(K^*)$. Then:*

$$max \left(min \{B_j \text{ such that } p_{ij} \neq 0 \ j=1...N\} \ i=1...N \right) \leq K^* \leq M-min\{B_i, i=1,...,N\}+1$$

Next, we present some equivalencies between closed queueing networks with respect to the buffer capacities and the number of jobs in the network. Two networks are said to be equivalent if they have the same steady state queue length distribution.

Under certain restrictions, the steady state queue length distribution of a closed queueing network under BAS or BBS-SO blocking is identical for a range of values of K. Consider a closed queueing network with exponential servers. If there is a node m with $B_m > \sum_{i=1}^N B_i - B_m$, i.e. the buffer capacity of node m is greater than the remaining capacity of the network, then the following lemma presents a sufficient condition for the network to have the queue length distribution for a range of values of K.

Lemma 12: *Consider an exponential closed queueing network with node capacities B_i. Let $B_m = max\{B_i, i=1,...,N\}$. If $B_m > \sum_{i=1}^N B_i - B_m$ then the network has the same steady state queue length distribution for all $K \in S$, where*

i) $S=\{L: \sum_{i=1}^N B_i - B_m + 1 \leq L \leq B_m \}$ in BAS blocking, and, ii) $S=\{L: \sum_{i=1}^N B_i - B_m \leq L \leq B_m \}$ in BBS-SO blocking.

Furthermore, a closed network under BAS blocking with $K=B_m+1$ jobs has the same *queue length distribution if*

$$K \geq \sum_{i=1}^{N} B_i - min\{B_j, j=1,...,N\}.$$

2.1.3. Other Results

Let $\lambda_i(K)$ and $\lambda(K)$ be respectively the throughput of node i and the throughput of the network when there are K customers in the network. By definition, $\lambda_i(K)=\{1-P_i^K(0)-P_i^K(b)\}\mu_i$, where μ_i is the service rate, $P_i^K(0)$ and $P_i^K(b)$ are the probabilities that node i is empty and blocked respectively given that there are K customers in the network. Shanthikumar and Yao [1989] considered exponential cyclic queueing networks under BBS-SO blocking and they identified the conditions under which the performance measures are monotone in service rate, node capacity, and population size. Let $\mu_i(k)$ be the load dependent service rate at station i. Furthermore, let $\underline{B}=(B_1,...,B_N)$ and $\underline{\mu}=(\mu_1(k),...,\mu_N(k))$ be the vector of node capacities and service rates respectively. The main properties obtained by Shanthikumar and Yao are given as follows:

Lemma 7: *Consider a cyclic network under BBS-SO blocking with two sets of service rates,* $\mu_i^1(k)$, $\mu_i^2(n)$. *If* $\mu_i^1(k) \geq \mu_i^2(n)$, $k \geq n$, $i=1,...,N$, *then*

$$Throughput(\mu^1,\underline{B},K) \geq Throughput(\mu^2,\underline{B},K)$$

Lemma 8: *Consider a cyclic network under BBS-SO blocking with two sets of buffer capacities,* $\underline{B}^1$, $\underline{B}^2$ *and assume that* $\mu_i(k)$ *is increasing in k for each i, i=1,...,N. If* $\underline{B}^1 \geq \underline{B}^2$ *then*

$$Throughput(\mu,\underline{B}^1,K) \geq Throughput(\mu,\underline{B}^2,K)$$

Lemma 9: *Let* $B^*=max\{B_i, i=1,...,N\}$. *Then, for* $0<K<B^*$,

$$Throughput(\mu,\underline{B},K+1) \geq Throughput(\mu,\underline{B},K)$$

Lemma 9 states that throughput is non-decreasing with respect to the number of customers as long as the number of customers is less than the maximum node capacity in the network. Similarly, lemmas 7 and 8 illustrate the monotonicity of the throughput with respect to service rates and node capacities, respectively. In particular, lemma 7 states that the throughput of the network does not decrease if the service rate of a node (or a group of nodes) increases. Similarly, lemma 8 states that the throughput of the network is non-decreasing as the buffer capacity of a node (or a group of nodes) increases.

The following lemma is a consequence of self-duality in cyclic networks conjectured by Persone and Grillo [1987] and Onvural [1987].

Lemma 10: *An exponential cyclic network under BBS-SO blocking has the same throughput with K and* $\sum_{j=1}^{N} B_j-K$ *customers in it.*

Lemma 11 below provides bounds on the maximum throughput and the number of customers, K*, that produces the maximum throughput (Onvural [1987]), which is

blocking another node are aggregated into one state.
We note that a closed network with exactly one node with an infinite capacity is a special case that satisfies this condition.
Now, consider a closed queueing network under BAS blocking with K jobs such that the node with the maximum buffer capacity can not be empty. Then, the following lemma illustrates that if the buffer capacity of this node and the number of jobs in the network are increased by the same amount, then both networks have the same steady state queue length distribution.

Lemma 13: Consider an exponential closed queueing network under BAS blocking (CQN-1) and let node m has the maximum buffer capacity, i.e. $B_m=max\{B_j; j=1,...,N\}$. Also, consider another network with the same parameters as the CQN-1 except that the buffer capacity of node m is increased to B_m^* (CQN-2). Furthermore, assume that the number of jobs in CQN-1 be such that no node can be empty, i.e.
$$K \geq \sum_{i=1}^{N} B_i - B_m + 1.$$ *Then, CQN-1 with K jobs have the same steady state queue length distribution as CQN-2 with $K^* = K + B_m^* - B_m$ jobs.*

The concept of duality as introduced by Gordon and Newell does not provide a product form solution for closed queueing networks under BAS blocking, as these networks could not be shown to have self-dual configurations. However, the following corollary, which is a special case of lemma 12, illustrates that two networks under BAS blocking has the same steady state queue length distribution if they have the same dual network.

Corollary 1: Consider a CQN-1 under BAS blocking with K_1 jobs and buffer capacities B_i. Also consider a CQN-2 identical to CQN-1 but with K_2 jobs and buffer capacities C_i. If K_1 and K_2 are such that no node can be empty, then the two networks have the same steady state queue length distribution if they have the same number of holes, i.e. $\sum_{i=1}^{N} B_i - K_1 = \sum_{i=1}^{N} C_i - K_2$.

Let us now consider a deadlock free open queueing networks with multiple arrival streams and exponentially distributed service times, and, let A be the set of nodes in which arrivals occur. For each node $i \epsilon A$, the interarrival times are assumed to be distributed exponentially with rate l_i. To find its equivalent closed queueing network, we will add a node (node 0) to this network with parameters $B_0^*=\infty$, $\mu_0^*=\lambda=\sum_{i \epsilon A} \lambda_i$, and $p_{0i}^*=\lambda_i /\lambda$, $i \epsilon A$.

The total number of customers, K, in the CQN-B is set to be equal to $\sum_{i=1}^{N} B_i$. Departures in the open network are routed back to node 0 in the closed network. Furthermore, let node 0 in the closed network be subject to RS-RD blocking independent of the blocking mechanism used in the open network. Hence, we might have two different blocking mechanisms in the equivalent CQN-B. Then, we have:

Lemma 14: Consider a deadlock free open network under type i blocking, i=BAS, BBS, RS, and consider a closed network constructed as above. Node 0 is subject to RS-RD blocking while all other nodes are subject to type i blocking, same as in the open network. Let $K=\sum_{i=1}^{N} B_i$. Then, the two networks have the same rate matrix.

For other types of equivalencies between open and closed networks, i.e. with single arrival streams and multiple classes of customers, an interested reader may refer to Onvural and Perros [1988].

The throughput of cyclic networks under BAS blocking with number of customers being equal to the capacity of the network can be calculated efficiently using the following lemma.

Lemma 15: Consider an exponential cyclic network under BAS blocking with node capacities B_i and K customers. If K=M then the throughput of the network is equal to $1/E[max(X_1,X_2,...,X_N)]$ where X_i is the service time at node i. Furthermore, assuming X_i's are distributed exponentially with rate μ_i, we have:

$$E[max(X_1,X_2,...,X_N)] = \int_0^\infty (1-\prod_{i=1}^{N}(1-e^{-\mu_i t}))\, dt.$$

For presentation purposes, let us consider a cyclic network with N=3, K=3, and $B_i=1$, i=1,2,3. Let X_i be the service time at node i and without loss of generality assume that $X_1 \leq X_2 \leq X_3$. Furthermore, assume that at t=0 all servers are busy working. Then, at $t=X_3$, all three servers will become blocked and a deadlock will occur. If we assume that deadlocks are detected immediately and resolved by instantaneously exchanging the blocked customers then at $t=X_3$, customer at node 1 will go to node 2, customer at node 2 will go to node 3, and customer at node 3 will go to node 1. At this point in time, all servers will start a new service. The points at which all three servers start a new service are the renewal points and the throughput of the cyclic network is 1/(expected time between arrivals) by definition.

2.1.4. Symmetric Networks

In this section, we discuss the concept of indistinguishable nodes as introduced by Onvural [1987] and Persone and Grillo [1987] in symmetric cyclic networks. When applicable, this notion allows the solution of the rate matrix of such networks on a reduced state space. It can be used as an efficient method to validate approximations as well as to study systems with symmetric parameters.

Consider an exponential cyclic network under BAS blocking with parameters $B_i=B$ and $\mu_i=\mu$, i=1,...,N. The algorithm presented next utilizes an aggregate state space obtained from the original state space after it is reduced by a factor of N. Consider this cyclic network under BAS blocking with B=2, K=4, and N=3. The state space of this network has the following structure with all transition rates being equal to μ.

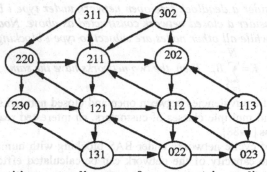

Figure 5: Transition rate diagram of a symmetric cyclic network under BAS blocking

with (n_1,n_2,n_3) denoting the state of the network and $n_i=B+1$ $(=3)$ denoting that node i is blocking preceding node. Let us define the following classes, where a state is a member of a class if that state has the same steady state probability as all the other states in the same class.

$$S_1=\{ (2,2,0),(0,2,2),(2,0,2) \}$$
$$S_2=\{ (2,3,0),(0,2,3),(3,0,2) \}$$
$$S_3=\{ (2,1,1),(1,2,1),(1,1,2) \}$$
$$S_4=\{ (3,1,1),(1,3,1),(1,1,3) \}$$

Then, we have the following state space structure for these equivalence classes with all transition rates being equal to μ.

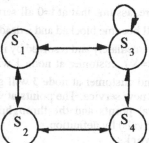

Figure 6: The transition rate diagram of the aggregated network

Then it can be shown that the respective steady state queue length distributions have the following relationship: $P(S_i)= \sum_{(i_1,i_2,i_3)\varepsilon S_i} P(i_1,i_2,i_3)$, $i=1,...,4$. Algorithm 1 summarizes the procedure to solve symmetric networks efficiently.

Algorithm 1:

S1. Generate the equivalence classes S_i, and set up the rate matrix.

S2. Solve the system numerically to obtain $P(S_i)$.

S3. Calculate the normalizing constant G_K for the original network as follows:

$$G_K =\sum_{i=1}^{S} R_i P(S_i)$$

where S is the number of equivalence classes and R_i is the number of states in the equivalence class i.

S4. $P(i_1,i_2,...i_N) = G_K^{-1} P(S_i)$.

Finally, we note that although the concept of indistinguishable nodes is discussed in cyclic networks under BAS blocking, it is also applicable to other blocking mechanisms defined in section 2 in cyclic exponential cyclic networks, and the central server model.

2.2. Open Networks

Unlike closed networks, open networks with blocking possess exact solutions in only a few special cases. Consider a tandem network with constant service times under BAS blocking. Arrivals occur only at the first node which has an infinite capacity. Interarrival times are assumed to be arbitrary. Then, we have (cf. Avi-Itzhak [1965]):

Lemma 16: i) The time spent in the system is independent of the order of the nodes and the capacity of nodes with finite capacities, and ii) the total time a customer spends in the network is the same as the same customer would spent waiting in a single server queue with a constant service time equal to the largest service time at the network, assuming that the service process in the equivalent single queue is the same as it is at the network.

Other than this result for tandem networks, the only other exact results in the literature, to the best of our knowledge, are reported in case of two node networks. A survey of two node open networks is given in Perros [1988]. In the following, the arrivals are assumed to occur at node 1 in a Poisson manner (with rate λ) which has an infinite capacity. The service times at each node is distributed exponentially with corresponding rates μ_1 and μ_2.

Konheim and Reiser [1976] obtained closed form expression for two node open networks under BBS blocking mechanisms assuming that a customer departing from the second server may be fed back to the first node.

Two limiting cases were investigated in Foster and Perros [1980], Konheim and Reiser [1976] and Hatcher [1969]. In the first case, it is shown that as $\mu_1 \to \infty$, the two node system is reduced to an M/M/1 queue with arrival rate 1 and service rate μ_2.

In the second case, it is assumed that the first node is saturated, an assumption often considered in production systems. In order for the first node to be saturated, its service rate should satisfy the condition $\mu_1 \leq \mu_0$, where μ_0 is the critical service rate at which the first queue becomes unstable. μ_0 is obtained numerically. Once μ_0 is known, the second queue is an M/M/1/B+1 queue with arrival rate μ_0 and service rate μ_2, where B is the capacity of node 2.

Asare [1978] considered two node networks under processor sharing discipline, where customers cycle between two nodes infinitely quickly receiving an infitestimal amount of service at each server and showed that the queue length distribution of this system has a closed form solution.

3. APPROXIMATIONS

As discussed in section 2, queueing networks with blocking do not, in general, have product or closed form solutions that can be used to solve such networks efficiently. Furthermore, numerical techniques are often restricted to small configurations, limiting their applicability. Hence, approximations are often used to investigate the performance characteristics of queueing networks with blocking.

3.1. Closed Queueing Networks

Akyildiz [1988a,b] developed approximation algorithms for the throughput of closed queueing networks with exponential and general service times. He approximates the throughput assuming that the throughput of a blocking network is approximately the same as an equivalent non-blocking network with product form queue length distribution. The equivalent network with infinite queue capacities has the same parameters as the blocking network except K. The number of customers in the non-blocking network is chosen such that the number of states of the blocking network is as close to the number of states of the non-blocking network as possible. The only assumption in the algorithm is that the network under consideration should be deadlock free.

Onvural and Perros [1989b] developed an approximation algorithm to calculate the throughput of large closed exponential queueing networks with finite queues. The algorithm approximately determines the number of customers such that the throughput of the network is maximum and fits a curve that passes through a number of known points to estimate the unknown throughput values as the number of customers in the network varies.

Perros, Nilsson, and Liu [1989] developed a numerical procedure for the approximate analysis of closed queueing networks in which some of the queues have finite capacities.

Suri and Diehl [1986] introduced the concept of *variable buffer size* and used it together with the *flow equivalent approximations* to approximate the throughput of cyclic networks with at least one node with an infinite capacity. The service time at each node is assumed to be exponentially distributed with rate μ_i, i=1,...,N.

Yao and Buzacott [1985] reported an approximation algorithm for analyzing closed queueing networks under RD-RS blocking. They considered networks of queues with each queue being served by multiple servers. Service times are assumed to follow arbitrary Coxian distributions. The topology of the network is such that if each service distribution is approximated by an exponential distribution with the same mean as the Coxian server, then the resulting exponential network is reversible and has a product form queue length distribution. The approximation is based on the notion of exponentialization.

Kouvatsos and Xenios [1989] used the principle of maximum entropy to find an approximate product form queue length distribution for closed queueing networks under RS-RD blocking. The algorithm requires the solution of non-linear equations using the principle of maximum entropy. An interested reader may refer to Kouvatsos [1983] for a detailed description of the maximum entropy principle. The procedure is based on decomposing the network into individual nodes and analyzing them in isolation with each node being studied as a GE/GE/1/B/FCFS queue, i.e. with generalized exponential arrival and service distributions. The service distribution at each queue is revised to accommodate the delays a customer might undergo due to blocking.

Dallery and Frein [1989] developed an approximation algorithm for the analysis of cyclic networks under BAS blocking in which there is at least one node with an infinite capacity. The approach is similar to the ones developed in the literature for open queueing networks with blocking. The algorithm decomposes the network into individual nodes with revised capacities, revised service rates, and revised arrival rates. The service and the interarrival times at each node in isolation are assumed to be exponentially distributed. The corresponding rates are determined iteratively assuming at each step that the network throughput is known. The algorithm was proven to be convergent. It produces both the throughput of the network and the mean queue lengths. Frein and Dallery [1989] extended this algorithm to cyclic networks under BBS-SO blocking.

We now discuss how a closed queueing network with blocking can be decomposed into individual nodes so that the marginal queue length probabilities obtained with these nodes analyzed in isolation are exact, i.e. the same as they are obtained from the joint steady state queue length distribution. Consider a cyclic network under BBS-SO blocking with N nodes, buffer capacities B_i, exponentially distributed service times, and K customers in it. Let $\underline{n}=\{n_1,...,n_N\}$ denote the state of this network, where n_i is the number of customers at node i and $P(\underline{n})$ be the steady state queue length distribution of the network. We have $0 \leq n_i \leq B_i$ and $\sum_{i=1}^{N} n_i = K$, $i=1,...,N$. Let us now partition the state space of the network into disjoint sets, $S_i(j)$, with respect to the number of customers, j, at node i. That is:

$$S_i(j) = \{\underline{n} \mid n_i = j \}, \quad j=0,...,B_i$$

Then, the behavior of node i in isolation can be readily obtained from the global balance equations by summing them over the sets $S_i(j)$, $j=0,...,B_i$.

For presentation purposes, consider a four node cyclic network with parameters $B_i=2$, $i=1,2,3,4$ and K=5. The global balance equations for the set $S_1(0)$ are given as follows:

$$\mu_4 \, P(0,1,2,2) = \mu_1 \, P(1,0,2,2) + \mu_2 \, P(0,2,1,2)$$
$$(\mu_2+\mu_4) P(0,2,1,2) = \mu_1 \, P(1,1,1,2) + \mu_3 \, P(0,2,2,1)$$
$$(\mu_3+\mu_4) P(0,2,2,1) = \mu_1 \, P(1,1,2,1)$$

Summing these equations side by side and canceling common terms, we have:

$$\mu_4 \, P_1(0) = \mu_1 \{ P_1(1) - P(1_1,2_2) \},$$

where $P\{k_i,n_j\}$ is the joint probability of having k and n customers at nodes i and j, respectively, and, $P_i(k)$ is the marginal probability of having k customers at node i. Similarly, for the other two sets $S_1(k)$, k=1,2 we have:

$$\mu_4 \{ P_1(1) - P\{1_1,0_4\} \} + \mu_1 \{ P_1(1) - P\{1_1,2_2\} \} =$$
$$\mu_4 \, P_1(0) + \mu_1 \{ P_1(2) - P\{2_1,2_2\}\}$$
$$\mu_1 \{ P_1(2) - P\{2_1,2_2\}\} = \mu_4 \{ P_1(1) - P\{1_1,0_4\} \}$$

These equations can equivalently be written as:

$$\mu_4 \, P_1(0) = \mu_1 \{ 1 - P(1_1,2_2) / P_1(1) \} P_1(1)$$
$$\mu_4 \{ 1 - P(1_1,0_4) / P_1(1)\} P_1(1) = \mu_1 \{1 - P(2_1,2_2) / P_1(2)\} P_1(2)$$

In this example, we observe that node 1 in isolation behaves like an M/M/1/B_i queue with state dependent arrival and service rates, which is generalized in the following lemma.

Lemma 17: Consider a deadlock free cyclic network under BBS-SO blocking with parameters B_i, K, μ_i, and p_{ij}; $i,j=1,...,N$. The service times are distributed exponentially. Then, the state dependent arrival, $\lambda_i(j)$, and service rates, $\mu_i(j)$, of a node *in isolation is given in terms of the joint steady state probabilities of the original network as follows:*

$$\lambda_i(j) = \mu_{i-1}\{1-P(0_k j_i) / P_i(j) \}, \qquad\qquad j=0,...,B_i-1;\; i=1,...,N$$

$$\mu_i(j) = \mu_i \{1 - P(j_i,B_k)) / P_i(j) \}, \qquad j=1,...,B_i$$

Furthermore, the marginal queue length probabilities of node i is obtained from the following set of equations:

$$\lambda_i(j)\, P_i(j) = \mu_i(j+1)\, P_i(j+1), j=0,...,B_i-1;$$

$$and \sum_{j=0}^{B_i} P_i(j)=1.$$

This result is rather surprising as a node of a closed queueing network under BBS-SO blocking in isolation behaves like an M/M/1/B queue. In particular, although the departure rate from a node of a blocking network is not Poisson, the above rate equations are the same rate equations of a $\lambda_i(j)/\mu_i(j)/1/B_i$ queue with state dependent Poisson arrivals and exponential service time distributions.

Although it is more involved than above construction, similar approach can be used to obtain the behavior of nodes in isolation in networks under BAS blocking. The decomposition approach for this type of blocking is discussed in the context of open networks.

Approximations developed for closed queueing networks in the literature are either based on some empirical observations or applications of approximations developed for open networks with blocking. Unlike open networks, the use of decomposition technique to approximately analyze closed networks is not a trivial task. In particular, in the simplest case, given the state of a node in isolation, i.e. the number of customers, the server may not be subject to blocking in closed networks depending on the total number of customers in the network whereas knowing the state of a node in isolation does not provide much information on the number of customers in other nodes of an open network. Hence, the state dependent arrival and service rates resulted by the exact decomposition appears to depend more strongly in closed networks on the number of customers at the node in isolation than they are in open networks, complicating the process.

3.2. Open Queueing Networks

Most approximations developed in the literature to analyze open queueing networks with blocking are based on decomposing the network into individual nodes and analyzing each node in isolation. In order to analyze a node in isolation, it is necessary to determine its arrival and service processes as well as its capacity.

In particular, consider a network under BAS blocking and let C be the capacity of a node with original capacity B in isolation. Furthermore, let the arrivals finding C customers at the node in isolation are assumed to be lost. In this case, if node i is blocked by node j, then the blocked customer is in fact can be viewed as a part of node j, i.e. joined queue j. This is because, when a departure occurs from node j then one of the blocked customers immediately joins node j. Hence, in general, C is equal to B plus the number of upstream servers connected directly to the node. However, if the node in isolation is analyzed with an arrival process which is subject to blocking then C=B. In this case, upon its attempt to enter the node, if the arriving customer finds B customers already in the queue then the arrival process is suspended. When a space becomes available, the blocked arriving customer joins the queue unblocking the arrival process.

In other types of blocking mechanisms, the blocked customer can not be viewed as part of its destination node as the blocked customer would be currently receiving service at its original node at a time a space becomes available at its destination. Hence, we have C=B in BBS and RS blocking mechanisms.

For presentation purposes, let us consider a tandem network under BAS blocking with N nodes, buffer capacities B_i, and exponentially distributed service times with corresponding rates μ_i. Arrivals are assumed to occur in a Poisson manner at the first node with rate 1. The exact behavior of a node in isolation can be obtained from the global balance equations, similar to the way it was done in the context of closed networks. Instead, we discuss intuitively how the arrival and service processes look like in isolation. Since node N is not subject to blocking, its service process in isolation is the same as it is in the original network. Node N-1, on the other hand, is subject to blocking and its service process in isolation should include the delay that a blocked customer goes through. In particular, if upon service completion at node N-1, there is no space available at node N then the customer is blocked and the service at node N-1 is suspended. The blocking delay in this case is the remaining service time at node N. However, due to the memoryless property of exponential distributions, this time is exponentially distributed with rate μ_N. Hence, the service process at node N-1 when analyzed in isolation is two phase Coxian, as illustrated in figure 7.

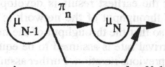

Figure 7: Service process at node N-1 in isolation.

The branching probability π_n depends on the state of the system and defined in terms of the joint queue length distribution of nodes N-1 and N-2. In particular, from the exact decomposition, we have π_n equal to the conditional probability that node N is full given that there are n customers at node N-1. Similarly, the blocking delay a customer goes through at node N-2 is given as follows: Upon service completion at node N-2, there are two possibilities. There is a space at node N-1 and the customer at node N-2 joins node N-1, or node N-1 is full at that time blocking node N-2. If blocked, there are two more possibilities. In the first case, node N-1 may be blocked by node N. Then, the blocking delay is the remaining service time at node N which is distributed exponentially. On the other hand, if node N-1 is busy serving then the blocked customer first has to wait for service completion at node N-1. Upon service completion at node N-1, customer at node N-1 may join node N, unblocking node N-2, or may get blocked by node N. Hence, the service process at node N-2 in isolation is phase type with three stages corresponding to servers N-2, N-1, and N, as illustrated in figure 8.

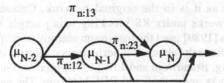

Figure 8: Service process at node N-2 in isolation.

The branching probabilities are now expressed in terms of the joint queue length distributions of nodes N-2, N-1, and N. For example, $\pi_{n:12}$ is the conditional probability that node N-1 is full and server N-1 is busy serving given that there are n customers at node N-2; $\pi_{n:23}$ is the conditional probability that node N is full given that there are n customers at node N-2 and node N-2 is blocked by node N-1; and $\pi_{n:13}$ is the probability that node N-1 is full and blocked by node N given that there are n customers at node N-2.

In general, the service process at node i includes all downstream servers with branching probabilities being positive for every j and k such that k>j.

The arrival process at a node in isolation "behaves like" a state dependent Poisson process. In particular the arrival rate to node i when it is in state (n,p) (i.e. there are n customers in it and service is in phase p) is equal to the product of the service rate at node i-1 and the conditional probability that node i-1 is not empty given that node i is in state (n,p). We note that the state (n,p) corresponds to, in general, nodes i to i+p-1 are blocked and node p is busy serving. Accordingly, the exact values of arrival rates at node i are given in terms of the joint queue length distributions of nodes i-1 to N.

An interested reader may refer to Perros [1989] for a survey of approximation algorithms reported in the literature for open networks with blocking. Tandem networks with blocking have been studied under a multiplicity of assumptions in the literature. Perhaps, one of the earliest result is developed by Hillier and Boiling [1967]. Assuming that the throughput of the network is known, the service rate at node i in isolation is fixed so that the throughput of the node is equal to the network throughput, whereas, the arrival rate is assumed to be equal to the throughput of the preceding node obtained at previous iteration. Further assuming that the corresponding distributions are distributed exponentially, each queue is analyzed as an $M/M/1/B_i+1$ queue. The algorithm iterates between nodes until a convergence on the network throughput is achieved.

Perros and Altiok [1986] developed an approximation in which each queue is analyzed as an $M/PH/1/B_i+1$ queue. The service process in isolation is obtained exactly the same way as they are in the exact decomposition except branching probabilities which are approximated by applying Little's relation to downstream queues. The arrival process to the queue is assumed to be Poisson and its rate is determined iteratively assuming the network throughput is known. We note that if the first queue is infinite then the network throughput is known. Otherwise, the network throughput has to be approximated iteratively. Over the years, this algorithm is extended to split and merge as well as arbitrary configurations, Coxian server and arrival processes, and tandem networks with Coxian arrivals, Coxian servers and multiple classes of customers.

Gershwin [1987, 1981] and Gun and Makowski [1989] studied tandem queues under BAS blocking where the arrival process is subject to blocking (as opposed to arrivals being lost in above cases). We note that in this case, the buffer capacity of a node in isolation is the same as it is in the original network. Caseau and Pujolle [1979] analyzed tandem networks under RS blocking using single node decomposition. Kouvatsos and Xenios [1989] used the maximum entropy principle to solve each node in isolation to approximately obtain the performance metrics of queueing networks under RS-RD blocking. Brandwajn and Jow [1988] used two node decomposition to analyze tandem networks under BAS and BBS blocking. The network is decomposed into N-1 subsystem with each subsystem i consisting of nodes i and i+1. To solve each subsystem, it is necessary to approximate the interaction between nodes i and i-1 for the arrival process and nodes i+1 and i+2 for the effective service time at node i+1, which are obtained from the analysis of subsystems i-1 and i+1. The algorithm, in general, captures more information than that can be obtained in a single decomposition and produces more accurate results. However, the solution of a subsystem numerically is more time consuming than it is to solve single nodes.

4. BUFFER ALLOCATION

The performance of a system highly depends on its topology, routing in the network, and the capacities of its queues. Although a single optimization model may be formulated, for practical purposes, the problem is generally decomposed into three interrelated optimization problems (Smith and Daskalaki [1988]): optimal topology problem, optimal routing problem, and optimal resource allocation problem.

In the buffer allocation problem, it is assumed that the topology of the system and the routing in the network are given. Then, the buffer capacities at service stations are determined such that the network throughput is close to its maximum value. This problem has a long history of research and development. However, most of the approximations reported in the literature considered tandem topologies of queueing networks in which service stations are connected in series (c.f. Buzacott and Shanthikumar [1992], Yamashita and Suzuki [1987] and Jafari and Shanthikumar [1989], Soyster. et. al. [1979], Sheskin [1976]). This model does not take the interactions between various tandem lines in the system into consideration. Smith and Daskalaki [1988] developed a heuristic to address the buffer allocation problem for tandem, merge. and split topologies of automated assembly lines. More recently, Yamashita and Onvural [1993]] proposed two approximation algorithms are developed to allocate the buffer capacities at each node such that the network throughput is close to its optimum value.

5. CONCLUSIONS

In this paper, we give a tutorial of queueing networks with blocking. Except for a few special cases, these networks could not be shown to have product form solutions. Although the steady state queue length distributions of these networks can, in theory, be calculated by solving the global balance equations together with the normalization equation numerically, this procedure can, in practice, be restrictive due to the time complexity of the procedure and the large storage required to store the rate matrices, particularly for large networks. Since exact values of their steady state queue length distributions are, in general, not attainable, good approximation algorithms are required to analyze queueing networks with finite queues.

REFERENCES

The list of references listed here by no means complete. They are the ones referred explicitly in the text and those of surveys, conference proceedings, and special issues for the interested reader to refer to. In particular, a bibliography of related papers on queueing networks with blocking can be found in Perros (1989).

Akyildiz, I.F. 1987, Exact Product Form Solutions for Queueing Networks with Blocking, IEEE Tran. Computers, 1, 121-126

Akyildiz, I.F. 1988b, On the Exact and Approximate Throughput Analysis of Closed Queueing Networks with Blocking, IEEE Trans. Software Engineering, SE-14-1, 62-71

Akyildiz, I.F. and Von Brand, H. 1989a, Exact Solutions for Open, Closed and Mixed Queueing Networks with Rejection Blocking, Theor. Comp. Sci. J., 64, 203-219

Akyildiz, I.F. and Perros, H.G. 1989, Special Issue of Performance Evaluation on Queuing Networks with Finite Capacity Queues, 10-3

Altiok, T. and Perros, H.G. 1987, Approximate Analysis of Arbitrary Configurations of Queueing Networks with Blocking, Annals of OR, 481-509

Asare, B. 1978, Queue networks with blocking, Ph.D. Thesis, Trinity College Dublin, Ireland, 1978.

Avi-Itzhak, B. 1965, A Sequence of Service Stations with Arbitrary Input and Regular Service Times, Management Science, 11, 565-571

Balsamo, S., Clo, M.C., and Donatiello, L. 1992, Cycle Time Distributions of Cyclic Networks with Blocking, Proc. Second Int. Workshop on Queueing Networks with Blocking, Onvural and Akyildiz (Eds.), North Holland

Balsamo, S. and Donatiello, L. 1988, Two-Stage Cyclic Network with Blocking: Cycle Time Distribution and Equivalence Properties, Proc. Modeling Tech. and Tools for Computer Perf. Eval., Potier and Puigjaner (Eds), 513-528

Balsamo, S., Persone V. De Nitto, and Iazeolla, G. 1986, Some Equivalencies of Blocking Mechanisms in Queueing Networks with Finite Capacity", Manuscript, Dipartimento di Informatica, Universite di Pisa, Italy

Balsamo, S. and Iazeolla, G. 1983, Some Equivalence Properties for Queueing Networks with and without Blocking", Performance'83, Agrawala and Tripathi (Eds), 351-360, North Holland Publishing Company, Amsterdam

Bocharov, P.P. and Albores, F.K. 1980, On Two-Stage Exponential Queueing System with Internal Losses or Blocking, Problems of Control and Information Theory, 9, 365-379

Boxma, O. and Konheim, A. 1981, Approximate Analysis of Exponential Queueing Systems with Blocking, Acta Informatica, 15, 19-66

Brandwajn, A. and Jow, Y.-L.L. 1988, An Approximation Method for Tandem Queues with Blocking, Operations Research, 36, 73-83

Caseau, P. and Pujolle, G. 1979, Throughput Capacity of a Sequence of Transfer Lines with Blocking Due to Finite Waiting Room", IEEE Trans. Software Engineering, 5, 631-642

Dallery, Y. and Frein, Y. 1989, A Decomposition Method for the Approximate Analysis of Closed Queueing Networks with Blocking, Proc. First International Workshop on Queueing Networks with Blocking, Perros and Altiok (Eds), 193-215, North Holland

Daskalaki, S. and MacGregor Smith, J. 1989, The Static Routing Problem in Open Finite Queueing Networks, Proc. First International Workshop on Queueing Networks with Blocking, Perros and Altiok (Eds), 193-215, North Holland

Foster, F.G. and Perros, H.G. 1980, On the Blocking Process in Queue Networks, Eur. J. Oper. Res., 5, 276-283

Frein, Y. and Dallery, Y. 1989, Analysis of Cyclic Queueing Networks with Finite Buffers and Blocking Before Service, Performance Evaluation, 197-210

Gershwin, S.B. 1987, An Efficient Decomposition Method for the Approximate Evaluation of Tandem Queues with Finite Storage Space and Blocking, Operations Research, 35, 291-305

Gershwin, S.B. 1987, An Efficient Decomposition Method for the Approximate Evaluation of Tandem Queues with Finite Storage Space and Blocking, Operations Research, 35, 291-305

Gordon, W.J. and Newell, G.F. 1967a, Cyclic Queueing Systems with Restricted Queues, Oper. Res., 15, 266-278

Gun, L. and Makowski, A.M. 1988, Matrix Geometric Solution for Finite Queues with Phase Type Distributions, Performance'87, Courtois and Latouche (Eds.), 269-282, North Holland

Hatcher, J.M. 1969, The Effect of Internal Storage on the Production Rate of a Series of Stages Having Exponential Service Times, AIIE Trans., 1, 150-156

Hillier, F.S. and Boling, R.W. 1967, Finite Queues in Series with Exponential or Erlang Service Times-A Numerical Approach, Operations Research, 15, 286-303

Hillier, F.S. and So, K.C. 1989, The Assignment of Extra Servers to Stations in Tandem Queueing Systems with Small or No Buffers, Performance Evaluation, 10-3, 219-232

Hordijk, A. and Van Dijk, N. 1981, Networks of Queues with Blocking, Performance'81, Klystra (Ed.), 51-65, Elsevier Science Publishers B.V. (North Holland)

Jafari, M.A. and Shanthikumar, J.G. 1984, Allocation of Buffer Storages Along a Multi-Stage Automatic Transfer Line, IE Rept. 84-003, Arizona University

Jafari, M.A. and Shanthikumar, J.G. 1985, Determination of Optimal Buffer Storage Capacities and Optimal Allocation in Multi-Stage Automatic Transfer Lines, IE&OR Rept. 85-011, Syracuse University

Kelly, F.P. 1984, Blocking, Reordering, and the Throughput of a Series of Buffers, Stochastic Processes and Their Applications, 17, 327-336

Kelly, K.P. 1979, Reversibility and Stochastic Networks, John Wiley and Sons Ltd., Chichester, England

Konheim, A.G. and Reiser, M. 1976, A Queueing Model with Finite Waiting Room and Blocking, J. ACM, 23, 328-341

Kouvatsos, D.D. 1983, Maximum Entropy Methods for General Queueing Networks, Modeling Tech. and Tools for Perf. Analysis, Potier (Ed.), 589-608, North Holland, Amsterdam

Kouvatsos, D.D. and Xenios, N.P. 1989, MEM for Arbitrary Queueing Networks with Multiple General Servers and Repetitive Service Blocking, Performance Evaluation, 10-3, 169-196

Labetoulle, J. and Pujolle, G. 1980, Isolation Method in a Network of Queues, IEEE Transactions on Software Engineering, SE-6, 373-381

Langaris, C. and Conolly, C. 1984, On the Waiting Time of a Two-Stage Queueing System with Blocking, J. Appl. Prob., 21, 628-638

Lavenberg, S.S. 1978, Stability and Maximum Departure Rate of Certain Open Queueing Networks Having Finite Capacity Constraints, RAIRO Informatique/Computer Science, 12, 353-370

MacGregor Smith, J. and Daskalaki, S. 1988, Buffer Space Allocation in Automated Assembly Lines, Operations Research, 36, 343-358

Mitra, D. and Mitrani, I. 1988, Analysis of a Novel Discipline for Cell Coordination in Production Lines, AT&T Bell Labs Res. Rep.

Onvural, R.O. 1987, Closed Queueing Networks with Finite Buffers, Ph.D. thesis, CSE/OR, North Carolina State University

Onvural, R.O. 1989a, On the Exact Decomposition of Exponential Closed Queueing Networks with Blocking, First International Workshop on Queueing Networks with Blocking, Perros and Altiok (Eds), 73-83, North Holland

Onvural, R.O. 1989b, A Note on the Product Form Solutions of Multi-Class Closed Queueing Networks with Blocking, Performance Evaluation, 10-3, 247-254

Onvural, R.O. 1990, A Survey of Closed Queueing Networks with Blocking, ACM Computing Surveys, 22-2, 83-122

Onvural, R.O. and Akyildiz, I.F. 1993, Proc. Second International Workshop on Queueing Networks with Finite Capacity, North Holland, 1993

Onvural, R.O. 1993, Queueing Networks with Finite Capacity (Ed.), Performance Evaluation, April 1993

Onvural, R.O. and Perros, H.G. 1986, On Equivalencies of Blocking Mechanisms in Queueing Networks with Blocking, Oper. Res. Letters, 5-6, 293-298

Onvural, R.O. and Perros, H.G. 1988, Equivalencies Between Open and Closed Queueing Networks with Finite Buffers, Performance Evaluation, 9, 263-269

Onvural, R.O. and Perros, H.G. 1989a, Some Equivalencies on Closed Exponential Queueing Networks with Blocking", Performance Evaluation, 9, 111-118

Onvural, R.O. and Perros, H.G. 1989b, Throughput Analysis in Cyclic Queueing Networks with Blocking, IEEE Trans. Software Engineering, SE 15-6, 800-808

Perros, H.G. 1984, Queueing Networks with Blocking: A Bibliography, ACM Sigmetrics, Performance Evaluation Review, 12-2, 8-12

Perros, H.G. 1989, A Bibliography of Papers on Queueing Networks with Finite Capacity Queues, Performance Evaluation, 10-3, 255-260

Perros, H.G. 1988, Two Node Open Networks with Finite Capacity Queues, CS Tech. Rep., North Carolina State University

Perros, H.G. and Altiok, T. 1986, Approximate Analysis of Open Networks of Queues with Blocking: Tandem Configurations, IEEE Trans. Software Engineering, SE-12, 450-461

Perros, H.G. 1989, Approximation Algorithms for Open Queueing Networks with Blocking, Chapter in Stochastic Analysis of Computer and Communications Systems, Takagi (Ed.), Elsevier SciencePublishers B.V. (north Holland)

Perros, H.G., Nilsson, A., and Liu, Y.C. 1989, Approximate Analysis of Product Form Type Queueing Networks with Blocking and Deadlock, Performance Evaluation, to appear

Persone, De Nitto, V., and Grillo, D. 1987, Managing Blocking in Finite Capacity Symmetrical Ring Networks, 3rd Conference on Data and Communication Systems and Their Performance, Rio de Jenerio, Brasil

Shanthikumar, G.J. and Yao, D.D. 1989, Monotonicity Properties in Cyclic Queueing Networks with Finite Buffers, First International Workshop on Queueing Networks with Blocking, Perros and Altiok (Eds), 325-344, North Holland

Sheskin, T. J. 1976, Allocation of Interstage Storage Along an Automated Production Line, AIIE Trans., 8, 146-152

Soyster, A.L., Schmidt, J.W., and Rohrer, M.W. 1979, Allocation of Buffer Capacities for a Class of Fixed Cycle Production Lines, AIIE Trans., 11, 140-146

Suri, R. and Diehl, G.W. 1986, A Variable Buffer Size Model and Its Use in Analytical Closed Queueing Networks with Blocking, Management Science, 32-2, 206-225

Takahashi, Y., Miyahara, H. and Hasegawa, T. 1980, An Approximation Method for Open Restricted Queueing Networks, Operations Research, 28, 594-602

van Dijk, N.M. **1989**, A Simple Throughput Bound for Large Closed Queueing Networks with Finite Capacities, Performance Evaluation, 10-3, 153-168

Van Dijk, N.M. and Tijms, H.C. **1986**, Insensitivity in Two Node Blocking Models with Applications, Teletraffic Analysis and Computer Performance Evaluation, Boxma, Cohen and Tijms (Eds), 329-340, Elsevier Science Publishers B.V. (North Holland), Amsterdam, The Netherlands

Yamashita, H. and Onvural, R.O. **1993**, Buffer Allocation in Queueing Networks with Arbitrary Topologies, to appear in Annals of OR on Queueing Networks, van Dijk (Ed.)

Yamashita, H. and Suzuki, S. **1987**, An Approximate Solution Method for Optimal Buffer Allocation in Serial n-stage Automatic Production Lines, Trans. Japan. Soc. Mech. Eng., 53-C, 807-814

Yao, D.D. and Buzacott, J.A. **1985**, Queueing Models for Flexible Machining Stations Part II: The Method of Coxian Phases, Eur. J. Operations Research, 19, 241-252

Real Time Systems: A Tutorial *

Fabio Panzieri and Renzo Davoli

Dipartimento di Matematica
Università di Bologna
Piazza di Porta S. Donato 5
40127 Bologna (Italy)

Abstract. In this tutorial paper, we introduce a number of issues that arise in the design of distributed real-time systems in general, and hard real-time systems in particular. These issues include time management, process scheduling, and interprocess communications within both local and wide area networks. In addition, we discuss an evaluation, based on a simulation model, of a variety of scheduling policies used in real-time systems. Finally, we examine some relevant examples of existing distributed real-time systems, describe their structuring and implementation, and compare their principal features.

1   Introduction

The principal responsibility of a real-time (RT) system can be summarized as that of producing correct results while meeting predefined deadlines in doing so. Hence, the computational correctness of the system depends on both the logical correctness of the results it produces, *and* the timing correctness, i.e. the ability to meet deadlines, of its computations.

Hard real-time (HRT) systems can be thought of as a particular subclass of RT systems in which lack of adherence to the above mentioned deadlines may result in a catastrophic system failure. In the following we shall use the phrase "soft real-time (SRT) systems" to indicate to those RT systems in which the ability to meet deadlines is indeed required; however, failure to do so does not cause a system failure.

The design complexity of HRT and SRT systems can be dominated by such issues as the application timing and resource requirements, and the system resource availability. In particular, in the design of a HRT system that support critical applications (e.g. flight control systems, nuclear power station control systems, railway control systems), that complexity can be exacerbated by such possibly conflicting application requirements as the demand for highly reliable and highly available services, under specified system load and failure hypotheses, and the need to provide those services while satisfying stringent timing constraints.

* Partial support for this work was provided by the Italian National Research Council (CNR) under contract N. 92.00069.CT12.115.25585.

In particular, as a HRT system has to provide services that be both timely and highly available, the design of any such system requires that appropriate fault tolerance techniques, capable of meeting hard real-time requirements, be deployed within that system.

Current technology allows the HRT system designer to implement cost-effective fault tolerance techniques, based on the use of redundant system components. However, the development of redundancy management policies, that meet real-time requirements, can introduce further complexity in the system design (and validation) process. Thus, in essence, the design of a HRT system requires that a number of performance/reliability trade-off issues be carefully evaluated.

Both HRT and SRT systems may well be constructed out of geographically dispersed resources interconnected by some communication network, so as to form a distributed RT system. (Conforming to the definition proposed in [8, 29, 36], distributed HRT systems can be classified as *responsive* systems, i.e. distributed, fault tolerant, real-time systems.)

In this tutorial paper, we shall focus on issues of design and implementation of distributed RT systems, and describe five operational examples of those systems, namely [52, 17, 33, 56, 47]. In particular, we shall discuss the key paradigms for the design of timely and available RT system services, and examine techniques for process scheduling, time management, and interprocess communications over local and wide area networks.

This paper is structured as follows. In the next Section, we discuss the principal issues arising in the design of RT systems. In Section 3, we examine a number of scheduling policies that are usually deployed in those systems. In addition, in that Section we introduce an evaluation of those policies, based on a simulation study, that allows one to asses the adequacy of those policies with respect to different parameters that can characterize the system load and its communication costs. Section 4 introduces the distributed RTOSs mentioned above. Finally, Section 5 proposes some concluding remarks.

2 Design Issues

A generic (i.e. hard or soft) real-time system can be described as consisting of three principal subsystems [23], as depicted in Figure 1 below.

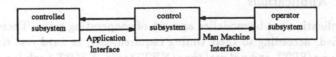

Fig. 1. Example of Real-Time System Organization

In Figure 1, the *controlled subsystem* represents the application, or environment (e.g. an industrial plant, a computer controlled vehicle), which dictates the real-time requirements; the *control subsystem* controls some computing and communication equipment for use from the controlled subsystem; the *operator subsystem* initiates and monitors the entire system activity. The interface between the controlled and the control subsystems consists of such devices as sensors and actuators. The interface between the control subsystem and the operator consists of a man-machine interface.

The controlled subsystem is implemented by tasks (termed *application tasks*, in the following) that execute using the equipment governed by the control subsystem. This latter subsystem can be constructed out of a possibly very large number of processors, equipped with such local resources as memory and mass storage devices, and interconnected by a real-time local area network (i.e. a local network that provides bounded maximum delay of a message exchange - see Subsection 2.4). Those processors and resources are governed by a software system that we term the Real-time Operating System (RTOS).

The deployment of RTOSs in safety critical environments (e.g. guidance and navigation systems) imposes severe reliability requirements on the design and implementation of those RTOSs [10]. As discussed in [26], these requirements can be defined in terms of maximum acceptable probability of system failure. Thus, for example, flight control systems, such as that used in the Airbus A-320, require 10^{-10} probability of failure per flight hour. Vehicle control systems in which the cost of a failure can be quantified in terms of an economic penalty, rather than loss of human lifes (e.g. systems for satellite guidance, unmanned underwater navigation systems), require 10^{-6} to 10^{-7} probabilities of failure per hour.

Fault tolerance techniques, based on the management of redundant hardware and software system components, are commonly used in order to meet these reliability requirements. However, it is worth pointing out that the implementation of these techniques, that indeed determine the system reliability, require that some of the system performance be traded for reliability. Methodological approaches that allow one to assess these trade-off issues are discussed in [1, 38, 57, 39].

The principal issues concerning the design of a RTOS are introduced below, in isolation. In particular, in the following we shall discuss (i) relevant characteristics of the RT applications that may use a RTOS, (ii) two general paradigms that can be applied to the design of a RTOS, (iii) time management, and (iv) interprocess communication issues in distributed RT systems.

2.1 RT Applications

A RT application can be modelled as a set of cooperating tasks. These tasks can be classified, according to their timing requirements, as *hard real time* (HRT), *soft real time* (SRT), and *not real time* (NRT) tasks. A HRT task is a task whose timely (and logically correct) execution is deemed as critical for the operation of the entire system. The deadline associated to a HRT task is conventionally termed *hard deadline*, owing to the critical nature of that task. As a consequence, it is assumed that missing a hard deadline can result in a catastrophic system failure. A **SRT task**, instead, is characterized by an execution deadline whose adherence is indeed desirable, although not critical, for the functioning of the system (hence, the SRT task deadline is usually termed *soft deadline*). **NRT tasks** are those tasks which exhibit no real-time requirements (e.g. system maintenance tasks that can run occasionally in the background).

Application tasks can be further classified as *periodic, aperiodic* (or *asynchronous* [60]), and *sporadic* tasks. **Periodic tasks** are those tasks that enter their execution state at regular intervals of time, i.e. every T time units. These tasks, generally used in such applications as signal processing and control, are typically characterized by hard deadlines [34]. **Aperiodic tasks** are those tasks whose execution time cannot be anticipated, as their execution is determined by the occurrence of some internal or external event (e.g. a task responding to a request from the operator). These tasks are usually characterized by soft deadlines. Finally, aperiodic tasks characterized by hard deadlines are termed **sporadic tasks** [30] (e.g. tasks dealing with the occurrence of system failures, or with emergency requests from the operator).

In view of the above classifications, one can observe that the principal responsibility of a RTOS is to guarantee that each individual execution of each application task meet the timing requirements of that task. However, it is worth noting that, in order to fulfil that responsibility, the objective of a RTOS cannot be stated just as that of minimizing the average response time of each application task; rather, as pointed out in [58, 60], the fundamental concern of a RTOS is that of being *predictable*, i.e. the functional and timing behaviour of a RTOS should be as deterministic as necessary to meet that RTOS specification. Thus, fast hardware and efficient algorithms are indeed useful, in order to construct a RTOS that meet real-time requirements; however, they are not sufficient to guarantee the predictable behaviour required from that system. .

2.2 RTOS Design Paradigms

Two general paradigms for the design of predictable RTOSs can be found in the literature. These paradigms have led to the development of two notably different RTOS architectures, termed Event-Triggered (ET) and Time-Triggered (TT) architectures [24], respectively. In essence, in ET RTOSs (e.g. [55]), any system activity is initiated in response to the occurrence of a particular event, caused by the system environment. Instead, in TT RTOSs (e.g. [21]), system activities are initiated as predefined instants of the *globally synchronized* time (see next Subsection) recur.

In both architectures, the RTOS predictability is achieved by using (different) strategies to assess, prior to the execution of each application task, the resource needs of that task, and the resource availability to satisfy those needs. However, in ET architectures, these resource needs and availability may vary at run-time, and are to be assessed dynamically. Thus, resource need assessment in ET architectures is usually based on parametric models [40]. Instead, in TT architectures these needs can be computed off-line, based on a pre-run time analysis of the specific application that requires the use of the TT architecture; if these needs cannot be anticipated, worst-case estimates are used.

TT architecture advocates criticize the ET architectural approach as the ET architectures, owing to their very nature, can be characterized by an excessive number of possible behaviors that must be carefully analyzed in order to establish their predictability [24]. In contrast, ET architecture advocates claim that these architectures are more flexible than TT architectures, and ideal for a large class of applications that do not allow to predetermine their resource requirements. In particular, they argue that TT architectures, owing to the worst case estimate approach mentioned above, are prone to waste resources in order to provide predictable behavior.

In both ET and TT architectures the resource need and availability assessment is to be carried out while taking into account the timing requirements of the applications. Hence, issues of time management, that characterize the system's temporal behaviour, are of crucial importance in the design of any RT system.

2.3   Time Management

One of the principal concerns, in the field of time management in RT systems, consists of providing adequate mechanisms for measuring (i) the time instants at which particular events must occur, and (ii) the duration of the time intervals between events. In a distributed RT system, these concerns become particularly critical, as the occurrence of the same event can be observed from such inherently asynchronous devices as a number of different processors.

However, this problem can be adequately dealt with by providing the RT applications with a common time reference of specified accuracy. This time reference can be constructed by synchronizing the values of the local real-time clocks, incorporated in each processor of the system, so as to obtain a global notion of time within that system.

A large variety of clock synchronization algorithms can be found in the literature, e.g. [28, 42, 27, 5, 50], based on the exchange of clock synchronization messages among the system nodes. We shall not describe these algorithms here, as they are discussed in detail in the already cited references. However, we wish to mention that, as pointed out in [41], any such algorithm has to meet the following four requirements:

1. the clock synchronization algorithm is to be capable of bounding, by a known constant, the maximum difference of the time values between the observation of the same event from any two different nodes of the system (measured according to the value of the local clock of each of these two nodes);

2. the notion of global time constructed by the synchronization algorithm is to be sufficiently accurate to allow one to measure small time intervals at any point in time;

3. the clock synchronization algorithm is to be capable of tolerating the possible fault of a local RT clock, or the loss of a clock synchronization message;

4. the overall system performance is not to be degraded by the execution of the clock synchronization algorithm.

In order to meet these requirements, either centralized or decentralized clock synchronization algorithms can be deployed. A centralized approach can be implemented by means of a central synchronization unit, e.g. a "time server" node responsible for periodically distributing time synchronization messages to the other nodes in the system; some such an approach can typically be very vulnerable to failures of the synchronization unit itself. Instead, a decentralized approach, owing to the redundancy inherent in the distributed infrastructure that can be used for its implementation, can offer better guarantees as to fault tolerance (provided that implementation be based on a realistic fault model).

As already mentioned, the clock synchronization algorithms in distributed RT systems can be implemented by message exchanges. However, it is worth pointing out that these implementations may introduce overheads that can affect the overall system performance, thus violating the requirement 4 above. In order to overcome this problem, a practical and effective solution has been proposed in [41] (and developed within the context of the MARS project [21]). This solution is based on the implementation of an accurate clock synchronization algorithm in a special-purpose VLSI chip; this chip can be incorporated in a subset of nodes of the system, and used by those nodes to exchange clock synchronization messages. The rest of the system nodes can maintain their clocks synchronized by monitoring the synchronization message traffic. This implementation notably reduces (to less than 1%, it is claimed in [41]) the CPU load and the network traffic caused by the clock synchronization algorithm.

2.4 Interprocess Communications

In view of the predictability requirement mentioned earlier, distributed RT systems require primarily that the communication support they use provide them with deterministic behaviour of the communication infrastructure. This behaviour can be achieved by constructing a communication protocol architecture characterized by such deterministic properties as *bounded channel access delay*, and *bounded message delay*.

The channel access delay is defined as the interval of time between the instant in which a task issues a request for sending a message, and the instant in which the communication interface, local to the node where that task is running, actually transmits that message on the communication channel. The message delay, instead, is defined as the interval of time between the instant in which a task requests the transmission of a message, and the instant in which that message is successfully delivered to its destination; hence, the message delay includes the channel access delay. If a message is delivered with a message delay that exceeds a target (e.g. application dependent) value, that message is considered lost.

It as been pointed out in [14] that, in such distributed RT applications as those based on non-interactive audio and video communications, an additional property that RT protocols are required to possess consists of the provision of bounded message delay *jitter*; this jitter is the absolute value of the difference between the actual message delay of a transmitted message, and the target message delay. Issues of delay jitter control in packet switching networks are discussed in [13]; protocols characterized by the bounded delay jitter property, for use for communications over those networks, are described in [14, 12, 11].

Further general properties that can be required from a RT protocol include stability, and fault tolerance. The former property refers to the ability of the protocol to continue to operate effectively in the presence of network traffic variations and temporary network overloading. The latter property refers to the protocol ability to survive communication channel failures (e.g. omission failures [6], such as those that can be caused by a noisy channel).

A survey of basic techniques for the design of protocols for distributed RT systems is discussed in [25]. In this paper, the authors examine time constrained protocols that can be deployed in distributed RT systems based on broadcast (both local and wide area) networks. In particular, they classify these protocols in *controlled access* and *contention based* protocols. The former class includes Time Division Multiple Access Protocols; the latter, instead, includes token based schemes. In addition, this paper points out a number of performance/reliability trade-off issues that arise in the design of these protocols. These issues include the relations among the message loss percentage, the message transmission rate, and the timing constraints associated to the messages.

Further work on RT communications, emphasizing HRT communication issues, can be found in [49, 61]. In [49], the author proposes a protocol for HRT communication in local area networks that provides bounded channel access delay. In [61], the authors evaluate the performance of four protocols for HRT communications, termed Virtual Time CSMA protocols. The performance metrics they use for this evaluation are based on the percentage of messages that miss their deadlines, and the effective channel utilization.

Finally, an interesting protocol for communications in distributed HRT systems has been recently proposed in [24]. This protocol, designed for the support of distributed TT architectures, provides principally (i) predictable message delay, (ii) group communications and membership service [7], (iii) redundancy management, and (iv) accurate clock synchronization. A further attractive (and unconventional) property of this protocol is that it is designed so as to be highly scalable, i.e. capable of operating efficiently on different communication media (e.g. twisted pairs as well as optical fibers).

3 Scheduling

In a RT system, the responsibility of the scheduling algorithm is to determine an order of execution of the RT tasks that be *feasible*, i.e. that meet the resource and timing requirements of those tasks. In the design of a RT system, the choice of an appropriate scheduling algorithm (or policy) may depend on several issues, e.g. the number of processors available in the system, their homogeneity or heterogeneity, the precedence relations among the application tasks, the task synchronization methods. In addition, application dependent characteristics of the RT tasks may contribute to determine the choice of the scheduling algorithm. For example, RT application tasks can be *preemptable*, or *non-preemptable*. A preemptable task is one whose execution can be suspended by other tasks, and resumed later; a non-preemptable task must run until it completes, without interruption. Thus, both preemptive and non-preemptive algorithms have been proposed. (However, for the purposes of this tutorial paper, non-preemptive scheduling will not be discussed as a large number of non-preemptive scheduling problems has been shown to be NP-hard [4].)

RT scheduling algorithms can be classified as either *static* or *dynamic* algorithms. A static scheduling algorithm is one in which a feasible schedule is computed off-line; one such algorithm typically requires a priori knowledge of the tasks' characteristics. In contrast, a dynamic scheduling algorithm determines a feasible schedule at run time. Thus, static scheduling is characterized by low run-time costs; however, it is rather inflexible, and requires complete predictability of the RT environment in which it is deployed. Instead, dynamic scheduling entails higher run-time costs; however, it can adapt to changes in the environment.

The literature on task scheduling algorithms is very vast (e.g. see [16, 4, 60]); a complete taxonomy of these algorithms and their properties is beyond the scope of this paper. Rather, we shall confine our discussion below to summarizing the most common scheduling algorithms that are used in the implementation of RT systems, and introduce the results obtained from a recent simulation study of these algorithms, that we have carried out.

3.1 Scheduling Algorithms

The scheduling of periodic tasks on a single processor is one of the most classical scheduling problems in RT systems [34]. Two alternative approaches have been proposed to solve this problem, based on the assignment of either a fixed or, alternatively, a dynamic priority value to each task. In the fixed priority approach, the task priority value is computed once, assigned to each task, and maintained unaltered during the entire task life time. In the dynamic priority approach (also termed deadline driven), a priority value is dynamically computed and assigned to each task, and can be changed at run-time. These approaches have led to the development of a variety of preemptive scheduling policies (preemption, in priority driven scheduling policies, means that the processing of a task can be interrupted by a request for execution originated from a higher priority task). These include the *Rate Monotonic* (RM), the *Earliest Deadline First* (EDF), and the *Least Slack Time First* (LSTF) policies, introduced below.

The RM policy assigns a fixed priority value to each task, according to the following principle: the shorter the task period, the higher the task priority. It has been shown in [34] that this policy is *optimal* among fixed priority policies (i.e. given a set of tasks, it always produces a feasible schedule of that set of tasks, if any other algorithm can do so).

The EDF and LSTF policies implement dynamic priorities. With the EDF policy, the earlier the deadline of a task, the higher the priority assigned to that task. Instead, with the LSTF policy, the smaller the *slack time* (see below) of a task, the higher the priority value assigned to that task. The task slack time is defined as the difference between the amount of time from the current time value to the deadline of a task, and the amount of time that task requires to perform its computation.

In order to deal with the scheduling of aperiodic tasks, the following five different policies have been proposed [30]. The first policy consists of scheduling the aperiodic tasks as background tasks, i.e. aperiodic tasks are allowed to make their computations only when no periodic tasks are active. The second policy, termed *Polling*, consists of creating a periodic process, characterized by a fixed priority, that serves the aperiodic task requests (if any). The main problem with this policy is the incompatibility between the cyclic nature of this policy, and the bursty nature of the aperiodic tasks.

The third and fourth policies are the *Priority Exchange* (PE) and the *Deferrable Server* (DS) policies. Both these policies aim to maximizing the responsiveness of aperiodic tasks by using a high priority periodic server that handles the aperiodic task requests. In both the PE and the DS policies, the server preserves the execution time allocated to it, if no aperiodic task requests are pending. (In fact, these policies are also termed *bandwidth preserving*, as they provide a mechanism for preserving the resource bandwidth allocated for aperiodic services if, when this bandwidth becomes available, it is not needed.)

The difference between these two policies is in the way they manage the high priority of their periodic servers. In the DS policy, the server maintains its priority for the duration of its entire period; thus, aperiodic task requests can be serviced at the server's high priority, provided that the server's execution time for the current period has not been exhausted. In contrast, in the PE policy, the server exchanges its priority with that of the pending, highest priority, periodic task, if no aperiodic task requests occur at the beginning of the server period.

The DS and PE policies have been developed in order to deal with sporadic tasks (i.e. aperiodic HRT tasks, as defined in Subsection 2.1 of this tutorial paper). The fifth policy that we consider, i.e. the *Sporadic Server* (SS) policy, has been designed to deal with the scheduling of aperiodic (SRT) tasks. This policy, yet again based on the creation of a periodic server of aperiodic requests, is characterized by a response time performance comparable to that of the DS and PE policies, and a lower implementation complexity than these two policies. The SS policy is discussed in detail in [30].

Task scheduling in tightly coupled distributed systems, such as a shared memory multiprocessor, can be governed by a single scheduler responsible for allocating the processing elements to the application tasks. McNaughton, in [37], has proposed an optimal, preemptive scheduling algorithm for independent tasks. This algorithm has been extended to deal with such different issues as tasks having DAG precedence graphs, and periodic executions (see [16] for a complete survey).

In loosely coupled distributed RT systems, owing to the high cost of process migration between processors, and to the loss of predictability that operation may entail, tasks can be statically assigned to the system processors. In these systems, the scheduler is usually structured in two separate components; namely, an *allocator*, and a *local scheduler*. The allocator is responsible for assigning tasks to the distributed system processors; the local scheduler (one for each processor) implements a single processor scheduling policy, such as those introduced earlier, to dispatch the (local) execution requests. It is worth mentioning that the allocation algorithms are usually based on some heuristic approach, as the problem of allocating tasks to processors can be very complex. (For example, it has been shown [3] that finding an optimal assignment of tasks, characterized by an arbitrary communication graph, to four or more processors with different speeds is an NP-hard problem.)

The I/O subsystem of a real-time system may require its own scheduler. The simplest way to access an I/O resource is by using a non-preemptive FIFO policy. However, the preemptive scheduling techniques introduced above for processor scheduling (i.e. RM, EDF, LSTF) can be implemented to schedule I/O requests.

Relevant figures of merit that can be used to assess the effectiveness of a scheduling policy include the *Breakdown Utilization* (BU), the *Normalized Mean Response Time* (NMRT), and the *Guaranteed Ratio* (GR), introduced below.

The BU, as defined in [30], is the degree of resource utilization at or below which the RTOS can guarantee that all the task deadlines will be met. This figure provides a metric for the assessment of the effectiveness of a scheduling policy, as the larger the breakdown utilization, the larger the cpu time devoted to task execution.

The NMRT is the ratio between the time interval in which a task becomes ready for execution and terminates, and the actual cpu time consumed for the execution of that task. Yet again, this figure provides a metric of the effectiveness of the selected scheduling policy as, the larger the NMRT, the larger the task idle time.

Finally, for dynamic algorithms, a relevant performance metric is the GR, i.e. the number of tasks whose execution can be guaranteed versus the total number of tasks that request execution.

3.2 Simulation Study

In order to evaluate the effectiveness of the algorithms introduced above, we have developed a distributed RT system simulation model that incorporates the majority of those algorithms, suitable for the scheduling of periodic, aperiodic, and sporadic tasks [43].

In particular, our model implements the RM, the EDF, and the LSTF algorithms, for the scheduling of periodic tasks.

Aperiodic task scheduling can be supported, in our model, by means of the background (BG), the Polling (PL), the DS, and the SS algorithms. The BG scheduling algorithm is implemented by executing aperiodic tasks in those time intervals in which no periodic tasks are active. The PL, DS, and SS algorithms are implemented by periodic servers that schedule aperiodic tasks at regular intervals of time, provided that no periodic task be in execution.

The scheduling of the sporadic tasks is simulated by implementing a periodic server, fully dedicated to the scheduling of those tasks, that is enabled sufficiently

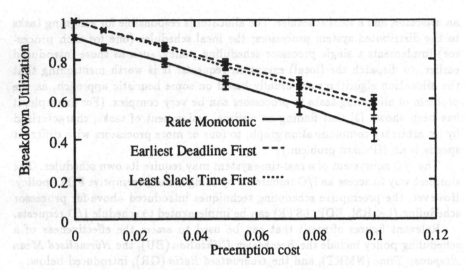

Fig. 2. RM, EDF, LSTF Performance

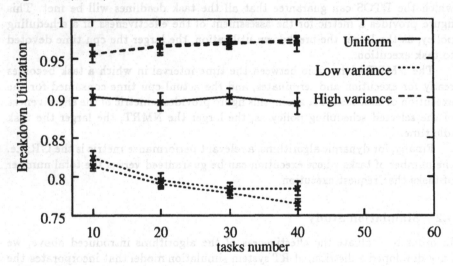

Fig. 3. RM Performance under different task period distributions

frequently to guarantee not to miss the sporadic task hard deadlines.

Moreover, in our model, the scheduling of tasks accessing I/O resources can be governed by one of the preemptive scheduling algorithms mentioned above (i.e. the RM, the EDF, and the LSTF algorithms). In addition, our model allows its user to choose a FIFO discipline for I/O resource management, and to specify arbitrary network delays.

Finally, our model embodies a number of task synchronization protocols that implement concurrency control mechanisms, and solve (or prevent [2]) the *priority inversion* problem [46].

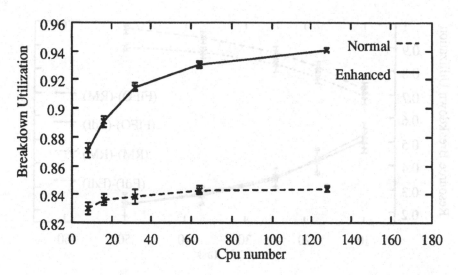

Fig. 4. Allocation algorithms performance

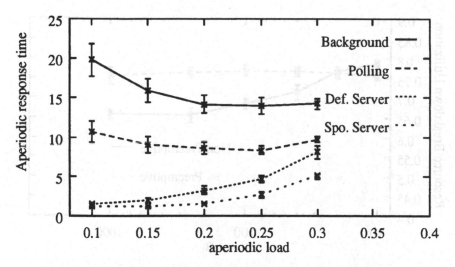

Fig. 5. Background, polling, DS, SS performance

The phrase 'priority inversion' is used to indicate the situation in which the execution of a higher priority task is delayed by lower priority tasks [9]. With priority driven RT schedulers, this problem can occur when there is contention for shared resources among tasks with different priorities. In order to simulate the mastering and control of that problem, our model implements the Basic Priority Inheritance (BPI), the Priority Ceiling (PC), the Priority Limit (PL), and the Semaphore Control (SC) protocols [51]. The principal scope of each of these four protocols is to minimize the so-called Worst Case Blocking Time, i.e. the time interval in which the execution of a higher priority task can be delayed

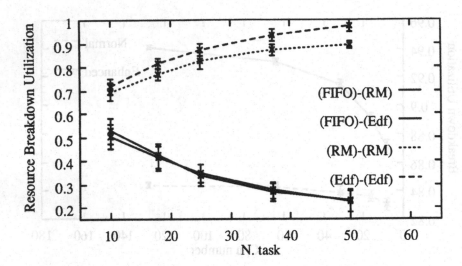

Fig. 6. I/O scheduling performance

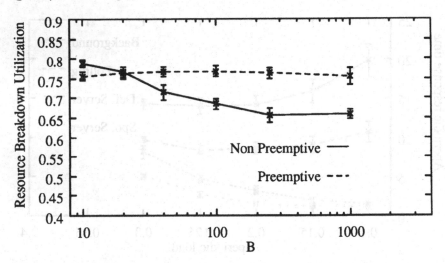

Fig. 7. Preemptive and non preemptive controller (uniform distribution case)

by lower priority tasks.

An alternative approach to the solution of the priority inversion problem has been proposed in [2], and is based on preventing the occurrence of that problem. In order to assess the effectiveness of that approach, our model incorporates a particular priority prevention protocol described in [2].

Our simulation model has been implemented, using the C programming language, so as to accept in input a description of the distributed RT system to simulate, and to produce, as output, statistical results of the simulation experiments.

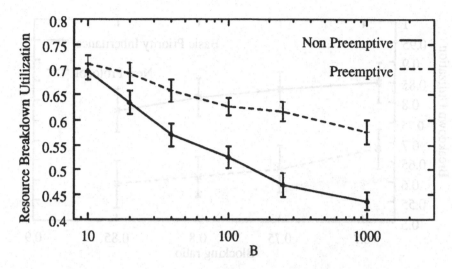

Fig. 8. Preemptive and non preemptive controller (high variance case)

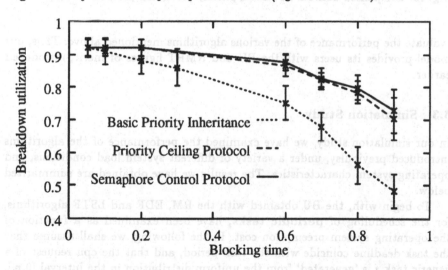

Fig. 9. Priority control protocols performance

The input DRTS description consists of the specification of both system load, and operating system parameters. The system load parameters include the following random variables: number of periodic (PT) and aperiodic tasks (AT) that may request execution, the task period (P), the CPU request (CR) and the deadline (D) of each task, and their probability distribution. The operating system parameters include the scheduling and task synchronization policies the operating system is to use, and the two random variables: operating system preemption cost (PrC), and network overhead (NO).

The output produced by our implementation is intended to allow one to

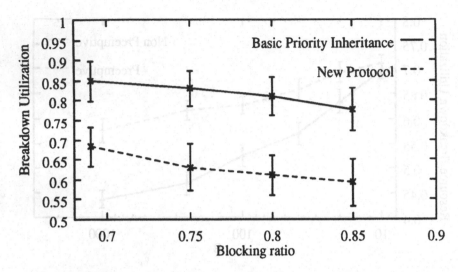

Fig. 10. Comparison between BPI and a priority prevention protocol

evaluate the performance of the various algorithms mentioned above. Thus, our model provides its users with the BU and NMRT figures of merit, introduced earlier.

3.3 Simulation Study

In our simulation study, we have examined the performance of the algorithms introduced previoulsy, under a variety of different system load conditions, and operating system characteristics. The results we have obtained are summarized below.

To begin with, the BU obtained with the RM, EDF and LSTF algorithms, for the scheduling of **periodic tasks**, have been examined as a function of the operating system preemption cost. In the following, we shall assume that the task deadline coincide with the task period, and that the cpu request of a generic task i is 'generated' from the uniform distribution in the interval $[0, p_i]$, where p_i denotes the task i period. The simulation results discussed in this Subsection have been obtained by using the method of independent replications (300 independent runs for each experiment), and 95% confidence intervals have been constructed for the performance indices.

Assuming that:

1. the PrC is the same for each one of these three algorithms,
2. PT is a constant, equal to 10,
3. P is uniformly distributed in the interval [1, 100],

our results show that the EDF and LSTF dynamic algorithms perform better than the RM static algorithm, as illustrated in Figure 2. However, in practice, the above assumption 1 can be unrealistic, as the dynamic algorithms must compute and assign the task priorities at run time, thus introducing additional overheads to the preemption cost; hence, the use of the RM algorithm can be favored to that of the dynamic algorithms, as its implementation is simpler, and the preemption cost it entails is lower.

This observation has led us to concentrate our investigation on the RM algorithm, as far as periodic task scheduling is concerned. Thus, we have examined its behavior as the number of tasks in execution grows. In addition, we have considered the following four different probability distributions of the random variable P:

1. Uniform distribution in [1, 100] (variance = 816.8),
2. Beta distribution with parameters a = 15 and b = 15 (variance = 79.4), and parameters a = 0.5 and b = 0.5 (variance = 1862.2),
3. Normal distribution with parameters mean = 50.5 and variance = 78.4,
4. Exponential distribution with parameter a = 0.5,

The Beta, Normal and Exponential distributions are scaled in the interval [1,100]. The results produced by our simulation model are illustrated in Figure 3.

This Figure shows that the RM algorithm is extremely sensitive to the variance of the random variable P. In particular, low variance of P can notably degrade the RM scheduling performance. In essence, this can be explained as follows. The RM algorithm assigns higher priority to tasks with shorter periods. Thus, if P has low variance, the different task periods are characterized by short time intervals between the periods' terminations. Owing to this observation, we have developed an algorithm that allocates independent tasks to the distributed RT system CPUs, so as to provide a high variance for P on each of these CPUs.

Figure 4 depicts the result produced by our model as a function of the number of CPUs. This Figure illustrates that a conventional task allocation algorithm (indicated as Normal in Figure 4), that ignores the task distribution issue by, for example, polling each CPU in the system until it finds one available for task execution, produces very low BU values compared to our allocation algorithm (indicated as Enhanced in Figure 4).

As to aperiodic tasks, the NMRT is the most relevant figure of merit when these tasks are introduced in a distributed RT system, and coexist with the periodic tasks. The experiment we have carried out consisted of simulating the presence (on the same CPU) of both periodic and aperiodic tasks. We assume that :

- the scheduling algorithm used is the RM algorithm,
- the periodic task load is about 69%, and the number of periodic tasks is 10, with period uniformly distributed in the interval [1,100],
- the number of aperiodic tasks is 10,
- the time between consecutive activations of each aperiodic task is exponentially distributed with mean equal to 20,
- the aperiodic task server is the task with highest priority.

The NMRT simulation results we have obtained, as a function of the aperiodic task load, show that the bandwidth preserving algorithms (i.e the DS, SS, IS algorithms) perform better than such traditional algorithms as polling and background, as depicted in Figure 5.

Essentially, this is because the aperiodic task execution can start any time during the server period. Thus complex algorithms, such as DS, SS, and IS, allow the scheduler to start rapidly the execution of the aperiodic tasks. Compared with easier methods, such as polling, these algorithms meet effectively the execution requirements of those aperiodic tasks that request short execution time (even if these requests are very frequent). However, we have observed that, when an aperiodic task requires an amount of CPU execution time close to that of the most time consuming task of the system, the differences among the various methods tend to disappear.

As pointed out in [45], I/O requests are scheduled, in general, according to a FIFO discipline; this can lead to a low resource utilization, as illustrated in Figure 6. The results shown in this Figure have been obtained by simulating a system characterized as follows :

1. a variable number of periodic tasks, with period P uniformly distributed in the interval [1,100], are concurrently running in the system,
2. every task is divided in three parts: input, processing, and output. We assume that the time spent during the I/O phase is the same consumed for processing data.

We have considered both non-preemptive and preemptive I/O controllers. A non preemptive controller is one that cannot interrupt an I/O operation once this has been started. With a preemptive controller, instead, a high priority I/O operation can preempt a lower priority one. Consequently, the use of a preemptive controller may appear to be more appropriate in a Real Time system. However, if the RM algorithm is implemented in order to assign priorities to the tasks (and hence to the task I/O requests) the following non obvious results can be observed.

We have carried out a number of simulations that show the performance differences (in terms BU) between the preemptive and the non preemptive controllers.

We have examined the behavior of these two controllers when the task periods are generated with a variety of different distributions. Figure 7 shows the BU values obtained when the task periods are uniformly distributed in the interval [1,B]. It can be seen that the preemptive controller can lead to a greater resource BU for a limited number of values of B, only. Using a low variance distribution (i.e. the normal distribution with variance equal to 78.4) for the period random variable P, we have obtained that, for all values of B, the BU achieved by the non preemptive controller is always greater than that achieved by the preemptive controller. In contrast, using a high variance distribution (i.e. a beta distribution with variance equal to 1862.2) the preemptive controller exhibits its superiority, as illustrated in Figure 8. Moreover, we have noted that the difference in terms of performance between the two kinds of controllers tend to disappear as the number of tasks grows. Thus, the benefits that can be obtained using a preemptive controller cannot be considered as absolute, as these benefits depend upon the system load.

The **priority inversion** problem can typically occur when RT tasks share data. Concurrent accesses to those data can be handled by means of concurrency control mechanisms such as semaphores. However, if a low priority task locks a semaphore, higher priority tasks which require that semaphore are forced to wait its release, thus incurring in a so-called blocking time overhead. Priority control protocols that limit this overhead in a RT system have been developed in order to guarantee the tasks deadlines (i.e. the BPI, SC, PL, and PC protocols already mentioned). As illustrated in Figure 9, these protocols exhibit different performance; in particular, as the blocking time grows, the BPI degrades notably. Instead, the performance of the PC, the SC, and the PL protocols maintain values which are very close to each other (the PL protocol performance results are omitted from Figure 9). However, the SC protocol is an optimal but hard to implement protocol; hence, a number of recent RT system implementations (e.g. Real Time MACH [59]) favor the use of the PC protocol.

Finally, our simulation model implements a recently proposed priority prevention protocol [2]. This protocol differs from the priority control protocols previously examined as it is capable of eliminating the priority inversion problem. Using this protocol, the analysis of a RT system is indeed easier, as less effort is required to construct a feasible schedule for that system. However, the performance of this priority prevention protocol turns out to be lower than that obtained with the priority control protocols discussed above, as illustrated in Figure 10.

4 Case Studies

In this Section we introduce five relevant examples of distributed RT systems; namely, the SPRING kernel, HARTS, MARS, MARUTI, and CHAOS. These systems are discussed below, in isolation.

4.1 SPRING

SPRING is a distributed RTOS kernel developed at the University of Massachusetts. The SPRING designers claim that the development of conventional RT systems has been often affected by a number of misconceptions and implementation deficiencies, as discussed at length in [58]. The SPRING kernel [48, 47] aims to overcoming those misconceptions and deficiencies. In particular, the key issues addressed in the SPRING design approach include *flexibility* and *predictability*, within the context of an ET distributed RT system.

In SPRING, tasks are classified as follows, on the basis of their relative costs of a deadline miss:

- Critical tasks (or HRT tasks) are those which must meet their deadlines, otherwise catastrophic failures may occur;
- Essential tasks are those which are indeed relevant to the operation of the system; however, in case of fault, they cannot cause dangerous situations to occur.
- Non-essential tasks may or may not have RT constraints. However, a non-essential task missing a deadline may cause only a poorer quality of service, as its timing constraints are very loose (i.e. those constraints specify a preferred answer time, only).

Each essential and non-essential task is characterized by a "criticalness" parameter associated with it. This parameter is used to quantify the relevance of a task, relative to the specific application it implements. The SPRING kernel executes essential and non-essential tasks by maximizing the value that can be obtained as the sum of the criticalness parameters of those tasks. (Critical tasks are outside the scope of this maximization process, as they are executed with the highest priority.)

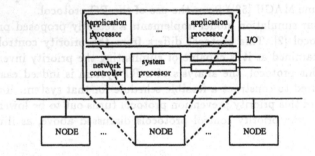

Fig. 11. A schematic view of the Springnet system

The hardware model for the SPRING kernel is a multiprocessor distributed system. Each node is composed by one (or more) application processors, one (or more) system processors and an I/O subsystem (see Fig. 11). Application processors execute critical and essential tasks; system processors run most of the operating system, as well as specific tasks which do not have deadlines. The I/O subsystem handles non-critical I/O, slow I/O devices and fast sensors.

The SPRING kernel is able to schedule task groups. A task group is a collection of tasks having precedence constraints among themselves but sharing a single deadline. Moreover, SPRING supports incremental tasks, i.e. tasks that compute an answer as soon as possible, and continue to refine the return value for the rest of their requested computation time. (A complete discussion on incremental tasks can be found in [35]).

In a loosely coupled processors environment, such as that used in SPRING, an optimal scheduling algorithm, in the worst case, may perform an exhaustive search on all the possible task partitions; this is a computationally intractable problem. SPRING addresses the scheduling problem by using a heuristic approach. In essence, whenever the execution of a task is requested, SPRING attempts to guarantee that execution locally, i.e. it tries to construct a feasible schedule that include that task in the same node where its execution request occurred. If that attempt fails, SPRING allocates a different node for that request. Finally, it is worth mentioning that fault tolerance issues have received little attention in the design of the SPRING Kernel.

4.2 HARTS

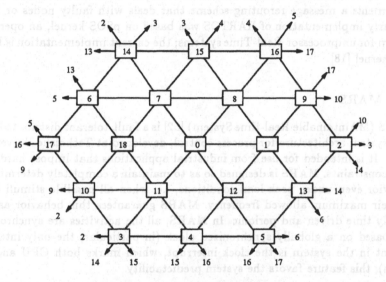

Fig. 12. An example of network mesh for HARTS: the hexagonal mesh of size 3

The distributed RT architecture of the HARTS project (Hexagonal Architecture for Real Time Systems [56]) is based on shared memory multiprocessor nodes interconnected by a wrapped hexagonal network (Fig.12 shows an example of the HARTS hexagonal network). This architecture aims to providing RT applications with high performance, reliability, and predictability.

The HARTS network can be conveniently implemented in hardware (e.g. by means of a VLSI chip), as it is planar, and characterized by a fixed number of connections. This network is scalable, and provides fault tolerance support.

One of the main research interests of the HARTS project is to focus onto low-level architectural issues, such as message routing and buffering, scheduling, and instruction set design. Moreover, as HARTS embodies both distributed system and multiprocessor architectural features, it allows one to evaluate the behavior of RT programs in both distributed and multiprocessor environments.

HARTOS [19] is the operating system developed for HARTS. The HARTOS kernel aims to providing a uniform interface for real-time communications between processes, regardless of their physical location. In particular, the HARTOS link-level protocol supports the co-existence, in the communication network, of a mix of normal and real time traffic. The application interface provides system calls for RT communications, as well as remote procedure calls, naming, and datagram delivery.

In addition, HARTOS supports fault tolerance, queued message passing, non queued event signals, and shared memory (between processors in the same node). Fault-tolerance is implemented at two separate levels of abstraction; namely, the task and network levels. At the task level, HARTOS provides replication features, and multicast communications; instead, at the network level, HARTOS implements a message rerouting scheme that deals with faulty nodes or links. An early implementation of HARTOS was based on pSOS kernel, an operating system for uniprocessor Real-Time systems; the current implementation is based on x-kernel [18].

4.3 MARS

MARS (MAintainable Real-time System) [52] is a fault-tolerant distributed real-time system architecture for process control, developed at Technishe Universität Wien. It is intended for use from industrial applications that impose hard-real-time constraints. MARS is designed so as to maintain a completely deterministic behavior even under peak-load conditions, i.e. when all possible stimuli occur at their maximum allowed frequency. MARS guarantees this behavior as it is strictly time driven and periodic. In MARS, all the activities are synchronous, and based on a globally synchronized clock (in particular, the only interrupt present in the system is the clock interrupt, which marks both CPU and bus cycles); this feature favors the system predictability.

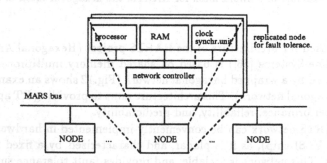

Fig. 13. A schematic view of a MARS cluster

The current implementation runs on a cluster of single-board mono-processor nodes (see Fig.13 for a schematic view of a MARS cluster). From a physical point of view the network hardware of the cluster is a standard ethernet; instead, the channel access protocol is based on a TDMA discipline (as the standard ethernet CSMA-CD (IEEE 802.3) protocol cannot guarantee peak-load timing correctness). As already discussed, a custom chip implements the clock synchronization protocol.

Key issues of this project include:

- fault tolerance: MARS can deal effectively with fail silent nodes and omission failures by using replicated hardware and messages;
- static scheduling: MARS implements static, pre-run time scheduling of the application tasks;
- repearability: in MARS, redundant components may be removed from a running cluster (e.g. for repair), and reintegrated later without affecting the system behavior,
- management of redundant networks (still under development).

Finally, an important development of this project, that is worth mentioning, is the real-time programming environment of MARS [44], a graphical based CASE for RT software development.

4.4 MARUTI

MARUTI [33, 32] is a hard-real-time, fault tolerant, distributed operating system developed at the Department of Computer Science of the University of Maryland. MARUTI is built as a modular system, using an object oriented approach; its architecture emphasizes the independence between the system elements. This system is driven by a time constrained model which imposes restrictions on both execution beginning and ending of the application tasks. In MARUTI, interrupt driven tasks can co-exist with conventional ones. A basic concept that MARUTI implements is that of the *calendar*; this is a data structure which is used to allow the verification of the schedulability of the application tasks, the reservation of guaranteed services, and the synchronization among tasks.

Jobs in MARUTI are invocations of executable objects. MARUTI accepts new jobs during the execution of already accepted jobs; it implements the following two different scheduling disciplines: the off-line and on-line disciplines. Tasks having non deterministic execution, as well as tasks which do not have timing constraints, are scheduled using the off-line discipline; instead, HRT tasks are executed in on-line mode. On-line tasks can preempt, if necessary, off-line ones.

The system provides the following two classes of objects: Kernel and Application level objects. At the Kernel level, MARUTI provides an Interrupt handler object, used to define a service object for any kind of interrupt in the system, a time service object, used for synchronization and ordering of events, and a scheduler. At the Application level, this system includes the allocator, which maps tasks (running in off-line mode) to processors, a file service, and a name service. Objects can communicate by either using shared buffers (if they are running at the same site), or message passing.

4.5 Chaos

CHAOS [17, 53] (Concurrent Hierarchical Adaptable Object System), is a complete programming and operating system for Real-Time applications.

Similar to MARUTI, CHAOS is object-based. The CHOS run-time system offers kernel level primitives which support the development of real-time software structured as a collection of interacting objects. CHAOS is particularly suitable for the development of large, complex real-time applications characterized by stringent timing constraints. Its goal is to support the programming of adaptable, efficient, predictable, and accountable applications.

Efficiency is important since RT applications are time-constrained; hence, system overload should be kept to a minimum so that these constraints can be satisfied. however, the system is to provide efficiency of execution, without compromising accountability, predictability, or reliability.

Accountability means that the kernel must either honor its critical commitments, or it has to report detected failure to the higher level software, before the system reach an unsafe state. (For example, in CHAOS an unanticipated change in the system environment, noted by the kernel, might cause that an invocation miss its hard deadline, and the kernel raise an appropriate exception.) Thus, one of the goals of accountability is to allow the application programmer to develop application specific methods for recovering from failures.

RT applications using CHAOS can be constructed using system provided primitives, customizing these primitives to the applications needs, or by defining new, application-specific primitive operations. CHAOS ensures the predictable behavior of all those synthesized primitives. In addition, it provides mechanisms by means of which the application programmer can monitor the application software, and adapt it to achieve the required performance. CHAOS is particularly suitable for supporting the implementation of robotics applications (the major test bed for CHAOS implementations is a 6-legged walking machine).

As to scheduling, CHAOS uses a two-level scheduling model [54, 15]. The higher level consists of the *object scheduler*; this scheduler receives the invocations and assigns them to specific threads of execution, on the basis of their attributes and processors' load. This scheduler (or allocator) is based on a heuristic greedy algorithm. At the processor level, scheduling is carried out by using an Earliest Deadline First dispatcher. Finally, CHAOS inherits, from the distributed database theory, the concept of atomicity. Transactional methods can be used to drive the invocation of recovery actions that avoid that partial execution results be permanently stored. Atomicity in Chaos refers to RT correctness, as recovery actions may be caused by timing faults.

To conclude this Section, we wish to point out that the five different systems we have introduced have been chosen as they are sufficiently representative of a rather wide spectrum of design choices that can be made in the design of a RT system.

For example, SPRING, although designed to provide ET applications with a predictable RT infrastructure, essentially neglects issues of fault tolerance; rather, its designers have favored the development of a flexible architecture that can accommodate application tasks characterized by different requirements (i.e. critical, essential, and non-essential tasks).

The design of HARTS emphasizes low level architectural issues, and investigates the use of a special-purpose network for distributed RT communications.

MARS is a predictable, time-triggered, distributed architecture; its design exploits the properties of the synchronous systems in order to provide its users with a dependable, real-time, distributed infrastructure for HRT applications.

Finally, MARUTI and CHAOS explore the use of an object oriented approach to the design of fault tolerant RTOSs. However, the design of MARUTI emphasizes issues of integration of conventional, and interrupt-driver RT tasks; instead, CHAOS emphasizes issues of accountability, and support for the development of application dependent fault tolerance techniques.

5 Concluding Remarks

In this tutorial paper we have discussed a number of RT system design issues, and described briefly five examples of distributed RT systems, that have been recently developed. To conclude this paper, we summarize below the principal criteria and metrics that can be used to evaluate RT systems in general, and distributed RT systems in particular.

To begin with, we have pointed out that "timeliness" is indeed a crucial requirement to be met in the design of a RT system; however, this requirement is not sufficient to guarantee the effectiveness of any such system, as a RT system is to be designed so as to be "predictable", primarily.

We have examined and contrasted two principal architectural paradigms for the design of predictable RT systems; namely, the Time Triggered and the Event Triggered paradigms. These two paradigms aim to meeting the predictability requirement mentioned above by implementing static or dynamic strategies, respectively, for the assessment of the resource and timing requirements of the RT application tasks.

Issues of clock synchronization in distributed RT systems have been introduced next. In this context, we have observed that the overhead introduced by the exchange of the clock synchronization messages is a relevant metric to assess the effectiveness of the clock synchronization algorithms that can be used in those systems.

We have then discussed interprocess communication design issues in RT systems. The principal requirements to be met by the communication infrastructure, in order to support RT applications, have been introduced (namely, bounded channel access delay, bounded message delay, and bounded delay jitter). Relevant figures of merit for the evaluation of RT communication mechanisms, that have emerged from our discussion, include: the message loss percentage, the message transmission rate, the deadline miss percentage, effective channel utilization, and the scalability of the mechanism.

Finally, we have examined issues of scheduling in RT systems, and discussed the results of a simulation study that we have carried out in order to assess a number of scheduling policies. The figures of merit that we have proposed for the assessment of the those policies include: the resource breakdown utilization, the normalized mean response time, and, for dynamic scheduling policies, the guaranteed ratio.

References

1. Anderson T., Lee P. A.: Fault Tolerance - Principles and Practice. London: Prentice-Hall International, 1981
2. Babaoglu O., Marzullo K., Schneider F. B.: A Formalization of Priority Inversion, Technical Report UBLCS-93-4 University of Bologna, March 1993.
3. Bokhari S. H., Shahid H. A Shortest Tree Algorithm for Optimal Assignements across Space and Time in a Distributed Processor System. IEEE Trans. on Software Engineering, SE-7(6), 1981.
4. Cheng S., Stankovic J. A.: Scheduling Algorithms for Hard Real-Time Systems: A Brief Survey. In Hard Real Time Systems, J. A. Stankovic and K. Ramamritham (Eds.), IEEE Computer Society Press, 1988, 150-173.
5. Cristian F., Aghili H., Strong R.: Clock Synchronization in the Presence of Omission and Performance Faults, and Processor Joins. In Proc. FTCS-16, Vienna, Austria, July 1986, 218-223.
6. Cristian F.: Understanding Fault Tolerant Distributed Systems. Comm. of the ACM, (34)2: February 1991, 56–78.
7. Cristian F.: Reaching Agreement on Processor Group Membership in Synchronous distributed Systems. Distributed Computing, 4: 1991, 175–187.
8. Cristian F.: Contribution to the panel: What are the Key Paradigms in the Integration of Timeliness and Availability? (position paper). In Proc. 2nd International Workshop on Responsive Computer Systems, Saitama, Japan, October 1-2 1992.
9. Davari S., Sha L.: Sources of Unbounded Priority Inversions in Real-time Systems and a Comparative Study of Possible Solutions. ACM Operating Systems Review, Vol. 26, N. 2, April 1992, 110-120.
10. Falcone M., Panzieri F., Sabina S., Vardanega T.: Issues in the design of a Real-time Executive for On-board Applications. in Proc. 6th IEEE Symp. on Real-time Operating System and Software, Pittsburgh, PA, May 1989.
11. Ferrari D., Verma D.: A Continuous Media Communication Service and its Implementation. Proc. GLOBECOM '92, Orlando, Florida, December 1992.
12. Ferrari D., Verma D.: A Scheme for Real-time Channel Establishment in Wide-area Networks. IEEE JSAC, (8)3: April 1990, 368–379.
13. Ferrari D.: Design and Applications of a Delay Jitter Control Scheme for Packet-switching Internetworks. In Network and Operating System Support for Digital Audio and Video. R.G. Herrtwich (Ed.), LNCS 614, Springer-Verlag, Berlin Heidelberg, 1992, 72–83.
14. Ferrari D.: Real-time Communication in Packet Switching Wide-Area Networks. Tech. Rep., International Computer Science Institute, Berkeley (CA), 1989.
15. Gheith A., Schwan K.: Chaos⁴rc: Kernel Support for Atomic Transactions in Real-Time Applications. In Proc. of Fault-Tolerant Computing Systems (FTCS), June 1989.
16. Gonzales, M. J. Jr.: Deterministic Processor Scheduling ACM Computing Surveys, 9(3): September 1977, 173–204.

17. Gopinath P., Schwan K.: Chaos: Why one cannot have only an Operating System for Real-Time Applications. ACM Operating System Review, 23(3): July 1989, 106–140.
18. Hutchinson N., Peterson L.: The x-kernel: An Architecture for Implementing Network Protocols. IEEE Trans. on Software Engineering, January 1991, 1–13.
19. Kandlur D. D., Kiskis D. L., Shin K. G.: Hartos: A Distributed Real-Time Operating System. ACM Operating System Review, 23(3): July 1989, 72–89.
20. Kopetz H. et al.: Real-time System Development: The Programming Model of MARS. Research Report N. 11/92, Institut für Informatik, Technische Universität Wien, Wien (Austria), 1992.
21. Kopetz H., Damm A., Koza C., Mulazzani M., Schwabl W., Senft C., Zainlinger R.: Distributed Fault Tolerant Real-Time Systems: The MARS Approach. IEEE Micro: February 1989, 25–40.
22. Kopetz H., G. Grünsteidl: TTP - A Time-triggered Protocol for Fault Tolerant Real-Time Systems. Research Report N. 12/92/2, Institut für Informatik, Technische Universität Wien, Wien (Austria), 1992.
23. Kopetz H., Kim K. H.. Temporal Uncertainties among Real-Time Objects. In Proc. IEEE Comp. Soc. 9th Symp. on Reliable Distributed Systems, Huntsville (AL), October 1990.
24. Kopetz H.: Six Difficult Problems in the Design of Responsive Systems. In Proc. 2nd International Workshop on Responsive Computer Systems, 2–7, Saitama, Japan, October 1-2 1992.
25. Kurose J. F., Schwartz M., Yemini Y.: Multiple Access Protocols and Time-constrained Communication. ACM Computing Surveys, 16(1), March 1984, 43–70.
26. Lala J., Harper R. E., Alger L. S.: A Design Approach for Ultrareliable Real-Time Systems. IEEE Computer, 24(5): May 1991, 12–22.
27. Lamport L., Melliar Smith L. M.: Synchronizing Clocks in the Presence of Faults. Journal of the ACM, 32: January 1985, 52-78.
28. Lamport L.: Time, Clocks and the Ordering of Events in a Distributed System. Comm. of the ACM, 21: July 1978, 558-565.
29. Le Lann G.: Contribution to the panel: What are the Key Paradigms in the Integration of Timeliness and Availability? (position paper). In Proc. 2nd International Workshop on Responsive Computer Systems, Saitama, Japan, October 1-2 1992.
30. Lehoczky J., Sprunt B., Sha L.: Aperiodic Task Scheduling for Hard Real-Time Systems. In Proc. IEEE Real Time Systems Symposium, 1988.
31. Lehocsky J.P., Sha L., Strosnider J.K.: Enhanced Aperiodic Resposiveness in Hard Real-Time Environments. In Proc. of 8th Real-time System Symposium, Dec.1987
32. Levi S. T., Agrawala A. K.: Real Time System Design. McGraw-Hill, 1990
33. Levi S. T., Tripathi S. K., Carson S. D., Agrawala A. K., The MARUTI Hard-Real-Time Operating System. ACM Operating System Review, 23(3): July 1989, 90–105.
34. Liu C. L., Layland J. W.: Scheduling Algorithms for Multiprogramming in a Hard-Real-Time Environment. Journal of the ACM, 20(1): January 1973, 46–61.
35. Liu J. W., Lin K. J., Shin W. K., Shi Yu A. C., Chung J. Y., Zhao W..: Algorithms for Scheduling Imprecise Computations. IEEE Computer: May 1991, 58–68.
36. Malek M.: Responsive Systems: A Challenge for the Nineties. In Proc. Euromicro 90, 16th Symp. on Microprocessing and Microprogramming. North Holland, August 1990.
37. McNaughton, R.: Scheduling with Deadline and loss Functions. Management Science 6(1), October 1969, 1–12.

38. Meyer J. F.: Closed Form Solutions of Performability. IEEE Trans. on Computers, C-31(7): July 1982, 648–657.

39. Muppala J. K. et al.: Real-time Systems Performance in the Presence of Failures. IEEE Computer, 24(5): May 1991, 37–47.

40. Natarajan S., Zhao W., Issues in Building Dynamic Real-Time Systems. IEEE Software, 9(5): September 1992, 16–21.

41. Ochsenreiter O., Kopetz H.: Clock Synchronization in Distributed Real-Time Systems. IEEE Transactions on Computers, C-36(8): August 1987, 933–940.

42. Owicki S., Marzullo K.: Maintaining Time in a Distributed System. In Proc. 2nd ACM Symp. on Principles of Distributed Computing: August 1983, 295–305.

43. Panzieri F., Donatiello L., Poretti L.: Scheduling Real Time Tasks: A Performance Study. In Proc. Int. Conf. Modelling and Simulation, Pittsburgh (PA), May 1993.

44. Posposchil G., Puschner P., Vrchotichy A., Zainlinger R.: Developing Real-Time Tasks with Predictable Timing. IEEE Software: September 1992, 35–44.

45. Rajkumar R., Sha L., Lehoczky J. P.: On Countering the Effects of Cycle-Stealing in Hard Real Time Environment. In Proc. IEEE Real Time Systems Symposium, 1987.

46. Rajkumar R., Sha L., Lehoczky J. P.: An Optimal Priority Inheritance Protocol for Real-Time Synchronization. ACM TOCS, 17 October 1988.

47. Ramamritham K., Stankovic J. A.: The Spring Kernel: a New Paradigm for Real-Time Systems. ACM Operating System Review, 23(3): July 1989, 54–71.

48. Ramamritham K., Stankovic J. A.: The Spring Kernel: a New Paradigm for Real-Time Systems. IEEE Software: May 1991, 62–72.

49. Ramamritham K.: Channel Characteristics in Local Area Hard Real-time Systems. Computer Networks and ISDN Systems, North-Holland, September 1987, 3-13.

50. Rangarajan S., Tripathi S. K.: Efficient Synchronization of Clocks in a Distributed System. in Proc. Real-time Systems Symposium, San Antonio, Texas, December 4-6, 1991, pp. 22-31.

51. Sha L., Lehoczky J. P., Rajkumar R.: Solution for Some Practical Problem in Prioritized Preemptive Scheduling. In Proc. IEEE Real-Time Systems Symposium, New Orleans, Luisiana, December 1986.

52. Schwabl W., Kopetz H., Damm A., Reisinger J.: The Real-Time Operating System of MARS. ACM Operating System Review, 23(3): July 1989, 141–157.

53. Schwan K., Gopinath P., Bo W.: Chaos: Kernel Support for Objects in the Real-Time Domain. IEEE Transactions on Computers, C-36(8): August 1987, 904–916.

54. Schwan K., Zhou H., Gheith A.: Multiprocessor Real-Time Thread. ACM Operating System Review, 26(1): January 1992, 54–65.

55. Seaton S., Verissimo P., Waeselnyk F., Powell D., Bonn G.: The Delta-4 Approach to Dependability in Open Distributed Computing Systems. In Proc. FTCS-18, 1988, 246–251.

56. Shin K. G.: Harts: A Distributed Real-Time Architecture. IEEE Computer: May 1991, 25–35.

57. Smith R. M., Trivedi K. S. , Ramesh A. V.: Performability Analysis: Measures, an Algorithm, and a Case Study. IEEE Trans. on Computers, C-37(4): April 1988, 406–417.

58. Stankovic J. A.: Misconceptions About Real-Time Computing: A Serious Problem for next-generation Systems. IEEE Computer, October 1988, 10–19.

59. Tokuda H., Nakajima T.: Evaluation of Real-Time Synchronization in Real-Time Mach. In Proc. Mach Symposium 1990, Monterey, CA.

60. Xu J., Parnas D. L.: On Satisfying Timing Constraints in Hard Real-Time Systems. IEEE Transactions on Software Engineering, 19(1): January 1993, 70–84.
61. Zhao W., Ramamritham K.: Virtual Time CSMA Protocols for Hard Real-time Communication. IEEE Trans. on Software Engineering, SE-13(8), August 1987, 938–952.

Performance Instrumentation Techniques for Parallel Systems

Daniel A. Reed*

Department of Computer Science
University of Illinois
Urbana, Illinois 61801

Abstract. Although the nascent state of parallel systems makes empirical performance measurement, analysis and tuning critical, rapid technological evolution, coupled with short product life cycles, has often made it difficult to isolate fundamental experimental principles from implementation artifacts. By definition, the apparatus for experimental performance analysis (i.e., instrumentation specification, data buffering, timestamp generation, and data extraction) is shaped by the intended experiment and the object of study. In some environments, certain experiments are not feasible. Balancing the volume of captured performance data against its accuracy and timeliness requires both appropriate tools and an understanding of instrumentation costs, implementation alternatives, and support infrastructure.

1 Introduction

The same production economics that have made personal computers so powerful, inexpensive and ubiquitous, are driving the development of scalable parallel systems. By exploiting commodity microprocessors and memory chips, it is now technically and economically feasible to build systems that scale from tens to hundreds or thousands of processors. However, achieving a large fraction of peak performance across a range of applications has proven much more difficult than first expected — many massively parallel systems exhibit performance instability (i.e., the variance in performance is high, both in a single application and across a group of applications). Even more distressing than performance instability is our current inability to predict the performance of a particular application on a given parallel system.

As an illustration of performance instability, consider a simple *gedanken* experiment involving workstations and parallel systems. Select ten application programs, measure their execution times on an arbitrarily chosen workstation, and

---

* This work was supported in part by National Science Foundation grants NSF CCR87-06653 and NSF CDA87-22836 (Tapestry), NASA ICLASS Contract No. NAG-1-613, DARPA Contract No. DABT63-91-K-0004, and by grants from the Digital Equipment Corporation External Research Program and the Intel Supercomputer Systems Division.

then rank the applications based on their measured execution times. Now repeat the process for another workstation with comparable peak performance and then compare the two rankings. Not only will the rankings be permuted, but the relative separation between ranked elements also will have changed. Finally, repeat the experiment using two parallel systems with comparable peak performance.[2] Not only will there be little correlation between rankings, but the differences in program execution times may well vary by multiple orders of magnitude.

Although single figures of merit (e.g., peak MIPS, MFLOPS, or clock rate) cannot be used to predict the performance of an isolated application code, for single processor systems they do provide rough performance guidelines, and one can be reasonably confident that a system with a 100 MHz clock will execute almost any application code faster than a comparable system with a 50 MHz clock. In contrast, a parallel system with lower peak performance may well execute a wide range of codes more quickly than another that has higher peak performance. Simply put, consistently achievable performance across a broad range of applications is the desired, though still elusive, goal.

The underlying causes of performance instability and low performance lie in the patterns of interaction among application software, the operating system, and the parallel hardware. For parallel systems, these interactions involve hundreds or thousands of processors and dynamic behavior on a microsecond time scale. Just as effective management techniques for small, human organizations do not readily scale to larger groups, well-understood techniques for harnessing the power of two or four processor systems are not directly extensible to massively parallel systems. In both contexts, accurate, timely information is the prerequisite to developing and implementing decision procedures that maximize performance. Obtaining this information is the goal of performance instrumentation.

Performance instrumentation itself is part of the larger discipline of experimental performance analysis. As Fig. 1 suggests, experimental performance analysis contains four phases: hypothesis construction, identifying measurement points, instrumentation and measurement, and data analysis.

All but instrumentation and measurement depend on the experimental goal. For example, an effective task scheduling strategy for a shared memory parallel system depends on the application programming model, the cost of task preemption, the expected multiprogramming level, and the hardware's memory hierarchy. Changes to any one of these will shift the scheduling strategy design point, the experimental hypothesis, the instrumentation points, and the data analysis, but usually not the instrumentation and data capture infrastructure.

Given the enormous breadth of possible performance analysis hypotheses, as well as space limitations, techniques for performance instrumentation and data capture are the primary focus of this survey. For lucid introductions to the broader issues of hypothesis testing and performance data analysis, see [2, 23, 24].

[2] In practice, conducting this experiment on two parallel systems is a formidable task. Programming models and system configurations differ so greatly that simply porting a code to multiple architectures is problematic.

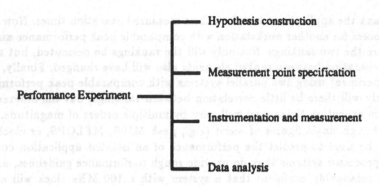

Figure 1 Experimental performance analysis phases

To provide a context for understanding experimental, parallel system performance analysis, §2 begins with a brief survey of parallel architectures and performance measurement levels, followed in §3 by a discussion of counting, timing, and tracing instrumentation. In §4, we compare hardware and software approaches to event tracing and discuss the importance of high resolution, low latency clocks. In §5 we describe potential performance instrumentation pitfalls and suggest guidelines for effective instrumentation, followed in §6 by a discussion of open problems and possible solutions. Finally, §7 concludes with a synopsis of our observations.

2 Parallel Processing and Instrumentation Levels

Although many of the techniques for experimental performance analysis apply generally to all classes of parallel systems, others are inextricably tied to particular classes of parallel architectures or particular programming models. Below, we briefly review common approaches to parallel processing, followed by a discussion of measurement levels and their instrumentation implications.

2.1 Parallel Architectures and Programming Models

Although a plethora of high-performance parallel systems have been proposed, the market is dominated by only three architecture classes: SIMD, shared memory MIMD, and distributed memory MIMD. Exemplars of these classes include the bit-serial SIMD Thinking Machines CM-2, the shared memory Cray C90 vector multiprocessor, and the Intel Paragon XP/S distributed memory multicomputer.[3] Not only does each have certain performance advantages and disadvantages, each also requires different performance measurements and differs in the ease of access to pertinent performance data.

[3] Other examples include, but are not limited to the SIMD Masspar MP-2, the Thinking Machines CM-5, Ncube/3, Cray T3D, and Convex MPP.

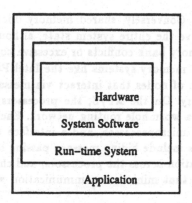

Figure 2 Performance instrumentation levels

The Thinking Machines CM-2 consists of up to 64K, one-bit processing elements (PEs), 2K high-speed floating point units, and a modest amount of local memory for each PE, all managed by a control processor that broadcasts instructions to the PEs. The PEs are connected by a two-dimensional mesh, for nearest neighbor communication, as well as a hypercube network, used for message routing to arbitrary destinations. The standard programming model is data parallel, arrays are distributed across the processors, and high-level array operations (e.g., array addition or reduction) are implemented by broadcasting instructions to the processor array. Key performance issues include maintaining a high degree of parallelism, minimizing delays for instruction broadcast, and minimizing interprocessor communication.

Because all instructions are issued by the control processor, capturing software performance data on a SIMD system is conceptually simple; one need only instrument instruction broadcast on the control processor to measure the execution time of particular operations (e.g., array or floating point operations). Moreover, because all PEs execute in lock step, one can halt instruction broadcast and interrogate the local memory of any PEs to extract additional data without perturbing the system state.

In striking contrast to the Thinking Machines CM-2, the Cray C90 contains up to 16 high-speed, pipelined vector processors that share access to a highly interleaved memory system. As a replacement for the Cray X/MP and Y/MP, the C90 relies on aggressive compilation of sequential Fortran codes to exploit vector operations, and on tasking directives to exploit multiple processors. Hardware semaphores provide synchronization for task scheduling. Key performance issues include maximizing vectorization, minimizing memory bank conflicts, and maintaining good load balance across the processors.

Shared memory simultaneously exacerbates and ameliorates performance instrumentation difficulties. The shared memory programming model encourages small, frequent state changes with synchronization only where necessary to ensure correctness. This makes it exceedingly difficult to capture the pattern of processor interactions. Conversely, shared memory does enable an instrumentation system to observe the entire system state, although care is necessary to avoid introducing memory bank conflicts or excessive context switching.

Finally, distributed memory systems like the Intel Paragon XP/S consist of hundreds or thousands of nodes that interact via message passing rather than through shared memory. On the XP/S, the processors are connected in two-dimensional mesh via a wormhole routing network. Each node contains a local memory, a commodity microprocessor, and a interface to the routing network. Key performance issues include hiding message passing latency by computation, balancing the computation across the processors, and choosing a distribution of data across processors that minimises communication while maximising parallelism.

In message passing, the interaction pattern among processors is explicit, and the maximum interaction frequency is low compared to that for shared memory systems. Although the relative isolation of the processors makes it easy to capture message passing performance data, the absence of a shared memory makes determining a global order for events difficult; see §4. Moreover, extracting performance data often must rely on the same network used to pass application messages; this can perturb the system.

The absence of a central control on both shared and distributed memory MIMD systems makes unobtrusive data capture and extraction more difficult than on SIMD systems. In consequence, the majority of vendor and research performance instrumentation efforts have focused on MIMD instrumentation implementations.

2.2 Performance Measurement Levels

The goal of performance instrumentation is to provide the requisite data to answer the basic question "How fast is it?" and its consequent "What should be modified to make it faster?" The meaning of the first question depends on its context. As Fig. 2 suggests, there are at least four potential instrumentation levels, namely hardware, system software, run-time software, and application code. In general, optimisation requires correlation of performance data across two or more of these levels. For example, maximising vector lengths is key to achieving good performance on most pipelined vector processors. An ideal performance instrumentation would include hardware support to count the number of scalar and vector floating point operations and software instrumentation in the application to record loop bounds and procedure call patterns. By combining hardware and application performance data, one could identify those code fragments that most need optimisation.[4]

From the instrumentation perspective, the techniques used to obtain performance data depend strongly on whether hardware, system software or application data are sought; see Table 1. Capturing hardware performance data without

---

[4] The Cray Hardware Performance Monitor (HPM) [9], together with application tracing, provides precisely this capability.

468

Table 1 Example performance measurements and instrumentation techniques

Level	Measurement	Example Technique	Support
Hardware	cache misses	counting	hardware
	network contention	timing	hardware
	instruction mix	counting	hardware
Operating system	system calls	counting/tracing	software/hardware
	context switches	counting/tracing	software/hardware
	page faults	counting	software
Run-time system	task creation	counting/tracing	software/hardware
	task synchronisation	counting/tracing	software
Application	procedure occupancy	profiling/timing	software
	message passing	tracing	software/hardware

hardware support is sometimes possible, though extremely difficult. Not only are many types of hardware data are not accessible via software (e.g., cache misses or pipeline stalls), but the trend is toward increasing inaccessibility. As microprocessors continue to replace discrete component designs, previously accessible measurement points are migrating onto the chip, and packaging constraints preclude the use of scarce pins for performance data extraction.[5] For example, it is not possible to capture a complete trace of physical memory references by monitoring memory accesses at a microprocessor's chip boundary; only misses to the on-chip cache are asserted on the chip's address pins.

Unfortunately, market pressures are unlikely to force microprocessor vendors to provide access to internal performance data. The parallel systems market, which increasingly relies on commodity processor building blocks, is a tiny fraction of the microprocessor market, and the predominant consumers of microprocessors, personal computer and workstation users, have not expressed interest in hardware instrumentation support.

Despite the lack of access to microprocessor internals, a plethora of hardware performance data remains accessible. Almost all parallel systems are constructed by augmenting microprocessors with ancillary logic to support either memory coherence (shared memory systems), message passing (distributed memory systems), or instruction issue (SIMD systems). By adding hardware counters and performance data extraction paths to these components, parallel systems vendors could provide ready access to a wealth of hardware performance data at minimal cost.

Hardware instrumentation can be unobtrusive, but is necessarily limited in scope and flexibility. The time scale for hardware events is small, their frequency is very high, and the number and type of instrumentation points must be chosen

---

[5] Increasing inaccessibility is a problem for chip testers as well. Builtin self-test (BIST) and scan logic for serial extraction of internal state are reactions to this limitation. See §4 for a discussion of clocks and clock access.

when the hardware is designed. In contrast, the software performance instrumentation options are much more rich and varied — both data capture techniques and instrumentation points can be changed long after the software has been designed.

The primary distinction between application instrumentation and that for operating system or run-time systems is the use of system services. Application instrumentation and data capture are free to use any system services if that use will not substantively change the application's performance or behavior. However, when designing operating system instrumentation and data capture, one must not use any system services that are potential instrumentation targets. For example, when measuring the performance of an input/output system, the performance data capture software must not rely on the input/output system for real-time data extraction. Similarly, a separate performance monitoring task can change the task scheduling pattern, and an instrumentation of a virtual memory system should not buffer performance data in virtual memory.

3 Performance Measurement Techniques

Regardless of the instrumentation level, there are four basic approaches to performance data capture: timing, counting, sampling, and tracing. Each represents a different balance between information volume, potential instrumentation perturbation, accuracy, and implementation complexity.

3.1 Timing

Speedup, the ratio of sequential to parallel execution time, relies on the simplest form of timing — a measure of aggregate execution time. If the execution time is sufficiently large, this measure requires no system support and introduces no perturbations, a simple stopwatch suffices. Aggregate system timing is a measure of success (i.e., it allows one to estimate how closely one approached the ideal), but it provides no insight when further performance optimization is required. Instead, one must measure the execution times of individual system components.

Although detailed timing data can identify *where* a system spends the majority of its time, it is insufficient to determine when or why. A procedure or hardware component may be in use a large fraction of time time, not because it was poorly optimised, but because some other component repeatedly and unnecessarily invokes it (i.e., timing can reveal proximate bottlenecks but not when or why particular hardware or software components were invoked).

To implement a timing facility, one needs only low latency access to a clock whose resolution is high compared to the elapsed time of the events being measured.[6] Both clock resolution and access latency are critical to accurate timing; the clock resolution limits the effective granularity of measurements, and the access latency bounds the instrumentation perturbation — access times for

---

[6] See §4 for a discussion of clocks and clock access.

a high latency clock can exceed the lifetime of the measured behavior. Finally, unless the number of timing points is large, the total volume of performance data produced by timing instrumentation is small.

3.2 Counting and Sampling

In contrast to timing, counting records the number of times an event occurred, but not where or why. Given both counts and total times, one can accurately compute average execution times. Unless the number of counters is exorbitant, counting is efficient, minimally intrusive, and produces only a modest amount of data. To implement a counting facility, one need only allocate sufficient storage for the array of counters, then during execution, index the counter array and increment the appropriate counter.

Sampling is an approximation to counting, obtained by periodically observing the system state and incrementing a counter that corresponds to the observed state. Standard profiles (e.g., Unix gprof [5]), sample the program counter at fixed time intervals, use the program counter as the index to a bin, and increment the associated counter. After program execution, the counter value in each bin is proportional to the total time spent executing code in the associated address range.

The primary limitations of profiling are its dependence on an external sampling task and the potential errors inherent in sampling. On single processor systems, the operating system implements profiling by sampling the task program counter at each clock tick, typically every 10–20 milliseconds. If the total program execution time is too low, the sampling error may be high. The operating system dependence of standard profiling techniques makes profiling operating system activity difficult.

On parallel systems, the existence of multiple processors can skew profiling statistics [16, 11]. Consider a code fragment that achieves linear speedup on P processors. The observed execution time for that code fragment is $\frac{1}{P}$ that for the comparable sequential code, and a program counter sample will underestimate its contribution to total execution time unless the samples across all P processors are combined.

3.3 Event Tracing

Event tracing is potentially the most invasive of the four instrumentation techniques, but it also is the most general and the most flexible. Event tracing generates a sequence of event records. Each event is some significant physical or logical activity, and the event record is an encoded instance of the action and its attributes. Each record typically includes the following.

1. *what* action occurred (i.e., an event identifier),
2. the time *when* the event occurred,
3. the location *where* the event occurred (e.g., a line number), and
4. any additional data that defines the event circumstances.

Not only does event tracing identify what happened and where it happened, the event timestamps impose an order on the events that defines control flow and system component interactions.

Event tracing subsumes timing, counting, and sampling; one can compute times and counts from trace data. For example, given a trace of procedure entries and exits, one can compute the total number of calls to each procedure by counting the number of instances of each event type, as well as the total procedure execution times by matching procedure entry and exit events, computing the difference in their event times, and adding the difference to a running sum for that procedure. In addition, the trace provides the dynamic procedure call graph Similarly, a trace of message passing events on a distributed memory parallel system defines the sequence of processor interactions, as well as load imbalances due to message waiting (i.e., by computing the waiting time to receive messages).

The disadvantage of tracing is its potential intrusion, the implementation complexity, and the large volume of generated performance data. Like timing, event tracing require low latency access to a high resolution clocks, but it also must unobtrusively buffer event data and extract it without excessively perturbing the measured system. Because software events can occur on a microsecond or millisecond time scale, and hardware events on an even smaller microsecond or even nanosecond scale, even on a single processor system, the data volume can exceed a megabyte per second. Fortunately, data rates for many common events are not that high, and, as we shall see, there are techniques to reduce the rate while retaining the advantages of tracing.

Despite its potential disadvantages, tracing is the software equivalent of a hardware logic analyzer. With tracing, one can capture component interactions, dynamic behavior, and transients. Too often, performance analysts treat software as a "black box" that can be stimulated externally but not probed internally. Event tracing allows users and performance analysts to study software and hardware interactions; in short, to understand *why* components perform as they do.

Because we believe event tracing is the most powerful tool for system understanding, and because the implementation issues for event tracing are a superset of those for counting and timing, tracing is the focus of the remainder of this survey. For a discussion of counting and timing facilities, see [23, 24].

4 Event Tracing

Event tracing is possible at either the hardware or software level. As discussed in §2.2, some components of hardware performance instrumentation (e.g., probe points) are inherently system dependent, and these dependences have profound implications for the other components. This is particularly true for event tracing, where the data rates are high and hardware solutions are closely linked to the intended application. In consequence, hardware event tracing is rarely used except in isolated circumstances (e.g., to obtain address traces). In contrast, software event tracing is effective with operating systems, run-time systems, and application codes. Moreover, the majority of the software implementation issues are independent of specific system idiosyncrasies. For this reason, our focus is support for capture of software events (i.e., events that occur in software).

Whether used with system or application software, any software event tracing implementation must resolve the following six issues:

1. timestamp generation,
2. trace buffer allocation,
3. event recording,
4. trace extraction,
5. data volume constraints, and
6. intrusion.

The expected data rates, system software environment, and the parallel architecture all constrain a particular implementation. To minimize the instrumentation intrusion, hardware support for some aspects of software data capture and extraction may be required.

As an example, on a distributed memory parallel system, event trace data can be buffered in individual processor processor memories, but when the volume of trace data exceeds the allocated storage, it must be removed from the node or some trace data must be discarded. Unless all nodes are preempted while the event trace data is extracted via the interprocessor communication network, using the network will interfere with system and application message passing and potentially change the timestamps or order of any events captured during the extraction. Given a separate, external performance data collection network, the data can be extracted from the system without using the standard communication network. However, writing the data to the collection network still consumes processor cycles. If the event data rate is extremely high, a data extraction co-processor may be needed as well.

In short, the instrumentation circumstances may dictate a software implementation, a hybrid of software and hardware, or a hardware implementation of software event tracing. Choosing an appropriate combination of hardware and software is part of the performance analyst's art.

4.1 Event Orders and Clocks

On a single processor system, sequential execution totally orders the event sequence — there is only one thread of control. For operating system or run-time systems, the event order is dependent on asynchronous events, and the event sequence may change across multiple executions. However, for most sequential application codes the event sequence is repeatable, given the same inputs. Moreover, at the application level, perturbations created by instrumentation can change the elapsed time between events, but they cannot change the event order; see Fig. 3.

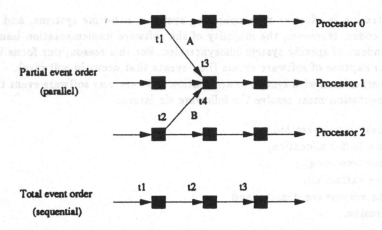

Figure 3 Partial and total event orders

On parallel systems, there are multiple threads of control, each potentially generating an event sequence. Just as for sequential execution, the event sequence for each thread is totally ordered. The global event order for the entire computation is obtained by merging the event orders from the individual event sequences.

If instrumentation differentially delays the threads, not only will the elapsed time between events change, but the global event order itself may change. Consider Fig. 3 where $t1$ and $t2$ denote the times that two different processors send messages to a third, $t3$ and $t4$ denote the times that those messages arrive, and the events A and B denote the two message arrivals. Delays on the parallel execution paths may result in the messages arriving in the order AB (i.e., $t3 < t4$) or the order BA (i.e., $t4 < t3$).

More perniciously, when merging the individual traces, it may be impossible to determine the correct event order. Continuing the example of Fig. 3, it may be impossible to determine which message was sent first (i.e., if $t1 < t2$). Three factors can prevent accurate event ordering: low resolution clocks, high latency clock access, and clock skew.

First and simplist, if the clock resolution is less than the nominal inter-event time, multiple events may have the same timestamp. On an individual processor or thread, these events still are totally ordered by the sequential execution, but across threads or processors they are unordered and apparently occur simultaneously. In the example of Fig. 3, if the measured times are such that $t1 = t2$, the order that the two message sends began cannot be resolved.

Unfortunately, many operating systems provide a user-accessible clock with a resolution equal to the power line frequency, either 50 or 60 Hz. In many cases, however, the hardware includes a higher resolution timer; it simply is not exported to the user by the system software. As processor speeds have increased, event frequencies have risen dramatically. This, coupled with low resolution clocks, has made accurate measurement of common software constructs

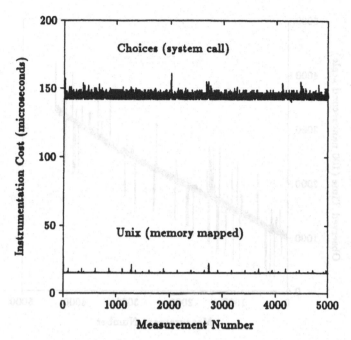

Figure 4 Encore Multimax event recording times

(e.g., procedure lifetimes) impossible.

Second, even if the clock resolution is high, a highly variable access cost can negate its effects. If events are timestamped under software control, a memory mapped clock that can be read by a single memory reference is imperative. As an example of its importance, Fig. 4 shows the cost to record an event on an Encore Multimax using two different operating systems, one with a memory mapped hardware clock and the other with the same clock accessible only via an operating system call [7]. With Encore's Unix implementation, accessing the clock requires only a memory read, and events can be recorded in as little as fifteen microseconds. Under the experimental *Choices* operating system, the system call not only increases the event recording time ten-fold, it also increases the access time variance. In addition to a protection boundary crossing, there are multiple procedure calls, memory references, and cache misses. Closely separated events on different processors may lie within the measurement uncertainty of the clock system call.

The third cause of uncertainties in global event orders is clock skew. Normally, we accept the classical physics view of time; we assume it flows at an equal rate at all locations, that it orders local and remote events, and that causality violations are impossible. Intuitively, an omniscient observer would see all events occurring in their "true" order with cause preceding effect.

Unfortunately, the classical view of time is inconsistent with reality on many parallel systems. If each processor has its own clock, measured time can po-

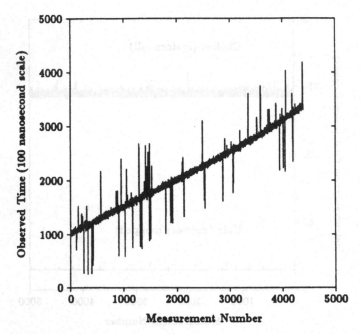

Figure 5 Clock drift in measured message transmission times

tentially flow at a different, non-uniform rate on each processor.[7] Non-uniform rates mean that the measured time between events on a single processor may be inaccurate. More troubling, however, is the effect of different rates — when comparing event timestamps on two different processors, causality violations can occur (i.e., effect can, based on timestamps, seem to precede cause).

Figure 5 illustrates the effect of inconsistent clocks on a Intel iPSC/860; each processor has a local clock with 100 nanosecond resolution. The figure shows a sequence of measured, message transmission times between a pair of nodes. The elapsed times were determined by computing the difference between the timestamp for a message send event on the transmitter and the timestamp on the associated message receive event on the receiver. The increasing time for a round trip message transmission is an artifact of clock drift, and the spikes are due to context switches on one or the other of the two processors. Near the beginning, the two clock values are nearly the same. As the measurement proceeds, the clocks drift apart. In this example, the separation is positive, but only a few of the estimates are accurate. If the identities of the receiver and sender were exchanged, the message transmission times would be negative.

Clock drift can be eliminated either by distributing the value of a single clock to all processors or by synchronizing all clocks to a master time base. Unless the clock resolution is very low, clock distribution requires hardware support via a

---

[7] This problem is not unique to parallel systems. The existence of unsynchronised local clocks motivated the creation of an international time base, Universal Time (UT).

clock distribution network. Even for a system with hundreds or thousands of processors, the cost of such a network is low.[8]

Software clock synchronization [3, 17] is the alternative to a global time base. Intuitively, one chooses one processor's clock as the master and synchronizes all other clocks to that master. To bound the potential difference between clocks, one initially measures the drift rate using measures similar to that in Fig. 5. and uses that to compute a resynchronization interval. The frequency of clock resynchronization depends on the drift rate, the desired error bound, and the tolerable synchronization cost, but it must be high enough to prevent causality violations in the measured event times.

To summarise, obtaining accurate, total event orders for parallel systems is dependent on high resolution, globally consistent, low latency clocks. Techniques for minimising instrumentation overhead may involve software, hardware, or a combination of the two. Failure in any area can lead to inaccurate data and incorrect event orders.

4.2 Software Support

Because software support for performance instrumentation can take many forms, implementation issues are best understood in a specific context. Hence, we describe three different software implementations of event tracing, Crystal, Pablo, and CTrace, each intended for a different environment. Crystal [20] supports operating system and application performance data capture on the Intel iPSC/2 hypercube, the Pablo instrumentation library [19] supports portable application event tracing, and the CTrace library [10] supports application and operating system tracing on a hierarchical, shared memory parallel system.

Crystal: Operating System Instrumentation. The Intel iPSC/2 hypercube typified second generation distributed memory systems. The iPSC/2 hypercube nodes were based on an Intel 80386/80387 pair, each node contained up to sixteen megabytes of memory, and the nodes sent messages via fixed path circuit-switching [1]. In addition, a subset of the nodes supported a parallel input/output system [15] with on commodity disks. Because the iPSC/2's salient features are an integral part of current systems (e.g., the Intel Paragon XP/S and Thinking Machines CM-5), most of the performance instrumentation issues are directly transferable to newer architectures.

Crystal [13, 20, 22, 21], based on a modified version of the Intel NX/2 operating system, was an event tracing facility designed to capture both application and operating system events. Application instrumentation could be inserted either manually by users or automatically by a compiler. In either case, the generated events were passed to a modified version of Intel's NX/2 operating system, which executed on each of the hypercube nodes.

---

[8] Despite its low cost, many commercial systems still lack a global time base.

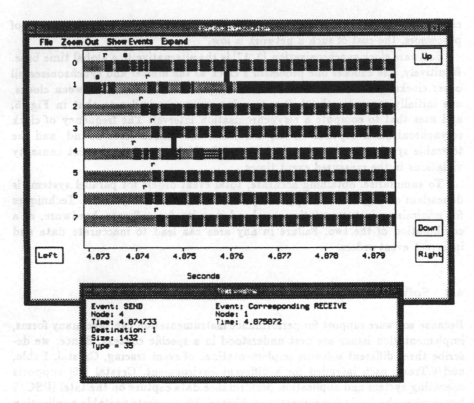

Figure 6 Crystal Intel iPSC/2 event time line

In addition to recording the application data, the modified NX/2 internally captured three classes of operating system events: message passing, process context switches, and all system calls. On each node, the application and operating system events were merged and stored in a trace buffer that was preallocated in the node's local memory. Because each node of the iPSC/2 had a local clock, the modified NX/2 synchronised all node clocks before event recording began and compensated for clock skew using the known clock drift rates.

Finally, when a node's trace buffer filled, tracing on that node normally was disabled. As a more intrusive alternative, a double buffering scheme allowed extraction of one trace buffer via the circuit-switched network while the other was being filled. The NX/2 operating system did not support virtual memory, and the Crystal instrumentation was a delicate balance between application memory needs and trace storage capacity. Allocating too much memory to trace capture left too little for the application code to execute. Allocating too little memory to trace buffers limited the amount of captured data.

Experience showed that the limited operating system instrumentation supported by Crystal was surprisingly powerful. Tracing the operating system message passing code showed the contributions of message buffer management, hardware setup, and transmission time to message latency, as well as the effects of the Intel iPSC/2 communication protocol.[9] Moreover, because all application file requests were realized using messages, the instrumented message passing showed all file-related communication traffic synthesized by the operating system. Finally, the context switch and system call data exposed the coupling of application requests for services with the operating system responses, as well as idle time due to load imbalances.

Figure 6 shows a portion of a graphical time line, constructed using trace data captured by Crystal. The event trace is from an eight processor execution of a parallel linear optimization code [25]. Notice the message send, highlighted on processor 4 and the corresponding receive, highlighted on processor 1. The series of parallel horizontal lines following the "s" are the hardware message transmission of a fixed size message header. Following this, the sending node is idle (indicated by light gray) while the receiver operating system on node 1 processes the message header (indicated by dark gray). Processor 4 then transmits the remainder of the message, shown by the second series of horizontal lines between times 4.875 and 4.876. More generally, the alternating light and dark gray pattern on the time line is a sequence of context switches between the application code and the operating system, as the application probes for message arrivals.

The primary strength of Crystal, its access to operating system internals, also proved to be its greatest weakness. Retrofitting instrumentation to a proprietary operating system required source code access, and licensing restrictions prevented redistribution of modified source code. Unless the operating system source code widely available (e.g., Mach or OSF/1), operating system instrumentation is best supported by a parallel systems vendor.

Pablo: Application Instrumentation. The Pablo Performance Analysis Environment[10] [19, 18] is a portable performance instrumentation and data analysis environment designed for large-scale parallel systems, with primary emphasis on the Intel Paragon XP/S and Thinking Machines CM-5. Unlike the Crystal instrumentation, Pablo's instrumentation software is designed to be architecture neutral and easily portable to new systems.[11]

Intended primarily for capturing application performance data, the Pablo instrumentation is implemented as a library that isolates architecture-independent data buffering and recording software from architecture-dependent aspects such as processor synchronization and timestamp acquisition. The data recording

---

[9] The iPSC/2 used a two-phase protocol to send messages longer than 100 bytes — first, a fixed size header was sent that contained the message length and an initial portion of the message. After the receiver acknowledged the receipt and its willingness to accept additional data, the sender transmitted the remainder of the message.

[10] Pablo is a trademark of the Board of Trustees of the University of Illinois.

[11] PICL, the portable, instrumented communication library [4], developed by the Oak Ridge National Laboratory, shares these attributes, though its primary focus is on portable message passing.

model is similar to that for the Crystal instrumentation; there is a separate trace buffer for each processor or thread of control, and performance data are written to these buffers. When any buffer fills, all processors are interrupted and all write their trace data to secondary storage. The cost of buffer dumping is recorded in the trace data, allowing buffering dumping overheads to be removed from the trace data during post-processing. For parallel systems that lack a global time base, the Pablo instrumentation periodically synchronizes the processors using an implementation of Dunigan's distributed synchronization algorithm [3].

The architecture-independent instrumentation interface supports counting, interval timing, and event tracing. Counts can be accumulated or periodically flushed to trace buffers. If they are flushed only once, at the end of data capture, the canonical definition of counting holds; conversely, flushing a count each time it changes is equivalent to event tracing. Periodic flushing of counts allows the performance analyst to balance data volume against instrumentation data granularity.

To further constrain data rates and to provide user control of instrumentation perturbations, the Pablo instrumentation library supports both user-specified and internal event rate controls. The instrumentation library monitors the data recording rate for each event. While the rate lies below a pre-specified event threshold, the event stream is recorded. However, when the rate exceeds the threshold, the instrumentation library substitutes less invasive data recording (.e.g., by converting trace events into periodic counts). When the event rate declines, more detailed data recording is re-enabled. By adjusting the event rate threshold, the user can balance data rates, event volume, and instrumentation perturbation against the need for specific performance data.

For counting, interval timing, and event tracing, the Pablo instrumentation library supports user-written extension functions. Because all event data is passed to these functions before being written to trace buffers, users can create higher-level events, selectively discard certain events, or modify the event data. For example, given a sequence of procedure entry and exit trace events, an extension function could replace the raw event trace with dynamic procedure profiles, a histogram of procedure lifetimes, or a matrix of procedure call transition probabilities.

To support user extensions and to maximize portability, Pablo generates performance data files in a self-describing data format (SDDF). These files include definitions of the record formats contained in the file; the definitions are then used to parse the record instances. Because new record definitions can be easily added, new types of performance data relevant to specific application or architecture contexts can be added without modifying the Pablo data capture library.

The strengthes of the Pablo instrumentation library's approach are its portability and extensibility. However, this emphasis does limit the library's ability to exploit system-specific features and to easily capture system-level performance data.

CTrace: Shared Memory Instrumentation. CTrace [10] is an event tracing system for the experimental Cedar multiprocessor. Cedar [8] consists of multiple processor clusters connected via a multistage Omega network to a global, shared memory. In turn, the individual clusters are modified Alliant FX/8 systems, each with eight vector processors, a shared cache, and a shared cluster memory.

Cedar programs are expressed in Cedar Fortran, a Fortran dialect that supports both loop and task parallelism. Parallel loop iterations can be either restricted to a particular cluster, or they can be distributed across multiple clusters. In either case, loop iterations can execute in parallel, vector, or parallel-vector mode. Parallel tasks executing on different clusters can cooperate via the global shared memory.

CTrace supports both operating system and application event tracing, with a default set of events captured by an instrumentation of the Cedar operating system and the Cedar Fortran run-time library. Specifically, operating system context switches are recorded by instrumenting the process switching code, and task creation, activation, suspension, and deletion, as well as invocations of synchronization primitives are captured by instrumenting the run-time library. Procedure, basic block, and loop entry/exit trace event instrumentation is generated on request by the Cedar Fortran compiler; additional trace events can be specified by manually by the user.

Like Crystal, Pablo, and PICL, CTrace is implemented as a library with multiple trace buffers to eliminate contention and synchronization when recording data. The Cedar hardware maintains a global time base across all clusters, no clock synchronization is required, and event causality is assured.

Unlike most distributed memory parallel systems, the shared memory Cedar system is multiprogrammed. Elapsed times, computed using the difference between to values of the real-time clock, may be inaccurate — a task may be forced to relinquish its processor during the measured interval. Using operating system context switch trace, elapsed times are adjusted to remove these anomalies and to correctly charge each task.

4.3 Hardware Support

When the event data rate is very high, trace buffer storage capacities are low, or clock synchronization costs are high, hardware support for performance data recording and extraction becomes essential. By shifting portions of the instrumentation implementation from software to dedicated hardware, larger event traces can be captured with lower overhead.

Ideally, the balance between hardware and software implementations is determined during system design. Unfortunately, many instrumentation systems are added late in the design process, necessitating accommodation with existing design features. Below, we describe two examples of hardware support for software performance data capture, Hypermon [11, 12], a retrofit to the Intel iPSC/2 hypercube, and Multikron [14], a performance data recording chip.

Hypermon: An Instrumentation Hardware Retrofit. Users of Crystal's software instrumentation on the Intel iPSC/2 often struggled to overcome its two major limitations: insufficient event data storage capacity and the lack of an accurate, global time base. In an attempt to remedy these limitations and to explore the feasibility of retrofitting an existing system with hardware support for performance data capture, Malony developed Hypermon [11, 12], a board set for hardware data buffering and timestamp generation.

Hypermon exploited a little-known feature of the Intel iPSC/2, a five bit interface from each node board to a spare node slot in the system cabinet. This interface was mapped to the input/output address space of each iPSC/2 node, with one bit used as a valid data strobe and four bits for input/output. By modifying the Crystal instrumentation to write performance data to this address, rather than buffering it in memory, performance data from all nodes was accessible at a single location.

The Hypermon hardware exploited the data collection interface to capture, buffer, and timestamp the four-bit event data. Crystal trace events normally included an event identifier and several bytes of ancillary data; transmitting these events from each node required several, four-bit writes to the memory-mapped interface. Because there was no hardware mechanism to identify event boundaries, Hypermon generated hardware event frames, rather than trace events, when one or more nodes wrote data to the interface within any 800 nanosecond window. Each frame contained four bits from each node, a bit vector indicating which nodes had sent valid data, and a timestamp. The resulting event frames were buffered and then transferred to a Intel iPSC/2 input/output node. Based on the event data rate, the frames could either be processed as they arrived or written to secondary storage for post-processing.

Hypermon performance measurements revealed two serious bottlenecks. The four-bit interface from the nodes proved debilitating. First, and not surprisingly, the nodes were forced to assert data validity via software strobing and to shift and mask the event bytes before writing to the data capture interface; this overhead proved two orders of magnitude higher than that for software data buffering. This was an unfortunate artifact of retrofitting. An eight bit wide interface with hardware strobing would have greatly reduced the overhead and made the overheads comparable to those for software event recording.

Second, event data rates were bursty; these bursts can lead to hardware buffer data overruns. Moreover, the total event data volume increased superlinearly with the number of nodes. As an example, Fig. 7, from [12], shows the Crystal event data rate, in one millisecond windows, for a standard cell placement code run on the Intel iPSC/2. The single processor trace includes only the context switch events that occur each fifty milliseconds. As the number of nodes increases, the number of message passing events increases and the data rate rises dramatically. In one second intervals, the data rate can exceed one megabyte/second for even a modest number of nodes.

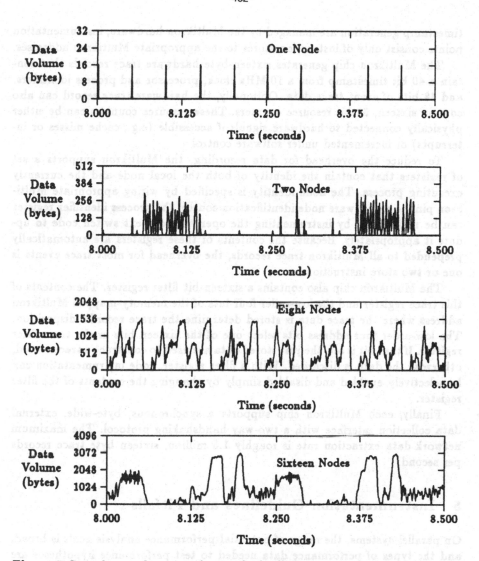

Figure 7 Crystal event data rates for standard cell placement

Multikron: A Performance Monitoring Chip. The NIST Multikron [14] integrates support for counting, event trace buffering, timestamp generation, and data extraction on a single chip. In its intended operational mode, each node or processor of a parallel system would include a Multikron chip for unobtrusive data recording.

Unlike Hypermon's constrained, four-bit interface, Multikron supports a set of 64-bit, memory-mapped interfaces that can be both read and written. Some of the interfaces are used for configuration commands, some to record event trace data, and some to query the Multikron state. Because the data recording and timestamp generation are managed by the Multikron hardware, instrumentation points consist only of instruction stores to the appropriate Multikron addresses.

The Multikron chip generates sixteen-byte hardware trace records that contain a 40 bit timestamp from a 10 MHz clock, processor and process identifiers, and 48 bits of event trace data. Optionally, the hardware trace record can also contain sixteen, 32-bit resource counters. These resource counters can be either physically connected to hardware signals if accessible (e.g., cache misses or interrupts) or incremented under software control.

To reduce the overhead for data recording, the Multikron supports a set of registers that contain the identity of both the local node and the currently executing process. The node identity is specified by wiring appropriate Multikron pins to a hardware node identification source; the process identifier register can be maintained by instrumenting the operating context switch code to update it appropriately. Because the contents of these registers are automatically prepended to all Multikron trace records, the overhead for most trace events is one or two store instructions.

The Multikron chip also contains a sixteen-bit filter register. The contents of this trace register and the low-order four bits of the memory-mapped Multikron address where the trace data is stored determine the trace record's disposition. The low-order four address bits select one of the sixteen bits in the trace filter register. If that bit is set, the just stored data are used to construct a trace record, otherwise the data is discarded. With a filter register, code instrumentation can be selectively enabled and disabled simply by changing the contents of the filter register.

Finally, each Multikron chip supports a synchronous, byte-wide, external data collection interface with a two-way handshaking protocol. The maximum network data extraction rate is roughly 1.5 million, sixteen byte trace records per second.

5 Instrumentation Guidelines and Pitfalls

On parallel systems, the range of potential performance analysis goals is broad, and the types of performance data needed to test performance hypotheses are equally diverse. To meet their instrumentation needs, vendors, performance analysts, researchers, and application software developers have all developed performance instrumentation hardware and software. Some instrumentation tools were designed to explore the design space for parallel computer systems, others to optimize system or application software performance.

Despite the diversity of intents and the variety of instrumentation techniques, several general lessons have emerged from the design, implementation, and use of multiple generations of performance instrumentation hardware and software. Succinctly,

1. instrumentation is best included early in a system's design, rather than retrofitted to an existing system,

2. performance data rates must be balanced against instrumentation overhead and data utility,
3. no single instrumentation technique is appropriate in all circumstances, and finally,
4. some aspect of the captured data usually surprises the analyst, motivating additional instrumentation.

Although these observations apply to performance instrumentation on any computer system, designing instrumentation for parallel systems poses special challenges. First, only a small portion of the large parallel system design space has been explored, and both hardware and software architectures for parallel systems are evolving rapidly. By the time instrumentation techniques for a particular parallel architecture are tested and well-understood, that architecture may have been abandoned in favor of another.[12] Second, parallelism introduces partial, rather than total, event orders and the data volume problems inherent with large numbers of processors. Below, we summarize some guidelines and pitfalls when developing instrumentation specifically for parallel systems.

5.1 Instrumentation Infrastructure

Implementation of a performance instrumentation system is necessarily dependent on extant hardware and software features and services. The absence of particular feature may preclude certain measurements. For example, measuring individual procedure invocation lifetimes is impossible with a clock whose resolution is equal to the power line frequency. To capture timestamped event traces on a parallel system, one minimally needs

1. high resolution clocks (i.e., microsecond or better),
2. memory-mapped, low latency clock access, and
3. global clock synchronization,

with the maximum allowable clock drift bounded by the clock resolution. For software events, the timestamp clock resolution need not be equal to that of the processor clock, but it should be close to an instruction execution time. When capturing hardware events, the clock resolution must equal or exceed that for the processor clock.

The data buffering and extraction facility must support bursty, potentially high volume, event data while minimizing the number of system services used. If the data rates are sufficiently high to perturb execution and stress a software data capture implementation, one should first ask if all the data is really necessary to understand the phenomenon being studied. If not, less invasive instrumentation (e.g., counting rather than tracing) is appropriate. Otherwise, hardware support for data buffering and extraction (e.g., like that provided by the NIST Multikron chip [14]) may be necessary.

---

[12] This temporal dependence is a cogent argument that vendors should include support for performance instrumentation early in their system designs.

Finally, quantifying instrumentation perturbation is difficult. To determine if instrumentation is perturbing system behavior, disable some subset of the instrumentation points or substitute less invasive instrumentation (e.g., counting rather than tracing). Where possible, compute equivalent performance metrics from both instrumentations and compare their values for consistency. Although this does not guarantee the absence of perturbation, it does lessen the likelihood that it is undetected.

5.2 Instrumentation Probes

Although choosing appropriate instrumentation points is constrained by the performance analysis goal, inappropriate instrumentation can grossly perturb system behavior and quickly generate large volumes of inaccurate performance data. Across a broad range of parallel architectures and performance experiments, capturing certain types of performance data has repeatedly proved valuable, while not excessively perturbing system activity.

In an operating system, capturing

1. processor context switches,
2. interrupts, and
3. system calls

provides the largest return on instrumentation investment. These instrumentation points capture the interactions of application code with system services, task scheduling patterns, busy and idle times, and many internal operating system component interactions. Moreover, only a few instrumentation points are required, and changes to system services (e.g., file systems or scheduling algorithms) normally do not affect the instrumentation.

In an application, standard instrumentation points include

1. procedure entries and exits,
2. loop entries and exists,
3. on shared memory systems, synchronisation and tasking primitives, and
4. on distributed memory systems, message passing primitives.

When inserting instrumentation, it is best to begin with the smallest possible set of instrumentation points, then insert additional points based on an analysis of the previously captured data. When instrumenting nested loops, ensure that lifetime of the inner loop is substantially larger than the instrumentation overhead; otherwise instrumentation will dominate the lifetime of the loop nest.

Finally, recognise that inserting instrumentation in source code can inhibit certain compiler optimisations. For example, bracketing the body of a procedure with two instrumentation points to capture its lifetime may prevent a compiler from inlining the code at the point of call. Similarly, source code instrumentation can prevent loop interchanges, change register allocations, and inhibit local code motion. To mitigate many of these effects, compilers should automatically generate standard types of instrumentation in response to user requests.

5.3 Instrumentation Scalability

Scalability is a key feature of most high-performance parallel systems. Using standard building blocks that contain a processor, local memory, and a network interface, a single parallel architecture can scale from tens to hundreds or thousands of processors. To achieve high performance and to exploit architectural scalability, system and application software must scale as well.

Regrettably, some instrumentation techniques do not scale to hundreds or thousands of processors. As an illustration, Table 2 shows the event data rates and expected event volumes when capturing processor utilizations and message send events on a 1024 processor system. Message tracing produces nearly 300K[13] bytes second, and even the simple processor utilization metric produces performance data at 32K bytes/second.

Moreover, as §4.3 illustrated, event data volume is not a linear function of the number of processors. For the example of Table 2, the time interval between message passing events will decrease as the number of processors increases, and the total data rate will increase. In small time intervals, the message passing event data rate might approach 3-5 megabytes/second for a thousand processor system.

Simply put, for systems with hundreds or thousands of processors, either hardware support for data capture or, preferably, real-time data reduction is imperative, For massively parallel systems, real-time data reduction is itself a parallel task. The number of data reduction processors must scale with the par-

Table 2 Example event data rates for 1024 processors

Processor Utilization	Message Traffic
processor identifier utilisation estimate	source processor source task destination processor destination task timestamp message length message type
Data capture interval (milliseconds)	
250	100
Total data rate (bytes/second)	
32K	287K
Total data volume (one hour)	
118 MB	1 GB

---

[13] fpractice, the actual amount is nearly twice this high because both message transmission and message receipt are traced.

allel system size, and a separate data extraction network must connect the data reduction processors to the data sources. Using the NIST Multikron chip as an example, one might place a Multikron chip on each processor, connect the external interfaces of each group of 8–16[14] Multikron chips to a single data reduction processor, and connect the set of data reduction processors via a high-speed network. In essence, one constructs two parallel systems, one executing the application and a second, smaller system, connected to the first via the Multikron chip external data collection interfaces.

6 Open Instrumentation Problems

Despite our breadth of experience with instrumentation techniques for sequential systems, and our growing experience with parallel systems, many open problems remain. Of these, two of the most pressing are those associated with data parallel languages and performance queries.

The tacit assumption underlying source code instrumentation is that the organisation and structure of the compiler-generated code are similar to that in the source code.[15] When this assumption is false, instrumentation may either inhibit or change the normal optimisations or it may measure something other than what might expected when examining the source code. Compilation of data parallel programs for distributed memory parallel systems is an apt illustration.

Historically, most distributed memory parallel systems were programmed in single program multiple data (SPMD) mode using an explicit message passing style, and standard workstation compilers were used to generate code. Data parallel languages like High-Performance Fortran (HPF) [6] express parallelism by specifying parallel operations on arrays that have been distributed across the memories of the system. Compilers for data parallel languages then create code that reads and writes the distributed arrays using compiler-synthesized message passing.

Not only must the translation from data parallel source code to message-based executable code bridge a large "semantic gap," but the translation procedure is hidden from the application programmer. Moreover, the translation is strongly dependent on how the arrays are distributed and accessed; small changes to either can dramatically alter the generated code.

Instrumenting the data parallel source code will not reveal the causes of poor performance; they lie in both the application source code and the compiler-synthesized code. Conversely, instrumenting the compiler-synthesized code provides accurate performance data but no mechanism to relate that data to source code constructs.

---

[14] The exact number depends on the event data rate, the complexity of the data reduction operations, and the speed of the data reduction processors.

[15] This assumption also underlies the implementation of most breakpoint debuggers. New techniques for debugging optimised code remain an active research topic, and only a few commercial debuggers now support it.

Obtaining accurate performance data that can be correlated with source code is an open research problem. However, it is clear that effective performance tuning and performance correlation for data parallel codes will require compiler support; it is not possible via standard source code instrumentation.

Ideally, the compiler would synthesise performance instrumentation and ancillary tools would reduce the resulting data to satisfy user performance queries. This query-response model differs from current approaches in two ways. First, the instrumentation points would be generated by the compiler, based on its knowledge of program structure and the synthesised code, and would not be visible to the user. Second, data analysis is inextricably tied to compilation and code generation. Only with access to program dependencies and generated data access patterns can query responses be computed. Implementing a query-response performance analysis model for data parallel languages will require close coupling of performance analysis tools, compiler-synthesised instrumentation, data capture libraries, and the compiler's program analysis data base.

7 Summary

Although parallel systems continue to change rapidly, a set of standard performance instrumentation techniques for parallel systems has begun to emerge. High resolution clocks with low access costs are fundamental to unobtrusive instrumentation. Similarly, data capture and extraction techniques must support high volume, bursty performance data rates. For massively parallel systems, hardware support for data extraction and real-time data reduction may be necessary if detailed event data are required.

Despite advances, many open issues remain, notably techniques for performance instrumentation and analysis of codes written in data parallel languages. To bridge the semantic gap between program source and generated code, performance analysis and instrumentation must be closely coupled with compilation.

Acknowledgments

My heartfelt thanks to the past and present members of the Pablo and Picasso research groups, without whom this work would not have been possible. Special thanks to Allen Malony, now at the University of Oregon, for many fruitful, pleasant discussions about instrumentation techniques.

References

1. ARLAUSKAS, R. iPSC/2 System: A Second Generation Hypercube. In *Proceedings of the Third Conference on Hypercube Concurrent Computers and Applications, Volume I* (Pasadena, CA, Jan. 1988), Association for Computing Machinery, pp. 38–42.

2. DONGARRA, J. J., AND TOURANCHEAU, B., Eds. *Environments and Tools for Parallel Scientific Computing*. North-Holland Publishing Company, 1992.

3. DUNIGAN, T. H. Hypercube Clock Synchronisation. *Concurrency: Practice and Experience 4*, 3 (May 1992), 258–268.

4. GEIST, G. A., HEATH, M. T., PEYTON, B. W., AND WORLEY, P. H. A User's Guide to PICL A Portable Instrumented Communication Library. Tech. Rep. ORNL/TM-11616, Oak Ridge National Laboratory, Aug. 1992.

5. GRAHAM, S., KESSLER, P., AND McKUSICK, M. gprof: A Call Graph Execution Profiler. In *Proceedings of the SIGPLAN '82 Symposium on Compiler Construction* (Boston, MA, June 1982), Association for Computing Machinery, pp. 120–126.

6. HPFF. High-Performance Fortran Language Specfication, version 1.0. Tech. rep., High Performance Fortran Forum, May 1993.

7. KOHR, D. R., ZHANG, X., REED, D. A., AND RAHMAN, M. Object-Oriented, Parallel Operating Systems: A Performance Study. Tech. rep., University of Illinois at Urbana-Champaign, Department of Computer Science, May 1993.

8. KUCK, D. J., DAVIDSON, E. S., LAWRIE, D. H., AND SAMEH, A. H. Parallel Supercomputing Today and the Cedar Approach. *Science 231* (February 28 1986), 967–974.

9. LARSON, J. Cray X-MP Hardware Performance Monitor. *Cray Channels* (1985).

10. MALONY, A. D. Multiprocessor Instrumentation: Approaches for Cedar. In *Instrumentation for Future Parallel Computing Systems*, M. Simmons, R. Koskela, and I. Bucher, Eds. Addison-Wesley, 1989, pp. 1–33.

11. MALONY, A. D. *Performance Observability*. PhD thesis, University of Illinois at Urbana–Champaign, Department of Computer Science, Aug. 1990.

12. MALONY, A. D., AND REED, D. A. A Hardware-Based Performance Monitor for the Intel iPSC/2 Hypercube. In *Proceedings of the 1990 ACM International Conference on Supercomputing* (June 1990), Association for Computing Machinery, pp. 213–226.

13. MALONY, A. D., REED, D. A., AND RUDOLPH, D. C. Integrating Performance Data Collection, Analysis, and Visualisation. In *Parallel Computer Systems: Performance Instrumentation and Visualization*, M. Simmons and R. Koskela, Eds. Addison-Wesley Publishing Company, 1990, pp. 73–97.

14. MINK, A., AND CARPENTER, R. J. Operating Principles of MULTIKRON Performance Instrumentation for MIMD Computer. Tech. Rep. NISTIR 4737, National Institute of Standards and Technology, Mar. 1992.

15. PIERCE, P. A Concurrent File System for a Highly Parallel Mass Storage Subsystem. In *Proceedings of the Fourth Conference on Hypercubes, Concurrent Computers and Applications* (Monterey, CA, Mar. 1989), Association for Computing Machinery, pp. 155–160.

16. PONDER, C., AND FATEMAN, R. Inaccuracies in Program Profiling. *Software: Practice and Experience 18*, 5 (May 1988), 459–467.

17. RAMANATHAN, P., SHIN, K. G., AND BUTLER, R. W. Fault-tolerant Clock Synchronisation in Distributed System. *IEEE Computer 23* (1990), 33–42.

18. REED, D. A., AYDT, R. A., MADHYASTHA, T. M., NOE, R. J., SHIELDS, K. A., AND SCHWARTZ, B. W. The Pablo Performance Analysis Environment. Tech. rep., University of Illinois at Urbana-Champaign, Department of Computer Science, Nov. 1992.

19. REED, D. A., OLSON, R. D., AYDT, R. A., MADHYASTHA, T. M., BIRKETT, T., JENSEN, D. W., NAZIEF, B. A. A., AND TOTTY, B. K. Scalable Performance Environments for Parallel Systems. In *Proceedings of the Sixth Distributed Memory Computing Conference* (1991), IEEE Computer Society Press, pp. 562–569.

20. REED, D. A., AND RUDOLPH, D. C. Experiences with Hypercube Operating System Instrumentation. *International Journal of High-Speed Computing 1*, 4 (Dec. 1989), 517–542.

21. RUDOLPH, D. C. Performance Instrumentation for the Intel iPSC/2. Master's thesis, University of Illinois at Urbana–Champaign, Department of Computer Science, July 1989.

22. RUDOLPH, D. C., AND REED, D. A. CRYSTAL: Operating System Instrumentation for the Intel iPSC/2. In *Proceedings of the Fourth Conference on Hypercube Concurrent Computers and Applications* (Monterey, CA, Mar. 1989), pp. 249–252.

23. SIMMONS, M., AND KOSKELA, R., Eds. *Parallel Computing Systems: Performance Instrumentation and Visualization*. Addison-Wesley Publishing Company, 1990.

24. SIMMONS, M., KOSKELA, R., AND BUCHER, I., Eds. *Instrumentation for Future Parallel Computing Systems*. Addison-Wesley Publishing Company, 1989.

25. STUNKEL, C. B., FUCHS, W. K., RUDOLPH, D. C., AND REED, D. A. Linear Optimisation: A Case Study in Performance Analysis. In *Proceedings of the Fourth Conference on Hypercube Concurrent Computers and Applications* (Monterey, CA, Mar. 1989), pp. 265–268.

A Survey of Bottleneck Analysis in Closed Networks of Queues *

P. J. Schweitzer

W. E. Simon Graduate School of Business Administration,
University of Rochester, Rochester, NY 14627, USA

G. Serazzi, M. Broglia

Politecnico di Milano, Dip. Elettronica e Informazione,
P.za L. da Vinci 32, 20133 Milano, Italy
serazzi@ipmel2.elet.polimi.it

Abstract

Several of the principal results in bottleneck analysis for closed queueing networks are surveyed. Both product-form closed queueing networks, where exact bottleneck analysis is possible, and non-product-form closed queueing networks, where approximations are given for asymptotic bottleneck behavior, are considered. Algorithms for the asymptotic bottleneck analysis are presented and the switching surfaces of bottlenecks are described.

1 Introduction and Scope

1.1 Importance

Identification of bottlenecks (BNs) in queueing networks is an important step in systems performance evaluation and upgrades: investing resources at a BN will have dramatic effect on systems performance; investing at a non-BN will have negligible benefit. However, over-investing at a BN is unwise because, beyond a certain point, the secondary (or tertiary) BN becomes the primary BN. Beyond this point, the investment should be split among the several near-ties for BN. This complication, along with the diminishing marginal benefits associated with investment, make BN analysis — especially of multiple BNs — somewhat complex.

*This work was partially supported by CNR "Progetto Finalizzato Sistemi Informatici e Calcolo Parallelo" by grant N. 92.01615.PF69.115.23757 and by M.U.R.S.T. 40% Project

In addition, BN analysis unavoidably leads to deep technical difficulties, because the creation of BNs is inherently a *non-linear* phenomenon: *small* changes in relative loads or capacities can lead to *large* shifts in BN locations. On the other hand, BN analysis can be simpler than a full performance analysis, because much less is being demanded, at the minimum merely requesting the location of the most-congested system resources. Furthermore, additional simplification is possible if one performs only *asymptotic* BN analysis, where the load on the system (e.g., customer population) approaches 100% saturation.

1.2 Purpose and Scope

The purpose of this paper is to survey several of the principal results in BN analysis for *closed* queueing networks (CQNs) (open queueing networks are much less challenging to analyze because knowledge of external arrival rates and visit ratios permits immediate prediction of resource utilizations).

We include both product-form closed queueing networks (PF-CQNs), where exact BN analysis are surveyed and non-product-form networks, where approximations are given for asymptotic BN behavior. However, there are several assumptions made to limit the scope, and thereby make the survey manageable in size:

- all servers are constant-rate, and either FCFS (no parallel servers) or ample server (AS);

- queue space is unlimited (no blocking) system;

- a customer is at only one resource at any given time, and makes *instantaneous* transfers from one resource to another (e.g., ignore bus transmission times);

- all customer classes are *closed*, and customers do not change class;

- only an equilibrium steady-state analysis is presented. This assumes, among other things, that loads (e.g., populations) remain constant over time, so that one does not have to forecast time-varying BNs;

- we do not distinguish between user-workload and system overhead.

1.3 Definition of Bottlenecks

At least two concepts of BNs are in common use:

- *physical bottleneck*:
  - resource with highest utilization;
  - resource with highest mean sojourn time;

- resource with highest mean queueing (delay) time;
- resource with highest mean queue length (queue length for us means number present either in service or in queue; this definition makes meaningful mean queue length at an AS (= mean number of customers present));
- device with highest 90% percentile (or other percentile) of sojourn time (or queue length);

- *economic bottleneck*:

  - resource with largest value of the derivative: rate of improvement in the system performance measure per dollar invested at the resource (the systems performance measure could be any scalar such as weighted average throughput, weighted average response time, etc.).

It is evident that many possible definitions of BNs exist, and that they are *not equivalent*: the device with highest utilization need not have highest response time, nor be the economic BN. However, in the case where one — and only one — device is running at a high level of congestion, all definitions will agree.

The device with highest value of the performance measure (e.g., highest utilization) is called the primary *bottleneck* (if more than one, we speak of the *BN set*). Next highest is called the secondary BN, etc.

It is noteworthy that physical BNs differ from economic BNs in two ways

- physical BN uses a *physical* measure of performance and does not involve money;

- physical BN looks at *average* level of performance while economic BN looks at *marginal return on performance*.

In this survey, we use *device with highest utilization* as our definition of BN. This is the most common approach, is the easiest to measure, and in any case acts as a reasonable surrogate for the congestion at the device.

1.4 Notation

To keep the presentation simple, in the sequel of the paper the index r will always be implicitly assumed to range from 1 to R and the indexes i, j to range from 1 to M.

1.4.1 Model Inputs

- M servers, labelled $\{1, 2, \ldots, M\} = SFCFS + SAS$, where $SFCFS = $ set of FCFS servers and $SAS = $ set of AS;

- customer classes labelled $\{1, 2, \ldots, R\}$;

- K_r = (fixed) population of class r;

- S_{ri} = mean service time of a class-r customer for each visit to server i (for product-form networks, S_{ri} is independent of r if i is FCFS);

- V_{ri} = mean number of visits a class-r customer makes to server i;

- $L_{ri} = V_{ri}S_{ri}$ = mean load a class-r customer makes to server i in all its visits.

We assume

- $\sum_r L_{ri} > 0 \quad 1 \le i \le M \qquad$ (otherwise delete server i);

- $\sum_i L_{ri} > 0 \quad 1 \le r \le R \qquad$ (otherwise delete class r);

- $K_r \ge 1 \quad 1 \le r \le R \qquad$ (otherwise delete class r);

- $R \ge 1$;

- $S_{ri}, V_{ri}, L_{ri} \ge 0 \quad 1 \le r \le R \quad 1 \le i \le M$;

- $K_{\text{sum}} \equiv \sum_r K_r$ = total customer population;

- $\beta_r = K_r / K_{\text{sum}}$ = fraction of population being of class $r \qquad 1 \le r \le R$;

- $\underline{\beta} = (\beta_1, \beta_2, \ldots, \beta_R)$ = mix vector;

- $\underline{K} = (K_1, K_2, \ldots, K_R) = \underline{\beta} K_{\text{sum}}$ = population vector.

1.4.2 Model Outputs

- W_{ri} = mean sojourn time;

- W_r = response time of class r;

- X_r = throughput of class r;

- X_{ri} = throughput of class-r customers at server i;

- Q_{ri} = mean queue length;

- Q_i = mean queue at server i;

- U_{ri} = utilization at server i due to class r;

- U_i = utilization of server i.

Only $\{W_{ri}\}$ are independent, the rest being obtained from

$$W_r = \sum_i V_{ri} W_{ri}$$

$$X_r = \frac{K_r}{W_r}, \qquad X_{ri} = X_r V_{ri} \quad \text{(forced-flow law)}$$

$$Q_{ri} = X_{ri} W_{ri} \quad \text{(Little's law)}, \qquad Q_i = \sum_r Q_{ri}$$

$$U_{ri} = X_{ri} S_{ri}, \qquad U_i = \sum_r U_{ri}$$

There are all nonnegative and also satisfy $W_{ri} \geq S_{ri}$ (so $W_r \geq \sum_i L_{ri} > 0$) and

$$\sum_i Q_{ri} = K_r.$$

2 Asymptotic Bottleneck Analysis

Here $K_{\text{sum}} \to \infty$, i.e., at least one customer class becomes very large. We assume that each class r with $K_r \to \infty$ also satisfies

$$\sum_{i \in SFCFS} L_{ri} > 0$$

i.e., class r visits at least one FCFS server. This means that at least one FCFS server will be saturated.

For product-form networks, where exact solutions are available (by looking, for example, at the integral representation of the generating function), one is interested in the asymptotic behavior of U_i, X_r, W_{ri}, Q_{ri} and Q_i as $K_{\text{sum}} \to \infty$. These are typically *asymptotic expansions* of the form

$$U_i = U_i^* + \frac{U_i^{**}}{K_{\text{sum}}} + O\left(\frac{1}{K_{\text{sum}}^2}\right) \qquad (U_i^* \leq 1)$$

$$X_r = X_r^* + \frac{X_r^{**}}{K_{\text{sum}}} + O\left(\frac{1}{K_{\text{sum}}^2}\right)$$

$$W_{ri} = K_{\text{sum}} W_{ri}^* + W_{ri}^{**} + O\left(\frac{1}{K_{\text{sum}}}\right)$$

$$Q_{ri} = K_{\text{sum}} Q_{ri}^* + Q_{ri}^{**} + O\left(\frac{1}{K_{\text{sum}}}\right)$$

$$Q_i = K_{\text{sum}} Q_i^* + Q_i^{**} + O\left(\frac{1}{K_{\text{sum}}}\right) \qquad \left(Q_i^* = \sum_r Q_{ri}^*\right)$$

Our notation uses * for the leading term, ** for the next term, etc. Note U_{ri} and X_{ri} approach finite limits (U_{ri}^* and X_{ri}^*) while Q_{ri} and W_{ri} diverge *linearly* with K_{sum} for at least one $i \in SFCFS$. Also note $0 \leq U_i^* \leq 1$, $Q_i^* = 0$ if i is an AS, $\sum\limits_{i \in SFCFS} Q_i^* = 1$.

The *asymptotic bottleneck set* $BN(\underline{\beta})$ is defined as the set of servers whose utilization approaches 100%:

$$BN(\underline{\beta}) \equiv \{i : i \in SFCFS \text{ and } U_i^* = 1\}$$

Note the set $\{i : i \in SFCFS \text{ and } Q_i^* > 0\}$ of servers whose queue length approaches infinity is a *subset* of $BN(\underline{\beta})$.

The primary goals of asymptotic BN analysis are to find

$$BN(\underline{\beta}) = \text{asymptotic bottleneck set}$$

and

$$\gamma_i(\underline{\beta}) = \frac{Q_i^*}{\sum\limits_{j \in SFCFS} Q_j^*} = Q_i^* = \text{asymptotic fraction of population at server } i$$

Note

$$\gamma_i(\underline{\beta}) = 0 \quad i \in SAS, \qquad \gamma_i(\underline{\beta}) \geq 0, \qquad \sum\limits_{i \in SFCFS} \gamma_i(\underline{\beta}) = 1$$

The remaining performance measures are then given by

$$W_{ri}^* = S_i \gamma_i \quad \text{(independent of } r\text{)}, \qquad W_r^* = \sum_i L_{ri} \gamma_i \tag{1a}$$

$$X_r^* = \frac{\beta_r}{\sum\limits_i L_{ri} \gamma_i}, \qquad X_{ri}^* = \frac{\beta_r V_{ri}}{\sum\limits_j L_{rj} \gamma_j} \tag{1b}$$

$$Q_{ri}^* = \frac{\beta_r L_{ri} \gamma_i}{\sum\limits_j L_{rj} \gamma_j}, \qquad Q_i^* = \gamma_i \sum_r \frac{\beta_r L_{ri}}{\sum\limits_j L_{rj} \gamma_j} \tag{1c}$$

$$U_{ri}^* = \frac{\beta_r L_{ri}}{\sum\limits_j L_{rj} \gamma_j}, \qquad U_i^* = \sum_r \frac{\beta_r L_{ri}}{\sum\limits_j L_{rj} \gamma_j} \tag{1d}$$

At least 4 different cases of asymptotic analysis must be distinguished

1. $K_{\text{sum}} \to \infty$, M fixed, at least one AS exists [RM82], [KB91];

2. $K_{sum} \to \infty$, $M \to \infty$, K_{sum}/M fixed [KT90];

3. $K_{sum} \to \infty$, $M \to \infty$, K_{sum}/M fixed (or has a limit), service in random order [BGPS87];

4. $K_{sum} \to \infty$, M fixed, no AS.

Case 1. is the best known due to the PANACEA code. A scheme is given to find as many terms as desired in the asymptotic expansion, along with a bound on the truncation error. However, due to the assumption of "normal usage", where all FCFS servers have utilizations bounded away from unity, the model is restricted to the case where an infinite number of customers accumulates at, and only at, the ample servers. These always act as "bottlenecks".

Case 2. models a computer network with a very large number of terminals. The asymptotic analysis is quite delicate.

Case 3. shows asymptotic normality of the joint queue lengths, and provides algorithms for the means and covariances.

Case 4. differs from Case 1 because customers demands must accumulate at, and only at, FCFS servers [BS93a], [BS93b], [SSB92] etc. It differs from Case 2 and 3 because M is fixed. Its extensions to ample servers is straightforward. This case is the least known, and therefore merits presentations of some of the technical details. It also leads to convenient approximations for the non-product-form case.

3 Algorithms for Asymptotic Bottleneck Analysis

3.1 Introduction

This section shows how to carry out the asymptotic BN analysis for CQN as $K_{sum} \to \infty$. In particular, we describe how to compute the asymptotic fractions

$$\gamma_i(\underline{\beta}) \equiv \lim_{K_{sum} \to \infty} \frac{Q_i(K_{sum}\underline{\beta})}{K_{sum}}$$

and the asymptotic bottleneck set $BN(\underline{\beta})$. Note that $\sum_i \gamma_i = 1$, $\gamma_i > 0$ implies $U_i^* = 1$.

Values of $\underline{\beta}$, $i \in BN(\underline{\beta})$ and $U_i^* = 1$ implies the converse, namely that $\gamma_i > 0$.

Note that the technical difficulty lies in computing $\gamma_i(\underline{\beta})$, since $BN(\underline{\beta})$ can then be easily computed from

$$BN(\underline{\beta}) = \{i \in SFCFS : U_i^* = 1\} = \left\{ i \in SFCFS : \sum_r \frac{\beta_r L_{ri}}{\sum_j L_{rj}\gamma_j(\underline{\beta})} = 1 \right\}$$

$$(2)$$

The algorithm include

1. fixed point methodology;

2. optimization methodology;

3. simultaneous non-linear equation methodology;

4. simultaneous linear equation methodology.

The remaining subsections discuss the higher order terms and the extensions to non-product form CQNs.

3.2 Fixed Point Methodology

This approach exploits the properties

$$\gamma_i(\underline{\beta}) \geq 0 \tag{3a}$$

$$U_i^*(\underline{\beta}) = \sum_r \frac{\beta_r L_{ri}}{\sum_j L_{rj} \gamma_j(\underline{\beta})} \leq 1 \tag{3b}$$

$$\gamma_i(\underline{\beta}) > 0 \implies U_i^*(\underline{\beta}) = 1 \tag{3c}$$

If we define the function

$$f_i(\underline{z}) \equiv \sum_r \frac{\beta_r L_{ri}}{\sum_j L_{rj} z_j} \qquad 1 \leq i \leq M, \quad \underline{z} \in [0,1]^M \tag{4}$$

where $\underline{z} = (z_1, z_2, \ldots, z_M)$ is constrained to satisfy $z_i \geq 0$ for all i and $\sum_j L_{rj} z_j > 0$ for all r, then (4) may be rewritten as the *non-linear complementarity problem*

$$\gamma_i \geq 0 \qquad 1 \leq i \leq M \tag{5a}$$

$$1 - f_i(\underline{\gamma}) \geq 0 \qquad 1 \leq i \leq M \tag{5b}$$

$$\gamma_i[1 - f_i(\underline{\gamma})] = 0 \qquad 1 \leq i \leq M \tag{5c}$$

(i.e., $\underline{\gamma} = (\gamma_1, \gamma_2, \ldots, \gamma_M)$ and $U_i^* = f_i(\underline{\gamma}) \quad 1 \leq i \leq M$).
Summation of the last of these shows that, as expected,

$$\sum_i \gamma_i = 1$$

In addition, the last may be understood as the *fixed point equation* for the γ's

$$\gamma_i = \gamma_i f_i(\underline{\gamma}) \qquad 1 \leq i \leq M \tag{6a}$$

subject to the side constraints

$$\gamma_i \geq 0 \qquad 1 \leq i \leq M \tag{6b}$$

$$\sum_i L_{ri}\gamma_i > 0 \qquad 1 \leq r \leq R \tag{6c}$$

$$f_i(\underline{\gamma}) \leq 1 \qquad 1 \leq i \leq M \tag{6d}$$

An alternate derivation of (5c) and (6a) is based directly upon the MVA recursion

$$Q_i(\underline{K}) = \sum_r \frac{K_r L_{ri}[1 + Q_i(\underline{K} - \underline{e}^r)]}{\sum_j L_{rj}[1 + Q_j(\underline{K} - \underline{e}^r)]} \qquad 1 \leq i \leq M \tag{7}$$

namely, divide both sides by K_{sum} and let $K_{\mathrm{sum}} \to \infty$.

The fixed point equation (6a) has been obtained by [Schw79], [Chow83]. In most cases it has a *unique* solution $\underline{\gamma}$. However there are some exceptional cases where (6a) does *not* have a unique solution, and one must go to higher order in the expansion

$$\frac{Q_i(K_{\mathrm{sum}}\underline{\beta})}{K_{\mathrm{sum}}} = \gamma_i(\underline{\beta}) + O\left(\frac{1}{K_{\mathrm{sum}}}\right)$$

in order to resolve ambiguities. Even in the case where the fixed point equation does not satisfy $\underline{\gamma}$ uniquely, it is possible to show that $f_i(\underline{\gamma})$ is unique for each i, hence $BN(\underline{\beta})$ is well-defined.

A convenient way to solve (6) is by *successive substitutions*

$$\gamma_i^{(n+1)} = \gamma_i^{(n)} f_i(\underline{\gamma}^{(n)}) \qquad 1 \leq i \leq M \tag{8}$$

starting from an initial guess which satisfies (6 c,d) but with (6b) replaced by $\gamma_i^{(0)} > 0$ (else $\gamma_i^{(n)}$ remain zero for all n). The scheme (8) is easy to program and usually has geometric convergence to $\underline{\gamma}$. However convergence is not guaranteed and sometimes the scheme fails. Ways of ensuring convergence are discussed in subsection 3.3 below, hence computation of $\gamma_i(\underline{\beta})$ and $BN(\underline{\beta})$ (and higher order terms) may be considered to be *routine*, except at (or near) the exceptional values of β where the fixed point is not unique. This algorithm appears to be *simpler* than other asymptotic expansions, such as those based upon integral representations.

3.3 Optimization Methodology

The scheme (8) may be shown [Schw79] to be a projected gradient approach for solving the concave optimization problem

$$\max\left\{ h(\underline{z}) : \underline{z} \in [0,1]^M, \quad z_i \geq 0 \text{ and } \sum_i L_{ri} z_i > 0 \right\} \tag{9}$$

where

$$h(\underline{z}) \equiv \sum_r \beta_r \log \left[\sum_i L_{ri} z_i \right] - \sum_i \gamma_i$$

and indeed, the complementary slackness conditions (6) are the Kuhn-Tucker conditions for (9), so (8) and (9) are equivalent characterizations of $\underline{\gamma}$.

The step-direction $\underline{\gamma}^{(n+1)} - \underline{\gamma}^{(n)}$ in successive substitutions is an *uphill* direction for maximizing h, i.e.,

$$\sum_i [\underline{\gamma}^{(n+1)} - \underline{\gamma}^{(n)}]_i \frac{\partial}{\partial z_i} h(\underline{\gamma}^{(n)}) = \sum_i \gamma_i^{(n)} [f_i(\underline{\gamma}^{(n)}) - 1]^2 > 0$$

However the step length could be too long, causing overshooting and lack of convergence of successive substitutions. To enforce convergence, one must merely check that $h(\underline{\gamma}^{(n+1)})$ is *strictly longer* than $h(\underline{\gamma}^{(n)})$, and if this is not so, one reduces the step length sufficiently that this criterion is met.

We found it simplest to repeatedly halve the step length (i.e., $\underline{\gamma}^{(n+1)} = \frac{1}{2}(\underline{\gamma}^{(n)} + \underline{\gamma}^{(n+1)})$) until $h(\underline{\gamma}^{(n+1)}) > h(\underline{\gamma}^{(n)})$ is met. This procedure works flawlessly, producing (at least) 6 digit accuracy without difficulty.

For other reduction of the leading asymptotic term to an optimization problem, see [Pitt79], [BGPS87], [PKT90].

3.4 Simultaneous Non-Linear Equation Methodology

Here one applies any root-finding technique for the M simultaneous equations (6a) and then checking for satisfaction of (6 b,c,d). For non-exceptional β, where $BN(\underline{\beta}) \equiv \{i : U_i^*(\underline{\beta}) = 1\} = \{i : \gamma_i(\underline{\beta}) > 0\}$, this is especially easy in the usual case where there is only a *small* set of bottlenecks $BN(\underline{\beta})$, because (6a) reduces to only $|BN(\underline{\beta})|$ simultaneous (non-linear) equations

$$1 = \sum_r \frac{\beta_r L_{ri}}{\displaystyle\sum_{j \in BN(\underline{\beta})} L_{rj} \gamma_j(\underline{\beta})} \qquad i \in BN(\underline{\beta}) \tag{10}$$

for $|BN(\underline{\beta})|$ unknowns $\{\gamma_i(\underline{\beta}) : i \in BN(\underline{\beta})\}$.

If $BN(\underline{\beta})$ can be guessed correctly, then (say) Newton's method applied to (10) gives $\{\gamma_i(\underline{\beta}) : i \in BN(\underline{\beta})\}$ while $\gamma_i(\underline{\beta}) = 0$ if $i \notin BN(\underline{\beta})$. One then checks if (6 b,c,d) hold in order to confirm the guess for $BN(\underline{\beta})$.

3.5 Simultaneous Linear Equation Methodology

This approach uses

$$X_r^* = \frac{\beta_r}{\displaystyle\sum_{i \in BN(\underline{\beta})} L_{ri} \gamma_i(\underline{\beta})} > 0 \qquad 1 \leq r \leq R \tag{11}$$

as primary unknowns, thereby transforming (10) into a set of *linear* equations

$$1 = \sum_r X_r^* L_{ri} \qquad i \in BN(\underline{\beta}) \qquad (= U_i^*) \tag{12}$$

for the X^*'s (if the X^*'s are under-determined, one adds additional equations involving the reciprocals of the X^*'s, to reflect the fact that the rows of $L(\underline{\beta}) \equiv [L_{ri}]$ $1 \le r \le R$, $i \in BN(\underline{\beta})$ may be linearly dependent). Once the X^*'s are known, the γ's can be chosen anywhere in the polytope

$$\left\{ \underline{\gamma} \in [0,1]^M \ : \ \gamma_i = 0 \text{ for } i \notin BN(\underline{\beta}), \quad \gamma_i \ge 0 \text{ for } i \in BN(\underline{\beta}), \right.$$

$$\left. \sum_i \gamma_i = 1, \quad \sum_i L_{ri} \gamma_i = \beta_r / X_r^* \text{ for all } r \right\} \tag{13}$$

preferably the *maximal* solution $\gamma_i > 0$ (strict) for all $i \in BN(\underline{\beta})$.

As the simplest illustration this, consider the most common case where there is just one BN, say

$$BN(\underline{\beta}) = \{b\}$$

Then

$$\gamma_i = \delta_{ib} \tag{14}$$

and (10) reduces to the identity

$$1 = \sum_r \frac{\beta_r L_{rb}}{L_{rb}}$$

Evidently

$$X_r^* = \frac{\beta_r}{L_{rb}} \qquad 1 \le r \le R$$

is easily determined from (11) and (14). Note $L(\underline{\beta})$ is a $R \times 1$ matrix, hence only one row of it is independent. Also, one must check that $U_i^* = \sum_r \frac{\beta_r L_{ri}}{L_{rb}} < 1 = U_b^*$ for $i \ne b$.

The next complicated case is of two BNs,

$$BN(\underline{\beta}) = \{b_1, b_2\}$$

This is most tractable if there are 2 types of customers, since (12) then consists of 2 simultaneous linear equations for the two y's. Finally, γ_{b_1} and γ_{b_2} are obtained from the latter two linear equations from the trio in (13)

$$\begin{cases} \gamma_{b_1} + \gamma_{b_2} = 1 \\ L_{rb_1} \gamma_{b_1} + L_{rb_2} \gamma_{b_2} = \beta_r / X_r^* \qquad r = 1, 2 \end{cases}$$

Assuming that the 2×2 matrix

$$L(\underline{\beta}) = \begin{bmatrix} L_{1b_1} & L_{1b_2} \\ L_{2b_1} & L_{2b_2} \end{bmatrix}$$

is non-singular, the result is

$$\begin{cases} \gamma_{b_1} = \dfrac{\beta_1 L_{2b_2}}{L_{2b_2} - L_{2b_1}} - \dfrac{\beta_2 L_{1b_2}}{L_{1b_1} - L_{1b_2}} \\[4mm] \gamma_{b_2} = \dfrac{\beta_2 L_{1b_1}}{L_{1b_1} - L_{1b_2}} - \dfrac{\beta_1 L_{2b_1}}{L_{2b_2} - L_{2b_1}} \end{cases}$$

More generally, this approach works if the number of bottlenecks $|BN(\underline{\beta})|$ agrees with the number of classes R, provided the $R \times R$ matrix

$$L(\underline{\beta}) \equiv \{L_{ri} : 1 \le r \le R, \quad i \in BN(\underline{\beta})\}$$

is non-singular.

3.6 Higher Order Terms

By inserting the asymptotic expansion

$$Q_i(K_{\text{sum}}\underline{\beta}) = K_{\text{sum}} Q_i^*(\underline{\beta}) + Q_i^{**}(\underline{\beta}) + O\left(\frac{1}{K_{\text{sum}}}\right) \tag{15}$$

into (7), one gets a *sequence* of fixed point problems for Q^*, Q^{**}, etc. We have already investigated the first of these, for Q^*. As long as β is not exceptional, the higher order terms can be evaluated recursively. The authors have obtained explicit expressions for Q^{**} and Q^{***}. We found that the first three terms in the series (15) are sufficient provided

- K_{sum} is sufficiently large (typically 1000's); the relatively slow convergence as $K_{\text{sum}} \to \infty$ was also noted in [Lave82] if ample servers occur;

- β is not too close to an exceptional value, where the asymptotic series becomes singular. The bad cases can usually be detected because of symptoms like $|Q_i^{**}|$ is very large for some $i \in BN(\underline{\beta})$, $\gamma_i(\underline{\beta})$ is very close to zero for some $i \in BN(\underline{\beta})$, some $\left|\dfrac{\partial}{\partial \beta_r} \gamma_i(\underline{\beta})\right|$ gets very large, etc. We call the set of β's where the expansions break down *switching surfaces* (i.e., singularities), because the set $BN(\underline{\beta})$ of BNs is discontinuous there.

3.7 Examples

Consider the case $M = 4$, $R = 2$ with

$$L_{ri} = \begin{bmatrix} 100 & 90 & 50 & 40 \\ 50 & 70 & 90 & 40 \end{bmatrix}$$

Server 4 can never be a bottleneck since it is masked-off by the other servers. Then, from (2), we have

$$BN(\underline{\beta}) = \begin{cases} \{3\} & 0 \leq \beta_1 < \frac{5}{23} \\ \{2,3\} & \frac{5}{23} \leq \beta_1 \leq \frac{9}{23} \\ \{2\} & \frac{9}{23} < \beta_1 < \frac{18}{25} \\ \{1,2\} & \frac{18}{25} \leq \beta_1 \leq \frac{4}{5} \\ \{1\} & \frac{4}{5} < \beta_1 \leq 1 \end{cases}$$

and $\beta_2 = 1 - \beta_1$.

The exceptional points (switching surfaces) are $\underline{\beta} = \left(\frac{5}{23}, \frac{18}{23}\right) \doteq (0.217, 0.783)$, $\underline{\beta} = \left(\frac{9}{23}, \frac{14}{23}\right) \doteq (0.391, 0.609)$, $\underline{\beta} = \left(\frac{18}{25}, \frac{7}{25}\right) = (0.72, 0.28)$ and $\underline{\beta} = \left(\frac{4}{5}, \frac{1}{5}\right) = (0.8, 0.2)$ where $BN(\underline{\beta})$ changes. The corresponding first terms in the asymptotic expansion are

$$\underline{\gamma}(\underline{\beta}) = \underline{Q}^*(\underline{\beta}) = \begin{cases} (0,0,1,0) & 0 \leq \beta_1 < \frac{5}{23} \\ \left(0, -\frac{5}{4} + \frac{23}{4}\beta_1, \frac{9}{4} - \frac{23}{4}\beta_1, 0\right) & \frac{5}{23} \leq \beta_1 \leq \frac{9}{23} \\ (0,1,0,0) & \frac{9}{23} < \beta_1 < \frac{18}{25} \\ \left(-9 + \frac{25}{2}\beta_1, 10 - \frac{25}{2}\beta_1, 0, 0\right) & \frac{18}{25} \leq \beta_1 \leq \frac{4}{5} \\ (1,0,0,0) & \frac{4}{5} < \beta_1 \leq 1 \end{cases}$$

The switching surfaces can be detected from the expressions for $Q_i^*(\underline{\beta})$, from (1c), that violate the requirements $0 \leq Q_i^* \leq 1$. In addition, at the switching surface we have the unusual situation where some server i has $U_i^* = 1$ but $\gamma_i = 0$.

As can be seen from Figure 1, the migration of the bottleneck from one server to another yields a bottleneck set in which both these servers saturate.

With $R = 3$ and K_{sum} constant all the possible mix vectors $\underline{\beta}$ belong to the triangle $\{\underline{\beta} : \beta_1 + \beta_2 + \beta_3 = 1 \text{ and } 0 \leq \beta_1, \beta_2, \beta_3 \leq 1\}$. The switching surfaces become straight lines identifying polyhedral regions in which one, two or (at most) three servers saturate. Each value of $BN(\underline{\beta})$ occurs only once, i.e., the regions are all connected sets. Bottleneck set switches from regions with one to regions with two and with three components.

504

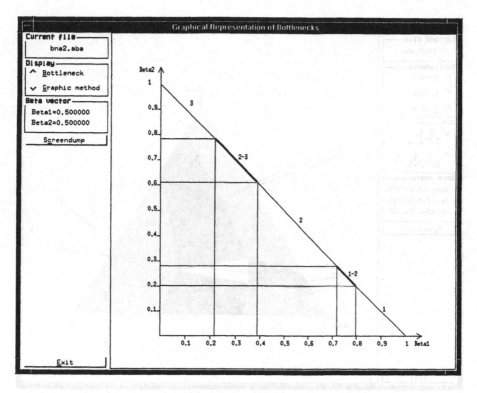

Figure 1: Bottleneck set $BN(\underline{\beta})$ vs. population mix $\underline{\beta}$ for $R = 2$.

Let us consider now the case $M = 5$, $R = 3$ with

$$L_{ri} = \begin{bmatrix} 90 & 50 & 60 & 80 & 70 \\ 40 & 80 & 30 & 40 & 30 \\ 50 & 80 & 90 & 50 & 70 \end{bmatrix}$$

Figure 2 represents the various bottleneck sets of this case. As can be seen, with the loading matrix considered we have only one bottleneck set in which three servers saturate together, i.e., the internal triangle. However, depending on the relative values of L_{ri} and on the number of servers none or several of such regions may exist. The regions with all the other bottleneck sets are also represented. A complete description of the switching surfaces can be found in [BS93b].

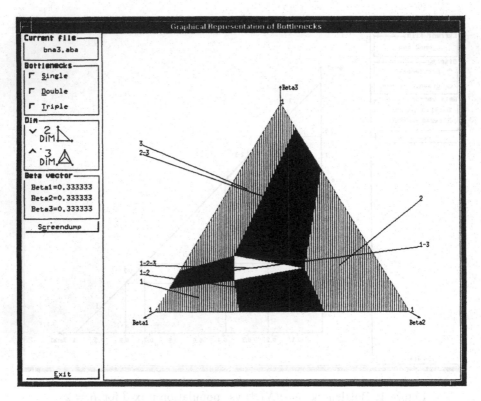

Figure 2: Bottleneck set $BN(\underline{\beta})$ vs. population mix $\underline{\beta}$ for $R = 3$.

3.8 Non-Product Form Networks

If S_{ri} depends upon r at one or more FCFS server i, the CQN lacks product-form. If we assume

$$W_{ri} \sum_t Q_{ti}S_{ti} + \mathrm{O}(1) \quad \text{for large } K_{\mathrm{sum}} \qquad (16)$$

$$\frac{Q_{ri}}{K_{\mathrm{sum}}} \to Q_{ri}^* \quad \text{as } K_{\mathrm{sum}} \to \infty$$

then

$$\frac{Q_i}{K_{\mathrm{sum}}} \to Q_i^* = \sum_r Q_{ri}^*$$

$$\frac{W_{ri}}{K_{\text{sum}}} \to W_i^* = \sum_t Q_{ti}^* S_{ti} \qquad \text{(independent of } r \text{ due to (16))}$$

$$X_{ri} = \frac{K_r V_{ri}}{\sum_j V_{rj} W_{rj}} \to \frac{\beta_r V_{ri}}{\sum_j V_{rj} W_j^*}$$

$$U_i = \sum_r X_{ri} S_{ri} \to U_i^* = \sum_r \frac{\beta_r L_{ri}}{\sum_j V_{rj} W_j^*}$$

We expect that $W_i^* > 0$ if and only if $Q_i^* > 0$ (since all throughputs X_{ri} are bounded, this follows from Little's law), so we still expect the relationships

$$W_i^* \geq 0 \qquad 1 \leq i \leq M$$

$$U_i^* \leq 1 \qquad 1 \leq i \leq M$$

$$W_i^* > 0 \implies U_i^* = 1 \qquad 1 \leq i \leq M$$

$$\sum_i V_{ri} W_i^* > 0 \qquad 1 \leq r \leq R$$

which is a non-linear complementarity problem for $\underline{W}^*$ similar to (3) and (5). It may still be solved by successive substitutions as in (8) or by a root-finder as in (10). However, we *lose* the interpretation of successive approximation being an optimization problem, and therefore lose the ability to force convergence by reducing the step length.

The one exception is if $S_{ri} = a_r b_i$ for all r and i, in which the optimization interpretation still survives [Schw79]. This case arises in models of telecommunications where r = message type, i = transmission link, and where the transmission time on a link depends on both on the (constant) message length S_r and the link speed b_i.

The empirical result is that successive substitution with stepsize reduction converges well, for arbitrary S_{ri}, despite the absence of an explanation. So asymptotic BN analysis is possible (for the dominant term) for general CQNs, although the accuracy of the higher-order terms (Q^{**}, Q^{***}, etc.) is doubtful.

Note that approximate MVA [Schw79], [Bard79] and both the linearizer [CN82] and Chow [Chow83] approximations will reduce to the fixed point problem when populations get very large. This help explains why all are accurate when the populations are very large.

4   Conclusions

One of the major problem that arise in modelling actual computer systems and networks is that the computational complexity of the exact solution techniques becomes prohibitively expensive as the number of classes, customers, and stations grows.

As a consequence, different methods are becoming fundamental for the future of systems modelling. Among them, approximation techniques and asymptotic bottleneck analysis techniques will play an important role in the near future.

In this paper several of the principal results in bottleneck analysis for closed queueing networks, either product-form and non product-form, are described. Algorithms for the asymptotic bottleneck set identification have been presented and their applicability has been shown through examples.

References

[Bard79] Y. Bard. Some extensions to multiclass queueing network analysis. In A. Butrimenko M. Arato and E. Gelenbe, editors, *Proceedings of the 4th International Symposium on Modelling and Performance Evaluation of Computer Systems*, Performance of Computer Systems, pages 51–62, Amsterdam, Netherlands, 1979. North Holland Publishing Company.

[BGPS87] O. Bronshtein, I. Gertsbakh, B. Pittel, and S. Shahaf. One-node closed multichannel service system: Several types of customers and service rates, and random pick-up from the waiting line. *Advanced Applied Probability*, 19:487–504, 1987.

[BS93a] G. Balbo and G. Serazzi. Asymptotic analysis of multiclass closed queueing networks: Common bottleneck. Submitted for publication, 1993.

[BS93b] G. Balbo and G. Serazzi. Asymptotic analysis of multiclass closed queueing networks: Multiple bottlenecks. Submitted for publication, 1993.

[Chow83] W. M. Chow. Approximations for large scale closed queueing networks. *Performance Evaluation*, 3:1–12, 1983.

[CN82] K. M. Chandy and D. Neuse. Linearizer: A heuristic algorithm for queueing network models of computing systems. *Communications of the ACM*, 25(2):126–134, February 1982.

[KB91] Y. Kogan and A. Birman. Asymptotic analysis of closed queueing networks with bottlenecks. In *Proceedings of International Conference Performance Distributed Systems and Integr. Comm. Networks*, Kyoto, Japan, September 1991.

[KT90] C. Knessl and C. Tier. Asymptotic expansions for large closed queueing networks. *Journal of the ACM*, 37(1):144–174, January 1990.

[Lave82]   S. S. Lavenberg. Closed multichain product form queueing networks
           with large population sizes. *Applied Probability*, pages 219–249, 1982.

[Pitt79]   B. Pittel. Closed exponential networks of queues with saturation:
           the jackson-type stationary distribution and its asymptotic analysis.
           Mathematics of Operations Research, 4(4):357–378, November 1979.

[PKT90]   K. R. Pattipati, M. M. Kostreva, and J. L. Teele. Approximate mean
           value analysis algorithms for queuing networks: Existence, unique-
           ness, and convergence results. *Journal of the ACM*, 37(3):643–673,
           July 1990.

[RM82]   K. G. Ramakrishnan and D. Mitra. An overview of PANACEA, a
           software package for analyzing markovian queueing networks. *Bell
           Systems Technical Journal*, 61(10):2849–2872, 1982.

[Schw79]   P. J. Schweitzer. Approximate analysis of multiclass closed networks
           of queues. In *Proceedings of International Conference on Stochastic
           Control and Optimization*, Free University, Amsterdam, Netherlands,
           April 1979.

[SSB92]   P. J. Schweitzer, G. Serazzi, and M. Broglia. A fixed-point ap-
           proximation to product-form networks with large population. Pre-
           sented at Second ORSA Telecommunications Conference, Boca Ra-
           ton, Florida, March 1992.

Software Performance Engineering

Connie U. Smith, Ph.D.

Performance Engineering Services
PO Box 2640
Santa Fe, NM 87504

Abstract. Software performance engineering (SPE) is a method for constructing software systems to meet performance objectives. It uses quantitative analysis techniques to predict and evaluate performance implications of design and implementation decisions. This tutorial introduces SPE then covers the evolution of SPE. It reviews the SPE process and the methods used in the software lifecycle. It presents general principles for performance oriented design, then it introduces the quantitative techniques for predicting and analyzing performance. The conclusion reviews the status and future of SPE.

1 Introduction

Software performance engineering (SPE) is a method for constructing software systems to meet performance objectives. The process begins early in the software lifecycle and uses quantitative methods to identify satisfactory combinations of requirements and designs, and to eliminate those that are likely to have unacceptable performance, before developers begin implementation. SPE continues through the detailed design, coding, and testing stages to predict and manage the performance of the evolving software, and to monitor and report actual performance against specifications and predictions. SPE methods cover performance data collection, quantitative analysis techniques, prediction strategies, management of uncertainties, data presentation and tracking, model verification and validation, critical success factors, and performance design principles.

The "performance balance" in Figure 1 depicts a balanced system: resource requirements match computer capacity, and software meets performance objectives. With SPE, analysts assess the "balance" *early in development*. If demand exceeds capacity, quantitative methods support cost-benefit analysis of hardware solutions versus software requirements or design solutions, versus a combination of the two. Developers select software or hardware solutions to performance problems before proceeding to the detailed design and implementation stages.

In this tutorial, *performance* refers to the response time or throughput as seen by the users. For real-time, or *reactive* systems, it is the time required to respond to events. Reactive systems must meet performance objectives to be correct. Other software has less stringent requirements, but responsiveness limits the amount of work processed, so it determines a system's effectiveness and the productivity of its users.

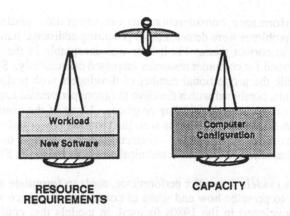

RESOURCE
REQUIREMENTS

CAPACITY

Fig. 1. Performance Balance

SPE is a *software-oriented* approach — it focuses on architecture, design, and implementation choices for managing performance. Other approaches have been proposed. For example, *system-oriented* approaches that focus on scheduling [SHA90; XU87], resource allocation, operating system executives [STAN91], total system approaches [KOPE85; KOPE91; LEVI90; POSP92; SHIN92] and so on are viable, supplemental methods for managing performance of real-time systems, but are outside the scope of the SPE approach defined here. Similarly, techniques that focus on timing requirements using temporal logic or fault-tree analysis [GABR90; JAFF91; JAHA87] are not within this SPE definition.

This tutorial first covers the evolution of SPE then it gives an overview of the SPE process and the SPE methods. It presents the general principles for performance-oriented design, then it introduces the quantitative techniques for predicting and analyzing performance. Finally, the conclusion reviews the status and future of SPE.

2 The Evolution of SPE

Performance was a principal concern in the early years of computing. Knuth's early work focused on efficient data structures, algorithms, sorting and searching [KNUT68; KNUT73]. The space and time required by programs had to be carefully managed to fit them on small machines. The hardware grew but, rather than eliminating performance problems, it made larger, more complex software feasible and programs grew into systems of programs. Software systems with strict performance requirements, such as flight control systems and other embedded systems used detailed simulation models to assess performance. Consequently creating and solving them was time-consuming, and updating the models to reflect the current state of evolving software systems was problematic. Thus, the labor-intensive modeling and assessment were cost-effective only for systems with strict performance requirements.

Authors proposed performance-oriented development approaches [BELL77; GRAH73; RIDD78; SHOL75] but most developers of non-reactive systems adopted the "fix-it-later" approach. It advocated concentrating on software correctness, deferring performance considerations to the integration testing phase and (if performance problems were detected then) procuring additional hardware or "tuning" the software to correct them. Fix-it-later was acceptable in the 1970s, but in the 1980s the demand for computer resources increased dramatically. System complexity increased while the proportional number of developers with performance expertise decreased. This, combined with a directive to ignore performance, made the resulting performance disasters a self-fulfilling prophecy. Many of the disasters could not be corrected with hardware – platforms with the required power did not exist. Neither could they be corrected with tuning – corrections required major design changes, and thus reimplementation. Meanwhile, technical advances led to the SPE alternative.

SPE uses *models* to predict performance, *tools* to formulate and solve models, and *methods* to prescibe how and when to conduct performance studies. The SPE techniques developed in the 1980s focused on models that could be solved with analytic techniques because the tools and the speed of the processors made analytic techniques more desirable than simulation techniques for early lifecycle design tradeoff studies. Consequently, the following sections on the SPE evolution focuses on these analytic techniques, tools, and methods. Later, section 2.3 presents recent developments that make other models, tools, and adaptations of the methods viable.

2.1 Modeling Foundations
In 1971, Buzen proposed modeling systems with queuing network models and published efficient algorithms for solving some important models [BUZE71]. In 1975, Baskett, et. al., defined a class of models that have efficient analytic solutions [BASK75]. The models are an abstraction of the computer systems they model, so they are easier to create than general purpose simulation models. Because they are solved analytically, they can be used interactively. Since then, many advances have been made in modeling computer systems with queuing networks, faster solution techniques, and accurate approximation techniques [JAIN90; LAZO84; MOLL89; SAUR81].

Queueing network models are commonly used to model computer systems for capacity planning. A capacity-planning model is constructed from specifications for the computer system configuration and measurements of resource requirements for each of the workloads modeled. The model is solved and the resulting performance metrics (response time, throughput, resource utilization, etc.) are compared to measured performance. The model is calibrated to the computer system. Then, it is used to study the effect of increases in workload and resource demands, and of configuration changes.

Initially, queueing network models were used primarily for capacity planning. For SPE they were sometimes used for feasibility analysis: request arrivals and resource requirements were estimated and the results assessed. More precise models were infeasible because the software could not be measured until it was implemented.

The second SPE modeling breakthrough was the introduction of analytical models for software [BEIZ78; BOOT79a; BOOT79b; BOOT80; SANG78; SMIT79a; TRIV82]. With them, software execution is modeled, estimates of resource requirements are made, and performance metrics are calculated. Software execution models yield an approximate value for best, worst, or average resource requirements (such as CPU usage or number of I/O operations). They provide an estimate for response time; they can detect response time problems, but because they do not model resource contention they do not yield precise values for predicted response time.

The third SPE modeling breakthrough was combining the analytic software models with the queueing-network system models to more precisely model execution characteristics [BGS; SMIT80b; SMIT80a]. Combined models more precisely model the execution. They also show the effect of new software on existing work and on resource utilization. They identify computer device bottlenecks and the parts of the new software with high use of bottleneck devices.

By 1980, the modeling power was established and modeling tools were available[1] [BGS; QSP; SES]. Thus, it became cost-effective to model large software systems early in their development.

2.2 SPE Methods

Early experience with a large system confirmed that sufficient data could be collected early in development to predict performance bottlenecks [SMIT82b]. Unfortunately, despite the predictions, the system design was not modified to remove them and upon implementation (approximately one year later) performance in those areas was a serious problem, as predicted. SPE methods were proposed [SMIT81] and later updated [SMIT90a] to address the reasons that early predictions of performance problems were disregarded. Key parts of the process are methods for collecting data early in software development, and critical success factors to ensure SPE success. The methods also address compatibility with software engineering methods, what is done, when, by whom, and other organizational issues. SPE methods are described in Section 3.

2.3 SPE Development

The 1980s brought advances in all facets of SPE. Software model advances were proposed by several authors [BEIZ84; BOOT86; ESTR86; QIN89; SAHN87; SMIT82a; SMIT90a; SMIT82c]. Martin proposed data-action graphs as a representation that facilitates transformation between performance models and various software design notations [MART88]. Opdahl and Sølvberg integrate information system models and performance models with extended specifications [OPDA92b]. Rolia extends the SPE models and methods to address systems of cooperating processes in a distributed and multicomputer environment with specific applications to Ada [ROLI92]. Woodside [WOOD86; WOOD89] proposes stochastic rendezvous networks to evaluate performance of Ada systems and Woodside and coworkers incorporate the analysis techniques into a software engineering tool [BUHR 89; WOOD91]. Opdahl [OPDA92a] describes SPE tools interfaced with the PPP (processes, phenomena, programs) CASE tool and the IMSE environment for performance modeling – both are part of the Esprit research initiative. Opdahl

---

[1] Many new tools are now available.

[OPDA92] develops analytic sensitivity analysis techniques to point out where refinement and parameter capture efforts should be focused, and to suggest improvements in the design specification. Lor and Berry [LOR91] automatically generate SARA (Systems ARchitects Apprentice) models from an arbitrary requirements specification language using a knowledge-based Design Assistant. Other tools that incorporate features to support SPE modeling are reported by numerous authors [BAGR91; BEIL88; GOET90; NICH90; NICH91; POOL91; SMIT91; SMIT90b].

Extensive advances have been made in computer system performance modeling techniques. A complete list of references is beyond the scope of this tutorial.

Bentley [BENT82] proposes a set of rules for writing efficient programs. A set of formal, general principles for performance-oriented design is reported by Smith [SMIT86b; SMIT88a; SMIT90a]. Software architects who are experts in formulating requirements and designs, and developers who are experts in data structure and algorithm selection, use intuition to develop their systems. The rules and principles formalize the expert knowledge developed through years of experience, for use by software developers with less experience. Additional information on the rules and principles and related work is in Section 4.

Fox [FOX87; FOX89] describes middle lifecycle SPE activities. He emphasizes that models alone are insufficient and that measurement and analysis of evolving software are essential to meeting performance objectives. Bell [BELL87] advocates techniques for *system* performance engineering. He covers middle lifecycle techniques and focuses on the overall system, not just the software.

Numerous authors relay experience with SPE [ALEX86; ALEX82; ANDE84; BELL88; BELL87; FOX87; FOX89; PATE91; SMIT85B; SMIT88B] The *Proceedings of the Computer Measurement Group Conferences* contain SPE experience papers each year [CMG].

SPE has also been adapted to real-time process control systems. When these systems must respond to events within a specified time interval, they are called *reactive systems*. Howes [HOWE90] prescribes principles for developing efficient reactive systems. Goettge applies SPE to a reactive system using a performance engineering tool with an expert system for suggesting performance improvements [BREH92; GOET90]. Williams and Smith describe the SPE process for a case study of a reactive system [SMIT93]. Sholl and Kim [SHOL86] adapt the computation-structure approach to real-time systems, and LeMer [LEME82] describes a methodology and tool. Joseph and Pandya claim a computationally efficient technique for finding the exact worst-case response time of real-time systems [JOSE86]. Valderruten and coworkers derive performance models from formal specifications [VALD92]. Chang and coworkers [CHAN89] use petri net model extensions to evaluate real-time systems. Baldasarri and coworkers integrate a petri net design notation into a CASE tool that provides performance results [BALD89]. As mentioned earlier, much of the other reported work on real-time systems is outside the scope of SPE's software-oriented work.

514

3 The SPE Process

Figure 2 depicts the SPE process; the following paragraphs explain the figure.

First, developers define the specific SPE assessments for the current software lifecycle phase. Assessments determine whether planned software meets its performance objectives, such as acceptable response times, throughput thresholds, or constraints on resource requirements. A specific, quantitative objective is vital if

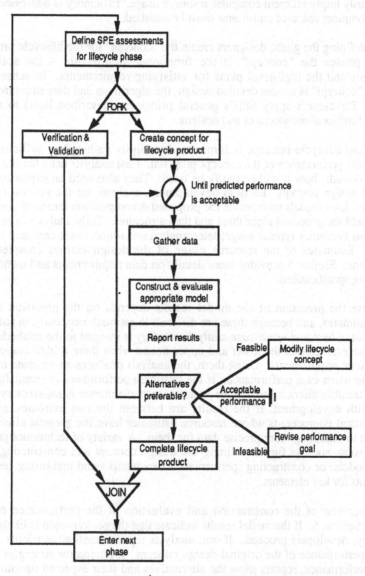

Fig. 2. Software Performance Engineering Process

analysts are to determine concretely whether that objective can be met. A crisp definition of the performance objectives lets developers determine the most appropriate means of achieving objectives, and avoid spending time overachieving them.

Business systems specify performance objectives in terms of *responsiveness* as seen by the system users. Reactive systems specify timing requirements for event responses. Both the response time for a task and the number of work units processed in a time interval (throughput) are measures of responsiveness. Responsiveness does not necessarily imply efficient computer resource usage. Efficiency is addressed only if critical computer resource constraints must be satisfied.

After defining the goals, designers create the "concept" for the lifecycle product. For early phases the "concept" is the functional architecture – the software requirements and the high-level plans for satisfying requirements. In subsequent phases the "concept" is a more detailed design, the algorithms and data structures, the code, etc. Developers apply SPE's general principles (described later) to create responsive functional architectures and designs.

Once the lifecycle concept is formulated, analysts gather data sufficient for estimating the performance of the concept proposal. First analysts need the projected system workload: how it will *typically* be used. They also need an explanation of the current design concept. Early in development, analysts use the general system architecture; later models incorporate the proposed decomposition into modules; still later, they add the proposed algorithms and data structures. Early analysis of reactive systems also examines typical usage; later analyses examine worst-case and failure scenarios. Estimates of the resource usage of the design entities complete the specifications. Section 5 provides more details on data requirements and techniques for gathering specifications.

Because the precision of the model results depends on the precision of the resource estimates, and because these are difficult to estimate very early in software development, a *best and worst-case analysis strategy* is integral to the methodology. Analysts use estimates of the lower and upper bound when there is high uncertainty about resource requirements. Using them, the analysis produces an estimate of both the best and worst-case performance. If the best-case performance is unsatisfactory, they seek feasible alternatives. If the worst-case performance is satisfactory, they proceed with development. If the results are between the two extremes, models identify critical components whose resource estimates have the greatest effect, and focus turns to obtaining more precise data for them. A variety of techniques provide more precision, such as further refining the design concept and constructing more detailed models, or constructing performance benchmarks and measuring resource requirements for key elements.

An overview of the construction and evaluation of the performance models follows in Section 5. If the model results indicate that the performance is likely to be satisfactory, developers proceed. If not, analysts report quantitative results on the predicted performance of the original design concept. If alternative strategies would improve performance, reports show the alternatives and their expected (quantitative) improvements. Developers review the findings to determine the cost-effectiveness of the alternatives. If a feasible and cost-effective alternative exists, developers modify the *concept* before the lifecycle product is complete. If none is feasible as, for example, when the modifications would cause an unacceptable delivery delay, developers explicitly revise the performance goal to reflect the expected degraded performance.

A vital and on-going activity of the SPE process is to *verify* that the models represent the software execution behavior, and *validate* model predictions against performance measurements. Reports compare the model specifications for the workload, software structure, execution structure, and resource requirements to actual usage and software characteristics. If necessary, analysts calibrate the model by adjusting model parameters until they represent the system behavior for a variety of loading conditions. They also examine discrepancies to update the performance predictions, and to identify the reasons for differences – to prevent similar problems occurring in the future. They produce reports comparing system execution model results (response times, throughput, device utilization, etc.) to measurements. Analysts study discrepancies, identify error sources, and calibrate the model as necessary. Model verification and validation (V&V) should begin early and continue throughout the lifecycle. In early stages, focus is on key performance factors; prototypes or benchmarks provide more precise specifications and measurements as needed. The evolving software becomes the source of the model verification and validation data.

This discussion outlined the steps for one design-evaluation "pass." The steps repeat throughout the lifecycle. For each pass the goals and the evaluations change somewhat. For additional information on SPE methods for lifecycle stages and the questions to be considered refer to [SMIT90a; SMIT93].

4 General Principles for Creating Responsive Systems

Engineering new software systems is an iterative process of refinement. At each refinement step, engineers *understand* the problem, *create* a hypothetical solution, describe or *represent* the proposed product of the creation step, and then *evaluate* that products' appropriateness. The evaluation assesses a design's *correctness* (adherence to specification), *feasibility* (cost, time, and technology to implement), and the *preferability* of one solution over another (simplicity, maintainability, usability, and so on). *Responsiveness* may be a correctness assessment (for reactive systems), or a feasibility assessment (will the architecture support the performance requirements), or a preferability assessment (when other requirements are met, engineers and users prefer a more responsive alternative).

Several software engineering methods advocate a software design process with these steps [ALFO85; BALD89; BELL77; RIDD78; WINC82]. Lampson [LAMP84] presents an excellent collection of hints for computer system design that addresses effectiveness, efficiency, and correctness. His efficiency hints are the type of folklore that has until recently been informally shared. Kopetz [KOPE86] presents principles for constructing real-time process control systems; some address responsiveness – all address performance in the more general sense.

Alter [ALTE79] and Kant [KANT81] take a different approach; they use program optimization techniques to generate efficient programs from logical specifications. Search techniques identify the best strategy from various alternatives for choices such as data set organizations, access methods, and computation aggregations.

Authors address program efficiency from three perspectives: efficient algorithms and data structures [BENT82; KNUT68; KNUT73]; efficient coding techniques [JALI77; MCNE80; VANT78]; and techniques for tuning existing programs to improve efficiency [BENT82; FERR78; FERR83b; KNUT71]. The program efficiency techniques evolved first. Later, the techniques evolved to address large-scale *systems* of programs in early life-cycle stages when developers seek requirements and design specifications that will lead to *systems* with acceptable responsiveness [SMIT86b; SMIT88a; SMIT90a]. During early stages, it is seldom the efficiency of machine resource usage that matters; it is the system *responsiveness*. Another distinction between system design and program tuning approaches is that program tuning transforms an inefficient program into a new "equivalent" program that performs the same function more efficiently. In system design, developers can transform *what* the software is to do as well as how it is to be done.

SPE uses both the early lifecycle system principles and the later lifecycle program design techniques. Section 4.1 gives a summary of general principles that apply to the requirements and design creation steps to identify alternatives that are likely to meet responsiveness objectives and to refine concepts that require improved responsiveness. Section 4.2 cites sources of principles that apply to implementation steps to identify desirable algorithms and data structures.

To experienced performance analysts, Lampson's hints, and these synthesis principles are not revolutionary new prescriptions. They are, however, a generalization and abstraction of the "expert knowledge" that performance specialists use in building or tuning systems.

The principles *supplement* performance assessment rather than replace it. Performance improvement has many tradeoffs – a local performance improvement may adversely affect overall performance. The quantitative methods covered in section 5 provide the data required to evaluate the net performance effect to be weighed against other aspects of correctness, feasibility, and preferability.

4.1 Early Lifecycle Performance Principles

Smith [SMIT90a] defines the following seven principles. A quantitative analysis of the performance results of three of them are in Smith [SMIT86b]. Both Smith [SMIT88a] and Smith [SMIT90a] give extensive explanations and examples for each principle.

Fixing-Point Principle. Fixing connects the desired action or function to the instructions that accomplish the action. Fixing also connects the desired result to the data used to produce it. The fixing "point" is a point in time. The latest fixing point is during execution immediately before the instructions or data are required. Fixing could establish connections at several earlier points: earlier in the execution, at program initiation time, at compilation time, or outside the software system.

Suppose users need summary data of multiple account detail records. The latest fixing point summarizes the data at the time users request summary-data screens; earlier fixing updates the summary data as account detail records arrive. The principle is as follows:

> *Fixing-Point Principle:* For responsiveness, fixing should establish connections at the earliest feasible point in time, such that retaining the connection is cost-effective.

It is cost-effective to retain the connection when the savings realized with it offset the retention cost. In the summary-data example, the retention cost is the cost of the storage to hold summary data. Assume that the data is saved for other purposes anyway, then there is no additional retention cost. The operational costs are roughly the same – to summarize upon request, the software must locate and read each detail record, then write one summary record. To update summary data as detail records arrive, there is one locate and one write per detail record. Thus, in this case early fixing is warranted because the responsiveness is better – users do not have to wait for the summary-data calculation.

Locality-Design Principle. Locality refers to the closeness of desired actions, functions, and results to physical resources. For example, if a desired screen result is identical to the physical database row that produces it, the locality is good. According to Webster, close means "being near in *time, space, effect* (that is, purpose or intent), or *degree* (that is, intensity or extent)."

The dictionary specification for *close* leads to four types of locality design for performance engineering. These are illustrated in the following example. Consider the logical task to sort a list of names. *Temporal locality* is better if the names are all sorted at the same time rather than sorting a few, and frequently adding a few more names to the list and sorting again. *Spatial locality* is better if the names are near the processor that conducts the sort, such as in the processor's local memory, rather than on a disk drive attached to a different machine. The sort can execute on different types of physical processors; *effectual locality* is better if the processor can sort long character strings directly, rather than breaking strings into smaller "processor-size" pieces (such as words or bytes). *Degree locality* is better if the entire list of names fits in memory rather than requiring intermediate storage on disk. The principle is as follows:

> *Locality Design Principle:* Create actions, functions, and results that are "close" to physical computer resources.

Processing Versus Frequency Tradeoff Principle. This principle addresses the amount of work done per processing request, and its impact on the number of requests made. The "tradeoff" looks for opportunities to reduce requests by doing more work per request and vice versa. The principle is as follows:

Processing versus Frequency Tradeoff Principle: Minimize the processing times frequency product.

When software adds many rows to a database, two design alternatives are (1) to execute the database load commands once per row; and (2) to collect the changes then execute the database load command once for the entire batch. The processing versus frequency tradeoff principle compares the total cost of the alternatives. If the software executes on a client platform, and the database resides on a server, the communication overhead processing is part of the total cost.

Shared-Resource Principle. Computer system resources are limited; thus, processes compete for their use. Some resources may be *shared:* Multiple processes can use the resource at the same time. Other resources require *exclusive use:* Processes take turns — each process has exclusive use of the resource, one at a time. Exclusive use affects performance in two ways: the additional processing overhead to schedule the resource and the possible contention delay to gain access to the resource. The contention delay depends on how many processes request exclusive use and the time they hold the resource. The shared-resource principle is of the *synergistic type:* it improves overall performance, through cooperation to reduce contention delays, rather than by reducing individual processing like the first three *independent-type* principles. The general principle is as follows:

> *Shared-Resource Principle:* Share resources when possible. When exclusive access is required, minimize the sum of the holding time and the scheduling time.

Resource sharing minimizes both the overhead for scheduling and the wait to gain access (there may be a wait if another process already has exclusive access even though the requester is willing to share). A database organization that keys on date and clusters transactions entered on the same date, does *not* promote "sharing when possible" because all additions during the day must lock the same portion of the database.

Parallel Processing Principle. Processing time can sometimes be reduced by partitioning a process into multiple concurrent processes. The concurrency can either be real concurrency in which the processes execute at the same time on different processors, or it can be apparent concurrency in which the processes are multiplexed on a single processor. For real concurrency, the processing time is reduced by an amount proportional to the number of processors. Apparent concurrency is more complicated: Although some of the processing may be overlapped (one process may use the CPU while another accesses the disk), each process may experience additional wait time. Both real and apparent concurrency require processing overhead to manage the communication and coordination between concurrent processes. The principle is as follows:

> *Parallel Processing Principle:* Execute processing in parallel (only) when the processing speedup offsets communication overhead and resource contention delays.

The parallel processing principle is another synergistic principle. SPE performance models assess speedup, contention delays, and communication delays.

Centering Principle. The five previous principles provide guidance for creating software requirements and designs. Their application improves the performance of the part of the system to which they are applied. Centering is different in that it leverages performance by focusing attention on the parts of software systems that have the greatest impact on responsiveness.[2] Centering identifies the subset ($\leq$ 20%) of the *system functions* that will be used most ($\geq$ 80%) of the time. These frequently used functions are the *dominant workload functions*.[3] Performance enhancements made to these key areas of the software system thus greatly affect the overall responsiveness of the system. The principle is as follows:

> *Centering principle:* Identify the dominant workload functions and minimize their processing.

That is, create special, streamlined execution paths for the dominant workload functions that are customized and trimmed to include only processing that *must* be part of the function. Use the five previous principles to minimize processing of the special paths. Create separate transactions for the workload functions that are used less frequently.

Design the dominant workload functions first to increase the liklihood that the data organization matches the access patterns. Even though the dominant workload functions are usually trivial transactions – not the essence of the software design – they will likely have the greatest effect on the overall responsiveness of the system. Thus, they require early resolution.

Instrumenting Principle. "Instrumenting software" means inserting code at key probe points to enable the measurement of pertinent execution characteristics. The principle is:

> *Instrumenting Principle:* Instrument systems *as you build them* to enable measurement and analysis of workload scenarios, resource requirements, and performance goal achievement.

This principle does not in itself improve performance, but is essential to *controlling* performance. It has its foundations in engineering, particularly process control engineering. Their rule of thumb is "if you can't measure it, you can't control it."

---

[2] Centering is based on the folkloric "80-20 rule" for the execution of code within programs (which claims that $\leq$ 20 percent of a program's code accounts for $\geq$ 80 percent of its computer resource usage).

[3] The dominant workload functions also cause a subset ($\leq$ 20%) of the programs or modules in the software system to be executed most ($\geq$ 80%) of the time, and the code within modules, and so forth.

Data collection mechanisms are part of the system requirements and design; it is much more difficult to add it after implementation. This is because of limitations in instrumenting technology - most external measurement tools collect system-level data, such as program execution time, rather than functional data such as end-to-end response time (for business units of work that require multiple transactions). To collect functional data, programmers must insert code to call system timing routines, and write key events and pertinent data to files for later analysis. *Define these probe points when defining the functions.*

Heuristics for Real-Time Systems Design. Howes develops design heuristics for "demonstrably efficient" real-time systems to be implemented in Ada. In Howes and Weaver [HOWE89] the authors introduce the

> *Structuring Principle of Physical Concurrency:* Introduce concurrency only to model physically concurrent objects or processes.

This is a specific instance of the earlier, more general parallel processing principle. This principle provides guidance to real-time system developers for the efficient use of Ada rendezvous. It is an alternative to maximum concurrency which advocates concurrency as a goal in itself, and conceptual concurrency which uses concurrency to simplify a design. Their paper compares the efficiency of the three concurrency approaches.

Howes [HOWE90] introduces the

> *Tuning Principle:* Reduce the mean service time of cyclic functions.

This is also a specific instance of the more general centering and processing versus frequency principles. It guides real-time system developers to identify the functions that execute at regular, specific time intervals and minimize their processing requirements.

Howes' 1990 paper applies both principles to a small design problem and compares the results to those achieved with other design heuristics that do not address performance. The paper's conclusion indicates that the investigation of other performance principles is underway.

Summary. A quantitative analysis of the performance effect of the fixing-point, processing versus frequency tradeoff, and centering principles is in Smith [SMIT86b]. While these three can be evaluated with simple, back-of-the-envelope calculations, the others require more sophisticated models. Section 4 reviews the quantitative methods for evaluating responsiveness of alternatives.

4.2 Implementation principles

Implementation principles apply during the detail-design stage to guide the selection and implementation of proper data structures and algorithms for the critical modules.

The *execution environment* defines the computer system configuration, such as the CPU, the operating system, and the I/O subsystem characteristics. It provides the underlying queueing network model topology and defines resource requirements for frequently used service routines. This is usually the easiest information to obtain. Performance modeling tools automatically provide much of it, and most capacity and performance analysts are familiar with the requirements.

Resource usage estimates determine the amount of service required of key devices in the computer system configuration. For each software component executed in the workload scenario, analysts need: the approximate number of instructions executed (or CPU time required); the number of physical I/O's; and use of other key devices such as communication lines (terminal I/O's and amount of data); memory (temporary storage, map and program size), etc. For database applications, the database management system (DBMS) accounts for most of the resource usage, so the number of database calls and their characteristics are usually sufficient. Early lifecycle requirements are tentative, difficult to specify, and likely to change, so SPE uses upper and lower bound estimates to identify problem areas or software components that warrant further study to obtain more precise specifications.

The number of times a component executes or its resource usage may vary significantly. To represent the variability, analysts identify the factors that cause the variability, use a data dependent variable to represent each factor, and specify the execution frequency and resource usage in terms of the data dependent variables. Later, the models study the performance sensitivity to various parameter values.

It is seldom possible to get precise information for all these specifications early in the software's lifecycle. Rather than waiting to model the system until it is available (i.e., in detailed design or later), SPE suggests gathering guesses, approximations, and bounded estimates to begin, then augmenting the models as information becomes available. This approach has the added advantage of focusing attention on key workload elements to minimize their processing (as prescribed by the "centering principle" in section 3). Otherwise, designers tend to postpone these important performance drivers in favor of designing more interesting but less frequently used parts of the software.

Because one person seldom knows all the information required for the software performance models, *performance walkthroughs* provide most of the data [SMIT90a]. Performance walkthroughs are closely modeled after design and code walkthroughs. In addition to software specialists who contribute software plans they bring together users who contribute workload and scenario information, and technical specialists who contribute computer configuration and resource requirements of key subsystems such as DBMS and communication paths. The primary purpose of a performance walkthrough is data gathering rather than a critical review of design and implementation strategy.

These topics are covered by a variety of data structure texts (see, for example, [KNUT68; KNUT73; SCHN78; STAN80]). Bentley [BENT82] provides a systematic methodology and specific efficiency rules for implementing the data structures and algorithms.

5 Quantitative Methods for SPE

The quantitative methods prescribe the data required to conduct the performance assessment and techniques for gathering the data; the performance models and techniques for adapting them to the system evolution; and techniques for verification and validation of the models.

5.1 Data Requirements

To create a software execution model analysts need: *performance goals, workload definitions, software execution characteristics, execution environment descriptions*, and *resource usage estimates*. An overview of each follows.

Performance goals, precise, quantitative metrics, are vital to determine concretely whether or not performance objectives can be met. For business applications, both on-line performance goals and batch window objectives must be met. For on-line transactions, the goals specify the response time or throughput required. Goal specifications define the external factors that impact goal attainment, such as the time of day, the number of concurrent users, whether the goal is an absolute maximum, a 90th percentile, and so on. For reactive systems, timing constraints specify the maximum time between an event and the response. Some reactive systems have throughput goals for the number of events processed in a time interval.

Workload definitions specify the key scenarios of the new software. For on-line transactions scenarios initially specify the transactions expected to be the most frequently used. Later in the lifecycle, scenarios also cover resource intensive transactions. On-line workload definitions identify the key scenarios and specify their workload intensity: the request arrival rates, or the number of concurrent users and the time between their requests (think time). Batch workload definitions identify the programs on the critical path, their dependencies, and the data volume to be processed. Reactive systems represent scenarios of time-critical functions, and worst-case operating conditions.

Software execution characteristics identify components of the software system to be executed for each workload scenario. The software execution scenario identifies: software components most likely to be invoked when users request the corresponding workload scenario; the number of times they are executed or their probability of execution; and their execution characteristics, such as the database tables used, and screens read or written. Reactive systems initially specify the likely execution paths, and later add less likely, but feasible execution paths.

5.2 Performance Models

Two models provide the quantitative data for SPE: the *software execution model* and the *system execution model*. The software execution model represents key facets of software execution behavior. The model solution quantifies the computer resource requirements for each workload scenario. The system execution model represents computer system resources with a network of queues and servers. The model combines the workload scenarios and quantifies overall resource utilization and consequent response times of each scenario.

Execution graph models are one type of software execution model. They are not the only option, but are convenient for illustration. A graph represents each workload scenario. Nodes represent functional components of the software; arcs represent control flow. The graphs are hierarchical with the lowest level containing complete information on estimated resource requirements [SMIT90a].

A static analysis of the graphs yields mean, best- and worst-case execution times of the scenarios. The static analysis makes the optimistic assumption that there are no other workloads on the host configuration competing for resources. Simple, graph-analysis algorithms provide the static analysis results [BEIZ78; BOOT79a; BOOT79b; SMIT90a].

Next, the system execution model solution yields the following additional information:

- The effect of resource contention on response times, throughput, device utilizations and device queue lengths.
- Sensitivity of performance metrics to variations in workload composition.
- Effect of new software on service level objectives of other existing systems.
- Identification of bottleneck resources.
- Comparative data on performance improvements to the workload demands, software changes, hardware upgrades, and various combinations of each.

To construct and evaluate the system execution model, analysts first represent the key computer resources with a network of queues, then use environment specifications to specify device parameters (such as CPU size and processing speed). The workload parameters and service requests come from the resource requirements computed from the software execution models. Analysts solve the model and check for reasonable results, then examine the model results. If the results show that the system fails to meet performance objectives, analysts identify bottleneck devices and correlate system execution model results with software components. After identifying alternatives to the software plans or the computer configuration, analysts evaluate the alternatives by making appropriate changes to the software or system model and repeating the analysis steps.

System execution models based on the network of queues and servers can be solved with analytic techniques in a few seconds. Thus analysts can conduct many tradeoff studies in a short time. Analytic solution techniques generally yield utilizations within 10 percent, and response times within 30 percent of actual. Thus, they are well-suited to early lifecycle studies when the primary objective is to identify feasible alternatives and rule out alternatives that are unlikely to meet performance goals. The resource usage estimates that lead to the model parameters are seldom sufficiently precise to warrant the additional time and effort required to produce more realistic models. Even reactive systems benefit from this intermediate step – it rules out serious problems before proceeding to more realistic models.

Early studies typically use simple SPE models. The SPE goal is to find problems with the simplest possible model. Experience shows that simple models can detect serious performance problems very early in the development process. The simple models isolate the problems and focus attention on their resolution (rather than on assumptions used for more realistic models). After they serve this primary purpose, analysts augment them as the software evolves to make more realistic performance predictions.

SPE calls for matching the modeling effort to the precision of the available data. The effort depends on the sophistication of the modeling tools available and their solution speed. As new tools become available and processor speeds increase, the shift from simple, optimistic models to more detailed, realistic models is adapted accordingly. Likewise, the shift from analytic to simulation solutions is adapted accordingly. Analytic solutions produce mean-value results which may not adequately reflect a system's performance if it has periodic problems or unusual execution characteristics.

Advanced system execution models are usually appropriate when the software reaches the detail-design lifecycle stage. Even when it is easy to incorporate the additional execution characteristics earlier, it is better to defer them to the advanced system execution model. It is seldom easy, however, and the time to construct and evaluate the advanced models usually does not match the input data precision early in the lifecycle.

The modeling difficulty arises from several sources. They are described next. First, advances in modeling technology follow the introduction of new hardware and operating system features. So accurate models of new computer system resources are active research topics. For example, I/O subsystems may have channel reconnect, path selection when multiple channel paths are available, disk cache controllers, etc. Models of these resources are evolving.

The second modeling difficulty is that special software features such as lock-free, acquire-release, etc., require *passive resources* – resources that are required for processing, but which do no work themselves. They are held while the software uses one or more active resources; the queueing delays for active resources influence the duration of passive resource usage. The impact of these passive resource delays is two-fold. The response of jobs forced to wait on the passive resource will be slower, but because these waiting jobs do not use active resources while they wait, other jobs may execute at a faster rate due to the decreased contention. Passive resource delays are difficult to quantify with analytic queueing network models: quantitative data for queueing delays requires a queue-server node, but its service time depends on the time spent in other queue-servers.

A third modeling difficulty is that computer system environment characteristics (such as distributed processing, parallel processing, concurrent and multi-threaded software, and memory management overhead) challenge model technology. They either use passive resources, have complex model topologies, or tightly couple the models of software and system execution.

These three facets of execution behavior are represented in the advanced system execution model. It augments the elementary system execution model with additional types of constructs. Then procedures specify how to calculate corresponding model parameters from software models, and how to solve the advanced models. SPE methods specify "checkpoint evaluations" to identify those aspects of the execution behavior that require closer examination [SMIT90a].

Recent modeling research results have simplified the analysis of advanced system execution models with passive resources [ROLI92; WOOD89; WOOD91]. Details of these models are beyond the scope of this tutorial. Information on system and advanced system execution models is available in books [JAIN90; LAZO84; MOLL89; SAUR81] as well as other publications. The *Proceedings of the ACM SIGMETRICS Conferences* and the *Performance Evaluation Journal* report recent research results in advanced systems execution models. The *Proceedings of the Performance Petri Net Conferences* also report relevant results.

5.3 Verification and Validation

Another vital part of SPE is continual verification of the model specifications and validation of model predictions (V&V). It begins early, particularly when model results suggest that major changes are needed. The V&V effort matches the impact of the results and the importance of performance to the project. When performance is critical, or major software changes are indicated, analysts identify the critical components, implement or prototype them, and measure. Measurements verify resource usage and path execution specifications and validate model results.

Early V&V is important even when predicted performance is good. Performance specialists influence the values that developers choose for resource usage estimates, and specialists tend to be optimistic about how functions will be implemented and about their resource requirements. Resource usage of the actual system often differs significantly from the optimistic specifications.

Performance engineers interview users, designers, and programmers to confirm that usage will be as expected, and that designed and coded algorithms agree with model assumptions. They adjust models when appropriate, revise predictions, and give regular status reports. They also perform sensitivity analyses of model parameters and determine thresholds that yield acceptable performance. Then, as the software evolves and code is produced, they measure the resource usage and path executions and compare with these thresholds to get early warning of potential problems. As software increments are deployed, measurements of the workload characteristics yield comparisons of specified scenario usage to actual and show inaccuracies or omissions. Analysts calibrate models and evaluate the effect of model changes on earlier results. As the software evolves, measurements replace resource estimates in the verification and validation process.

V&V is crucial to SPE. It requires the comparison of multiple sets of parameters, for heavy and light loads, to corresponding measurements. The model precision depends on how closely the model represents the key performance drivers. It takes constant vigilance to make sure they match.

6 Lifecycle SPE

The previous sections outline the SPE steps: define objectives, apply principles to formulate performance-oriented concepts, gather data, model, evaluate, and measure to verify model fidelity, validate model predictions, and confirm that software meets performance objectives. The steps are repeated throughout the lifecycle. The goals and the evaluation of the objectives change somewhat for each pass.

System performance engineering techniques evaluate the overall end-to-end performance to ensure that performance objectives will be met when all subsystems are combined. Systems with complex combinations of software, networks, and hardware have many potential pitfalls in addition to application software choices.

During later lifecycle stages performance engineers adapt the SPE methods to the lifecycle stage. As more information about the proposed software becomes available, the quantitative methods produce more precise performance metrics and support implementation trade-off decisions. Performance measurements confirm that the software performs as expected and augment earlier model estimates. Refer to [SMIT93] for more information on activities in later lifecycle stages.

7 Status and Future of SPE

Since computers were invented, the attitude persists that the next hardware generation will offer significant cost-performance enhancements, so it will no longer be necessary to worry about performance. There was a time, in the early 1970's, when computing power exceeded demand in most environments. The cost of achieving performance goals, with the tools and methods of the era, made SPE uneconomical for many batch systems – its cost exceeded its savings. Today's methods and tools make SPE the appropriate choice for many new systems. Will tomorrow's hardware solve all performance problems and make SPE obsolete? It has not happened yet. Hardware advances merely make new software solutions feasible, so software size and sophistication offset hardware improvements. There is nothing wrong with using more powerful hardware to meet performance objectives, but SPE suggests evaluating all options early, and selecting the most effective one. Thus hardware may be the solution, but it should be explicitly chosen – early enough to enable orderly procurement. SPE still plays a role.

The three primary elements in SPE's evolution are the *models* for performance prediction, the *tools* that facilitate the studies, and the *methods* for applying them to systems under development. With these the *use* of SPE increases, and new design *concepts* develop that lead to high-performance systems. Future evolution in each of these five areas will change the nature of SPE but not its underlying philosophy to build performance into systems. The following paragraphs speculate on future developments in each of these areas.

Both research and development will produce the *tools* of the future. We seek better integration of the models and their analysis with software engineering tools such as specification languages, CASE tools, and automatic program generators. Then software changes automatically update prediction models. Simple models can be transparent to designers – designers could click a button while formulating designs and view automatically generated performance predictions. Expert systems could suggest performance improvements [GOET90]. Visual user interfaces could make analysis and reporting more effective. Software measurement tools could capture, reduce, interpret, and report data at a level of detail appropriate for designers. Measurement tools could automatically generate performance tests and compare specifications to measurements, compare predictions to actual performance, and report discrepancies. Each of these tools could interface with an SPE database to store evolutionary design and model data and support queries against it.

While simple versions of each of these tools are feasible with today's technology, research must establish the framework for fully functional versions. For example, if a CASE tool supports data flow diagrams and structure charts, how does software automatically convert them to software models? How should performance models integrate with specification languages or automatic program generators – should one begin with models and generate specifications or code from them, or should one write the specifications and let underlying models select efficient implementations, or some other combination? How can expert systems detect problems? Can software automatically determine from software execution models where instrumentation probes should be inserted? Can software automatically reduce data to appropriate levels of detail? Can software automatically generate performance tests? Each of these topics represents extensive research projects.

Performance models currently have limits in their ability to analytically solve models of tomorrow's complex environments. Models of extensive parallel or distributed environments must be hand-crafted, with many checkpoint evaluations tailored to the problem. More automatic solutions are desired. Secondly, the analytic queueing network models yield only mean value results. Analysts need to quickly and easily model transient behavior to study periodic behavior or unusual execution characteristics. For example, averaged over a 10-hour period, locking effects may be insignificant, but there may be short 1 minute intervals in which locks cause all other active jobs to "log jam," and it may take 30 minutes for the log jam to clear. Mean value results do not reflect these after-effects; transient behavior models could. Petri nets and simulation offer more of the desired capabilities than analytical methods. Finally, as computer environments evolve, model technology must also develop. Thus, research opportunities are rich in software and computer environment models.

Technology transfer suggests that the *use of SPE* is likely to spread. More literature documenting SPE experiences is likely to appear. As it is applied to new, state-of-the-art software systems, new problems will be discovered that require research solutions. Future SPE applications will require skills in multiple domains and offer many new learning opportunities. As quantitative models evolve, so will the use of SPE for new problem domains. For example, models of software reliability have matured enough to be integrated with other SPE methods. Similarly, models can also support hardware-software codesign and enable software versus hardware implementation choices early in development [FRAN85].

The *concepts for building high performance systems* will evolve as SPE use spreads. Experience will lead to many examples illustrating the difference between high and low- performance software that can be used to educate new software engineers. SPE quantitative techniques should be extended to build in other quality attributes, such as reliability, availability, testability, maintainability, etc. Research in these areas is challenging – for example: Do existing software metrics accurately represent quality factors? Can one develop predictive models? What design data will drive the models? What design concepts lead to improved quality?

SPE methods should undergo significant change as its usage increases. The methods should be better integrated into the software development process, rather than an add-on activity. SPE should become better integrated into capacity planning as well. As they become integrated, many of the pragmatic techniques should be unnecessary (how to convince designers there is a serious problem, how to get data, etc.). The nature of SPE should then change. Performance walkthroughs will not be necessary for data gathering; they may only review performance during the course of regular design walkthroughs. The emphasis will change from finding and correcting design flaws to verification and validation that the system performs as expected. Additional research into automatic techniques for measuring software designs is needed, for calibrating models, and for reporting discrepancies.

SPE methods need to evolve from a general methodology with numerous examples (many in the business systems area) to a more exhaustive set of procedures based on system types. For a particular type of system: Is a standard set of performance requirements appropriate? Which performance metrics are relevant? Which design principles and rules of thumb are most important? What specific SPE steps should be conducted at each lifecycle stage? Which modeling techniques and tools are most appropriate to represent pertinent system characteristics? What specific measurements are needed and which tools provide the data?

For certain real-time systems, particularly those with mission-critical or safety-critical performance requirements, SPE procedures must be rigorously defined. The SPE results must also be defined and *reviewable* so inspectors can determine that SPE was properly conducted and the system will meet its performance requirements [SMIT92b].

Thus, the research challenges for the future are to extend the quantitative methods to model the new hardware-software developments, to extend hardware-software measurement technology to support SPE, and to develop interdisciplinary techniques to address the more general definition of performance. The challenges for future technology transfer are to automate the sometimes cumbersome SPE activities, and to evolve SPE to make it easy and economical for future environments.

Acknowledgement

This tutorial is an excerpt from the article "Software Performance Engineering" that appears in *The Encyclopedia of Software Engineering*, John Wiley and Sons, 1993.

BIBLIOGRAPHY

[ALEX86] C.T. Alexander, "Performance Engineering: Various Techniques and Tools," *Proceedings Computer Measurement Group Conference*, Las Vegas, NV, Dec. 1986, pp. 264-267.

[ALEX82] William Alexander and Richard Brice, "Performance Modeling in the Design Process," *Proceedings National Computer Conference*, Houston, TX, June 1982.

[ALFO85] M. Alford, "SREM at the Age of Eight: The Distributed Computing Design System," *IEEE Computer*, vol. 18, no. 4, April 1985.

[ALTE79] S. Alter, "A Model for Automating File and Program Design in Business Application Systems," *Communications of the ACM*, vol. 22, no. 6, June 1979, pp. 345-353.

[ANDE84] Gordon E. Anderson, "The Coordinated Use of Five Performance Evaluation Methodologies," *Communications of the ACM*, vol. 27, no. 2, Feb. 1984, pp. 119-125.

[BAGR91] R.L. Bagrodia and C. Shen, "MIDAS: Integrated Design and Simulation of Distributed Systems," *IEEE Transactions on Software Engineering*, vol. 17, no. 10, Oct. 1991, pp. 1042-58.

[BALD89] M. Baldassari, et al., "PROTOB: A Hierarchical Object-Oriented CASE Tool for Distributed Systems," *Proceedings European Software Engineering Conference - 1989*, Coventry, England, Sept. 1989.

[BASK75] F. Baskett, et al., "Open, Closed, and Mixed Networks of Queues with Different Classes of Customers," *Journal of the ACM*, vol. 22, no. 2, Apr. 1975, pp. 248-260.

[BEIL88] Heinz Beilner, J. Mäter, and N. Weissenburg, "Towards a Performance Modeling Environment: News on HIT," *Proceedings 4th International Conference on Modeling Techniques and Tools for Computer Performance Evaluation*, Plenum Publishing, 1988.

[BEIZ78] Boris Beizer, *Micro-Analysis of Computer System Performance*, New York, NY, Van Nostrand Reinhold, 1978.

[BEIZ84] Boris Beizer, "Software Performance," in *Handbook of Software Engineering*, C.R. Vicksa and C.V. Ramamoorthy, ed., New York, NY, Van Nostrand Reinhold, 1984, pp. 413-436.

[BELL88] Thomas E. Bell, guest editor, *Computer Measurement Group Transactions*, Spring, 1988.

[BELL77] Thomas E. Bell, D.X. Bixler, and M.E. Dyer, "An Extendible Approach to Computer-aided Software Requirements Engineering," *IEEE Transactions on Software Engineering*, vol. 3, no. 1, Jan. 1977, pp. 49-59.

[BELL87] Thomas E. Bell and A.M. Falk, "Performance Engineering: Some Lessons From the Trenches," *Proceedings Computer Measurement Group Conference*, Orlando, FL, Dec. 1987, pp. 549-552.

[BENT82] Jon L. Bentley, *Writing Efficient Programs*, Englewood Cliffs, NJ, Prentice-Hall, 1982.

[BGS] BGS Systems, Inc., 128 Technology Center, Waltham, MA 02254, (617)891-0000.

[BOOT79a] Taylor L. Booth, "Performance Optimization of Software Systems Processing Information Sequences Modeled by Probabilistic Languages," *IEEE Transactions on Software Engineering*, vol. 5, no. 1, Jan. 1979, pp. 31-44.

[BOOT79b] Taylor L. Booth, "Use of Computation Structure Models to Measure Computation Performance," *Proceedings Conference on Simulation, Measurement, and Modeling of Computer Systems*, Boulder, CO, Aug. 1979.

[BOOT86] Taylor L. Booth, R.O. Hart, and Bin Qin, "High Performance Software Design," *Proceedings Hawaii International Conference on System Sciences*, Honolulu, HI, Jan. 1986, pp. 41-52.

[BOOT80] Taylor L. Booth and C.A. Wiecek, "Performance Abstract Data Types as a Tool in Software Perfromance Analysis and Design," *IEEE Transactions on Software Engineering*, vol. 6, no. 2, Mar. 1980, pp. 138-151.

[BREH92] Eric W. Brehm, Robert T. Goettge, and Frederick W. McCaleb, "START/ES — An Expert System Tool for System Performance and Reliability Analysis," *Proceedings Modelling Techniques and Tools for Computer Performance Evaluation*, Rob Pooley and Jane Hillston, ed., Edinburgh Scotland, September 1992, pp. 151-165.

[BUHR 89] R.J. Buhr, et al., "Software CAD: A Revolutionary Approach," *IEEE Transactions on Software Engineering*, vol. 15, no. 3, Mar. 1989, pp. 234-249.

[BUZE71] Jeffrey P. Buzen, "Queueing Network Models of Multiprograming," Ph.D. Dissertation, Harvard University, 1971.

[CHAN89] C.K. Chang, et al., "Modeling a Real-Time Multitasking System in a Timed PQ Net," *IEEE Transactions on Software Engineering*, vol. 6, no. 2, March 1989, pp. 46-51.

[CMG] Computer Measurement Group, 414 Plaza Dr. Suite 209, Westmont, IL 60559, (708)655-1812.

[ESTR86] G. Estrin, et al., "SARA (System ARchitects' Apprentice): Modeling, Analysis, and Simulation Support for Design of Concurrent Systems," *IEEE Transactions on Software Engineering*, vol. SE-12, no. 2, Feb. 1986, pp. 293-311.

[FERR78] Domenico Ferrari, *Computer Systems Performance Evaluation*, Englewood Cliffs, NJ, Prentice-Hall, 1978.

[FERR83b] Domenico Ferrari, Giuseppe Serazzi, and Alessandro Zeigner, *Measurement and Tuning of Computer Systems*, Englewood Cliffs, NJ, Prentice-Hall, 1983.

[FOX87] Gregory Fox, "Take Practical Performance Engineering Steps Early," *Proceedings Computer Measurement Group Conference*, Orlando, FL, Dec. 1987, pp. 992-993.

[FOX89] Gregory Fox, "Performance Engineering as a Part of the Development Lifecycle for Large-Scale Software Systems," *Proceedings 11th International Conference on Software Engineering*, Pittsburgh, PA, May 1989, pp. 85-94.

[FRAN85] Geoff A. Frank, Connie U. Smith, and John L. Cuadrado, "Software/Hardware Codesign with an Architecture Design and Assessment System," *Proceedings Design Automation Conference*, Las Vegas, NV, 1985.

[GABR90] Armen Gabrielian and Matthew K. Franklin, "Multi-Level Specification and Verification of Real-Time Software," *Proceedings Twelfth International Conference on Software Engineering*, Nice, France, Apr. 1990, pp. 52-62.

[GOET90] Robert T. Goettge, "An Expert System for Performance Engineering of Time-Critical Software," *Proceedings Computer Measurement Group Conference*, Orlando FL, 1990, pp. 313-320.

[GRAH73] R.M. Graham, G.J. Clancy, and D.B. DeVaney, "A Software Design and Evalation System," *Communications of the ACM*, vol. 16, no. 2, Feb. 1973, pp. 110-116.

[HOWE90] Norman R. Howes, "Toward a Real-Time Ada Design Methodology," *Proceedings Tri-Ada 90*, Baltimore, MD, Dec. 1990.

[HOWE89] Norman R. Howes and Alfred C. Weaver, "Measurements of Ada Overhead in OSI-Style Communications Systems," *IEEE Transactions on Software Engineering*, vol. 15, no. 12, Dec. 1989, pp. 1507-1517.

[JAFF91] Matthew S. Jaffe, et al., "Software Requirements Analysis of Real-Time Process Control Systems," *IEEE Transactions on Software Engineering*, vol. 17, no. 3, Mar. 1991, pp. 241-258.

[JAHA87] Farnam Jahanian and Aloysius K.L. Mok, "A Graph-Theoretic Approach for Timing Analsis and its Implementation," *IEEE Transactions on Computers*, vol. C-36, no. 8, Aug. 1987, pp. 961-975.

[JAIN90] R. Jain, *Art of Computer Systems Performance Analysis*, New York, NY, John Wiley, 1990.

[JALI77] Paul J. Jalics, "Improving Performance The Easy Way," *Datamation*, vol. 23, no. 4, Apr. 1977, pp. 135-148.

[JOSE86] M. Joseph and P. Pandya, "Finding Response Times in a Real-Time System," *The Computer Journal*, vol. 29, no. 5, 1986, pp. 390-395.

[KANT81] Elaine Kant, *Efficiency in Program Synthesis*, Ann Arbor, MI, UMI Research Press, 1981.

[KNUT68] Donald E. Knuth, *The Art of Computer Programming, Vol.1: Fundamental Algorithms*, Reading, MA, Addison-Wesley, 1968.

[KNUT71] Donald E. Knuth, "An Empirical Study of FORTRAN Programs," *Software Practice & Experience*, vol. 1, no. 2, Apr. 1971, pp. 105-133.

[KNUT73] Donald E. Knuth, *The Art of Computer Programming, Vol.3: Sorting and Searching*, Reading, MA, Addison-Wesley, 1973.

[KOPE86] Herman Kopetz, "Design Principles of Fault Tolerant Real-Time Systems," *Proceedings Hawaii International Conference on System Sciences*, Honolulu, HI, Jan. 1986, pp. 53-62.

[KOPE85] H. Kopetz and W. Merker, "The Architecture of Mars," *Proceedings FTCS 15*, Ann Arbor, MI, IEEE Press, June 1985, pp. 274-279.

[KOPE91] H. Kopetz, et al., "The Design of Real-Time Systems: From Specification to Implementation and Verification," *Software Engineering Journal*, 1991, pp. 72-82.

[LAMP84] Butler W. Lampson, "Hints for Computer System Design," *IEEE Software*, vol. 2, no. 1, Feb 1984, pp. 11-28.

[LAZO84] Edward D. Lazowska, et al., *Quantitative System Performance: Computer System Analysis Using Queuing Network Models*, Englewod Cliffs, NJ, Prentice-Hall, Inc., 1984.

[LEME82] Eric LeMer, "MEDOC: A Methodology for Designing and Evaluating Large-Scale Real-Time Systems," *Proceedings National Computer Conference, 1982*, Houston, TX, 1982, pp. 263-272.

[LEVI90] S. Levi and A.K. Agrawala, *Real-Time System Design*, New York, NY, McGraw-Hill, 1990.

[LOR91] K. Lor and D.M. Berry, "Automatic Synthesis of SARA Design Models from System Requirements," *IEEE Transactions on Software Engineering*, vol. 17, no. 12, Dec. 1991, pp. 1229-1240.

[MART88] Charles R. Martin, "An Integrated Software Performance Engineering Environment," Masters Thesis, Duke University, 1988.

[MCNE80] M. McNeil and W. Tracy, "PL/I Program Efficiency," *SIGPLAN Notices*, vol. 15, no. 6, June 1980, pp. 46-60.

[MOLL89] Michael K. Molloy, *Fundamentals of Performance Modeling*, MacMillan, 1989.

[NICH90] Kathleen M. Nichols, "Performance Tools," *IEEE Software*, vol. 7, no. 3, May 1990, pp. 21-30.

[NICH91] Kathleen M. Nichols and Paul Oman, "Special Issue in High Performance," *IEEE Software*, vol. 8, no. 5, 1991.

[OPDA92a] A. Opdahl, "A CASE Tool for Performance Engineering During Software Design," *Proceedings Fifth Nordic Workshop on Programming Environmental Research*, Tampere, Finland, Jan. 1992.

[OPDA92b] A. Opdahl and A. Sølvberg, "Conceptual Integration of Information System and Performance Modeling," *Proceedings Working Conference on Information System Concepts: Improving the Understanding*, 1992.

[OPDA92] Andreas L. Opdahl, "Sensitivity Analysis of Combined Software and Hardware Performance Models: Open Queueing Networks," *Proceedings Modelling Techniques and Tools for Computer Performance Evaluation*, Rob Pooley and Jane Hillston, ed., Edinburgh, September 1992, pp. 257-271.

[PATE91] M. Paterok, R. Heller, and H. deMeer, "Performance Evaluation of an SDL Run Time System - A Case Study," *Proceedings 5th International Conference on Modeling Techniques and Tools for Computer Performance Evaluation*, Torino, Italy, Feb. 1991, pp. 86-101.

[POOL91] R. Pooley, "The Integrated Modeling Support Environment," *Proceedings 5th International Conference on Modeling Techniques and Tools for Computer Performance Evaluation*, Torino, Italy, Feb. 1991, pp. 1-15.

[POSP92] Gustav Pospischil, et al., "Developing Real-Time Tasks with Predictable Timing," *IEEE Software*, vol. 9, no. 5, Sept. 1992, pp. 35-50.

[QIN89] Bin Qin, "A Model to Predict the Average Response Time of User Programs," *Performance Evaluation*, vol. 10, 1989, pp. 93-101.

[QSP] Quantitative System Performance, 7516 34th Ave N., Seattle, WA 98117-4723.

[RIDD78] W.E. Riddle, et al., "Behavior Modeling During Software Design," *IEEE Transactions on Software Engineering*, vol. 4, 1978.

[ROLI92] J.A. Rolia, "Predicting the Performance of Software Systems," University of Toronto, 1992.

[SAHN87] Robin A. Sahner and Kishor S. Trivedi, "Performance and Reliability Analysis Using Directed Acyclic Graphs," *IEEE Transactions on Software Engineering*, vol. 13, no. 10, Oct. 1987, pp. 1105-1114.

[SANG78] John W. Sanguinetti, "A Formal Technique for Analyzing the Performance of Complex Systems," *Proceedings Performance Evaluation Users Group 14*, Boston, MA, Oct. 1978.

[SAUR81] C.H. Sauer and K.M. Chandy, *Computer Systems Performance Modeling*, Englewood Cliffs, NJ, Prentice-Hall, 1981.

[SCHN78] G.M. Schneider, S.W. Weingart, and D.M. Perlman, *An Introduction to Programming and Problem Solving with Pascal*, New York, NY, John Wiley and Sons, 1978.

[SES] Scientific and Engineering Software, 4301 West Bank Drive, Bldg A., Austin, TX 78746, (512)328-5544.

[SHA90] Lui Sha and John B. Goodenough, "Real-Time Scheduling Theory and Ada," *IEEE Computer*, vol. 23, no. 4, Apr. 1990, pp. 53-62.

[SHIN92] Kang G. Shin, et al., "A Distributed Real-Time Operating System," *IEEE Software*, vol. 9, no. 5, Sept. 1992, pp. 58-68.

[SHOL86] H. Sholl and S. Kim, "An Approach to Performance Modeling as an Aid in Structuring Real-time, Distributed System Software," *Proceedings Hawaii International Conference on System Sciences*, Honolulu, HI, Jan. 1986, pp. 5-16.

[SHOL75] H.A. Sholl and Taylor L. Booth, "Software Performance Modeling Using Computation Structures," *IEEE Transactions on Software Engineering*, vol. 1, no. 4, Dec. 1975.

[SMIT79a] Connie U. Smith and J.C. Browne, "Performance Specifications and Analysis of Software Designs," *Proceedings ACM Sigmetrics Conference on Simulation Measurement and Modeling of Computer Systems*, Boulder, CO, Aug. 1979.

[SMIT80a] Connie U. Smith and J.C. Browne, "Aspects of Software Design Analysis: Concurrency and Blocking," *Proceedings ACM Sigmetrics Conference on Simulation Measurement and Modeling of Computer Systems*, May 1980.

[SMIT80b] Connie U. Smith, "The Prediction and Evaluation of the Performance of Software from Extended Design Specifications," Ph.D. Dissertation, University of Texas, 1980.

[SMIT81] Connie U. Smith, "Software Performance Engineering," *Proceedings Computer Measurement Group Conference XII*, Dec. 1981, pp. 5-14.

[SMIT82a] Connie U. Smith, "A Methodology for Predicting the Memory Management Overhead of New Software Systems," *Proceedings Hawaii International Conference on System Sciences*, Honolulu, HI, Jan. 1982, pp. 200-209.

[SMIT82b] Connie U. Smith and J.C. Browne, "Performance Engineering of Software Systems: A Case Study," *Proceedings National Computer Conference*, Houston, TX, vol. 15, June 1982, pp. 217-224.

[SMIT82c] Connie U. Smith and David D. Loendorf, "Performance Analysis of Software for an MIMD Computer," *Proceedings ACM Sigmetrics Conference on Measurement and Modeling of Computer Systems*, Seattle, WA, Aug. 1982, pp. 151-162.

[SMIT85b] Connie U. Smith, guest editor, *Computer Measurement Group Transactions*, 1985.

[SMIT86b] Connie U. Smith, "Independent General Principles for Constructing Responsive Software Systems," *ACM Transactions on Computer Systems*, vol. 4, no. 1, Feb. 1986, pp. 1-31.

[SMIT88a] Connie U. Smith, "Applying Synthesis Principles to Create Responsive Software Systems," *IEEE Transactions on Software Engineering*, vol. 14, no. 10, Oct. 1988, pp. 1394-1408.

[SMIT88b] Connie U. Smith, "Who Uses SPE?," *Computer Measurement Group Transactions*, Spring 1988, pp. 69-75.

[SMIT90a] Connie U. Smith, *Performance Engineering of Software Systems*, Reading, MA, Addison-Wesley, 1990.

[SMIT90b] Connie U. Smith and Lloyd G. Williams, "Why CASE Should Extend into Software Performance," *Software Magazine*, vol. 10, no. 9, 1990, pp. 49-65.

[SMIT91] Connie U. Smith, "Integrating New and 'Used' Modeling Tools for Performance Engineering," *Proceedings 5th International Conference on Modeling*

Techniques and Tools for Computer Performance Evaluation, Torino, Italy, Feb. 1991.

[SMIT92b] Connie U. Smith, "Software Performance Engineering in the Development of Safety-Critical Systems," No.92-03, L&S Computer Technology, November, 1992.

[SMIT93] Connie U. Smith, "Software Performance Engineering," in *The Encyclopedia of Software Engineering*, John Wiley and Sons, 1993.

[SMIT93] Connie U. Smith and Lloyd G. Williams, "Software Performance Engineering: A Case Study with Design Comparisons," *IEEE Transactions on Software Engineering*, to appear 1993.

[STAN80] T.A. Standish, *Data Structure Techniques*, Reading, MA, Addison-Wesley, 1980.

[STAN91] John A. Stankovic and Krithi Ramamritham, "The Spring Kernel: A New Paradigm for Real-Time Systems," *IEEE Software*, vol. 8, no. 3, Mar. 1991, pp. 62-72.

[TRIV82] Kisor S. Trivedi, *Probability and Statistics With Reliability, Queueing, and Computer Science Applications*, Englewood Cliffs, NJ, Prentice-Hall, 1982.

[VALD92] Alberto Valderruten, et al., "Deriving Queueing Networks Performance Models from Annotated LOTOS Specifications," *Proceedings Modelling Techniques and Tools for Computer Performance Evaluation*, Rob Pooley and Jane Hillston, ed., Edinburgh, September 1992, pp. 167-178.

[VANT78] D. Van Tassel, *Program Style, Design, Efficiency, Debugging, and Testing*, Englewood Cliffs, NJ, Prentice-Hall, 1978.

[WINC82] J.W. Winchester and G. Estrin, "Methodology for Computer-based Systems," *Proceedings National Computer Conference*, vol. 51, 1982, pp. 369-79.

[WOOD86] C.M. Woodside, "Throughput Calculation for Basic Stochastic Rendezvous Networks," Technical Report, Carleton University, Ottawa, Canada, April, 1986.

[WOOD89] C.M. Woodside, "Throughput Calculation for Basic Stochastic Rendezvous Networks," *Performance Evaluation*, vol. 9, 1989.

[WOOD91] C.M. Woodside, et al., "The CAEDE Performance Analysis Tool," *Ada Letters*, vol. XI, no. 3, Spring 1991.

[XU87] J. Xu and D.L. Parnas, "On Satisfying Timing Constraints in Hard Real-Time Systems," *Proceedings ACM SIGSOFT 91 Conference on Software for Critical Systems*, New Orleans, LA, vol. 16, 1991, pp. 132-145.

Performance Measurement
Using System Monitors

Erwin M. Thurner

Siemens AG, ZFE ST SN 13
D - 81730 München

Abstract: *System monitors record inner states of computing systems. They are required for the debugging of computer systems as well as for the measurement of performance and they are used for the verification of system models, too. This paper first discusses the area of application of system monitors, and afterwards it introduces measurement-principles of the different monitor types:*
- *Software monitors, that either analyze the account-log, or that are available as event-driven monitors, as samplers or as profiling-monitors.*
- *Hardware monitors, using the measurement-principles logic-analyzer, events, sampling, and constructing classes of states.*
- *Hybrid monitors, which use the measurement-principles of hardware-monitors on the hardware part, but differ by the software part that generates the signals to be measured.*

At last, connections to performance-analysis based on models are discussed.

Key words: *System Monitor, Bus Monitor, Software Monitor, Hardware Monitor, Hybrid Monitor, Measurement of Performance, Debugging, Performance Models, Event Monitor, Sampling Monitor, Monitor based on Classes of States*

1 What does "System Monitor" mean?

1.1 Usage of System Monitors

A system monitor has the task to protocol inner states of a computing system. The results that can be obtained by system monitors allow to solve problems in a broad area of application:
- to find some errors in a computing system (debugging),
- to check the resource utilization and the job load of system components,
- to say something about the performance of the systems,

- to provide a base for building models of the computing system,
- to find system bottlenecks.

The broadness of the requirements necessitates that more than only one type of monitors is offered on the market. In the next sections, we will classify these different kinds of monitors under aspects of objects of measurement, type and principles of measurement.

1.2 Measurement Objects of System Monitors

For system monitors, typical objects of measurement are:

- *Bus Monitors:*
  The buses of a computer are the central connection elements between its system components. The bus activity is an indication of the sytem components' activity. By measuring the bus, we can make statements
  - about errors in the bus protocol,
  - about the kind and the amount of communication on the bus,
  - about system bottlenecks,
  - (indirectly) about the load of the sytem components.

- *Cache Monitors:*
  The behaviour of the cache is very important for the overall performance of high-performance-sytems. If the real system behaviour is known, one is able to tune the system purposefully.

- *CPU Monitoring:*
  By doing this, one can directly measure the CPU load. Measurements like these are particularly important for multi-processor systems, because the process scheduling depends on it. That is why the system must be checked continuously for busy and idle processors and which of them are able to perform a waiting task.

- *I/O Monitoring:*
  The I/O-system plays an important role for the overall-performance of a computer, as pointed out by Hennessy and Patterson [14]. Besides this, I/O-operations are very costly and therefore they are important for the accounting of the system. For this reason, I/O-operations are measured either via the system bus or on the components, via the working time of an I/O-processor or the duration of moving the harddisk arm.

- *Other System Monitors:*
  Basically, the performance of any system component can be measured by a particular monitor. In practice, only such components are measured which are suspected of being faulty or retarding for the overall-performance of the system.

1.3 Types of System Monitors

The types of system monitors are distinguished by the realization of their detecting element into: software monitors, hardware monitors, and hybrid monitors.
The evaluation on the one hand and the display of the measured system parameters can basically be done independently of the measurement itself. This fact enables the user to select the detecting element and the evaluation programs separately. Furthermore, the evaluation tools must be adapted both to the detecting element and the requirements.

2. Usage and Requirements of System Monitors

In this chapter, a survey is given about the usage of system monitors. The results will be summarized in a table at the end of this chapter.

2.1 Debugging of System Components and Interconnections

Particularly in the test-phase of the system components, system monitors are very often used for the debugging of system components and their connections.

- *Debugging of System Components:*
  Here, both the faults of the system components and faults that happen by the cooperation of the components in a system are analyzed. Due to the progress in simulation, a lot of faults of the system components can already be discovered and corrected in the design phase of the system. Nevertheless, in complex systems many faults of system components and their cooperation are not discovered before their integration into the system.
- *Debugging of Connections (Buses) and Protocols:*
  When system components are connected with the standard backplane bus of computing systems, the exact obediance to the bus protocol has to be verified. The same is true for other connections like LANs and wires. Besides a careful testing (e. g. by using a test suite, cf. [1]), Formal Description Techniques (FDTs) are used for this purpose. FDTs are available in languages Estelle, SDL or LOTOS (see [5] and [7]). FDTs are being developed even for bus protocols [30]. Also Petri Nets are used successfully for the verification of protocols [6].

For debugging, a *high temporal resolution* of the monitor is necessary, i.e. a sampling frequency that is as fast as the bus clock. A good *selectivity* is very useful, i. e. the monitor only records data when errors occur, but then the erroneous data have to be recorded with as many details as necessary. For debugging monitors, a long record-time is usually not very important. For this purpose mostly event hardware-monitors or logic analyzers are used.

2.3 Load of System Components and Performance Measurement

To measure the load of system components, "software probes" are injected into the source code of device drivers. These probes measure when an I/O-operation is started and when it has been terminated (e. g. [9] and [24]).
The monitoring of system components can be done for several reasons:
- Accounting of the used CPU and the I/O computing power, to determine the cost of the computing for every user.
- The load distribution, the allocation and the migration of tasks in a multi-processor system or within loosely coupled systems.
- Optimization of the system performance by optimizing frequently used system resources or parts of a program.
- To get a performance profile of a system, i. e. continuous watching of interesting parts of a system and the overall-performance of the system.
- Response times of a system.

For load monitors, mostly *statistical* statements are made about a longer duration, rather than to get measurement values that are as exact and have as many details as possible. For load and performance monitors, event hybrid and software-monitors are mostly used; but there are also hardware monitors available e.g. the idle counter.

2.4 Building a System Model

The evaluation of the performance of computer systems requires the usage of system models, which describe the system's behaviour. These models are to represent realistically on the one hand all the system parameters of the computer system and on the other hand the system load. For the construction and the verification of system models, some data are to be measured concerning the characteristic load and the behaviour.
The evaluation of the system performance and other system parameters is unavoidable, if the system is not yet available as hardware, but some claims are to be made about it to make architectural decisions. This way is gone frequently nowadays for the analysis and evaluation of new architectural approaches, and the quantitative influence of architectural parameters on the system performance. Due to this, the load profile of this system must be available.
To make statements about the whole system, classes-of-states hardware monitors are very well suited. For partial aspects, event or sampling hybrid monitors or profiling software monitors are used. Table 1 gives a survey of the typical usage of the monitor principles.

Type of Monitor / *Usage*	Hardware Monitor	Hybrid Monitor	Software Monitor
Debugging	event monitors, logic analyzers, classes-of-states monitor with attribute memory	—	—
System Load and System Performance	classes-of-states monitor, idle counter	event monitors, sampling monitors	analysis acc.-log, event-driven, sampling and profiling
System Bottlenecks	classes-of-states monitor, big logic analyzers	event monitors	profiling
Model Building	classes-of-states monitor	event monitors, sampling monitors	profiling

Table 1: Types of Monitors and Typical Usage

2.5 Classifying System Monitors

As mentioned above, the different classes of system monitors differ by
- their *temporal resolution*,
- their *duration of measurement*, and
- the *amount of measured data*.

So the selection of a monitor can be made by constructing a coordinate frame with the axes temporal resolution, duration of measurement, and amount of measured data (fig. 1). In this coordinate frame, the desired place of one's monitor can be determined. Of course, the cost of a monitor grows with growing coordinates.

Using this categorization, the different variants of monitors can be shown very well. The monitor with the best cost-performance-ratio for a distinct usage can be determined easily by assigning one's requirements in this parameter space to a suitable monitor in this space.

Let us illustrate the classification of monitors by looking at some examples, which are drawn in fig. 1: A *logic analyzer* has a temporal resolution of

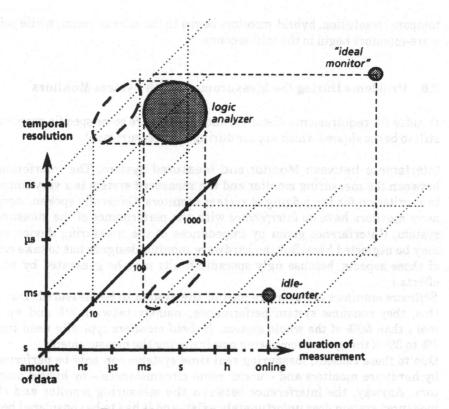

Fig. 1: Classification of System Monitors

some nanoseconds, a measurement duration of some microseconds, and it can display some 10 or 100 signals. An *idle counter* has the temporal resolution of about one millisecond, a very long duration of measurement (up to "online"), and it supports only one signal, namely idle. An *"ideal monitor"*, i. e. a monitor that records and displays everything that happens within a computer system, would be drawn into the right upper corner of fig. 1. But: "Ideal monitors" like this are virtually never realized due to the enormous amount a data one has to cope with. Furthermore, the measurement results obtained by this method are not so much better than results that can be gained by monitors with reasonable limitations. That is why "ideal monitors" actually have a very bad price-performance ratio. This approach to collect as much data as possible and to reduce the amount of data not before the evaluation has been realized only in the very first generation of system monitors. Modern research in this area has the target of successive limitation, where the exact formulation of the data to be gained and the parts to be examined plays an essential role. Using the classification-diagram of fig. 1, also software and hybrid monitors can be categorized easily: At the temporal resolution, hybrid-monitors begin in the microseconds, while software-monitors begin in the milliseconds.

2.6 Problems During the Measurement with System Monitors

Besides the requirements discussed above, there are some specific problems still to be considered which appear during the measurement.

Interference between Monitor and Measured System. The interference between the measuring monitor and the measured system is a very important criterion for the judging of system monitors. Generally spoken, *hardware monitors* have *no interference* with the performance of the measured system. (Interference given by impedances of the measuring device etc. may be neglected here. But the hardware monitor designer has to take care of these aspects, because ugly sporadic faults may be generated by such effects.)

Software monitors however are part of the system to be measured. Due to this, they consume system performance, namely between 3% and up to more than 50% of the whole system. *Hybrid monitors* typically need from 1% to 3% of the system computing power during the measurement.

Due to these reasons, measuring real time systems can only be performed by hardware monitors and – under some circumstances – by hybrid monitors. Anyway, the interference between the measuring monitor and the measured system does unfortunately exist, and it has to be considered both at the evaluation and when load models of the system are based on these measurements.

Measuring of Time. Another problem of system monitors is the measuring of time: The used time slots must be fine enough to record every single activity of a system. For hardware monitors and hybrid monitors, this is not a real problem, because an external clock can be provided, which can be selected freely. With software monitors however, the system clock is used for all purposes in the computer and it provides in many cases only the resolution of one second. This problem can be solved by introducing an additional process clock, which can be read via a special register (cf. [26] and [10], section 5.2.2).

An additional problem arises with multi processor system: Here, a global system clock must be provided, to correlate the activities of the processors. [15] proposes a synchronization signal, which is sent to the measuring devices via Ethernet. For other monitors, cables with exactly the same length from the measured system parts to the recording device are enough.

2.7 Other Criteria for the Judging of System Monitors

Evaluation Tools. After measurement, the collected data must be evaluated. So one can ask which criteria suitable evaluation tools have to fulfill:
- How good do the tools work together with the measuring devices?
- How can they be handled?
- Generally: How fast can I say something about the system's behaviour?

The requirements of the evaluation are hard to quantify. It seems that there is no alternative to considering every evaluation tool to be used, if it is really able to display what is needed for the desired application.

Flexibility. At system monitors, flexibility can be useful. Flexibility in this context means, that one type of monitor can be adapted easily to more than one bus or to more than only one object to be measured. So the user has to learn only one concept, one user menu etc. The manufacturer could offer only one type of monitors for a whole class of requirements.

Documentation and Archive Procedure of the Measurement Results. The ability for documentation and the functionality of the archive procedure of the measurement results is important, because usually many more than one measurement must be performed to say something about the behaviour of a computing system under several aspects.

3. Types of System Monitors

The types of system monitors are divided into
- software monitors (and firmware monitors),
- hardware monitors, and
- hybrid monitors.

For these types, the measurement principles and some typical implementation examples are given in this chapter.

3.1 Software Monitors

Software monitors were the first types of system monitors that have been developed. Their first task was to measure, how much of computing time, I/O throughput etc. are needed for a particular user resp. for each particular task. Based on this, the cost for the computer usage are assigned to the users. Aspects like performance came much later. In this section, first common principles and problems of software monitors are sketched. Afterwards, the measurement principles of software monitors are explained.

Principles and Problems of Software Monitors. Generally spoken, software monitors are a part of the measured system and it is unavoidable, that they interfere with it: They need memory, they use the CPU, and they perform I/O-operations. This fact must be considered when using software monitors. That is why there are several approaches to minimize the general load or one of the discussed parameters caused by the monitor.

For a software monitor, additional program code must be inserted into the system to be measured. Inserting additional code into the examined places of a program is called *instrumentation*. This can be done by three methods (cf. [10]):

- To use an additional program in the computing system:
  Such a program can cyclically evaluate data of the operating system and analyze them under some aspects. This approach is followed by sampling monitors and by the analysis of the account-log.
- Modification of the program to be measured:
  This method is mostly used by modern software and hybrid monitors. Here, the examined parts of a program – like procedure calls, basis blocks, program line, etc. – are "instrumented" by additional code, which produces a protocol about the dynamic run of the program. This method is used for the principles profiling and for event-driven software monitors.
- Modification of the operating system:
  This method is the least portable one, because it uses the internal data of the operating system. This approach is used for generating the account-log, but also for the interrupt-intercept approach at event-driven monitors.

When measuring multi processor systems, the problem of the global time for the whole system comes up once more. This problem can be solved either by some hardware measure such as a system-wide common clock, or by a synchronization signal for start and stop, from which the correct times can be computed.

Analyzing the Account-Log. The data of the account-log are recorded regularly at multi user systems. They include some details about duration of tasks, process load, usage of peripheral devices, login times etc. So the account-log can be used as a source for some statistics about the load of the computing system. It shows load peaks and it is a first indication for system bottlenecks. It has the advantage of giving no additional load to the system, because these values are always measured. This methods depend very much on the examined machine and the operating system.

In [25] a software monitor is introduced, which reads the account-log every day and computes the difference to the last account-log. Based on this, the monitor compiles some daily statistics about the usage of the hardware resources, like CPU, I/O, paging etc., and the offered "service", here defined as the response times at multi user mode.

Event-Driven, Interrupt-Intercept. An event is defined in [10] as any change of the state of a computing system. (This definition must not be confused with the notion of "event" at a hardware monitor!) An event-driven software monitor is a machine that records changes of the states of a computing system in a so-called event-trace. This approach has the disadvantage, that a complete trace *("full trace monitoring")* generates an enormous amount of data, so that the data flood is to be reduced by limitation on distinct aspects.

It suggests itself only to consider important actions of the operating system in the event-trace such as task switches or I/O-requests. Particularly for this request, interrupt-intercept monitors are used. In these kind of monitors the addresses of the interrupt routines are changed, so that every interrupt-call in reality first calls a monitoring routine and then jumps to the subroutine which actually handles the interrupt [17]. With this monitor, meaningful traces about important actions of the operating system can be captured.

Sampling Software Monitor. Sampling Monitors perform measurements in periodical time slots. The monitor is subdivided into two parts (cf. [10], section 5.2.1):

– The Extractor:
   It periodically generates an interrupt, say 1 to 20 times per second. In the software routine that handles the interrupt data are collected, which are meaningful for the system state. This interrupt needs a high priority, so that the interrupt routine cannot be interrupted and the watched system data cannot become corrupted by that interrupt.
– The Analyzer:
   It evaluates the data from the extractor under some aspects and shows relevant system data.

It is clear, that sampling monitors can make only *statistical* statements about system data. The exactness can be influenced in a broad range by the sampling frequency.

Profiling Monitor. Profiling is the *dynamical analysis* of a program. See the description of the tools prof, pixie, pixstats in [22] and prof, lprof in [27]. The opposite is the *static analysis* of the assembler-code, which provides the relative frequency of one instruction. The instrumentation of the examined program can be performed automatically and can simply be chosen by a compiler option.

In most cases, the time used to execute a procedure is measured, or the number of runs of every line or basic block of a program. By using data gained this way, frequently used procedures and program parts can be found, at which tuning will make sense. In addition, subroutines can be found which are not called at all. This may be an indication of an error or of a lack of fault coverage.

With this kind of monitors, data or instruction profiling can be executed: With the MIPS-tool `pixie` traces can be made, which list the virtual addresses of program data and instructions in the temporal sequence they appear when the program is run. This list can be used as a base for a cache simulator (e. g. `cache2000` for MIPS computers), which computes the hit rates of the caches.

3.2   Hardware Monitors

Hardware monitors measure electrical signals, which come from distinct points of a computer (fig. 2). Such measuring points may be: bus signals, critical signals within a computing system, control signals of peripheral devices, e. g. the positioning arm of harddisks (see [10]), or even more complex signals, like the well-known "wait"-light of IBM /360 computers, (cf. [23], p. 54).

Due to the amount of data becoming huge, if all signals in every bus cycle are measured, after the probes of a hardware monitor a filter is installed, which limits the amount of data. This filter moves a real hardware monitor away from the "ideal monitor" of fig. 1 in at least one axis. The limitation can be performed either by limiting the recorded period of time, or by considering only a subset of the signals to be measured, or by reduction of the recorded number of cycles, or by limitation on some events etc. It must be guaranteed by this filter, that even in the worst case all measured parameters are recorded without loss. The overflow of an intermediate buffer may make a full measurement invalid.

For the *online evaluation* it must be ensured that the measured values can be read continuousely from the intermediate buffer and that they can be computed for the display. After displaying them, the computed values can be stored. The continuous display requires a high data reduction, because human watchers cannot follow fast changes of many signals. The *offline evaluation* uses stored data as a base. These data can be computed and displayed under a broad range of aspects.

The measured signals usually change with a frequency of some megahertz (signals inside a computer or bus signals), sometimes in the range of kilohertz (composed or peripheral signals). At the online evaluation the display typically changes once a second.

With hardware monitors *only low-level signals* can be measured. If statements about high-level processes are to be made, e. g. idle of the operating system, subroutine calls, duration of I/O-operations, task switch etc.), then the measured signals can be postprocessed or concentrated by suitable tools, or they must have been preprocessed before the measured value is

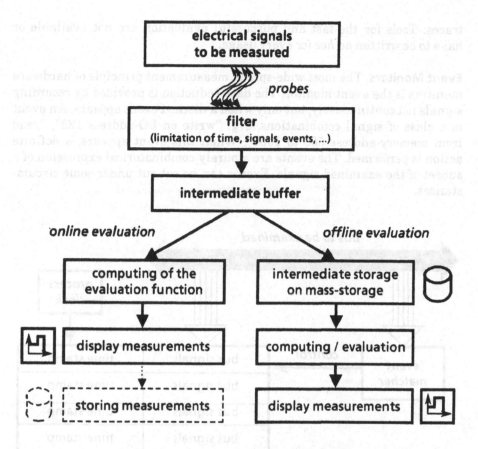

Fig. 2: Principle of a Hardware Monitor

taken, e. g. the wait-signal mentioned above or by the software part of hybrid monitors.

Logic Analyzer. A logic analyzer is the simpliest form of a hardware monitor: It records the signals to be examined with a variable resolution. The data are displayed on a screen, which represents the signals as a sequence of 0s and 1s. There are also triggering conditions available. With logic analyzers, it is possible not only to record the signals *after* the triggering conditions, but even *before* it. Progress in logic analyzers resulted in higher temporal resolution, more signals, longer traces, and the support of more complex triggering conditions.

For the measurement of the system load, these devices are not very suitable: On the one hand, every measurement causes a huge amount of data, on the other hand, the evaluation only consists in looking through the traces. Tools for the fast and purposeful evaluation are not available or have to be written *ad hoc* for every usage.

Event Monitors. The most wide-spread measurement principle of hardware monitors is the event monitor. The data reduction is provided by recording signals not continuousely, but only when a distinct event appears. An event is a class of signal combinations, e. g. "write on I/O-address 123", "read from memory-address 500 to 1000". When this event appears, a definite action is performed. The events are a purely combinatorical expression of a subset of the examined signals. Events can be cut out under some circumstances.

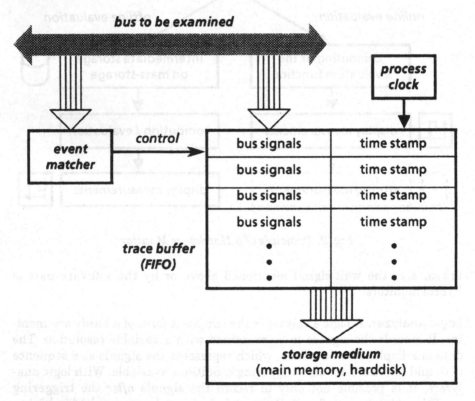

Fig. 3: Principle of an Event Hardware Monitor, Time Mode

If an event happens, then all the signals are stored in a FIFO, which is called *trace-buffer*. To get a temporal relationship, a *time stamp* is stored together with the event data. The events and the actions to be performed must be defined before the measurement takes place. The data reduction of event monitors happens by the fact, that due to their triggering conditions only 1% to 0.1% of the cycles are recorded. The trace-buffer FIFO is necessary to deal with short peak-loads.

The action that is performed mostly at event monitors is to record all the signals or a subset of them when the event occurs (so-called *time mode*). Fig. 3 shows the principle of an event monitor: The event-matcher of the monitor recognizes the signals, adds a time stamp and stores them into the trace-buffer FIFO. The trace-buffer is read out either after the measurement or – for online and long-time measurements – during the measurement. The content of the trace-buffer is stored into a storage medium. The time mode needs about 64 to 128 bits for every line of the trace-buffer, and its length is about 8 K to 64 K entries. Instead of using the time mode it is possible only to count the number of events. This is performed by the *count mode*.

It is also possible to make this monitor programmable. When an event happens, one of a broad range of actions may be started. Anderson et al. [3] introduce a monitor, which performs the following actions:

– Increment or reset external or internal counters.
– Buffering of signals, maybe with a time stamp (similar to time mode).
– Writing data from the buffer to an external storage-medium.
– Set and reset of the event counter.

With these measures, an event monitor can be made very flexible.

Sampling and Cumulation. At the sampling mode of system monitors, significant values of the measured system are recorded in equidistant intervals – e. g. every millisecond, see fig. 4 – or in stochastic intervals.

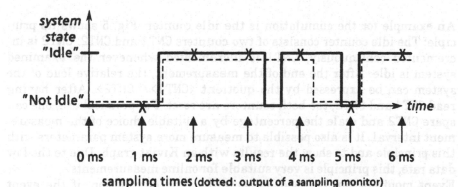

Abb. 4: Principle of a Sampling Monitor

With this kind of measurement, only statistical statements about the system can be made. Furthermore, measurement values are neglected. In fig. 4 the system is not idle between 3 and 4 ms, but this is not noticed by a sampling monitor, on the other hand it records the short not-idle at 5 ms. The measured signals are shown by the thin broken line. With sampling monitors, long measurements and even online-measurement is possible.

A typical sampling monitor is described by Hattenbach [13]: Here every millisecond a measurement takes place. Recorded values are: the current op-code in the instruction register, i. e. which operation is being executed at the time of the recording, and the physical address of the main memory, to get an impression of the usage of the main memory. The measurements lasted over several hours resp. days. Based on this measurement data, claims are made about the floating-point load of the computer and the efficiency of paging. With these measurements some questions were to be made clear, e. g. if an additional CPU is necessary. Furthermore, a software monitor was checked by this sampling monitor.

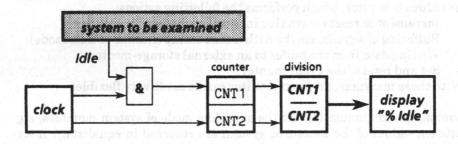

Fig. 5: Principle of an Idle Counter (Cumulation)

An example for the cumulation is the idle counter. Fig. 5 shows its principle: The idle counter consists of two counters CNT1 and CNT2. CNT2 is incremented continuously, CNT1 is incremented whenever the examined system is idle. After the end of the measurement, the relative load of the system can be expressed by the quotient ⟨CNT1⟩/⟨CNT2⟩. After having read CNT1 and CNT2, the both counters are reset. For practical use, one can spare CNT2 and scale the percentage by a suitable choice of the measurement interval. It is also possible to measure more system parameters with this principle and to show the results with an Kiviat graph. Due to the low data rate, this principle is very suitable for online measurements.

Event monitors can be used for sampling and cumulation, if the event matcher is substituted by a timer-clock. The mesurement can be done without the time stamp then.

Classes-of-States Monitor. The principles eventing and sampling are not very suitable to find system bottlenecks and to look for their reasons. With these monitors it may happen, that short state changes of the examined object are averaged or vanish completely (sampling monitor), or state-changes that are important for the performance are not recorded at all (event monitor), or the measurement interval is too short to answer the questions asked by this measurement (logic analyzer). So it is necessary to record every state-change of the system, i. e. to measure with the system clock, and a longer time interval, say one second or more, has to be recorded and analyzed. Therefore a Classes-of-States Monitor is very suitable (see [29]).

Multibus II

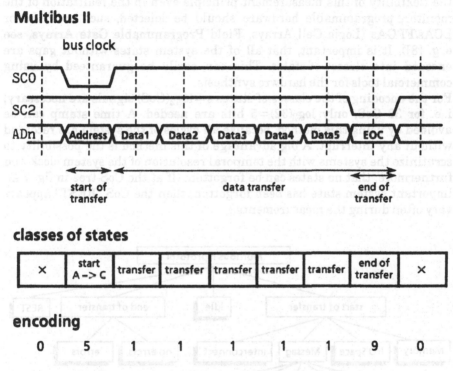

Fig. 6: Message Passing Protocol of the Multibus II

The basic idea of this monitoring principle is to look at the actions, which take place on a processor, on a bus or in a cache system, as a sequence of states. The Multibus II in a message passing operation has the state-sequence "idle, start of transfer A→C, transfer data1, transfer data2, transfer end, idle" (fig. 6, cf. [16]). A selected set of these states can be clustered to a class-of-states (CoS). The states in a class-of-states are different only by their attributes, which are neglected by this method. In the example of fig. 6 "start of transfer A→C" is shown as CoS 5, "transfer" as CoS 1, EOC (End-Of-Cycle, transfer end) as CoS 9, and the classes-of-states out of the transfer as as CoS 0. In the evaluation, the "Transfer A→C" can be searched by searching for the regular expression "5 [1]+ 9". The acquisition of the measurement values at classes-of-states monitor consists of storing the sequence of CoS in a memory; at 32 CoS, 5 bits for the encoding are necessary. The evaluation consists of the search for the patterns. The occurence of these patterns can be shown by histograms and load-diagrams. By this method the whole protocol of a bus – or all the states of a computing system – can be represented as a sequence of CoS. The definition of the CoS – i. e. the clustering of a set of states to one class-of-state – can be done as the user likes. Due to this, it can be adapted to every requirement. To keep the flexibility of this measurement principle even in the realization of the monitor, programmable hardware should be selected, such as PALs or LCAs/FPGAs (Logic Cell Arrays, Field Programmable Gate Arrays, see e. g. [8]). It is important, that all of the system states without gaps are encoded into classes-of-states. This can easily be guaranteed by using commercial tools for the hardwre synthesis.

For the encoding of the classes-of-states $s = \log_2(CoS)$ signals are necessary, i. e. for 32 CoS, only $\log_2(32) = 5$ bits are needed. A time stamp can be avoided by using this method, because all cycles of the system are recorded without any interrupt. A big advantage of this method is the possibility to scrutinize the systems with the temporal resolution of the system clock and furthermore, that no states can be forgotten. (If at the CoS-tree in fig. 7 an important system state has been forgotten, then the CoS "REST" appears very often during the measurements.)

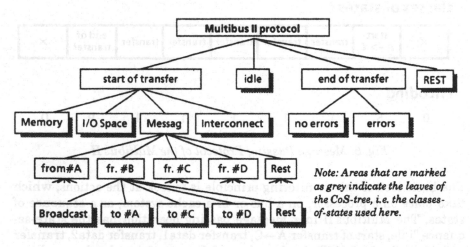

Fig. 7: CoS-tree of the Multibus II Protocol (32 CoS)

Fig. 7 shows as an example, how the protocol of the Multibus II can be divided into classes-of-states: First idle and transfer are distinguished. The transfer is subdivided into three parts (cf. fig. 5): the start of transfer, transfer itself, and the transfer end. At the start of transfer the address space can be distinguished etc. This refinement is performed as long as the protocol is subdivided into all the CoS to be differentiated. Of course, every other CoS-tree than this one may be constructed as well as the one of fig. 7. Using this scheme, the CoS-tree can be constructed for any bus protocol, and even for the states of a computer system or of a processor cache.

Based on this principle, one can go one step ahead and record the *attributes* – i. e. the contents of address – in a special storage, the attribute-storage. By doing this, the amount of data increases, but the advantage of a simple and fast evaluation remains, and the debugging of systems becomes possible.

3.3 Hybrid Monitors

Hybrid monitors are hardware monitors with a software front-end (fig. 8). This software front-end generates some signals – in fig. 8 with the sub-routine monitor() – and the hardware part records these signals. If an event monitor is used as hardware part, then every call of the function monitor() can be considered as an event and can be recorded.

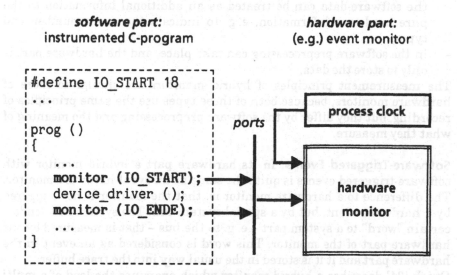

Fig. 8: Principle of a Hybrid Monitor

From the software part, the hardware of a hybrid monitor is a device which can be called by the C-function monitor(). The hardware part, however, only sees a lot of signals, which appear on a bus or on a port of the computer. That is why only the software part of a hybrid monitor – i. e. the procedure-call and the driver-part of the call – interferes with the system. The transfer of the signal, e. g. to a computer port, lasts some microseconds. The system load caused by a hybrid monitor is about 1% to 3%.

The examined software has to be instrumented, before a measurement can take place. Exactly spoken, in front of every interesting system-call, access to variables etc. the call monitor() has to be set. To differentiate the calls, a value is given with them, in fig. 8 the values IO_START and IO_END. If not only the starting time of a call is to be considered, but also the duration of system-calls, then the program has to be instrumented in front of the call and behind it. The instrumentation should be done automatically.

By the interconnection with the software it becomes possible to watch even high-level informations of the program, such as task switches, begin and end of subroutines, duration of I/O-operations (i. e. I/O-drivers), how much time a LAN-software needs in which OSI-levels (i. e. I/O-drivers), idle of the operating system, writing onto (shared memory) variables, etc.

Hybrid monitoring is not limited to the recording of software-triggered events. Virtually every hardware monitor can be used as a hybrid monitor, if a port for the output of the software information is provided. The software part can be used for a broad range of applications:

- as a single signal, e. g. as an event or as a trigger for the start and the end of the data record of a hardware monitor;
- the software-data can be treated as an additional information to the pure hardware information, e. g. to indicate the event number and types;
- in the software preprocessing can take place, and the hardware part is only to store the data.

The measurement principles of hybrid monitors are similar to those of hardware monitors, because both of these types use the same principles of recording, but they differ by the software preprocessing and the meaning of what they measure.

Software-Triggered Events. In its hardware part a hybrid monitor with software-triggered events is quite the same as an event hardware monitor. The difference to a hardware monitor is, that the monitor is not triggered by a hardware event, but by a special system-call. The system-call sends a certain "word" to a system part – e. g. to the bus – that is measured by the hardware part of the monitor. This word is considered as an event in the hardware part and it it is stored in the usual way into the trace buffer.

Quick [24] describes a hybrid monitor which examines the load of a multi processor system by setting software-probes to relevant parts in the operating system. The "relevant parts" are selected on the basis of the UNIX process model. The record (event lane) has 9 bits width and is recorded by a hardware monitor, whose clock has a temporal resolution of one microsecond. The execution of one measurement lasts between 7 µs and 15 µs. The interference with the measured system of course strongly depends on the frequency of the system-calls. Usually it ranges from 0.1% to 10%. The results of the measurement are displayed in several Gantt-diagrams. Hofmann [15] introduces the next version of this monitor: The trace-buffer has been enlarged to 96 Bit (40 Bit time stamp, 8 bit flags, 48 bit data) and has the length of 32 K entries. The trace-buffer can be transfered stage-by-stage, with a maximum of 10,000 events per second. The causal interdependencies between the activities of the processor – such as send and receive mechanisms – were considered as to be important. Due to this, the temporal resolution of the time stamp has been increased to 400 ns, and the clocks of the submonitors in every processor are synchronized via Ethernet by a special synchronization pulse and a pseudo-event.

In [11] the commercial "Software Analysis Workstation" of CADRE/Micro-CASE is used. The port to the monitor is a so-called "monitor-register", which can be accessed by special functions, i. e. software calls write into this register during the measurement, and the hardware parts read the words provided by the calls. One measuring event last "few microseconds". The program to be measured is instrumented by the function "write to monitor-register".

Cumulation. At the cumulation the measuring takes place in equidistant points of time. The difference to the sampling consists in the evaluation by the host before the measurement. Typically the load percentage of the system states "idle", "CPU busy" etc. is measured.

Software-Triggered Classes-of-States. The classes-of-states approach can also be used for hybrid monitoring, after some slight changes. In this case, the software-trigger is used to start and to terminate the measuring at a definite place. Between these points, the usual functions of the classes-of-states monitor are given. As long as no measurement takes place, a "pseudo class-of-states" PAUSE is written into the CoS-memory. This class-of-state PAUSE is used to keep the time correlation.

This measure makes sense if only some parts of a program, e. g. device-drivers, are to be examined. By the pseudo class-of-states PAUSE, combined with an efficient coding of the run length, the duration of the measurement can be enlarged very much.

4. System Monitors and Measuring of Performance

Considered historically, the usage of system monitors has changed its main focus: System monitors used to be used mostly for the accounting and for the debugging. Today, they are mostly used to measure the performance of a system. Even the measuring of performance has changed: Nowadays, performance measuring is not only done in computing centers, who want to have data about the system load of their machines, but more and more by programmers and system designers, who want to find performance bottlenecks in their system or program. A new usage arises to multi processor systems and LAN-coupled computers: To control efficiently the task migration to a processor or computer in idle, a continuous survey about the system load has to be provided.

In parallel to the developments in the field of system monitors, many methods have been developed, which can be used to make statements about systems that not yet exist and to influence the design of this system before its developement. To do this, models of computing systems are built, which can be evaluated with several methods.

● *Simulation:*

Bemmerl et al. [4] use models on which the run of several benchmarks is simulated. By varying some architectural parameters some claims about the effect of these parameters for the performance of the computing system can be made.

● *Analytical Evaluation:*

Besides queuing models (see [12] and [2]), Timed Petri Nets are used to evaluate the performance and the reliability of new system architectures (cf. [2]). The tool which has been introduced by Klas and Lepold in [18] supports the definition and the analytical evaluation of Generalized Stochastic Petri Nets (GSPN). In [19], [20], [21] several examples are described for the usage of GSPNs for the analysis of performance and reliability of computing systems.

A problem that arises both at the simulation and at the analytical evaluation is the validation of the load profiles: How can I know that I really use a model which is near to reality? By the comparison with measured load profiles – measured by system monitors – these methods have been enhanced very much. Finally, the agreement resp. the difference to the assumptions made in the model with the real system has to be shown. Also for this case measurement data are necessary, which can be gained by system monitors.

References

[1]   Adams, M.; Qian, Y.; Tomaszunas, J.; Burtscheid, J.; Kaiser, E.; Juhász, C.: Conformance Testing of VMEbus and Multibus II Products. IEEE Micro, February 1992, pp. 57-64

[2]   Ajmone Marsan, M.; Balbo, G.; Conte, G.: Performance Models of Multiprocessor Systems. The MIT Press: Cambridge (Mass.), 1986

[3]   Anderson, C. S.; Armstrong, K. J.; Borriello, G.: Proceedings of CS 586. PHM – A Programmable Hardware-Monitor. Technical Report # 89-09-11, University of Washington, Seattle (WA). August 1989

[4]   Bemmerl, Th.; Karl, W.; Luksch, P.: Evaluierung von Architekturparametern verschiedener Rechnerstrukturen mit Hilfe von CAE-Workstations. In: Müller-Stoy, P. (Hrsg.): Architektur von Rechen-

558

systemen. 11. GI/ITG-Fachtagung. VDE-Verlag: Berlin 1990, S. 255-273

[5]   Brinksma, E.: A Tutorial on LOTOS. Protocol Specification, Testing, and Verification, V, 1986, pp. 171-194

[6]   Civera, P.; Conte, G.; del Corso, D.; Maddaleno, F.: Petri Net Models for the Description and Verification of Parallel Protocols. In: Barbacci, M. R.; Koomen, C. J. (Eds.): Computer Hardware Description Languages and their Applications. North-Holland 1987, pp. 309-325

[7]   Dembinski, P.; Budkowski, S.: Specification Language Estelle. In: Diaz, M.; Ansart, J.-P.; Courtiat, J.-P.; Azema, P.; Chari, V.: The Formal Description Technique Estelle. Results of the ESPRIT/ SEDOS Project. North-Holland 1989, pp.35-76

[8]   Conner, D.: High-Density PLDs. EDN, January 2, 1992, pp. 76-88

[9]   Fehlau, F.; Simon, Th; Spaniol, O.; Suppan-Borowka, J.: Messungen des Leistungsverhaltens Lokaler Netze mit einem Software-Monitor. Informatik Forsch. Entwick. (1987) 2: 55-64

[10]   Ferrari, D.; Serazzi, G.; Zeigner, A.: Measurement and Tuning of Computer Systems. Prentice-Hall: Englewood Cliffs 1983

[11]   Föckeler, W.; Rüsing, N.: Aktuelle Probleme und Lösungen zur Leistungsanalyse von modernen Rechensystemen mit Hardware-Werkzeugen. In: Informatik-Fachberichte 218, 1989, S. 39-50

[12]   Gross, D.; Harris, C. M.: Fundamentals of Queuing Theory. Wiley and Sons: New York 1985

[13]   Hattenbach, J.: Hardware-Monitor-Messungen an einer SPERRY 1100/83. GWDG-Bericht Nr. 26, 1983, S. 1-21

[14]   Hennessy, J. L.; Patterson, D. A.: Computer-Architecture: A Quantitative Approach. San Mateo (CA) 1990

[15]   Hofmann, R.: Gesicherte Zeitbezüge beim Monitoring von Multiprozessorsystemen. In: Müller-Stoy, P. (Hrsg.): Architektur von Rechensystemen. 11. GI/ITG-Fachtagung. VDE-Verlag: Berlin 1990, S. 389-401

[16]   Intel: Multibus II Bus Architecture Specification Handbook. Santa Clara (CA), 1984

[17]   Keefe, D. D.: Hierarchical Control Programs for System Evaluation. IBM Systems Journal, Vol. 7, No. 2, 1968, pp. 123-133

[18]   Klas, G.; Lepold, R.: TOMSPIN, a Tool for Modeling with Stochastic Petri Nets. Proc. CompEuro 92, The Hague (The Netherlands), May 1992

[19]   Klas, G.; Wincheringer, Ch.: A Generalized Stochastic Petri net Model of Multibus II. Proc. CompEuro 92, The Hague (The Netherlands), May 1992

[20]   Lepold, R.: Performability Evaluation of a Fault-Tolerant Multiprocessor Architecture Using Stochastic Petri Nets. Proc. 5th Int. Conf. on Fault-Tolerant Computing Systems. Nürnberg, September 1991

[21]   Lepold, R.; Klas, G.: Generierung und analytische Auswertung stochastischer Petri-Netz-Modelle zur Bewertung komplexer Rechensysteme. In: Müller-Stoy, P.: Architektur von Rechensystemen. Tagungsband 11. GI/ITG-Fachtagung. vde-Verlag: Berlin 1990

[22]   MIPS Computer Systems Inc.: RISC/os User's Reference manual, Vol. I (System V). Sunnyvale (CA), June 1990

[23]   Nutt, G.: Tutorial: Computer System Monitors. IEEE Computer, November 1975, pp. 51-61

[24]   Quick, A.: Synchronisierte Software-Messung zur Bewertung des dynamischen Verhaltens eines UNIX-Multiprozessor-Betriebssystems. In: Informatik-Fachberichte 218, 1989, S. 142-158

[25]   Richter, E.: LS2 – Software-Monitor und Steuersystem für SVM. rechentechnik / datenverarbeitung 26 (1989) 3, S. 19-22

[26]   Rosenbohm, W.: Messung von SVC-Ausführungszeiten mit Hilfe eines Software-Monitors. In: Mertens, B. (Hrsg.): Messung, Modellierung und Bewertung von Rechensystemen. Springer: Berlin, Heidelberg 1981, S. 58-72

[27]   SCO (The Santa Cruz Operation): SCO Open Desktop Development System, Programmer's Guide, ch. 9: C Programmer's Productivity Tools. Santa Cruz (CA) 1989

[28]   Svoboda, L.: Software Performance Monitors: Desing Trade-Offs. In: CMG VII Conference Proceedings, 1976, pp. 211-220

[29]   Thurner, E. M.: Hardware-Monitor Using Classes of States to Detect Performance-Bottlenecks in Computer Systems. In: Krupat, C.: Proc. Supercomputing Symposium '92, Montreal 1992, pp. 328-339

[30]   Thurner, E. M.: Formal Specification of Bus-Protocols and a Way to their Automatic Implementation. In: Eck, Ch. et al. (Eds.): Proc. Open Bus Systems '92. Zürich (Schweiz), 1992, pp. 123-128

Providing Quality of Service in Packet Switched Networks[1]

Don TOWSLEY

Dept. of Computer Science
University of Massachusetts
Amherst, MA 01003
U.S.A.

Abstract

Increases in bandwidths and processing capabilities of future packet switched networks will give rise to a dramatic increase in the types of applications using them. Many of these applications will require guaranteed quality of service (QOS) such as a bound on the maximum end-to-end packet delay and/or on the probability of packet loss. This poses exciting challenges to network designers. In this paper we discuss the QOS requirements of different applications and survey recent developments in the areas of call admission, link scheduling, and the interaction between the provision of QOS and call routing and traffic monitoring and policing. We identify what some of the important issues are in these areas and point out important directions for future research efforts.

Keywords : quality of service, call admission, real-time services, link scheduling.

1 Introduction

Networking is evolving at a rapid pace these days. Only ten years ago, wide area network bandwidths were in the range of 56Kbs and less. Typical applications were electronic mail, file transfers and remote login. Present day wide area networks have bandwidths in the order of 45Mbs (NSFnet backbone) and applications include, in addition to those listed above, digitized voice and low rate video. In addition, there exist several experimental networks that are operating in the gigabit range. Work is underway on a wide variety of high bandwidth applications such as HDTV, medical diagnosis, multimedia conferencing, etc..

One of the burning issues in this evolution deals with the provision of adequate service for these new applications. Recent experience on the internet indicates that it is ill suited to handle time and loss sensitive applications such as voice and video. This is due not only to the inadequate bandwidth provided by the internet but, more importantly, because the internet does not provide the

---

[1] This work was supported in part by the National Science Foundation under grant NCR-9116183.

right support in the form of end-to-end protocols and switch scheduling policies. It is the aim of this paper to describe issues and problems that arise in providing quality of service (QOS) to applications along with several approaches that have been proposed and studied in the literature.

We will discover that the problem of providing quality of service to B-ISDN applications is complex and that it cannot be solved satisfactorily without also dealing with numerous other problems such as routing, congestion control, link scheduling, traffic shaping and monitoring, etc... We will briefly discuss the realtionship between these problems and that of providing quality of service. We will observe that the solutions to some of these problems such as traffic shaping and link scheduling are intricately related to the design of algorithms for providing QOS. Other problems, such as routing can be treated in a more detached manner.

The remainder of this paper is structured in the following way. Section 2 introduces a sample of B-ISDN applications focussing primarily on their QOS requirements. A discussion of how they are typically modelled and their salient workload parameters is also included in section 2. Section 3 describes the problem of providing QOS in greater detail including a discussion of a number of issues that must addressed by any network architecture supporting QOS guarantees. Section 4 will discuss the problems of traffic shaping and monitoring and will describe the rate control paradigm commonly included as a component of a network architecture that provides for QOS. A description and discussion of several link scheduling algorithms, which can be used to support applications having diffeent QOS requirements is found in section 5. The primary focus of the paper is on call admission which is the subject of section 6. Section 7 summarizes the main ideas and lists a number of directions for further research.

2 Applications and their QOS Requirements

Applications can be divided broadly into two classes, those without real-time constraints and those with. Traditional networking applications such as file transfer, electronic mail, and remote login do not have real-time constraints. The performance metrics of interest for these applications are typically average packet delay and throughput. They also require full reliability which is provided by high level end-to-end protocols.

Of more interest to us are those applications having real-time constraints. These include voice and video. Such applications are characterized by a bound, D, on the time, T, allowed to transmit a packet across the network. Thus, a deadline is associated with each packet and, if the packet reaches its destination after its deadline, it may be considered useless and discarded.

The following two QOS requirements have been proposed for real-time applications in the literature,

$$(Q1) \qquad T \leq D,$$
$$(Q2) \qquad \Pr[T > D] < \epsilon.$$

The first of these metrics requires that the application suffer no packet loss. Clearly this is impossible to achieve given that network components can fail and communication links can corrupt packets. Hence, it is normally interpreted to mean that the application requires no losses beyond what may be introduced by component failures and link noise. Henceforth, we ignore link noise and component failures and assume a fully reliable network. Fortunately, the most common real-time applications, voice and video can tolerate some fraction of either lost or delayed packets, (approximately $10^{-6} - 10^{-2}$). Here losses occur as a result of buffer overflow.

For some applications, such as voice and video, there is no benefit to having packets arrive far ahead of their deadlines. This is because the receiver is required to store these packets until the deadline at which point the data can be played out. Thus the following QOS requirement has also been considered

$$(Q3) \qquad T_{max} - T_{min} \leq J.$$

Figure 1 illustrates the first and third criteria (Q1 and Q3).

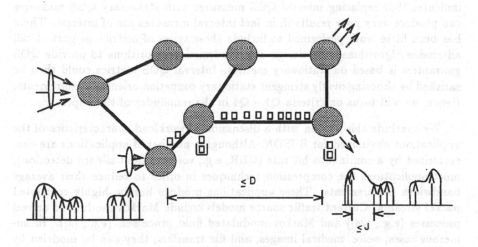

Figure 1: End-to-end delay and jitter bounds.

The fourth QOS requirement commonly treated in the literature is

$$(Q4) \qquad \Pr[\text{end-to-end packet loss}] < \epsilon$$

This may be appropriate for real-time applications such as voice operating on networks where packets that, because of their architecture, guarantee that any packet reaching its destinationhas an end-to-end delay less than D. It may also be appropriate for non-real-time applications as it bounds the number of retransmissions that are required to ensure lossless data transfer.

Based on these QOS requirements, we divide applications into three classes,

- deterministic (Q1, Q3),

- statistical (Q2, Q4), and

- best effort (no requirement).

Although, these are the QOS metrics typically considered in the literature on provision of QOS, they may not be the most appropriate metrics, [39, 40, 6, 43, 30, 5, 37]. For example, consider the requirement that packet loss not exceed 1% for a voice application. If the application ultimately transmits 100,000 packets, then there is a considerable difference in the user's perception of the quality of the voice if the first packet out of each group of 100 are lost rather than the first 100 packets out of each group of 10,000. Thus a number of papers propose QOS requirements based on intervals of time, e.g., 1% loss over a talkspurt in audio applications [40, 6], over a frame in video [43, 30, 5, 37]. Recent work [36] indicates that replacing interval QOS measures with stationary QOS measures can produce very poor results if, in fact interval measures are of interest. There has been little work performed to include these types of metrics as part of call admission algorithms. The design of call admission algorithms to provide QOS guarantees is based on stationary metrics. Interval QOS metrics could then be satisfied by choosing overly stringent stationary connetion oriented requirements. Hence, we will focus on criteria Q1 – Q4 in the remainder of the paper.

We conclude this section with a discussion of workload characteristics of the applications envisioned for B-ISDN. Although a number of applications are characterized by a continuous bit rate (CBR, e.g., voice without silence detection), most applications use compression techniques in order to reduce their average bandwidth requirements. These applications produce bursty, highly correlated packet streams. Current traffic source models include Markov modulated arrival processes (e.g., [24]) and Markov modulated fluid processes, (e.g., [3]). In numerous cases, voice, medical images, and file transfers, they can be modeled by two state on-off models. If the process is in an off state, no packet is generated and if it is in an on state, packets are generated with at constant intervals of time. We will not discuss these models farther except to state that the typical statistics associated with these processes that are used in provision of QOS include x_{min}, the minimum interarrival time between packets, L_{max}, the maximum packet size, R_{peak}, the peak rate, b, the expected burst length, and u, the fraction of time the source is on. The problem of modeling packet streams for different applications is far from having been solved. Future work in this area will undoubtedly impact ways for providing QOS.

3   Overview of Providing QOS

QOS requirements are typically specified on an *end-to-end* basis. This imposes requirements on the hosts at each end as well as the network connecting them. We will only focus on the network QOS requirements in this paper (although many of the ideas could be applied to the hosts). QOS requirements are best satsisfied through connection oriented services. A connection consists of three phases, call setup, data transport, and call breakdown. In the preceding section, we discussed different potential data transport QOS requirements. However, the setup and breakdown phases can have their own requirements. For example, setup requirements typically include constraints on connection blocking probability and connection setup delay and breakdown requirements typically include constraints on breakdon delay. We will focus on the provision of QOS during the transport phase.

Call set up is concerned with answering the following question,

The question: Can the call be admitted so that its QOS requirements are met without violating the QOS requirements of any existing call in the network?

This involves choosing a physical path between the two end nodes. Next a call setup control packet is sent along this path to determine whether it can meet the QOS requirements without violating those of any existing call in the network. This involves checking at each node whether sufficient resources exist to do so. If the determination is made that each node can do so, then the resources are reserved and the call accepted.

We are concerned with answering "the question" with repect to a single physical path. Although path selection (routing) is extremely important in obtaining good performance, its solution is, to some extent, orthogonal to the design of good algorithms for provision of QOS on a single path. Various aspects of the routing problem and its relationship to the provision of QOS can be found in [26]. Solutions to the routing problem will undoubtedly borrow from routing in circuit-switched networks, [18].

Consider the problem of answering the question whether or not the QOS requirements of a new call can be satisfied while continuing to provide the QOS of other calls. In its general form, this is an extremely difficult question to answer as the admission of a call has the potential of affecting every session currently using the network. In order to mitigate this problem most approaches follow the *principle of nodal isolation*; namely that the behavior of the nodes on the path should be isolated from each other and from that of the remaining nodes in the network. This can be accomplished in one of two ways, 1) statically partitioning resources among connections, or 2) imposing local QOS requirements on each node so that each node on the path determines independently whether it can satisfy these local QOS requirements. We shall refer to the former as the *principle of connection isolation*and will examine approaches based on both as well as a hybrid. The reader is referred to [49] for further design principles for call admission algorithms.

In order to answer "the question", a connection must provide workload descriptors along with its QOS requirements. The previous section described some proposed descriptors and requirements. A successful call setup corresponds to a contract between the application and network. In order to prevent an application from breaking its part of the contract, i.e., that it will behave according to the description that it provided the network, the network should provide a traffic monitoring and policing mechanism at the edge of the network. An example of such a mechanism is the leaky bucket [46]. Further details are found in section 4. A second reason for monitoring the traffic of a connection would be to provide adaptivity. If the traffic characteristics of a connection change, then the network could note these changes and make use of them when setting up additional calls. This approach is taken in [22, 11].

Most of the work in this area is based on the underlying assumption that bursts generated by sources are typically small compared to the buffer capacity of each node in the network. Most of the approaches that we will focus on in this paper will not work well if bursts are comparable in size or larger than buffer sizes. If the buffer size is much smaller than the burst size, then the only solution may be to perform fast circuit switching at a burst level. An example of this approach is found in [47].

4 Traffic Shaping and Monitoring

As we have observed in section 3, a traffic shaping mechanism may be necessary to ensure that a source behaves according to the characterization that it provides the network at the time that it establishes its session. Traffic shaping mechanisms come in many different flavors. However, they are mostly variations of the *leaky bucket* rate control mechanism originally proposed by Turner, [46]. We briefly describe one variation which is used by a number of different proposed bandwidth allocation policies.

Briefly, a leaky bucket consists of a data buffer and a finite capacity token buffer. Packets enter the data buffer from the source. Tokens are generated deterministically at rate rho and immediately enter the token buffer. Whenever a packet containing p bits enters the data buffer and finds at least p tokens in the token buffer, the packet immediately is released to the network. Otherwise it queues up in the data buffer and waits until it is the oldest packet and p tokens have accumulated. At that time, the packet is allowed to enter the network. The capacity of the token buffer is σ and is used to control the burst length of the source. Last, a peak bandwidth enforcer is used to ensure that the peak bandwidth never exceeds C. The leaky bucket is illustrated in Figure 2.

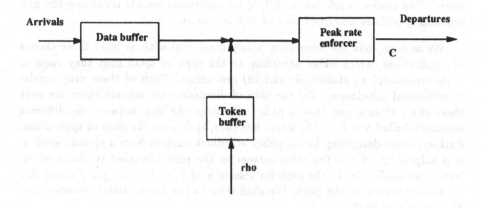

Figure 2: Leaky Bucket Functional Diagram.

As mentioned before, many variations of this mechanism exist. One variation, suited to ATM, allows packets to always enter the network without delay. However, if the packet arrives to find an insufficient number of tokens, it is marked before being released. Coupling this with a link scheduling policy that is allowed to drop marked packets in the case of congestion, can yield performance improvements over the standard leaky bucket, [16]

A source is said to be a (σ, ρ, C) *linearly bounded arrival process (LBAP)* if, when fed through a leaky bucket with parameters σ, ρ, and C, none of the packets ever incur a delay. The leaky bucket always guarantees that the network will see a (σ, ρ, C) LBAP. Often times C is taken to be ∞. In that case the peak rate parameter will be omitted, e.g., (σ, ρ) LBAP instead of (σ, ρ, ∞) LBAP.

Before ending this section, we mention that the leaky bucket has been the subject of many studies. Most have focussed on evaluating its performance, either in isolation, e.g., [44], or feeding one or more downstream queues, e.g., [41]. More recent work has focussed on formally stating and proving a number of burst reduction properties exhibited by this mechanism. These include burstiness exhibited by the departure process, or by its effects on delays and/or losses at downstream queues [35, 34].

5 Link Scheduling Policies

In a high speed network setting, link scheduling policies must allow different classes of applications having different quality of service requirements to share a link. In this section, we describe some of the issues that arise in designing multiclass scheduling policies and how they have been treated by network designers. The reader is referred to [23, 4] for additional details regarding the link scheduling policies described here as well as others.

We assume that the scheduling policy must deal with at least three classes of applications which differ according to the type of QOS that they require, *i*) deterministic, *ii*) statistical, and *iii*) best effort. Each of these may consist of additional subclasses. For the sake of discussion we assume there are only these three classes and that a policy schedules the link between S_k different sessions labelled $s = 1, \ldots, S_k$ where $k \in \{d, s, b\}$ denotes the class of application. Further, when describing how a policy schedules packets from a specific session, it is helpful to refer to the other servers on the path allocated to that session. Hence, we shall refer to the path for session s as $\Gamma_s = (j_{i,1}, \ldots, j_{i,n_s})$ where $J_{i,k}$ is the k-th server on the path. We shall refer to the server under consideration as l_s in this context.

A scheduling policy has to deal with several issues. First, to what extent will it isolate the effects of different classes of applications from each other? Second, to what extent will it isolate the effects of different sessions within the same class from each other? This suggests that a policy has a hierarchic structure. At the top level of the hierarchy is a mechanism for scheduling between different classes of sessions. At the second level will be a mechanism for scheduling sessions from the same class. This, of course may differ from class to class. If one of the classes is further subdivided into additional subclasses, then the policy may contain three or more levels.

The issue of whether or not to isolate sessions/classes from each other is an extremely important one. Traditional circuit switching is characterized by absolute session isolation; each session is given a fixed fraction of the bandwidth and is never aware of other sessions. Such isolation can be emulated in B-ISDN by a careful implementation of space division/ time division multiplexing where each session obtains a fraction of the bandwidth corresponding to its *peak rate*. This policy has the advantage that it simplifies the problem of making deterministic guarantees. However, it may provide very inefficient use of the bandwidth if the applications are bursty. Such a philosophy, with some modifications to provide flexibility lies behind three recently proposed policies, Hierarchical round robin (HRR) ([29]), Stop-and-Go (SG) ([20], and Weighted fair queueing (WFQ) ([13, 32]). We will describe these later in this section.

It is worth pointing out that the ATM standard provides for virtual paths [7, 8] between source-destination pairs. Briefly, a virtual path can be viewed as a dedicated bandwidth channel between a pair of nodes. Hence, it is a mechanism that can be used to isolate different classes of service from each other.

A second approach to session/class isolation is to assign static priorities to different sessions. Thus, for example priority could be given in decreasing order to deterministic, statistical, and best effort service. This appears at first sight to be a good solution as it appeals to our intuition regarding the relative importance and urgency of the three classes of services. However, as a general multiclass scheduling policy it has been found wanting in several respects. First, it is very inflexible. It has been observed in that policies that attempt to cooperatively share the bandwidth between statistical and best effort classes of service can provide better performance for the latter class of service with either no or marginal degradation in the QOS of the former class. Second, it may provide overkill to the class of service receiving the highest priority of service. For example, there is no benefit in transmitting a packet far ahead of its deadline. Instead, it may be possible to provide better performance to the other classes of service packets by delaying the packet's transmission for awhile and allocating the link instead to these other classes of service. These have been illustrated in [10].

It is important to point out that most proposed algorithms provide higher priority to packets generated by deterministic and statistical applications than to best effort packets.

There have been some attempts to develop high level scheduling policies that attempt to share the link cooperatively between different classes of service rather than to isolate them, [27]. We will survey these policies later in this section.

Last, a scheduler has to be chosen to schedule packets belonging to the same class of service on the link. Clearly, any policy that provides class isolation can be used to provide session isolation. If this is the choice, then FIFO is often used to schedule packets belonging to a single session. Such an approach suffers because no benefit is obtained (statistical multiplexing gain) from sharing the link between a group of sessions. To ameliorate this problem, several policies have been proposed for scheduling sessions belonging to the same class of service. These include FIFO, Earliest-due-date (EDD), FIFO+, and Jitter earliest due date (J-EDD). We will discuss each of these in turn later in this section.

Before beginning our description and discussion of class isolating policies and intra class scheduling policies, we briefly mention that policies can be further characterized as either idling or non-idling policies. Here a policy is said to be non-idling if it never allows the server to idle when there are packets queued at that server. A policy is said to be an idling policy if it is allowed to idle the server while there are packets queued for it. Although idling appears to be wasteful, it provides *predictability* which simplifies the problem of providing deterministic delay bounds as we will see shortly. Figure 3 provides a high level functional diagram of a link scheduler.

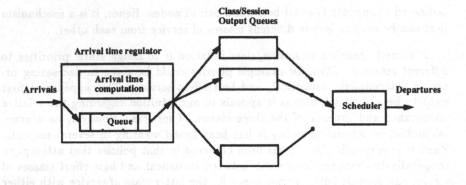

Figure 3: Link scheduler.

5.1 Class isolating scheduling policies

Hierarchical round robin (HRR): In its simplest form HRR is time division multiplexing. Time is divided into periods of constant length F and each session is given a fixed number of slots within that frame. Consequently, HRR is an idling policy. The maximum packet delay for a session can be bounded by $2F$ by choosing the fraction appropriately, provided that the source is described as a LBAP.

Sessions can be placed into groups with each group being assigneda fraction of the frame. The groups can then handled using round robin and each group can have its own scheduler for scheduling packets belonging to that group. One choice fo a group scheduler is the round robin policy. This provides the basis for HRR in its most general form.

In its most general form, HRR consists of $N > 1$ levels. Associated with level i , $1 \leq i \leq N$, is a set of sessions, a frame size F_i, and parameter b_i. Consider the operation of level i. During the first b_i slots of that frame, the server is dedicated to the sessions associated with levels $i + 1$ and above. During the remaining $F_i - b_i$ slots of the frame, the server is assigned to sessions belonging to level i. The packets belonging to levels $i + 1$ and above are scheduled using HRR having levels $i + 1, \ldots, N$. Thus multilevel HRR can be recursively defined in this way. Note that HRR operating at level N can provide all of the slots within its frame to the sessions assigned to that level.

Multilevel HRR provides suficient flexibility to provide different determinstic guarantees to different applications. Furthermore, due to the fact that a session may not use more than its share of slots within a frame, determinstic jitter guarantees can be made as well.

Although, as defined, HRR seems to be geared to applications with determinstic QOS requirements, in fact, best effort applications can be easily introduced by assigning it a priority lower than the determinstic class. In particular, best effort packets can use slots that would normally go idle.

Last, This policy is easy to implement. See [29] for further details on its implementation and performance.

Stop and Go Queueing (SG): This policy is similar to HRR with one important distinction. In addition to associating a frame to the outgoing link, a frame of the same length is also associated with each incoming link. These frames are then mapped to frames on the outgoing link by introducing a constant delay θ, where $0 \leq \theta < F$. This has the advantage that the end-to-end jitter can never exceed $2F$, no matter how long the path traversed by a session. The maximum delay on a link is $2F$ as under HRR.

As with HRR, it is possible to define a multiple level Stop-and-Go policy. Here F_i is assumed to be a multiple of F_{i+1}. Thus, an application having a delay bound of D at the node would be assigned to level $J = \arg\min\{i : 2F_{i-1} < D \leq 2F_i\}$. See [20] for further details and [19] for a description of how it can be integrated with other traffic classes

Weighted Fair Queuing: This policy was first introduced as a mechanism to ensure fairness between different sessions in traditional data networks[13]. It is most easily described under the assumption that workloads generated by sessions can be treated as infinitely divisible fluids. Let S sessions labelled $i = 1, \ldots, S$ share a link with capacity r. Associated with the sessions are parameters $\{\phi_i\}_{i=1}^{S}$ which determine the rates at which they receive service. Each session sees a link with capacity at least as large as $\phi_i / \sum_{j=1}^{S} \phi_j$. More precisely, if the set of sources with queued packets at time t is $\mathcal{S}(t) \subseteq \{1, \ldots, S\}$, then source $i \in \mathcal{S}(t)$ receives service at rate $\phi_i / \sum_{j \in \mathcal{S}(t)} \phi_j$. This policy ensures that, if a source has data to send during the period $[s, t]$, then the amount of its data transmitted is at least as large as $(t - s)\phi_i / \sum_{j=1}^{S} \phi_j$.

As described above, this policy is not implementable since the smallest unit of data transfer is a packet. However, it is not too difficult a task to accurately approximate the above policy by a dynamic priority policy. In particular, a packet is assigned a priority equal to the time that it would complete under WFQ. Let $\hat{T}_i$ an T_i denote the response times of the i-th packet under the preemptive WFQ and the non-preemptive version of WFQ respectively. If r denotes the rate of the server and L_{max} the maximum packet length, then it has been shown ([38]) that $|T_i - \hat{T}_i| \leq L_{max}/r$.

This policy was originally proposed and studied in [13] with $\phi_i = 1/S$ for the purposes of providing fair service to traditional data traffic in the internet. However, it has recently been shown that, if a source is a (σ, ρ) LBAP, it is possible to choose values for ϕ so that the maximum delay at the server is bounded [38]. In particular, if $\phi_i = \rho_i$, then

$$T_i \leq \frac{\sigma_i}{\rho_i} + L_{max}/r \tag{1}$$

It is unnecessary for other sessions to behave as LBAP's. Thus this policy can be used to share the server among applications requiring hard real time guarantees, statistical guarantees, and no guarantees. We will observe in the next section that this policy is the cornerstone of an approach proposed by Clark, et al. for providing QOS in an integrated digital services network.

5.2 Intra-class scheduling policies

The most commonly used policy in this group is FIFO. This is due to several reasons. First, it is extremely easy to implement. Second, it exhibits a number of important properties. For example, it is known to minimize the variance in the delay through a node and, in certain cases, the end-to-end delays through a tandem network [45]. It is also known to stochastically minimize the maximum end-to-end delay. These two features make it the policy of choice within a session and an option to consider for scheduling packets from different sessions belonging to the same class of service.

It is not clear that FIFO is an appropriate policy for scheduling packets belonging to either the deterministic or statistical service classes. Recently, a number of deadline based policies have been proposed. All of these are based on classical real-time scheduling policies such as rate monotonic (RM) and earliest due date (EDD).

Under EDD, each packet has associated with it a *due date*, typically interpreted as the time by which to complete transmission of the packet. At the time that the server becomes available, it is assigned the packet with the smallest (earliest) due date to transmit. Ferrari and Verma [15] propose this policy as part of a QOS provision mechanism where the due-date associated with a session is negotiated at the time that a call is admitted. It is also a component of the MARS approach [27].

A problem inherent in FIFO and EDD is that end-to-end jitter tends to grow as a function of the path length in networks. As a consequence, Verma and Ferrari [48] proposed an idling version of EDD, Jitter-EDD (J-EDD) which has the provable property that end to end jitter never exceeds that for a single node, regardless of path length. This property results from the addition of an input regulator (see Figure 3) which holds a packet until the time it is expected to arrive at the node. At that time it is released into the node to be scheduled.

More recently, Clarke, Shenker, and Zhang proposed a non-idling policy for controlling end-to-end jitter over long paths ([11]). Unlike J-EDD which holds a packet at a server until its expected arrival time, FIFO+ attempts to reduce jitter by giving higher priority to packets that have taken an inordinately long time in reaching the server and low priority to those that have arrived more quickly. Consider session s. Associated with server j_k on its path is a target delay $t_{s,k}$. Let $T_{s,k,j}$ be the actual delay incurred by the j-th packet from session s at server j_k. Then packet j is given a due-date of $\sum_{u=1}^{k-1} T_{s,u,j} - \sum_{u=1}^{k} t_{s,u}$ at server j_k. It is suggested that $t_{s,k}$ be set to the expected packet delay for session s and that it be updated as it changes. Very preliminary results indicate that it appreciably reduces the variance in the end-to-end response time over a policy such as FIFO. Last, it can be used in combination with other policies such as WFQ.

5.3 Inter class sharing policies

Minimum laxity threshold (MLT): The policies so far either partition the bandwidth between different classes of applications or even sessions (WFQ) or apply to a single application class. Recently, several policies have been proposed that attempt to deal with the QOS requirements of two or more distinct classes of applications in a complementary manner. One of the earliest such policies, Minimum Laxity with Threshold (MLT), introduced by Chipalkatti, et al. [10] deals with an application in which the QOS metric is the fraction of packets whose delay exceeds a deadline D and another application whose QOS metric is expected delay. They propose a policy that schedules the first class of packets whenever one or more of them are within d units of time from their deadline and serves the second class of packets otherwise. Their preliminary results show that a threshold can be chosen that tradeoffs the QOS of both classes thus yielding better performance than what mght be achieved by either a static priority scheme or FIFO.

More recently, Lazar, et al. [27], have proposed a more sophisticated variation of MLT that interleaves the transmission of deterministic and statistical packets in such a way that statistical packets are given priority so long as no deterministic packet is allowed to miss its deadline [27].

5.4 Buffer management policies

So far no mention has been made of the fact that buffer capacity at the link is finite in capacity, much less the impact that this has on link scheduling (if any). For the most part, the problem of buffer management is orthogonal to the subject of this paper. We assume that there are sufficient buffers for applications requiring deterministic QOS provided that other resources are available. In the case of applications requiring statistical guarantees, overflow is possible. The problem of choosing a packet discard policy has received less attention than it deserves. However, the proper choice must address two questions. Which session to choose from and, within a session, which packet to choose. The first question has not been satisfactorily answered. If there are best effort packets available, then discards should be made from them. If not, then there is the question of whether to spread discards over many statistical sessions or over a few.

6 Call Admission

The problem of how to do call admission is very complex and has generated a number of potential solutions. As described in section 3, a complete solution may require rate control/traffic shaping mechanisms, new link scheduling policies, routing policies and traffic monitoring mechanisms. Furthermore, call admission must also account for the different classes of traffic that are envisioned. These include minimally

1. deterministic,

2. statistical, and

3. best effort

as described in section 2. These may further subdivide into subclasses that differ from each other according to their associated QOS metrics.

Rather than attempt to provide complete solutions from the outset, we will focus on the problem of call admission for each class separately.

6.1 Deterministic guarantees

We begin with a discussion of how deterministic guarantees can be made for networks using session isolating schedulers such as HRR and SG. Consider the case where a deterministic session traverses a path Γ, consisting of h hops. If the frame size at each link is F, then the end-to-end delay is bounded by $2hF$ under both HRR and SG. Multilevel versions of these policies can provide different delay bounds, one for each level. Thus deterministic applications can be divided into subclasses associated with the level that provides the appropriate delay bound. One problem with call admission based on HRR and SG is that it is not possible to decouple the delay bounds from bandwidth allocations. Applications requiring tight delay bounds will tend tobe allocated high bandwidths and vice versa. aathis is less true for HRR than for SG but is present nevertheless. Table 1 compares these two policies.

	Delay Bound	Jitter Bound
HRR	2hF	-
SG	2hF	2F

Table 1: Comparison between SG and HRR.

We turn our attention to call admission in the case that local schedulers use deadline based policies (EDD, J-EDD). Recall that these policies require that each session have a local deadline associated with it. Hence a responsibility of the connection set up phase is the choice of these local deadlines. The use of local deadlines also provides nodal isolation. Hence, checking on whether or not the establishment of a connection will affect other sessions need not proceed outside of the path in question.

Consider a new session, s, desiring to establish a connection on path Γ_s. During the first phase of call admission, each node determines whether or not there exists a local deadline which it can guarantee the delays of session s to fall below while maintaining the local guarantees for all other sessions. Examples of such calculations along with their computaional costs can be found in [15, 48]. Let d_k denote this minimum local deadline at node j_k. If all nodes on the path are able to calculate such deadlines, then the destination checks whether or not the end-to-end deadline can be met, i.e., is $\sum_{k=1}^{n_s} d_k \leq D_s$? If so, then the destination allocates local deadlines, D_k to the nodes on Γ_s sothat $d_k \leq D_k$ and $\sum_{k=1}^{n_s} D_k = D_s$. Several ways of allocating end-to-end deadline to local deadlines are described in [15]. This approach can produce provable guarantees using EDD and J-EDD as the local schedulers. The latter provides lower jitter guarantees than the former.

The following question arises: is it possible to provide guarantees under non-idling policies other than EDD? The answer is yes. In a very interesting series of papers, Cruz [12] shows that delays are bounded for a set of (possibly non-identical) sessions under *any set of non-idling policies* traversing a feed forward network provided that 1) each session (i) is described by a LBAP with parameters (σ_i, ρ_i) and for each link k, $r_k > \sum_{m \in S_k} \rho_m$ where S_k is the set of sessions traversing link k. These results also apply to some non-feed-forward networks.

Unfortunately, the bounds are not useful for call admission. The bounds can be very very loose. For example, consider an h hop path consisting of T1 links shared by 48 32Kbs voice calls (see Table 2. The bounds appear to grow exponentially as a function of the path length. In addition, the bounds are not easy to compute and the results for non-feed-forward networks incomplete.

Following in the footsteps of Cruz, Parekh developed end-to-end delay bounds for a session s described by an LBAP in an arbitrary network operating under

h	WFQ	FIFO	SG
1	16	16	48
2	32	48	80
3	49	115	113
4	65	264	145
5	81	623	177
6	98	1,572	210
7	114	4,382	242
8	130	13,835	274
9	147	50,676	307
10	163	220,010	339

Table 2: Comparison of bounds for FIFO, SG, and WFQ.

WFQ under very reasonable assumptions. The theory exhibits the folllowing important properties.

- Networks can be non-feed-forward,

- In the case that $\phi_k = \rho_s$ for $j_k \in \Gamma_s$, the delay bound is given by

$$T \leq \frac{\sigma_s}{\rho_s} + \text{propagation delay} \qquad (2)$$

which is independent of the path length.

Clarke, et al., [11] have proposed WFQ as the scheduler in their architecture for providing deterministic QOS. The quality of the bounds provided by WFQ can be found in Table 2 and can be compared with those of FIFO and SG for our voice example.

6.2 Statistical guarantees

Considerable work has been conducted on the design and evaluation of call admission policies for sessions requiring one or the other of the following two guarantees,

$$\Pr[T \leq D] < \epsilon$$
$$\Pr[\text{packet loss}] < \epsilon.$$

We will consider each of these in turn.

6.2.1 Statistical deadline guarantees

Consider a session that requires a guarantee on the tail of the end-to-end delay distribution. One approach to handling this session is to treat it as if it has the following deterministic QOS requirement, $T \leq D$. However, there is considerable evidence that such an approach will result in extremely poor performance, i.e., the number of sessions permitted to use the network will be considerably lower than necessary. We illustrate this with an example taken from [51].

Figure 4 illustrates a network (labelled M4) of 3×3 switches connected by T1 rate lines. The network has been configured so that each communication link carries 48 32Kbs voice calls where each voice call generates a packet every 16ms during a talkspurt. Talkspurt lengths are assumed to be exponentially distributed random variables with mean 352 ms and silence periods are assumed to be exponentially distributed rv's with mean 6.5 ms. (Silence periods are typically much larger. This mean was chosen so that the link utilizations would be all approximately 98%.)

Figure 5 shows simulation results for the distribution of the end-to-end delay of a session traversing links S1 - S4. The estimate for the distribution is taken from ten independent simulation runs, each of which simulated approximately 1/2 million packets for those sessions whose path length was four. Also shown are the bounds obtained for WFQ, SG, and FCFS. The results illustrate how poorly the bounds on maximum delay can be for the tail of the end-to-end delay distribution.

Consequently, a different approach is required for performing call admission when applications require statistical guarantees. In this section we describe several such approaches and discuss their advantages and disadvantages. These include

- provable guarantees,

- and approximate guarantees.

The first approach is an extension of the work of Cruz for bounding maximum end-to-end delay to bounding the tail of the end-to-end delay distribution. Kurose [33] provides tail bounds for the same network as Cruz under the assumption that busy periods at each node are finite and bounded in duration. Inherent in the model is the asumption that sources are described by LBAP's. Yaron and Sidi [50] and Chang [9] consider more general arrival processes for which the peak rate is unbounded and, based on Chernoff's bound, develop bounds on the end-to-end delay distribution. Although these models can be used to provide tighter bounds than the model of Cruz, preliminary evidence indicates that they remain still too loose to be of practical use in call admission. Furthermore, they share some of the problems inherent in Cruz's model, high computational complexity, not suitable for most general networks, etc...

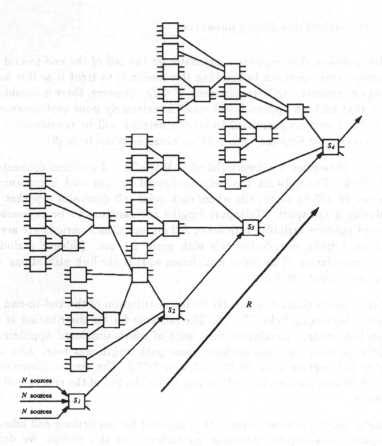

Figure 4: M4 Network.

This brings us to the approach most prevalent in the literature, namely to develop call admission policies that *approximately* provide statistical guarantees. Two approaches have been taken in this direction. The first is to develop heuristic models for estimating the tails of delay distributions [15, 28]. The latter approach actually measures current network behavior and uses this to parameterize the model. The second is to classify applications into different classes and perform analysis or simulations off-line to determine the number of statistical sessions that can be admitted and, more generally, the number of statisical sessions that can be combined with different numbers of deterministic sessions. This is exemplified in the work described in [27].

6.2.2 Statistical loss guarantees

We begin the discussion of how to provide statistical loss guarantees by first noting that a solution to this problem often automatically solves the problem of

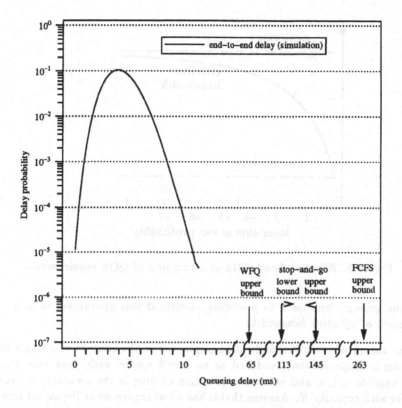

Figure 5: Delay comparison for M4 network.

providing statistical deadline guarantees in many high speed networks. Consider a network with links having bandwidths of 150Mbs. Let the scheduler at each link be FIFO and let the buffer capacity be 800Kb (approximately 100 1Kbyte packets). The delay through a 5 hop path is bounded by 30ms (excluding propagation delay) which is tolerable for real-time applications such as voice and video. Hence, the event $T > D$ corresponds to the event of a packet that is lost due to buffer overflow in this case.

Unlike deadlines, there is no general method for obtaining provable bounds on packet loss probabilities except in the case of a single link. Saito [42] provides bounds on cell loss probabilities for an ATM switch using a FIFO scheduler. The bounds require the average rate and the peak rate for each source over an interval of length $K/2$ where K is the buffer capacity. As the model does not derive expressions of this peak rate at the output of the switch, it is not able to handle more than one multiplexer.

Once we relax our requirement that the guarantee be provable, then we find

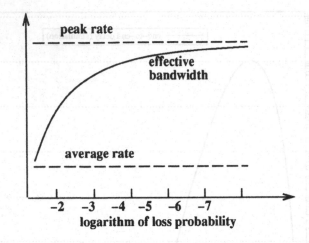

Figure 6: Effective bandwidth as a function of QOS requirement.

that the primary approach to providing statistical loss guarantees is based on the *theory of effective bandwidths*.

The theory of effective bandwidths originated in the context of a single link. Consider a single session, modelled as an on-off source with peak rate R_{peak}, mean burst length b, and utilization (fraction of time in the on state) u feeding a buffer with capacity K. Assume that it has a loss requirement $\Pr[\text{packet loss}] \leq \epsilon$. The effective bandwidth $\hat{c}$ is the service rate required to serve this source so that its QOS requirement is met. The effective bandwidth as a function of the QOS requirement is illustrated in Figure 6. It falls between the peak and average rates and increases as the QOS requirement becomes more stringent.

Assume for now that the effective bandwidth of a source is easily calculated and that the effective bandwidth corresponding to a set of sources can be expressed as the sum of their individual effective bandwidths, i.e., $\sum_{i \in \mathcal{S}} \hat{c}_i$. Then, the problem of call admission is simplified tremendously. The decision to accept a new call s requires the following test, is $r - \sum_{i \in \mathcal{S}} \hat{c}_i > \hat{c}_s$? This approach was first proposed in [21] where the following heuristic expression was given to compute the effective bandwidth of an on-off source,

$$\hat{c} = R_{peak} - \frac{x - \sqrt{[\alpha b(1-u)R_{peak} - K]^2 + 4K\alpha bu(1-u)R_{peak}}}{2\alpha b(1-u)} \tag{3}$$

where $\alpha = \ln(1/\epsilon)$. This expression was derived from a fluid model of an off-on source, [3], and developed to be 1) simple to compute, depending on only three parameters and 2) generally pessimistic.

One problem with this approach is that it ignores the possible multiplexing gains achieved by sharing the link among a number of sources. Hence, the following expression in [21] was proposed for the effective bandwidth of a collection of sources $\mathcal{S}$,

$$\hat{C} = \min \left\{ m + \alpha'\sigma, \sum_{i \in \mathcal{S}} \hat{c}_i \right\} \tag{4}$$

where m is the average aggregate rate of the sources in $\mathcal{S}$, σ is the standard deviation in the aggregate rate, and $\alpha' = \sqrt{-2\ln\epsilon - \ln(2\pi)}$. The first expression in the min is based on a Gaussian approximation of the aggregate bit rate. Such approximations have been shown to accurately model the stationary bit rate when the number of sources is sufficiently large (¿10 is suggested in [22]).

This has been extended to a network setting by assuming that the source traffic characteristics are relatively unaffected much when passing through a link (see [22] for evidence for the validity of this assumption) and through an application of the principle of nodal isolation, i.e., allocating the end-to-end packet loss requirement among the nodes on a path. See [22] for details of this approach.

There is currently insufficient experience with this approach to determine how well it will work. As mentioned earlier, the guarantees are approximate. In order to compensate for this, they have been chosen to be very conservative. However it is not known how conservative they are. Further work is required to evaluate this approach.

There have been several other proposals on how to calculate effective bandwidth for the case of identical sources sharing identical loss requirements. They are based on the following approach - for a given loss requirement, determine the maximum number of sources, n_{max}, that can share a link so that they all satisfy their requirements. Then $\hat{c} = r/n_{max}$. This can be obtained either through analysis, [1], or simulation, [16].

Observe that the test for call admission can be stated in the following equivalent form, is $n + 1 \leq n_{max}$? Here n denotes the number of sessions currently using the link. Two types of sessions can be handled in this way by calculating a feasible region (see Figure 7) which indicates the different combinations of sessions of the two types that can be accommodated while satisfying the loss requirements of both. Again, a call can be admitted if the combined populations fall within the feasible region. Such an approach has been sggested and studied in [25]. in the context of loss requirements and in the context of different types of QOS requirements [27].

Last, the work of Guerin, et al., which first proposed and developed the theory of effective bandwidths through simple heuristic arguments has been placed on a solid mathematical basis by several recent papers, [17, 14, 31]. This work has resulted in two types of results. The first is the derivation of the effective bandwidth of a single source for a large class of queueing systems and traffic models. Typically these relate to the dominant eigenvalue of the rate matrix associated with a Markovian model of the source. Second, it has been shown in

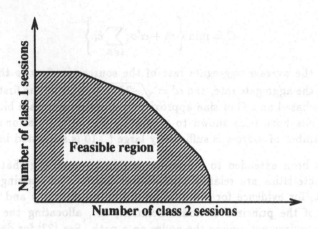

Figure 7: Feasible region for call admission.

the limit as $K \to \infty$ and $\epsilon \to 0$ that the effective bandwidth corresponding to a collection of sessions is equal to the sum of the effective bandwidths asociated with the sources for Markovian arrival processes. Hence, the assumption that the effective bandwidth of a collection of sessions can be approximated by the sum of the effective bandwidths of the individual sources is quite reasonable for low loss probabilities.

6.3 Best effort

This class of applications is easily handled. In a real implementation it may be useful to allocate a fraction of the bandwidth to best effort traffic. This is easily done with most of the approaches that we have described as they either are based on the principle of session isolation or they require knowledge of peak rates.

6.4 Other issues

There are a number of issues and problems that have not been adequately addressed, either in this section or in the literature. These ibclude

- allocation of end-to-end QOS requirements to nodal QOS requirement,
- adaptivity to changes in link loads, and
- adaptivity to changes in session characteristics.

Although several proposed call admission algorithms require the allocation of end-to-end QOS requirements to nodal requirements, e.g., [15, 22], the problem has not been thoroughly addressed. One exception is the work of Nagarajan [36] which compares an optimal allocation to the simple heuristic of equal allocation. This study shows that, if the QOS requirement is low loss, then little is gained in using the optimal allocation over the equal allocation. On the other hand, is the QOS requirement is a mean delay bound, then an optimal allocation can provide significantly better performance than an equal allocation. A sensitivity measure, the relative gain ratio, is proposed which can be used to perform a quick test to determine whether it is useful to try to find the optimal allocation.

A second issue that is only now beginning to receive attention is that of changes in network loads, source characteristics, etc.. Is the contract negotiated between network and user static during the life of the session or can it be renegotiated? For example, if a user declares itself as being characterized by a high value of R_{peak} but the network determines through measurements that it is considerably lower, can the network take advantage of it? Several proposed algorithms allow the network to modify network resource allocations to sessions in order to account for changes in traffic characteristics, see [2].

7 Summary and Future Work

In this paper we have presented the state of the art of provision of QOS in integrated digital services networks. We have focussed primarily on the problem of call admission, and specifically the question *can a new call be admitted with the QOS that it desires while maintaining the QOS of all sessions presently in the network?* We have seen how this is intricately related to the choice of scheduling policy at each link. We have described a number of approaches to solving the problem of call admission based on the principles of nodal and session isolation as well as approaches that attempt to share resources between sessions of different classes. At this point in time there is has been very little comparison between different approaches - either from the point of view of assumptions regarding the underlying network architecture or from the point of view of performance. Much remains to be done in this area.

One interesting dichotomy exists in the different approaches reported on how to provide QOS that has yet to be dealt with satisfactorily. This is the division between the approaches that deal primarily with delay and those that ignore delay but deal with buffer overflow. It seems clear that the current real-time applications such as voice and video can be handled in a satisfactory manner by the latter approach provided that raw bandwidth is at least 100Mbs. It remains to be seen whether applications will be developed which will require deadline constraints that are only slightly larger than propagation delays or whether there will be a large number of low speed networks for which the algorithms providing delay guarantees will be required. This is an area worth investigating.

Another area worth investigating is the application of some of the approximate guarantee techniques developed for delays [28] to the problem of packet loss. Another fruitful area of research is that of either developing call admission algorithms based on interval QOS metrics or trelating such metrics more closely to stationary metrics such as Q2 and Q4 so as to use existing approaches for dealing with interval metrics.

Last, the development of protocols for dealing with call admission or the data transport is in its infancy. Furthe work is required in this area.

Acknowledgments: I would like to acknowledge Ramesh Nagarajan for the endless discussions regarding the behavior and underlying assumptions of different scheduling algorithms and call admission algorithms. I would also like to thank David Yates for supplying me with the numerical and simulation results comparing different call admission policies.

References

[1] S. Akhtar. Congestion control in a fast packet switching network. Master's thesis, Washington University, St. Louis, Missouri, 1987.

[2] J.-T. Amenyo, A.A. Lazar, and G. Pacific. Cooperative distributed scheduling for ats-based broadband networks. In *INFOCOM'92*, pages 333–342, May 1992.

[3] D. Anick, D. Mitra, and M. M. Sondhi. Stochastic theory of a data-handling system with multiple sources. *Bell System Technical Journal*, 61:1871–1894, 1982.

[4] Caglan M. Aras, Jim Kurose, Douglas Reeves, and Henning Schulzrinne. Real-time communication in packet-switched networks. To Appear in Proceedings of the IEEE, January 1994.

[5] Ernst Biersack. Error recovery in high-speed networks. In *Second International Workshop on Network and Operating System Support for Digital Audio and Video*, page 222, 1991.

[6] Hugh S. Bradlow. Performance measures for real-time continuous bit-stream oriented services: Application to packet reassembly. *Computer Networks and ISDN systems*, 20:15–26, 1990.

[7] CCITT. Rec. I.121: Recommendation on broadband aspects of ISDN. 1988.

[8] CCITT. Rec. I.371: Recommendation on traffic control and congestion control in B-ISDN. 1992.

[9] C.-S. Chang. Stability, queue length and delay, part ii:stochastic queueing networks. Technical Report RC 17709, IBM.

[10] R. Chipalkatti, J.F. Kurose, and D. Towsley. Scheduling policies for real-time and non-real-time traffic in a statistical multiplexer. In *IEEE INFO-COM'89*, pages 774–783, April 1989.

[11] D.D. Clark, S. Shenker, and L. Zhang. Supporting real-time applications in an integrated services packet network: architecture and mechanism. In *ACM SIGCOMM'92*, pages 14–26, 1992.

[12] Rene Cruz. A calculus for network delay, part II: Network analysis. *IEEE Transactions on Information Theory*, 37:132–141, 1991.

[13] A. Demers, S. Keshav, and S. Shenker. Analysis and simulation of a fair queueing algorithm. *Internetworking:Research and Experience*, 1:3–26.

[14] Anwar Elwalid and Debasis Mitra. Effective bandwidth of general Markovian traffic sources and admission control of high-speed networks. Submitted to ACM-IEEE Transactions on Networking, July 1992.

[15] Domenico Ferrari and Dinesh Verma. A scheme for real-time channel establishment in wide-area networks. *IEEE J.Select.Areas Commun.*, 8:368–379, April 1990.

[16] G. Gallassi, G. Rigolio, and L. Fratta. ATM:bandwidth assignment and bandwidth enforcement policies. In *GLOBECOM'89*, pages 1788–1793, December 1989.

[17] R. J. Gibbens and P. J. Hunt. Effective bandwidths for multi-type uas channel. *QUESTA*, 9:17–28, 1991.

[18] André Girard. *Routing and Dimensioning in Circuit-Switched Networks*. Addison Wesley, 1990.

[19] S. J. Golestani. A stop-and-go queueing framework for congestion management. In *Proc. 1990 SIGCOMM*, pages 8–18.

[20] S. J. Golestani. Congestion-free transmission of real-time traffic in packet networks. In *IEEE INFOCOM'90*, pages 527–536, June 1990.

[21] Roch Guerin et al. Equivalent capacity and its application to bandwidth allocation in high-speed networks. *IEEE J.Select.Areas Commun.*, 9(7):968–981, 1991.

[22] Roch Guerin and Levent Gun. A unified approach to bandwidth allocation and access control in fast packet-switched networks. In *INFOCOM'92*, pages 01–12, 1992.

[23] S. Keshav H. Zhang. Comparison of rate-based service disciplines. In *SIGCOMM*.

[24] Harry Heffes and David Lucantoni. A markov modulated characterization of voice and data traffic and related statistical multiplexer performance. *IEEE J.Select.Areas Commun.*, SAC-4:856–867, September 1986.

[25] Joseph Y. Hui. Resource allocation for broadband networks. *IEEE J.Select.Areas Commun.*, 6(9):1598–1608, December 1988.

[26] Ren-Hung Hwang. *Routing in high-speed networks*. PhD thesis, University of Massachusetts, Amherst, 1993.

[27] Jay M. Hyman et al. Real-time scheduling with quality of service constraints. *IEEE J.Select.Areas Commun.*, 9(7):1052–1063, September 1991.

[28] S. Jamin, S. Shenker, L. Zhang, and D.D Clark. An admission control algorithm for predictive real-time service(extended abstract). In *Third International Workshop on network and operating system support for digital audio and video*, pages 308–315, November 1992.

[29] C.R. Kalmanek, H. Kanakia, and S. Keshav. Rate controlled servers for very high-speed networks. In *Globecom'90*, December 1990.

[30] Gunnar Karlsson and Martin Vetterli. Packet video and its integration into the network architecture. *IEEE J.Select.Areas Commun.*, 7(5):739–751, June 1989.

[31] F. P. Kelly. Effective bandwidths at multi-class queues. *QUESTA*, 9:5–16, 1991.

[32] S. Keshav. On the efficient implementation of fair queueing. *Internetworking:Research and Experience*, 2:157–173.

[33] Jim Kurose. On computing per-session performance bounds in high-speed multi-hop computer networks. In *ACM SIGMETRICS'92*, pages 128–139, June 1992.

[34] Z. Liu and D. Towsley. Burst reduction properties of the token bank in ATM networks. In *IFIP workshop on modeling and performance evaluation of ATM technology*.

[35] Zhen Liu and Don Towsley. Burst reduction properties of rate-control throttles:departure process. To Appear in *Annals of Operations Research*.

[36] Ramesh Nagarajan. *Quality-of-service issues in high-speed networks*. PhD thesis, University of Massachusetts, Amherst, 1993.

[37] Pramod Pancha and Magda El Zarki. Bandwidth requirements of variable bit rate MPEG sources in ATM networks. In *IFIP workshop on modeling and performance evaluation of ATM technology*, pages 5.2.1–5.2.25, January 1993.

[38] Abhay Parekh and Robert Gallager. A generalized processor sharing approach to flow control in integrated services networks - the single node case. In *INFOCOM'92*, pages 915–924, 1992.

[39] V. Ramaswamy. Traffic performance modeling for packet communication whence, where and wither. In *Third Australian Teletraffic Seminar*, November 1988. Keynote Address.

[40] V. Ramaswamy and Walter Willinger. Efficient traffic performance strategies for packet multiplexers. *Computer Networks and ISDN systems*, 20:401–407, 1990.

[41] J.-F. Ren, J.W. Mark, and J.W. Wong. Performance analysis of a leaky-bucket controlled ATM multiplexer. To Appear in *Performance Evaluation*.

[42] H. Saito. Call admission control in an ATM network using upper bound of cell loss probability. *IEEE Transactions on Communications*, 40(9):1512–1521, September 1992.

[43] Nachum Shacham. Packet recovery in high-speed networks using coding and buffer management. In *INFOCOM*, pages 124–131, 1990.

[44] M. Sidi, W. Liu, I.Cidon, and I. Gopal. Congestion control through input rate regulation. In *GLOBECOM'89*.

[45] D. Towsley and F. Baccelli. Comparisons of service disciplines in a tandem queueing network with real-time constraints. *OR Letters*, 10.

[46] J. Turner. New directions in communications (or which way to the information age). *IEEE Communications Magazine*, 24:8–15, 1986.

[47] J.S. Turner. Managing bandwidth in ATM networks with bursty traffic. *IEEE Network*, 6(5):50–59, September 1992.

[48] Dinesh Verma, Hui Zhang, and Domenico Ferrari. Delay jitter control for real-time communication in a packet switching network. In *IEEE Tricomm'91*, April 1991.

[49] G.M. Woodruff and R. Kositpaiboon. Multimedia traffic management principles for guaranteed ATM network performance. *IEEE J.Select.Areas Commun.*, 8.

[50] Opher Yaron and Moshe Sidi. Calculating performance bounds in communication networks. In *IEEE INFOCOM'93*, pages 539–546, April 1993.

[51] David Yates et al. On per-session end-to-end delay and the call admission problem for real-time applications with qos requirements. To appear in SIGCOMM'93.

Dependability and Performability Analysis*

Kishor S. Trivedi[1], Gianfranco Ciardo[2], Manish Malhotra[3], Robin A. Sahner[4],

[1] Department of Electrical Engineering, Duke University
[2] Department of Computer Science, College of William and Mary
[3] AT&T Bell Laboratories, Holmdel, NJ 07733
[4] Urbana, IL, 61801

Abstract. In this tutorial, we discuss several practical issues regarding specification and solution of dependability and performability models. We compare model types with and without rewards. Continuous-time Markov chains (CTMCs) are compared with (continuous-time) Markov reward models (MRMs) and generalized stochastic Petri nets (GSPNs) are compared with stochastic reward nets (SRNs). It is shown that reward-based models could lead to more concise model specification and solution of a variety of new measures. With respect to the solution of dependability and performability models, we identify three practical issues: largeness, stiffness, and non-exponentiality, and we discuss a variety of approaches to deal with them, including some of the latest research efforts.

1 Introduction

Dependability, performance, and performability evaluation techniques provide a useful method for understanding the dynamic behavior of a computer or communication system. To be useful, the evaluation should reflect important system characteristics such as fault-tolerance, automatic reconfiguration, and repair; contention for resources; concurrency and synchronization; deadlines imposed on the tasks; and graceful degradation. Furthermore, complexity of current-day systems and corresponding system evaluation should be explicitly addressed.

Traditional performance evaluation is concerned with contention for system resources. Performance evaluation of parallel and distributed systems also address concurrency and synchronization of tasks. Real-time system performance evaluation takes into account various hard and soft deadlines on task exection times.

Reliability, availability, safety, and related measures are collectively known as dependability. Dependability evaluation encompasses fault-tolerance, reconfiguration, and repair aspects of system behavior. More recently, interest in combining performance and dependability evaluation has grown. Such performability

* This research was partially supported by the National Aeronautics and Space Administration under NASA Contract No. NAS1-19480 while the first two authors were in residence at the Institute for Computer Applications in Science and Engineering (ICASE), NASA Langley Research Center, Hampton, VA 23681.

evaluation considers the graceful degradation of the system in addition to the dependability aspects.

While measurement is an attractive option for assessing an existing system or a prototype, it is not a feasible option during the system design and implementation phases. Model-based evaluation has proven to be an attractive alternative in these cases. A model is an abstraction of a system that includes sufficient detail to facilitate an understanding of system behavior. Several types of models are currently used in practice. The most appropriate type of model depends upon the complexity of the system, the questions to be studied, the accuracy required, and the resources available for the study.

Discrete-event simulation is the most commonly used modeling technique in practice but it tends to be relatively expensive. Analytical modeling provides a cost-effective alternative to simulation for studying the performance and dependability of computer and communication systems. Due to recent developments in model generation and solution techniques and automated tools, large and realistic models can be developed and studied. In this tutorial we concentrate on such analytic models. The rest of this tutorial is organized as follows. In the next section, we present an overview of various approaches to dependability and performance modeling. In Section 3, we show how performability analysis can be carried out using MRMs. We also show how dependability measures can be obtained via performability analysis using special reward rate assignment.

In Section 4, we compare GSPNs and stochastic reward nets. In Section 5, we discuss in detail some practical issues in solving dependability and performability models: largeness, stiffness, and non-exponentiality.

2 Approaches to Modeling

2.1 Dependability Modeling

Reliability block diagrams, fault trees, and reliability graphs are commonly used to study the dependability of systems [59]. Although these models are concise and have efficient solution methods, they cannot represent dependencies among components [56] as easily as CTMC models can [21, 23].

We begin by considering a fault-tolerant, multi-processor computer with multiple, shared memory modules. The system is able to detect a processor or memory module failure and reconfigure itself to continue operation without the failed component. The system can operate with just one processor and one memory module.

Our first model of this system is the reliability block diagram in Figure 1. We could attach to each component the probability of having failed by a particular time. In a more general parameterization, a failure time distribution function, rather than a probability value, can be attached to each component. For example, one can assign the exponential distribution $F_p(t) = 1 - e^{-\lambda_p t}$ to processors and $F_m(t) = 1 - e^{-\lambda_m t}$ to memories. We can request the system failure time distribution as a function of the time variable t. For a system with

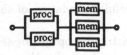

Fig. 1. A reliability block diagram model.

two processors and three memory modules,

$$F_{sys}(t) = 1 - (1 - (1 - e^{-\lambda_p t})^2)) \cdot (1 - (1 - e^{-\lambda_m t})^3)) \ .$$

We can also ask for the mean time to system failure,

$$MTTF_{sys} = \int_0^\infty (1 - F_{sys}(t)dt$$

$$= \frac{6}{\lambda_p + \lambda_m} - \frac{3}{2\lambda_p + \lambda_m} - \frac{6}{\lambda_p + 2\lambda_m} + \frac{3}{2\lambda_p + 2\lambda_m} + \frac{2}{\lambda_p + 3\lambda_m} - \frac{1}{2\lambda_p + 3\lambda_m} \ .$$

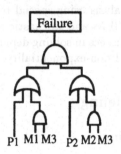

Fig. 2. A fault tree model.

Now suppose we want to investigate a different computer design where the two processors have fast private memory modules and the system has slower, shared memory modules. We assume that the system operates as long as there is at least one operational processor with access to either a private or shared memory. We cannot model this system with a block diagram, because there is no way to model how the shared memories are connected to all processors while private memories are connected to particular processors. So, we turn to a fault tree model, shown for two processors and three memory modules in Figure 2. We could also use a reliability graph, where time-to-failure distributions are assigned to the edges. The system is operational as long as there is a path from source (src) to sink. In this particular model (Figure 3), processor failures happen along the edges labeled *P1* and *P2* and memory failures happen along the edges *M1*, *M2*, and *M3*. The edges *I1* and *I2* do not represent system components; they represent the structure of the system (the sharing of *M3*). We assign the "infinite" distribution, defined by $I(t) = 0$, to them. There is a path from source to sink if *P1* and *M1* are up or if *P1* and *M3* are up, and similarly for paths involving *P2*. Analysis of the reliability graph results in the same failure time distribution as the fault tree analysis.

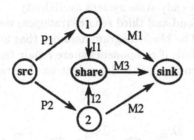

Fig. 3. A reliability graph model.

Now we extend our models to take into account repair or replacement of parts. We calculate the "availability" of the system, the (transient or steady-state) probability that the system is functioning. We examine the all-shared-memory system and look at three repair strategies:

1. There are enough repair resources to repair all components at the same time, if necessary.
2. There are two repair facilities, one for processors and one for memory modules, each able to handle one component at a time.
3. There is one repair facility, able to handle one component at a time. Processor repair has preemptive priority over memory repair.

For the first strategy, the state of the components (either up or down) are mutually independent, since the failure and repair of each component does not depend on that of any other component. Because of this independence, we can use the block diagram used to model reliability (Figure 1) to model availability as well. Instead of assigning to each component the time-to-failure distribution, we use the transient unavailability. If the ith component has exponentially distributed failure behavior with rate λ_i and repair is also exponentially distributed with rate μ_i, its unavailability at time t is

$$U_i(t) = \frac{\lambda_i}{\lambda_i + \mu_i} - \frac{\lambda_i}{\lambda_i + \mu_i} e^{-(\lambda_i + \mu_i)t} \qquad (1)$$

and the steady-state unavailability is given by

$$\lim_{t \to \infty} U_i(t) = \frac{\lambda_i}{\lambda_i + \mu_i}$$

These expressions can be derived by solving the two-state (up/down) CTMC for a component [62].

If we analyze the reliability block diagram of Figure 1 with the assignment of distribution functions of Equation 1 to the components, the resulting function is the system unavailability at time t, $U_{sys}(t)$, and the "mass at infinity" $(1 - \lim_{t \to \infty} U_{sys}(t))$ is the steady-state system availability.

To deal with the second and third repair strategies, we can no longer use the block diagram model. The block diagram assumes that all components are statistically independent, but, if components share repair facilities, the failure and repair behavior of one component is dependent on the state of all components.

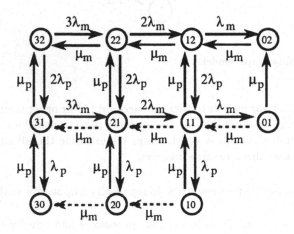

Fig. 4. A CTMC model.

If the failure and repair distributions are exponential, we can use a CTMC model. Consider the CTMC in Figure 4. State mp represents the system when m memory units and p processors are functional. The model with all of the solid and dashed-line transitions is for the second repair strategy (one repair facility for processors and one for memories). The model for the third strategy (only one repair facility giving priority to the processors) is obtained by excluding the dashed lines, since no memory is repaired while there are failed processors.

We note that we could have used a CTMC for the first repair strategy as well. We would have assigned different transition rates to the repair transitions to reflect the fact that more than one component can be repaired at a time. As an example, the rate for the transition from 02 to 12 would be $3 * \mu_m$ rather than μ_m. The block diagram model, though, is both easier to construct and more efficient to analyze.

Before leaving the subject of unavailability, we illustrate the use of one more model type, the GSPN. For a discussion of this model type, the reader is referred to [1]. Modeling the availability of this system with a GSPN does more than just give us another validity check. It allows us to find the unavailability for a system with any number of processors and memories without having to construct a separate model for each number of components. The GSPN in Figure 5 is a model of the system in which there is one repair facility to be shared for all components.

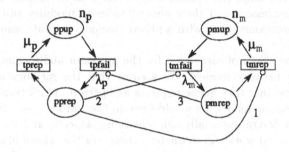

Fig. 5. A GSPN model.

There is a token for each processor and each memory. Initially, there are n_p tokens in the place *ppup* (place: processors up) and n_m tokens in the place *pmup* (place: memories up). When a processor fails, its token moves from place *ppup* through transition *tpfail* (transition: processor fails) to place *pprep* (place: processor waiting for repair). Processor repair is represented by a token moving from place *pprep* through transition *tprep* to place *ppup*. The inhibitor arcs from *pprep* to *tmfail* and *pmrep* to *tpfail* reflect the assumption that if the system has already failed because all processors or all memories have failed, the remaining working components do not fail while they are not running. This aspect of the system was modeled only implicitly in the CTMC model, by the absence of failure transitions from the places with either no operating processors or no operating memory modules. The inhibitor arc from *pprep* to *tmrep* is the one that represents our assumption that there is only one repair facility; if there are any failed processors, there can be no memory repair.

We can verify that analyzing this GSPN with $n_p = 2$ and $n_m = 3$ gives the same result for system steady-state unavailability as the CTMC model. We note that the GSPN, although a more efficient specification, is no more efficient to analyze than the CTMC, since analysis of a GSPN involves translating the GSPN into a CTMC. However, dependability modeling with GSPN tends to be clumsy [41]. Stochastic reward nets remove this restriction from GSPN models. We elaborate more on this in Section 4.

2.2 System Performance Models

In this section, we look at aspects of system performance, including performance of gracefully degraded systems. In the performance domain, task precedence graphs [31, 55] can be used to model the performance of concurrent programs with unlimited resources. Product form queueing networks [35, 36], on the other hand, can represent contention for resources. However they cannot model concurrency within a job, synchronization, or server failures, since these violate the product form assumptions.

We consider the same two system architectures as in Section 2.1: the first containing two processors and three shared memory modules and the second containing two processors, each with a private memory module, and one shared memory module.

To capture the effects of contention for the processor and memory resources, we use queueing network models. We assume that the memory modules are servers in the sense that they queue requests and perform block transfers. To set up a realistic queueing model, we would have to take into account the proposed operating system design, especially the scheduling aspects, and we would need some kind of expected workload characterization. For the sake of illustration, we use the closed queueing network models shown in Figures 6 and 7.

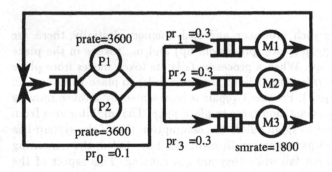

Fig. 6. A product form queueing network for the system with three shared memories.

The network in Figure 6 is for the design containing two processors and three shared memory modules. We model the two processors by a multiple-server station. That is, jobs wait in a single queue and enter whichever server becomes

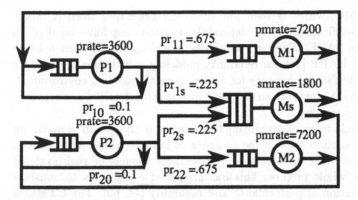

Fig. 7. A product form queueing network for the system with one shared memory and two local memories.

free. When a job wants to access the memory, it requires memory module Mi with probability pr_i. After some visits to the processor, a job finishes: pr_0 is the probability that a job is finished when it leaves one of the processors. As is usual for closed queueing networks, the assumption is that each finished job is replaced by a statistically identical new job.

The network in Figure 7 is for the design containing two private memory modules. For this system, we assume that jobs are targeted to particular processors. This is reasonable, since, once a job starts on a processor, we want it to continue where it has access to that processor's private memory. We carry out this assumption by making the queueing network a "multiple-chain" queueing network, in this case having two "chains", or classes of jobs. Jobs in the first class go from $P1$ to either $M1$ or Ms and back to $P1$ and jobs in the second class go from $P2$ to either $M2$ or Ms and back to $P2$.

As expected, the system with private memories provides higher system throughput as opposed to that for the shared-memory system.

To model the systems when one memory has failed, we remove the server $M1$ (and its queue) from each of the models and adjust the probabilities pr_i and pr_{ij} appropriately.

Queueing models are able to capture the effects of resource contention, but measures related to the total number of jobs serviced do not capture the performance of the system as seen by a single parallel program: series-parallel acyclic graph models [55] can be used for this purpose.

Also CTMCs provide a useful framework to model system performance, but a detailed CTMC model is often large and complex and its construction is an error-prone process. Hence there is a need for a higher-level model-type having an underlying CTMC, which is then automatically generated from it. Some attempts in the specific instance of dependability modeling have resulted in useful packages like SAVE [23], for availability modeling, which uses a block diagram input, and HARP [21], for reliability modeling, which uses a fault-tree input. A suitable interface is necessary for a more general modeling environment. GSPNs [1] and SRNs [13] provide an excellent interface for detailed performance modeling of complex systems.

The advent of fault-tolerant computing has resulted in the design of machines which continue to function even in the presence of failures, albeit at a reduced level of performance. Pure reliability or performance models of such systems do not capture the whole picture. This has prompted researchers to consider the combined evaluation of performance and reliability [44, 63]. The CTMC is extended by associating rewards with its states to obtain a "Markov reward process", or "Markov reward model" (MRM). This process not only facilitates modeling of performance and reliability but also the combined evaluation of performance and reliability. Since this paper considers the automatic generation of the CTMC from the GSPN description of the model, the reward structure must also be defined in terms of the GSPN entities. Consequently the GSPN description is modified to obtain "stochastic reward nets" [13] which can be automatically transformed to obtain the underlying MRM.

3 CTMCs versus MRMs

CTMCs have been traditionally used to model dependability. MRMs [25] are CTMCs in which reward rates may be associated with states of the CTMC (*rate-type* rewards) or with transitions of the CTMC (*impulse-type* rewards) or both. We consider MRMs with rate-type rewards. MRMs have been successfully used for performability analysis [44, 63] according to the following methodology. Initially, a dependability model (also known as *structural model*) of the system is constructed. Assuming the dependability model is state-space type (such as a CTMC), a performance measure is obtained (possibly by solving a performance model) for each state of the dependability model. This performance measure becomes the reward rate of that state in the dependability model. With the reward-rate assignment, the dependability model becomes an MRM which may then be solved for various performability measures. There is an approximation involved in this decomposition of performance and dependability models: the system is assumed to have attained (quasi-)steady-state in each state of the dependability model, so that the reward rate for each state of the reliability model is a steady-state performance measure. Transient or steady-state analysis of the dependability model with rewards is then carried out. The justification for this decomposition lies in the fact that the performance activities are much faster than the dependability events.

CTMCs can also be used for performability analysis if a monolithic model is constructed which combines both the dependability and performance model of the system. However, the state-space of this model is approximately the cross-product of state-spaces of the dependability and performance models. In addition, this monolithic model is stiff because of extreme disparity between the transition rates (job arrival rates could be 10^9 times or more than the fault occurrence rates). One may argue that this approach is more accurate than the MRM approach since no approximation is involved. However, this gain in accuracy may well be negated due to the computational problems posed by largeness and stiffness of the monolithic model. We focus more on these two problems, largeness and stiffness, in later sections. The MRM approach has another significant advantage. No assumptions are made about how the reward rates are obtained. The reward rates may be obtained by simulation, by solving a queuing network, or by solving a semi-Markov process (SMP), etc.

It is easy to see that CTMCs are special cases of MRMs and therefore dependability analysis becomes a special case of performability analysis. In this section, we briefly show how various dependability measures can be analyzed as performability measures when the MRM has a special reward-rate assignment. Let $\{\Theta(t), t \geq 0\}$ be an MRM with state space Ψ and constant reward rate r_i associated with each state i of the CTMC. If the MRM spends τ_i units of time in state i, then $r_i\tau_i$ is the reward accumulated during this sojourn. Let $\mathbf{Q}$ be the generator matrix and $\mathbf{P}(t)$ be the state probability vector of the MRM. Here $P_i(t)$ denotes the transient probability of the MRM being in state i at time t. The transient behavior of this MRM is given by the Kolmogorov differential equation:

$$\frac{d\mathbf{P}(t)}{dt} = \mathbf{P}(t)\mathbf{Q} \ , \tag{2}$$

given the initial state probability vector $\mathbf{P}(0)$. The steady-state probability vector π (assuming that it exists and is unique) is obtained by setting the l.h.s. in Equation 2 to zero:

$$\pi\mathbf{Q} = 0 \ , \ \sum_{i \in \Psi} \pi_i = 1 \ ,$$

The cumulative state probability vector of the MRM is defined as $\mathbf{L}(t) = \int_0^t \mathbf{P}(x)dx$, where $L_i(t)$ denotes the expected total time spent by the MRM in state i during the interval $[0, t)$. To compute $\mathbf{L}(t)$, we integrate Equation 2:

$$\frac{d\mathbf{L}(t)}{dt} = \mathbf{L}(t)\mathbf{Q} + \mathbf{P}(0) \ .$$

The reward rate at time t for the MRM is given by $\Upsilon(t) = r_{\Theta(t)}$. The accumulated reward over the interval $[0, t)$ is given by:

$$\Phi(t) = \int_0^t \Upsilon(x)dx = \int_0^t r_{\Theta(x)}dx \ .$$

The expected reward rate at time t of the MRM is:

$$E[\Upsilon(t)] = \sum_{i \in \Psi} r_i P_i(t) \ .$$

The expected reward rate in steady-state for the MRM is:

$$E[\Upsilon_{ss}] = \sum_{i \in \Psi} r_i \pi_i .$$

To compute availability measures, the state-space of the MRM is partitioned into two: a set of system-up states, with reward rate 1, and a set of system-down states, with reward rate 0. We term this a *0-1 reward assignment*. The *transient availability* of the system is given by $E[\Upsilon(t)]$ and *steady-state availability* is given by $E[\Upsilon_{ss}]$.

The expected accumulated reward over the interval $[0, t)$ is:

$$E[\Phi(t)] = \sum_{i \in \Psi} r_i L_i(t) .$$

The expected time-averaged reward rate over the interval $[0, t)$ is given by $\sum_i r_i L_i(t)/t$. In an availability model with 0-1 reward assignment, the *total uptime* of the system over the interval $[0, t)$ is $E[\Phi(t)]$. *Interval availability* is the proportion of time a system is up in a given interval of time and it is given by $E[\Phi(t)]/t$ for the interval $[0, t)$.

For MRMs with absorbing states, the state-space Ψ is partitioned into two: Ψ_A (set of absorbing states) and Ψ_T (set of transient states). Let $\mathbf{Q}_T$ be the submatrix of $\mathbf{Q}$ corresponding to the transitions between transient states. The mean time spent by the MRM in state $i \in \Psi_T$ before absorption is given by $\tau_i = \int_0^\infty P_i(x)dx$, which is obtained by integrating Equation 2 from 0 to ∞:

$$\tau \mathbf{Q}_T + \mathbf{P}_T(0) = 0 .$$

The mean time to absorption is given by:

$$MTTA = \sum_{i \in \Psi_T} \tau_i .$$

To compute reliability measures, all the system-down states are made absorbing states (transitions leaving from them are deleted). The same 0-1 reward assignment is used. The *reliability* is given by $E[\Upsilon(t)]$. The *lifetime* (similar to total uptime) [20] of the system over the interval $[0, t)$ is $E[\Phi(t)]$. The expected accumulated reward until absorption is:

$$E[\Phi(\infty)] = \sum_{i \in \Psi_T} r_i \tau_i .$$

and the *mean time to failure* (MTTF) of the system is $E[\Phi(\infty)]$.

The distribution of the reward rate at time t, $\Upsilon(t)$, is computed as:

$$P[\Upsilon(t) \le \psi] = \sum_{r_i \le \psi, i \in \Psi} P_i(t) .$$

The distribution of accumulated reward until absorption or a finite period can also be computed. If the time to accumulate a given reward r is $\Gamma(r)$, then the distribution of $\Gamma(r)$ is known once the distribution of accumulated reward is known [32]:

$$P[\Gamma(r) \leq t] = 1 - P[\Phi(t) < r] \ . \tag{3}$$

For instance, the distribution of time to complete a job that requires r units of processing time on a system which is modeled by an MRM can be computed in this fashion.

From the above discussion, it is clear that dependability analysis can be carried out using MRMs with special reward rate assignment to various system states. This analysis can also be carried out using CTMCs (without rewards) in an equally efficient manner. However, performability analysis, which can be easily carried out using MRMs, becomes cumbersome if rewards are not used.

4 SPNs versus SRNs

CTMCs modeling real systems tend to be large, sometimes with hundreds of thousands states. A higher-level specification mechanism is thus needed for the concise description of the model and the automatic conversion into a CTMC. Stochastic Petri nets (SPNs) provide such a mechanism. Molloy [48] used SPNs for performance analysis and showed that they are isomorphic to CTMCs. Since then, several extensions have been made to SPNs. Some of these extensions have enhanced the flexibility of use and allowed for even more concise description of performance and reliability models. Some other extensions have enhanced the modeling power by allowing for non-exponential distributions (see Section 5.3).

In this section, we compare SPNs with and without rewards. Specifically, we compare SRNs as defined by Ciardo et al. [13] and GSPNs as defined by Ajmone-Marsan et al. [2]. SRNs are an extension of GSPNs, since they include all the features of GSPNs and add more features. There are several structural extensions such as guards (earlier known as enabling functions), priorities with timed transitions, marking-dependent arc cardinalities, and halting condition. Besides the structural extensions, a reward rate function associates a reward rate with each reachable marking. GSPNs and SRNs have been shown to be isomorphic to CTMCs and MRMs respectively. However, we show in this section that SRNs allow a much more concise description of system behavior than GSPNs. This is particularly true for dependability models. Furthermore, certain reward-based measures as described in Section 3 can be computed using SRNs but cannot be computed using GSPNs.

To compare GSPNs and SRNs, we present an example. Consider a simple network between *src* and *sink* nodes consisting of three links (Figure 8). The network is operational as long as link A and at least one of the links B or C is operational. Assuming that each link has its independent repairperson, the availability of the network can be modeled by the GSPN shown in Figure 9. A token in places pA, pB, and pC respectively indicates that links A, B, and C are operational. A token in place pF implies that the network is failed. A token in place pR implies that, due to repair of one or more links, the component is ready to be operational again. The firing of transition tR removes the token from pF, signifying that the network is operational. The steady-state (transient) probability of a token being in place pF gives the steady-state (transient) unavailability of the network.

The availability of this network can also be modeled by an SRN as shown in Figure 10. The reward rate function is as shown in the table. The expected value of reward rate r in steady-state (or at time t) gives the steady-state (transient) availability of the network. Let us now compare the GSPN and SRN models. A GSPN model requires a mesh of immediate transitions, places, and inhibitor arcs to capture the operational dependence of the network on the links. Part of this mesh captures the dependence such as the subsystem of links B and C fails only when both B and C have failed. The other part of the mesh captures the impact of repairs of links which reflect complementary conditions, such as removal of a token from place pBC as soon as either B or C is repaired. As the systems grow in complexity, this mesh becomes very complex and unwieldy. On the other hand, an SRN captures the operational dependence of the network on links by reward rate function. This results in a simpler and more manageable net.

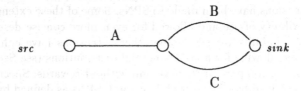

Fig. 8. A simple network

5 Computational Problems

In modeling practice, it is often the case that no single model is adequate to solve a problem. Different parts or levels of detail in a system may require different modeling techniques. In cases where a single model type can be used, it may be too large (a problem both for specification and analysis) or intractable ("stiff" or ill-conditioned). Three main difficulties in analytic models include largeness, stiffness, and the need to model non-exponential distributions. We explore these topics in the following subsections.

5.1 Largeness

The problem of model largeness can be handled in two ways: it can be avoided or it can be tolerated.

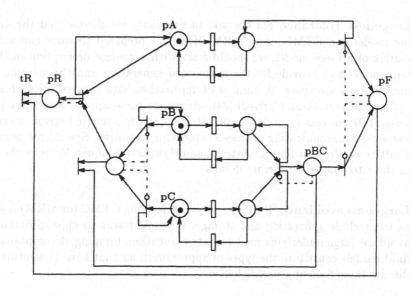

Fig. 9. GSPN availability model of the network

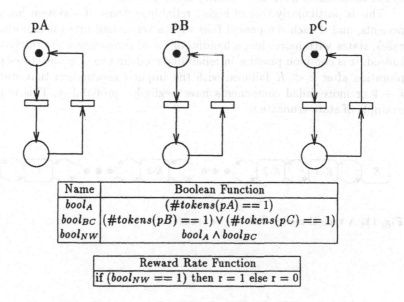

Name	Boolean Function
$bool_A$	$(\#tokens(pA) == 1)$
$bool_{BC}$	$(\#tokens(pB) == 1) \lor (\#tokens(pC) == 1)$
$bool_{NW}$	$bool_A \land bool_{BC}$

Reward Rate Function
if $(bool_{NW} == 1)$ then $r = 1$ else $r = 0$

Fig. 10. SRN availability model of the network

Largeness Tolerance For the sake of simplicity we assume that the underlying model is a CTMC or an MRM. If we are prepared to store and solve the matrix of a large model, we should start with a concise description of the system model and provide for the automated generation and the solution of the underlying state space. A number of approaches have evolved for such specifications. Haverkort and Trivedi [24] summarize these approaches. They present seven different classes of specification techniques: Stochastic Petri nets and their variants, Communicating processes, Queueing networks, Specialized languages, Fault-trees, Production rule systems, and Hybrid techniques. We refer the reader to the cited paper for further details.

Largeness avoidance If the size of the underlying CTMC (or MRM) is so large as to preclude generation and storage, we must resort to approximations that avoid the large underlying model. State truncation, lumping, decomposition and fluid models constitute the types of approximations that have been utilized. We discuss these four approaches below.

Truncation For many practical systems, the exact number of structural states in a corresponding model might be extremely large, or even infinite. State-space based approaches, then, cannot be applied directly to the model. In many cases, though, the system spends most of the time in a small subset of the entire state space; most states have an extremely small probability.

This is particularly true of highly reliable systems: if a system has K components, and if each component fails with a very small rate (as is normally the case), states with more than a handful of failed components are rarely reached. Indeed, it is common practice in reliability modeling to stop the state-space exploration after $k \ll K$ failures, with the implicit assumption that states with $k + 1$ or more failed components have negligible probability. This is just one example of state truncation.

Fig. 11. A typical model that can be truncated.

Fig. 12. Strict truncation.

Fig. 13. Aggregation truncation.

As an example, consider a K-processor system, where nodes fail and are repaired with rate λ and μ, respectively. We want to compute the expected cumulative computational capacity during the time interval $[0, t)$, $C(t)$, that is, the expected number of non-failed processors as a function of time, integrated between 0 and t. If the state is characterized by the number of working processors, the model corresponds to a birth-death process with state space $\{K, K-1, \ldots 0\}$ (Figure 11). If the processors have different failure and repair behaviors, the identity of the failed processors must be recorded in the state and the size of the state space grows, dramatically, from $K + 1$ to 2^K.

Formally, given a reachability graph $(\mathcal{S}, \mathcal{A})$, a state truncation results in a truncated reachability graph $(\mathcal{S}', \mathcal{A}')$.

If $(\mathcal{S}', \mathcal{A}')$ is a subgraph of $(\mathcal{S}, \mathcal{A})$, the exact state-space exploration algorithm, or the model, is simply modified to ignore certain arcs which lead to states in $\mathcal{S} \setminus \mathcal{S}'$. In our example, we can prevent a $k + 1$-th failure in a state which already has k failed components. We call this case "strict truncation" (Figure 12).

Alternatively, $(\mathcal{S}', \mathcal{A}')$ might be composed by a subgraph of $(\mathcal{S}, \mathcal{A})$, augmented with one or more states and arcs. In our example, we might add a new state u (for unknown), and an arc from each state with k failed components to u, corresponding to further failures of the non-failed components. Strictly speaking, this is more an "aggregation", so we call this approach an "aggregation truncation" (Figure 13).

The two approaches often allow us to obtain upper and lower bounds on the measure of interest. In our example, we can solve the two CTMCs of Figures 12 and 13, obtaining two transient probability vectors:

$$\pi^s(t) = [\pi^s_K(t), \ldots \pi^s_{K-k}(t)]$$

and

$$\pi^a(t) = [\pi^a_K(t), \ldots \pi^a_{K-k}(t), \pi^a_u(t)]$$

respectively. If we associate the reward rates

$$\rho^s = [\rho^s_K = K, \ldots \rho^s_{K-k} = K - k]$$

and

$$\rho^a = [\rho^a_K = K, \ldots \rho^a_{K-k} = K - k, \rho^a_u = 0]$$

with the states of the two CTMCs, we obtain the inequalities

$$C^s(t) = \sum_{i \in \{K, \ldots K-k\}} \rho^s_i \pi^s_i \geq C(t) \geq \sum_{i \in \{K, \ldots K-k, u\}} \rho^a_i \pi^a_i \geq= C^a(t)$$

If we are interested in the expected instantaneous computational capacity in steady state, c, that is, the expected number of non-failed processors in the long run, the CTMC in Figure 12 still offers an upper bound, but the one in Figure 13 is of no use, since state u has probability one in steady state, which would simply result in the trivial lower bound 0 for c. In any case, our ability to obtain useful bounds is normally tied to our a priori knowledge of aspects of the CTMC structure and values of the reward rates. In our example, we can prove that $C^s(t)$ is an upper bound on $C(t)$ because we know that

- Removing the set of states $\{K-k-1,\ldots0\}$ does not decrease the probability of any of the states in $\{K,\ldots K-k\}$
- The maximum reward rates of the states in $\{K-k-1,\ldots0\}$ is not larger than the minimum reward rates of the states in $\{K,\ldots K-k\}$.

and we can prove that $C^a(t)$ is a lower bound on $C(t)$ because we know that

- Aggregating the set of states $\{K-k-1,\ldots0\}$ into a single absorbing state u does not increase the probability of any of the states in $\{K,\ldots K-k\}$
- The minimum reward rates of the states in $\{K-k-1,\ldots0\}$ is not smaller than 0, the reward rate of states u.

For steady state analysis, more sophisticated arguments based on [17] can be used [49]. We conclude by observing that simulation is, in a probabilistic sense, a form of automatic truncation, since the most likely states are visited frequently while unlikely states may not be visited at all.

Lumping Most complex systems (models) consist of a large set of systems (submodels), many of them of the same type. The state of the system is then obtained by composing the state of each subsystem. When performing state-space exploration, though, there are simplifications which might lead to a smaller state space while still allowing an exact solution. For example, in our system with K processors, we could model each of them as an independent subsystem which can be in one of two states, *up* or *down*. The entire system can then be viewed as composed of K such subsystems, thus having 2^K states. This approach is wasteful, though, since it is not necessary to distinguish between processors, if they all have the same failure and repair behavior. Rather, we can represent the state of the system as the number of subsystems in each state (*up* or *down*, but, since the total number of processors is known, we can simply remember the number of *up* processors).

This application of lumping [30, 53] is indeed so natural that we used it in conjunction with truncation, without even justifying its adoption. In real systems, though, the reachability graph of a subsystem might be quite complex. The general algorithm to obtain the lumped state space for a system consisting of K independent subsystems can be easily expressed making use of SPNs [13] (see also [29] for an example of use of this algorithm):

1. Generate the reachability graph for a single subsystem. Markings and arcs are labeled with the number of tokens in each place and the name of the corresponding transition, respectively.

2. Transform the reachability graph into a SPN: for each marking i, add a place p_i, initially empty; for each arc from state i labeled by transition t, add a transition t_i with marking-dependent rate equal $\#(p_i)$ times the rate of t_i in marking i for a single subsystem, an input arc from p_i to t_i, and an output arc from t_i to p_j ($\#(p_i)$ is the number of tokens in place p_i).

3. Set the initial marking of the SPN: for each subsystem, if its initial state is i, add a token in p_i. Note that the subsystems can start in a different initial state without affecting the correctness of lumping.

4. Generate the CTMC underlying this SPN.

Figure 14 shows the application of the algorithm to a system composed of K dual-redundant subsystems, where repair is initiated only when both units have failed. Each subsystem is described by a SPN whose reachability graph has four markings. If no lumping is applied, the total number of states is 4^K. The application of our algorithm, instead, results in a SPN with $(K+3)(K+2)(K+1)/6$ states.

In general, if there are K subsystems with N states each, the size of state space with and without lumping is

$$N^K = \underbrace{N \times \cdots \times N}_{K \text{ terms}} \quad \text{vs.} \quad \binom{N+K-1}{K} = \underbrace{\frac{N+K-1}{K} \times \cdots \times \frac{N+1}{2}\frac{N}{1}}_{K \text{ terms}}$$

Each of the K terms in the second case is smaller than N, with the exception of the last one, which is N, so this approach is always guaranteed to reduce the size of the state space. The reduction is particularly sizable when N is small and K is large: for example, when $N = 2$ we have 2^K vs. $K + 1$.

In practice, the submodels have some interaction, so independence does not hold. If the interaction is limited to a "rate dependence" [14] where the transition rates in a subsystem depend on the number of subsystems in certain states, but not on their identity, the algorithm can still be applied: only a different specification of the firing rates for the resulting SPN is needed. In our example, the repairperson could be a shared resource, so the rate of transition *repair* in each subsystem could be $\lambda/f^{1.1}$, where f is the total number of subsystems being repaired, and the exponent 1.1 models the inherent inefficiency due to resource sharing. The rate of transition $repair_{1010}$ in the resulting SPN should then be specified as $\lambda/\#(p_{1010})^{1.1}$, where $\#(p_{1010})$ indicates the number of tokens in p_{1010} or, in other words, f.

Other types of dependence are structural: often, tokens might have to move from a submodel to another portion of the global model. With some care, lumping might still be possible [57].

Composition In this approach, the overall model is composed of a set of submodels. Construction and generation of a large model is avoided and the solution is obtained by interactions among the submodels. Interactions imply exchange of information between the submodels. Reward based performability analysis [44, 63] is an example of composition of reliability and performance models. The

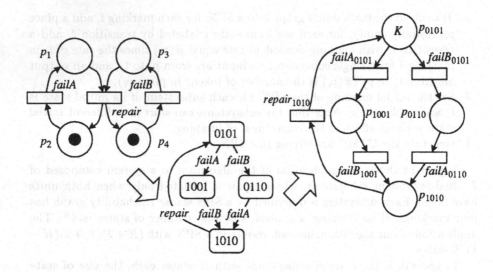

Fig. 14. Lumping of a model.

performance submodel is solved and its results are passed as reward rates to the reliability submodel. In general, quantities such as probability distributions, mean, variance, or numerical values of reliability and availability are exchanged among submodels.

Other examples of composition include flow-equivalent server approximation introduced by Chandy et al [10], behavioral decomposition used in the software tool HARP [21], composition of GSPNs and queuing networks proposed by Balbo et al [3], and hybrid hierarchical composition employed in the software tool SHARPE [56]. These approaches can be classified as *hierarchical composition* techniques. Hierarchical composition approaches differ not only in the way the model is constructed but also in the way the model is solved. The set of submodels can be solved iteratively using a fixed-point iteration scheme (a cyclic dependence exists among the submodels) [12, 14, 47, 61] or in a non-iterative fashion (a strict hierarchy exists among the submodels) [43, 56]. For a unified view of these seemingly different approaches to hierarchical composition, refer to [42].

Fluid Models As the number of tokens in a place or the number of jobs in a queue becomes large, the size of the underlying CTMC grows. It may be possible to approximate the number of tokens in the place, or the number of jobs in the queue, as a non-negative real number. It is then possible to write the differential equations for the dynamic behavior of the model and, in some cases, provide solution. Mitra has developed models along these lines [46]. More recently, Kulkarni and Trivedi have proposed fluid stochastic Petri nets (FSPNs) [33].

5.2 Stiffness

CTMC stiffness is a computational problem which adversely affects the stability, accuracy, and efficiency of a numerical solution method unless that method has been specially designed to handle it. CTMC stiffness is caused by extreme disparity between transition rates. In a reliability model, repair rates could be 10^6 times the failure rates. In a monolithic performability model, the job arrival rates could be 10^9 times the component failure rates. In this section, we discuss how stiffness can be overcome. To begin with, we describe how the extreme disparity between transition rates translates into a computational problem for numerical solution methods.

Let us consider the linear system of differential equations in Equation 2. This system is considered stiff if the solution has components whose rates of change (decay or gain) differ greatly. The rate of change of each solution component is governed by the magnitude of an eigenvalue of the generator matrix $\mathbf{Q}$. This system is considered stiff if for $i = 2, ..., m$, $Re(\lambda_i) < 0$ and

$$\max_i |Re(\lambda_i)| >> \min_i |Re(\lambda_i)| \, ,$$

where λ_i are the eigenvalues of $\mathbf{Q}$. The rate of change of a solution component is defined relative to the solution interval, hence Miranker [45] gave the following definition: "a system of differential equations is said to be stiff in the interval $[0, t)$ if there exists a solution component of the system which has variation in that interval that is large compared to $1/t$". However, the CTMC attains numerical steady-state at some finite time t_{ss}: within the specified accuracy (or error tolerance) the state probability vector does not change with increase in time. Hence we may redefine stiffness: "the system of differential equations in Equation 2 is said to be stiff in the interval $[0, t)$ if there exists a solution component of the system which has variation in that interval that is large compared to $1/\min\{t, t_{ss}\}$. The large difference in transition rates of the CTMC approximately translates into large difference in magnitude of the eigenvalues of the generator matrix.

Stiffness could cause numerical instability and make the solution methods inefficient if the methods are not designed to handle stiffness. Like largeness, two basic approaches to overcome stiffness are: stiffness avoidance or stiffness tolerance.

Stiffness Avoidance According to this approach, stiffness is eliminated from a model by applying some approximation scheme. This results in a set of non-stiff models which are then solved to obtain the overall solution. Bobbio and Trivedi [8] have designed one such technique based on aggregation. Most of these approaches avoid largeness as well, since some kind of model decomposition or aggregation is involved.

Stiffness Tolerance Special solution methods that are designed to handle stiffness are used in this approach. The two most commonly used methods for transient analysis of CTMCs are uniformization and numerical ODE solution methods. It has been shown [54, 40] that uniformization is inefficient for stiff CTMCs. A modified implementation of uniformization which incorporates steady-state detection of the underlying discrete-time Markov chain (DTMC) [50] was shown to be more efficient than the standard implementation when the solution interval was larger than t_{ss}. However, uniformization remains much more inefficient than L-stable ODE methods [38]. L-stable ODE methods [34] are recommended for stiff CTMCs. Among these, second-order TR-BDF2 [54] is efficient for low accuracy requirements and third order implicit Runge-Kutta method [40] is efficient for high accuracy requirements. Recently, more efficient methods based on stiffness detection [37] have been proposed.

5.3 Non-exponential distributions

Phase Approximations The basic methodology of phase approximations is to replace a non-exponential distribution in a model by a set of states and transitions between those states such that the holding time in each state is exponentially distributed. This follows from Cox [18], who showed that any non-exponential probability distribution with rational Laplace Steiltjes transform (LST) can be represented by a series of exponential stages with complex valued transition rates. Each stage is entered with some probability and exited (the process stops) with complementary probability. However, conditions to determine whether the resulting function is a proper cdf or not are not known. To overcome this problem, Neuts [52] restricted the Coxian representation by defining phase type distributions as absorbing-time distributions of a CTMC with at least one absorbing state. Non-exponential distributions can be approximated by phase type distributions (also known as phase approximations when used in this context). Distributions without rational LSTs can be approximated by distributions having rational LSTs, although, arbitrarily close approximations may require a CTMC with a large state space.

A complete approach to phase approximations is discussed in [39]. This approach consists of a few basic steps:

- *Selecting a phase approximation class for a given distribution.* One of the most commonly used phase approximation classes is a mixture of Erlang distributions [9]. It has been used in [26, 39, 60] and good fits to some commonly occurring distributions such as Weibull, deterministic, lognormal, and uniform have been obtained. Schmickler [58] has used mixtures of Erlang distributions to fit empirical functions. Bobbio et al. [6, 4, 5] have used a different kind of acyclic phase approximation and obtained good fits to several distributions.
- *Obtaining the parameters of phase approximations.* Once a suitable phase approximation has been chosen for a given distribution (which may be in

empirical form), the next step is to fit the parameters of this phase approximation. The choices include moment matching, function (cdf or pdf) fitting, maximum likelihood estimation (in case of empirical distributions), or a combination of these [9, 39]. Johnson and Taffe [27, 28] have considered matching the first three moments of mixtures of two Erlang distributions. For more references on this topic, refer to [7].

- *Generation of the overall CTMC.* After the parameters of phase approximations for all the non-exponential distributions have been fitted (or estimated), the overall CTMC is generated. This may require the cross-product of phase approximations [39].

A few software packages implementing this approach have been developed. Phase approximations were used in the SURF package [16], although SURF was intended only for a restricted class of reliability models. Cumani [19] has designed the software package ESP for evaluation of SPNs with phase-type distributed firing times. Phase approximations for a class of non-Markovian models have been implemented in GSHARPE [39]. GSHARPE is a front end for a general purpose performance and reliability modeling toolkit called SHARPE [56]. It accepts a non-Markovian model and converts it into a CTMC in SHARPE syntax after applying phase approximations.

Non-homogeneous CTMCs If transition rates in a CTMC are allowed to be time-dependent, where time is measured from the beginning of system operation, the model becomes a non-homogeneous CTMC. Such models are used in software reliability under the name of NHPP (Non-Homogeneous Poisson Process) [51] and in hardware reliability models of non-repairable systems [22]. Tools such as CARE III and HARP allow component failure distributions to be Weibull using this approach.

Markov regenerative processes (MRGPs) The use of non-homogeneous CTMC allows transition rates to be globally time-dependent while the use of SMPs allow the time dependence to be local (since the entry into the state). Both of these are often inadequate in practice. While, in principle, the phase approximations allow more general time dependence, their practical usefulness is limited by the increased size of the underlying stochastic process, which further exacerbates the largeness problem. MRGPs seem to provide a useful time-dependence that can capture many interesting practical scenarios. The basic idea is that not every state change is required to be a regeneration point. Thus, in a multi-component system with each component having exponential time-to-failure distribution and a generally distributed repair with a single repairperson (FCFS), the underlying stochastic process is a MRGP (but not a SMP or a CTMC). Recent work on this topic can be found in [11, 15].

References

1. M. Ajmone-Marsan, G. Balbo, and G. Conte. *Performance Models of Multiprocessor Systems.* MIT Press, Cambridge, MA, 1986.

2. M. Ajmone-Marsan, G. Conte, and G. Balbo. A class of Generalized Stochastic Petri Nets for the performance evaluation of multiprocessor systems. *ACM Transactions on Computer Systems*, 2(2):93–122, 1984.

3. G. Balbo, S. C. Bruell, and S. Ghanta. Combining queuing networks and GSPN's for the solution of complex models of system behavior. *IEEE Transactions on Computers*, 37:1251–1268, 1988.

4. A. Bobbio and A. Cumani. A Markov approach to wear-out modeling. *Microelectronics and Reliability*, 23(1):113–119, 1983.

5. A. Bobbio and A. Cumani. ML estimation of the parameters of a PH distribution in triangular canonical form. Technical Report R.T. 393, Istituto Elettrotecnico Nazionale Galileo Ferraris, Torino, Italy, 1990.

6. A. Bobbio, A. Cumani, A. Premoli, and O. Saracco. Modeling and identification of non-exponential distributions by homogeneous Markov processes. In *Proc. of the Sixth Advances in Reliability Symposium*, Apr. 1980.

7. A. Bobbio and M. Telek. Parameter estimation of phase type distributions. In *20th European Meeting of Statisticians*, Bath, UK, Sept. 1992.

8. A. Bobbio and K. Trivedi. An aggregation technique for the transient analysis of stiff Markov chains. *IEEE Transactions on Computers*, C-35(9):803–814, Sept. 1986.

9. W. Bux and U. Herzog. The phase concept: approximation of measured data and performance analysis. In K. Chandy and M. Reiser, editors, *Computer Performance*, pp. 23–38. North-Holland, Amsterdam, 1977.

10. K. M. Chandy, U. Herzog, and L. S. Woo. Parametric analysis of queuing networks. *IBM Journal of Research and Development*, 19:43–49, 1975.

11. H. Choi, V. G. Kulkarni, and K. S. Trivedi. Markov Regenerative Stochastic Petri Nets. In *16th IFIP W.G. 7.3 Int'l Sym. on Computer Performance Modelling, Measurement and Evaluation (Performance'93)*, Rome, Italy, Sept. 1993.

12. H. Choi and K. S. Trivedi. Approximate performance models of polling systems using stochastic Petri nets. In *Proc. of IEEE Infocom 92*, pp. 2306–2314, Florence Italy, May 1992.

13. G. Ciardo, A. Blakemore, P. F. Chimento, J. K. Muppala, and K. S. Trivedi. Automated generation and analysis of Markov reward models using Stochastic Reward Nets. In C. Meyer and R. J. Plemmons, editors, *Linear Algebra, Markov Chains, and Queueing Models, IMA Volumes in Mathematics and its Applications*, volume 48. Springer-Verlag, Heidelberg, Germany, 1993.

14. G. Ciardo and K. Trivedi. A decomposition approach for stochastic reward net models. *To appear in Performance Evaluation.*

15. G. Ciardo, R. German, and C. Lindemann. A characterization of the stochastic process underlying a stochastic Petri net. In *Proc. of the Fifth Int. Workshop on Petri Nets and Performance Models (PNPM93)*, Toulouse, France, Oct. 1993.

16. A. Costes, J. Doucet, C. Landrault, and J. C. Laprie. SURF: A program for dependability evaluation of complex fault-tolerant computing systems. In *Proc. 11th Intl. Symposium on Fault-Tolerant Computing*, pp. 72–78, 1981.

17. P. Courtois. Computable bounds for conditional steady-state probabilities in large Markov chain and queueing models. *IEEE J. Sel. Areas in Comm.*, SAC-4(6):926–937, 1986.

18. D. Cox. A use of complex probabilities in the theory of stochastic processes. *Proc. of the Cambridge Philosophical Society,* 51:313–319, 1955.

19. A. Cumani. ESP – A package for the evaluation of stochastic Petri nets with phase-type distributed transition times. In *Proc. of International Workshop on Timed Petri Nets,* pp. 144–151, Torino, Italy, July 1985.

20. E. de Souza e Silva and H. R. Gail. Performability analysis of computer systems: from model specification to solution. *Performance Evaluation,* 14:157–196, 1992.

21. J. Dugan, K. Trivedi, M. Smotherman, and R. Geist. The hybrid automated reliability predictor. *AIAA Journal of Guidance, Control and Dynamics,* pp. 319–331, May-June 1986.

22. R. Geist and K. Trivedi. Ultra-high reliability prediction for fault-tolerant computer systems. *IEEE Transactions on Computers,* C-32(12):1118–1127, Dec. 1983.

23. A. Goyal, W. Carter, E. de Souza e Silva, S.S, Lavenberg, and K. Trivedi. The system availability estimator. In *Proc. of IEEE 16th Fault-Tolerant Computing Symposium,* pp. 84–89, July 1986.

24. B. Haverkort and K. Trivedi. Specification and generation of Markov reward models. *Discrete-Event Dynamic Systems: Theory and Applications 3* , pp.219–247, 1993.

25. R. A. Howard. *Dynamic Probabilistic Systems, Vol.II: Semi-Markov and Decision Processes.* John Wiley & Sons, New York, 1971.

26. M. Johnson. Selecting parameters of phase distributions: combining nonlinear programming, heuristics, and Erlang distributions. To appear in ORSA JOC.

27. M. Johnson and M. Taffe. Matching moments to phase distributions: mixtures of Erlang distribution of common order. *Stochastic Models,* 5:711–743, 1989.

28. M. Johnson and M. Taffe. Matching moments to phase distributions: density function shapes. *Stochastic Models,* 6:283–306, 1990.

29. H. Kantz and K. Trivedi. Reliability modeling of MARS system : A case study in the use of different tools and techniques. In *International Workshop on Petri Nets and Performance Models,* Melbourne, Australia, 1991.

30. J. Kemeny, J. Snell, and A. Knapp. *Denumerable Markov Chains.* Springer-Verlag, 1976.

31. W. Kleinoder. Evaluation of task structures for hierarchical multiprocessor. In D. Potier, editor, *Modeling Techniques and Tools for Performance Analysis.* North-Holland, 1985.

32. V. Kulkarni, V. Nicola, R. Smith, and K. Trivedi. Numerical evaluation of performability measures and job completion time in repairable fault-tolerant systems. In *Proc. 16th Intl. Symp. on Fault Tolerant Computing,* Vienna, Austria, July 1986. IEEE.

33. K.S. Trivedi and V. G. Kulkarni, "Fluid Stochastic Petri Nets," *Proc. 14th International Conference on Applications and Theory of Petri Nets,* Chicago, June 1993.

34. J. Lambert. *Numerical Methods for Ordinary Differential Systems.* John Wiley and Sons, 1991.

35. S. Lavenberg. *Computer Performance Modeling Handbook.* Academic Press, 1983.

36. E. D. Lazowska, J. Zahorjan, G. S. Graham, and K. C. Sevcik. *Quantitative System Performance.* Prentice-Hall, Englewood Cliffs, NJ, USA, 1984.

37. M. Malhotra. A computationally efficient technique for transient analysis of repairable Markovian systems. To appear in *Performance Evaluation* subject to revision, 1993.

38. M. Malhotra, J. K. Muppala, and K. S. Trivedi. Stiffness-tolerant methods for transient analysis of stiff Markov chains. Technical Report DUKE-CCSR-92-003, Center for Computer Systems Research, Duke University, 1992.

39. M. Malhotra and A. Reibman. Selecting and implementing phase approximations for semi-Markov models. To appear in *Stochastic Models*, 1993.

40. M. Malhotra and K. Trivedi. Higher-order methods for transient analysis of stiff Markov chains. In *Third international conference on Performance of Distributed Systems and Integrated Communication Networks*, Kyoto, Japan, 1991.

41. M. Malhotra and K. Trivedi. Dependability modeling using Petri-net based models. Technical Report DUKE-CCSR-92-012, Center for Computer Systems Research, Duke University, 1992.

42. M. Malhotra and K. S. Trivedi. A methodology for formal expression of hierarchy in model specification and solution. In *Proceedings of Fifth Intl. Workshop on Petri Nets and Performance Models*, 1993.

43. M. Malhotra and K. S. Trivedi. Reliability analysis of redundant arrays of inexpensive disks. *Journal of Parallel and Distributed Computing*, 17:146–151, Jan. 1993.

44. J. Meyer. On evaluating the performability of degradable computer systems. *IEEE Transactions on Computers*, C-29:720–731, Aug. 1980.

45. W. Miranker. *Numerical Methods for Stiff Equations and Singular Perturbation Problems*. D. Reidel, Dordrecht, Holland, 1981.

46. D. Mitra, "Stochastic Theory of Fluid Models of Multiple Failure-Susceptible Producers and Consumers Coupled by a Buffer," *Advances in Applied Probability*, Vol. 20, pp. 646-676, 1988.

47. I. Mitrani. Fixed-point approximations for distributed systems. In G. Iazeolla, P. J. Courtois, and A. Hordijk, editors, *Mathematical Computer Performance and Reliability*, pp. 245–258. North-Holland, 1984.

48. M. Molloy. Performance analysis using stochastic Petri nets. *IEEE Transactions on Computers*, C-31(9):913–917, Sept. 1982.

49. R. R. Muntz, E. de Souza e Silva, and A. Goyal. Bounding availability of repairable computer systems. *IEEE Transactions on Computers*, C-38(12):1714–1723, Dec. 1989.

50. J. Muppala and K. Trivedi. Numerical transient analysis of finite Markovian queueing systems. In U. Bhat and I. Basawa, editors, *Queueing and Related Models*, pp. 262–284. Oxford University Press, 1992.

51. J. Musa, A. Iannino, and K. Okumoto, *Software Reliability; Measurement, Prediction, Application*, McGraw-Hill, 1987.

52. M. Neuts. *Matrix-Geometric Solutions in Stochastic Models*. Johns Hopkins University Press, Baltimore, MD, 1981.

53. V. Nicola. Lumping in Markov reward processes. In W. Stewart, editor, *Numerical Solution of Markov Chains*, pp. 663–666. Marcel Dekker Inc, New York, 1991.

54. A. Reibman and K. Trivedi. Numerical transient analysis of Markov models. *Computers and Operations Research*, 15(1):19–36, 1988.

55. R. Sahner and K. Trivedi. Performance and reliability analysis using directed acyclic graphs. *IEEE Transactions on Software Engineering*, 14(10):1105–1114, Oct. 1987.

56. R. Sahner and K. Trivedi. A software tool for learning about stochastic models. *IEEE Transactions on Education*, 36(1):56–61, Feb. 1993.

57. W. Sanders and J. Meyer. Reduced base model construction methods for stochastic activity networks. *IEEE Selected Areas of Communications*, pp. 25–36, Jan. 1991.

58. L. Schmickler. MEDA – mixed Erlang distributions as phase-type representation of empirical functions. *Stochastic Models*, 8(1):131–156, Aug. 1992.

59. M. L. Shooman. *Probabilistic Reliability: An Engineering Approach*. McGraw-Hill, New York, 1968.

60. C. Singh, R. Billinton, and S. Lee. The method of stages for non-Markovian models. *IEEE Transactions on Reliability*, R-26(1):135–137, June 1977.

61. L. A. Tomek and K. S. Trivedi. Fixed point iteration in availability modeling. In M. D. Cin and W. Hohl, editors, *Proc. of the 5th International GI/ITG/GMA Conference on Fault-Tolerant Computing Systems*, pp. 229–240, Berlin, Sept. 1991. Springer-Verlag.

62. K. Trivedi. *Probability and Statistics with Reliability, Queuing, and Computer Science Applications*. Prentice-Hall, Englewood-Cliffs, NJ, 1982.

63. K. Trivedi, J. Muppala, S. Woolet, and B. Haverkort. Composite performance and dependability analysis. *Performance Evaluation*, 14:197–215, 1992.

Architectures and Algorithms for Digital Multimedia On-Demand Servers*

P. Venkat Rangan

Multimedia Laboratory
Department of Computer Science and Engineering
University of California at San Diego
La Jolla, CA 92093-0114
E-mail : venkat@cs.ucsd.edu; Phone: (619) 534-5419

Abstract. Future advances in networking coupled with the rapid advances in storage technologies will make it feasible to build multimedia on-demand servers that provide services similar to those of neighborhood videotape rental stores on a metropolitan-area network. A critical requirement in building a multimedia server is the need for guaranteeing continuous playback of media streams. Hence, there are two important questions that need to be addressed in designing a multimedia server: (1) how should media streams be laid out on disk so as to guarantee their continuous retrieval, and (2) how can multiple clients be serviced simultaneously by a multimedia server? In order to address the first question, we propose a constrained block placement policy, in which separations between successive media blocks on disk are bounded so as to guarantee their continuous retrieval at real-time rates. To enable the multimedia server to support multiple clients, we study various policies (such as, round robin and quality proportional) for servicing multiple clients, and propose admission control algorithms for determining whether a new client can be admitted without violating the real-time requirements of any of the clients already being serviced. Finally, we capture the multiplicity of media streams characterizing multimedia objects by defining a multimedia rope abstraction, and describe techniques for their efficient storage on disk, as well as address the problem of servicing multiple rope retrieval requests simultaneously.

1 Introduction

Future advances in networking will make it feasible for computer networks to support digital multimedia transmission. Coupled with the rapid advances in storage technologies, they can be used to build multimedia on-demand services over metropolitan-area networks (such as B-ISDN) that are expected to permeate residential and commercial premises in a manner similar to existing cable TV and telephone networks [12]. A multimedia on-demand server, which we will refer to as a *Multimedia Server* in the rest of this paper, provides services similar to those of a neighborhood videotape rental store. It digitally stores media information such as entertainment movies, educational documentaries, advertisements, etc., on a large array of extremely high-capacity storage

---

* This tutorial is based on work done by the author and his student, Harrick M. Vin, at the UCSD Multimedia Laboratory

devices such as optical or magnetic disks, that are random accessible with a short seek time and are permanently on-line. The multimedia server is connected to *display sites* belonging to clients via a *high-speed network subsystem*. Clients can make a selection of a multimedia object through a variety of indices such as the object's name, and request its retrieval for real-time playback on their display sites. The multimedia server, if it has the necessary resources (such as service time and buffer space), services the client's request by connecting to his/her chosen display site(s), and transmitting the chosen multimedia segment. The retrieval can be interactive, in the sense that clients can stop, pause, resume, and even record and edit the media information if they have permissions to do so. Thus, the multimedia server subsumes the functions of VCRs, videotapes, audio recorders, etc., and can serve varying sizes of clientele: from individual households to entire neighborhoods, and from commercial organizations and educational institutions to national services.

A critical requirement in building a multimedia on-demand service is the need for guaranteeing continuous playback of media streams (since media quanta, such as video frames or audio samples, convey meaning only when presented continuously in time, unlike text in which spatial continuity is sufficient). In order to guarantee continuous playback, (1) the multimedia server must support continuous retrieval from the disk, (2) the network subsystem must guarantee timely delivery of media quanta to the display sites, and (3) the display sites must avoid buffer overruns or starvations. Specifically:

- The multimedia server organizes the storage of media streams in terms of blocks on its disk. In order to guarantee continuous retrieval of a media stream from disk, the multimedia server must constrain the separations between successive media blocks of the media stream so as not to exceed the media blocks' playback durations. Furthermore, servicing multiple clients simultaneously may require that the multimedia server reserve disk access bandwidth for each client prior to rendering the service.
- In order to guarantee timely delivery of media quanta to the display sites, the network subsystem may have to reserve network resources for each client so as to ensure bounds on delay jitter.
- In the absence of variations in playback rates at display sites, ensuring continuous playback at display sites requires that the sites prefetch sufficient number of media quanta, whose total playback duration equals at least the network delay jitter. In the presence of non-deterministic playback rate variations, however, additional mechanisms are essential to enable the multimedia server to detect overruns or starvations of media units at the display sites, and to preventively readjust the transmission rate of media units so as to avoid playback discontinuities.

In this paper, we focus on the first item above, i.e., a multimedia server for supporting continuous retrieval of media streams from disk. The second item, namely the design of a network subsystem for continuous delivery of media quanta has been dealt with by Ferrari and Verma [3]. The last item, i.e., the problem of avoiding overruns and starvations at the display sites in the presence of non-deterministic playback rate variations, has been addressed by Ramanathan and Rangan [7].

Multimedia server designs for guaranteeing continuous retrieval of digital video and audio have, however, remained relatively unexplored. Most of the past work on

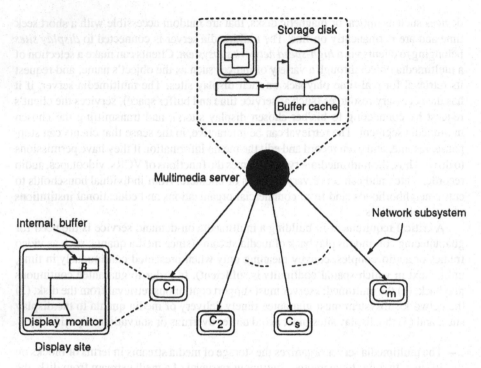

Fig. 1. Configuration of a multimedia on-demand service

multimedia storage systems is restricted to still images and/or audio [1, 5, 6]. Recently, Gammell et al. [4] have described file system designs for supporting audio playback, but they do not address multi-user video on-demand services. A qualitative design for a file system offering video services is presented by the author in [8]. A quantitative model for the design of a file system for storing real-time video and audio streams on disks have been presented by Rangan and Vin [10, 11]. Admission control algorithms for multi-user video on-demand servers are presented by Vin and Rangan [13]. A review of these architectures and algorithms for designing a high-performance, multimedia server capable of servicing a large number of clients is the subject matter of this paper.

First, we address the problem of storing multiple media *strands*, each of which denotes a sequence of continuously recorded video frames or audio samples. We propose a constrained block allocation policy, in which separations between successive media blocks on disk are bounded so as to guarantee their continuous retrieval at real-time rates.

Then, we address the question of servicing multiple clients by a multimedia server. Given the maximum rate of disk data transfer, the multimedia server can only service a limited number of clients simultaneously. We study various policies (such as, round robin and quality proportional) for servicing multiple clients, and propose *admission control algorithms* for determining whether a new client can be admitted without violating the real-time requirements of any of the clients already being serviced. In the quality proportional servicing (QPMS) algorithm proposed in this paper, the number of media blocks of a strand retrieved during each service round is proportional on an average to the the strand's playback rate, and successive number of media blocks retrieved are fine tuned individually to achieve the servicing of an optimal number of clients.

We capture multiplicity of media streams constituting a multimedia object by defining a *multimedia rope* abstraction, which represents a collection of media strands tied together by synchronization information. We propose a merging algorithm for efficient storage and retrieval of media strands constituting a rope, and describe techniques for servicing multiple rope retrieval requests simultaneously.

The rest of this paper is organized as follows: Constrained placement policies are developed in Section 2. The admission control algorithm is described in Section 3. Merged storage and retrieval of ropes are addressed in Section 4. Section 5 presents performance evaluation, and finally, Section 6 concludes the paper.

2 Managing Storage of Digital Multimedia

Digitization of video yields a sequence of frames, and that of audio yields a sequence of samples. We refer to a sequence of continuously recorded video frames or audio samples as a *Strand*. A multimedia server must divide video and audio strands into blocks while storing them on a disk. Continuous playback of media strands requires that the time for retrieving a media block of a strand from disk does not exceed the media block's playback duration.

Most existing storage server architectures employ unconstrained placement of blocks on disk. In such storage servers, reserving computational cycles to meet real-time requirements is not sufficient to support continuous retrieval of media strands. This is because, separations between blocks of a strand may not be constrained enough to guarantee bounds on seek and rotational latencies incurred while accessing successive blocks of the strand. Contiguous placement of media blocks, on the other hand, guarantees that successive blocks can be retrieved without incurring any seek or rotational latency. However, contiguous placement of media blocks is fraught with inherent problems of fragmentation, and can entail enormous copying overheads during insertions and deletions.

Constrained block placement maintains the access time of media blocks within the real-time playback requirements of strands by bounding the separation between successive media blocks on disk. Even the projected speeds of future fast disk configurations are not sufficient to ensure that unconstrained separations between blocks lie within the requirements of high performance video applications. Hence, constrained block placement is not an artifact of today's storage performance, but a fundamental problem that is not likely to be obviated by the availability of faster storage devices in the near future.

There are two questions that need to be answered in constrained placement of media blocks on disk: (1) What should the size of the blocks (i.e. the *granularity*) be? and (2) What should the separation between successive blocks (i.e. the *scattering*) of a strand be? Together, they define the *storage pattern* of a media strand (see Figure 2). Whereas granularity can be determined using the available buffer space at display sites, upper and lower bounds on scattering can be derived using the requirements of continuous playback, and maximizing the data transfer rate, respectively. In this section, we determine these parameters for digital video (which is the most demanding medium with respect to performance and storage space requirements); the analysis for audio can be carried out in a similar manner.

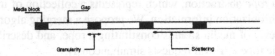

Fig. 2. Storage pattern of a media strand

2.1 Determining Granularity and Scattering

During playback, media blocks are transmitted by a multimedia server to display sites belonging to clients. Consequently, the sizes of internal buffers available at the display sites can be used to determine granularity. For instance, if internal buffers available at display sites can store multiple video frames (say f), then the buffers can be partitioned into two sets (each capable of holding $f/2$ frames): one set to hold the blocks being transmitted by the multimedia server, and another set to hold the blocks being displayed. Hence, each media block may contain $f/2$ frames, yielding $\eta_{vs} = f/2$.

Symbol	Explanation	display unit
$\mathcal{R}_{vp}$	Video playback rate	frames/sec
$\mathcal{R}_{dr}$	Disk data transfer rate	bits/sec
η_{vs}	Granularity of video storage	frames
s_{vf}	Size of a video frame	bits/frame
l_{ds}^{l}	Lower bound on scattering	sec
l_{ds}^{u}	Upper bound on scattering	sec

Table 1. Symbols used in this paper

The guiding factor in determining the upper bound on scattering is the requirement of continuous playback. Whereas playback durations of media blocks of a strand depend on the playback rate of the strand, the time for retrieving a sequence of blocks is a function of their placement on disk. Table 1 defines the symbols used for the parameters governing continuity requirements, using which, it can be seen that the playback duration of a media block is given by $\frac{\eta_{vs}}{\mathcal{R}_{vp}}$. Continuous playback at the media playback rate requires that the time to access each media block from disk (given by $l_{ds}^{u} + \frac{\eta_{vs} * s_{vf}}{\mathcal{R}_{dr}}$) be bounded by its playback duration, yielding:

$$l_{ds}^{u} + \frac{\eta_{vs} * s_{vf}}{\mathcal{R}_{dr}} \leq \frac{\eta_{vs}}{\mathcal{R}_{vp}} \tag{1}$$

which we refer to as the *continuity equation*. Thus, having determined the granularity, the upper bound on scattering l_{ds}^u can be determined by direct substitution in the continuity equation.

Even though bounding the separation between successive media blocks so as not to exceed l_{ds}^u ensures continuous retrieval of media strands, the value of l_{ds}^u derived from the continuity equation may, in general, be significantly larger than the time to read a media block from disk (namely, $\frac{\eta_{gs} * s_{vl}}{\mathcal{R}_{dr}}$). Hence, if a placement policy is based solely on l_{ds}^u, then only a small fraction of the time required to access a media block may be spent in reading its contents from disk, thereby yielding low data transfer rates. In order to maximize the data transfer rate, it is essential that media blocks be placed on disk in a *rotationally optimal* manner. The rotationally optimal separation between media blocks depends on the characteristics of the multimedia server (such as, the delay incurred in initiating a new disk block access after having completed a previous request). If the separation between successive media blocks on disk is smaller than rotationally optimal separation, then while accessing each pair of successive media blocks, the disk head may go past the location on disk containing the next media block after having retrieved the previous media block, before the next read operation read can be initiated. Consequently, maximum rotational latency may be incurred in accessing the next media block. Thus, rotationally optimal separation defines a lower bound on scattering between successive media blocks, and is denoted by l_{ds}^l.

2.2 Constrained Placement of Media Strands

Consider the problem of placing a media strand on disk. Assume that the storage space of the disk is divided into tracks, each track is subdivided into several disk blocks, and accessing a disk block requires positioning the disk head on the track containing the disk block (thereby incurring seek latency), and then waiting for the block to rotate under the disk head (thereby incurring rotational latency). The seek time is assumed to vary linearly with the seek distance (expressed in terms of number of tracks), and the maximum rotational latency is assumed to be bounded by l_{rot}^{max}. The goal of the constrained placement algorithm is to allocate disk blocks to media blocks such that the separation between successive media blocks on disk conforms to the bounds on scattering.

Specifically, given that a media block B_i of a strand S, with bounds on scattering $[l_{ds}^l, l_{ds}^u]$, is placed in disk block d on track t, the algorithm determines disk block d_{new} on track t_{new} for storing media block B_{i+1} of strand S, such that the seek and rotational latencies incurred while moving the disk head from media block B_i to B_{i+1} is within $[l_{ds}^l, l_{ds}^u]$. Once a disk head is positioned on track t_{new}, since any block on that track can be retrieved within time l_{rot}^{max}, the feasibility of storing media block B_{i+1} on track t_{new} depends on $(l_{ds}^l - l_{seek})$ and $(l_{ds}^u - l_{seek})$, where l_{seek} denotes the time to seek from track t to t_{new}. We refer to $(l_{ds}^l - l_{seek})$ and $(l_{ds}^u - l_{seek})$ as the *residual lag time* (r_{lag}) and *residual slack time* (r_{slack}), respectively. Clearly, if $r_{slack}, r_{lag} > l_{rot}^{max}$ or if $r_{slack}, r_{lag} < 0$, then it is not possible to place block B_{i+1} on track t_{new}. In all other cases, the disk blocks on track t_{new} can be partitioned into feasible and infeasible sets such that allocating any disk block from the feasible set guarantees that the separation between media blocks B_i and B_{i+1} is within $[l_{ds}^l, l_{ds}^u]$. None of the blocks from the infeasible set can be allocated to B_{i+1}, and hence, remain available for allocation to future media blocks. Thus, given the disk characteristics (namely, a, b, and l_{rot}^{max}), as well as the strand characteristics (namely, l_{ds}^l and l_{ds}^u), the constrained placement algorithm determines a track and a disk block within that track where media block B_{i+1} can be stored.

A *strict* placement algorithm guarantees that the separation between each pair of successive media blocks is within $[l_{ds}^l, l_{ds}^u]$ (i.e., $r_{lag} < 0$ and $r_{slack} > 0$). On the contrary, an *adaptive* placement algorithm may accommodate occasional violations of the bounds on scattering (yielding $r_{lag} > 0$ or $r_{slack} < 0$), as long as the average separation between successive media blocks over a finite window of blocks is within $[l_{ds}^l, l_{ds}^u]$. Whereas strict placement of a media strand on disk permits its playback to be initiated from an arbitrary block without any read-ahead, an adaptive placement may require a read-ahead equal to the number of media blocks within an averaging window. The adaptive placement algorithm, however, is much more flexible since it may succeed in placing media blocks on disk even when the strict algorithm fails to do so.

3 Servicing Multiple Clients Simultaneously

Till now, we have investigated techniques for placing a media strand on disk so as to guarantee its continuous retrieval in isolation. However, in practice, a multimedia server has to process requests from several clients simultaneously. In the best scenario, all the clients may request the retrieval of the same media strand, in which case, the multimedia server needs only to retrieve the strand once from the disk and then multicast it to all the clients. However, more often than not, different clients may request the retrieval of different strands; and even when the same strand is being requested by multiple clients (such as a popular movie), there may be phase shifts among their requests (e.g., each client viewing a different part of the movie at the same time). A simple mechanism to guarantee that the real-time requirements of none of the clients are violated is to dedicate a disk head to each client, which, however, limits the total number of clients to the number of disk heads. On the other hand, if the data transfer rate of the disk is higher than the requirements of a single client, then the number of clients that can be serviced simultaneously can be significantly increased by multiplexing a disk head among several clients. However, given the maximum rate of disk data transfer, the multimedia server can only service a limited number of clients. Hence, a multimedia server must employ admission control algorithms to decide whether a new client can be admitted without violating the continuity requirements of any of the clients already being serviced.

3.1 Formulating the Admission Control Problem

Continuous playback of a media strand involves a sequence of periodic tasks with deadlines, where tasks correspond to retrievals of media blocks from disk, and deadlines correspond to the scheduled playback times of media blocks. Thus, servicing multiple strand retrieval requests requires the derivation of a real-time schedule, for which the complexity of the best known algorithms show quadratic dependence on the number of tasks. Since strands usually consist of a large number of media blocks (e.g., if each media block contains one video frame, then a five minute clip of a HDTV video strand recorded at 60 frames/s contains 18000 blocks), the number of tasks can be very large. Hence, direct application of traditional real-time scheduling techniques is out of question.

Consider a multimedia server that is required to concurrently service requests for strands $S_1, S_2, ..., S_n$. Since each request is periodic, the multimedia server can service them by proceeding in *rounds*. Suppose that, during each round, the multimedia server retrieves a sequence of k_1 media blocks of strand S_1, and k_2 media blocks of strand S_2, ..., and k_n media blocks of strand S_n. The total time required to complete the round should not exceed the minimum of the playback durations of $k_1, k_2, ...,$ or k_n blocks. Whereas the playback duration of a sequence of media blocks of a strand is a function of the playback rate of that strand, the retrieval rate of media blocks is a function of their placement on disk. Thus, the policies for servicing multiple clients can be classified into two main categories: *deadline based* and *placement based*. Whereas the former retrieves media blocks based on the earliest deadline first scheduling policy, the latter retrieves media blocks from disk so as to minimize the total seek and rotational latencies incurred during retrieval. Servicing policies can be applied either to the media blocks within a strand (yielding a *local schedule*) or the global pool of media blocks from all the strands (yielding a *global schedule*). Clearly, when servicing policies are applied among media blocks within a strand, the multimedia server has to employ ordering techniques (such as, round robin ordering) to switch from one strand to next during each round. We will now formulate the problem of servicing multiple strand retrieval requests assuming a deadline based servicing policy for deriving local schedules and round robin ordering of strands, and describe an admission control algorithm which a multimedia server can employ to decide whether a new client request can be admitted without violating the real-time requirements of the clients already being serviced.

Let us suppose that a multimedia server is servicing n client, each retrieving a different media strand (say, $S_1, S_2, ..., S_n$, respectively). Let $\eta_{vs}^1, \eta_{vs}^2, ..., \eta_{vs}^n$ denote the granularities of the n strands being retrieved, $l_{ds}^1, l_{ds}^2, ..., l_{ds}^n$ denote the upper bounds on scattering, and $\mathcal{R}_{vp}^1, \mathcal{R}_{vp}^2, ..., \mathcal{R}_{vp}^n$ their playback rates. Assuming round-robin ordering of strands, the multimedia server retrieves a finite number of media blocks k_i of each strand S_i, $i \in [1, n]$ in accordance with the earliest deadline first policy, before switching to the next strand. Whereas the rate of transfer of successive blocks of a strand is governed by its granularity and scattering, switching from one strand to another may entail an overhead of up to the maximum seek and rotational latencies (since the layout does not constrain the relative positions of two different strands). The continuity requirement for each strand can be satisfied if and only if the service time per round does not exceed the minimum of the playback durations of $k_1, k_2, ...,$ or k_n blocks. That is,

$$n * (l_{seek}^{max} + l_{rot}^{max}) + \sum_{i=1}^{n} \sum_{j=1}^{k_i-1} \left(l_{ds}^i + \frac{\eta_{vs}^i * s_{vf}^i}{\mathcal{R}_{dr}} \right) \leq \min_{i \in [1,n]} \left(k_i * \frac{\eta_{vs}^i}{\mathcal{R}_{vp}^i} \right) \quad (2)$$

Clearly, evaluating the validity of Equation (2) for each round, using the precise values of media block sizes and the separation between successive media blocks for each strand, is computationally infeasible. Hence, in order to provide *deterministic* service guarantees to each of the n clients, the values of l_{ds}^i and s_{vf}^i, in Equation (2), $\forall i \in [1, n]$, must be set to their respective maximum values. However, this may be very pessimistic, since constrained block placement algorithm and variable rate compression techniques (such as, JPEG and MPEG) may yield l_{ds} and s_{vf} significantly smaller than their respective maximum values. Consequently, the multimedia server can service a larger number of clients by exploiting the variable reductions in l_{ds} and s_{vf}, and providing *statistical* service guarantees to each of the clients. Specifically, if l_{ds}^i and s_{vf}^i represent random variables characterizing the separation between successive media blocks, and the bit size distribution of frames yielded by compression techniques such as JPEG and MPEG, respectively, then the term

$$\sum_{i=1}^{n} \sum_{j=1}^{k_i-1} \left(l_{ds}^i + \frac{\eta_{vs}^i * s_{vf}^i}{\mathcal{R}_{dr}} \right)$$

in Equation (2) represents the sum of $2 * \sum_{i=1}^{n}(k_i - 1)$ independent random, and can be denoted as a random variable χ. Hence, Equation (2) reduces to:

$$\chi \leq \min_{i \in [1,n]} \left(k_i * \frac{\eta_{vs}^i}{\mathcal{R}_{vp}^i} \right) - n * (l_{seek}^{max} + l_{rot}^{max}) \tag{3}$$

If F_χ is the distribution function of χ, then guaranteeing continuous playback of n video strands with a probability greater than π necessitates that:

$$F_\chi \left(\min_{i \in [1,n]} \left(k_i * \frac{\eta_{vs}^i}{\mathcal{R}_{vp}^i} \right) - n * (l_{seek}^{max} + l_{rot}^{max}) \right) \geq \pi \tag{4}$$

The multimedia server can service all the n clients simultaneously if and only if $k_1, k_2, ..., k_n$ can be determined such that either Equation (2) (in the case of deterministic guarantees) or Equation (4) (in the case of statistical guarantees) is satisfied. Since both of these formulations contain n parameters and only one equation, determination of the values of $k_1, k_2, ..., k_n$ require additional techniques. The simplest technique for the choice of $k_1, k_2, ..., k_n$ is to use the same value for all of them, yielding what is generally referred to as a *round robin servicing algorithm with fixed quanta*. However, this certainly may not be the optimal number of clients, because, whereas the strand with the maximum playback rate will have retrieved exactly the number of media blocks it needs for the duration of a service round, other strands with smaller playback rates will have retrieved more media blocks than they need in each service round (thereby, leading to accumulation of media blocks at display sites). Consequently, by reducing the number of media blocks retrieved per service round for such strands, it may be possible to accommodate more number of clients. We now propose a *quality proportional multi-client servicing algorithm* that allocates values to k_i proportional to the playback rate of the strand S_i, and is guaranteed to yield values of k_i so as to satisfy Equation (2) whenever a solution exists for the given number of clients.

3.2 Quality Proportional Multi-client Servicing

In the *Quality Proportional Multi-client Servicing (QPMS)* algorithm, the number of blocks accessed during each round for each strand is proportional to its playback rate. That is,

$$\forall i \in [1, n]: \quad k_i \propto \mathcal{R}_{vp}^i$$

If k is the proportionality constant, using which, we get, $k_1 = k * \mathcal{R}_{vp}^1$, $k_2 = k * \mathcal{R}_{vp}^2$, ..., $k_n = k * \mathcal{R}_{vp}^n$. Under these conditions, Equation (2) reduces to:

$$n*(l_{seek}^{max}+l_{rot}^{max})+k*\sum_{i=1}^{n}\mathcal{R}_{vp}^i*(l_{ds}^i+\frac{\eta_{vs}^i*s_{vf}^i}{\mathcal{R}_{dr}})-\sum_{i=1}^{n}(l_{ds}^i+\frac{\eta_{vs}^i*s_{vf}^i}{\mathcal{R}_{dr}}) \leq k*\eta_{vs} \quad (5)$$

Given the granularity and scattering parameters for each strand, Equation (5) can be used to determine k, from which, the number of blocks retrieved during each service round can be obtained as: $k_1 = k*\mathcal{R}_{vp}^1$, $k_2 = k*\mathcal{R}_{vp}^2$, ..., $k_n = k*\mathcal{R}_{vp}^n$. It can be shown that this algorithm always yields values of k_i so as to satisfy Equation (2) whenever a solution exists for the given number of clients [13].

Notice, however, that the values of k_i's obtained using the QPMS algorithm may not be integral. Since the display of media strands proceeds in terms of quanta such as frames, if k_i is not an integer, then retrieval of a fraction of a frame cannot be used for display, causing the display to starve until the remaining fraction arrives, possibly in the next service round. Such scenarios can be avoided if k_i's are all integers, techniques for deriving which we now elaborate, starting from the real values yielded by the QPMS algorithm.

Let the values of $\{k_1, k_2, ..., k_n\}$ yielded by the QPMS algorithm be given by: $\forall i \in [1, n]$: $k_i = I_i + F_i$, where I_i and F_i are the integer and the fractional parts of k_i, respectively. If $I = \sum_{i=1}^{n} I_i$ and $F = \sum_{i=1}^{n} F_i$, then $(I + F)$ denotes the average number of blocks that need to be retrieved in each service round. In the technique that we present, the number of blocks of strand S_i retrieves during a service round toggles between $\lfloor k_i \rfloor$ and $\lceil k_i \rceil$, so that on an average, the transfer rate for each strand S_i is k_i blocks/round. Specifically, for each round r, the multimedia server must determine the set $\mathcal{K}^r = \{k_1^r, k_2^r, \cdots k_n^r\}$ of the sequence of number of blocks of the n strands to be retrieved during round r, where k_i^r can equal either $\lfloor k_i \rfloor$ or $\lceil k_i \rceil$. However, in doing so, both the service time and buffer space constraints, that would have been met had k_i blocks been retrieved for every round, must continue to be satisfied. Maintenance of the continuity requirement requires that the cumulative slack time at the multimedia server, which is the sum of the differences between the RHS and the LHS of Equation (2) for each round, must be non-negative so as to ensure that none of the clients are starved during a service round. Similarly, the buffer space constraint requires that the slack buffer space at the multimedia server, which is the difference between the available buffer space and the used buffer space, must be non-negative. To ensure that both the constraints are not violated, the toggling of $\lfloor k_i \rfloor$ to $\lceil k_i \rceil$ for strands must be dynamically staggered. The order of toggling can be determined as follows:

Since during every round, k_i blocks of strand S_i are consumed on an average, during rounds in which $\lfloor k_i \rfloor$ blocks are retrieved, there must be sufficient accumulation of data at display sites belonging to clients to maintain continuity of playback, and the accumulation is resumed during rounds in which $\lceil k_i \rceil$ blocks are retrieved. Furthermore, an initial prefetching of blocks is also necessary to guarantee continuity during the first few rounds (since not all strands S_i can have $\lceil k_i \rceil$ blocks retrieved during the first few rounds). Thus, the accumulation at the end of round R for client i is the sum of differences between k_i^r and k_i during the R rounds plus the prefetched number of blocks

$\mathcal{P}_i$, and is given by:

$$\mathcal{D}_i(R) = \mathcal{P}_i + \sum_{r=1}^{R}(k_i^r - k_i) \tag{6}$$

During a round R, if $\mathcal{D}_i(R) < F_i$, a shortage of blocks would occur during the next round; hence, round R is the *deadline* for accessing $\lceil k_i \rceil$ blocks of strand S_i. During each round, if there is sufficient slack time available to transfer extra blocks, strands are ordered with earliest deadline round first, and $\lceil k_i \rceil$ blocks are retrieved for each such strand S_i until the exhaustion of the slack time. During each service round, if for all the strands, k_i^r is set to I_i, then the multimedia server can retrieve the extra blocks of at least $\lfloor \sum_{i=1}^{n}(k_i - I_i) \rfloor = \lfloor F \rfloor$ strands in the order of earliest occurring deadline first, and whenever sufficient slack time accumulates, retrieve the extra blocks of $\lceil F \rceil$ strands. Such a policy allows the deadline requirements of the maximum number of strands to be satisfied as much in advance as possible, while at the same time limiting the maximum extra buffering needed during each round to $\lceil F \rceil$.

4 From Media Strands to Multimedia Ropes

A multimedia object consists of several media components (such as, audio and video). We refer to a collection of media strands tied together by synchronization information as a *multimedia rope*. Synchronization information among media strands constituting a rope can be expressed by relating the playback intervals of media strands in one of thirteen possible ways [2]: *before, meets, overlaps, during, starts, ends, equals*, plus the inverse relations - except *equals*. In this section, we first describe techniques for efficient storage and retrieval of multimedia ropes on disk, and then address the problem of servicing multiple rope retrieval requests.

4.1 Efficient Storage of Multimedia Ropes

Consider a multimedia rope M consisting of strands $S_1, S_2, ..., $ and S_n. A straightforward approach for storing these strands is to permit each disk block to contain media samples from various strands (i.e., *heterogeneous* blocks). For instance, if S_1 and S_2 denote a video and an audio strand, respectively, then a video frame and corresponding audio samples can be stored in the same disk block. Whereas such a storage scheme affords the advantage that it provides implicit inter-media synchronization, it entails additional processing for combining these media during storage, and for separating them during retrieval.

A better approach is to restrict each disk block to contain exactly one medium (i.e., *homogeneous* blocks). Such a scheme permits the multimedia server to exploit the properties of each medium to independently optimize the storage of each media strand. However, the multimedia server must maintain explicit relationships among the playback intervals of strands so as to ensure their synchronous retrieval.

Using homogeneous blocks, a simple scheme for storing a multimedia rope is to independently layout blocks of each of its constituent strands. However, playback of such a rope may incur significant seek and rotational latencies while concurrently accessing media blocks of its constituent strands. Since media blocks of all the strands constituting a rope may be concurrently available at the time of storage, the multimedia server can minimize the overhead due to seek and the rotational latencies incurred during retrieval, due to switching between strands, by filling up the gaps between media blocks of one strand with media blocks of other strands. We refer to the process of storing media blocks of a strand in the gaps between successive blocks of other strands as *merging*.

Intuitively, the storage of n strands S_1, S_2, ..., S_n can be merged together if the sum of the fractions of space occupied by their media blocks does not exceed 1. Thus, if η_{ms}^1, η_{ms}^2, ..., η_{ms}^n denote the granularities, and l_{ds}^1, l_{ds}^2, ..., l_{ds}^n denote the upper bounds on scattering, for strands S_1, S_2, ..., S_n, respectively, then the condition for merging their storage can be formally stated as:

$$\sum_{i=1}^{n} \left(\frac{\eta_{vs}^i * s_{vf}^i}{\eta_{vs}^i * s_{vf}^i + l_{ds}^i * \mathcal{R}_{dr}} \right) \le 1 \tag{7}$$

where $\eta_{vs}^i * s_{vf}^i$ and $(\eta_{vs}^i * s_{vf}^i + l_{ds}^i * \mathcal{R}_{dr})$ denote the sizes (in terms of bits) of media blocks and storage pattern of strand S_i, respectively.

Suppose that media strands are placed on disk such that chunks of k_1 blocks of S_1, k_2 blocks of S_2, ..., and k_n blocks of S_n follow each other, and the sequence repeats (see Figure 3). Consequently, guaranteeing retrieval of each strand S_i at its playback rate requires that the space occupied by blocks of all the other strands S_j $(j \ne i)$, between two successive chunks of blocks of S_i, does not exceed the total gap space permitted for k_i blocks (present in each chunk) of S_i. That is,

$$\forall \text{ strands } S_i, i \in [1, n]: \sum_{j \in [1,n], j \ne i} k_j * \left(\eta_{vs}^j * s_{vf}^j \right) \le k_i * \left(l_{ds}^i * \mathcal{R}_{dr} \right) \tag{8}$$

Fig. 3. Merged storage of media strands

The values of k_1, k_2, ..., k_n satisfying the above system of n equations define a *merge cycle*. As a solution to the above system of equations, we now propose a *scaled placement policy*, in which the number of consecutive blocks k_i of a strand S_i placed in a merge cycle is inversely scaled by the length of its storage pattern (i.e., $\eta_{vs}^i * s_{vf}^i + l_{ds}^i * \mathcal{R}_{dr}$). That is, $\forall i \in [1, n]$:

$$k_i = \frac{k}{\left(\eta_{vs}^i * s_{vf}^i + l_{ds}^i * \mathcal{R}_{dr} \right)} \tag{9}$$

where, k is a constant. Substituting the values of k_i's obtained from Equation (9), and rearranging the terms of Equation (8), it can be shown that the scaled placement policy is guaranteed to yield a merge cycle whenever the merge condition (Equation (7)) is satisfied [9].

When $k_1, k_2, ..., k_n$ in a merge cycle satisfy Equation (8), for each strand S_i, fetching its k_i blocks within each merge cycle is sufficient to guarantee continuous retrieval for the duration of the merge cycle. Hence, at a display site, up to $2 * k_i$ buffers may be required for strand S_i: one set of k_i buffers to hold the blocks being transferred, and another set to hold the blocks being displayed. In turn, given the bounds on buffering available at display devices (which is in fact the case in most hardware environments), bounds on the values of k_i can be fixed, from which, bounds on the values of k can be determined by Equation (9). Among all such bounds of k, the lowest is chosen as the value of k, from which the tightest values of k_i are recomputed, again by using Equation (9).

Notice, however, that the values of k_i's so obtained may not be integral (unless k is chosen to be an integral multiple of the LCM of the storage pattern lengths, which, of course, can be very large). In order to ensure continuous retrieval of media strands, the values of k_i's must be integral. By using a technique similar to one presented in Section 3.2 for the QPMS algorithm, the integral number of media blocks required to be stored in each merge cycle can be derived by toggling between $\lfloor k_i \rfloor$ and $\lceil k_i \rceil$ for each strand in a staggered manner between successive merge cycles, so that on an average, the number of blocks of strand S_i stored in a merge cycle equals k_i.

4.2 Admission Control Algorithm for Multimedia Ropes

Playback of a multimedia rope may require simultaneous or sequential display of its constituent media strands. Hence, the data transfer requirement of a rope may vary during its playback. The admission control algorithms described in Section 3 have assumed a fixed data transfer requirement for each strand throughout the duration of its playback. In this section, we present a technique for partitioning the playback duration of a rope into intervals, each with fixed data transfer requirements, thereby reducing the problem of servicing a rope retrieval request to a set of problems for servicing multiple strand retrieval requests.

Given the relationship between the playback intervals of media strands, the data transfer requirement of a multimedia rope can be completely characterized by maintaining: (1) the time instants at which the playback of its constituent media strands begin and end during the playback of the rope, and (2) the extent of increase or decrease in the data transfer requirement. Formally, for a multimedia rope M_l, we define *alteration points* (denoted by a_l^i) as the time instants at which the playback of its constituent strands either begin or end. We refer to an ordered set (sorted in the increasing order of time) of alteration points as an *alteration set*, and denote it by $\mathcal{A}_l$. We refer to the time interval between successive pairs of alteration points (namely, $\forall i \in [1, n_l] : [a_l^i, a_l^{i+1}]$ where $n_l = |\mathcal{A}_l|$) as an *alteration interval*. Since each alteration interval may involve simultaneous playback of multiple strands, the data transfer requirement for each alteration interval can be represented as a set of the data transfer requirements of strands (defined by the 4-tuple $\{\eta_{vs}, s_{vf}, l_{ds}, \mathcal{R}_{vp}\}$), and is referred to as the *playback set* (denoted by ψ^i). Thus, the data transfer requirement of a rope M_l can be uniquely represented as a pair $\{\mathcal{A}_l, \Psi_l\}$, where $\mathcal{A}_l$ denotes the alteration set and Ψ_l denotes a sequence of playback sets.

Consider the process of initiating simultaneous playback of multimedia ropes M_1 and M_2. Let the data transfer requirements of ropes M_1 and M_2 be characterized by $\{A_1, \Psi_1\}$ and $\{A_2, \Psi_2\}$, respectively. Let $|A_1| = n_1$ and $|A_2| = n_2$, and let

$$A_1 = \{a_1^1, a_1^2, ..., a_1^{n_1}\}$$

$$A_2 = \{a_2^1, a_2^2, ..., a_2^{n_2}\}$$

Similarly, let

$$\Psi_1 = \{\psi_1^0, \psi_1^1, ..., \psi_1^{n_1-1}, \psi_1^{n_1}\}$$

$$\Psi_2 = \{\psi_2^0, \psi_2^1, ..., \psi_2^{n_2-1}, \psi_2^{n_2}\}$$

where $\psi_1^0 = \psi_1^{n_1} = \psi_2^0 = \psi_2^{n_2} = \emptyset$. If the playback of ropes M_1 and M_2 are initiated simultaneously, then the data transfer requirement will change at each of the alteration points of M_1 and M_2. Consequently, the cumulative alteration set $A = \{a^1, a^2, ..., a^{n_1+n_2}\}$ can be obtained by performing a *merge sort* operation on A_1 and A_2. Furthermore, simultaneous playback of ropes M_1 and M_2 yields at most (n_1+n_2+1) alteration intervals, the playback set ψ^i for each interval can be determined using an *iterative algorithm*:

- If $\exists j_1 \in [1, n_1]$ such that $a^i = a_1^{j_1}$, then

$$\psi^i = (\psi^{i-1} - \psi_1^{j_1-1}) \cup \psi_1^{j_1}$$

- If $\exists j_2 \in [1, n_2]$ such that $a^i = a_2^{j_2}$, then

$$\psi^i = (\psi^{i-1} - \psi_2^{j_2-1}) \cup \psi_2^{j_2}$$

Thus, playback of ropes M_1 and M_2 can be initiated simultaneously if and only if the multimedia server can satisfy the data transfer requirements of each of the cumulative alteration intervals. If, however, the multimedia server is unable to meet the data transfer requirement of any one of the intervals, the earliest time instant at which the playback of M_2 can be initiated, given that the playback of M_1 has already been scheduled, can be determined by delaying the initiation of M_2 by an alteration interval of M_1, and repeating the analysis.

5 Experience and Performance Evaluation

A prototype multimedia server is being implemented at the UCSD Multimedia Laboratory in an environment consisting of multimedia stations connected to a multimedia server through Ethernet and FDDI networks. Each multimedia station consists of a computing workstation, a PC-AT, a video camera, and a TV monitor. The PC-ATs are equipped with digital video processing hardware that can digitize and compress motion video at real-time rates, and audio hardware that can digitize voice at 8 KBytes/sec. The multimedia server is implemented on a 486-PC equipped with multiple gigabytes of storage.

The software architecture of the prototype multimedia server consists of two functional layers: the *Storage Manager* and the *Rope Server* (see Figure 4). The storage manager is responsible for physical storage of strands on disk, and handles determination of granularity and scattering parameters for strands, constrained placement of media blocks on disk, and merged storage of strands constituting a rope. The rope server, on the other hand, handles maintenance of synchronization relationships between strands, and admission control. The rope server also provides facilities for users to create, edit, and retrieve multimedia ropes.

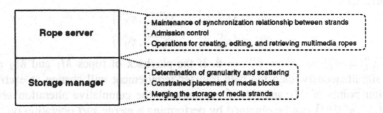

Fig. 4. Software architecture of the prototype multimedia server

We have carried out simulations to evaluate the performance of various media block placement policies. Our simulations have shown that the data transfer bandwidths yielded by both unconstrained and constrained placement policies improve with increase in disk block size. This is because, increasing the disk block size results in a reduction in the number of disk blocks required to store a media strand, thereby reducing the total seek and rotational latency overhead. However, even at large disk block sizes, unconstrained placement policy can achieve only about 3% of the maximum data transfer bandwidth. The performance of the constrained placement policy, on the other hand, depends on the average separation between successive media blocks. As the average separation approaches l_{ds}^{l} (derived using the rotationally optimal separation), the data transfer bandwidth yielded by the constrained placement policy approaches the maximum data transfer bandwidth of the disk.

We have also evaluated the relative performance various deterministic and statistical admission control algorithms. Our analysis demonstrates that providing statistical service guarantees to video strands encoded using JPEG or MPEG compression techniques yields smaller values of k_i's (and hence, imposes smaller buffer space requirement), and can service a larger number of clients simultaneously, as compared to its deterministic counterpart (see Figure 5). These experiments also illustrated the gain in the maximum number of simultaneous clients in the QPMS as compared to the round-robin algorithm. Higher the asymmetry among the playback rates of the client requests, greater is the advantage of employing the QPMS algorithm. When the playback rates of all the clients are the same, the performance of the QPMS algorithm degenerates to that of the round-robin algorithm.

6 Concluding Remarks

Constrained placement of media blocks on disk does not entail the disadvantages of contiguous and unconstrained placement policies, and ensures that the access time of

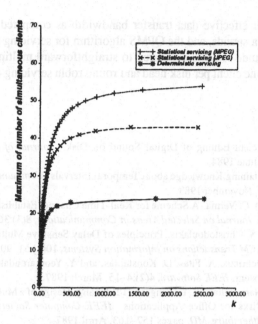

Fig. 5. Relative variations in the number of clients (n) that can be serviced with the length of a service round (in number of media blocks k) for deterministic servicing and statistical servicing (JPEG and MPEG) of video requests.

media blocks within the real-time playback requirements of strands. However, multimedia servers employing constrained placement policy may be required to fill gaps between media blocks of one strand with media blocks of other strands, so as to utilize the storage space efficiently.

Whereas constrained placement of a media strand can only guarantee its continuous retrieval in isolation, a multimedia server, in practice, has to service multiple clients simultaneously. Given the maximum rate of disk data transfer, the multimedia server can only service a limited clients without violating the continuity requirements of any one of them. The admission control algorithm depends on: (1) the real-time requirements imposed by each client, (2) the type of service rendered by the multimedia server (i.e., deterministic or statistical), (3) the servicing policy (namely, deadline based or placement based), and (4) whether the servicing policy is applied to media blocks within a request (yielding a local schedule) or to the global pool of media blocks from all the requests (yielding a global schedule).

We have studied several policies for (such as, round robin and quality proportional) for servicing multiple clients, and have proposed algorithms by which a multimedia server can enforce these policies without violating the real-time retrieval rates of any of the clients. The quality proportional servicing algorithm retrieves media blocks at a rate proportional on an average to the media playback rates of requests, but uses a staggered toggling technique by which successive numbers of retrieved media blocks are fine tuned individually to achieve the servicing of an optimal number of clients. Our performance analysis illustrates that the constrained placement policy achieves significantly higher effective data transfer bandwidth as compared to unconstrained placement of media strands, and the QPMS algorithm for servicing multiple clients is an order of magnitude scalable compared to straightforward multiplexing techniques such as servicing one client per disk head and round robin servicing of clients.

References

1. C. Abbott. Efficient Editing of Digital Sound on Disk. *Journal of Audio Engineering*, 32(6):394–402, June 1984.
2. J.F. Allen. Maintaining Knowledge about Temporal Intervals. *Communications of the ACM*, 26(11):832–843, November 1983.
3. D. Ferrari and D. C. Verma. A Scheme for Real-Time Channel Establishment in Wide-Area Networks. *IEEE Journal on Selected Areas in Communications*, 8(3):368–379, April 1990.
4. J. Gemmell and S. Christodoulakis. Principles of Delay Sensitive Multimedia Data Storage and Retrieval. *ACM Transactions on Information Systems*, 10(1):51–90, 1992.
5. S. Gibbs, D. Tsichritzis, A. Fitas, D. Konstantas, and Y. Yeorgaroudakis. Muse: A Multi-Media Filing System. *IEEE Software*, 4(2):4–15, March 1987.
6. B.C. Ooi, A.D. Narasimhalu, K.Y. Wang, and I.F. Chang. Design of a Multi-Media File Server using Optical Disks for Office Applications. *IEEE Computer Society Office Automation Symposium, Gaithersburg, MD*, pages 157–163, April 1987.
7. Srinivas Ramanathan and P. Venkat Rangan. Adaptive Feedback Techniques for Synchronized Multimedia Retrieval over Integrated Networks. *IEEE/ACM Transactions on Networking*, 1(2):246–260, April 1993.
8. P. Venkat Rangan. Video Conferencing, File Storage, and Management in Multimedia Computer Systems. *Computer Networks and ISDN Systems*, 25:901–919, March 1993.
9. P. Venkat Rangan, Thomas Kaeppner, and Harrick M. Vin. Techniques for Efficient Storage of Digital Video and Audio. In *Proceedings of 1992 Workshop on Multimedia Information Systems (MMIS'92), Tempe, Arizona*, pages 68–85, February 1992.
10. P. Venkat Rangan and Harrick M. Vin. Designing File Systems for Digital Video and Audio. In *Proceedings of the 13th Symposium on Operating Systems Principles (SOSP'91), Operating Systems Review, Vol. 25, No. 5*, pages 81–94, October 1991.
11. P. Venkat Rangan and Harrick M. Vin. Efficient Storage Techniques for Digital Continuous Multimedia. *To appear in the IEEE Transactions on Knowledge and Data Engineering*, August 1993.
12. P. Venkat Rangan, Harrick M. Vin, and Srinivas Ramanathan. Designing an On-Demand Multimedia Service. *IEEE Communications Magazine*, 30(7):56–65, July 1992.
13. Harrick M. Vin and P. Venkat Rangan. Designing a Multi-User HDTV Storage Server. *IEEE Journal on Selected Areas in Communications*, 11(1):153–164, January 1993.

ANALYSIS AND CONTROL OF POLLING SYSTEMS

Uri Yechiali

Department of Statistics & Operations Research, School of Mathematical Sciences,
Sackler Faculty of Exact Sciences, Tel Aviv University, Tel Aviv 69978, Israel
Email: uriy@math.tau.ac.il

Abstract. We present methods for analyzing continuous-time multi-channel queueing systems with Gated, Exhaustive, or Globally-Gated service regimes, and with Cyclic, Hamiltonian or Elevator-type polling mechanisms. We discuss issues of dynamically controlling the server's order of visits to the channels, and derive easily implementable index-type rules that optimize system's performance. Future directions of research are indicated.

Keywords: Multi-channel queueing systems, polling, gated, exhaustive, globally-gated, conservation laws, Hamiltonian tours, Elevator polling, dynamic control.

1 Introduction

Queueing systems consisting of N queues (channels) served by a single server which incurs switch-over periods when moving from one channel to another have been widely studied in the literature and used as a central model for the analysis of a wide variety of applications in the areas of computer networks, telecommunication systems, multiple access protocols, multiplexing schemes in ISDNs, reader-head's movements in a computer's hard disk, flexible manufacturing systems, road traffic control, repair problems and the like. Very often such applications (e.g. Token Ring networks in which N stations attempt to transmit their messages by sharing a single transmission line) are modeled as a polling system where the server visits the channels in a cyclic routine or according to an arbitrary polling table.

In many of these applications, as well as in most polling models, it is customary to control the amount of service given to each queue during the server's visit. Common service policies are the Exhaustive, Gated and Limited regimes. Under the Exhaustive regime, at each visit the server attends the queue until it becomes completely empty, and only then is the server allowed to move on. Under the Gated regime, all (and only) customers (packets, jobs) present when the server starts visiting (polls) the queue are served during the visit, while customers arriving when the queue is attended will be served during the next visit. Under the K_i-Limited service discipline only a limited number of jobs (at most K_i) are served at each server's visit to queue i. There is extensive literature on the theory and applications of these models. Among the first works are Cooper & Murray [1969] and Cooper [1970] who studied the cyclic Exhaustive and Gated regimes with no switchover times. Eisenberg [1972] generalized the results of Cooper & Murray by allowing changeover times and by considering a *general* polling table, i.e., by allowing a general configuration of the server's (periodic) sequence of visits to the channels. Many other authors have investigated various aspects of polling systems, and for a more detailed description the reader is referred to a book [1986] and an update [1990] by Takagi, and to a survey by Levy & Sidi [1990].

Recently, Globally-Gated regimes were proposed by Boxma, Levy & Yechiali [1992], who provided a thorough analysis of the *cyclic* Globally-Gated (GG) scheme. . Under the Globally-Gated regime the server uses the instant of cycle beginning as a reference point of time, and serves in each queue only those jobs that were present there at the cycle-beginning.

A special, yet important, polling mechanism is the so-called Elevator (or scan)-type (cf. Shoham & Yechiali [1992], Altman, Khamisy & Yechiali [1992]): instead of moving cyclically through the channels, the server first visits the queues in one direction, i.e. in the order $1, 2, \ldots, N$ ('up' cycle) and then reverses its orientation and serves the channels in the opposite direction ('down' cycle). Then it changes direction again, and keeps moving in this manner back and forth. This type of service regime is encountered in many applications, e.g. it models a common scheme of addressing a hard disk for writing (or reading) information on (or from) different tracks. Among its advantages is that it saves the return walking time from channel N to channel 1.

All the above models studied *open* systems with external arrivals, where jobs exit the system after service completion. Altman & Yechiali [1992] studied a *closed* system in which the number of jobs is fixed. They analyzed the Gated, Exhaustive, Mixed and Globally-Gated regimes and derived measures for system's performance.

One of the main tools used in the analysis of polling systems is the derivation of a set of multi-dimensional Probability Generating Functions (PGS_i's) of the number of jobs present in the various channels at a polling instant to queue i ($i = 1, 2, \ldots, N$). The common method is to derive PGF_{i+1} in terms of PGF_i and from the set of N (implicit) dependent equations in the unknown PGF_i's one can obtain expressions which allow for *numerical* calculation of the mean queue size or mean waiting time at each queue. The Globally-Gated regime stands out among the various disciplines as it yields a *closed-form* analysis and leads to *explicit* expressions for performance measures, such as mean and second moment of waiting time at each queue, as well as the Laplace-Stieltjes Transform (LST) of the cycle duration.

Most of the work on polling systems has been concentrated on obtaining equilibrium mean-value or approximate results for the various service disciplines. Browne & Yechiali [1989a], [1989b] were the first to obtain *dynamic* control policies for systems under the Exhaustive, Gated or Mixed service regimes. At the beginning of each cycle the server decides on a *new* Hamiltonian tour and visits the channels accordingly. Browne & Yechiali showed that if the objective is to minimize (or maximize) cycle-duration, then an index-type rule applies. Such a rule makes it extremely easy for practical implementations. For the Globally-Gated regime Boxma, Levy & Yechiali [1992] showed that minimizing weighted waiting costs for each cycle *individually*, minimizes the long-run average weighted waiting costs of all customers in the system. A surprising result holds for the Globally-Gated Elevator-type mechanism (Altman, Khamisy & Yechiali [1992]): mean waiting times in *all* channels are the *same*.

In this tutorial we present and discuss (i) *analytical* techniques used in studying polling systems, and (ii) methods derived and applied for *dynamic control* of such systems.

In sections 3 and 4 we present the basic tools for analyzing polling systems with Gated or with Exhaustive service regimes, respectively. Section 5 discusses conservtion laws and optimal visit frequencies. In section 6 we address the issue of dynamic control of polling systems having service regimes with linear growth of work. Secion 7 studies the Globally-Gated regime, and in section 8 the Elevator-type polling mechanism is analyzed. Future directions of research are indicated in section 9.

2   Models and Notation

A polling system is composed of N channels (queues), labeled $1, 2, \ldots, N$, where 'customers' (messages, jobs) arrive at channel i according to some arrival process, usually taken as an independent Poisson process with rate λ_i. There is a single server in the system which moves from channel to channel following a prescribed order ('polling table'), most-commonly cyclic, i.e., visiting the queues in the order $1, 2, , \ldots, N - 1, N, 1, 2, \ldots$. The server stays at a channel for a length of time determined by the service discipline and then moves on to the next channel.

Each job in channel i $(i = 1, 2, \ldots, N)$ carries an independent random service requirement B_i, having distribution function $G_i(\cdot)$, Laplace-Stieltjes Transform $\widetilde{B}_i(\cdot)$, mean b_i, and second moment $b_i^{(2)}$. The queue discipline determines how many jobs are to be served in each channel. The disciplines most often studied are the *Exhaustive, Gated* and *Limited* service regimes. To illustrate these regimes, assume the server arrives to channel i to find m_i jobs (customers) waiting. Under the *Exhaustive* regime, the server must service channel i until it is empty before it is allowed to move on. This amount of time is distributed as the sum of m_i ordinary *busy periods* in an $M/G_i/1$ queue. Under the *Gated* regime, the server 'gates off' those m_i customers and serves only them before moving on to the next channel. As such, the total service time in channel i is distributed as the sum of m_i ordinary *service requirements*. Under *Limited service* regimes, the server must serve either 1 job, at most K_i jobs, or deplete the queue at channel i by 1 (i.e., stay one busy period of $M/G_i/1$ type). According to the recently introduces Globally-Gated service regime, at the *start* of the cycle *all* channels are 'gated off' *simultaneously*, and only customers gated at that instant will be served during the coming cycle.

Typically, the server takes a (random) *non-negligible* amount of time to switch between channels. This time is called 'walking' or 'switchover' period. The switchover duration from channel i to the next is denoted by D_i, with LST $\tilde{D}_i(\cdot)$, mean d_i, and second moment $d_i^{(2)}$. In some applications (e.g. star configuration) the time to move from channel i to channel j $(j \neq i)$ is composed of a switch over time D_i, out of channel i, *plus* a switch-in period to channel j, R_j. In other applications, even for a cyclic polling procedure, the switch-in time R_j is incurred *only* if there is *at least* one message in queue i (see Altman, Blanc, Khamisy & Yechiali [1992]), thus saving the switching time into an empty channel.

We will discuss here only systems where each channel has an *infinite buffer* capacity, assuming *steady state* conditions, and we focus on *continuous-time* models where channel i is an $M/G_i/1$ queue with Poisson arrival rate λ_i and service requirements B_i. The analysis will concentrate on *three main service regimes*: Gated, Exhaustive and Globally-Gated.

3 Analysis of the Gated Regime

Let X_i^j denote the number of jobs present in channel j $(j = 1, 2, \ldots, N)$ when the server arrives at (polls) channel i $(= 1, 2, \ldots, N)$. $\mathbf{X}_i = (X_i^1, X_i^2, \ldots, X_i^N)$ is the state of the system at that instant. Let $A_i(T)$ be the number of Poisson arrivals to channel i during a (random) time interval of length T. Then, for the Gated service regime, the evolution of the state of the system is given by

$$X_{i+1}^j = \begin{cases} X_i^j + A_j\left(\sum_{k=1}^{X_i^i} B_{ik} + D_i\right), & j \neq i \\ A_i\left(\sum_{k=1}^{X_i^i} B_{ik} + D_i\right), & j = i \end{cases} \tag{1}$$

where B_{ik} are all distributed as B_i.

One of the basic tools of analysis is to derive the multidimensional Probability Generating Function (PGF$_i$) of the state of the system at the polling instant to channel i $(i = 1, 2, \ldots, N)$. PGF$_i$ is defined as

$$G_i(\mathbf{z}) = G_i(z_1, z_2, \ldots, z_{i-1}, z_i, z_{i+1}, \ldots, z_N) = E\left[\prod_{j=1}^N z_j^{X_i^j}\right]. \tag{2}$$

Then, for the *Gated* regime, while using (1),

$$G_{i+1}(\mathbf{z}) = E\left[\prod_{j=1}^N z_j^{X_{i+1}^j}\right]$$

$$= E_{\mathbf{X}_i}\left[\prod_{\substack{j=1 \\ j \neq i}}^N z_j^{X_i^j} E\left[\prod_{j=1}^N z_j^{A_j(\sum_{k=1}^{X_i^i} B_{ik})} \bigg| \mathbf{X}_i\right]\right] \cdot E\left[\prod_{j=1}^N z_j^{A_j(D_i)}\right] \tag{3}$$

For a Poisson random variable $A_j(T)$, and with $\tilde{T}(\cdot)$ denoting the Laplace-Stieltjes Transform (LST) of T, we have

$$E[z_j^{A_j(T)}] = E_T[e^{-\lambda_j(1-z_j)T}] = \tilde{T}[\lambda_j(1-z_j)]$$

and

$$E\left[\prod_{j=1}^{N} z_j^{A_j(T)}\right] = \tilde{T}\left[\sum_{j=1}^{N}\lambda_j(1-z_j)\right].$$

Therefore

$$G_{i+1}(\mathbf{z}) = E_{\mathbf{X}_i}\left[\prod_{\substack{j=1 \\ j\neq i}}^{N} z_j^{X_i^j}\left(\tilde{B}_i\left[\sum_{j=1}^{N}\lambda_j(1-z_j)\right]\right)^{X_i^i}\right]\cdot\tilde{D}_i\left[\sum_{j=1}^{N}\lambda_j(1-z_j)\right].$$

Thus, for $i = 1, 2, \ldots, N-1, N$ (where we take $N+1$ as 1)

$$G_{i+1}(\mathbf{z})=G_i\left(z_1, z_2, \ldots, z_{i-1}, \tilde{B}_i\left[\sum_{j=1}^{N}\lambda_j(1-z_j)\right], z_{i+1}, \ldots, z_N\right)\cdot\tilde{D}_i\left[\sum_{j=1}^{N}\lambda_j(1-z_j)\right] \tag{4}$$

Equations (4) define a set of N relations between the various PGFs which are used to derive moments of the variables X_i^j, as follows.

Moments The mean number of messages, $f_i(j) = E(X_i^j)$, present in channel j at a polling instant to channel i is obtained by taking derivatives of the PGFs, where

$$f_i(j) = E(X_i^j) = \left.\frac{\partial G_i(\mathbf{z})}{\partial z_j}\right|_{\mathbf{z}=1} \tag{5}$$

A set N^2 linear equations in $\{f_i(j) : i, j = 1, 2, \ldots, N\}$ determines their values:

$$f_{i+1}(j) = \begin{cases} f_i(j) + \lambda_j b_i f_i(i) + \lambda_j d_i & j \neq i \\ \lambda_i b_i f_i(i) + \lambda_i d_i & j = i \end{cases} \tag{6}$$

Indeed, equations (6) could be obtained *directly* from (1).

Set $\rho_k = \lambda_k b_k$, $\rho = \sum_{k=1}^{N}\rho_k$, $d = \sum_{k=1}^{N}d_k$. Then, the solution of (6) is given by

$$f_i(j) = \begin{cases} \lambda_j\left(\sum_{k=j}^{i-1}\left[\rho_k\left(\frac{d}{1-\rho}\right) + d_k\right]\right) & j \neq i \\ \lambda_i\left(\frac{d}{1-\rho}\right) & j = i \end{cases} \tag{7}$$

The explanation of (7) is the following. It will be shown shortly that the mean cycle time is $E[C] = d/(1-\rho)$. During that time the mean number of arrivals to channel i is $\lambda_i E[C]$. Also, during a cycle the server renders service to channel k for an average length of time $\rho_k E[C]$. Thus, the elapsed time since the last gating instant of channel j ($j \neq i$) until the polling instant of channel i, is

$\sum_{k=j}^{i-1} [\rho_k E[C] + d_k]$. Within that time-interval the mean number of arrivals to channel j is $f_i(j)$, as given by (7).

The second moments of the X_i^j are also derived from the set of PGFs (4). Let

$$f_i(j,k) = E[X_i^j X_i^k] = \frac{\partial^2 G_i(\mathbf{z})}{\partial z_j \, \partial z_k}\bigg|_{\mathbf{z}=1} \quad (i,j,k = 1,2,\ldots,N \text{ not all equal})$$

$$f_i(i,i) = E[X_i^i(X_i^i - 1)]] = \frac{\partial^2 G_i(\mathbf{z})}{\partial z_i^2}\bigg|_{\mathbf{z}=1} \tag{8}$$

Clearly, $\mathrm{Var}[X_i^i] = f_i(i,i) + f_i(i) - \big(f_i(i)\big)^2$.

Taking derivatives, the solution of (8) is given (see, Takagi [1986]) as a set of N^3 linear equations in the N^3 unknowns $\{f_i(j,k)\}$.

Cycle Time The mean cycle time is obtained from the balance equation $E[C] = \rho E[C] + d$. Hence,

$$E[C] = \frac{d}{1-\rho}.$$

The mean sojourn time of the server at channel i is $f_i(i)b_i = \rho_i E[C]$, and the number of jobs served in a cycle is clearly, $\sum_{i=1}^{N} f_i(i) = \big(\sum_{i=1}^{N} \lambda_i\big) E[C]$.

The PGF of L_i and Waiting Times

Consider the probability generating function, $Q_i(z) = E(z^{L_i})$, of the number of customers, L_i, left behind by an arbitrary departing customer from channel i in a polling system with arbitrary service regime. As the distributions of the number of customers in the system at epochs of arrival and epochs of departure are identical, then by the well known PASTA phenomenon (Poisson Arrivals See Time Averages), $Q_i(z)$ also stands for the generating function of the number of customers at channel i in a steady state condition at an arbitrary point of time.

Let T_i be the total number of customers served in channel i during a visit of the server to that channel, and let $L_i(n)$ $(n = 1,2,\ldots,T_i)$, be the sequence of random variables denoting the number of customers that the n-th departing customer from channel i (counting from the moment that the channel was last polled) leaves behind it. Then the PGF of L_i is given by (see, Takagi [1986], p. 78)

$$Q_i(z) = \frac{E\big(\sum_{n=1}^{T_i} z^{L_i(n)}\big)}{E(T_i)}. \tag{9}$$

As $L_i(n) = X_i^i - n + A_i\big(\sum_{k=1}^{n} B_{ik}\big)$, the evaluation of the expression for $Q_i(z)$ becomes

$$Q_i(z) = \frac{1}{E(T_i)} E\left(\sum_{n=1}^{T_i} z^{X_i^i - n + A_i(\sum_{k=1}^{n} B_{ik})}\right) = \frac{1}{E(T_i)} E\left(z^{X_i^i} \sum_{n=1}^{T_i} z^{-n + A_i(\sum_{k=1}^{n} B_{ik})}\right)$$

$$= \frac{1}{E(T_i)} E\left(z^{X_i^i} \sum_{n=1}^{T_i} z^{-n} e^{-\lambda_i (\sum_{k=1}^{n} B_{ik})(1-z)}\right) = \frac{1}{E(T_i)} E\left(z^{X_i^i} \sum_{n=1}^{T_i} \left[\frac{\tilde{B}_i(\lambda_i(1-z))}{z}\right]^n\right)$$

$$= \frac{1}{E(T_i)} E\left(z^{X_i^i} \cdot \frac{\tilde{B}_i(\lambda_i(1-z))}{z} \cdot \frac{1 - \left[\frac{\tilde{B}_i(\lambda_i(1-z))}{z}\right]^{T_i}}{1 - \frac{\tilde{B}_i(\lambda_i(1-z))}{z}}\right)$$

$$= \frac{\tilde{B}_i(\lambda_i(1-z))}{E(T_i)[z - \tilde{B}(\lambda_i(1-z))]} E[z^{X_i^i - T_i}(z^{T_i} - [\tilde{B}_i(\lambda_i(1-z))]^{T_i})] . \qquad (10)$$

Let W_{q_i} denote the *queueing* time of an arbitrary message at queue i, and let $W_i = W_{q_i} + B_i$ denote the sojourn (residence) time of a message in the system. As the messages left behind by a departing message from channel i have *all* arrived during its residence time W_i, we have

$$Q_i(z) = \sum_{k=0}^{\infty} P\left(\begin{matrix} \text{number of messages} \\ \text{at channel } i = k \end{matrix}\right) z^k = \sum_{k=0}^{\infty} z^k \int_0^{\infty} e^{-\lambda_i w} \frac{(\lambda_i w)^k}{k!} dP(W_i \le w)$$

$$= \widetilde{W}_i[\lambda_i(1-z)] = \widetilde{W}_{q_i}[\lambda_i(1-z)] \tilde{B}_i[\lambda_i(1-z)]$$

Hence,

$$\widetilde{W}_{q_i}(s) = \frac{Q_i(1 - s/\lambda_i)}{\tilde{B}_i(s)} \qquad (11)$$

For the Gated regime, $X_i^i = T_i$, and therefore

$$Q_i(z) = \frac{\tilde{B}_i(\lambda_i(1-z))}{E(T_i)[z - \tilde{B}_i(\lambda_i(1-z))]} \left(E[z^{X_i^i}] - E[(\tilde{B}_i(\lambda_i(1-z)))^{X_i^i}]\right) \qquad (12)$$

(see also Takagi [1986], p. 109).

As $E(T_i) = E(X_i^i) = \lambda_i E[C]$, using (11) and (12) leads to

$$E(W_{q_i}) = \frac{E((X_i^i)^2) - E(X_i^i)}{2\lambda_i E(X_i^i)}(1 + \rho_i) = \frac{(1 + \rho_i)f_i(i,i)}{2\lambda_i^2 E[C]} \qquad (13)$$

By Little's law, $E[L_i] = \lambda_i[E(W_{q_i}) + b_i]$.

4 Exhaustive Regime

To derive the PGF of the state of the system at a polling instant to channel $i+1$ we use the law of motion

$$X_{i+1}^j = \begin{cases} X_i^j + A_j\left(\sum_{k=1}^{X_i^i} \Theta_{ik} + D_i\right), & j \ne i \\ A_i(D_i), & j = i \end{cases} \qquad (14)$$

where Θ_i denotes the length of a *regular* busy period in an $M/G_i/1$ queue, and Θ_{ik} are all distributed as Θ_i. Then,

$$G_{i+1}(\mathbf{z}) = E\left[\prod_{j=1}^{N} z_j^{X_{i+1}^j}\right]$$

$$= E_{\mathbf{X}_i}\left[\prod_{\substack{j=1 \\ j\neq i}}^{N} z_j^{X_i^j} \cdot E\left[\prod_{\substack{j=1 \\ j\neq i}}^{N} z_j^{A_j(\sum_{k=1}^{X_i^i}\theta_{ik})}\Big|\mathbf{X}_i\right]\right] \cdot E\left[\prod_{j=1}^{N} z_j^{A_j(D_i)}\right]$$

$$= E_{\mathbf{X}_i}\left[\prod_{\substack{j=1 \\ j\neq i}}^{N} z_j^{X_i^j} \left(\tilde{\theta}_i\left[\sum_{\substack{j=1 \\ j\neq i}}^{N} \lambda_j(1-z_j)\right]\right)^{X_i^i}\right] \tilde{D}_i\left[\sum_{j=1}^{N} \lambda_j(1-z_j)\right]$$

Hence,

$$G_{i+1}(\mathbf{z}){=}G_i\left(z_1, z_2, \ldots, z_{i-1}, \tilde{\theta}_i\left[\sum_{\substack{j=1 \\ j\neq i}}^{N} \lambda_j(1{-}z_j)\right], z_{i+1}, \ldots, z_N\right) \cdot \tilde{D}_i\left[\sum_{j=1}^{N} \lambda_j(1{-}z_j)\right]$$

$$(15)$$

To get the N^2 values of $f_i(j)$ one can differentiate (15) or use directly (14). The result is

$$f_{i+1}(j) = \begin{cases} f_i(j) + \lambda_j E(\Theta_i)f_i(i) + \lambda_j d_i & j \neq i \\ \lambda_j d_i & j = i \end{cases} \qquad (16)$$

where $E(\Theta_i) = b_i/(1 - \rho_i)$ is the mean duration of a regular busy period at channel i.

The solution of (16) is

$$f_i(j) = \begin{cases} \lambda_j\left(\sum_{k=j+1}^{i-1} \rho_k\left(\frac{d}{1-\rho}\right) + \sum_{k=j}^{i-1} d_k\right) & j \neq i \\ \lambda_i(1 - \rho_i)\left(\frac{d}{1-\rho}\right) & j = i \end{cases} \qquad (17)$$

The interpretation of (17) is the following. The mean cycle time is *again* $E[C] = d/(1 - \rho)$, which is derived from the *same* balance equation as for the Gated regime. The fraction of time that the server stays at channel i is ρ_i, hence, during the time interval since the server leaves (an empty) channel i until it arrives there again, the mean number of accumulated messages at i is $\lambda_i(1 - \rho_i)E[C]$. For channel $j \neq i$, the total switchover times from the moment the server last exited the channel until it enters channel i is $\sum_{k=j}^{i-1} d_k$, and the mean time spent in each of the channels $k = j + 1, j + 2, \ldots, i - 1$, is $\rho_k E[C]$. Thus, the expected number of jobs accumulated at channel j when the server polls channel i is given by $\lambda_j\left(\sum_{k=j}^{i-1} d_k + \sum_{k=j+1}^{i-1} \rho_k\left(\frac{d}{1-\rho}\right)\right)$. The PGF of the number of messages at channel i can be obtained by using result (10). For the Exhaustive case, the number of customers served during a visit to channel i is $T_i = X_i^i + A_i\left(\sum_{k=1}^{X_i^i} \Theta_{ik}\right)$, so that $E(T_i) = f_i(i) + \lambda_i f_i(i)E(\Theta_i) = f_i(i)/(1 - \rho_i)$, and by using (17), $E(T_i) = \lambda_i E[C]$.

The PGF of the number of messages at channel i at an arbitrary point of time is given by Takagi [1986], p. 79:

$$Q_i(z) = \frac{1}{\lambda_i E[C]} \cdot \frac{\widetilde{B}_i[\lambda_i(1-z)]}{z - \widetilde{B}_i[\lambda_i(1-z)]} \big[E[Z^{X_i}] - 1\big] \tag{18}$$

The mean number of messages at channel i and the mean queueing times are derived from (18),

$$E[L_i] = \rho_i + \frac{\lambda_i^2 b_i^{(2)}}{2(1-\rho_i)} + \frac{f_i(i,i)}{2\lambda_i(1-\rho_i)E[C]}$$

$$E[W_{q_i}] = \frac{\lambda_i b_i^{(2)}}{2(1-\rho_i)} + \frac{f_i(i,i)}{2\lambda_i^2(1-\rho_i)E[C]}$$

Again, the values of $f_i(i,i)$ have to be calculated numerically by solving a set of N^3 linear equations in the unknowns $f_i(j,k)$ derived (see (8)) by differentiating the PGFs in (15).

Remarks on Computational Methods

Several numerical procedures have been proposed for computing the mean waiting times in polling systems with Gated or with Exhaustive service regimes. The procedure mentioned above of determining the mean delay in various channels by solving a set of N^3 linear equations is called the Buffer Occupancy method. It is of high computational complexity, but can also be applied to solve models with switch-in times or with limited-service regimes. A more efficient procedure is known as the Station Time method (see Ferguson & Aminetzah [1985]). This is an iterative procedure which has been applied to a number of polling systems, but cannot be directly used for closed networks or for open systems with customers' routing. Sarkar & Zangwill [1989] have developed an algorithm for cyclic (Exhaustive or Gated) systems were the mean waiting times are obtained by solving a set of only N linear equations (thus requiring $O(N^3)$ computational steps). Recently, Konhein, Levy & Srinivasan [1993a] introduced a Descendant Set (DS) approach which is based on counting the number of descedants generated in the system by each customer. The method can be applied to variations of Exhaustive or Gated polling systems which are based on *fixed order* of visits, and can also be used to derive second and higher delay moments. It is claimed that the DS is superior to other methods due to its low computational complexity, even though it is based on the buffer occupancy variables. In a further effort to develop efficient computational methods, the same authors [1993b] introduced the Individual Station (IS) technique which, like the DS procedure, allows for the determining of mean waiting time at one or more selected nodes without having to obtain mean waiting times at all channels simultaneously. The IS is superior to the DS for systems with high utilization factor, while the DS would be preferred for systems with very large N.

5 Conservation Laws and Visit Frequencies

In an arbitrary single-server system (with single or multiple queues) when no work is generated or lost within the system, the amount of work present does not depend on the order of service – and hence equals the amount of work in the 'corresponding' system with a single queue and FCFS service discipline. This 'principle' of work conservation yields useful expression which we now discuss. Suppose that no switching times are incurred in our polling system, and assume cyclic or any order of the server's visits. Then it is well known (see, Kleinrock [1975]) that the expected amount of work in the system is constant, i.e.,

$$\sum_{i=1}^{N} b_i E[L_i] = \sum_{i=1}^{N} \rho_i E(W_i) = \rho \frac{\sum_{i=1}^{N} \lambda_i b_i^{(2)}}{2(1-\rho)} \equiv \overline{W} . \tag{19}$$

When switching times are incurred, Boxma & Groenendijk [1987] and Boxma [1989] have derived the so called 'pseudo-conservation laws' and showed that for an arbitrary polling system with *mixed* channels

$$\sum_{i=1}^{N} \rho_i E(W_i) = \overline{W} + \rho \frac{d^{(2)}}{2d} + \frac{d}{2(1-\rho)} \left[\rho^2 - \sum_{i=1}^{N} \rho_i^2 \right] + \sum_{i=1}^{N} EM_i^{(1)} \tag{20}$$

where $EM_i^{(1)}$ is the expected *unfinished* work at the ith queue at an (arbitrary) instant of departure of the server from that queue. Result (20) holds for any service regime, and $EM_i^{(1)}$ depends *only* on the service discipline in channel i. For the Exhaustive service regime $EM_i^{(1)} = 0$ for every i, so that

$$\sum_{i=1}^{N} \rho_i E(W_i) = \overline{W} + \rho \frac{d^{(2)}}{2d} + \frac{d}{2(1-\rho)} \left[\rho^2 - \sum_{i=1}^{N} \rho_i \right] . \tag{21}$$

For the Gated regime, we use (7) and write

$$EM_i^{(1)} = [(f_i(i)b_i)\lambda_i] b_i = \rho_i^2 \left(\frac{d}{1-\rho} \right) .$$

Hence, for the Gated,

$$\sum_{i=1}^{N} \rho_i E(W_i) = \overline{W} + \rho \frac{d^{(2)}}{2d} + \frac{d}{2(1-\rho)} \left[\rho^2 + \sum_{i=1}^{N} \rho_i^2 \right] . \tag{22}$$

It follows that for the *same* set of parameters, whenever switchover times are incurred the mean amount of work in the system under the Exhaustive regime is *smaller* then that under the Gated discipline. Furthermore, expressions (21) and (22) enabled Boxma, Levy & Weststrate (see, Boxma [1991]) to develop 'good' visit frequencies of the server to the various channels so as to construct a polling table that will *reduce* the value of the expected amount of work in the system, as expressed in (20). For the Exhaustive and for the Gated regimes the visit frequencies v_i^{exh}, and v_i^{gated} are given by

$$v_i^{\text{exh}} = \frac{\sqrt{\rho_i(1-\rho_i)/d_i}}{\sum_{j=1}^N \sqrt{\rho_j(1-\rho_j)/d_j}}$$

$$v_i^{\text{gated}} = \frac{\sqrt{\rho_i(1+\rho_i)/d_i}}{\sum_{j=1}^N \sqrt{\rho_j(1+\rho_j)/d_j}}$$

For example, in a 3-channel case for which the calculated visit frequencies are 0.52, 0.32 and 0.16, the approximate visit frequencies are 1/2, 1/3 and 1/6, respectively, such that a (periodic) polling table of size 6 is constructed with the order of visits [1,2,1,3,1,2].

Another approach in the attempt to control and otimize the visit frequencies of the server to the various channels is the Cyclic Bernoulli Polling (CBP) introduced by Altman & Yechiali [1993]. The server moves *cyclically* among the N channels where *change-over* times between stations are composed of two parts: *walking* times required to 'move' from one channel to another and *switch-in* times that are incurred *only* when the server actually enters a station to render service. Upon arrival to channel i the server switches in with probability p_i, or moves on to the next channel (with probability $1 - p_i$) without serving any customer. Altman & Yechiali analyzed the Gated and Exhaustive regimes and defined a mathematical program to find the *optimal* values of the switch-in probabilites $\{p_i\}_{i=1}^N$ so as to *minimize* the expected amount of unfinished work in the system. Any CBP scheme for which the optimal p_i's are not equal to 1 yields a *smaller* amount of expected unfinished work in the system than that in the standard cyclic procedure with equivalent parameters. They showed that even in the case of a *single queue*, it is *not always* true that $p_1 = 1$ is the best strategy, and derived conditions under which it is optimal to have $p_1 < 1$.

6 Dynamic Control of Server's Visits: Hamiltonian Tours

A basic question that arises when planning efficient polling systems concerns the order of visits performed by the server. For *static* order one can think of a 'good' polling table that optimizes some measure of effectiveness. Steps in this direction were taken, as mentioned in section 5, by various authors. However, a more reaching goal is to control the system *dynamically*, so that the server will modify its order of visits in response to the stochastic evolution of the system. In other words, the general control problem facing the server when it exits a specific channel, is *"which of the channels to visit next?"*. In trying to solve this problem Browne & Yechiali [1989a], [1989b] developed and formulated semi-Markov Decision Processes (SMDP) for the Gated and for the Exhaustive regimes. They derived a set of optimality equations where the objective is to minimize mean weighted waiting costs. However, these equations are non-tractable, so that one should look for alternative methods. An appealing approach is to look for semi-dynamic control schemes. The idea is to dispatch the server to perform Hamiltonian tours, each tour different from its previous one, depending on the state of the system at the *beginning* of the tour, so as to optimize some measure of effectiveness.

Specifically, suppose that at the beginning of a cycle the state of the system is $(n_1, n_2, \ldots, n_N)$, where n_i is the number of jobs waiting in channel i ($1 \leq i \leq N$). Assume for the moment that switching times between channels are negligible. The objective is to choose a path (Hamiltonian tour) through the queues so as to *minimize* the expected time of traversing this path. It was shown by Browne & Yechiali [1989a], [1989b] that for *both* service disciplines – the fully Gated and the fully Exhaustive – this measure of effectiveness is *minimized* if the channels are ordered by *increasing* values of the *index* n_i/λ_i. This is a *surprising* result, as the index n_i/λ_i *does not include the service times* at the various channels. It is surprising as well that the *same* index-rule holds for *both* service regimes (although, obviously, the *duration* of a Gated-type cycle that starts with $(n_1, n_2, \ldots, n_N)$ differs from its Exhaustive counter-part starting with the same system-state).

The dynamics of the control are such that at the *end* of each Hamiltonian cycle a *new* system-state is observed, say $(n'_1, n'_2, \ldots, n'_N)$, and the server follows a *new* path governed by a new order: increasing values of n'_i/λ_i, etc. This is an extremely simple rule which can be directly implemented. Moreover, suppose that, for one reason or another, there are systems where the objective is to *maximize* the duration of each cycle. Then, the index-rule that determines the order of visits to the channels is simply *reversed*: the server completes a Hamiltonian tour determined by a *decreasing* order of n_i/λ_i.

To understand the above surprising result Browne & Yechiali [1990] studies a *general* scheduling problem with a *linear growth of work*, as follows.

Consider a single-processor system with N jobs waiting to be performed sequentially. Let a_i be the *initial* (expected) processing time requirement of job i ($i = 1, 2, \ldots, N$), called the 'core'. If job i is delayed and is started at time t, then its processing requirement *grows linearly* with the delay to

$$Y_i(t) = a_i + \alpha_i t$$

where α_i is the *growth rate* of work requirement by job i. Consider the processing order $\pi_0 = (1, 2, \ldots, N)$, and let Y_i denote the *actual* processing length of job i under π_0. Let $S_k = \sum_{i=1}^{k} Y_i$ be the completion time of job k under π_0 ($S_0 = 0$). Then $Y_j = a_j + \alpha_j S_{j-1}$. By adding S_{j-1} to both sides we obtain a set of difference equations

$$S_j - (1 + \alpha_j) S_{j-1} = a_j \qquad (j = 1, 2, \ldots, N) \tag{23}$$

The solution of (23) is

$$S_j = \sum_{i=1}^{j} a_i \prod_{r=i+1}^{j} (1 + \alpha_r) \qquad (j = 1, 2, \ldots, N) \tag{24}$$

so that the *makespan* is $S_N = S_N(\pi_0) = \sum_{i=1}^{N} a_i \prod_{r=i+1}^{N}(1 + \alpha_r)$.

The objective is to find a visit order π that *minimizes the makespan* $S_N(\pi)$ over all $n!$ possible permutations π.

Consider now the processing sequence $\pi_1 = (1, 2, \ldots, j - 1, j + 1, j, j + 2, \ldots, N)$, where the order of jobs j and $j + 1$ is interchanged. The corresponding makespan is $S_N(\pi_1)$. Then, it is easy to show that $S_N(\pi_0) < S_N(\pi_1)$ iff $a_j/\alpha_j < a_{j+1}/\alpha_{j+1}$. That is, the makespan is *minimized* (maximized) if we process the jobs in an increasing (decreasing) order of the ratio index a_i/α_i, i.e., 'core' divided by 'growth rate'.

Consider again the Gated regime. If $(n_1, n_2, \ldots, n_N)$ is the state of the system at the *start* of the Hamiltonian tour, then $a_i = n_i b_i$. The growth rate (i.e., the amount of work flowing to channel i per unit of time) is ρ_i. Hence,

$$\frac{a_i}{\alpha_i} = \frac{n_i b_i}{\lambda_i b_i} = \frac{n_i}{\lambda_i}.$$

For the Exhaustive regime, $a_i = n_i E(\Theta_i) = n_i\left(\frac{b_i}{1-\rho_i}\right)$, whereas $\alpha_i = \frac{\rho_i}{1-\rho_i}$ (the duration of time that the server has to stay in channel i grows linearly at a rate of $\frac{b_i}{1-\rho_i}$ for each new arrival. As the rate of arrivals is λ_i, we have $\alpha_i = \frac{\rho_i}{1-\rho_i}$). Thus, for the Exhaustive case

$$\frac{a_i}{\alpha_i} = \frac{n_i\left(\frac{b_i}{1-\rho_i}\right)}{\left(\frac{\rho_i}{1-\rho_i}\right)} = \frac{n_i b_i}{\rho_i} = \frac{n_i}{\lambda_i}$$

which is the *same* index as for the Gated regime.

We can now reintroduce the switchover and switch-in times. For illustration, assume a star-configuration of the system. Recall that D_i is the switchover time out of i and R_j denotes the switch-in duration into j. Then, for the Gated regime, assuming gating occurs after switch-in is completed,

$$a_i = n_i b_i + (1 + \rho_i)r_i + d_i$$
$$\alpha_i = \rho_i \ ,$$

so that $a_i \alpha_i = [n_i b_i + (1 + \rho_i)r_i + d_i]/\rho_i$. For the Exhaustive

$$a_i = \frac{r_i}{1 - \rho_i} + \frac{n_i b_i}{1 - \rho_i} + d_i$$
$$\alpha_i = \rho_i/(1 - \rho_i) \ ,$$

so that $a_i/\alpha_i = [r_i + n_i b_i + d_i(1 - \rho_i)]/\rho_i$.

It should be emphasized that the scheduling principle a_i/α_i can be applied to *any* system with a mixed set of service regimes among the channels: Gated, Exhaustive, Binomial or Bernoulli Gated, Binomial or Bernoulli Exhaustive, etc. (see, Yechiali [1991]). All that one has to do is to calculate (once) α_i for every channel, and then, at the beginning of each new Hamiltonian tour, to calculate the current 'core' a_i at each channel. Then, performing a visit tour that follows an *increasing* (decreasing) order of a_i/α_i will *minimize* (maximize) cycle duration.

Browne & Yechiali [1991] further employed the above ideas to achieve dynamic scheduling in systems with only a unit buffer at each channel.

7 The Globally-Gated Regime

A drawback both of the Gated and the Exhaustive regimes is that they are not 'fair' with regard to the FCFS principle. To help resolve this dichotomy, Boxma, Levy & Yechiali [1992] introduced a (cyclic) Globally Gated (GG) service scheme which uses a time-stamp mechanism for its operation: the server moves cyclically among the queues, and uses the instant of cycle-beginning as a reference point of time; when it reaches a queue it serves there all (and only) customers who were present at that queue at the cycle-beginning. This strategy can be implemented by marking all customers with a time-stamp denoting their arrival time. In its nature the GG policy resembles the regular Gated policy. However, the GG policy leads to a mathematical model which allows for derivation of closed-form expressions for the mean delay in the various queues. As a result, the operation of the polling system by the GG policy is easy to control and optimize. As in earlier sections, the system consists of N infinite-buffer channels, the rate of offered load to queue i is $\rho_i = \lambda_i b_i$ and the total system load-rate is $\rho \equiv \sum_{i=1}^{N} \rho_i$. When leaving queue i and before starting service at the next queue, the server incurs a random switchover period D_i. The total 'walking' time in a cycle is $D \equiv \sum_{i=1}^{N} D_i$. (Clearly, other 'Global' versions, such as Globally Exhaustive, can be easily imagined and analyzed.)

Cycle Time

Assume, without loss of generality, that a cycle starts from channel 1. Let $(X_1^1, X_1^2, \ldots, X_1^j, \ldots, X_1^N) = (X_1, X_2, \ldots, X_j, \ldots, X_N)$ be the state of the system at the beginning of the cycle. Then, the cycle duration is

$$C = D + \sum_{j=1}^{N} \sum_{k=1}^{X_j} B_{jk} .$$

The LST of C is derived as follows

$$E\left(e^{-wC} \mid (X_1, X_2, \ldots, X_N)\right) = \tilde{D}(w) \prod_{j=1}^{N} \left(B_i(w)\right)^{X_j} . \tag{25}$$

On the other hand, the length of a cycle determines the joint queue-length distribution at the beginning of the next cycle. Hence

$$E\left[\prod_{j=1}^{N} z_j^{X_j}\right] = E_C\left[E\left[\prod_{j=1}^{N} z_j^{X_j} \mid C\right]\right] = E_C\left[\exp\left[-\sum_{j=1}^{N} \lambda_j(1-z_j)C\right]\right]$$

$$= \tilde{C}\left[\sum_{j=1}^{N} \lambda_j(1-z_j)\right] . \tag{26}$$

Combining (25) and (26)

$$\tilde{C}(w) = \tilde{D}(w)\tilde{C}\left[\sum_{j=1}^{N} \lambda_j \left(1 - \tilde{B}_j(w)\right)\right] . \tag{27}$$

The mean cycle time is derived from (27)

$$E[C] = d + \left(\sum_{j=1}^{N} \lambda_j b_j\right) E[C] .$$

That is, $E[C] = d/(1 - \rho)$, as for the Gated and the Exhaustive regimes. The second moment of C is derived from (27)

$$E[C^2] = \left[d^{(2)} + \left(2d\rho + \sum_{j=1}^{N} \lambda_j b_j^{(2)}\right) E[C]\right] \bigg/ (1 - \rho^2) . \tag{28}$$

Let C_P and C_R denote, respectively, the past and residual duration of a cycle. It is well known that

$$\tilde{C}_P(w) = \tilde{C}_R(w) = \frac{1 - \tilde{C}(w)}{w E[C]}$$

and $E[C_P] = E[C_R] = \frac{E[C^2]}{2E[C]}$.

Pseudo-Conservation law

To derive a pseudo-conservation law we use (20) and the observation that for the cyclic GG regime, $E(X_j) = \rho_j E[C]$ and

$$EM_j^{(1)} = \rho_j \left[\sum_{i=1}^{j} \left[E(X_i) b_i + \sum_{i=1}^{j-1} d_i\right]\right] = \rho_j \sum_{i=1}^{j-1} \left(\rho_i \frac{d}{1-\rho} + d_i\right) + \rho_j^2 \frac{d}{1-\rho} . \tag{29}$$

Substituting (29) in (20) yields

$$\sum_{j=1}^{N} \rho_j E(W_j) = \overline{W} + \rho \frac{d^{(2)}}{2d} + \frac{d}{1-\rho} \rho^2 + \sum_{j=2}^{N} \rho_j \sum_{i=1}^{j-1} d_i . \tag{30}$$

Waiting Times

Consider an arbitrary job K at channel k. The cycle age at the job's arrival instant is C_P. The job's waiting time is composed of (i) the residual cycle time C_R, (ii) the service times of all customers who arrive at channels 1 to $k - 1$ during the cycle in which K arrives, (iii) the switchover times of the server through channels 1 to k, and (iv) the service times of all customers that arrive at channel k during the past part of the cycle, C_P. Then

$$E(W_k) = E[C_R] + \sum_{j=1}^{k-1} \rho_j \left(E[C_P] + E[C_R]\right) + \sum_{j=1}^{k-1} d_j + \rho_k E[C_P]$$

$$= \left(1 + 2\sum_{j=1}^{k-1} \rho_j + \rho_k\right) E[C_R] + \sum_{j=1}^{k-1} d_j . \tag{31}$$

It readily follows that

$$E(W_{k+1}) - E(W_k) = (\rho_{k+1} + \rho_k)E[C_R] + d_k$$

so that, for the cyclic GG regime, we *always* have

$$E(W_1) < E(W_2) < \ldots < E(W_N) . \tag{32}$$

Boxma, Weststrate & Yechiali [1993] extended the cyclic GG model to the case where the server suffers periods of breakdown, and applied the results to real-world repairman problems where both preventive and corrective maintenance actions are considered.

Static Optimization

Let c_k be the cost rate of a waiting job at queue k. Then, the mean weighted waiting cost of an arbitrary job in the system is

$$\sum_{k=1}^{N} \left(\lambda_k \bigg/ \sum_{j=1}^{N} \lambda_j\right) c_k E(W_k) . \tag{33}$$

By substituting (31) into (33) and using an interchange argument it follows that the cycle which *minimized* (33) is determined by an *increasing* order of the index

$$u_j = \frac{2E[C_R]\rho_j + d_j}{\lambda_j c_j}$$

If d_j is negligible, the above index reduces to the index b_j/c_j, which is the well known "$c\mu$" rule.

Dynamic Control

An important characteristic of the GG regime is that the order of visits selected for one cycle *does not affect* the future stochastic behaviour of the system. Moreover, *any* Hamiltonian tour that starts from state $(n_1, n_2, \ldots, n_M)$ yields the *same* cycle duration $C(n_1, n_2, \ldots, n_N)$. Thus, if we consider the costs incurred *during the cycle* by the customers *present* at its initiation and add to it the costs incurred along that cycle by the *new* arrivals, then the *long-run miminal cost* can be achieved by determining a new optimal Hamiltonian tour for each cycle *independently*.

The mean total weighted cost incurred during a cycle starting with $(n_1, n_2, \ldots, n_N)$ is

$$\sum_{k=1}^{N} c_k \left[n_k \sum_{j=1}^{k-1}(n_j b_j + d_j) + b_k \sum_{i=1}^{n_k-1} i \right] \qquad (34)$$

$$+ \sum_{k=1}^{N} c_k \lambda_k E\left[C(n_1, n_2, \ldots, n_N)^2 \right]/2$$

where the first term is the contribution to total cost incurred by the customers present at the cycle beginning, and the second term is due to the customers arriving during that cycle (see, Yechiali [1976]). The only term in (34) that depends on the order of visits is $\sum_{k=}^{N} c_k n_k \sum_{j=1}^{k-1}(n_j b_j + d_j)$. It follows (by an interchange argument) that the optimal order of visits that minimizes expected total costs of the coming cycle is determined by an *increasing* order of the (Gittins) index

$$\frac{n_j b_j + d_j}{n_j c_j}.$$

Again, for negligible d_j this index reduces to the "$c\mu$" rule (i.e., b_j/c_j).

8 Elevator-Type Polling

In an Elevator-type (scan) polling mechanism the server alternates between 'up' and 'down' cycles. In an 'up' cycle it visits the channels in the order $1, 2, \ldots, N-1, N$, and in a 'down' cycle the order of visits is reversed to $N, N-1, \ldots, 2, 1$. This type of polling procedure is encountered in many applications, e.g., it models a common scheme of addressing a hard disk for writing (reading) information on (from) different tracks. It is important to note that the Elevator-type polling saves the return walking time from channel N to channel 1. A comprehensive analysis of Elevator-type polling with four different service regimes can be found in Shoham & Yechiali [1992]. Here we present the Globally-Gated (GG) regime as discussed in Altman, Khamisy & Yechiali [1992].

According to the Elevator-type polling with GG service regime all channels are gated off at the beginning of the 'up' cycle, where the system-state is $(n_1^{\mathrm{up}}, n_2^{\mathrm{up}}, \ldots, n_N^{\mathrm{up}})$, and the server resides in channel i for n_i^{up} regular service durations. At the end of the up cycle all channels are gated again, the system-state is $(n_1^{\mathrm{down}}, n_2^{\mathrm{down}}, \ldots, n_N^{\mathrm{down}})$, and the server starts its down cycle, serving n_i^{down} customers in channel i. We assume that the down walking time from channel $i+1$ to channel i has the same distribution as the up walking time D_i from channel i to channel $i+1$. A key observation is that arbitrary up and down cycles have the *same* distribution, which differs from its *cyclic* GG counter-part only in that it is smaller by the 'saved' walking time D_N. Hence, the results derived for the cycle time distribution (27) and for mean waiting times (31) in a *cyclic* GG regime are directly applicable to the Elevator case, with $D_N = 0$.

Waiting Times

Consider an arbitrary job at channel k. Since all cycles are distributed *alike*, the job arrives during an up or a down cycle with equal probabilites, 0.5. Hence, its mean waiting time is given by

$$E(W_k) = 0.5E\left(W_k \,\middle|\, \begin{matrix} \text{server} \\ \text{moves down} \end{matrix}\right) + 0.5E\left(W_k \,\middle|\, \begin{matrix} \text{server} \\ \text{moves up} \end{matrix}\right) . \tag{35}$$

The expression for $E\left(W_k \,\middle|\, \begin{matrix} \text{server} \\ \text{moves down} \end{matrix}\right)$ is given by (31), with $d_N = 0$, whereas, by reversing the order of visits, we have

$$E\left(W_k \,\middle|\, \begin{matrix} \text{server} \\ \text{moves up} \end{matrix}\right) = \left(1 + 2\sum_{j=k+1}^{N} \rho_j + \rho_k\right)E[C_R] + \sum_{j=k}^{N-1} d_j . \tag{36}$$

Combining (35) with (31) and (36) yields the *surprising result*

$$E(W_k) = (1 + \rho)E[C_R] + 0.5d . \tag{37}$$

That is, expected waiting times are *equal* in *all channels*. This is the only-known non-symmetric polling system that exhibits such a "fairness" phenomenon. An explanation of result (37) is the following. An arbitrary arrival has to wait, on the average, $E[C_R]$ units of time until the cycle (up or down) in which it arrives terminates. Then, it waits until the server moves back to channel k, which requires, on the average (taking into account both directions), $\frac{1}{2}[(E[C_R] + E[C_p])\rho + d]$ units of time.

Optimal Arrangement of Channels The interesting result that $E(W_k)$ is the same for all channels, independent of their location, leads to considering channels' arrangement such that the *variation* in waiting times will be small.

Let $a_i = 2E[C_R]\rho_i + d_i$ $(i = 1, 2, \ldots, N)$. Then

$$E\left(W_k \,\middle|\, \begin{matrix} \text{server} \\ \text{moves down} \end{matrix}\right) = E[C_R](1 + \rho_k) + \sum_{i=1}^{k-1} a_i$$

$$E\left(W_k \,\middle|\, \begin{matrix} \text{server} \\ \text{moves up} \end{matrix}\right) = E[C_R](1 + \rho_k) + \sum_{i=k+1}^{N} a_i + d_k$$

Let $\Delta_k = E(W_k \mid \text{down}) - E(W_k \mid \text{up}) = \sum_{i=1}^{k-1} a_i - \sum_{i=k+1}^{N} a_i - d_k$. Now, $\Delta_1 = -\sum_{i=2}^{N} a_i - d_1 < 0$, $\Delta_N = \sum_{i=1}^{N-1} a_i > 0$ (recall that $d_N = 0$), and Δ_k is a monotone increasing function of k.

One goal is to arrange the channels such that $\max_{1 \le k \le N}\{|\Delta_k|\}$ is as small as possible. Clearly

$$\max_{1 \le k \le N}\{|\Delta_k|\} = \max\{|\Delta_1|, |\Delta_N|\}$$

$$= \max\left\{\sum_{i=1}^{N} a_i - 2E[C_R]\rho_1, \sum_{i=1}^{N} a_i - 2E[C_R]\rho_N\right\} \tag{38}$$

It follows from (38) that $\max_{1 \leq k \leq N} \{|\Delta_k|\}$ is *minimized* if channel 1 is the one with the *highest* value of ρ_i and channel N is the one with the *second highest* value of ρ_i (or vice versa).

9 Future Directions of Research

We have presented methods of analysis for single-server, continuous-time, infinite buffers polling systems, and studied several control and optimization problems. Difficult problems are finite-capacity models and limited service regimes, for which only partial solutions are given in the literature (see, bibliography in Takagi [1990]). A few authors have studied polling systems with multiple servers, and recently Browns & Weiss [1992] investigated dynamic priority rules for a system with parallel servers.

All the systems mentioned above are *open*, with external arrivals, where jobs exit the system after service completion. Closed systems should also be investigated, and only recently Altman & Yechiali [1992] analyzed such systems with Gated, Exhaustive or Globally-Gated service regimes.

For other future directions of research we state a recent 'call for papers' on "Discrete-Time Models and Analysis Methods":

"The past few years have seen an increasing interest in discrete-time models and their solution techniques. One of the driving forces behind this area has been new developments in telecommunications, espacially in high-speed metropolitan area and wide area networks. Tehcnological advances and user demands have shifted the evolution of telecommunication systems towards integrated networks where information is transferred in small, ofted fixed-size, packets, slots or cells (e.g., ATM networks, high-speed LANs and MANs such as DQDB, etc...), operting in a discrete-time environment. The resulting mathematical models of such slotted systems, crucial for the evaluation of design alternatives and their dimensioning, are discrete-time models. The complexity of the stochastic processes involved (e.g., arrival and departure processes) and of the system operation mechanisms (e.g., service mechanism, access protocol, etc...) pose an exciting challenge for the development of efficient and tractable methods for deriving the main performance measures of these systems.

Papers are solicited on discrete-time models and their analysis methods, in particular on, but not restricted to, the following topics:

— Discrete-time queueing models (polling systems, priority systems, multiserver systems, vacation models, etc...).

— Exact and approximate solution methods for discrete-time queueing models, with emphasis on the efficiency and the numerical tractability of these methods.

— Stochastic processes as traffic models for performance studies (taking into account the diversity of time scales, correlations between arrivals, etc...)

— Discrete-time markov chains and their analysis methods".

Naturally, we add to the above topics the interesting and challenging problems of control and optimization of such systems.

Bibliography

1. Altman, E., Blanc, H., Khamisy, A., Yechiali, U.: Gated-type polling systems with walking and switch-in times. Technical Report, Dept. of Statistics & OR, Tel Aviv University 1992.
2. Altman, E., Khamisy, A., Yechiali, U.: On elevator polling with globally-gated regime. Queueing Systems 11 (1992) 85-90.
3. Altman, E., Yechiali, U.: Polling in a closed network. Technical Report SOR-92-14, Dept. of Statistics & OR, New York University 1992.
4. Altman, E., Yechiali, U.: Cyclic Bernoulli polling. ZOR-Methods and Models of Operations Research 38 (1993).
5. Boxma, O.J.: Workloads and waiting times in single-server systems with multiple customer classes. Queueing Systems 5 (1989) 185-214.
6. Boxma, O.J.: Analysis and optimization of polling systems. In: Cohen, J.W., Pack, C.D. (Eds.) Queueing, Performance and Control in ATM. North-Holland, 1991, pp.173-183.
7. Boxma, O.J., Groenendijk, W.P.: Pseudo conservation laws in cyclic service systems. Journal of Applied Probability 24 (1987) 949-964.
8. Boxma, O.J., Levy, H., Yechiali, U.: Cyclic reservation schemes for efficient operation of multiple-queue single-server Systems. Annals of Operations Research 35 (1992) 187-208.
9. Boxma, O.J., Weststrate, J.A., Yechiali, U.: A globally gated polling system with server interruptions, and applications to the repairman problem. Probability in the Engineering and Informational Sciences 7 (1993).
10. Browne, S., Yechiali, U.: Dynamic priority rules for cyclic-type queues, Advances in Applied Probability 21 (1989a) 432-450.
11. Browne, S., Yechiali, U.: Dynamic routing in polling systems. In: M. Bonatti (Ed.) Teletraffic Science for New Cost-Effective Systems, Networks and Services. North-Holland, 1989b, pp.1455-1466.
12. Browne, S., Yechiali, U.: Scheduling deteriorating jobs on a single processor. Operations Research 38 (1990) 495-498.
13. Browne, S., Yechiali, U.: Dynamic scheduling in single-server multiclass service systems with unit buffers. Naval Research Logistics 38 (1991) 383-396.
14. Browne, S., Weiss, G.: Dynamic priority rules when polling with multiple parallel servers. Operations Research Letters 12 (1992) 129-137.
15. Cooper, R.B. Murray, G.: Queues served in cyclic order. Bell System Technical Journal 48 (1969) 675-689.
16. Cooper, R.B.: Queues served in cyclic order: waiting times. Bell System Technical Journal 49 (1970) 399-413.
17. Eisenberg, M.: Queues with periodic service and changeover time. Operations Research 20 (1972) 440-451.
18. Ferguson, M.J., Aminetzah, Y.J.: Exact results for nonsymmetric token ring systems. IEEE Transactions on Communications 33 (1985) 223-231.
19. Kleinrock, L.: Queueing Systems, Vol. 1: Theory. John Wiley, 1975.

20. Konheim, A.G., Levy, H., Srinivasan: Descendant set: an efficient approach for the analysis of polling systems. IEEE Transactions on Communications (to appear 1993a).

21. Konheim, A.G., Levy, H., Srinivasan: The individual station technique for the analysis of polling systems. Technical Report, 1993b.

22. Levy, H., Sidi, M.: Polling systems: applications, modeling and optimization. IEEE Transactions on Communications 8 (1990) 1750-1760.

23. Sarkar, D., Zangwill, W.I.: Expected waiting time for nonsymmetric cyclic queueing systems – exact results and applications. Management Science 35 (1989) 1463-1474.

24. Shoham, R., Yechiali, U.: Elevator-type polling systems. Technical Report, Dept. of Statistics & OR, Tel Aviv University, 1992.

25. Takagi, H.: Analysis of Polling Systems. MIT Press, 1986.

26. Takagi, H.: Queueing analysis of polling models: an update. In: Takagi, H. (ed.) Stochastic Analysis of Computer and Communications Systems. North Holland, 1990, pp.267-318.

27. Yechiali, U.: A new derivation of the Khintchine-Pollaczek formula. In: Haley, K.B. (Ed.) Operational Research '75. North Holland, 1976, pp.261-264.

28. Yechiali, U.: Optimal dynamic control of polling systems. In: Cohen, J.W., Pack, C.D. (Eds.) Queueing, Performance and Control in ATM. North Holland, 1991, pp.205-217.

Modeling and Analysis of Transaction Processing Systems

Philip S. Yu

IBM Research Division, T. J. Watson Research Center
Yorktown Heights, NY 10598

Abstract. In recent years, the demand for on-line transaction processing systems has grown rapidly with ever stringent performance requirements. In this paper, we examine several issues encountered in designing transaction processing systems and report some of the recent advancements in analytical performance modelling methodology on analyzing alternative design trade-offs. First of all, the Concurrency Control (CC) scheme employed can profoundly affect the performance of transaction processing systems. A general analytic modelling approach is presented that can be applied to analyze the various CC schemes under a unified framework, including locking, various optimistic schemes, and hybrid schemes. The analysis can capture the effect of skewed data access, different lock modes, variable length transactions and the buffer retention effect on rerun transactions. Next we consider the analysis of buffer hit probability. In a multi-node environment, whether in a cluster or client server environment, buffer coherency needs to be addressed. The cross invalidation phenomenon can have an adverse effect on the buffer hit probability. A general methodology to analyze various coherency control schemes is examined to predict the buffer hit probability. A hierarchical approach is used to decompose the modelling of transaction processing systems into three components: hardware resource, concurrency control and buffer models. The interaction among the components is then captured through a fixed point iteration.

1. Introduction

In recent years, the demand for on-line transaction processing systems has grown rapidly with ever stringent performance requirement. With the advent of VLSI technology, coupling multiple micro-processors to support high transaction rates has been pursued by various vendors [KRON86, YU92B,C]. Furthermore, client-server architectures have increasingly become a common approach to support transaction processing [KIM90, DEUX90, HORN87]. There has also been considerable interest in geographically distributed transaction processing systems, in which the databases may be distributed among regional systems [GRAY86]. In this paper, we examine several issues encountered in designing transaction processing systems to accommodate these requirements and report some of the recent advancement in analytical modelling methodology on analyzing performance trade-offs of alternative designs to address these issues.

First of all, the Concurrency Control (CC) scheme employed can profoundly affect the performance of transaction processing systems. This is particularly so as the demand for transaction throughput increases leading to greater data contention. There have been numerous analytical studies of the performance of CC schemes. A survey of the analysis of locking in centralized databases can be found in [TAY84,TAY90], while [SEVC83] examines early analytical work on the performance of different CC schemes in distributed databases. More recent work includes [CHES83, MORR85, TAY85A,B, THOM85, YU85, RYU87, YU87, CELL88, SING88, HSU88,

DAN88, HART89, CICI90A,B, SING91, THOM91, YU91, CICI92, HSU92, YU92A,93]. While there have been numerous simulation studies of concurrency control performance, we do not mention them here since the focus of this paper is on analytical methodology. Here a general analytic modelling framework is presented which can be applied to analyze the performance trade-offs of various CC schemes under a unified methodology, including locking, various optimistic schemes, and hybrid schemes. This is based on the methodology developed in [YU93] which is derived and extended from a number of specific studies we have done, e.g. [YU85, CORN86, YU87, CICI92,90A,B, YU90,91,92A]. The analysis can capture the effect of skewed data access, different lock modes, and variable length transactions.

Next we consider the analysis of buffer hit probability. In a multi-node environment, whether in a cluster or client-server environment, buffer coherency control needs to be addressed. The cross invalidation phenomenon can have an adverse effect on the buffer hit probability. In the literature, there have been few studies based on analytic models for this. Recently, a general methodology has been developed in [DAN90,91,92A,93A,B] to model the effects of various coherency control schemes on buffer hit probability. Here we present the buffer modeling methodology based on these works. We note that coherency control can be provided by generalizing the CC manager function to track the buffer contents [DIAS89]. Various lock retention schemes have also been proposed to support coherency control [RAHM86, RAHM88, MOHA91, DAN92A,93A, WILK90, FRAN92, CARE91], although most of the performance studies are based on simulations.

The execution time of a transaction depends on three main factors: 1) the concurrency control protocol used for resolving conflict in accessing data pages (waiting, abort etc.), 2) the buffer hit probability that determines the number of I/O operations to be performed by the transaction, and 3) the processing time and the queueing delay in accessing system resources such as CPU, etc.. We model the concurrency control, buffer hit probability and system resource access times separately and capture their interactions via a higher level model. This higher level model relates quantities from the lower level models through a set of non-linear equations. The solution of the higher level model corresponds to the solution of a fixed point problem which we solve through an iterative process. The transaction execution time depends on the buffer hit probability estimated by the buffer model, and by the queueing and services estimated by the CPU model. The CC model estimates the data conflict probability based on the transaction execution time, and this in turn affects both the buffer and resource models.

In Section 2 we discuss the workload model. In Section 3 we discuss the general methodology for analyzing concurrency control schemes. We apply this methodology in Section 4 to analyze various CC schemes. For optimistic schemes the effect of changed buffer hit probability when a transaction is rerun is handled in the analysis. For locking we provide a simple approximate expression for the mean lock waiting time. In Section 5 we present the methodology to analyze the buffer hit probability under various coherency control schemes. In Section 6, generalization of the methodology in Section 5 is considered. Concluding remarks appear in Section 7.

2. Workload Model

In this section, we briefly discuss the issue on how to provide characterization of database workload. There are two entities involved. One is the transaction and the other is the database. The transactions can generally be characterized by the number of granules accessed, the mode of each access (i.e. share vs exclusive), the instructions executed between granule accesses, etc. The database is characterized by its size, i.e. the number of granules in the database. If the system studied is in operation, all these parameters can often be measured from some tracing facilities.

To model the progression of a transaction, our transaction model can be described as follows. Assume that N_L is the number of granules accessed by a transaction. The transaction model would consist of $N_L + 2$ states or stages, (We use the term granule to refer to the unit of data to which concurrency control is applied.) The transaction has an initial setup phase (including program fetch, and message processing), state 0. Following the initial setup, a transaction progresses to states 1, 2, ... , N_L, in that order. This is the execution phase. At the start of each state, i, the transaction begins to access a new granule and moves to state $i + 1$ when the next new granule access begins. At the end of state N_L, if successful, the transaction enters into the commit phase at state $N_L + 1$.

We still need to specify the granule accessed at each state. This is where the complexity of the workload characterization lies. We make the following assumption which is used in obtaining all the analytical results:

• All granule access requests are independent. While it is reasonable to assume that granule access requests from different transactions are independent, independence cannot hold within a transaction if a transaction's granule accesses are distinct. However, we use this assumption as an approximation for the granule accesses from the same transaction. If the probability of accessing any particular granule is small, e.g. when the number of granules in the database is large and the the number of granules accessed by each transaction is small, this approximation should be very accurate. A similar approximation is also made in [TAY84,85A,B].

(Note that this assumption is certainly not appropriate for query scanning through a large portion of the databases sequentially.) The frequencies that granules accessed by transactions are generally skewed as observed in real workload analysis [DAN93C]. An example of a skewed access pattern often used in the literature is the 80-20 access rule where 80% of the references access 20% of the granules (i.e., the hot set), while the remaining 20% of the references access the rest of of the granules (i.e., the cold set).

Here we use a generalized skewed access model which covers the 80-20 access pattern as a special case. In this model, based on the frequency of data access, the data granules are logically grouped into M partitions,[1] such that the probability of accessing any granule within a partition is uniform. Let β_i denote the fractional size of partition i. Let α_i denote the probability that any data access lies in partition i. An example of this type of logical grouping is the 80-20

---

[1] This logical grouping is done for computation purpose only, since granules with the same frequency of access has the same buffer hit probability under the LRU replacement policy.

access pattern where $K = 2$, $(\alpha_1, \alpha_2) = (0.8, 0.2)$, and $(\beta_1, \beta_2) = (0.2, 0.8)$. The uniform access model is another special case with $M = 1$, $\alpha_1 = 1$ and $\beta_1 = 1$. Even if each transaction application follows the 80-20 access pattern on some relations, multiple transaction applications may have different hot sets and cold sets, and different access rates. Overall this can result in a larger number of logical partitions with different access frequencies and partition sizes. In [DAN93C], real workload traces are analyzed to fit this kind of skewed access model. It was found that with a small number of partitions, the matching of the buffer hit prediction based on this model with the trace driven simulation can be very close.

We note that skewed access pattern has different effects on data contention and buffer hit probability [DAN90B]. The presence of skew increases the data contention probability. This would have a negative effect on the the transaction response time. On the other hand, the skewed accesses improve the buffer hit probability. This would have a positive effect on the response time. However, in a multi-node environment, the skewed accesses also makes the buffer invalidation effect more severe, and thus negatively affects the buffer hit probability. The analytic modelling methodology would need to capture all these effects.

3. Concurrency Control: General Methodology

In an environment with no data contention, the transaction response time is determined by the queueing and processing delay in accessing hardware resources such as CPU, I/O, etc.. In the presence of data contention, the transaction response time further depends upon the occurrence of data conflict in accessing the database. The probability of data conflict for any transaction depends not only on the CC scheme itself but also on the transaction response time which in turn depends on the conflict probability. For example, when locking is used, if the lock contention probability increases, the transaction response time increases due to additional lock waits. In turn, longer transaction response time leads to a longer lock holding time, and hence to a higher lock contention probability. Similarly, when an optimistic CC scheme is used if the transaction abort rate increases, there is a concomitant increase in the CPU utilization causing longer response and data holding times, and therefore a higher probability of abort. We model hardware resource access times and the effect of CC separately and then we solve the models simultaneously using an iteration to estimate the mean transaction response time. We assume here an open model with Poisson transaction arrivals, but the analysis can be extended to a closed model as shown in [YU93]. The hardware resource contention can be modeled by conventional queueing models with CPU servers and disk servers. Since this is rather straightforward, we will only briefly outline it for the case of analyzing optimistic CC (Section 4.1.2).

In this and the next section, we will concentrate on how to estimate the data conflict probability and mean lock waiting time. A model for predicting buffer hit probability can also be incorporated to provide a more accurate estimate of the number of IO's and will be discussed in Section 5.

3.1 Conflict Analysis

A conflict is defined to be an event in which a transaction accesses a data granule that is currently accessed or in use by another transaction in an incompatible mode. The result of a conflict is either a transaction wait or transaction abort. We assume that there is only one transaction type. (Generalization to multiple transaction types is straightforward and can be found in

[YU93].) We also make the following additional assumptions and then show how they can be relaxed at the end of this section:

• The granule access distribution is uniform over the set of granules.

• All accesses to granules are exclusive or update.

Let λ be the transaction arrival rate, N_L be the mean number of granule accesses by each transaction, and L be the number of granules in the database. Let T_H denote the mean holding time of a granule, that is the period of time from when the granule is first accessed until the end of the transaction.

Consider a generic locking scheme. We assume that the probability of deadlock is negligible compared to lock contention as shown in [GRAY81, TAY85B, YU93]. Before a granule can be accessed, a transaction needs to acquire a lock on that granule. A lock request can be made right before each granule is accessed as in dynamic locking, or all lock requests can be made at the beginning of a transaction as in static locking. Each time a lock request is made the corresponding entry in the lock table is examined. If no other transactions hold an incompatible lock on that entry, the granule is locked and the access is granted. The granule is locked until it is released by the transaction. If the granule has already been locked in an incompatible mode, lock contention occurs. (Note that for now we are considering only exclusive granule access so that all accesses to the same granule are incompatible.) Due to the assumption that deadlocks do not occur and the assumption of uniform granule access distribution, the arrival rate of lock requests for a particular granule is $\lambda N_L/L$. We have

Conflict probability under Locking: Assume that the lock request times form a Poisson process and that lock contention events for a transaction are independent. Then the probability of contention on any lock request, P_W, is given by

$$P_W = \frac{\lambda N_L T_H}{L} , \tag{3.1}$$

and the probability, P_{CONT}, that a transaction encounters lock contention is upper bounded as follows:

$$P_{CONT} \leq 1 - (1 - \frac{\lambda N_L T_H}{L})^{N_L} . \tag{3.2}$$

The derivation is straightforward for the case of fixed length transactions. As shown in [YU93], this is also true for the case of variable length transactions.

We will use the upper bound in Equation (3.2) as an approximation to P_{CONT}, i.e.

$$P_{CONT} \approx 1 - (1 - \frac{\lambda N_L T_H}{L})^{N_L} . \tag{3.3}$$

An $O(1/L)$ approximation to Equation (3.3) is given by

$$P_{CONT} \approx \frac{\lambda N_L^2 T_H}{L} . \tag{3.4}$$

We next consider a generic Optimistic CC (OCC) scheme. Transactions access granules as they progress. At the end of execution, if all granules accessed are the up-to-date versions, the transaction will commit and reflect the updated values into the database.[2] In this generic OCC scheme, the commit is assumed to be instantaneous. The effect of non-zero commit time is addressed in the next section when specific certification schemes are considered. At the end of the commit phase, for each granule updated, any transaction accessing the granule is notified that the granule is invalid. Transactions accessing invalid granules are aborted at commit time (referred to as pure OCC). (Later we will consider the case where transactions accessing invalid granules are aborted immediately, referred to as broadcast OCC.) The rate of invalidation to a particular granule is equal to the transaction throughput multiplied by the mean number of granules updated per transaction and divided by the database size, i.e. it is given by $\lambda N_L/L$. From [YU93], we have

Conflict Probability under OCC: Assume that the invalidation times for a given granule form a Poisson process and that all such processes (to different granules) are independent. Then the probability, P_A, that a transaction is aborted when it first tries to commit is upper bounded as follows:

$$P_A \leq 1 - exp\left(-\frac{\lambda N_L^2 T_H}{L}\right) \tag{3.5}$$

where in Equation (3.5) T_H is the mean granule holding time for transactions during their first run only.

Note that Equation (3.5) need not hold for rerun transactions since the mean length of rerun transactions need not equal that of first run transactions except if all transactions have the same fixed length. We will use the upper bound in Equation (3.5) as an approximation to P_A, i.e.

$$P_A \approx 1 - exp\left(-\frac{\lambda N_L^2 T_H}{L}\right) \tag{3.6}$$

An $O(1/L)$ approximation to Equation (2.10) is

$$P_A \approx \frac{\lambda N_L^2 T_H}{L} \tag{3.7}$$

We next consider the case of non-uniform accesses to the database. Assume that the database consists of multiple (M) sets or partitions of granules with α_i fraction of the references go to β_i fraction of the granules. Let T_{Hi} be the mean granule holding time for partition i. The lock utilization for partition i is $\lambda \alpha_i N_L T_{Hi}/\beta_i L$. Assume Poisson arrivals of lock requests and that lock contention events for a transaction are independent, a similar expression can be obtained as in (3.3). In the same way that the approximation in Equation (3.4) was shown to follow from the expression, it follows that

---

[2] We assume that during the course of a transaction any updates are kept in a private buffer, and are only made visible to other transactions after a successful commit, as in [BERN87, KUNG81].

$$P_{CONT} \approx \sum_{i=1}^{M} \frac{\lambda \alpha_i^2 N_L^2 T_{H_i}}{\beta_i L} \ . \tag{3.8}$$

As we assume that each lock request independently references partition i with probability α_i, the mean lock holding times are the same for each partition i, i.e. $T_{H_i} = T_H$, $1 \leq i \leq M$. Under OCC in this environment, a similar development to that for a single partition of granules gives,

$$P_A \approx \sum_{i=1}^{M} \frac{\lambda \alpha_i^2 N_L^2 T_{H_i}}{\beta_i L} \ . \tag{3.9}$$

Finally we illustrate how the case of different access modes can be handled by considering the case of exclusive and shared modes. Assume that each data access has probability p^u of being in exclusive mode and that the mode of each access is independent. Again we consider the case of uniform accesses to the database. First consider the generic locking case, similar to Equation (3.3), we can get,

$$P_{CONT} \leq 1 - (1 - \frac{\lambda N_L T_H}{L})^{N_L p^u} (1 - \frac{\lambda N_L p^u T_H}{L})^{N_L(1 - p^u)} \ .$$

An approximation similar to that in Equation (3.4) is,

$$P_{CONT} \approx \frac{\lambda N_L^2 T_H p^u (2 - p^u)}{L} \ . \tag{3.10}$$

Under the OCC environment, a similar development leads to

$$P_A \approx \frac{\lambda N_L^2 T_H p^u}{L} \ . \tag{3.11}$$

3.2 Conservation Property of Conflict

The approximate expressions for the transaction abort/invalidation probability when using the generic OCC scheme given in Equation (3.7) and for the transaction contention probability when using the generic locking CC scheme given in Equation (3.4) are the same for the case of a single transaction type with exclusive access mode. (These approximations contain only the dominant term, which is $O(1/L)$ in the approximations in Equations (3.6) and (3.3) respectively. However, we believe that the $O(1/L)$ expressions provide insight into the effects of data conflicts for the various CC schemes we consider, and thus we discuss them in this section.) This is true even if the database consists of multiple partitions of granules with different access probabilities as shown in Equations (3.8) and (3.9). This is referred to as the **conservation property of conflict** in [YU93]. Note, however, that the mean granule holding times, T_H, will in general not be equal for the two schemes, as discussed later in this section, so that the conflict probabilities will differ.

In the optimistic case, the abort probability affects the number of reruns and hence the CPU utilization which affects T_H. In the dynamic locking case, the contention probability increases the transaction response time, and consequently, the mean granule holding time, T_H. If the CPU resource is unlimited, the optimistic approach provides lower conflict since T_H is close to the processing time. If the CPU resource is very limited, static locking tends to provide lower conflict. (In static locking, a transaction tries to acquire all locks at once at the beginning. If it cannot get all of them, it does not hold on to any locks, but tries later or waits until they all become available.) In this case, the wait time to get the locks does not enlarge the granule holding time. In [YU90], a CC scheme using a combination of locking and OCC is proposed, and is shown to improve the performance over both OCC and locking schemes by striking a balance between the effect of transaction aborts and lock waits as discussed in Section 4.3.1.

Finally, a word of caution. If we allow for different access modes like shared and exclusive, the conservation property may no longer hold. This is clear by comparing Equations (3.10) and (3.11). This is due to the fact that the concept of access modes is a further optimization to reduce conflicts between transactions and different CC schemes like locking and OCC, depending upon the specific implementation, can have different capabilities to exploit it. Another case where the conservation property is violated is when transactions which may not be successfully committed abort conflicting transactions, or when transactions wait for subsequently aborted transactions, as in wound wait [ROSE78], locking with no-waiting [TAY85A], various running priority schemes in [FRA85], and wait depth limited concurrency control in [FRA92]. These schemes produce unnecessary aborts or waits. On the other hand, these schemes may result in smaller values for T_H compared to locking.

4. Analysis of Various CC schemes

In this section, we demonstrate how to apply the methodology just presented to approximate the mean response time for optimistic and locking CC schemes. Unless stated otherwise, for simplicity we will assume that there is only one transaction type, the granule access distribution is uniform and all accesses are exclusive. Relaxing these constraints can be similarly addressed as in Section 3. Furthermore, only the case of fixed length transactions is considered and a centralized lock manager is assumed. Generalization of the methodology to handle variable length transactions and distributed environments with database replications can be found in [YU93].

4.1 Optimistic Protocols

In this subsection, we consider the OCC schemes. Various OCC schemes have been proposed in the literatures. Two commonly considered variations are the **pure OCC** scheme where a transaction is aborted only at certification time, and the **broadcast OCC** scheme where a transaction is aborted as soon as any granule it has accessed is made obsolete by a committing transaction. Most previous analyses on OCC schemes ignored the fact that due to buffering in main memory rerun transactions may not need to re-access from disk all the granules brought in during previous runs and therefore came out in favor of broadcast OCC. In [YU93], the analysis specifically captures this **buffer retention** effect and is able to show that pure OCC can in fact outperform broadcast OCC. A combination of the pure OCC and broadcast OCC, referred to as **OCC with broadcast during rerun** is proposed and analyzed in [YU92A]. In this scheme, a transaction uses pure OCC for its first run, and employs the early abort of broadcast OCC for any subsequent reruns. Compared with pure OCC, the immediate abort during rerun reduces wasted CPU instruction, hence improves the performance. In the following, we present the analysis for the OCC with broadcast during rerun to illustrate the methodology. The analysis of the pure OCC follows directly from that of the first run of this scheme. The analysis of the broadcast OCC can be generalized from that of the rerun transactions, albeit using a more complex set of difference equations [YU93].

4.1.1 OCC with Broadcast During Rerun

In Section 3 when we analyzed the pure OCC scheme we assumed that commit processing was instantaneous. We now approximate the abort probability in a more realistic setting. We assume that each transaction at the beginning of each state of its execution phase informs the CC manager of its request to access to a new granule. The CC manager keeps a list of transactions accessing each granule, and also maintains locks for granules held by transactions in commit. During the first run, if a transaction requests access to a granule for which an incompatible lock is held by a transaction in commit, it is marked for abort. At commit time, the CC manager checks if a transaction has been marked for abort. If so, the CC manager removes the transaction from the list of granules accessed, and the transaction restarts after a backoff interval with mean duration $T_{Backoff}$. Otherwise, the transaction enters commit processing, and the CC manager grants locks for the granules accessed by the transaction and marks for abort any transactions that have conflicting access. The transaction then writes commit records to the log and propagates the updates to the disk, modeled as taking a mean time of T_{Commit}, following which locks are released. Let N_L denote the (fixed) number of granules accessed by a transaction. The initial setup phase of the transaction consists of execution of a mean of P_{INPL} instructions and a mean of I_{INPL} I/O's. In the first run of a transaction, the mean time in each state i, $1 \leq i \leq N_L$, is assumed to be the same and is denoted by $\hat{R}$. $\hat{R}$ corresponds to execution of a mean of $\hat{P}$ instructions, and a mean of $(1 - H)$ I/Os, where H denotes the (buffer hit) probability that the accessed granule is found in a main memory buffer.

Assuming instantaneous commit processing, Equation (3.6) approximates the invalidation probability on the first run P_A as $1 - exp(-\lambda N_L^2 T_H/L)$, where T_H is the mean granule holding time and is equal to $(N_L + 1)\hat{R}/2$. This corresponds to the probability that a transaction is marked for abort by a transaction that enters commit processing after the invalidated transaction accessed a conflicting data granule. Recall that transactions are also aborted when the new granule accessed at any stage is already locked by a transaction in commit; the probability that this occurs is approximated by Equation (3.3) with T_{Commit} replacing T_H. Transactions (in the process of commit) that hold a lock on the new granule requested and transactions that initiate commit during the i-th state of the transaction being considered are different sets of transactions. We assume that invalidations due to these two cases are independent events since they arise from conflicts from different sources. Thus, the probability of transaction abort is approximated as,

$$P_A \approx 1 - exp\left(-\lambda N_L^2 T_H/L\right)\left(1 - \frac{\lambda N_L T_{Commit}}{L}\right)^{N_L}. \tag{4.1}$$

This can be further approximated as,

$$P_A \approx \frac{\lambda N_L^2 (T_H + T_{Commit})}{L}. \tag{4.2}$$

While we can derive Equation (4.2) from Equation (4.1), what is interesting to note is that we can directly write down the expression by adding together the conflict terms from the two different sources, i.e. conflicting with transactions already in commit, and aborting by transactions initiating commit. This is referred to as the **additive approximation** property in [YU93]. In doing this, it is important to identify the sources of abort. In this case there are two: one is from invalidation and the other is from lock contention. Taking advantage of the additive approximation, we can estimate each term separately based on Equations (3.4) and (3.7) and sum them.

We next consider the rerun transactions. After state $N_L + 1$, if the transaction is aborted, it returns to state 1. During reruns, upon entering state i, the transaction not only informs the concurrency control manager of its access to the i-th granules, but also checks to see if it has already been marked for abort. If already marked for abort, the transaction is immediately aborted and returns to state 1.

To analyze the abort probability of rerun transactions, recall that all read I/Os are assumed to be done in the first run; hence, there is no I/O during rerun. The mean time at each state i, $1 \le i \le N_L$, is assumed to be the same and is denoted by R' corresponding to execution of P' instructions. The probability of abort $A(i)$ in the i-th state of a rerun is estimated as,

$$A(i) = 1 - exp\left(-iN_L\lambda R'/L\right)\left(1 - \frac{N_L\lambda T_{Commit}}{L}\right). \tag{4.3}$$

The remaining response time at the start of a rerun (if any) is estimated as,

$$B = \sum_{i=1}^{N_L}\left\{\prod_{k=1}^{i-1}(1-A(k))\right\}A(i)\{B + T_{Backoff} + (i-1)R'\} + \left\{\prod_{k=1}^{N_L}(1-A(k))\right\}N_L R'. \tag{4.4}$$

In the first summation term of Equation (4.4), $\{\prod_{k=1}^{i-1}(1-A(k))\}A(i)$ corresponds to the abort probability after advancing to state i in a rerun and $\{B + T_{Backoff} + (i-1)R'\}$ is the expected response time measured at the start of this rerun. In the second term of (4.4), $\prod_{k=1}^{N_L}(1 - A(k))$ is the probability that a rerun completes and commits, while $N_L R'$ is the corresponding response time. The expected remaining instructions executed by a rerun transaction is estimated as,

$$
D = \begin{aligned}
&\sum_{i=1}^{N_L} \{\prod_{k=1}^{i-1}(1-A(k))\}A(i)\{D + T_{Backoff} + (i-1)P'\}\\
&+ \{\prod_{k=1}^{N_L}(1-A(k))\}N_L P'\,.
\end{aligned}
\tag{4.5}
$$

This equation is similar to (4.4) with B replaced by D, and R' by P'.

4.1.2 Hardware Resource Model

We now describe the hardware resource model and show how it can be coupled with the data contention model through an iteration. We assume that the system consists of a single CPU and a database that is spread over multiple disks. Assuming Poisson arrivals of transactions, we model the processors as an M/M/1 queue with FCFS discipline and the disks as an infinite server. Other open queueing network models could be used; we chose this one for simplicity. The processor utilization is given by

$$
\rho = \frac{\lambda \times \{P_A D + P_{INPL} + N_L \hat{P}\}}{MIPS}
\tag{4.6}
$$

where MIPS is the processor speed. Then the mean times in different states are given by as,

$$
R_{INPL} = \frac{P_{INPL}}{MIPS(1-\rho)} + I_{INPL} \times IOTIME
$$
$$
\hat{R} = \frac{\hat{P}}{MIPS(1-\rho)} + \hat{I} \times IOTIME
\tag{4.7}
$$
$$
R' = \frac{P'}{MIPS(1-\rho)}
$$

where $\hat{I} = 1 - H$ is the average number of I/Os per state in the first run (respectively any subsequent run). We will discuss how to estimate H in Section 6. The overall mean transaction response time is given by

$$
R = R_{INPL} + N_L \hat{R} + T_{Commit} + P_A (T_{Backoff} + B).
\tag{4.8}
$$

From Section 4.1.1, we know P_A and $A(i)$ depend upon $\hat{R}$ and R', respectively, whereas $\hat{R}$ and R' depend upon the CPU utilization ρ which in turn depends upon P_A and $A(i)$. There clearly is an interdependency. We can first pick some arbitrarily small abort probabilities, P_A and $A(i)$, and calculate the mean response times, $\hat{R}$ and R'. The mean response times are then used to calculate a new set of abort probabilities. The process continues and typically converges in a few iterations.

4.2 Standard Locking

We now show how the methodology can be applied to analyze the standard two-phase locking (2PL) scheme. Let N_L be the (fixed) number of granules accessed by a transaction. In our transaction model, transactions make lock requests at the beginning of states $1, ..., N_L$. If the granule has already been locked in an incompatible mode, the transaction is enqueued at the CC manager and waits till the lock becomes available. As before for locking, we neglect the probability of deadlock. For locking each state i, $1 \leq i \leq N_L$, is divided into two substates $\bar{i}$ and $\hat{i}$. In substate $\bar{i}$ the transaction holds $i - 1$ locks and is waiting for its i-th lock request to be satisfied. In substate $\hat{i}$ it holds i locks and is executing. Let a denote the mean time in substate $\hat{i}$ which is assumed to be independent of i and is obtained from the hardware resource model as discussed later in this section. The probability that substate $\bar{i}$ is entered upon leaving substate $\hat{i} - 1$ is the lock contention probability for a lock request, P_w, which is given in Equation (3.1) and assumed to be independent of i. The time spent in substate $\bar{i}$, given it is entered, is the lock waiting time whose mean we denote by R_w which is also assumed to be independent of i. The unconditional mean time in substate $\bar{i}$ is therefore $b = P_w R_w$. R_w can be approximated as follows. The mean number of transactions in substate $\bar{i}$ (respectively $\hat{i}$) is λb (respectively λa). Since a transaction in substate $\bar{i}$ (respectively $\hat{i}$) holds $i - 1$ locks and is waiting for its i-th lock (respectively holds i locks) and the granule access distribution is uniform, the probability that a lock request contends with a transaction in substate $\bar{i}$ (respectively $\hat{i}$) is $(i - 1)\lambda b/L$ (respectively $i\lambda a/L$), $1 \leq i \leq N_L$. Similarly, the probability that a lock request contends with a transaction in state $N_L + 1$ is $\lambda N_L c/L$ where $c = T_{Commit}$. Let

$$G = \{ \sum_{i=1}^{N_L} (ia + (i-1)b) \} + N_L c \ . \tag{4.9}$$

(Note that since i locks (respectively $i - 1$ locks) are held in substate $\hat{i}$ (respectively substate $\bar{i}$) with a mean sojourn time of a (respectively b), G is the sum of the (mean) lock holding time for each granule over all N_L granules and G/N_L is the mean lock holding time averaged over all N_L granules.) Then,

$$R_W \approx \sum_{i=1}^{N_L} \left(\frac{(i-1)b}{G} \{ \frac{R_W}{f_1} + a + s_i \} + \frac{ia}{G} \{ \frac{a}{f_2} + s_i \} \right) + \frac{N_L c}{G} \{ \frac{c}{f_3} \}. \tag{4.10}$$

In the above expression $(i - 1)b/G$ (respectively ia/G) is the conditional probability that a lock request contends with a transaction in substate $\bar{i}$ (respectively $\hat{i}$) given that lock contention occurs, $1 \leq i \leq N_L$, and $N_L c/G$ is the similar expression for state $N_L + 1$. The quantity s_i is the mean time from leaving state $\hat{i}$ until the end of commit and is given by

$$s_i = (N_L - i)(a + b) + c \ . \tag{4.11}$$

The quantity R_W/f_1 (respectively a/f_2) is the mean remaining time in substate $\bar{i}$ (respectively $\hat{i}$) given that the transaction contended with was in that state, $1 \leq i \leq N_L$, and similarly for c/f_3. Note that in obtaining Equation (4.10) we have assumed that when a transaction T_1 encounters contention for a lock held by another transaction T_2, then no other transaction T_3 can be waiting for this same lock, i.e. the queue length for any lock never exceeds two. Thus, when T_2 commits and releases the lock T_1 acquires it without further waiting. Note, however, that T_2 can be waiting for a lock held by yet another transaction T_4, and T_4 can also be waiting, etc. Thus, wait chains can build up due to waits for different locks, and this is captured by the analysis. Since transactions typically hold several locks, wait chains of this type (rather than for the same granule) predominate. The factors f_1, f_2 and f_3 depend on the distributions of the times in substates $\bar{i}$, $\hat{i}$ and $N_L + 1$ respectively. Substate $\hat{i}$ corresponds to the CPU execution time and the I/O time if the granule accessed in the state is not found in memory (recall that H denotes the probability that a granule accessed in any state is found in a main memory buffer). Assuming that H is not very close to one and that I/O time is constant and much larger than the processing time (this is true for typical parameter values), then it is easy to show that $f_2 \approx 2(1 - H)$. In our studies we will assume that $f_3 = 2$ corresponding to a constant time in the the commit state and that $f_1 = 1$ corresponding to exponential lock waiting times. Comparison with simulations [YU92A] indicated that $f_1 = 1$ yields good results. At low contention levels, the estimates from $f_1 = 1$ are a little pessimistic. Equation (4.10) can be simplified to yield,

$$R_W \approx \frac{\dfrac{(a+b)^2(N_L+1)(N_L-1)}{6} + \dfrac{(N_L+1)(\dfrac{a^2}{f_2}+ab+ac+bc)}{2} + \dfrac{c^2}{f_3} - ab - bc}{a(\dfrac{N_L+1}{2}) + c + b(\dfrac{N_L-1}{2})(1-\dfrac{1}{f_1})} . \tag{4.12}$$

For large N_L, small c, and small b compared to a, the right side of Equation (4.12) is approximately equal to $((a+b)(N_L-1)+c)/3$. This is the approximation used in [YU87]. Furthermore, it follows from using Equation (3.1) and computing the mean lock holding time T_H from Equation (4.9) that

$$P_W = \frac{\lambda G}{L} . \tag{4.13}$$

The mean response time can be estimated as

$$R = R_{INPL} + R_E + N_L P_W R_W + T_{Commit} \tag{4.14}$$

where $R_E = N_L \times a$ is the mean duration of the execution phase, which can be approximated using a hardware resource model similar to that in Section 4.1.2. Since both R_W and P_W in Equations (4.12) and (4.13), respectively, depend upon $b = P_W R_W$, we need to solve for them through an iteration. Starting with $b = 0$, we can get initial values for R_W and P_W, and thus a new b value. The process continues and typically converges in a few iterations.

4.3 Extensions to Other CC Schemes

4.3.1 Hybrid CC Schemes

Locking tends to suffer form cascade blocking while OCC may suffer from wasting resources due to transaction aborts. Various combinations of locking and OCC schemes have been considered in the literature. One type of hybrid CC schemes is to use pure OCC for the first run and locking for the second run. As the second run will be shorter due to the buffer retention effect, the blocking effect would be minimized. This would also greatly reduce the number of reruns. If static locking is used for the second run, there can be at most one rerun. These types of schemes are analyzed in [YU92A] based on a similar analytic approach presented here.

Another type of hybrid scheme, referred to as locking with deferred blocking, is to divide transaction execution into a non-blocking phase and a blocking phase. At the start of the execution, a transaction is in the non-blocking phase similar to OCC. After a transaction has accessed a predefined number of granules, it tries to enter the blocking phase by obtaining locks on the granules already accessed and if successful, it will request locks for all subsequent granule accesses. This would avoid costly abort at the later states of a transaction execution and avoid long waits as transactions only hold locks at the later states. This scheme is analyzed in [YU90] using similar approach presented here. These hybrid schemes have been shown to lead to better performance than the conventional locking and OCC schemes and are especially attractive for real-time CC [YU94].

4.3.2 Dynamic Timestamp Certification

The OCC schemes considered in Section 4.1 attempt to serialize transactions using certification times as the timestamps [BERN87]. Other OCC certification schemes using dynamically derived timestamps or interval of timestamps have been proposed [BAYE82, BOKS87, YU91]. This type of schemes is effective in reducing the read write conflict. Consider the following scenario. Assume that transaction X reads granule A and transaction Y subsequently updates granule A and commits before transaction X completes. If OCC (pure or broadcast) is used, transaction X will be aborted. This type of conflict is referred to as rw-conflict. However, transaction X can in fact be committed with a back-shifted timestamp earlier than that of transaction Y. This is what the dynamic timestamp certification scheme offers. Note that shifting timestamp backward would not be allowed if it would cause conflict with other committed transactions. For example, if transaction X further updates granule C and some other transaction Z already read the old value of C and committed after transaction Y, giving transaction X a back-shifted timestamp before transaction Y would cause a conflict, referred to as a wr-conflict, with transaction Z and hence violate the serializability constraint.

The methodology presented here has been extended in [YU91] to analyze the dynamic timestamp certification scheme based on timestamp history. In [YU91], a discrete time approach is adopted to simplify the analysis. A transaction goes through discrete stages (or states) as explained before. We use the mean sojourn time at each state as the basic time unit. The timestamp assigned dynamically at certification time to each transaction can get back-shifted several stages. That is, the back-shift is approximated as a multiple of stages in the analysis. We therefore introduce, pb_i ($i = 0, 1, \ldots$) as the probability that a committed transaction is back-shifted i stages, i.e., the timestamp given to a committing transaction is i stages prior to the actual commit time of the transaction. No back-shift occurs if the transaction has incurred no conflict. (This happens with probability pb_0.) Let P_A be the transaction abort probability,

$$1 = P_A + pb_0 + \sum_{i=1}^{\infty} pb_i . \tag{4.15}$$

The pb_i for an arbitrary transaction X satisfies the following equation

$$pb_i \approx \sum_{j=1}^{\min\{i,L\}} P\{ \text{ rw-conflict exactly at stage } L - j + 1 \text{ with a committing transaction}\}$$

$$\times P\{\text{conflicting (committing) transaction back-shifted } i - j \text{ stages }\}$$

$$\times P\{ \text{ no wr-conflict preventing this transaction backshifting i stages }\} .$$

Assuming transaction Y is the conflicting transaction, the first term in the product represents the probability that a transaction Y committing during stage $L - j + 1$ of transaction X has updated a data granule read by transaction X. The second term is the conditional probability that transaction Y needs to be back-shifted $i - j$ stages assuming it can be committed. All rw-conflicts summed up in this equation will lead to the conflicting transaction Y getting a timestamp during the interval of stage $L - i + 1$ and thus cause the running transaction X to get a timestamp back-shifted i stages. The first term in the right hand side can be obtained based on the conflict analysis in Section 3. Similarly, the third term can be derived with the back-shift probability taken into account.

For the back-shift distribution of committed transactions, we estimate

$$P\{ \text{ conflicting (committing) transaction back-shifted } i - j \text{ stages }\} = \frac{pb_{i-j}}{1 - P_A} .$$

Note that the back-shift probabilities have to be normalized by $1 - P_A$ because we consider only the case of successful completion in the conditional probabilities.

5. Buffer Coherency Control and Buffer Hit Modelling

We next consider the issue of buffer hit analysis. The problem becomes more complex in a multi-node environment where buffer invalidation can occur. (Here a multi-node environment can mean either a cluster-like environment, or a client-server like environment. The modelling methodology described below is applicable to both environments, albeit the parameter values in the two environments can be different.) Various buffer coherency control schemes have been proposed in the literature [DIAS89, RAMA89, WILK90, CARE91, DAN93B]. In [DAN93B], these are classified into three approaches: **detection** of invalidated granules, **notification** of invalidated granules, and **propagation** of updated granules. These schemes show different trade-offs on the buffer hit probability and CPU overhead. A general modeling methodology is developed in [DAN93B] to analyze six different coherency schemes under the three approaches.

The buffer hit analysis under the LRU replacement policy can be analyzed based on two simple principles: (1) **conservation of flow on LRU substack composition** and (2) **location content probability proportional to relative push down rate**, as explained later. These have been applied to analyze the single node environment in [DAN90A] and the multi-node environment in [DAN93B, DAN92A,B]. We will use the multi-node environment to illustrate the ideas as the single node case can be considered to be a degenerate case of $N = 1$ in the multi-node environment. Two commonly used coherency control schemes are examined: the check-on-access (CA) and the broadcast or selective invalidation notification (IN) schemes, where CA follows a detection oriented approach and IN uses a notification oriented approach. (Note that the buffer hit probability under the propagation oriented approach is not affected by the the invalidation effect as the invalidated granules are immediately replaced.)

Under the IN approach, an invalidation message containing a list of granules modified by the committing transaction is broadcast to all other nodes during transaction commit [STRI82, DAN90B]. Each node upon receiving the invalidation message will check for the updated granules and mark them invalid if present in its local buffer. This immediately frees up the buffer space occupied by the obsolete granules which are brought to the bottom of the LRU stack. A variation of the scheme is to selectively notified only the nodes with a copy of the invalidated granules

Under the CA approach, the obsolete granules are detected at the granule access time by a transaction. We assume that the coherency control function is integrated with the CC manager/controller [DIAS89] which not only provides the traditional concurrency control service, but also tracks which node has a valid copy of a granule. The lock table entry can contain an additional **valid bit** for each node to indicate whether it has a valid copy. Before accessing any granule, the processing node of the transaction makes a lock request to the integrated CC manager. In response, the integrated CC manager returns not only the requested lock, but also the result of the associated buffer validation check based on the valid bit. Note that if the valid bit is off, it will be turned on after the status of the valid bit is returned as invalidation has now been accomplished. At the lock release time, if the granule has been updated, the valid bits of all other nodes except the updating node (which is the only node with an up-to-date version of that granule) will be turned off. The CA scheme certainly saves the overhead of sending immediate notification of invalidated granules, but it also reduces the buffer hit probability as the obsolete granules continue to reside in the local buffer.

We consider the case of a homogeneous multi-node environment where the access pattern to the database is the same from all nodes. Generalization to the case where each node has its own affinity data set which is accessed less often by others can be found in [DAN92B, DAN93A,B].

Since the multi-node is assumed to be homogeneous, we focus our attention to a single buffer. We first look at the buffer hit probability under the detection oriented approach (CA), which is more difficult to analyze as both valid and invalid granules are mixed together in the buffer, based on the approach in [DAN93B]. To estimate the steady state probability of buffer hit, we first derive the average number of valid granules of each partition in the local buffer of any node. Let $V_i(j)$ denote the average number of valid granules of partition i in the top j locations of the LRU stack. Therefore, the buffer hit probability of the i-th partition is $h_i = V_i(B)/(\beta_i L)$, and the overall buffer hit probability for a granule requested by a transaction is estimated as

$$H^{ca} = \sum_{i=1}^{M} \alpha_i h_i. \tag{5.1}$$

Let $p_i(j)$ be the probability that the j-th buffer location from the top of the LRU stack contains a granule of partition i. Let $p_i^v(j)$ be the probability that the granule is valid given that the granule belongs to the i-th partition. Then,

$$V_i(j) = \sum_{l=1}^{j} p_i(l) p_i^v(l). \tag{5.2}$$

Also, let $Y_i(j)$ denote the average number of (both valid and invalid) granules of partition i in the top j locations of the LRU stack. Then,

$$Y_i(j) = \sum_{l=1}^{j} p_i(l). \tag{5.3}$$

We will set up a recursive formulation to determine $p_i(j+1)$ and $p_i^v(j+1)$ for $j \geq 1$ given $p_i(l)$ and $p_i^v(l)$ for $l = 1,...,j$. Consider a smaller buffer consisting of the top j locations only. The buffer location $(j+1)$ receives the granule that is pushed down from location j. Let $r_i(j)$ be the rate at which granules of partition i are pushed down from location j. Similarly, let $r_i^v(j)$ be the rate at which valid granules of partition i are pushed down from location j. Our estimation of $p_i(j)$ and $p_i^v(j)$ are based on the following two observations.

- Conservation of flow: Under steady state conditions, the long term rate at which granules of the i-th partition get pushed down from the top j locations of the buffer equals the rate at which they are brought into the top j locations. Note that if the new access is a hit on an invalid granule present in the top j buffer locations, the granule simply will be refreshed with a valid copy and will not cause a replacement from the top j locations. Hence, the push down rate, $r_i(j)$ is given by

$$r_i(j) = \lambda N_L \alpha_i (1 - \frac{Y_i(j)}{\beta_i L}).$$ (5.4)

Using a similar conservation of flow argument for the valid granules, we equate the long term rate at which valid granules of the i-th partition get pushed down from the top j locations of the buffer, $r_i^v(j)$, to the difference of the rate at which they are brought into the top j locations, and the rate they become invalid. Hence, $r_i^v(j)$ is given by

$$r_i^v(j) = \lambda N_L \alpha_i (1 - \frac{V_i(j)}{\beta_i L}) - (N-1)\lambda N_L \alpha_i p_i^u \frac{V_i(j)}{\beta_i L}.$$ (5.5)

- Relative push down rate: The expected value of finding a granule of the i-th partition in the $(j+1)$-st buffer location over all time, $p_i(j+1)$, is approximately the same as the probability of finding a granule of the i-th partition in the $(j+1)$-st buffer location in the event that a granule is pushed down from location j to location $(j+1)$.

$$p_i(j+1) \approx \frac{r_i(j)}{\sum_{l=1}^{M} r_l(j)}.$$ (5.6)

Note that instantaneous value of $r_i(j)$ is dependent on the content of the top j buffer locations, and the more accurate estimation of $p_i(j)$ requires the precise distribution of the content of j buffer locations. Similarly,

$$p_i^v(j+1) \approx \frac{r_i^v(j)}{r_i(j)}, \quad j = 1...B-1.$$ (5.7)

Equations (5.2)-(5.7) can be solved iteratively, with the base condition of $p_i(1) = \alpha_i$ and $p_i^v(1) = 1$. Note that, although $r_i(j)$ is a function of the transaction rate (λ), $p_i(j)$, $p_i^v(j)$ and therefore, h_i and H^{ca} are independent of λ, because λ cancels out in Equations (5.6) and (5.7).

Let H^{bi} be the buffer hit probabilities under IN. H^{bi} can be estimated in a similar way as H^{ca} by setting the push down rate, $r_i(j)$, in Equation (5.4) as the difference of miss rate and invalidation rate (buffer purge rate).

$$r_i(j) = \lambda N_L \alpha_i (1 - \frac{Y_i(j)}{\beta_i L}) - (N-1)\lambda N_L \alpha_i p_i'' \frac{Y_i(j)}{\beta_i L}. \tag{5.8}$$

(Note that there are no invalid granules under IN.) Together with Equations (5.6) and (5.3), it can be solved iteratively with the initial condition of $p_i(1) = \alpha_i$. Hence,

$$H^{bi} = \sum_{i=1}^{M} \alpha_i Y_i(B)/(\beta_i L). \tag{5.9}$$

It was found in [DAN93B] that the difference in buffer hit probabilities between CA and IN to be very sensitive to the data access pattern. For skewed data accesses, the difference tends to be small, as under IN the immediate identification of invalidated granules for buffer reuse results mainly in more cold granules being buffered. In the presence of invalidation effect, as the buffer increases, a saturation point on buffer hit probability will be reached even under IN. This occurs at the point where the replacement rate is zero, i.e., at a buffer size of $L/(1 + (N-1)p'')$ as can be derived from (5.8). Furthermore, from (5.8), it can be shown that the buffer hit probability at this point is roughly $1/(1 + (N-1)p'')$ for each partition, cold or hot. This upper limit on buffer hit probability is independent of the access pattern, uniform or skew. This is in contrast to the single node case where with sufficient buffer, the buffer hit probability can go to one.

6. Extensions on Buffer Modeling

6.1 Lock Retention, Deferred Writes, and Remote Caching

The buffer modelling methodology can be extended to study various other buffer related issues. In a single node environment, deferred write policy, where the dirty granules are not forced to disk at commit time, is often used to save write IO's as in IBM DB2. The number of write IO's is reduced if a granule can get multiple updates from different transactions before it is flushed out from the buffer and written to disks. The write IO rate under the deferred write policy can be determined by the rate that dirty granules are flushed out from the buffer, i.e. the dirty fraction of $\sum_{i=1}^{M} r_i''(B)$. The write I/O reduction can be analyzed by extending the above methodology to distinguish between clean and dirty granules [DAN93A].

The two principles on conservation of flow and relative push down rate still hold for the dirty (respectively, the clean) granules of each partition. However, there is an additional complexity. Consider the CA (similarly for the IN) scheme. In the previous section, Equations (5.2)-(5.7) form a set of forward recurrence relations. This is due to the fact that in Equation

(5.5) for the conservation of flow, only the content in the top stack j positions matters. This is referred to as the substack decomposable property in [DAN92B]. However, if we apply the conservation of flow to the dirty pages of partition i, the first term on the right hand side of Equation (5.5) is no longer the miss probability at the top j stack positions. Instead, it is now the probability that the remaining stack positions (from location $j + 1$ to B) containing the dirty granule requested. (In the previous section, we only need to know that the requested granule is missing from the top substack. Now the fact that the requested granule is missing from the top substack does not imply that a dirty granule would be brought to the top of the stack. This can only occur if the requested granule is already present in the bottom portion of the buffer and is dirty.) We thus lose the substack decomposable property. This makes the recurrence relations more complex to solve.

In a multi-node environment, the delaying propagation of dirty granules to disks or server nodes can cause coherency problem for other nodes trying to access these dirty granules. This problem can be solved via **lock retention** on dirty granules where locks are continued to be held after commit by the buffering node as long as the granules are in the buffer. The lock manager can thus identify the node owning the most up-to-date version of a granule and properly direct a requesting node where to obtain the up-to-date version of a granule. With the ever increasing gap between memory and disk access times, the concept of remote caching has been pursued by various researchers [LEFF91, LI89, FRAN92, MOHA91]. Under remote caching, granules can be directly transferred between buffers. (In essence, the buffers of all the other nodes become another level of the storage hierarchy between local buffer and disks.) Note that although delaying propagation of dirty granules to disks can improve normal performance, it can prolong the recovery time upon system failure as all dirty granules need to be derived from the database log and applied to the database. For the multi-node environment, the recovery process can be further complicated as log entries from all nodes need to be merged and applied in order, if dirty granules can be transferred to multiple nodes via the remote caching mechanism before writing to disks [MOHA91].

Generalizations of the buffer coherency schemes to support lock retention, remote caching and delayed dirty page propagations have been proposed in [MOHA91, DAN92A,93A] for a data-sharing like environment and for a client-server like environment in [FRAN92]. The buffer analysis presented here can be extended to study the performance improvement of these schemes [DAN92A, DAN93A] and their recovery time trade-offs [DAN93B]. The extension needs to track the buffer composition in terms of the lock mode held in each buffer location, in addition to the partition type of a granule. The two principles on conservation of flow and relative push down rate still hold for granules of each lock mode held, but again we lose the substack decomposable property.

6.2 Shared Buffer

As pointed out in the previous section, in a multi-node environment, the cross invalidation effect puts a upper limit on the attainable buffer hit probability and the usable amount of local buffer. Furthermore, granule replications among the local buffers also reduce the effectiveness of buffer usage as compared to a single node environment. Shared buffer has been considered as a means of providing more effective buffering, e.g. [DAN91, YU92B,C, FRAN92]. In [DAN91], a unified analytical modelling methodology is developed to study various shared buffer placement polices. These polices differ on the types of granules selected to place in the shared buffer, such as updated granules, missed granules, replaced granules from the local buffer, and any combinations of these three types of granules. Note that in the shared buffer, only the granules that are not already duplicated in the local buffer can help improve the overall buffer hit probability. The analysis in [DAN91] captures the dependency between local and shared buffer contents under each policy.

7. Summary and Conclusion

In transaction processing, the complexity of the system makes it difficult to understand the trade-offs between the various design alternatives without detailed analysis. Simulation models of transaction processing systems can often be very time consuming to run. Therefore, for exploring a wide variety of design alternatives it would be useful to have a unified analytical methodology. Furthermore, from simulation studies, it is generally hard to pinpoint the causality of the results, extrapolate the findings from the environment studied to other environments, and reconcile the differences among other related studies, as the large number of parameters can interact in very complex ways. On the other hand, an analytic expression can provide far more insight into the causality effect of the various parameters, and be used by other practitioners to study different environments under another sets of parameter values.

In this paper we reported some recent advancement in analytical modelling methodology for transaction processing systems. A unified approximate analytical methodology is reported to study various aspects of the transaction processing systems, including the effects of different CC schemes and coherency control schemes over a spectrum of environments including single node, to multi-node cluster or client-server environment. The methodology presented decomposes the model into submodels for hardware resource contention, for data contention and for buffer hit. We focus on the data contention model and buffer model. The data contention model is applicable to various CC schemes, including locking, different OCC and hybrid schemes. The buffer model can be applied to various buffer coherency schemes, including check on access scheme, broadcast or selective notification scheme, and other extensions with lock retention to support remote caching and delayed dirty page propagations.

References

[BERN87] Bernstein, P.A., Hadzilacos, V., and Goodman, N., "Concurrency Control and Recovery in Database Systems", Addison Wesley, 1987.

[BAYE82] Bayer, R., et al., "Dynamic Timestamp Allocation for Transactions in Database Systems", In H.-J. Schneider, editor, Proc. of 2nd Intl. Symp. on Distributed Data Bases, pp. 9-21, North Holland, 1982.

[BOKS87] Boksenbaum, C., et al., "Concurrent Certifications by Intervals of Timestamps in Distributed Database Systems", IEEE Transactions on Software Engineering, Vol. SE-13, No. 4, April 1987, pp. 409-419.

[CARE91] Carey, M.J., et al., "Data Caching Tradeoffs in Client-Server DBMS Architectures", ACM SIGMOD, Denver, CO, May 1991, pp. 357-366.

[CELL88] Cellary, W., Gelenbe, E., and Tadeusz, M., "Concurrency Control in Distributed Database Systems", North-Holland, 1988.

[CHES83] Chesnais, A., Gelenbe, E., and Mitrani, I., "On the Modeling of Parallel Access to Shared Data", Comm. ACM, Vol. 26, No. 3., Mar. 1983, pp. 196-202.

[CICI90A] Ciciani, B., Dias, D.M., and Yu, P.S. "Analysis of Replication in Distributed Database Systems", IEEE Transactions on Knowledge and Data Engineering, Vol. 2, No. 2, June 1990, pp. 247-261.

[CICI90B] Ciciani, B., Dias, D.M., Iyer, B.R., and Yu, P.S., "A Hybrid Distributed Centralized System Structure for Transaction Processing", IEEE Transactions on Software Engineering, Vol. 16, No. 8, Aug. 1990, pp. 791-806.

[CICI92] Ciciani, B., Dias, D.M., and Yu, P.S. "Analysis of Concurrency-Coherency Control Protocols for Distributed Transaction Processing with Regional Locality", IEEE Transactions on Software Engineering, Vol. 18, No. 10, Oct. 1992, pp. 899-914.

[CORN86] Cornell, D.W., Dias, D.M. and Yu, P.S., "On Multisystem Coupling Through Function Request Shipping", IEEE Transactions on Software Engineering, Vol. SE-12, No.10, October 1986, pp. 1006-1017.

[DATE83] Date, C.J., "An Introduction to Database Systems", Vol. 2, Addison Wesley, Reading, MA, 1983.

[DAN88] Dan, A., Towsley, D.F., and Kohler, W.H., "Modeling the Effects of Data and Resource Contention on the Performance of Optimistic Concurrency Control Protocols", Proc. 4th Intl. Conf. on Data Engineering, Los Angeles, CA, Feb. 1988, pp. 418-425.

[DAN90A] Dan, A., and Towsley, D., "An Approximate Analysis of the LRU and FIFO Buffer Replacement Schemes", ACM SIGMETRICS, Denver, CO, (Performance Evaluation Review, Vol. 18, No. 1), May 1990, pp. 143-152.

[DAN90B] Dan, A., Dias, D. M. and Yu, P. S., "The Effect of Skewed Data Access on Buffer Hits and Data Contention in a Data Sharing Environment", Proc. 16th Intl. Conf. on Very Large Databases, Brisbane, Australia, Aug. 1990, pp. 419-431.

[DAN91] Dan, A., Dias, D.M., and Yu, P.S., "Analytic Modelling of a Hierarchical Buffer for a Data Sharing Environment", Proc. 1991 ACM SIGMETRICS Conference, San Diego, CA, May 1991, pp. 156-167.

[DAN92A] Dan, A., and Yu, P.S., "Performance analysis of coherency control policies through lock retention", Proc. of the ACM SIGMOD Intl. Conf. on Management of Data, San Diego, CA, June 1992, pp. 114-123.

[DAN92B] Dan, A., Yu, P.S. and Jhingran, A. "Recovery Analysis of Data Sharing Systems under Deferred Dirty Page Propagation Policies", IBM research Report RC 18553, Yorktown Heights, 1992.

[DAN93A] Dan, A. and Yu, P.S., "Analytic Modeling and Comparison of Buffer Coherency Policies based on Lock Retention", IBM research Report RC 18664, Yorktown Heights, 1993.

[DAN93B] Dan, A., and Yu, P.S., "Performance Analysis of Buffer Coherency Policies in a Multi-System Data Sharing Environment," IEEE Transactions on Parallel and Distributed Systems, Vol. 4, No. 3, March 1993.

[DAN93C] Dan, A., Yu, P.S., and Chung, J-Y., "Database Access Characterization for Buffer Hit Prediction", Proc. 9th Intl. Conf. on Data Engineering, Vienna, Austria, April 1993.

[DIAS88] Dias, D. M., Iyer, B. R. and Yu, P. S., "Trade-offs Between Coupling Small and Large Processors for Transaction Processing", IEEE Transactions on Computers, Vol. 37, No. 3, March 1988, pp. 310-320.

[DEUX90] Deux, O., et al, "The Story of O_2", IEEE Transactions on Knowledge and Data Engineering, Vol. 2, No. 1, March, 1990, pp. 91-108.

[FRA85] Franaszek, P.A. and Robinson, J.T., "Limitations of Concurrency in Transaction Processing", ACM Transactions on Database Systems, Vol. 10, No. 1, March 1985, pp. 1-28.

[FRA92] Franaszek, P.A., Robinson, J.T. and Thomasian, A., "Concurrency Control for High Contention Environments", ACM Transactions on Database Systems, Vol. 17, No. 2, June 1992, pp. 304-345.

[FRAN92] Franklin, M.J., and Carey, M.J. and Livny, M., "Global Memory Management in Client Server DBMS Architectures", Proc. 18th Intl. Conf. on Very Large Databases, Vancouver, Canada, Aug. 1992, pp. 596-609.

[GRAY81] Gray, J., Homan, P., Obermarck, R. and Korth, H., "A Straw Man Analysis of Probability of Waiting and Deadlock", IBM Research Report RJ 3066, San Jose, CA, 1981.

[GRAY86] Gray, J.N., "An Approach to Decentralized Computer Systems", IEEE Transactions on Software Engineering, Vol SE-12, No. 6, June 1986, pp. 684-692.

[HART89] Hartzman, C. S., "The Delay Due to Dynamic Two-Phase Locking", IEEE Transactions on Software Engineering, Vol. 15, No. 1, Jan. 1989, pp. 72-82.

[HORN87] Hornick, M., and Zdonik, S., "A Shared, Segmented Memory System for an Object-Oriented Database", ACM Transactions on Information Systems, Vol. 5, No. 1, Jan, 1987.

[HSU88] Hsu, M., and Shang, B., "Modeling Performance Impact of Hotspots", Technical Report TR-08-88, Aiken Computation Lab., Harvard University, April 1988.

[HSU92] Hsu, M., and Zhang, B., "Performance Evaluation of Cautious Waiting", ACM Transactions on Database Systems, Vol. 17, No. 3, Sept. 1992. pp. 477-512.

[KIM90] Kim, W., et al, "The Architecture of the ORION Next Generation Database System", IEEE Transactions on Knowledge and Data Engineering, Vol. 2, No. 1, March 1990, pp. 109-124.

[KRON86] Kronenberg, N., Levy, H., and Strecker, W.D., "VAXcluster: a Closely-Coupled Distributed System", ACM Transactions on Computer Systems, Vol. 4, No. 2, May 1986, pp. 130-146.

[KUNG81] Kung, H.T. and Robinson, J.T., "On Optimistic Methods for Concurrency Control", ACM Transactions on Database Systems, Vol. 6, No. 2, June 1981, pp. 213-226.

[LAVE83] Lavenberg, S.S. (Ed.), "Computer Performance Modeling Handbook", Academic Press, 1983.

[LEFF91] Leff, A., Yu, P.S., and Wolf, J.L, "Policies for Efficient Memory Utilization in a Remote Caching Architecture", Proc. 1st Intl. Conf. on Parallel and Distributed Information Systems, Miami Beach, Florida, Dec. 1992, pp. 198-205.

[LI89] Li, K., and Hudak, P., "Memory Coherence in Shared Virtual Memory Systems," ACM Transactions on Computer System, Vol. 7, Nov. 1989, pp. 321-359.

[MOHA91] Mohan, C., and Narang, I., "Recovery and Coherency Control Protocols for Fast Intersystem Page Transfer and Fine Granularity Locking in a Shared Disks Transaction Environment", Proc. 17th Intl. Conf. on Very Large Databases, Barcelona, Spain, Sept. 1991, pp. 193-207.

[MORR85] Morris, R.J.T., Wong, W.S., "Performance Analysis of Locking and Optimistic Concurrency Control Algorithms", Performance Evaluation, Vol. 5, 1985, pp. 105-118.

[RAHM86] Rahm, E., "Primary Copy Synchronization for DB-Sharing", Information Systems, Vol. 11, No. 4, 1986, pp. 275-286.

[RAHM88] Rahm, E., "Emprical Performance Evaluation of Concurrency and Coherency Control Protocols for Data Sharing", IBM Research Report RC 14325, 1988.

[RAMA89] Ramachandran, U., Ahamad, M. and Khalidi, M.Y.A., "Coherence of Distributed Shared Memory: Unifying Synchronization and Data Transfer", Proc. 18th Intl. Conf. on Parallel Processing, St. Charles, Ill, Aug. 1989, pp. II-160--II-169.

[RYU87] Ryu, I. K. and Thomasian, A., "Performance Analysis of Centralized Databases with Optimistic Concurrency Control", Performance Evaluation, Vol. 7, 1987, pp. 195-211.

[ROSE78] Rosenkrantz, D.J., Stearns, R.E., and Lewis, P.M., II. "System Level Concurrency Control for Distributed Database Systems", ACM Transactions on Database Systems, Vol. 3, No. 2, June 1978, pp. 178-198.

[SEVC83] Sevcik, K. C., "Comparison of Concurrency Control Methods Using Analytic Models", Information Processing 83, R.E.A. Mason (ed.), North Holland, 1983, pp. 847-858.

[SING88] Singhal, M. and Yesha, Y., "A Polynomial Algorithm for Computation of the Probability of Conflicts in a Database under Arbitrary Data Access Distribution", Information Processing Letters, Vol. 27, No., 2, Feb. 1988, pp. 69-74.

[SING91] Singhal, M., "Analysis of the Probability of Transaction Abort and Throughput of Two Timestamp Ordering Algorithms for Database Systems", IEEE Transaction on Knowledge and Data Engineering, Vo. 3, No. 2, June 1991, pp. 261-266.

[TAY84] Tay, Y.C., "A Mean Value Performance Model for Locking in Databases", Ph.D. Dissertation, Harvard University, Cambridge, MA, Feb. 1984.

[TAY85A] Tay, Y.C., Suri, R. and Goodman, N., "A Mean Value Performance Model for Locking in Databases: The No-Waiting Case", Journal of the ACM, Vol. 32, No. 3, July 1985, pp. 618-651.

[TAY85B] Tay, Y.C., Goodman, N., and Suri, R., "Locking Performance in Centralized Databases", ACM Transactions on Database Systems, Vol. 10, No. 4, Dec. 1985, pp. 415-462.

[TAY90] Tay, Y.C., "Issues in Modelling Locking Performance", in "Stochastic Analysis of Computer and Communication Systems, H. Takagi (Ed.), North-Holland, 1990, pp. 631-655.

[THOM85] Thomasian, A. and Ryu, I.K., "Analysis of Some Optimistic Concurrency Control Schemes Based on Certification", Performance Eval. Review, 13, 2 (Proc. of 1985 ACM SIGMETRICS), pp.192-203.

[THOM91] Thomasian, A. and Ryu, I.K., "Performance Analysis of Two-Phase Locking", IEEE Transactions on Software Engineering, Vol. 17, No. 5, May 1991, pp. 386-401.

[WILK90] Wilkinson, K., and Neimat, M.A., "Maintaining Consistency of Client-Cached Data" Proc. 16th Very Large Database Conf., Brisbane, Australia, August 1990, pp. 122-133.

[YU85] Yu, P.S., Dias, D.M., Robinson, J.T., Iyer, B.R. and Cornell, D.W., "Modelling of Centralized Concurrency Control in Multi-System Environment", Performance Eval. Review, 13, 2 (Proc. of 1985 ACM SIGMETRICS), pp.183-191.

[YU87] Yu, P.S., et al., "On Coupling Multi-Systems Through Data Sharing", Proceedings of the IEEE, Vol. 75, No. 5, May 1987, pp. 573-587.

[YU90] Yu, P.S. and Dias, D.M., "Concurrency Control Using Locking with Deferred Blocking", Proc. 6th Intl. Conf. on Data Engineering, Los Angeles, CA, 1990, pp.30-36.

[YU91] Yu, P.S., Heiss, H. and Dias, D.M., "Modelling and Analysis of a Time-Stamp History Based Certification Protocol for Concurrency Control", IEEE Transactions on Knowledge and Data Engineering, Vo. 3, No. 4, Dec. 1991, pp. 525-537.

[YU92A] Yu, P.S. and Dias, D.M., "Analysis of Hybrid Concurrency Control Schemes for a High Data Contention Environment", IEEE Transactions on Software Engineering, Vol. 18, No. 2, Feb. 1992, pp. 118-129.

[YU92B]   Yu, P.S. and Dan, A., "Effect of System Dynamics on Coupling Architectures for Transaction Processing", Proc. 8th Intl. Conf. on Data Engineering, Tempe, AZ, Feb. 1992, pp. 458-469.

[YU92C]   Yu, P.S., and Dan, A., "Impact of Workload Partitionability on the Performance of Coupling Architectures for Transaction Processing", Proc. 4th IEEE Symposium on Parallel and Distributed Processing, Dec. 1992, pp. 40-49.

[YU93]   Yu, P.S., Dias, D., and Lavenberg, S.S., "On the Analytical Modeling of Database Concurrency Control", Journal of the ACM, Sept. 1993.

[YU94]   Yu, P.S., K.L. Wu, K.J. Lin, and S.H. Son, "On Real-time Databases: Concurrency Control and Scheduling", (to appear) Proceedings of the IEEE, Jan. 1994.

Springer-Verlag
and the Environment

We at Springer-Verlag firmly believe that an international science publisher has a special obligation to the environment, and our corporate policies consistently reflect this conviction.

We also expect our business partners — paper mills, printers, packaging manufacturers, etc. — to commit themselves to using environmentally friendly materials and production processes.

The paper in this book is made from low- or no-chlorine pulp and is acid free, in conformance with international standards for paper permanency.

Springer-Verlag
and the Environment

We at Springer-Verlag firmly believe that an international science publisher has a special obligation to the environment, and our corporate policies consistently reflect this conviction.

We also expect our business partners – paper mills, printers, packaging manufacturers, etc. – to commit themselves to using environmentally friendly materials and production processes.

The paper in this book is made from low- or no-chlorine pulp and is acid free, in conformance with international standards for paper permanency.

Lecture Notes in Computer Science

For information about Vols. 1–655
please contact your bookseller or Springer-Verlag